D0124507

WITHDRAWN

THE
CORNELL WORDSWORTH
COLLECTION

Cornell University. Library

THE CORNELL
WORDSWORTH
COLLECTION

A CATALOGUE OF
BOOKS AND MANUSCRIPTS
PRESENTED TO THE UNIVERSITY
BY
MR VICTOR EMANUEL
CORNELL 1919

COMPILED BY
GEORGE HARRIS HEALEY

ITHACA · NEW YORK
CORNELL UNIVERSITY PRESS
1957

120097

Try L.C.

CORNELL UNIVERSITY PRESS
LONDON: OXFORD UNIVERSITY PRESS

PUBLISHED 1957
EDITION LIMITED TO 750 COPIES

ALL RIGHTS RESERVED

PR
5881
.Z99
C81
1957

Printed in Great Britain at the University Press, Cambridge
(Brooke Crutchley, University Printer)

PREFACE

THE collection of books and manuscripts here catalogued had its beginning in the St John Collection of Wordsworth, which was acquired in 1925 by Mr Victor Emanuel and presented to Cornell University. That collection represented forty years of devoted attention by Mrs Cynthia Morgan St John of Ithaca. Long before the end of her life she had assembled a Wordsworth library fine enough to attract the attention of scholars on both sides of the ocean and full enough to form the basis of her projected bibliography of Wordsworth.

Mrs St John collected Wordsworth simply because she admired the poet and his poetry. She was not a wealthy woman, and at least in the beginning wealth was not necessary to her purpose. When she started her library, in the late 1870's, Wordsworth was an esteemed author but too modern to be a 'collected' one. Her competitors in the field, also admirers of the poet rather than professional book collectors, were not so numerous as to bid prices up. Furthermore, her few rivals soon became her fast friends. The trouble was not in meeting the cost of the books she wanted to buy, but rather in finding dealers who bothered to offer them. Since prices were not high enough to unearth the books, she relied confidently upon her friends to do so, and of helpers she had many. William Knight, Thomas Hutchinson, Edward Dowden, Dykes Campbell, John R. Tutin, and many lesser-known Wordsworthians posted intelligence reports to her and even gave her volumes from their own shelves.

Like all collectors, she often wished ruefully that she had seized some earlier opportunities. In 1885 she could have bought her *Lyrical Ballads*, 1800, for ten shillings; she later paid eight dollars for her set. In 1885 she could have got *Peter Bell* for twelve and six; her copy later cost her twenty-five shillings. But from the perspective of her late years she could of course take satisfaction in having formed her collection as early as she had. Her *Convention of Cintra*, for instance, inscribed by Wordsworth to Southey, had come to her for £2; her London *Lyrical Ballads*, 1798, for $25; her *Evening Walk*, 1793, for £15; and her triumphant Bristol *Lyrical Ballads*, 1798, at a time when only two other copies of this 'black tulip' were known, for $375.

By 1909, after thirty years of cultivation, her library was complete enough to supply most of the material for the bibliography of Words-

v

worth upon which she had long been engaged. But in the summer of that year, at a time when she was correcting the first galleys of the book, a fire completely destroyed her country house near Ithaca, and with the house went the entire manuscript of the bibliography. The loss was cruel, to be sure, but it might have been worse: that summer, for the first time, she had not moved the Wordsworth collection itself into the country house. She did not attempt to rewrite her book. At about that time T. J. Wise informed her that he was doing a similar work. She abandoned the bibliography to him but continued, though at a slower pace, to extend her library.

Upon the death of Mrs St John in 1919, the collection was offered for sale. No immediate purchaser appeared; the price, quite justly, was high. The books were removed from Ithaca to be exhibited elsewhere, and a number of rival institutions appointed committees, summoned supporters, and began to collect funds. At that point Mr Emanuel came forward, acquired the library, and returned it to Ithaca as a gift to his university.

Fortunately, the generous enthusiasm that led Mr Emanuel to obtain the St John collection also prompted him to sustain and extend it. For thirty-two years now he has presided genially over its steady development. During much of this time he was aided diligently by the first curator of the Cornell Wordsworth Collection, the late Professor L. N. Broughton. Later, for a brief but flourishing period, he was advised by Professor R. C. Bald. The collection was and is, however, an abiding personal interest of his own, and, though one of the busiest of men, he is never too busy to see a manuscript or to place a bid at Sotheby's. In depression and in prosperity, in wartime and in peacetime, in Charing Cross and on Fourth Avenue, he has cheerfully but determinedly seen to it that the resources of the collection were constantly widened and deepened. The result of that persistence is evident. The St John library of 1925 consisted of about a thousand pieces; the Cornell Wordsworth Collection today (catalogued as 3206 items, some of them multiple) comes to about 3500 pieces.

Wordsworth is the most voluminously studied of all the Romantic poets. As might be expected then, the largest division of the collection is that here catalogued as Part V, 'Wordsworthiana.' The aim has been to make available at Cornell, either within the collection or within the University Library that shelters it, a record of everything significant that has been written about Wordsworth or that is likely to help in understanding him. That goal recedes endlessly, of course, but it always remains a goal. Of the Romantic poets, Wordsworth is also the most frequently published. The divisions that perhaps approach nearest to the unattainable hope of completeness are Parts I and II, those containing the editions of his works. In Part II, the editions published since the poet's death, gaps still are occasionally filled, and still occasionally discovered. In Part I, the editions issued during Wordsworth's lifetime, the gaps are fortunately few and not very important. Those few are now filled by means of photostatic facsimiles, but always with the hope that an original will someday turn up. This section is the heart of the collection. These are the books in which the author presented himself to the public. They show in many instances his successive and interminable revisions, and they provide much of the material from which the critic makes his judgment and the editor his text. Because of the importance of these books to scholars, collectors, and bookmen generally, they have first place in the collection and in the *Catalogue*. And because the bibliographies of Wordsworth in which some of them have been set forth are either out of date or otherwise unpopular, they are described here (in accordance with Fredson Bowers's *Principles of Bibliographical Description*, 1949) with particular fullness and care.

Part III, 'Early Periodicals,' is a small division, both because Wordsworth wrote but little for the journals and because that little is not often procurable in its original form. Part IV, 'Early Anthologies,' is likewise small, but for a different reason. Since Wordsworth is the most abundantly anthologized of all the English poets, to admit every anthology in which he appeared would flood the collection. Older and hence rarer anthologies find a place here; of the others, many can be found in the general holdings of the University Library. Part VI, 'Coleridge and His Family,' was begun as a support for Wordsworth studies, but in view of the continuing acquisition of Coleridge books and manuscripts, it may well one day stand in its own right. Likewise Part VII, 'The Lake District,' intended originally as an adjunct, has lately begun to find use as a primary collection. 'Books of Associative Interest,' Part VIII, though not long, brings warmth and sentiment into the collection. Here are the books that were close to Wordsworth and his friends, books that they read, or received, or gave, or annotated. Of all these divisions, however, the one showing the most comprehensive development over the past few years is surely Part IX, 'Manuscripts.' Indeed, piece for piece, the manuscripts now comprise almost a third of the collection. Of major importance are the 243 letters of Wordsworth, ranging from 1796 to 1850, and the 79 letters of Coleridge, ranging from 1796 to 1834. Also worthy of special notice are the substantial number of literary manuscripts of both poets, the large number of letters written to and about them by their friends and acquaintances, and the several albums of miscellanies, most notably perhaps that kept by Joseph Cottle of Bristol from 1796.

In manuscript and print, then, every succeeding year brings valuable accessions to each part of the collection. And, of a different order of importance and satisfaction, every succeeding year brings to the collection a greater number of scholarly visitors, the furtherance of whose work is its principal purpose and its happiest one.

For counsel during the preparation of this *Catalogue* I am indebted to Professor R. C. Bald of the University of Chicago.

I am happy to record my thanks to Miss Georgia Coffin, rare books librarian at Cornell, for her daily kindnesses and to Dr Paul M. Zall, formerly of Cornell, for his expert assistance.

For bibliographical information and for help of other kinds I am obliged to Mr L. E. Bliss, the Huntington Library; Mr Herbert Cahoon, the Pierpont Morgan Library; Miss Martha A. Connor, Swarthmore College; Miss Helen Darbishire, Grasmere; Mr David Foxon, the British Museum; Miss Hannah D. French, Wellesley College; Dr John D. Gordan, the New York Public Library; Professor E. L. Griggs, the University of California at Los Angeles; Miss Phoebe Johnson, Grasmere; Mr Herman W. Liebert, Yale University; Dr Stephen A. McCarthy, Cornell University; Mr N. F. McKeon, Amherst College; Dean Francis E. Mineka, Cornell University; Mr J. H. P. Pafford, the University of London; Dr Felix Reichmann, Cornell University; Professor W. M. Sale, Jr., Cornell University; Mr C. R. H. Taylor, the Alexander Turnbull Library; Dr F. M. Todd, Canberra University College; Miss Geneva Warner, Indiana University; Mr F. P. White, St John's College, Cambridge; Mr J. C. Wyllie, the University of Virginia; and Miss Marjorie Wynne, Yale University.

I am grateful too for courtesies granted me at Amherst College; the British Museum; the Bodleian Library; the Cambridge University Library; Columbia University; the Dove Cottage Library; the University of Edinburgh; Harvard University; the University of London; Indiana University; the University of Pennsylvania; Princeton University; St John's College, Cambridge; Swarthmore College; Trinity

College, Dublin; the Victoria and Albert Museum; Wellesley College; and Yale University.

My deepest thanks, and the thanks of many others I am sure, go to Mr Victor Emanuel, who in every sense made this *Catalogue* possible. He merits the good opinion of all good men for his abiding interest in university education, for his earnest support of research in the humanities, and for his long years of devotion to Wordsworth and to Wordsworth scholarship.

G. H. H.

CORNELL UNIVERSITY
May 1957

CONTENTS

LIST OF ILLUSTRATIONS

PART I

WRITINGS OF WORDSWORTH IN BOOK FORM
1793–1850

1 AN | EVENING WALK. | *An EPISTLE*; | In VERSE. | ADDRESSED to a Young LADY, | FROM THE | *LAKES* | OF THE | NORTH of ENGLAND. | BY | W. WORDSWORTH, B.A. | Of St. JOHN's, CAMBRIDGE. | *LONDON:* | Printed for J. Johnson, St. Paul's Church-Yard. | 1793.

Special imprint. None.
Collation (10¼ × 8⁵⁄₁₆ in.). [A]² χ1 B–D⁴ E².
Pagination. [i–vi], [1] 2–27 [28].
Contents. [i] title-page; [ii] blank; [iii] 'ARGUMENT.'; [iv] blank; [v] 'ERRATA.'; [vi] blank; [1] text; [28] advertisement for *Descriptive Sketches*.
$1, 2 signed, at center of foot. Pagination in square brackets centered at top. Laid paper, with fleur-de-lis watermark; chain-lines 1¹⁄₁₆ in. apart. Three stab holes at inner margin. Inserted in plain modern wrappers. The lines of verse are numbered throughout; line 425 is misnumbered '525'.

First edition. In some copies the word 'night,' on p. 3, line 1, is corrected by erasure or deletion to 'nigh,'.

2 DESCRIPTIVE SKETCHES. | IN VERSE. | TAKEN DURING A | PEDESTRIAN TOUR | IN THE | ITALIAN, GRISON, SWISS, AND SAVOYARD | *ALPS.* | BY | W. WORDSWORTH, B.A. | Of St. JOHN's, CAMBRIDGE. | [rule] | —Loca pastorum deserta atque otia dia. | Lucret. | Castella in tumulis— | —Et longe saltus lateque vacantes. | Virgil. | [rule] | *LONDON:* | Printed for J. Johnson, St. Paul's Church-Yard. | 1793.

Special imprint. None.
Collation (10¾ × 8¾ in.). [A]² B–H⁴.
Pagination. 4 pp. unnumbered, [i] ii, [3–5] 6–55 [56].
Contents. Title-page, verso blank; blank page, with 'ERRATA.' on verso; [i] dedication to Robert Jones; [3] 'ARGUMENT.'; [4] blank; [5] text; [56] advertisement for *An Evening Walk*.
$1, 2 signed, at center of foot. Pagination in square brackets centered at top. Laid paper, with fleur-de-lis watermark; chain-lines 1¹⁄₁₆ in. apart. Three stab holes at inner margin.
Binding. Three-quarter brown calf over marbled boards; uncut.

First edition. Both the page of Errata and the title-page are printed on the same side of a half sheet. Hence, as that sheet is folded, the title-page is on the recto of A1, the page of Errata is on the verso of A2, and the two facing pages between them are awkwardly blank. In some copies A2 has been removed, turned round, and re-inserted so that the page of Errata becomes a recto.

Samuel Taylor Coleridge's copy, with an inscription on the title-page in the hand of Dorothy Wordsworth: 'To S. T. Coleridge from D Wordsworth.' On a blank leaf is a full-page inscription by Henry Reed, Wordsworth's American editor, dated 3 November 1850, presenting the volume to Sara Coleridge and explaining that Reed acquired it from a bookseller in Bristol. Another leaf bears the signature of Sara's daughter, Edith Coleridge.

3 LYRICAL BALLADS, | WITH | *A FEW OTHER POEMS.* | BRISTOL: | PRINTED BY BIGGS AND COTTLE, | FOR T. N. LONGMAN, PATERNOSTER-ROW, LONDON. | 1798.

Special imprint. None.
Collation (6¼ × 3⅝ in.). π1 2π⁴ [A]⁸ B–C⁸ D⁸(–D8) χ⁴ [E]⁸(–E1, 2) F–N⁸ O⁴(–O4).
Pagination. 2 pp. unnumbered, [i] ii–v [vi–viii], [1–5] 6–51 [52–3] 54–8 [59] 60–2 [63] 64–9, 2 pp. unnumbered, 70–84 [85] 86–93 [94–5] 96–7 [98] 99–104 [105] 106–9 [110] 111–14 [115] 116 [117] 118–46 [147–8] 149–210 [211–14].

Contents. Title-page, verso blank; [i] '*ADVERTISEMENT.*'; [vi] blank; [vii] '*CONTENTS.*'; [viii] blank; [1] fly title: 'THE RIME | OF THE | ANCYENT MARINERE, | IN | SEVEN PARTS.'; [2] blank; [3] '*ARGUMENT.*'; [4] blank; [5] text; [52] blank; [53] text; unnumbered verso of 69, blank; unnumbered recto of 70, text; [94] blank; [95] text; [147] fly title: 'THE | IDIOT BOY.'; [148] blank; 149 text; [211] 'ERRATA.'; [212] blank; [213–14] advertisement for fourteen books published for Joseph Cottle by T. Longman, and Lee & Hurst.

$1 signed, at center of foot; cancellans E1 unsigned. Pagination centered at top. Wove paper, water-marked 'LLOYD 1795'. Sheets bulk $\frac{5}{8}$ in.

Binding. Full green morocco, panelled back; all edges gilt; marbled end-papers. De Ricci says the original binding of the Bristol issue was drab boards; apparently no copy in that condition survives.

First edition, first issue. As originally printed, *Lyrical Ballads* contained Coleridge's Lewti, on pp. 63–7. That poem was suppressed before publication, however, and was replaced by Coleridge's Nightingale. This substitution required the cancellation of D8, E1, and E2, and the insertion in their place of χ^4. The original, uncancelled leaves bearing Lewti survive in four copies of the book. Furthermore, since the original page of Contents listed Lewti—three examples of the page survive—that had to be changed, too. But either the change was made in the press, or else the whole gathering 2π was reprinted, for $2\pi4$, the revised page of Contents, is not a cancel, though often called such. In one known copy of the book, perhaps experimental, there appears in addition to The Nightingale another poem, Thomas Beddoe's Domiciliary Verses. It is printed on a separate leaf, paged 62* and 63*, and inserted between D7 and $\chi1$.

The number of surviving copies of the Bristol issue has been estimated so variously that a specific listing, even though perhaps incomplete, may prove useful. The following thirteen examples are known to me. Containing Lewti, four copies: (1) British Museum, (2) Berg Collection, New York Public Library, (3) Mr. Robert H. Taylor, Yonkers, New York, (4) Yale University. Containing The Nightingale *and* Domiciliary Verses, one copy: the Ashley Library of the British Museum. Containing The Nightingale, eight copies: (1 and 2) Lord Rothschild, (3) Alexander Turnbull Library, Wellington, New Zealand, (4) Berg Collection, New York Public Library, (5) Cornell, (6) Harvard, (7) Indiana, (8) Yale.

This copy has the two pages of advertisements at the end, and the following variants. On p. 19, line 10, the misprint 'Oft' is uncorrected; in some copies (of both the Bristol and London issues) the word is corrected with a pen to 'Off'. P. 204, line 26 has 'woods,' where in some copies it has deteriorated to 'woods' and in others to 'wood'. Similarly, on p. 204, line 28 has 'thought,' where some copies have 'thought' and others 'though'. See D. F. Foxon, 'The Printing of *Lyrical Ballads*', *The Library*, IX (1954), 221–41; R. W. Daniel, 'The Publication of the *Lyrical Ballads*', *Modern Language Review*, XXXIII (1938), 406–10; J. E. Wells, 'Variants in the *Lyrical Ballads* of 1798', *Times Literary Supplement*, 23 June 1932, p. 464; and J. E. Wells, '*Lyrical Ballads*, a Variant?', *Review of English Studies*, IX (1933), 199–201.

4 LYRICAL BALLADS, | WITH | *A FEW OTHER POEMS.* | LONDON: | PRINTED FOR J. & A. ARCH, GRACECHURCH-STREET. | 1798.

Special imprint. None.

Collation ($6\frac{1}{16} \times 3\frac{11}{16}$ in.). $\pi1(\pm)$ $2\pi^4$ [A]^8 B–C^8 D^8(–D8) χ^4 [E]^8(–E1, 2) F–N^8 O^4(–O4).

Pagination. 2 pp. unnumbered, [i] ii–v [vi–viii], [1–5] 6–51 [52–3] 54–8 [59] 60–2 [63] 64–9, 2 pp. unnumbered, 70–84 [85] 86–93 [94–5] 96–7 [98] 99–104 [105] 106–9 [110] 111–14 [115] 116 [117] 118–46 [147–8] 149–210 [211–14].

Contents. Title-page, verso blank; [i] '*ADVERTISEMENT.*'; [vi] blank; [vii] '*CONTENTS.*'; [viii] blank; [1] fly title: 'THE RIME | OF THE | ANCYENT MARINERE, | IN | SEVEN PARTS.'; [2] blank; [3] '*ARGUMENT.*'; [4] blank; [5] text; [52] blank; [53] text; unnumbered verso of 69, blank; unnumbered recto of 70, text; [94] blank; [95] text; [147] fly title: 'THE | IDIOT BOY.'; [148] blank; 149 text; [211] 'ERRATA.'; [212] blank; [213–14] Cottle's advertisements.

$1 signed, at center of foot; cancellans E1 unsigned. Pagination centered at top. Wove paper, water-marked 'LLOYD 1795'. Sheets bulk $\frac{1}{2}$ in.

Binding. Three-quarter blue morocco over marbled boards; marbled end-papers. Other copies survive in drab boards with lighter drab backstrip (London bookseller), pink boards rebacked with blue paper (Ashley Library in the British Museum), and blue boards rebacked with white paper (Berg Collection, New York Public Library). I have seen no copy with an original paper label.

First edition, second issue. Except for the title-page, the London issue does not differ from the Bristol. At some time in the history of one copy of the London issue, now No. 2251 of the Ashley Library, a false leaf was printed and inserted in place of its original leaf G1. The purpose supposedly was to make up a complete copy from a defective one. Unfortunately, this unrepresentative copy, its spurious leaf mistaken for a cancel, was set forth in a bibliography as the standard example of the

London issue. Among the unhappy effects was the immediate elevation of all ordinary copies of the book to the unreal distinction of preserving 'G1 in original uncancelled state.' The error dies hard, and it is still necessary to warn that Ashley 2251 is an aberrant copy, that G1 therein is not a cancel but a sophistication, and that uncancelled G1 in *Lyrical Ballads* is unremarkable.

This copy has the two pages of advertisements; 'Oft' uncorrected (p. 19, line 10); 'woods' with the 's' deteriorating (p. 204, line 15); and 'thought' with a defective final 't' and no comma (p. 204, line 17).

5 Another copy.

$6\frac{1}{16} \times 3\frac{5}{8}$ in. This copy lacks the two pages (O3) of advertisements. Sheets bulk $\frac{9}{16}$ in. Bound in full green morocco; maroon end-papers; all edges gilt. P. 19, line 10 has 'Oft' corrected with a pen to 'Off'; p. 204, line 15 has 'woods'; p. 204, line 17 has 'though'.

1800

6 LYRICAL BALLADS, | WITH | *OTHER POEMS.* | IN TWO VOLUMES. | By W. WORDSWORTH. | [thick-and-thin rule] | Quam nihil ad genium, Papiniane, tuum! | VOL. I. | SECOND EDITION. | *LONDON:* | PRINTED FOR T. N. LONGMAN AND O. REES, PATERNOSTER-ROW, | BY BIGGS AND CO. BRISTOL. | 1800.

LYRICAL BALLADS, | WITH | *OTHER POEMS.* | IN TWO VOLUMES. | By W. WORDSWORTH. | [thick-and-thin rule] | Quam nihil ad genium, Papiniane, tuum! | VOL. II. | *LONDON:* | PRINTED FOR T. N. LONG-MAN AND O. REES, PATERNOSTER-ROW, | BY BIGGS AND CO. BRISTOL. | 1800.

Special imprints. Vol. 1 (on p. 215): [thick-and-thin rule] | Printed by BIGGS and COTTLE, St. Augus-tines-Back, Bristol,
    Vol. 2 (on p. 228): [ornamental rule] | Printed by BIGGS and Co. Bristol.
Collation ($6\frac{1}{4} \times 3\frac{3}{4}$ in.). Vol. 1: [*a*]⁸ *b–c*⁸ A–N⁸ O⁴. Vol. 2: π² A–O⁸ P².
Pagination. Vol. 1: [i–v] vi–xlvi [xlvii–xlviii], 1–104 [105–6] 107–50 [151–4] 155–99 [200] 201–10 [211–16]. P. ix misnumbered 'xi'.
    Vol. 2: [i–iv], [1] 2–15 [16–18] 19–99 [100–2] 103–48 [149–50] 151–74 [175–8] 179–96 [197–8] 199–227 [228].
Contents. Vol. 1: [i] title-page; [ii] blank; [iii] '*CONTENTS.*'; [iv] blank; [v] 'PREFACE.'; [xlvii–xlviii] blank; 1 text; [105] fly title: 'THE | IDIOT BOY.'; [106] blank; 107 text; [151] fly title: 'THE | ANCIENT MARINER, | A POET'S REVERIE.'; [152] blank; [153] '*ARGUMENT.*'; [154] blank; 155 text; [200] blank; 201 text; [211] '*NOTES.*'; [216] blank.
    Vol. 2: [i] title-page; [ii] blank; [iii] '*CONTENTS.*'; [1] text; [16] blank; [17] fly title: 'THE | BROTHERS, | A PASTORAL POEM.'; [18] blank; 19 text; [100] blank; [101] fly title: 'RUTH.'; [102] blank; 103 text; [149] fly title: 'THE OLD | CUMBERLAND BEGGAR. | *A DESCRIP-TION.*'; [150] blank; 151 text; [175] fly title: 'POEMS | ON THE | *NAMING OF PLACES.*'; [176] blank; [177] 'ADVERTISEMENT.'; [178] blank; 179 text; [197] fly title: 'MICHAEL, | *A PASTORAL POEM.*'; [198] blank; 199 text; 226 notes on The Brothers; 227 notes on Michael; [228] 'ERRATA.'.
$1 signed, at center of foot. Running title 'PREFACE.' appears in vol. 1, pp. vi–xlvi; no running titles elsewhere. Pagination of Preface set in outer margin of headline; elsewhere centered at top. Wove paper, watermarked 'LLOYD 1795', or 'LLOYD 1', or 'LLOYD'. Vol. 1 sheets bulk $\frac{11}{16}$ in.; vol. 2, $\frac{9}{16}$ in.
Binding. Contemporary green half leather over marbled boards. The original binding varied. Copies survive in drab boards with lighter drab backstrip (Pierpont Morgan Library), blue boards with drab backstrip (London bookseller), drab boards with blue backstrip (Swarthmore College), and pink boards with drab backstrip (Cornell). No copy with paper labels entirely intact is known to me, but the surviving fragments suggest the following: 'LYRICAL BALLADS. | [rule] | BY WORDS-WORTH. | [rule] | VOL. I[II].'

Second edition. But 'Second Edition' appears on the title-page of vol. 1 only; vol. 2, which contained new matter, was considered to be a first edition. Similarly, in the 1802 edition vol. 1 was designated 'third edition' and vol. 2 'second edition.' In the edition of 1805, however, the distinction was abandoned; both volumes were labelled 'fourth edition.' Hence no edition of vol. 2 was labelled as the third edition.

In this 1800 edition the author's name on the title-page of vol. 2 is set in type smaller than that of the comparable line in vol. 1. In all states of this edition p. ix of vol. 1 is misnumbered 'xi'; vol. 1, p. 149, line 11 has 'teaah' for 'teach'; and vol. 2, page of Contents has 'The two Theives.'

This edition of *Lyrical Ballads* is bibliographically the most complex of all Wordsworth's books and appears in a number of different states. In most copies, leaf a_3 of vol. 1, which carries pp. v and vi of Wordsworth's celebrated Preface, is cancelled. Three known copies, however, preserve leaf a_3 uncancelled. In that state the following announcement is found on p. vi: 'For the sake of variety and from a consciousness of my own weakness I have again requested the assistance of a Friend who contributed largely to the first volume, and who has now furnished me with the Poem of Christabel, without which I should not yet have ventured to present a second volume to the public.' But Coleridge never succeeded in finishing Christabel, the book had to be printed without it, and a_3 was cancelled so that the Preface could be revised accordingly.

But even this revised leaf itself appears in two different states, each printed from a different setting of type. Both settings give the same text, but slight typographical variations between them are numerous. In one state, for instance, the opening words of the Preface are 'The first Volume'; in the other, 'The First Volume'. The verso of the leaf shows differences, too. Where p. v has 'The first Volume', lines 13–14 of p. vi divide as follows: 'FOSTER-MOTHER's TALE, the NIGHTINGALE, | the DUNGEON, and the Poem entitled LOVE.' |. But when p. v has 'The First Volume', then those same lines divide in this way: 'FOSTER-MOTHER's TALE, the NIGHTINGALE, the | DUNGEON, and the Poem entitled LOVE. I' |.

Again, in some copies of vol. 1, leaves I3 and I4 (pp. 133–6) are cancelled and replaced by a fold. But this cancellans fold was printed from the same type-setting as that of the uncancelled pages; pp. 133–6 are precisely identical in both states. Why, then, were the four pages cancelled? Just as strangely, these cancels—with one exception—are found only in copies that exhibit on the next page following them two typographical errors: 'becn' for 'been' at line 9, and 'te' for 'to' at line 13 (p. 137). When the cancels are present, the misspellings are present; when the cancels are absent, the misspellings are corrected. (One copy has both the cancels *and* the corrected spellings.) For this puzzling situation, no satisfactory explanation has yet appeared. Two possibilities, however, have been advanced. R. W. Chapman suggested the following sequence: (1) Sig. I without cancels but with 'becn' and 'te' on p. 137 (no copy in this state is known); (2) for reasons now unknown, pp. 133–6 cancelled and replaced by a fold; (3) to get rid of 'becn' and 'te' on p. 137 the whole of gathering I abandoned and completely reprinted, using the same type-settings as for stage 2 except that 'becn' and 'te' were corrected. Copies representing stages 2 and 3 are common. But Chapman rejected the notion because it did not account for the single copy showing both the cancels *and* the correct spellings. On the other hand, John Edwin Wells suggested that 'becn' and 'te' were discovered and corrected while the sheet was going through the press, that a cancellans fold was ordered to be printed with the view of replacing the offending page in the sheets already printed, and that through an error the cancellans reprinted the wrong set of pages and hence missed its mark.

Cancellation produces variant states also in vol. 2. As originally printed, p. 210 has but ten lines and omits fifteen lines of Michael. This is the state in which the volume is usually found. But in a very few extant copies the omission is corrected by the cancellation of leaves O1 and O2 and the substitution of three leaves, $O(O1) + \chi^2$. In such copies the pagination of the cancelled section runs as follows: 209, 210, *209 (with six lines only, at the top), *210 (with three lines only, at the foot), 211, 212. In copies so corrected, yet another cancellation and substitution was made. At the end of the volume, leaf P2 (pp. 227–8) was cancelled so that the three-item Errata on p. 228 could be extended to list twenty-seven items. In the process, a change was made also on the other side of the leaf, p. 227; there, the word 'END.' in the cancellandum became '*FINIS*.' in the cancellans. The Michael-cancels and the Errata-cancel were doubtless printed together as a half sheet. They are always found together.

John Edwin Wells believed that in vol. 2, E1 (or E8) might be a cancel, at least in some copies. To be sure, in his own copy (now at Swarthmore College) E1 and E8 do not seem to be conjugate, yet they are typographically identical with conjugate E1.8 in other volumes. At any rate I have seen no copy in which either E1 or E8 was clearly and certainly a cancel in the usual meaning of the word.

In two known copies (Swarthmore College and the Huntington Library) the missing lines of Michael are supplied not by cancellation and substitution but rather by means of a small slip, like an errata slip, inserted between pp. 210 and 211.

Some other variants, these not involving cancellation, remain to be noted. In vol. 1, p. 196, line 14, some copies read erroneously 'That agency returns'; in others the line has been corrected to 'That agony returns'. In vol. 2, p. 64, line 1, some copies have 'Oft had I heard of Lucy Gray', while other copies have 'Oft I had heard of Lucy Gray'. Copies with 'Oft had I' in line 1 invariably have 'She dwelt on a wide Moor' in line 6; copies with 'Oft I had' in line 1 invariably have 'She dwelt on a wild

Moor' in line 6. In vol. 2, p. 83, line 6, the words 'last days' are followed in some copies by a comma, in others by a period. In vol. 2, p. 92, line 2, some copies have 'the skill which he', while others have 'the skill which He'. Finally, in vol. 2, p. 129, line 11, some copies show normal spacing of the words 'when they please'; others show 'when t hey please' (some of them with attempted correction in manuscript); and Ashley 2254 shows a middle state in the deterioration of the line. See R. W. Chapman, '*Lyrical Ballads*, 1800', *Book Collector's Quarterly*, II (1932), 25–6; E. L. McAdam, 'The Publication of *Lyrical Ballads*, 1800', *Yale University Library Gazette*, VIII (1933), 43–6; J. E. Wells, '*Lyrical Ballads*, 1800: a Paste-in', *The Library*, XIX (1939), 486–91; and J. E. Wells, '*Lyrical Ballads*, 1800: Cancel Leaves', *PMLA*, LIII (1938), 207–29.

The most remarkable feature of this particular copy is the presence in vol. 1 of the extremely rare uncancelled first leaf of Wordsworth's Preface, with its reference to Coleridge's Christabel. Only two other copies are known (Ashley Library, and Professor C. B. Tinker, of Yale). The other variants in this copy follow. In vol. 1, I3, 4 are uncancelled; p. 137, line 9 has 'been' and line 13 has 'to'; p. 196, line 14 has 'That agency returns'. In vol. 2, O1, 2 are uncancelled; P2 is uncancelled; p. 64, line 1 has 'Oft had I heard' and line 6 has 'a wide Moor'; p. 83, line 6 has 'last days.'; p. 92, line 2 has 'the skill which He'; p. 129, line 11 has 'when they please' spaced correctly; and p. 210 has ten lines only.

7 Another copy.

$6\frac{5}{8} \times 4$ in. Original pink boards with drab backstrips, vestiges of labels; uncut. Collation of vol. 1: $[a]^8(\pm a3)$ b–c^8 A–N^8 O^4; of vol. 2: π^2 A–O^8 P^2. This is a common collation for *Lyrical Ballads*, 1800, and it describes the copies that follow in this Catalogue unless otherwise noted. In vol. 1 of this copy, I3, 4 are uncancelled; p. v, line 1 has 'The first Volume'; p. 137, line 9 has 'been' and line 13 has 'to'; p. 196, line 14 has 'agency'. In vol. 2, O1, 2 and P2 are uncancelled; p. 64, line 1 has 'Oft I had' and line 6 has 'wild Moor'; p. 83, line 6 has 'last days.'; p. 92, line 2 has 'which He'; p. 129, line 11 is normal; and p. 210 has ten lines only.

8 Another copy.

$6 \times 3\frac{1}{2}$ in. Contemporary calf. In vol. 1, I3, 4 are uncancelled; p. v, line 1 has 'The First Volume'; p. 137, line 9 has 'been' and line 13 has 'to'; p. 196, line 14 has 'agency'. In vol. 2, O1, 2 and P2 are uncancelled; p. 64, line 1 has 'Oft had I' and line 6 has 'wide Moor'; p. 83, line 6 has 'last days,'; p. 92, line 2 has 'which he'; p. 129, line 11 is normal; and p. 210 has ten lines only.

9 Another copy.

$6\frac{1}{4} \times 3\frac{13}{16}$ in. Contemporary half green calf over marbled boards. In vol. 1, I3, 4 are uncancelled; p. v, line 1 has 'The first Volume'; p. 137, line 9 has 'been' and line 13 'to'; p. 196, line 14 has 'agency'. In vol. 2, O1, 2 and P2 are uncancelled; p. 64, line 1 has 'Oft had I' and line 6 has 'wide Moor'; p. 83, line 6 has 'last days,'; p. 92, line 2 has 'which he'; p. 129, line 11 is normal; and p. 210 has ten lines only.

J. Dykes Campbell's copy, with his annotations in both volumes explained by the following note in vol. 1: 'The pencilled notes in this volume—except where otherwise referenced—are all from Mr. Longman's copy of this edition corrected for the 1802 edition. J.D.C. Augt 91. See also my copy of 1802 & notebook on the corrected copy. I began on this book systematically with p. 1 of text of Poems. J.D.C. As a rule mere changes in punctuation & cap initials not noted.' That is, Campbell has copied into these volumes the corrections made by Wordsworth in that copy of the 1800 edition that formed the printer's copy for the edition of 1802.

10 Another copy.

$6 \times 3\frac{5}{8}$ in. Full blue morocco, marbled end-papers; all edges gilt. In vol. 1, I3, 4 are cancelled; p. v, line 1 has 'The first Volume'; p. 137, line 9 has 'been' and line 13 'te'; p. 196, line 14 has 'agency'. In vol. 2, O1, 2 and P2 are uncancelled; p. 64, line 1 has 'Oft had I' and line 6 has 'wide Moor'; p. 83, line 6 has 'last days,'; p. 92, line 2 has 'which he'; p. 129, line 11 is normal; and p. 210 has ten lines only.

The collation of vol. 1, a variant, follows: $[a]^8$ b–c^8 A–H^8 I^8(–I3, 4+χ^2) K–N^8 O^4.

11 Another copy.

$6\frac{1}{8} \times 3\frac{3}{4}$ in. Three-quarter brown calf over marbled boards; all edges stained yellow. In vol. 1, I3, 4 are uncancelled; p. v, line 1 has 'The First Volume'; p. 137, line 9 has 'been' and line 13 'to'; p. 196, line 14 has 'agency'. In vol. 2, leaves O1, 2 and P2 are cancelled, and are replaced by O(O1)+χ^2 and by P(P2); p. 64, line 1 has 'Oft I had' and line 6 has 'wild Moor'; p. 83, line 6 has 'last days,'; p. 92, line 2 has 'which he'; and p. 129, line 11 is normal.

The remarkable feature of this copy is the presence in vol. 2 of the cancels whereby the omission on p. 210 of fifteen lines from Michael was corrected and the three-item list of errata on p. 228 was extended to twenty-seven items. The pagination of the cancelled portion of Sig. O runs as follows: 209, 210, *209, *210, 211, 212. On p. 209, the word 'shearing', the last word on the page, lies at the extreme left margin (on the uncancelled page it lies at the center). P. 210 has nineteen lines (the uncancelled page has but ten). P. *209 has six lines only, set at the top of the page, the remainder blank. P. *210 has three lines only, set at the bottom of the page, the remainder blank. P. 211 has eighteen lines and begins 'Distressful tidings. Long before the time' (the uncancelled page has nineteen lines and begins 'While this good household thus were living on'). P. 212 has eighteen lines and begins 'Two evenings after he had heard the news' (the uncancelled page has nineteen lines and begins 'And his heart fail'd him. "Isabel," said he'). In cancellans leaf P2, p. 227 concludes with the word '*FINIS.*' (the uncancelled page has 'END.'); p. 228 is headed '*ERRATA AND CORRECTIONS.*' and lists twenty-seven items (the uncancelled page is headed 'ERRATA.' and lists three items). Since these changes were made only after most of the edition was sold, copies of this state of the book are rare indeed. Only two other examples are known to me (Swarthmore College, and St. John's College, Cambridge). This copy bears the bookplate of William B. Scott, Scottish poet and painter. A later owner, John C. Foster, notes that the book passed from Scott to Canon Alfred Ainger, the editor of Charles Lamb.

The collation of vol. 2, a variant, follows: π^2 A–N^8 O^8(–O1, 2+O1, χ^2) P^2($\pm$P2).

1802

12 LYRICAL BALLADS, | WITH | PASTORAL | AND OTHER | 𝔓oems. | IN TWO VOLUMES. | By W. WORDSWORTH. | [thick-and-thin rule] | Quam nihil ad genium, Papiniane, tuum! | VOL. I. | THIRD EDITION. | *LONDON:* | PRINTED FOR T. N. LONGMAN AND O. REES, PATERNOSTER-ROW, | BY BIGGS AND COTTLE, CRANE-COURT, FLEET-STREET. | [thin-and-thick rule] | 1802.

LYRICAL BALLADS, | WITH | PASTORAL | AND OTHER | 𝔓oems. | IN TWO VOLUMES. | By W. WORDSWORTH. | [thick-and-thin rule] | Quam nihil ad genium, Papiniane, tuum! | VOL. II. | SECOND EDITION. | *LONDON:* | PRINTED FOR T. N. LONGMAN AND O. REES, PATERNOSTER-ROW, | BY BIGGS AND COTTLE, CRANE-COURT, FLEET-STREET. | [thin-and-thick rule] | 1802.

Special imprints (on last page of both volumes). [double rule] | PRINTED BY BIGGS AND COTTLE, CRANE-COURT.

Collation ($6\frac{5}{8} \times 4\frac{3}{16}$ in.). Vol. 1: π^2 a–d^8 e1 A–M^8 N^4 O^2. The signature of e1 is defectively printed.
    Vol. 2: π^2 A–P^8 Q^4 R1.

Pagination. Vol. 1: 4 pp. unnumbered, [i] ii–lxiv [lxv–lxvi], 1–31 [32–4] 35–63 [64–6] 67–96 [97–8] 99–142 [143–4] 145–89 [190] 191–200 [201–4].
    Vol. 2: [i–iv], [1] 2–15 [16–18] 19–63 [64] 65–98 [99–100] 101–48 [149–50] 151–72 [173–6] 177–206 [207–8] 209–36 [237] 238–47 [248] 249–50.

Contents. Vol. 1: Title-page, verso blank; '*CONTENTS.*', verso blank; [i] 'PREFACE.'; [lxv] fly title: 'LYRICAL BALLADS, | WITH | PASTORAL | AND | *OTHER POEMS.*' | [thick-and-thin rule]| [three lines of Latin] | [thin-and-thick rule]; [lxvi] blank; 1 text; [32] blank; [33] fly title: 'THE | THORN.'; [34] blank; [35] text; [64] blank; [65] fly title: 'THE | FEMALE VAGRANT.'; [66] blank; 67 text; [97] fly title: 'THE | IDIOT BOY.'; [98] blank; 99 text; [143] fly title: 'THE | ANCIENT MARINER, | A POET'S REVERIE.'; [144] blank; 145 text; [190] blank; 191 text of Tintern Abbey; [201] 'NOTES.'.
    Vol. 2: [i] title-page; [ii] blank; [iii] '*CONTENTS.*'; [1] text; [16] blank; [17] fly title: 'THE | BROTHERS, | A PASTORAL POEM.'; [18] blank; 19 text; [64] blank; 65 text; [99] fly title: 'RUTH.'; [100] blank; 101 text; [149] fly title: 'THE OLD | CUMBERLAND BEGGAR. |

A DESCRIPTION.'; [150] blank; 151 text; [173] fly title: 'POEMS | ON THE | *NAMING OF PLACES.*'; [174] blank; [175] 'ADVERTISEMENT.'; [176] blank; 177 text; [207] fly title: 'MICHAEL, | A | *PASTORAL POEM.*'; [208] blank; 209 text; [237] 'APPENDIX.'; [248] blank; 249 notes on The Brothers; 250 notes on Michael.

\$1 signed, at center of foot. Running title 'PREFACE.' appears in vol. 1, pp. ii–lxiv; no running titles elsewhere. Pagination of the Preface set in outer margin of headline; elsewhere centered at top. Wove paper, watermarked '1800' or '1801'. Vol. 1 sheets bulk $\frac{11}{16}$ in.; vol. 2, $\frac{5}{8}$ in.

Binding. Blue boards with drab backstrips; no labels; uncut. A copy of vol. 1 at Swarthmore College has blue boards and paper label: [ornamental rule] | 'LYRICAL | BALLADS. | [thick-and-thin rule] | BY | WORDSWORTH[ ] | [thin-and-thick rule] | VOL. I.' | [ornamental rule].

Third edition.

13 Another copy.

$6\frac{1}{16} \times 3\frac{11}{16}$. Three-quarter plum calf over marbled boards.

14 LYRICAL BALLADS, | WITH | *OTHER POEMS:* | IN TWO VOLUMES. | BY W. WORDSWORTH. | [ornamental rule] | Quam nihil ad genium, Papiniane, tuum! | [rule] | VOL. I [II]. | [rule] | FROM THE LONDON SECOND EDITION. | 𝔓𝔥𝔦𝔩𝔞𝔡𝔢𝔩𝔭𝔥𝔦𝔞: | PRINTED AND SOLD BY JAMES HUMPHREYS. | At the N.W. Corner of Walnut and Dock-street. | [line of dots] | 1802.

Special imprint. None.
Collation ($6\frac{5}{8} \times 4$ in.). Vol. 1: [a]² b–c⁶ B–N⁶ O².
 Vol. 2: [A]⁴ B–O⁶ P⁴.
Pagination. Vol. 1: [i–v] vi–xxii, 1–5 [6] [13] 14–49 [50] 51–3 [54] 55–73 [74] 75–137 [138] 139–59 [160]. Gap in pagination pp. [6] to [13]; p. 96 misnumbered '78'.
 Vol. 2: [1–6] 7–168 [169] 170–2. P. 96 misnumbered '57'.
Contents. Vol. 1: [i] title-page; [ii] blank; [iii] '*CONTENTS.*'; [iv] 'ADVERTISEMENT.'; [v] 'PREFACE.'; 1 text; [6] title and argument of The Ancient Mariner; [13] text; [50] blank; 51 text; [54] blank; 55 text; [74] blank; 75 text; [138] blank; 139 text; [160] blank.
 Vol. 2: [1] title-page; [2] blank; [3] '*CONTENTS.*'; [5] fly title: 'HART-LEAP WELL.'; [6] blank; 7 text; [169] 'NOTES.'.
\$1, 3 signed, at center of foot; \$3 signed '2' throughout. Running title 'PREFACE.' in vol. 1, pp. vi–xxii; no running titles elsewhere. Pagination of Preface set in outer margin of headline; elsewhere centered at top. Laid paper, without watermark; chain-lines run horizontally, $1\frac{1}{8}$ in. apart. Vol. 1 sheets bulk $\frac{3}{4}$ in.; vol. 2, $\frac{3}{4}$ in.
Binding. Contemporary tan calf with red leather label; two volumes in one.

First American edition. The book was advertised in Relf's *Philadelphia Gazette* on 16 January 1802. For a variant imprint, see the following copy.

15 Another copy.

LYRICAL BALLADS, | WITH | *OTHER POEMS:* | IN TWO VOLUMES | BY W. WORDSWORTH. | [ornamental rule] | Quam nihil ad genium, Papiniane, tuum! | [rule] | VOL. I [II]. | [rule] | FROM THE LONDON SECOND EDITION. | 𝔓𝔥𝔦𝔩𝔞𝔡𝔢𝔩𝔭𝔥𝔦𝔞: | PRINTED BY JAMES HUM-PHREYS. | FOR JOSEPH GROFF, | At No. 75, South Second-street. | [line of dots] | 1802.

$6\frac{1}{4} \times 3\frac{1}{2}$ in. Bound two volumes in one, in modern buckram. The imprint on the title-page differs from that of the preceding copy; otherwise the two sets are identical except that in vol. 2 of this copy p. 96 is correctly numbered. The title-pages are not cancels in either set.

16 Another copy.

$6\frac{3}{8} \times 3\frac{7}{8}$ in. Bound two volumes in one, in tan calf by Max Adjarian. This set combines both title-pages. Vol. 1 has 'PRINTED AND SOLD BY JAMES HUMPHREYS. | At the N.W. Corner of Walnut and Dock-street.'; vol. 2 has: 'PRINTED BY JAMES HUMPHREYS. | FOR JOSEPH GROFF, | At No. 75, South Second-street.'

1805

17 LYRICAL BALLADS, | WITH | PASTORAL | AND OTHER | 𝔓𝔬𝔢𝔪𝔰. | IN TWO VOLUMES. | BY W. WORDSWORTH. | [rule] | Quam nihil ad genium, Papiniane, tuum! | [rule] | VOL. I [II]. | FOURTH EDITION. | [thick-and-thin rule] | LONDON: | PRINTED FOR LONGMAN, HURST, REES, AND ORME, | *By R. Taylor and Co.* 38, *Shoe-Lane.* | [rule] | 1805.

Special imprint. Vol. 1 (on p. 204): [rule] | *R. Taylor and Co. Printers, 38, Shoe-Lane.*
    Vol. 2 (on p. 248): [rule] | *R. Taylor and Co. Printers, 38, Shoe-Lane.*
Collation ($6\frac{11}{16} \times 4\frac{1}{8}$ in.). Vol. 1: π^2 *a–l*^{12} *m*^{4}.
    Vol. 2: π^2 *a–k*^{12} *l*^{4}.
Pagination. Vol. 1: 4 pp. unnumbered, [i] ii–lxiv [lxv–lxvi], 1–32 [33–4] 35–63 [64–6] 67–96 [97–8] 99–142 [143–4] 145–89 [190] 191–200 [201–4].
    Vol. 2: [i–iv], [1] 2–15 [16–18] 19–63 [64] 65–98 [99–100] 101–48 [149–50] 151–72 [173–6] 177–206 [207–8] 209–36 [237] 238–48. P. 76 misnumbered '79'.
Contents. Vol. 1: title-page, verso blank; 'CONTENTS.', verso blank; [i] 'PREFACE.'; [lxv] fly title: 'LYRICAL BALLADS, | WITH | PASTORAL | AND | *OTHER POEMS.*' | [thick-and-thin rule] | [three lines of Latin] | [thin-and-thick rule]; [lxvi] blank; 1 text; [33] fly title: 'THE | THORN.'; [34] blank; 35 text; [64] blank; [65] fly title: 'THE | FEMALE VAGRANT.'; [66] blank; 67 text; [97] fly title: 'THE | IDIOT BOY.'; [98] blank; 99 text; [143] fly title: 'THE | ANCIENT MARINER. | A POET'S REVERIE.'; [144] blank; 145 text; [190] blank; 191 text; [201] '*NOTES.*'
    Vol. 2: [i] title-page; [ii] blank; [iii] '*CONTENTS.*'; [1] text; [16] blank; [17] fly title: 'THE | BROTHERS: | A PASTORAL POEM.'; [18] blank; 19 text; [64] blank; 65 text; [99] fly title: 'RUTH.'; [100] blank; 101 text; [149] fly title: 'THE OLD | CUMBERLAND BEGGAR. | *A DESCRIPTION.*'; [150] blank; 151 text; [173] fly title: 'POEMS | ON THE | *NAMING OF PLACES.*'; [174] blank; [175] 'ADVERTISEMENT.'; [176] blank; 177 text; [207] fly title: 'MICHAEL, | A | *PASTORAL POEM.*'; [208] blank; 209 text; [237] 'APPENDIX.'; 248 Notes to The Brothers and Michael.
$1, 2, 5 signed, at center of foot. Running title 'PREFACE.' appears in vol. 1, pp. ii–lxiv; 'NOTES.' in vol. 1, pp. 202–4; no running titles elsewhere. Pagination set in outer margin of headline when running titles are present; otherwise centered at top. Wove paper, watermarked '1804'. Vol. 1 sheets bulk $\frac{5}{8}$ in.; vol. 2, $\frac{1}{2}$ in.
Binding. Tan boards, without labels; uncut. A copy at Yale has blue boards and gray backstrips. No copy with labels intact is known to me.
    Fourth edition.

18 Another copy.

$6\frac{1}{8} \times 3\frac{7}{8}$ in. Three-quarter tan leather over marbled boards, by Max Adjarian.

1807

19 POEMS, | IN | *TWO VOLUMES,* | BY | WILLIAM WORDSWORTH, | AUTHOR OF | *THE LYRICAL BALLADS.* | *Posterius graviore sono tibi Musa loquetur* | *Nostra: dabunt cum securos mihi tempora fructus.* | VOL. I [II]. |

LONDON: | PRINTED FOR LONGMAN, HURST, REES, AND ORME, | PATERNOSTER-ROW. | 1807.

Special imprints. Vol. 1 (p. ii and on p. 158): *Wood & Innes,* | *Printers, Poppin's Court, Fleet Street.* Second imprint set beneath a rule.

Vol. 2 (p. ii and on p. 170): *Wood & Innes,* | *Printers, Poppin's Court, Fleet Street.* Second imprint set beneath a rule.

Collation (7 × 4$\frac{7}{16}$ in.). Vol. 1: [A]^4 B–C^{12} D^{12}(–D11, 12+'D11'.1) E–G^{12} H^8.

Vol. 2: [A]^4 B^{12}(±B2) C–H^{12} I1.

Pagination. Vol. 1: [i–viii], [1] 2–6 [7] 8 [9] 10–13 [14] 15 [16] 17–18 [19] 20–1 [22] 23–6 [27] 28–30 [31] 32–6 [37] 38–44 [45] 46–9 [50] 51–7 [58] 59–62 [63] 64–5 [66] 67 [68] 69 [70] 71–4 [75–6] 77–97 [98–100] 101 [102–4] 105–24 [125–6] 127–52 [153–5] 156–8 [159–60].

Vol. 2: [i–viii], [1–3] 4–35 [36–8] 39–62 [63–4] 65–144 [145–6] 147–58 [159–61] 162–70.

Contents. Vol. 1: [i] half title: 'POEMS.'; [ii] printer's imprint; [iii] title-page; [iv] blank; [v] '*CONTENTS.*'; [1] text; [75] fly title: 'POEMS | COMPOSED | DURING A TOUR, CHIEFLY ON FOOT.'; [76] blank; 77 text; [98] blank; [99] fly title: 'SONNETS.'; [100] blank; 101 '*PREFATORY SONNET.*'; [102] blank; [103] fly title: 'PART THE FIRST. | [rule] | MISCEL-LANEOUS SONNETS.'; [104] blank; 105 text; [125] fly title: 'PART THE SECOND. | [rule] | SONNETS | DEDICATED | TO LIBERTY.'; [126] blank; 127 text; [153] fly title: '*NOTES* | *to the* | *FIRST VOLUME.*'; [154] blank; [155] '*NOTES.*'; [159] 'ERRATUM.'; [160] blank.

Vol. 2: [i] half title: 'POEMS.'; [ii] printer's imprint; [iii] title-page; [iv] blank; [v] '*CON-TENTS.*'; [viii] blank; [1] fly title: 'POEMS | *WRITTEN DURING A TOUR* | IN | SCOTLAND.'; [2] blank; [3] text; [36] blank; [37] fly title: 'MOODS OF MY OWN MIND.'; [38] blank; 39 text; [63] fly title: 'THE | BLIND HIGHLAND BOY; | WITH | *OTHER POEMS.*'; [64] blank; 65 text; [145] fly title: 'ODE.'; [146] '*Paulò majora canamus.*'; 147 text; [159] fly title: '*NOTES* | *to the* | *SECOND VOLUME.*'; [160] blank; [161] '*NOTES.*'.

$1, 2, 5 signed, at center of foot; cancellandum D11 is signed; E2, F2, and H5 are unsigned. The running title 'CONTENTS.' appears in vol. 1, pp. [vi–viii]; no running titles elsewhere. Pagination of the Contents pages is set in the outer margin of the headline; elsewhere centered at the top. Wove paper, watermarked 'HS | 1807'. Vol. 1 sheets bulk $\frac{1}{2}$ in.; vol. 2, $\frac{1}{2}$ in.

Binding. Original blue boards; vestiges of labels; uncut. Copies survive also in drab boards (London bookseller), gray-green boards (Berg Collection, New York Public Library), blue boards with drab backstrips (London Bookseller), pink boards with blue backstrips (New Haven bookseller), and drab boards with red backstrips (Pierpont Morgan Library). The paper labels have: 'WORDSWORTH's| POEMS. | [rule] | Vol. I[II].' In one of the Berg copies, the labels are set sidewise, to read from bottom to top.

In all copies known to me, D11 and D12 of vol. 1, and B2 of vol. 2 are cancels. Southey preserved the cancellanda leaves, however, and they survive bound into his copy, now in the British Museum. In vol. 1, when leaves D11 and D12 are cancelled the first verse on p. [70] is: 'Stern Daughter of the Voice of God!'; when they are uncancelled that verse is: 'There are who tread a blameless way.' In vol. 2, when B2 is cancelled the last line on p. [3] is: 'Or keep his Friends from harm.'; when B2 is uncancelled the line is: 'In Honour of that Hero brave!'. In some copies of vol. 1, on p. [103] the period following 'SONNETS' is clear; in some it is defective; in some it is absent. In some copies of vol. 2, p. 98, line 15 has 'Thy fnuction'; in others, 'Thy function'. In this particular copy, the pagination of vol. 1, p. 107 failed to print. Vol. 2, p. 98, line 15 has 'Thy function'.

20 Another copy.

6$\frac{1}{8}$ × 3$\frac{13}{16}$ in. Full crimson morocco; marbled end-papers; all edges gilt. In vol. 1, p. [103], the period following 'SONNETS' has entirely disappeared. In vol. 2, p. 98, line 15 has 'fnuction'.

21 Another copy.

6 × 3$\frac{7}{8}$ in. Three-quarter brown calf over brown cloth. Lacks the half titles. In vol. 1, p. [103], the period following 'SONNETS' is defectively printed. In vol. 2, p. 98, line 15 has 'fnuction'. Inserted between pp. [160] and [161] of vol. 2 is a single leaf, not part of the book, upon which is printed Wordsworth's Sonnet to B. R. Haydon (see No. 37).

Both volumes are inscribed: 'To Hannah Burchell from her affectionate friend Jane Reynolds.' On the fly leaf of vol. 1 appears John Hamilton Reynolds's Sonnet to Wordsworth, in the hand of the author and signed by him. Jane Reynolds, the sister of John Hamilton Reynolds, later married Thomas Hood.

1809

22 CONCERNING | THE RELATIONS | OF | GREAT BRITAIN, | SPAIN, AND PORTUGAL, | TO EACH OTHER, AND TO THE COMMON ENEMY, | AT THIS CRISIS; | AND SPECIFICALLY AS AFFECTED BY | THE | CONVENTION OF CINTRA: | *The whole brought to the test of those Principles, by which | alone the Independence and Freedom of Nations | can be Preserved or Recovered.* | [thick-and-thin rule] | Qui didicit patriæ quid debeat; — — | Quod sit conscripti, quod judicis officium; quæ | Partes in bellum missi ducis. | [thin-and-thick rule] | BY WILLIAM WORDSWORTH. | [rule] | 𝕷𝖔𝖓𝖉𝖔𝖓: | PRINTED FOR LONGMAN, HURST, REES, AND ORME, | PATERNOSTER-ROW. | [rule] | 1809.

Special imprints. (On pp. ii and 216): [thick-and-thin rule] | C. and R. Baldwin, Printers, | New Bridge-street, London. | [thin-and-thick rule].

(On p. 191): [thick-and-thin rule] | *C. and R. Baldwin, Printers,* | *New Bridge-street, London.*| [thin-and-thick rule].

Collation ($8\frac{1}{4} \times 4\frac{7}{8}$ in.). $\pi^2(\pi 1 + 1)$ A⁴(–A1) B–2D⁴.

Pagination. 4 pp. unnumbered, [1–3] 4–191 [192–3] 194–216.

Contents. [i] title-page; [ii] six-line quotation from Bacon, and printer's imprint; [iii] 'ERRATA.'; [iv] blank; [1] 'ADVERTISEMENT.'; [3] text; [192] blank; [193] 'APPENDIX.'.

$1, 2 signed, at center of foot. Running title 'APPENDIX.' appears pp. 194–216; no running titles elsewhere. Pagination of Appendix set in outer margin of the headline; elsewhere centered at top. Wove paper; sheets watermarked variously '1808', '808', '08', '1809', or not at all. Sheets bulk $\frac{1}{2}$ in.

Binding. Contemporary full tan calf; gilt spine, with 'S' (for Southey) at the foot; marbled end-papers. All the copies known to me have three stab holes at the inner margin. In several examples the title-page and p. 216 are soiled, as if those copies had once been without any kind of covering. A copy in drab boards is in the Berg Collection, New York. Wordsworth speaks of a copy in green paper, and green wrappers are bound in with a copy at Swarthmore College.

As first printed, the title-page of this tract read: 'CONCERNING | THE | CONVENTION OF CINTRA, | *IN RELATION TO* | THE PRINCIPLES BY WHICH THE INDEPENDENCE OF | NATIONS MUST BE PRESERVED OR RECOVERED. | [thin-and-thick rule] | LONDON: | Printed for Longman, Hurst, Rees, and Orme, | Paternoster Row. | [rule] | 1809.'. That title-page was cancelled before the book was issued; but it has survived in three known examples, each bound into a copy containing the revised title-page, one in the British Museum (De Quincey's copy), one at Swarthmore College (also De Quincey's), and one in the Berg Collection, New York (Charles Lloyd's copy). The old title-page was A1 of a quarto gathering. It was replaced not by a single leaf but by a two-leaf fold; the second leaf carried a new addition to the book, the 'Advertisement'. Furthermore, an errata leaf was printed and inserted in the middle of this new fold. Cancellandum A1 was replaced, therefore, by three leaves. Another cancellation took place after the book was issued. At that time N1 was cancelled and replaced in order to soften a passage that Wordsworth feared might be libellous. But some copies escaped before that change was made. When N1 is uncancelled, p. 97, lines 14–17 read: 'for what punishment could be greater than to have brought upon themselves the unremoveable contempt and hatred of their countrymen?'. When N1 is cancelled, however, the passage reads: 'for what punishment could be greater than to have brought upon themselves the sentence passed upon them by the voice of their countrymen?'. The book is not well printed, was re-written constantly while going through the press, and shows many errors, of which the errata leaf corrects but a few. On p. 8, line 31 has deteriorated in all the copies I have seen.

This was Southey's copy and contains his bookplate. The title-page is inscribed by Wordsworth: 'Robert Southey from William Wordsw[ ]'; the margin is cropped. The following corrections are entered, in the hand of Southey: verso of title-page, 'zeal' deleted and replaced by 'hate'; p. 12, line 26, the first 'to' deleted; p. 96, line 10, 'destroying' altered to 'destroyed'; p. 123, line 9, 'to itself' changed to 'of itself'; p. 123, line 20, 'would' changed to 'could'; p. 169, line 30, 'loves' changed to 'love'; p. 178, line 17, 'nature. It' changed to 'nature, it'; p. 184, line 32, 'calenture' changed to 'calenture of fancy'; p. 186, line 16, 'abuses' changed to 'abusers'; p. 188, line 9, 'act' changed to 'word'; p. 191, line 14, 'explete' changed to 'expleti'. See J. E. Wells, 'The Story of Wordsworth's *Cintra*', *Studies in Philology*, XVIII (1921), 15–77; and, same author, 'Printer's Bills for Coleridge's *Friend* and Wordsworth's *Cintra*', *Studies in Philology*, XXXVI (1939), 521–3.

23 Another copy.

$8\frac{1}{8} \times 4\frac{15}{16}$ in. Tan calf over marbled boards, by Max Adjarian. Leaf N1 in uncancelled state. No manuscript corrections in the text.

Benjamin Bailey's copy, with his bookplate, his signature on the title-page, and marginal notes in his hand.

1814

24 THE EXCURSION, | BEING A PORTION OF | THE RECLUSE, | *A POEM.* | [thick-and-thin rule] | BY | WILLIAM WORDSWORTH. | [thin-and-thick rule] | LONDON: | PRINTED FOR LONGMAN, HURST, REES, ORME, AND BROWN, | PATERNOSTER-ROW. | 1814.

Special imprints (at lower left of p. iv). [rule] | T. Davison, Lombard-street, | Whitefriars, London.
(Center of p. 448): [thick-and-thin rule] | T. DAVISON, Lombard-street, | Whitefriars, London. | [thin-and-thick rule].

Collation ($10\frac{1}{2} \times 8\frac{1}{8}$ in.). [a]⁴ b⁴ c² B–3L⁴ χ1. a1 and χ1 lacking in this copy.

Pagination. [i–vii] viii–xiv [xv] xvi–xx, [1–3] 4–49 [50–1] 52–93 [94–5] 96–140 [141] 142–200 [201] 202–47 [248–9] 250–308 [309] 310–57 [358–9] 360–86 [387] 388–423 [424–5] 426–47 [448–50]. Pp. [i–ii] lacking in this copy.

Contents. [i] half title (lacking in this copy): [thick-and-thin rule] | 'THE | EXCURSION.' | [thin-and-thick rule]; [ii] blank; [iii] title-page; [iv] printer's imprint; [v] dedication to the Earl of Lonsdale; [vi] blank; [vii] 'PREFACE.'; [xv] 'SUMMARY OF CONTENTS.'; [1] fly title: [thick-and-thin rule] | 'THE | EXCURSION.' | [thin-and-thick rule]; [2] blank; [3] text of Book 1; [50] blank; [51] text of Book 2; [94] blank; [95] text of Book 3; [141] text of Book 4; [201] text of Book 5; [248] blank; [249] text of Book 6; [309] text of Book 7; [358] blank; [359] text of Book 8; [387] text of Book 9; [424] blank; [425] 'NOTES.'; [448] printer's imprint; [449] 'ERRATA.'; [450] blank (these two pages lacking in this copy).

\$1 signed, at center of foot; G1 signed an inch to the right of center; Y2 signed. No running titles. Pagination centered at top. Wove paper, each sheet watermarked in three places: '1813'; 'HS'; '1813.' Sheets bulk $1\frac{3}{4}$ in.

Binding. Full brown morocco, by Max Adjarian. A second copy at Cornell has blue-gray boards, and the Ashley copy in the British Museum has drab boards; the paper label of these copies reads: 'THE | EXCURSION, | BEING A PORTION OF | THE RECLUSE, | A POEM. | [rule] | BY W. WORDSWORTH.'.

When sheet Y was printed, two lines of verse were omitted at the end of p. 162. To restore these lines ('Depresses the Soul's vigour. Quit your couch— | Cleave not so fondly to your moody Cell;') leaf Y1 was cancelled and replaced. When Y1 is in uncancelled state, p. 161 has twenty-three lines and concludes 'That seek yon Pool, and there prolong their stay', and p. 162 has twenty-two lines, begins 'In silent congress; or together rouzed' and concludes 'Infect the thoughts; the languor of the Frame'. When Y1 is in cancelled state, however, p. 161 has twenty-four lines and concludes 'In silent congress; or together rouzed', and p. 162 has twenty-three lines, begins 'Take flight; while with their clang the air resounds.', and concludes 'Cleave not so fondly to your moody Cell;'. In the second Cornell copy the Errata leaf is inserted at the end of the volume. In copies at Cambridge University and at Swarthmore College the leaf is inserted as pp. [xxi–xxii] following the preliminary 'Summary of Contents.' In the Ashley copy, however, it follows the text of the poem, after p. [424], and is joined there by the 'Summary of Contents,' which follows the Errata leaf and precedes the 'Notes.' This arrangement is found also in the Yale copy, except that no Errata leaf is present.

This copy has Y1 in uncancelled state; it lacks the half title and the page of errata. It belonged to Benjamin Robert Haydon and contains his marginalia and underscoring in the text, and his signature and monogram stamp on the title-page. A correction in Wordsworth's hand appears on p. 149, line 17, where 'sleep' is changed to 'rapt'. Beneath that correction Haydon wrote: 'This Wordsworth corrected himself, the day he sat to me for My Picture—that is to be put in by Newton & Voltaire—Dec. 22, 1817 while he was reading the passage aloud.' (Wordsworth appears as one of the figures in Haydon's Christ's Entry into Jerusalem.) On p. 179, opposite the lines 'Even from the blazing Chariot of the Sun, | A beardless Youth, who touched a golden lute, | And filled the illumined groves with ravishment' Wordsworth has written: 'Poor Keats used always to prefer this passage to all others—.'

25 Another copy.

11 × 8¾ in. Blue-gray boards with white end-papers watermarked 'W | 1812'; uncut. White paper label reads: 'THE | EXCURSION, | BEING A PORTION OF | THE RECLUSE, | A POEM. | [rule] | BY W. WORDSWORTH.'. In this copy, leaf Y1 is in cancelled state. Both the half title and the page of Errata are present.

1815

26 THE | WHITE DOE | OF | RYLSTONE; | OR | *THE FATE OF THE NORTONS.* | A POEM. | [thick-and-thin rule] | BY | WILLIAM WORDS-WORTH. | [thin-and-thick rule] | LONDON: | [thick-and-thin rule] | PRINTED FOR | LONGMAN, HURST, REES, ORME, AND BROWN, | PATERNOSTER-ROW, | BY JAMES BALLANTYNE AND CO., EDIN-BURGH. | [thin-and-thick rule] | 1815.

Special imprint (on p. 162). [thick-and-thin rule] | EDINBURGH: | Printed by James Ballantyne & Co.
Collation (11¼ × 8⅝ in.). [a]⁴ b² A–U⁴ X1.
Pagination. [i–ix] x–xi [xii], [1–3] 4–21 [22–5] 26–39 [40–3] 44–61 [62–5] 66–77 [78–81] 82–93 [94–7] 98–107 [108–11] 112–30 [131–3] 134–7 [138–41] 142–62.
Contents. [i] half title: [rule] | 'THE | WHITE DOE OF RYLSTONE. | A POEM.' | [rule]; [ii] blank; engraved frontispiece by J. C. Bromley of a painting of the White Doe by Sir George Beaumont, dated May 1815; [iii] title-page; [iv] blank; [v] 'ADVERTISEMENT.'; [vi] blank; [vii] sonnet ('*Weak is the will of Man, his judgement blind*') and nine-line quotation from Bacon; [viii] blank; [ix] dedicatory poem to Mary Wordsworth ('In trellis'd shed with clustering roses gay'); [xii] blank; [1] fly title: [rule] | 'THE | WHITE DOE OF RYLSTONE. | CANTO FIRST.' | [rule]; [2] blank; [3] text; [22] blank; [23] fly title, canto second; [24] blank; [25] text; [40] blank; [41] fly title, canto third; [42] blank; [43] text; [62] blank; [63] fly title, canto fourth; [64] blank; [65] text; [78] blank; [79] fly title, canto fifth; [80] blank; [81] text; [94] blank; [95] fly title, canto sixth; [96] blank; [97] text; [108] blank; [109] fly title, canto seventh; [110] blank; [111] text; [131] fly title: [rule] | 'THE | FORCE OF PRAYER; | OR | THE FOUNDING OF BOLTON PRIORY.' | [rule]; [132] blank; [133] text; [138] blank; [139] fly title: [rule] | NOTES. | [rule]; [140] blank; [141] 'NOTES.'; +16 octavo pp. (folded quarto) of Longman's advertisements, dated March 1815. $1 signed, at center of foot. Running titles as follows: pp. 4–130, 'THE WHITE DOE OF RYL-STONE.', with 'CANTO I [etc.].' set at the inner margin; pp. 134–7, 'THE FORCE OF PRAYER.'; pp. 142–62, recto 'NOTES.', verso 'THE WHITE DOE OF RYLSTONE.'. Pagination set in outer margin of headline. Wove paper, watermarked variously '1814 | H SMITH 1814', or '1815 | H SMITH 1815', or '1814'. Sheets bulk ⅝ in.
Binding. Drab boards; uncut. Paper label (flaked): [thick-and-thin rule] | 'THE | *WHITE DOE*[,] | A POEM. | BY | *W. Wordsworth*[.]' | [thin-and-thick rule]. Other copies in original bindings show drab boards with green cloth backstrip (Dove Cottage Library); blue boards with drab paper backstrip (Dyce Collection, Victoria and Albert Museum); blue-gray boards with blue-green paper backstrip (Berg Collection, New York Public Library); and green boards with gray paper backstrip (Berg Collection).
First edition.

27 Another copy.

11⅛ × 8⅝ in. Three-quarter calf over marbled boards; uncut. Sig. b misbound between A4 and B1. With the half title but without the advertisements. Some leaves have been removed; see below.

This copy belonged to Sara Coleridge, who received it from Thomas Monkhouse (a cousin of Mary Wordsworth) and later presented it to her cousin Henry Nelson Coleridge during the period of her long engagement to him. The book contains copious notes written by Sara and clearly intended for the eye of Henry Nelson Coleridge only, in which she freely expresses both her judgment of Wordsworth and her affection for the man she was waiting to marry. On a fly leaf is the following note by Edith Coleridge, daughter of Sara and Henry: 'This book was given by Sara Coleridge "to her beloved and respected friend" Henry Nelson Coleridge, on Friday 9th February 1827. Five letters to my father, written to her on the fly leaves, have been removed to me, to be preserved among her other letters to H.N.C.

E.C. May 18th 1899.' Underneath the foregoing is an earlier inscription: 'Edith Coleridge, presented to her by her dear Sister, Ellen P. Coleridge, Christmas, 1895.' Ellen Phillips Coleridge was Edith's sister-in-law, the widow of her brother Herbert.

28 Another copy.

11$\frac{3}{16}$×8$\frac{5}{8}$ in. Drab boards, spine and label flaked; uncut. Half title and advertisements present.

This copy belonged to John Hamilton Reynolds, editor of *The Keepsake* and author of a parody of Wordsworth's Peter Bell, and has his signature on the half title.

29 Another copy.

10$\frac{1}{2}$×8$\frac{1}{4}$ in. Full contemporary calf. Half title and advertisements lacking.

From the library of Wordsworth's friend Sir George Beaumont, whose painting of the White Doe was reproduced as the frontispiece of the book.

30 POEMS | BY | WILLIAM WORDSWORTH: | INCLUDING | LYRICAL BALLADS, | AND THE | MISCELLANEOUS PIECES OF THE AUTHOR. | WITH ADDITIONAL POEMS, | A NEW PREFACE, AND A SUPPLEMENTARY ESSAY. | [thick-and-thin rule] | IN TWO VOLUMES. | [thin-and-thick rule] | VOL. I [II]. | [rule] LONDON: | PRINTED FOR LONGMAN, HURST, REES, ORME, AND BROWN, | PATERNOSTER-ROW. | [rule] | 1815.

Special imprints. Vol. 1 (p. ii): [rule] | T. DAVISON, Lombard-street, | Whitefriars, London. (p. 376): [thick-and-thin rule] | T. DAVISON, Lombard-street, | Whitefriars, London. | [thin-and-thick rule].
Vol. 2 (p. ii): [rule] | T. DAVISON, Lombard-street, | Whitefriars, London. (p. [400]): [rule] | T. DAVISON, Lombard-street, | Whitefriars, London.
Collation (8$\frac{5}{8}$×5$\frac{1}{16}$ in.). Vol. 1: a–c⁸ d² B–P⁸ Q⁸(–Q1, 2, 3, 4+χ⁴) R–2A⁸ 2B⁴.
Vol. 2: [A]1 B–Z⁸ 2A⁸(±2A5) 2B–2C⁸.
Pagination. Vol. 1: [engraved frontispiece], [i–iii] iv–v [vi–vii] viii–xlii [xliii] xliv–xlv [xlvi] xlvii–li [lii], [1–3] 4–60 [61–3] 64–90 [91–3] 94–232 [233–5] 236–93 [294–6] 297–337 [338–41] 342–75 [376]. P. xvii misnumbered 'xvi'.
Vol. 2: [i–ii], [1–2] 3–80 [81–3] 84–156 [157–8] 159–95 [196–8] 199–224 [225–6] 227–58 [259–61] 262–79 [280–3] 284–93 [294–7] 298–323 [324–7] 328–44 [345–7] 348–55 [356–7] 358–61 [362–3] 364–94 [395] 396–400. P. 144 misnumbered '145'; p. 383 misnumbered '382'; p. 400 misnumbered '440'.
Contents. Vol. 1: frontispiece, illustrating Lucy Gray, engraved by J. C. Bromley from a painting by Sir George Beaumont; dated 1 March 1815; [1] title-page; [ii] printer's imprint; [iii] 'DEDICATION.'; [vi] blank; [vii] 'PREFACE.'; [xliii] 'CONTENTS OF VOLUME I.'; [xlvi] 'CONTENTS OF VOLUME II.'; [lii] '*ERRATA AND CORRECTIONS*.'; [1] fly title: [thick-and-thin rule] | 'POEMS | REFERRING TO THE PERIOD OF CHILDHOOD.' | [thin-and-thick rule]; [2] blank; [3] text; [61] fly title: [thick-and-thin rule] | 'JUVENILE PIECES.' | [thin-and-thick rule]; [62] blank; [63] text; [91] fly title: [thick-and-thin rule] | 'POEMS | FOUNDED ON THE AFFECTIONS.' | [thin-and-thick rule]; [92] blank; [93] text; [233] fly title: [thick-and-thin rule] | 'POEMS | OF THE FANCY.' | [thin-and-thick rule]; [234] blank; [235] text; [294] blank; [295] fly title: [thick-and-thin rule] | 'POEMS | OF THE IMAGINATION.' | [thin-and-thick rule]; [296] blank; 297 text; [338] blank; [339] 'NOTES TO VOLUME I.'; [340] blank; [341] 'ESSAY, | SUPPLEMENTARY TO THE PREFACE.'; [376] printer's imprint.
Vol. 2: frontispiece, Peel Castle, engraved by S. W. Reynolds from a painting by Sir George Beaumont; [i] title-page; [ii] printer's imprint; [1] fly title: [thick-and-thin rule] | 'POEMS | OF THE IMAGINATION | CONTINUED.' | [thin-and-thick rule]; [2] blank; 3 text; [81] fly title: [thick-and-thin rule] | 'POEMS | PROCEEDING FROM SENTIMENT | AND REFLECTION.' | [thin-and-thick rule]; [82] blank; [83] text; [157] fly title: [thick-and-thin rule] | 'MISCELLANEOUS SONNETS.' | [thin-and-thick rule]; [158] blank; 159 text; [196] blank; [197] fly title: [thick-and-thin rule] | 'SONNETS | DEDICATED | TO LIBERTY. | PART FIRST.' | [thin-and-thick rule]; [198] blank; 199 text; [225] fly title: [thick-and-thin rule] | 'SONNETS | DEDICATED | TO LIBERTY. | PART SECOND.' | [thin-and-thick rule]; [226] blank; 227 text;

[259] fly title: [thick-and-thin rule] | 'POEMS | ON THE | NAMING OF PLACES.' | [thin-and-thick rule]; [260] 'ADVERTISEMENT.'; [261] text; [280] blank; [281] fly title: [thick-and-thin rule] | 'INSCRIPTIONS.' | [thin-and-thick rule]; [282] blank; [283] text; [294] blank; [295] fly title: [thick-and-thin rule] | 'POEMS | REFERRING TO THE PERIOD | OF OLD AGE.' | [thin-and-thick rule]; [296] blank; [297] text; [324] blank; [325] fly title: [thick-and-thin rule] | 'EPITAPHS | AND | ELEGIAC POEMS.' | [thin-and-thick rule]; [326] blank; [327] text; [345] fly title: [thick-and-thin rule] | 'ODE. | INTIMATIONS OF IMMORTALITY FROM | RECOLLECTIONS OF EARLY | CHILDHOOD.' | [thin-and-thick rule]; [346] three lines from My Heart Looks Up; [347] text; [356] blank; [357] 'NOTES TO VOLUME II.'; [362] blank; [363] 'PREFACE' [to the second edition of *Lyrical Ballads*]; [395] 'APPENDIX.'

$1, 2 signed, toward outer margin of foot. No running titles. Pagination centered at top. Wove paper, watermarked '1814' or 'L | 1814.' Vol. 1 sheets bulk $\frac{7}{8}$ in.; vol. 2, 1 in.

Binding. Brown calf, rebacked. The Ashley Library copy (British Museum) is in blue boards with drab backstrip; the paper labels read: 'WORDSWORTH's | POEMS: | INCLUDING | LYRICAL BALLADS. | [rule] | VOL. I[II].'.

In vol. 1, leaves Q1, 2, 3, 4 were cancelled to permit a number of revisions in Laodamia; these leaves, however, are preserved in uncancelled state in a copy at Wellesley College. When p. 225 is cancelled, the second stanza begins: 'So speaking, and by fervent love endowed'; when it is uncancelled, the second stanza begins: 'O terror! what doth she perceive?—O joy!'. When cancelled, p. 227 begins: 'Thou know'st, the Delphic oracle foretold'; when uncancelled, it begins: 'And forth I leapt upon the sandy plain'. When cancelled, p. 229 has a two-line footnote; when uncancelled, it has no footnote. When cancelled, p. 231 has a full page of text and no footnote; when uncancelled, it has a half page of text and a three-line footnote. Why in vol. 2 leaf 2A5 (pp. 361–2) was cancelled remains unknown to me; no example of that page in uncancelled state has come to my notice. With this two-volume set of 1815 is sometimes found a third volume, with a collective title-page dated 1820, made by binding together The River Duddon, Peter Bell, The Waggoner, and Thanksgiving Ode. For an example see No. 56.

31 Another copy.

$8\frac{5}{8} \times 5$ in. Diced calf, marbled end-papers. Bound in at the end of vol. 1 is Wordsworth's Thanksgiving Ode, 1816.

Dorothy Wordsworth's copy, with her signature on the fly leaves of both volumes. The text contains a few corrections, in an unidentified hand, some of them incorporated into later editions, some not.

32 Another copy.

$8\frac{7}{8} \times 5\frac{3}{8}$ in. Original blue boards, rebacked with green cloth; uncut.

Each volume is inscribed: 'F. E. Merewether, The Gift of Lady Beaumont.' Sir George Beaumont, husband of the donor, painted the originals from which the two frontispieces of this edition were engraved. Merewether was the pastor at Coleorton.

33 Another copy.

$8\frac{1}{4} \times 5\frac{1}{4}$ in. Tan calf over marbled boards, by Max Adjarian. With 'VOL. III', consisting of The River Duddon, Peter Bell, The Waggoner, and Thanksgiving Ode bound together, with the collective title-page.

1816

34 A | LETTER | TO | A FRIEND OF ROBERT BURNS: | OCCASIONED BY | AN INTENDED REPUBLICATION | OF | THE ACCOUNT OF THE LIFE OF BURNS, | BY DR. CURRIE; | AND | OF THE SELECTION MADE BY HIM FROM | HIS LETTERS. | [thick-and-thin rule] | BY WILLIAM WORDSWORTH. | [thin-and-thick rule] | *LONDON:* | PRINTED FOR LONGMAN, HURST, REES, ORME, AND BROWN, | PATERNOSTER-ROW. | [rule] | 1816.

AN

EVENING WALK.

An EPISTLE;

IN VERSE.

ADDRESSED TO A YOUNG LADY,

FROM THE

LAKES

OF THE

NORTH OF ENGLAND.

BY

W. WORDSWORTH, B. A.

Of St. JOHN's, CAMBRIDGE.

LONDON:

PRINTED FOR J. JOHNSON, St. PAUL's CHURCH-YARD.
1793.

Wordsworth's First Book.   No. 1

To S. T. Coleridge from D. Wordsworth

DESCRIPTIVE SKETCHES.

IN VERSE.

TAKEN DURING A

PEDESTRIAN TOUR

IN THE

ITALIAN, GRISON, SWISS, AND SAVOYARD

A L P S.

BY

W. WORDSWORTH, B. A.

Of St. JOHN's, CAMBRIDGE.

—Loca paſtorum deſerta atque otia dia.

LUCRET.

Caſtella in tumulis—
—Et longe ſaltus lateque vacantes.

VIRGIL.

L O N D O N:
PRINTED FOR J. JOHNSON, ST. PAUL's CHURCH-YARD.
1793.

Coleridge's Copy of *Descriptive Sketches*, the Gift of Dorothy Wordsworth. No. 2

Special imprints (at lower left of p. i). [rule] | T. Davison, Lombard-street, | Whitefriars, London.
(At center of p. 40): [thick-and-thin rule] | T. DAVISON, Lombard-street, | Whitefriars, London. | [thin-and-thick rule].

Collation ($8\frac{3}{16} \times 4\frac{15}{16}$ in.). [A]² B–C⁸ D⁴.

Pagination. [i–iv], [1] 2–37 [38–40].

Contents. [i] half title: 'A | LETTER | TO | A FRIEND OF ROBERT BURNS.' [and printer's imprint]; p. [ii] blank; [iii] title-page; [iv] blank; [1] text; [38–9] blank; [40] printer's imprint.

$1, 2 signed, toward outer margin of foot. No running titles. Pagination centered at top. Wove paper, watermarked 'W Balston & Cº | 1814', or 'W Balston & Cº | 1815', or '7 | W Balston & Cº | 1815'. Leaves have five stab holes at inner margin; bulk ⅛ in.

Binding. Three-quarter green morocco over marbled boards by Riviere. The Yale copy is stitched into drab paper wrappers. Some copies show five stab holes, some three. John Wordsworth's copy, now in the Ashley Library of the British Museum, has the drab wrappers and two leaves of advertisements dated March 1816; it is mostly unopened. (That copy is not the one described in the published catalogue of the Ashley Library.) The Amherst College copy is in gray wrappers. In addition to the watermarks listed above, two others have been noted in other copies: '5 | W Balston & Cº | 1815' and '6 | W Balston & Cº | 1815'.

First edition.

35 Another copy.

$8 \times 4\frac{15}{16}$ in. Half tan calf over marbled boards, by Max Adjarian. Leaf D4 (blank) removed. Three stab holes at inner margin.

Benjamin Bailey's copy, with his signature on the half title.

36 Another copy.

$8\frac{1}{8} \times 5\frac{1}{8}$ in. Binding removed. [A]² and D4 lacking. Three stab holes.

37 A single leaf with the following caption: 'ORIGINAL POETRY. | [thick-and-thin rule] | *SONNET*, | ADDRESSED IN A LETTER (AND PUBLISHED BY THE | POET'S PERMISSION) | TO B. R. HAYDON, PAINTER. | *BY WORDSWORTH*.'

The leaf is now $5\frac{7}{8} \times 3\frac{3}{4}$ in., having been bound into a set of Wordsworth's *Poems in Two Volumes*, 1807. The poem appeared in *The Examiner* on 31 March 1816, and in *The Champion* on that same day (not 4 February as generally stated). This leaf is printed from the same type-setting as that used for *The Champion*. The paper, however, is not newsprint. Verso blank. No other copy is known.

38 THANKSGIVING ODE, | JANUARY 18, 1816. | WITH | OTHER SHORT PIECES, | CHIEFLY REFERRING TO RECENT PUBLIC EVENTS. | [thick-and-thin rule] | BY WILLIAM WORDSWORTH. | [thin-and-thick rule] | *LONDON: | Printed by Thomas Davison, Whitefriars;* | FOR LONGMAN, HURST, REES, ORME, AND BROWN, | PATERNOSTER-ROW. | [rule] | 1816.

Special imprint (on p. 52, lower left). [rule] | T. Davison, Lombard-street, | Whitefriars, London.

Collation ($9 \times 5\frac{5}{8}$ in.). [A]⁶ B–D⁸ E².

Pagination. [i–iii] iv–ix [x–xii], [1–3] 4–21 [22–5] 26–32 [33–5] 36–52.

Contents. [i] title-page; [ii] blank; [iii] 'ADVERTISEMENT.'; [x] six-line suggestion for binding with *Poems* of 1815; [xi] 'CONTENTS.'; [xii] blank; [1] fly title: 'THANKSGIVING ODE, | *January* 18, 1816.'; [2] blank; [3] text; [22] blank; [23] fly title: 'ODE, | COMPOSED IN JANUARY 1816.'; [24] nine lines from Horace; [25] text; [33] fly title: 'MISCELLANEOUS PIECES, | REFERRING CHIEFLY TO RECENT PUBLIC EVENTS.'; [34] blank; [35] text; two leaves of advertisements dated April 1816.

$1, 2 signed, toward outer margin of foot. No running titles. Pagination centered at top. Wove paper, with various watermarks: 'W Balston & Cº | 1814', or '8 | W Balston & Cº | 1814', or 'o | W Balston & Cº | 1815', or '5 | W Balston & Cº | 1815'.

Binding. Blue-green paper wrappers, lined with white; uncut. White paper label on front cover: [thick-and-thin rule] | 'THANKSGIVING ODE. | BY | W. WORDSWORTH.' | [thin-and-thick rule].

First edition. In addition to the watermarks listed above, two others have been noted in other copies: '7 | W Balston & Cº | 1815', and '10 | W Balston & Cº | 1815'.

39 Another copy.

8⅜ × 5⅛ in. Dorothy Wordsworth's copy, bound into vol. 2 of her set of *Poems*, 1815.

40 Another copy.

8⅛ × 4¾ in. Benjamin Bailey's copy, bound with some other pieces, with his signature on the title-page and a few notes in the text.

41 Another copy.

8⅞ × 5½ in. Half brown morocco over marbled boards, by Max Adjarian; uncut.

1818

42 TWO | ADDRESSES | TO THE | FREEHOLDERS | OF | WEST-MORLAND. | [thin-and-thick rule] | 𝕶enɗal: | PRINTED BY AIREY AND BELLINGHAM. | [rule] | 1818.

Special imprint. None.
Collation (8¾ × 5½ in.). [A]⁴(A1+1) B–I⁴ K⁴(–K4).
Pagination. [i–ii], [1–3] 4–18 [19] 20–74 [75–8].
Contents. [i] title-page; [ii] blank; [1] '*ADVERTISEMENT.*'; [2] 'TO THE READER.'; [3] text; [19] 'SECOND ADDRESS.'; [75] 'NOTE.'.
$1 signed, at center of foot. Running title 'NOTE.' appears on pp. [76–8]; no running titles elsewhere. Pagination centered at top. Wove paper, some sheets without watermark, some watermarked 'WP | 1815'. Three stab holes at the inner margin. Sheets bulk 3/16 in.
Binding. Three-quarter brown-green morocco over blue paper boards; blue end-papers; uncut.

First edition. This copy contains the following corrections, perhaps in the hand of Wordsworth: p. 13, last line, 'men' changed to 'man'; p. 64, second line from bottom, 'Places, Pensions, and Taxes' is changed to 'Places and Pensions'; p. 72, last line, 'Country' is changed to 'County'.

43 Caption: 'TO THE | *FREEHOLDERS* | OF | WESTMORLAND.' | [thin-and-thick rule].

Imprint (lower right corner). *Airey and Bellingham, Printers, Kendal.* A single sheet, 16¾ × 10½ in., printed in three columns, dated 28 February 1818, and signed 'A FREEHOLDER.'. The text is a part of Wordsworth's *Two Addresses to the Freeholders of Westmorland*. The excerpt begins 'The Freeholders of past times knew, that their rights were most likely to repose in safety, under the shade of rank and property.'. The final words are '...in the situation of a Man whose words are equally to be mistrusted, whether they disavow his past, assert his present, or promise for his future proceedings.'. A photostat of the original at Yale University.

1819

44 PETER BELL, | A | 𝕮ale in 𝔙erse, | BY | WILLIAM WORDSWORTH. | [rule] | *LONDON:* | Printed by Strahan and Spottiswoode, Printers-Street; | FOR LONGMAN, HURST, REES, ORME, AND BROWN, | PATERNOSTER-ROW. | 1819.

Special imprint (on p. 88). [rule] | Printed by Strahan and Spottiswoode, | Printers-Street, London.
Collation ($7\frac{15}{16} \times 4\frac{15}{16}$ in.). [A]⁴ B–F⁸ G⁴.

Pagination. 2 pp. unnumbered, [i–iii] iv–v [vi], [1] 2–14 [15] 16–40 [41] 42–55 [56] 57–82 [83–5] 86–8. Pagination of p. iv defective in some copies.

Contents. Half title: 'PETER BELL.' [the period after 'BELL' is often missing]; verso blank; frontispiece engraved by J. C. Bromley after a painting by Sir George Beaumont, entitled '*PETER BELL.*' and dated 1 March 1819; [i] title-page; [ii] blank; [iii] dedication to Southey; [vi] blank; [1] 'PROLOGUE.'; [15] 'PART FIRST.'; [41] 'PART SECOND.'; [56] 'PART THIRD.'; [83] fly title: 'SONNETS, | SUGGESTED BY | Mr. W. WESTALL'S VIEWS OF THE CAVES, &c. | IN YORKSHIRE.'; [84] two-line note in italics; [85] text.

$1, 2, 3, 4 signed, at center of foot. Only G1 signed in Sig. G. Running titles as follows: 'DEDICATION.' pp. iv–v; 'PETER BELL.' centered, 'Prologue.' at the inner margin, pp. 2–14; 'PETER BELL.' centered, 'Part I [II, III].' at the inner margin, pp. 16–82; 'SONNETS.' centered, pp. 86–8. Pagination at outer margin of headline, without watermark.

Binding. Three-quarter crimson morocco over marbled boards; all edges gilt. The Ashley Library copy in the British Museum has drab paper wrappers, four leaves of Longman advertisements at the end, and the paper label (flaked) reading vertically: [thick-and-thin rule] | 'PETER BELL, | [*BY*] W. WORDSWORTH.' | [thin-and-thick rule].

First edition.

45 Another copy.

$8\frac{1}{16} \times 4\frac{3}{4}$ in. Benjamin Bailey's copy, bound with some miscellaneous pieces, with two marginal notes in his hand.

46 Another copy.

$8\frac{3}{4} \times 5\frac{5}{8}$ in. Quarter brown cloth over green paper boards.

47 PETER BELL, | A | 𝕮𝖆𝖑𝖊 𝖎𝖓 𝖁𝖊𝖗𝖘𝖊, | BY | WILLIAM WORDS-WORTH. | [rule] | *SECOND EDITION.* | LONDON: | Printed by Strahan and Spottiswoode, Printers-Street; | FOR LONGMAN, HURST, REES, ORME, AND BROWN, | PATERNOSTER-ROW. | 1819.

Special imprint (p. 88). [rule] | Printed by Strahan and Spottiswoode, | Printers-Street, London.
Collation ($8\frac{5}{8} \times 5\frac{11}{16}$ in.). [A]⁴ B–F⁸ G⁴.
Pagination. [i–v] vi–vii [viii], [1] 2–14 [15] 16–40 [41] 42–55 [56] 57–82 [83–5] 86–8.
Contents. [i] half title: 'PETER BELL.'; [ii] announcement of 'Benjamin the Waggoner,' to be published 'in a few days'; Frontispiece engraved by J. C. Bromley after a painting by Sir George Beaumont, entitled '*PETER BELL.*' and dated 1 March 1819; [iii] title-page; [iv] blank; [v] dedication to Southey; [viii] blank; [1] 'PROLOGUE.'; [15] 'PART FIRST.'; [41] 'PART SECOND.'; [56] 'PART THIRD.'; [83] fly title: 'SONNETS.'; [84] two-line note in italics; [85] text.
$1, 2, 3, 4 signed, at center of foot. Only G1 signed in Sig. G. Running titles as follows: 'DEDICATION.' pp. vi–vii; 'PETER BELL.' centered, 'Prologue.' at the inner margin, pp. 2–14; 'PETER BELL.' centered, 'Part I [II, III].' at the inner margin, pp. 16–40, 42–55, 57–82; 'SONNETS.' centered, pp. 86–8. Pagination in outer margin of headline. Wove paper, without watermark. Sheets bulk $\frac{1}{4}$ in.
Binding. Original drab wrappers, lined with white. Label on spine reads (bottom to top): [thick-and-thin rule] | 'PETER BELL, | *BY W. WORDSWORTH.*' | [thin-and-thick rule].

Second edition.

48 Another copy.

$8\frac{3}{4} \times 5\frac{1}{2}$ in. Half brown morocco over marbled boards, by Max Adjarian. Frontispiece lacking.

49 THE | WAGGONER, | 𝕬 𝕻𝖔𝖊𝖒. | TO WHICH ARE ADDED, | SONNETS. | BY | WILLIAM WORDSWORTH. | [thick-and-thin rule] | "What's in a NAME?" | [line of dashes] | "Brutus will start a Spirit as soon as

Cæsar!" | [thin-and-thick rule] | LONDON: | Printed by Strahan and Spottiswoode, Printers-Street; | FOR LONGMAN, HURST, REES, ORME, AND BROWN, | PATERNOSTER-ROW. | 1819.

Special imprint (on p. 68). [rule] | Printed by Strahan and Spottiswoode, | Printers-Street, London.
Collation ($8\frac{3}{4} \times 5\frac{1}{2}$ in.). [A]² B–E⁸ F².
Pagination. [i–iii] iv, [1] 2–18 [19] 20–9 [30] 31–8 [39] 40–54 [55–7] 58–68.
Contents. [i] title-page; [ii] blank; [iii] dedication to Charles Lamb; [1] text; [55] fly title: 'SONNETS.'; [56] blank; [57] text.
$1, 2, 3, 4 signed, at foot of center. Pagination set in outer margin of headline. Running titles as follows: p. iv, 'DEDICATION.'; pp. 2–54 'THE WAGGONER.' at the center and 'Canto I [II, III, IV].' at the inside margin; pp. 58–68, 'SONNETS.'; no headline on pp. [19, 30, 39]. Wove paper, without watermark. Sheets bulk $\frac{5}{16}$ in.
Binding. Drab wrappers, lined with white; uncut. Paper label on spine, flaked, set vertically: [thick-and-thin rule] | 'THE WAGGONER, | *BY W. WORDSWORTH.*' | [thin-and-thick rule].

First edition.

50 Another copy.

$8\frac{5}{8} \times 5\frac{3}{8}$ in. Half brown morocco over marbled boards, by Max Adjarian.

51 Another copy.

$8\frac{1}{16} \times 4\frac{3}{4}$ in. Benjamin Bailey's copy with marginal notes in his hand. Bound with three other pieces.

1820

52 THE | RIVER DUDDON, | A SERIES OF | 𝔖onnets: | VAUDRACOUR AND JULIA: | AND | *OTHER POEMS.* | TO WHICH IS ANNEXED, | A TOPOGRAPHICAL DESCRIPTION | OF THE | Country of the Lakes, | *IN THE NORTH OF ENGLAND.* | [thick-and-thin rule] | By WILLIAM WORDSWORTH. | [thin-and-thick rule] | LONDON: | PRINTED FOR LONGMAN, HURST, REES, ORME, AND BROWN, | PATERNOSTER-ROW. | 1820.

Special imprints (p. ii and on pp. 322 and 324). [rule] | Printed by A. and R. Spottiswoode, | Printers-Street, London.
Collation ($8\frac{13}{16} \times 5\frac{1}{2}$ in.). A⁴ B–L⁸ M⁸(±M6) N–X⁸ Y1 χ1.
Pagination. [i–vii] viii, [1–3] 4–35 [36–7] 38–9 [40–1] 42–68 [69–71] 72–86 [87] 88–91 [92] 93–5 [96] 97–8 [99] 100–1 [102] 103 [104] 105–9 [110] 111–12 [113] 114–17 [118] 119–20 [121] 122 [123] 124 [125] 126–32 [133] 134–7 [138] 139–53 [154] 155–6 [157] 158 [159–64] 165–72 [173–5] 176–86 [187] 188 [189] 190–2 [193] 194–7 [198] 199–200 [201] 202–5 [206] 207–12 [213–15] 216–321 [322–4].
Contents. (i) title-page; (ii) printer's imprint; [iii] dedication to Christopher Wordsworth; [iv] blank; [v] 'ADVERTISEMENT.'; [vi] blank; [vii] 'CONTENTS.'; [1] fly title: 'THE | RIVER DUDDON. | A SERIES OF | *SONNETS.*'; [2] six-line note in italics; [3] text; [36] blank; [37] 'POST-SCRIPT.'; [40] blank; [41] 'NOTES.'; [69] fly title: 'VAUDRACOUR AND JULIA.'; [70] four-line note in italics; [71] text; [87] miscellaneous poems; [173] fly title: 'THE PRIORESS'S TALE, | (FROM CHAUCER.)'; [174] eleven-line note in italics; [175] text; [187] miscellaneous poems; [213] fly title: 'TOPOGRAPHICAL DESCRIPTION | OF | THE COUNTRY OF THE LAKES | IN | 𝔗he 𝔑orth of 𝔈ngland.'; [214] eight-line note in italics; [215] text; [322] 'ERRATA.'; [323] collective title-page; [324] printer's imprint; plus an inserted slip bearing a title-label, and four pages of advertisements dated April 1820.
$1, 2, 3, 4 signed, at center of foot. M(M6) is signed '*M6'. Most pages have running titles and are paginated in outer margin of headline. Wove paper, without watermark. Sheets bulk 1 in.

Binding. Original drab boards; uncut. Paper label (flaked) reads: [thick-and-thin rule] | '*Wordsworth's* | RIVER | DUDDON, | &c.' | [thin-and-thick rule]. The Amherst copy has light gray boards with a dark gray backstrip, and a copy at Yale has blue boards with a tan backstrip.

First edition. Leaf M6 was cancelled probably to allow for revision; both pages (171–2) of that leaf show important variations from the manuscript. I have seen no example of the cancellandum. Inserted at the end of the text is a collective title-page (χ1, not Y2 as often said) for the use of those who wished to bind together The River Duddon, Peter Bell, The Waggoner, and Thanksgiving Ode, and thus form a third volume to be added to the two-volume *Poems* of 1815. (For an example of this procedure, and for the text of the collective title-page, see No. 56.) After this leaf there is inserted a slip upon which is printed a label for the spine of the collective volume: 'WORDSWORTH's | POEMS: | INCLUDING THE | RIVER DUDDON, | &c. &c. | [rule] | VOL. III.'

This copy is from Wordsworth's library and was presented by Mary Wordsworth to the poet's grandson John Wordsworth.

53 Another copy.

$8\frac{13}{16} \times 5\frac{1}{2}$ in. Drab boards, uncut, with paper label intact. Leaf M6 in cancelled state. Without the collective title-page and the inserted title-label.

54 Another copy.

$8\frac{3}{16} \times 5\frac{1}{8}$ in. Three-quarter brown calf over marbled boards. Leaf M6 in cancelled state. Without the collective title-page and the inserted title-label.

55 Another copy.

$8\frac{1}{16} \times 4\frac{7}{8}$ in. Modern cloth. M6 in cancelled state. Without the collective title-page and the inserted title-label.

Benjamin Bailey's copy, with a few marginal notes in his hand. Bailey removed pp. 213–322 and bound them into another volume.

56 POEMS | BY | WILLIAM WORDSWORTH: | INCLUDING | THE RIVER DUDDON; | VAUDRACOUR AND JULIA; | PETER BELL; THE WAGGONER; | A THANKSGIVING ODE; | AND | MISCELLANEOUS PIECES. | [rule] | VOL. III. | [rule] | *LONDON:* | PRINTED FOR LONGMAN, HURST, REES, ORME, AND BROWN, | PATERNOSTER-ROW. | 1820.

A bound volume of the following publications, each described separately elsewhere in this *Catalogue*:
(1) The River Duddon; (2) Peter Bell (second edition); (3) The Waggoner; (4) Thanksgiving Ode.
Collation ($8\frac{1}{4} \times 5\frac{1}{16}$ in.). The River Duddon: A⁴($\pm$A1) B–L⁸ M⁸($\pm$M6) N–X⁸ Y1.
 Peter Bell: [A]⁴(–A2) B–F⁸ G⁴.
 The Waggoner: [A]²(–A1) B–E⁸ F².
 Thanksgiving Ode: [A]⁶(–A1) B–D⁸ E².
The collective title-page transcribed above was inserted (as a separate leaf) at the end of The River Duddon for the use of those who wished to bind with it Peter Bell, The Waggoner, and Thanksgiving Ode, and thus form a third volume, to be added to their sets of *Poems*, 1815. This volume is an example. The title-page of The River Duddon has been cancelled and replaced by the collective title-page; the other separate title-pages have been removed. For the set of which this copy became vol. 3, see No. 33.
Binding. Half tan calf over marbled boards by Max Adjarian.

57 THE | LITTLE MAID | AND | The Gentleman; | OR, | WE ARE SEVEN. | [rule] | EMBELLISHED WITH ENGRAVINGS. | [rule] | YORK: | Printed by J. Kendrew, 23, Colliergate.

Special imprint (on p. 15). [rule] | J. Kendrew, Printer, York.
Collation ($3\frac{13}{16} \times 2\frac{1}{2}$ in.). Eight leaves, quired.

Pagination. [1–5] 6–15 [16].

Contents. [1] cover (recto yellow, verso white): [thick-and-thin rule] | [ornamental cut inscribed:] 'KENDREW'S EDITION | [regular type:] OF | WE ARE SEVEN.' | [thin-and-thick rule]; [2] 'FRONTISPIECE.' | [rule] | [woodcut of a man and woman] | [four lines from Isaac Watts]; [3] title-page; [4] blank; [5] text; [16] cover (recto white, verso yellow), with a woodcut of a young man and woman.

The text begins: 'A simple child dear brother Jim.' A woodcut appears on each page except the title-page and its verso. Other surviving copies are at Amherst, Yale, British Museum, and the Bodleian. The date of publication has not been established, but the British Museum copy is bound with nineteen other Kendrew chapbooks into a volume labelled '*York Chap-books 1820.*' This copy is unbound. See Helen Hughes, 'Two Wordsworth Chapbooks', *Modern Philology*, xxv (1927), 207–10.

58 Fly title: TOPOGRAPHICAL DESCRIPTION | OF | THE COUNTRY OF THE LAKES | IN | The North of England.

Pp. 213–322 of The River Duddon, 1820; excerpted from a bound volume of miscellaneous items of Wordsworth once owned by Benjamin Bailey. Rebound, 8 × 5 in.

59 LYRICAL BALLADS, | WITH | *OTHER POEMS.* | BY W. WORDSWORTH. | [thick-and-thin rule] | Quam nihil ad genium, Papiniane, tuum! | *LONDON:* | PRINTED FOR LONGMAN, HURST, REES, ORME, AND BROWNE. | 1820.

Special imprint (on p. 228). [ornamental rule] | Printed by BIGGS and Co. Bristol.

Collation ($6\frac{11}{16}$ × 4 in.). $\pi^2(\pm\pi 1)$ A–O^8 P^2.

Pagination and *Contents* are those of vol. 2 of *Lyrical Ballads*, 1800; this volume is made up of the sheets of that edition. The following variants are present: p. 64, line 2 has 'Oft had I' and line 7 has 'a wide Moor'; p. 83, line 6 has 'last days,'; p. 92, line 2 has 'the skill which he'; p. 129, line 11 has normal spacing; and p. 210 has ten lines only.

Binding. Modern green boards; uncut. Copies in original bindings show blue boards with drab backstrips (St. John's, Cambridge and Cornell), light drab boards with dark drab backstrip (Cornell), and drab boards with green cloth backstrip (Swarthmore College).

Of how or why this book came into being, nothing is known. It is not a new edition of *Lyrical Ballads*, but rather a new and dubious title-page attached to the sheets of vol. 2 only of *Lyrical Ballads* 1800. That title-page fails to indicate that only half the *Lyrical Ballads* are in fact present in the volume, and it misspells as 'Browne' the final name in the Longman partnership. In some other copies this title-page is followed by the sheets of vol. 2 of the 1805 edition. I have noted no example of its use with vol. 2 of the 1802 edition, or with vol. 1 of any edition. John Edwin Wells suggested that some person may have obtained remainder sheets of the second volume of *Lyrical Ballads* and offered them for sale under this deceptive and presumably unauthorized title-page. The evidence of bindings and inscriptions supports the date on the title-page; the books were put together about 1820. Only six copies are known to me. Of these, two have the sheets of 1800 (Amherst and Cornell); the remaining four have the sheets of 1805 (St. John's College, Cambridge; Swarthmore College; and Cornell, two copies). None of these has a printed label. See J. E. Wells, 'Wordsworth's *Lyrical Ballads*, 1820', *Philological Quarterly*, xvii (1938), 398–402; and Hugh MacDonald, '*Lyrical Ballads*', *Times Literary Supplement*, 17 March 1932, p. 202.

60 Another copy.

Imprint (on p. 248). [rule] | *R. Taylor and Co. Printers, 38, Shoe-Lane.*

Collation ($6\frac{3}{4}$ × $4\frac{1}{4}$ in.). $\pi 1$, 2 a–k^{12} l^4.

Pagination and *Contents* are those of vol. 2 of *Lyrical Ballads*, 1805; these are the sheets of that edition.

Binding. Old light drab boards, dark drab backstrip; uncut. Title inked on spine, though deteriorated, probably read 'Wordsworth's Ballads.'.

The gift of Miss Helen Darbishire.

61 Another copy.

$6\frac{3}{4}$ × $4\frac{1}{4}$ in. Like the preceding copy, this has the sheets of vol. 2 of *Lyrical Ballads*, 1805. Blue boards, drab paper backstrip; uncut.

62 THE | EXCURSION, | BEING A PORTION OF | THE RECLUSE, | 𝕬 𝔭𝔬𝔢𝔪. | BY | WILLIAM WORDSWORTH. | [rule]| *SECOND EDITION.* | [rule] | LONDON: | PRINTED FOR LONGMAN, HURST, REES, ORME, AND BROWN, | *PATERNOSTER-ROW.* | 1820.

Special imprints (p. iv). [rule] | Printed by A. and R. Spottiswoode, | Printers-Street, London.
(P. 452). [rule] | Printed by A. and R. Spottiswoode, | Printer's Street, London.
Collation ($8\frac{13}{16} \times 5\frac{1}{2}$ in.). A⁸ *a*² B–2F⁸ 2G².
Pagination. [i–vii] viii–xiv [xv] xvi–xx, [1–3] 4–49 [50–1] 52–93 [94–5] 96–140 [141] 142–200 [201] 202–47 [248–9] 250–308 [309] 310–57 [358–9] 360–86 [387] 388–423 [424–5] 426–52.
Contents. [i–ii] blank; [iii] title-page; [iv] printer's imprint; [v] dedication to the Earl of Lonsdale; [vi] blank; [vii] 'PREFACE.'; [xv] 'SUMMARY OF CONTENTS.'; [1] fly title: [thick-and-thin rule] | 'THE EXCURSION.' | [thin-and-thick rule]; [2] blank; [3] 'BOOK FIRST.'; [50] blank; [51] 'BOOK THE SECOND.'; [94] blank; [95] 'BOOK THE THIRD.'; [141] 'BOOK THE FOURTH.'; [201] 'BOOK THE FIFTH.'; [248] blank; [249] 'BOOK THE SIXTH.'; [309] 'BOOK THE SEVENTH.'; [858] blank; [359] 'BOOK THE EIGHTH.'; [387] 'BOOK THE NINTH.'; [424] blank; [425] 'NOTES.'. Preceding p. i are 8 pp. of Longman advertisements dated December 1821.
$1, 2, 3, 4 signed, at center of foot. Running titles throughout. Pagination set in outer margin of headline. Wove paper, without watermark. Sheets bulk 1 in.
Binding. Drab boards; uncut. Paper label reads: [thick-and-thin rule] | 'THE | EXCURSION[ ] | A POEM, | BY | [W.] WORDSWORTH[ ] | [rule] | *Second Edition.*' | [thin-and-thick rule].
Second edition.

63 Another copy.

$8\frac{1}{4} \times 5\frac{5}{16}$ in. Green morocco over marbled boards. Leaf [A]1 (a blank) lacking.

64 THE | MISCELLANEOUS | POEMS | OF | WILLIAM WORDS-WORTH. | [rule] | 𝔍𝔫 𝔉𝔬𝔲𝔯 𝔙𝔬𝔩𝔲𝔪𝔢𝔰. | [rule] | Vol. I[etc.]. | LONDON: | PRINTED FOR LONGMAN, HURST, REES, ORME, AND BROWN, | PATERNOSTER-ROW. | 1820.

Special imprints (verso of first leaf and at end of text of each volume). [rule] | Printed by A. and R. Spottiswoode, | Printers-Street, London.
Collation ($6\frac{7}{16} \times 3\frac{11}{16}$ in.). Vol. 1: A¹² *a*¹² B–O¹² P⁴(–P4) χ1.
  Vol. 2: [A]⁴ B–P¹² Q⁶.
  Vol. 3: A⁶ B–P¹² Q1.
  Vol. 4: [A]² *a*² B–O¹² P¹⁰.
Pagination. Vol. 1: [i–iii] iv–v [vi–ix] x–xliv [xlv] xlvi–xlvii [xlviii], [1–3] 4–61 [62–4] 65 [66–8] 69–88 [89–91] 92 [93–4] 95–140 [141–2] 143–278 [279–80] 281–317 [318–20].
  Vol. 2: [i–v] vi–vii [viii], [1–5] 6 [7] 8–113 [114–16] 117–275 [276–9] 280–1 [282] 283–342 [343] 344–7 [348]. P. 24 misnumbered '4'.
  Vol. 3: [i–v] vi–xi [xii], [1–4] 5–99 [100] 101–12 [113–14] 115–26 [127–8] 129–61 [162–4] 165–201 [202–4] 205–30 [231–2] 233–71 [272–5] 276–338. P. 179 misnumbered '79' in some copies.
  Vol. 4: [i–iii] iv–viii, [1–3] 4–6 [7] 8–37 '39' (for 38) '40' (for 39) [40–1] 42–3 [44] 45–72 [73–4] 75–170 [171–2] 173–92 [193–5] 196–217 [218–21] 222–46 [247–9] 250–72 [273–5] 276–84 [285–7] 288–324 [325] 326–31 [332]. P. 259 misnumbered '229'; between pp. 37 and 42 the pagination is confused.
Contents. Vol. 1: Frontispiece illustrating Lucy Gray, engraved by J. C. Bromley from a painting by Sir George Beaumont; [i] title-page; [ii] printer's imprint; [iii] dedication to Sir George Beaumont; [vi] blank; [vii] 'ADVERTISEMENT.'; [viii] blank; [ix] 'PREFACE.'; [xlv] 'CONTENTS OF VOLUME I.'; [xlviii] blank; [1] fly title: [thick-and-thin rule] | 'POEMS | REFERRING TO CHILDHOOD AND EARLY | YOUTH.' | [thin-and-thick rule]; [2] blank; [3] text; [62] blank; [63] fly title: [thick-and-thin rule] | 'JUVENILE PIECES.' | [thin-and-thick rule]; [64] eleven-line note in italics; 65 introductory poem; [66] blank; [67] fly title: 'AN EVENING WALK, | ADDRES-SED TO | *A YOUNG LADY,* | FROM THE LAKES OF THE NORTH OF ENGLAND.'; [68] 'ARGUMENT.'; 69 text; [89] fly title: 'DESCRIPTIVE SKETCHES | TAKEN DURING | *A PEDESTRIAN TOUR* | AMONG | THE ALPS.'; [90] blank; [91] dedication to Robert Jones;

[93] 'ARGUMENT.'; [94] blank; 95 text; [141] fly title: [thick-and-thin rule] | 'POEMS | FOUNDED ON THE AFFECTIONS.' | [thin-and-thick rule]; [142] blank; [143] text; [279] fly title: [thick-and-thin rule] | 'VAUDRACOUR AND JULIA.' | [thin-and-thick rule]; [280] four-line note in italics; 281 text; 317 'NOTE.'; [318] blank; [319] 'ERRATA.'; [320] blank.

Vol. 2: [i] half title: 'THE | MISCELLANEOUS | POEMS | OF | WILLIAM WORDS-WORTH. | [rule] | VOL. II.'; [ii] printer's imprint; frontispiece illustrating Peter Bell, engraved by J. C. Bromley from a painting by Sir George Beaumont; [iii] title-page; [iv] blank; [v] 'CON-TENTS OF VOLUME II.'; [viii] blank; [1] fly title: [thick-and-thin rule] | 'POEMS | OF THE FANCY.' | [thin-and-thick rule]; [2] blank; [3] fly title: 'THE WAGGONER.'; [4] blank; [5] dedication to Charles Lamb; [7] text; [114] blank; [115] fly title: [thick-and-thin rule] | 'POEMS | OF THE IMAGINATION.' | [thin-and-thick rule]; [116] blank; 117 text; [276] blank; [277] fly title: 'PETER BELL, | A TALE.'; [278] blank; [279] dedication to Robert Southey; [282] blank; 283 text; [343] 'NOTES TO VOLUME II.'; [348] blank.

Vol. 3: [i] half title; [ii] printer's imprint; frontispiece illustrating The White Doe of Rylstone, engraved by J. C. Bromley from a painting by Sir George Beaumont; [iii] title-page; [iv] blank; [v] 'CONTENTS OF VOLUME III.'; [xii] blank; [1] fly title: 'THE | WHITE DOE | OF | RYLSTONE; | OR | *THE FATE OF THE NORTONS*.'; [2] six-line note in italics; [3] twelve-line quotation from Bacon; [4] introductory sonnet; 5 dedicatory poem to Mary Wordsworth; 9 text; [100] 'NOTES.'; [113] fly title: [thick-and-thin rule] | 'THE PRIORESS'S TALE. | (FROM CHAUCER.) | [thin-and-thick rule]; [114] twelve-line note in italics; 115 text; [127] fly title: [thick-and-thin rule] | MISCELLANEOUS SONNETS. | PART FIRST.' | [thin-and-thick rule]; [128] blank; 129 text; [162] blank; [163] fly title: [thick-and-thin rule] | 'MISCELLANEOUS SONNETS. | PART SECOND.' | [thin-and-thick rule]; [164] blank; 165 text; [202] blank; [203] fly title: [thick-and-thin rule] | 'SONNETS | DEDICATED | TO LIBERTY. | PART FIRST.' | [thin-and-thick rule]; [204] blank; 205 text; [231] fly title: [thick-and-thin rule] | 'SONNETS DEDICATED | TO LIBERTY. | PART SECOND.' | [thin-and-thick rule]; [232] blank; 233 text; [272] blank; [273] fly title: 'ODE | COMPOSED IN JANUARY, 1816.'; [274] nine-line quotation from Horace; [275] 'ADVERTISEMENT.'; 281 text; 299 'ESSAY; | SUPPLEMENTARY TO THE PREFACE.'.

Vol. 4: Frontispiece illustrating Peel Castle, engraved by S. W. Reynolds from a painting by Sir George Beaumont; [i] title-page; [ii] printer's imprint; [iii] 'CONTENTS OF VOLUME IV.'; [1] fly title: 'THE | RIVER DUDDON. | A SERIES OF | *SONNETS*.'; [2] six-line note in italics; [3] dedication to Christopher Wordsworth; [7] text; [40] blank; [41] 'POSTSCRIPT.'; [44] 'NOTES.'; [73] fly title: [thick-and-thin rule] | 'POEMS | OF SENTIMENT AND REFLEC-TION.' | [thin-and-thick rule]; [74] blank; 75 text; [171] fly title: [thick-and-thin rule] | 'POEMS | ON THE NAMING OF PLACES.' | [thin-and-thick rule]; [172] 'ADVERTISEMENT.'; 173 text; [193] fly title: [thick-and-thin rule] | 'INSCRIPTIONS.' | [thin-and-thick rule]; [194] blank; [195] text; [218] blank; [219] fly title: [thick-and-thin rule] | 'POEMS | REFERRING TO THE PERIOD OF OLD AGE.' | [thin-and-thick rule]; [220] blank; [221] text; [247] fly title: [thick-and-thin rule] | 'EPITAPHS | AND | ELEGIAC POEMS.' | [thin-and-thick rule]; [248] blank; [249] text; [273] fly title: [thick-and-thin rule] | 'ODE. | INTIMATIONS OF IMMORTALITY FROM | RECOLLECTIONS OF EARLY | CHILDHOOD.' | [thin-and-thick rule]; [274] three lines of verse ('The Child is Father of the Man'); [275] text; [285] 'NOTES.'; [286] blank; [287] 'PREFACE' [to *Lyrical Ballads*, 1800]; [325] 'APPENDIX.'; [332] blank.

$1, 2, 3, 4, 5, 6 signed, at center of foot. Pagination in outer margin of headline when running titles are present; elsewhere centered at top. Wove paper, without watermark. Sheets of each volume bulk ¾ in.

Binding. Three-quarter brown calf over marbled boards. The Swarthmore copy is in blue boards, with paper labels. A copy at Yale is in drab boards, with labels. The labels read: [thick-and-thin rule] | '*Wordsworth's* | MISCELLANEOUS | POEMS. | [rule] | *In four volumes*. | VOL. I [etc.].' | [thin-and-thick rule].

Presentation set from Wordsworth to W. Strickland Cookson, with an inscription in each volume.

1822

65 A | DESCRIPTION | OF THE | SCENERY OF THE LAKES | IN | *THE NORTH OF ENGLAND*. | [rule] | THIRD EDITION, | (NOW FIRST PUBLISHED SEPARATELY) | *WITH ADDITIONS*, | AND

ILLUSTRATIVE REMARKS UPON THE | 𝔖𝔠𝔢𝔫𝔢𝔯𝔶 𝔬𝔣 𝔱𝔥𝔢 𝔄𝔩𝔭𝔰. | [rule] | By WILLIAM WORDSWORTH. | [rule] | *LONDON:* | PRINTED FOR | LONGMAN, HURST, REES, ORME, AND BROWN, | PATERNOSTER-ROW. | 1822.

Special imprints (pp. ii and on 156). LONDON: | Printed by A. & R. Spottiswoode, | New-Street-Square.
Collation (6½ × 4 in.). [A]² B–G¹² H⁶.
Pagination. [i–iii] iv, [1] 2–156.
Contents. Folding map; [i] title-page; [ii] printer's imprint; [iii] 'CONTENTS.'; [1] text.
\$1, 2, 3, 4, 5, 6 signed, at center of foot. Headlines throughout. Pagination set in outer margin of headline. Wove paper, without watermark. Sheets bulk $\frac{7}{16}$ in.
Binding. Original green paper wrappers; front cover reproduces the title-page within a border of rules; back cover contains Longman's advertisement. Title printed vertically on spine: '*WORDSWORTH*[ ]| DESCRIPTION OF THE LAKES[ ]'; back flaked.

First separate edition. The work had first appeared as the anonymous Introduction of Joseph Wilkinson's *Select Views in Cumberland, Westmoreland, and Lancashire*, 1810; and had been reprinted as 'A Topographical Description of the Country of the Lakes in the North of England' in Wordsworth's *The River Duddon*, 1820.

66 Another copy.

6½ × 4 in. Green wrappers, rebacked.

67 ECCLESIASTICAL | SKETCHES | BY | WILLIAM WORDSWORTH. | [rule] | *LONDON:* | PRINTED FOR | LONGMAN, HURST, REES, ORME, AND BROWN, | PATERNOSTER-ROW. | 1822.

Special imprints (pp. ii and 123). LONDON: | Printed by A. & R. Spottiswoode, | New-Street-Square.
Collation (8⅞ × 5½ in.). A⁶(–A6) B–H⁸ I⁴ K².
Pagination. [i–v] vi [vii] viii–x, [1–3] 4–40 [41–3] 44–78 [79–81] 82–108 [109–11] 112–23 [124]+4 pp. advertisements.
Contents. [i] half-title: 'ECCLESIASTICAL | SKETCHES.'; [ii] printer's imprint; [iii] title-page; [iv] blank; [v] 'ADVERTISEMENT.'; [vii] 'CONTENTS.'; [1] fly title: 'ECCLESIASTICAL | SKETCHES. | PART I. | FROM THE INTRODUCTION OF CHRISTIANITY INTO BRITAIN, | TO THE CONSUMMATION OF THE PAPAL DOMINION.'; [2] blank; [3] text; [41] fly title: 'ECCLESIASTICAL | SKETCHES. | PART II. | TO THE CLOSE OF THE TROUBLES IN THE REIGN | OF CHARLES I.'; [42] blank; [43] text; [79] fly title: 'ECCLE-SIASTICAL | SKETCHES. | PART III. | FROM THE RESTORATION, TO THE PRESENT TIMES.'; [80] blank; [81] text; [109] fly title: 'NOTES.'; [110] blank; [111] text; [124] blank; 4 pp. Longman's advertisements, dated March 1822.
\$1, 2, 3, 4 signed, at center of foot. Running titles as follows: p. vi 'ADVERTISEMENT.'; pp. viii–x 'CONTENTS.'; pp. 4–40, 44–78, 82–108 'ECCLESIASTICAL SKETCHES.'; pp. 112–23 'NOTES.'. Pagination set at outer margin of headline. Wove paper, without watermark. Sheets bulk ¼ in.
Binding. Drab boards; uncut. Paper label on spine, flaked, reads vertically: [thick-and-thin rule] | '*WORDSWORTH'S* | ECCLESIASTICAL SKETCHES.' | [thin-and-thick rule]. A copy at Yale has blue boards with drab backstrip.

First edition.

68 Another copy.

8⅛ × 5$\frac{1}{16}$ in. Three-quarter tan calf over marbled boards, by Max Adjarian. Without the advertisements.

69 Another copy.

8¼ × 5 in. Half brown morocco over brown cloth. Without the half title and advertisements.

70 MEMORIALS | OF A | TOUR ON THE CONTINENT, | 1820. | [rule] | By WILLIAM WORDSWORTH. | [rule] | LONDON: | PRINTED FOR |

LONGMAN, HURST, REES, ORME, AND BROWN, | PATERNOSTER-ROW. | 1822.

Special imprints (p. ii and on 103). LONDON: | Printed by A. & R. Spottiswoode, | New-Street-Square.
Collation ($8\frac{13}{16} \times 5\frac{7}{16}$ in.). [A]⁴ B–G⁸ H⁴.
Pagination. [i–vii] viii, [1] 2–67 [68–71] 72–9 [80–3] 84–91 [92–4] 95–100 [101] 102–3 [104].
Contents. [i] half title: 'MEMORIALS.'; [ii] printer's imprint; [iii] title-page; [iv] blank; [v] 'DEDI-CATION.'; [vi] blank; [vii] 'CONTENTS.'; [1] text; [68] blank; [69] fly title: 'TO ENTER-PRIZE.'; [70] two-line note in italics; [71] text; [80] blank; [81] fly title: 'NOTES.'; [82] blank; [83] text; [92] blank; [93] fly title: 'DESULTORY STANZAS.'; [94] blank; 95 text; [101] 'NOTES.'; [104] blank.
$1, 2, 3, 4 signed, at center of foot, or to left of center. Running titles as follows: viii 'CONTENTS.'; 1–67 none; 72–9 'TO ENTERPRIZE.'; 84–91 'NOTES.'; 96–100 'DESULTORY STANZAS.'; 102–3 'NOTES.'. Pagination set at outer margin of headline when running title present; otherwise centered at top. Wove paper, without watermark. Sheets bulk $\frac{3}{16}$ in.
Binding. Drab boards; uncut. With the paper label, which reads: [thick-and-thin rule] | '*WORDS-WORTH'S* MEMORIALS | OF A TOUR ON THE CONTINENT.' | [thin-and-thick rule]. A copy at Amherst has blue boards and gray backstrip, with label; one at Harvard has gray-green boards, with label; one at Yale has drab boards, without label.

First edition. Inserted before the front fly leaf is a two-page advertisement for the *Literary Gazette*.

71 Another copy.

$8\frac{5}{8} \times 5$ in. Three-quarter green calf over marbled boards. Half title lacking.

72 Another copy.

$8\frac{3}{4} \times 5\frac{7}{16}$ in. Full brown calf. Half title lacking.

1823

73 A | DESCRIPTION | OF THE | SCENERY OF THE LAKES | IN | *THE NORTH OF ENGLAND.* | [rule] | FOURTH EDITION, | (NOW FIRST PUBLISHED SEPARATELY) | *WITH ADDITIONS*, | AND ILLUSTRATIVE REMARKS UPON THE | 𝔖𝔠𝔢𝔫𝔢𝔯𝔶 𝔬𝔣 𝔱𝔥𝔢 𝔄𝔩𝔭𝔰. | [rule] | By WILLIAM WORDSWORTH. | [rule] | *LONDON:* | PRINTED FOR | LONGMAN, HURST, REES, ORME, AND BROWN, | PATERNOSTER-ROW. | 1823.

Special imprint (pp. ii and on 144). LONDON: | Printed by A. & R. Spottiswoode, | New-Street-Square.
Collation ($5\frac{15}{16} \times 3\frac{11}{16}$ in.). [A]² B–G¹².
Pagination. [i–iii] iv, [1] 2–144.
Contents. Folding map; [i] title-page; [ii] printer's imprint; [iii] 'CONTENTS.'; [1] text.
$1, 2, 3, 4, 5, 6 signed, at center of foot. Headlines throughout. Pagination in outer margin of headline. Wove paper, without watermark. Sheets bulk $\frac{5}{16}$ in.
Binding. Three-quarter plum calf over marbled boards; ivory end-papers. The Ashley Library copy is in reddish wrappers; the front cover carries the same copy as the title-page and the back cover carries advertisements. A copy at Yale has drab wrappers, printed as above, with a vertical label on the spine which, though flaked, suggests the following reading: '*WORDSWORTH'S* | DESCRIPTION OF THE LAKES.' No copy with a perfect label is known to me.

Second separate edition; reset, revised, and enlarged.

1824

74 THE | POETICAL WORKS | OF | WILLIAM WORDSWORTH. | [rule] | IN FOUR VOLUMES. | [rule] | VOL. I [etc.]. | BOSTON: | PUBLISHED BY CUMMINGS, HILLIARD & CO. | [rule] | HILLIARD AND MET-CALF, PRINTERS. | 1824.

Special imprints (last p. of vols. 1, 2, 3). UNIVERSITY PRESS,—CAMBRIDGE. | *Hilliard and Metcalf, Printers.*

Collation (7¾ × 4½ in.): Vol. 1: *a–i*⁶ *k*⁴ 1–26⁶ 27⁴.

Vol. 2: π⁴ 1–30⁶ 31–32².

Vol. 3: *a*⁶ 1–32⁶.

Vol. 4: π² 1–32⁶.

Pagination. Vol. 1: [i–iii] iv [v] vi–xxvii [xxviii] xxix–lxviii [lxix] lxx–cv [cvi] cvii–cxii [cxiii] cxiv–cxv [cxvi], [1–3] 4–43 [44–6] 47 [48–50] 51–65 [66–9] 70 [71–2] 73–108 [109–10] 111–207 [208–10] 211–38 [239–45] 246–319 [320].

Vol. 2: [i–iii] iv–viii, [1–3] 4–112 [113–15] 116–59 [160–4] 165–7 [168] 169–236 [237] 238–49 [250–2] 253–61 [262–4] 265–86 [287–8] 289–313 [314–16] 317–34 [335–6] 337–63 [364–8].

Vol. 3: [i–iii] iv–xii, [1–3] 4–7 [8] 9–21 [22–4] 25–8 [29] 30–50 [51] 52–3 [54–5] 56–82 [83–4] 85–150 [151–3] 154–66 [167–8] 169–82 [183–4] 185–202 [203–4] 205–19 [220–2] 223–30 [231–3] 234 [235] 236–60 [261] 262–85 [286–7] 288–305 [306–7] 308–17 [318–23] 324–62 [363–5] 366–70 [371] 372–81 [382] 383–4.

Vol. 4: 4 pp. unnumbered, [i–v] vi–xi [xii–xiii] xiv–xix [xx], [21] 22–57 [58–9] 60–92 [93] 94–128 [129] 130–76 [177] 178–213 [214–15] 216–61 [262–3] 264–301 [302–3] 304–24 [325] 326–53 [354–5] 356–82 [383–4].

Contents. Vol. 1: inserted slip, 'NOTE OF THE PRINTERS.', announcing that 'the latest English edition has been carefully followed'; [i] title-page; [ii] blank; [iii] dedication to Sir George Beaumont; [v] 'PREFACE.'; [xxviii] blank; xxix 'ESSAY;'; [lxix] 'PREFACE' [to *Lyrical Ballads*, 1800]; [cvi] 'APPENDIX.'; cxiii 'CONTENTS OF VOLUME I.'; [cxvi] blank; [1] fly title: [rule] | 'POEMS | REFERRING TO CHILDHOOD AND EARLY | YOUTH.' | [rule]; [2] blank; [3] text; [44] blank; [45] fly title: [rule] | 'JUVENILE PIECES.' | [rule]; [46] nine-line note in italics; 47 introductory poem; [48] blank; [49] fly title: 'AN EVENING WALK, | ADDRESSED | TO A YOUNG LADY, | FROM THE LAKES OF THE NORTH OF ENGLAND.'; [50] 'ARGUMENT.'; 51 text; [66] blank; [67] fly title: 'DESCRIPTIVE SKETCHES | TAKEN DURING | *A PEDESTRIAN TOUR* | AMONG | THE ALPS.'; [68] blank; [69] dedication to Robert Jones; [71] 'ARGUMENT.'; [72] blank; [73] text; [109] fly title: [rule] | 'POEMS | FOUNDED ON THE AFFECTIONS.' | [rule]; [110] blank; [111] text; [208] blank; [209] fly title: [rule] | 'VAUDRACOUR AND JULIA.' | [rule]; [210] four-line note in italics; 211 text; [239] fly title: [rule] | 'POEMS | OF THE FANCY.' | [rule]; [240] blank; [241] fly title: 'THE WAGGONER.'; [242] blank; [243] dedication to Charles Lamb; [244] blank; [245] text; [320] 'NOTE.'.

Vol. 2: [i] title-page; [ii] blank; [iii] 'CONTENTS OF VOLUME II.'; [1] fly title: [rule] | 'POEMS | OF THE IMAGINATION.' | [rule]; [2] blank; [3] text; [113] fly title: 'PETER BELL, | A TALE.'; [114] blank; [115] dedication to Southey; 117 text; [160] blank; [161] fly title: 'THE | WHITE DOE | OF | RYLSTONE; | OR | *THE FATE OF THE NORTONS.*'; [162] six-line note in italics; [163] eleven-line quotation from Bacon; [164] introductory sonnet; 165 dedicatory poem to Mary Wordsworth, in italic; [168] blank; 169 text; [237] 'NOTES.'; [250] blank; [251] fly title: [rule] | 'THE PRIORESS'S TALE. | (FROM CHAUCER.)' | [rule]; [252] twelve-line note in italics; 253 text; [262] blank; [263] fly title: [rule] | 'MISCELLANEOUS SONNETS. | PART FIRST.' | [rule]; [264] blank; 265 text; [287] fly title: [rule] | 'MISCELLANEOUS SONNETS. | PART SECOND.' | [rule]; [288] blank; 289 text; [314] fly title: [rule] | 'SONNETS | DEDICATED | TO LIBERTY. | PART FIRST.' | [rule]; [316] blank; 317 text; [335] fly title: [rule] | 'SONNETS | DEDICATED | TO LIBERTY. | PART SECOND.'; [336] blank; 337 text; [364] 'END OF VOL. II.'; [365] 'NOTES TO VOLUME II.'. Final gathering, pp. [365–8], lacking in this copy.

Vol. 3: [i] title-page; [ii] blank; [iii] 'CONTENTS OF VOLUME III.'; [1] fly title: 'ODE | COMPOSED IN JANUARY, 1816.'; [2] nine-line quotation from Horace; [3] 'ADVERTISEMENT.'; [8] blank; 9 text; [22] blank; [23] fly title: 'THE | RIVER DUDDON. | A SERIES OF | *SONNETS.*'; [24] six-line note in italics; 25 dedicatory poem in italics to Christopher Wordsworth; [29] text; [51] 'POSTSCRIPT.'; [54] blank; [55] 'NOTES.'; [83] fly title: [rule] | 'POEMS | OF SENTIMENT AND REFLECTION.' | [rule]; [84] blank; 85 text; [151] fly title: [rule] | 'POEMS |

ON THE NAMING OF PLACES.' | [rule]; [152] 'ADVERTISEMENT.'; [153] text; [167] fly title: [rule] | 'INSCRIPTIONS.' | [rule]; [168] blank; 169 text; [183] fly title: [rule] | 'POEMS | REFERRING TO THE PERIOD OF OLD AGE.' | [rule]; [184] blank; 185 text; [203] fly title: [rule] | 'EPITAPHS | AND | ELEGIAC POEMS.' | [rule]; [204] blank; [205] text; [220] blank; [221] fly title: [rule] | 'ODE. | INTIMATIONS OF IMMORTALITY FROM RECOLLEC- TIONS | OF EARLY CHILDHOOD.' | [rule]; [222] three lines of verse; 223 text; [231] fly title: [rule] | 'ECCLESIASTICAL SKETCHES.' | [rule]; [232] blank; [233] 'ADVERTISEMENT.'; [235] text; [286] blank; [287] text; [306] blank; [307] 'NOTES TO PART I.'; [318] blank; [319] fly title: [rule] | 'MEMORIALS | OF A | TOUR ON THE CONTINENT, | 1820.' | [rule]; [320] blank; [321] 'DEDICATION.'; [322] blank; [323] text; [363] fly title: [rule] | 'TO ENTER- PRIZE.' | [rule]; [364] two-line note in italics; [365] text; [371] 'NOTES.'; 378 'DESULTORY STANZAS'; [382] 'NOTES.'.

    Vol. 4: title-page, verso blank; blank leaf; [i] fly title: 'THE | EXCURSION, | BEING A PORTION OF | THE RECLUSE, | A Poem.'; [ii] blank; [iii] dedication to the Earl of Lonsdale; [iv] blank; [v] 'PREFACE.'; [xii] blank; [xiii] 'SUMMARY OF CONTENTS.'; [xx] blank; [21] 'BOOK FIRST.'; [58] blank; [59] 'BOOK THE SECOND.'; [93] 'BOOK THE THIRD.'; [129] 'BOOK THE FOURTH.'; [177] 'BOOK THE FIFTH.'; [214] blank; [215] 'BOOK THE SIXTH.'; [262] blank; [263] 'BOOK THE SEVENTH.'; [302] blank; [303] 'BOOK THE EIGHTH.'; [325] 'BOOK THE NINTH.'; [354] blank; [355] 'NOTES.'; [383–4] blank.

$1, 2 signed, at center or sometimes at left of center of foot. $3 signed with the signature designation preceded by an asterisk. Running titles throughout. Pagination set in outer margin of headline. Wove paper, without watermark. Vol. 1 sheets bulk $1\frac{3}{16}$ in.; vol. 2, 1 in.; vol. 3, $1\frac{1}{8}$ in.; vol. 4, 1 in. *Binding.* Original drab boards; rebacked with white cloth; uncut.

First American collective edition. According to the 'NOTE OF THE PRINTERS.' inserted on a slip in vol. 1, 'In printing this work, the latest English edition has been carefully followed; and whatever is peculiar in Orthography, Punctuation, and the Use of Capital Letters, is copied from the same without change.'

75 Another copy.

$7 \times 4\frac{3}{8}$ in. Three-quarter black calf over black cloth.

1827

76 THE | POETICAL WORKS | OF | WILLIAM WORDSWORTH. | [rule] | In Five Volumes. | [rule] | VOL. I [etc.]. | LONDON: | PRINTED FOR | LONGMAN, REES, ORME, BROWN, AND GREEN, | PATERNOSTER- ROW. | 1827.

Special imprints (verso of title-page and on final page of each vol.). LONDON: | Printed by A. & R. Spottiswoode, | New-Street-Square.
Collation ($6\frac{7}{16} \times 3\frac{7}{8}$ in.). Vol. 1: A¹² a¹² B–P¹² Q¹⁰.
    Vol. 2: A⁴ B–R¹² S² T².
    Vol. 3: A⁶ a² B–U¹².
    Vol. 4: A⁴ B–R¹² S⁸(–S8).
    Vol. 5: A⁶(±A3.4) a⁴(–a4) B–S¹² T⁸.
Pagination. Vol. 1: [i–ix] x–xliv [xlv] xlvi–xlvii [xlviii], [1–3] 4–47 [48–50] 51–71 [72–5] 76–120 [121–2] 123–268 [269–71] 272–312 [313–14] 315–54 [355–6]. No pagination on p. 207.
    Vol. 2: [i–iii] iv–viii, [1–3] 4–39 [40–2] 43–186 [187–9] 190–1 [192] 193–251 [252–5] 256–301 [302–4] 305–49 [350–1] 352–6 [357] 358–91 [392]. Pagination defectively printed on p. 82.
    Vol. 3: [i–v] vi–xvi, [1–2] 3–55 [56–8] 59–78 [79–80] 81–100 [101–2] 103–23 [124–6] 127–55 [156–8] 159–233 [234–5] 236 [237–40] 241–313 [314–15] 316–22 [323–5] 326 [327] 328–64 [365–6] 367–405 [406–8] 409–44 [445] 446–55 [456]. No pagination on p. 62; defectively printed pagination on pp. 335 and 340.
    Vol. 4: [i–iii] iv–vii [viii], [1–3] 4–5 [6–7] 8–103 [104–5] 106–16 [117–19] 120–2 [123] 124–56 [157] 158 [159] 160–85 [186–8] 189–295 [296–8] 299–318 [319–21] 322–55 [356–7] 358–89 [390–1] 392–7 [398]. No pagination on p. 15.

Vol. 5: [i–ix] x–xvi [xvii–xviii], [1–3] 4–43 [44–6] 47–84 [85–6] 87–128 [129–30] 131–85 [186–8] 189–230 [231–2] 233–82 [283–4] 285–328 [329–30] 331–56 [357–8] 359–91 [392–3] 394–421 [422]. Lacking: [423–4].

Contents. Vol. 1: [i] title-page; [ii] printer's imprint; [iii] dedication to Sir George Beaumont; [vi] blank; [vii] 'ADVERTISEMENT.'; [viii] blank; [ix] 'PREFACE.'; [xlv] 'CONTENTS OF VOLUME I.'; [xlviii] blank; inserted slip: 'ERRATA IN VOL. I.'; [1] half title: [rule] | 'POEMS | REFERRING TO THE PERIOD OF CHILDHOOD.' | [rule]; [2] blank; [3] text; [48] blank; [49] fly title: [rule] | 'JUVENILE PIECES.' | [rule]; [50] eleven-line note in italics; 51 introductory poem; 52 text; [72] blank; [73] fly title: 'DESCRIPTIVE SKETCHES | TAKEN DURING | *A PEDESTRIAN TOUR* | AMONG | THE ALPS.'; [74] blank; [75] dedication to Robert Jones; 77 text; [121] fly title: [rule] | 'POEMS | FOUNDED ON THE AFFECTIONS.' | [rule]; [122] blank; 123 text; [269] fly title: [rule] | 'THE WAGGONER.' | [rule]; [270] blank; [271] dedication to Charles Lamb; 273 text; [313] fly title: [rule] | 'POEMS | OF THE FANCY.' [no closing rule]; [314] blank; 315 text; [355–6] blank.

Vol. 2: [i] title-page; [ii] printer's imprint; [iii] 'CONTENTS OF VOLUME II.'; inserted slip: 'ERRATA IN VOL. II.'; [1] fly title: [rule] | 'POEMS OF THE FANCY | *CONTINUED.*' | [rule]; [2] blank; [3] text; [40] blank; [41] fly title: [rule] | 'POEMS | OF THE IMAGINATION.' | [rule]; [42] blank; 43 text; [187] fly title: [rule] | 'PETER BELL, | A TALE. | What's in a *Name?* | [row of asterisks] | Brutus will start a Spirit as soon as Cæsar!' | [rule]; [188] blank; [189] dedication to Southey; [192] blank; 193 text; [252] blank; [253] fly title: [rule] | 'MISCELLANEOUS SONNETS. | PART FIRST.' | [rule]; [254] blank; [255] text; [302] blank; [303] fly title: [rule] | 'MISCELLANEOUS SONNETS. | PART SECOND.' | [rule]; [304] blank; 305 text; [350] blank; [351] 'NOTES TO VOLUME II.'; [357] 'ESSAY, | SUPPLEMENTARY TO THE PREFACE.'; [392] printer's imprint.

Vol. 3: [i] half title: 'WORDSWORTH'S | POETICAL WORKS. | VOL. III.'; [ii] printer's imprint; [iii] title-page; [iv] blank; [v] 'CONTENTS OF VOLUME III.'; inserted slip: 'ERRATA IN VOL. III.'; [1] fly title: [no opening rule] 'MEMORIALS | OF | A TOUR IN SCOTLAND, | 1803.' | [rule]; [2] blank; 3 text; [56] nine-line note; [57] fly title: [rule] | 'MEMORIALS | OF | A TOUR IN SCOTLAND. | 1814.' | [rule]; [58] blank; 59 text; [79] fly title: [rule] | 'POEMS | ON THE NAMING OF PLACES.' | [rule]; [80] 'ADVERTISEMENT.'; 81 text; [101] fly title: [rule] | 'INSCRIPTIONS.' | [rule]; [102] blank; 103 text; [124] blank; [125] fly title: [rule] | 'SONNETS | DEDICATED TO LIBERTY. | PART FIRST.' | [rule]; [126] blank; 127 text; [156] blank; [157] fly title: [rule] | 'SONNETS | DEDICATED TO LIBERTY. | PART SECOND.' | [rule]; [158] blank; 159 text; [234] blank; [235] 'NOTES.'; [237] fly title: [rule] | 'MEMORIALS | OF | A TOUR ON THE CONTINENT. | 1820.' | [rule]; [238] blank; [239] 'DEDICATION.'; [240] blank; 241 text; [314] blank; [315] 'NOTES.'; [323] fly title: [rule] | 'ECCLESIASTICAL | SKETCHES. | PART I. | FROM THE INTRODUCTION OF CHRISTIANITY INTO BRITAIN, TO THE | CONSUMMATION OF THE PAPAL DOMINION.' | [rule]; [324] three lines of verse; [325] 'ADVERTISEMENT.'; [327] text; [365] fly title: [rule] | 'ECCLESIASTICAL | SKETCHES. | PART II. | TO THE CLOSE OF THE TROUBLES IN THE REIGN OF CHARLES I.' | [rule]; [366] blank; 367 text; [406] blank; [407] fly title: [rule] | 'ECCLESIASTICAL | SKETCHES. | PART III. | FROM THE RESTORATION TO THE PRESENT TIMES.' | [rule]; [408] blank; 409 text; [445] 'NOTES.'; [456] printer's imprint.

Vol. 4: [i] title-page; [ii] printer's imprint; [iii] 'CONTENTS OF VOLUME IV.'; [viii] blank; inserted slip: 'ERRATA IN VOL. IV.'; [1] fly title: [rule] | 'THE | WHITE DOE OF RYLSTONE; | OR, | THE FATE OF THE NORTONS.' | [rule]; [2] 'ADVERTISEMENT.'; [3] introductory poem to Mary Wordsworth; [6] twelve-line quotation from Bacon; [7] text; 93 'NOTES.'; [104] blank; [105] 'THE PRIORESS'S TALE.'; [117] fly title: [rule] | 'THE | RIVER DUDDON. | A SERIES OF | SONNETS.' | [rule]; [118] five-line note; [119] dedication to Christopher Wordsworth; [123] text; [157] 'POSTSCRIPT.'; [159] 'NOTES.'; [186] blank; [187] fly title: [rule] | 'POEMS | OF SENTIMENT AND REFLECTION.' | [rule]; [188] blank; 189 text; [296] blank; [297] fly title: [rule] | 'POEMS | REFERRING TO THE PERIOD OF OLD AGE.' | [rule]; [298] blank; 299 text; [319] fly title: [rule] | 'EPITAPHS | AND | ELEGIAC POEMS.' | [rule]; [320] blank; [321] text; [356] blank; [357] 'PREFACE' [to *Lyrical Ballads*, 1800]; [390] blank; [391] 'APPENDIX.'; [398] printer's imprint.

Vol. 5: [i] half title: 'WORDSWORTH'S | POETICAL WORKS. | VOL. V.'; [ii] printer's imprint; [iii] title-page; [iv] blank; [v] fly title: [rule] | 'THE | EXCURSION, | BEING A PORTION OF | THE RECLUSE.' | [rule]; [vi] blank; [vii] dedication to the Earl of Lonsdale; [viii] blank; [ix] 'PREFACE.'; [xvii] 'CONTENTS OF VOLUME V.'; [xviii] blank; inserted slip: 'ERRATUM IN VOL. V.'; [1] fly title: 'THE EXCURSION. | [rule] | BOOK I. | THE WANDERER.'; [2] 'ARGUMENT.'; [3] text; [44] blank; [45] fly title: 'THE EXCURSION. | [rule] | BOOK II. | THE SOLITARY.'; [46] 'ARGUMENT.'; 47 text; [85] fly title: 'THE EXCURSION. | [rule] | BOOK III. | DESPONDENCY.'; [86] 'ARGUMENT.'; 87 text; [129]

fly title: 'THE EXCURSION. | [rule] | BOOK IV. | DESPONDENCY CORRECTED.'; [130] 'ARGUMENT.'; 131 text; [186] blank; [187] fly title: 'THE EXCURSION. | [rule] | BOOK V. | THE PASTOR.'; [188] 'ARGUMENT.'; 189 text; [231] fly title: 'THE EXCURSION. | [rule] | BOOK VI. | THE CHURCH-YARD AMONG THE MOUNTAINS.'; [232] 'ARGUMENT.'; 233 text; [283] fly title: 'THE EXCURSION. | [rule] | BOOK VII. | THE CHURCH-YARD AMONG THE MOUNTAINS | CONTINUED.'; [284] 'ARGUMENT.'; 285 text; [329] fly title: 'THE EXCURSION. | [rule] | BOOK VIII. | THE PARSONAGE.'; [330] 'ARGUMENT.'; 331 text; [357] fly title: 'THE EXCURSION. | [rule] | BOOK IX. | DISCOURSE OF THE WANDERER &c.'; [358] 'ARGUMENT.'; 359 text; [392] blank; [393] 'NOTES.'; [422] printer's imprint; [423] advertisement for *A Description of the Scenery of the Lakes*; [424] blank. The last two pages are lacking in this copy.

$1, 2, 3, 4, 5, 6 signed, at center of foot. Unsigned: vol. 1, C4 and P5; vol. 2, D6 and I1; vol. 4, B3. Pagination set in outer margin of headlines when running titles are present; otherwise centered at top. Wove paper, with a very faint laid surface; no watermark. Vol. 1 sheets bulk 1 in.; vol. 2, 1 in.; vol. 3, $1\frac{3}{16}$ in.; vol. 4, 1 in.; vol. 5, $1\frac{1}{16}$ in.

Binding. Green cloth with pebble surface, white end-papers. The Sir John Sterling copy has gray boards, green cloth backstrip, white end-papers, and labels as follows: [thick-and-thin rule] | 'Wordsworth's | POETICAL | WORKS. | [rule] | VOL. I [etc.].' | [thin-and-thick rule].

Why fold A3.4 of vol. 5 was cancelled is unknown; no example of those leaves in uncancelled state has come to my notice. But the fact of cancellation seems reasonably clear, for in many copies those leaves are short, or long, or loose, or pasted in, not sewn.

77 Another copy.

$6\frac{3}{16} \times 3\frac{5}{8}$ in. Contemporary calf, rebacked; leather lettering pieces; white end-papers. Lacking the errata slips.

78 THE | EXCURSION, | BEING A PORTION OF | THE RECLUSE, | A POEM. | BY | WILLIAM WORDSWORTH. | [rule] | LONDON: | PRINTED FOR | LONGMAN, REES, ORME, BROWN, AND GREEN, | PATERNOSTER-ROW, | 1827.

Special imprint (verso of title-page). LONDON: | Printed by A. & R. Spottiswoode, | New-Street-Square.

Collation ($6\frac{5}{8} \times 4\frac{7}{8}$ in.). A⁶(−A1 ± A2, 3.4) a⁴(−a4) B–S¹² T⁸. (T8 lacking in this copy.)

Pagination and *Contents* are identical with those of vol. 5 of the collective edition of 1827, the sheets of which are here bound under a different title-page.

Third edition.

1828

79 THE | POETICAL WORKS | OF | WILLIAM WORDSWORTH. | COMPLETE IN ONE VOLUME. | [woodcut] | PARIS | PUBLISHED BY A. AND W. GALIGNANI, | Nº 18, RUE VIVIENNE. | [rule] | 1828.

Special imprint (p. ii). [rule] | PRINTED BY JULES DIDOT, SENIOR, | PRINTER TO HIS MAJESTY, RUE DU PONT-DE-LODI, Nº 6.

Collation ($9\frac{1}{4} \times 5\frac{13}{16}$ in.). π² 2π⁴ a² 1–42⁴ 43².

Pagination. [i–vii] viii–xii [xiii] xiv–xvi, [1] 2–340.

Contents. [i] half title: 'THE | POETICAL WORKS | OF WILLIAM WORDSWORTH.', [ii] printer's imprint; frontispiece, portrait of Wordsworth engraved by J. J. Wedgwood from the painting by R. Carruthers, dated 1828; [iii] title-page; [iv] blank; [v] 'ADVERTISEMENT.'; [vi] blank; [vii] '𝕮𝖔𝖓𝖙𝖊𝖓𝖙𝖘.'; [xiii] '𝕸𝖊𝖒𝖔𝖎𝖗 𝖔𝖋 𝖂𝖎𝖑𝖑𝖎𝖆𝖒 𝖂𝖔𝖗𝖉𝖘𝖜𝖔𝖗𝖙𝖍, 𝕰𝖘𝖖.'; [1] title, dedication to Sir George Beaumont, and Preface; on 15 '𝕻𝖔𝖊𝖒𝖘 | REFERRING TO THE PERIOD OF CHILD-HOOD.'; on 22 '𝕵𝖚𝖇𝖊𝖓𝖎𝖑𝖊 𝕻𝖎𝖊𝖈𝖊𝖘.'; on 35 '𝕻𝖔𝖊𝖒𝖘 𝖋𝖔𝖚𝖓𝖉𝖊𝖉 𝖔𝖓 𝖙𝖍𝖊 𝕬𝖋𝖋𝖊𝖈𝖙𝖎𝖔𝖓𝖘.'; 67 '𝕻𝖔𝖊𝖒𝖘 𝖔𝖋 𝖙𝖍𝖊 𝕱𝖆𝖓𝖈𝖞.'; on 78 '𝕻𝖔𝖊𝖒𝖘 𝖔𝖋 𝖙𝖍𝖊 𝕴𝖒𝖆𝖌𝖎𝖓𝖆𝖙𝖎𝖔𝖓.'; on 113 '𝕸𝖎𝖘𝖈𝖊𝖑𝖑𝖆𝖓𝖊𝖔𝖚𝖘 𝕾𝖔𝖓𝖓𝖊𝖙𝖘.'; on 125 '𝕸𝖊𝖒𝖔𝖗𝖎𝖆𝖑𝖘 𝖔𝖋 𝖆 𝕿𝖔𝖚𝖗 𝖎𝖓 𝕾𝖈𝖔𝖙𝖑𝖆𝖓𝖉, 1803.'; on 137 '𝕻𝖔𝖊𝖒𝖘 𝖔𝖓 𝖙𝖍𝖊 𝕹𝖆𝖒𝖎𝖓𝖌 𝖔𝖋 𝕻𝖑𝖆𝖈𝖊𝖘.'; 141 '𝕴𝖓𝖘𝖈𝖗𝖎𝖕𝖙𝖎𝖔𝖓𝖘.'; 144

'𝕾𝖔𝖓𝖓𝖊𝖙𝖘 𝕯𝖊𝖉𝖎𝖈𝖆𝖙𝖊𝖉 𝖙𝖔 𝕷𝖎𝖇𝖊𝖗𝖙𝖞.'; on 159 '𝕸𝖊𝖒𝖔𝖗𝖎𝖆𝖑𝖘 𝖔𝖋 𝖆 𝕿𝖔𝖚𝖗 𝖔𝖓 𝖙𝖍𝖊 𝕮𝖔𝖓𝖙𝖎𝖓𝖊𝖓𝖙, 1820.'; 172 '𝕰𝖈𝖈𝖑𝖊𝖘𝖎𝖆𝖘𝖙𝖎𝖈𝖆𝖑 𝕾𝖐𝖊𝖙𝖈𝖍𝖊𝖘.'; on 189 '𝕿𝖍𝖊 𝖂𝖍𝖎𝖙𝖊 𝕯𝖔𝖊 𝖔𝖋 𝕽𝖞𝖑𝖘𝖙𝖔𝖓𝖊;'; 209 '𝕿𝖍𝖊 𝕻𝖗𝖎𝖔𝖗𝖊𝖘𝖘'𝖘 𝕿𝖆𝖑𝖊.'; on 211 '𝕿𝖍𝖊 𝕽𝖎𝖛𝖊𝖗 𝕯𝖚𝖉𝖉𝖔𝖓.'; on 224 '𝕻𝖔𝖊𝖒𝖘 𝖔𝖋 𝕾𝖊𝖓𝖙𝖎𝖒𝖊𝖓𝖙 𝖆𝖓𝖉 𝕽𝖊𝖋𝖑𝖊𝖈𝖙𝖎𝖔𝖓.'; on 241 '𝕻𝖔𝖊𝖒𝖘 | REFERRING TO THE PERIOD OF OLD AGE.'; on 245 '𝕰𝖕𝖎𝖙𝖆𝖕𝖍𝖘 𝖆𝖓𝖉 𝕰𝖑𝖊𝖌𝖎𝖆𝖈 𝕻𝖔𝖊𝖒𝖘.'; 251 'OBSERVA-TIONS' [i.e., Preface to *Lyrical Ballads*, 1800]; on 260 '𝕿𝖍𝖊 𝕰𝖝𝖈𝖚𝖗𝖘𝖎𝖔𝖓,'. Preceding the half title is a page of advertisements.

$1 signed, at lower left, just inside the frame of rules that surrounds each page. Running titles throughout. Pagination set in outer margin of headline. Printed in double column. Laid paper, chainlines 1 in. apart. Watermarked 'CS', the letters within a mantling; and '251' or '252', the numbers set above a horizontal brace. Sheets bulk 1 in.

Binding. Original gray boards, with white laid end-papers; uncut. Paper label on spine reads: [thick-and-thin rule] | 'WORDSWORTH'S | 𝕻𝖔𝖊𝖙𝖎𝖈𝖆𝖑 | WORKS. | [thick-and-thin rule] | IN ONE VOLUME. | [thin-and-thick rule] | 1828.' | [thin-and-thick rule].

80 Another copy.

$9\frac{1}{4} \times 5\frac{13}{16}$ in. Original binding as above. With four pp. of advertisements.

1831

81 SELECTIONS | 𝔉𝔯𝔬𝔪 𝔱𝔥𝔢 𝔓𝔬𝔢𝔪𝔰 | OF | WILLIAM WORDSWORTH, ESQ. | CHIEFLY FOR THE USE OF | SCHOOLS AND YOUNG PERSONS. | [three lines from Rasselas] | LONDON: | EDWARD MOXON, 64, NEW BOND STREET. | [rule] | 1831.

Special imprints (p. ii). LONDON: | BRADBURY AND EVANS, PRINTERS, | BOUVERIE STREET.
    (On p. 365): [rule] | BRADBURY AND EVANS, PRINTERS, | BOUVERIE STREET.
Collation ($7\frac{1}{2} \times 4\frac{1}{2}$ in.). a⁸ B–Q¹² R⁴(–R4).
Pagination. [i–v] vi–xii [xiii] xiv–xvi, [1] 2–250 [251] 252–365 [366].
Contents. [i] title-page; [ii] printer's imprint; [iii] dedication to the admirers of Wordsworth's poetry; [iv] blank; [v] 'PREFACE.'; [xiii] 'CONTENTS.'; inserted slip: 'ERRATA.'; [1] text; [366] blank.

$1, 2, 5 signed, at center of foot; $5 signed '3'; R2 unsigned. Running titles throughout. Pagination set in outer margin of headline. Wove paper, without watermark. Sheets bulk $\frac{15}{16}$ in.

Binding. Bright blue cloth; blue end-papers watermarked '1848'; uncut. The copy at Dove Cottage (formerly William A. Knight's) is in reddish-brown cloth with paper label. That at Swarthmore College has drab boards and paper label; the label reads: [thick-and-thin rule] | 'SELECTIONS | FROM | WORDSWORTH | [rule] | *Price 5s.*' | [thin-and-thick rule].

First edition. Edited by Joseph Hine.

82 Another copy.

$7\frac{3}{16} \times 4\frac{1}{8}$ in. Full tan calf, gilt, marbled end-papers.

1832

83 THE | POETICAL WORKS | OF | WILLIAM WORDSWORTH. | [rule] | A NEW EDITION. | [rule] | IN FOUR VOLUMES. | VOL. I [etc.] | LONDON: | PRINTED FOR | LONGMAN, REES, ORME, BROWN, GREEN, & LONGMAN, | PATERNOSTER-ROW. | 1832.

Special imprints (verso of first page and at end of each volume). LONDON: | Printed by A. & R. Spottiswoode, | New-Street-Square.

Collation ($6\frac{1}{16} \times 3\frac{15}{16}$in.). Vol. 1: A⁸ a–b⁸ B–Y⁸ Z⁴.

Vol. 2: A–2A⁸ 2B⁴ 2C1. F3 and L4 unsigned.

Vol. 3: A⁶ B–Z⁸ 2A⁴. F4 unsigned.

Vol. 4: [A]⁴ B–Z⁸ 2A⁴.

Pagination. Vol. 1: [i–v] vi–vii [viii–xi] xii–xli [xlii–xliii] xliv–xlvii [xlviii], [1–3] 4–32 [33–4] 35–49 [50–3] 54–86 [87–8] 89–188 [189–90] 191–218 [219–20] 221–70 [271–2] 273–85 [286–7] 288–300 [301] 302–10 [311] 312–42 [343–4].

Vol. 2: [i–v] vi–xv [xvi], [1–2] 3–104 [105–7] 108–47 [148–9] 150–73 [174–5] 176–99 [200–1] 202–35 [236–7] 238–50 [251] 252–66 [267] 268–311 [312–13] 314 [315–16] 317–64 [365] 366–77 [378].

Vol. 3: [i–iii] iv–xi [xii], [1–3] 4–6 [7] 8–24 [25] 26 [27] 28–51 [52–5] 56–7 [58–9] 60–130 [131–3] 134–281 [282–3] 284–322 [323] 324–52 [353] 354–8 [359–60]. P. 155 paginated '155'.

Vol. 4: [i–viii], [1–3] 4–9 [10–15] 16–46 [47–8] 49–78 [79–80] 81–113 [114–16] 117–59 [160–3] 164–95 [196–8] 199–237 [238–40] 241–75 [276–8] 279–98 [299–300] 301–26 [327] 328–34 [335] 336–57 [358–60].

Contents. Vol. 1: [i] half title: 'THE | POETICAL WORKS | OF | WILLIAM WORDSWORTH.'; [ii] printer's imprint; [iii] title-page; [iv] blank; [v] dedication to Sir George Beaumont; [viii] blank; [ix] 'ADVERTISEMENT.'; [x] blank; [xi] 'PREFACE.'; [xlii] blank; [xliii] 'CONTENTS OF VOLUME I.'; [xlviii] blank but for a paste-on slip: 'ERRATA IN VOL. I.'; [1] fly title: 'POEMS | REFERRING TO THE PERIOD OF CHILDHOOD.'; [2] blank; [3] text; [33] fly title: 'JUVENILE PIECES.'; [34] eleven-line note in italics; 35 text; [50] blank; [51] fly title: 'DESCRIPTIVE SKETCHES | TAKEN DURING | A PEDESTRIAN TOUR | AMONG | THE ALPS.'; [52] blank; [53] dedication to Robert Jones; 55 text; [87] fly title: 'POEMS | FOUNDED ON THE AFFECTIONS.'; [88] blank; 89 text; [189] fly title: 'THE WAGGONER.'; [190] dedication to Charles Lamb; 191 text; [219] fly title: 'POEMS OF THE FANCY.'; [220] blank; 221 text; [271] fly title: 'POEMS | ON THE NAMING OF PLACES.'; [272] 'ADVERTISE-MENT.'; 273 text; [286] blank; [287] 'INSCRIPTIONS.'; [301] 'THE PRIORESS'S TALE.'; [311] 'ESSAY,'; [343] 'NOTE TO VOLUME I.'; [344] printer's imprint.

Vol. 2: [i] half title: 'THE | POETICAL WORKS | OF | WILLIAM WORDSWORTH. | VOL. II.'; [ii] printer's imprint; [iii] title-page; [iv] blank; [v] 'CONTENTS OF VOLUME II.'; [xvi] blank but for a paste-on slip: 'ERRATA IN VOL. II.'; [1] fly title: 'POEMS OF THE IMAGINATION.'; [2] blank; 3 text; [105] fly title: 'PETER BELL. | A TALE. | What's in a *Name?* | [row of asterisks] | Brutus will start a Spirit as soon as Cæsar!'; [106] blank; [107] dedication to Southey; 109 text; [148] blank; [149] 'MISCELLANEOUS SONNETS.'; [174] blank; [175] 'MISCELLANEOUS SONNETS. | [rule] | PART SECOND.' | [rule]; [200] blank; [201] 'MEMORIALS | OF | A TOUR IN SCOTLAND, 1803.'; [236] blank; [237] 'MEMORIALS | OF | A TOUR IN SCOTLAND, 1814.'; [251] 'SONNETS | DEDICATED TO LIBERTY. | [rule] | PART FIRST.' | [rule]; [267] 'SONNETS | DEDICATED TO LIBERTY. | [rule] | PART SECOND.' | [rule]; [312] blank; [313] 'NOTES.'; [315] 'MEMORIALS | OF | A TOUR ON THE CONTINENT, | 1820.'; [316] 'DEDICATION.'; 317 text; [365] 'NOTES TO VOLUME II.'; [378] printer's imprint.

Vol. 3: [i] title-page; [ii] printer's imprint; [iii] 'CONTENTS OF VOLUME III.'; [xii] blank but for a paste-on slip: 'ERRATA IN VOL. III.'; [1] fly title: 'THE | RIVER DUDDON. | A SERIES OF | SONNETS.'; [2] five-line note; [3] dedication to Christopher Wordsworth; [7] text; [25] 'POSTSCRIPT.'; [27] 'NOTES.'; [52] blank; [53] fly title: 'THE | WHITE DOE OF RYLSTONE; | OR, | THE FATE OF THE NORTONS.'; [54] 'ADVERTISEMENT.'; [55] dedicatory poem; [58] twelve-line quotation from Bacon; [59] text; 120 'NOTES.'; [131] fly title: 'ECCLESIASTICAL SKETCHES, | IN A SERIES OF SONNETS. | PART I. | FROM THE INTRODUCTION OF CHRISTIANITY INTO BRITAIN, TO | THE CONSUMMATION OF THE PAPAL DOMINION.'; [132] three lines of verse; [133] 'ADVERTISEMENT.'; 135 text; 155 'ECCLESIASTICAL SKETCHES. | [rule] | PART II. | TO THE CLOSE OF THE TROUBLES IN THE REIGN OF CHARLES I.' | [rule]; 175 'ECCLESIASTICAL SKETCHES. | [rule] | PART III. | FROM THE RESTORATION TO THE PRESENT TIMES.' | [rule]; 194 'NOTES.'; 205 'POEMS | OF SENTIMENT AND REFLECTION.'; [282] blank; [283] 'POEMS | REFERRING TO THE PERIOD OF OLD AGE.'; 297 'EPITAPHS AND ELEGIAC POEMS.'; [323] 'PREFACE' [to *Lyrical Ballads*, 1800]; [353] 'APPENDIX.'; [359–60] blank.

Vol. 4: [i–ii] blank; [iii] half title: 'THE | POETICAL WORKS | OF | WILLIAM WORDS-WORTH. | VOL. IV.'; [iv] printer's imprint; [v] title-page; [vi] blank; [vii] 'CONTENTS OF VOLUME IV.'; [viii] blank but for a paste-on slip: 'ERRATA IN VOL. IV.'; [1] fly title: 'THE EXCURSION, | BEING A PORTION OF | THE RECLUSE.'; [2] blank; [3] 'PREFACE.'; [10] blank; [11] dedication to the Earl of Lonsdale; [12] blank; [13] fly title: 'THE EXCURSION. | [rule] | BOOK I. | THE WANDERER.'; [14] 'ARGUMENT.'; [15] text; [47] fly title: 'THE EXCURSION. | [rule] | BOOK II. | THE SOLITARY.'; [48] 'ARGUMENT.'; 49 text; [79] fly

LYRICAL BALLADS,

WITH

A FEW OTHER POEMS.

BRISTOL:

PRINTED BY BIGGS AND COTTLE,

FOR T. N. LONGMAN, PATERNOSTER-ROW, LONDON.

1798.

LYRICAL BALLADS,

WITH

A FEW OTHER POEMS.

LONDON:

PRINTED FOR J. & A. ARCH, GRACECHURCH-STREET.

1798.

The Bristol and London Issues of *Lyrical Ballads*, 1798.   Nos. 3 and 4

LYRICAL BALLADS,

WITH

OTHER POEMS.

IN TWO VOLUMES.

By W. WORDSWORTH.

Quam nihil ad genium, Papiniane, tuum!

VOL. I.

SECOND EDITION.

LONDON:

PRINTED FOR T. N. LONGMAN AND O. REES, PATERNOSTER-ROW,

BY BIGGS AND CO. BRISTOL.

1800.

LYRICAL BALLADS,

WITH

OTHER POEMS.

IN TWO VOLUMES.

By W. WORDSWORTH.

Quam nihil ad genium, Papiniane, tuum!

VOL. II.

LONDON:

PRINTED FOR T. N. LONGMAN AND O. REES, PATERNOSTER-ROW,

BY BIGGS AND CO. BRISTOL.

1800.

title: 'THE EXCURSION. | [rule] | BOOK III. | DESPONDENCY.'; [80] 'ARGUMENT.'; 81 text; [114] blank; [115] fly title: 'THE EXCURSION. | [rule] | BOOK IV. | DESPONDENCY CORRECTED.'; [116] 'ARGUMENT.'; 117 text; [160] blank; [161] fly title: 'THE EXCUR- SION. | [rule] | BOOK V. | THE PASTOR.'; [162] 'ARGUMENT.'; [163] text; [196] blank; [197] fly title: 'THE EXCURSION. | [rule] | BOOK VI. | THE CHURCH-YARD AMONG THE | MOUNTAINS.'; [198] 'ARGUMENT.'; 199 text; [238] blank; [239] fly title: 'THE EXCUR- SION. | [rule] | BOOK VII. | THE CHURCH-YARD AMONG THE MOUNTAINS | CON- TINUED.'; [240] 'ARGUMENT.'; 241 text; [276] blank; [277] fly title: 'THE EXCURSION. | [rule] | BOOK VIII. | THE PARSONAGE.'; [278] 'ARGUMENT.'; 279 text; [299] fly title: 'THE EXCURSION. | [rule] | BOOK IX. | DISCOURSE OF THE WANDERER, &c.'; [300] 'ARGUMENT.'; 301 text; [327] 'NOTES.'; 335 'ESSAY UPON EPITAPHS.'; 356 'NOTES.'; [358] printer's imprint; [359] advertisement; [360] blank.

$1, 2, 3, 4 signed, at center of foot. Running titles throughout (but unaccountably absent in vol. 1, pp. 120–9). Pagination set in outer margin of headline when running titles are present; otherwise centered at top. Wove paper, without watermark. Vol. 1 sheets bulk 1 in.; vol. 2, 1 in.; vol. 3, $\frac{7}{8}$ in.; vol. 4, 1 in.

Binding. Green cloth, pebble surface; white end-papers. Paper labels read: [thick-and-thin rule] | 'Wordsworth's | POETICAL | WORKS. | [rule] | IN FOUR VOLUMES. | VOL. I [etc.]. | [rule] | £1 4s.' | [thin-and-thick rule]. Swarthmore College has two sets in original bindings, one in gray boards, the other in blue-gray boards; both have the labels as above. Some copies of vol. 4, with appropriate half title and title-page, were issued as a separate edition of *The Excursion*.

1834

84 SELECTIONS | 𝔉rom the 𝔓oems | OF | WILLIAM WORDSWORTH, ESQ. | CHIEFLY FOR THE USE OF SCHOOLS AND | YOUNG PERSONS. | [rule] | [three-line quotation from Rasselas] | A NEW EDITION. | LONDON: | EDWARD MOXON, DOVER STREET. | [rule] | MDCCCXXXIV.

Special imprints (p. ii). LONDON: | PRINTED BY BRADBURY AND EVANS, | WHITEFRIARS. (On p. 326): [rule] | BRADBURY AND EVANS, PRINTERS, WHITEFRIARS.

Collation ($6\frac{3}{4} \times 4$ in.). [A]⁸ B–X⁸ Y⁴.

Pagination. [i–v] vi–xii [xiii] xiv–xvi, [1] 2–216 [217] 218–326 [327–8].

Contents. [i] title-page; [ii] printer's imprint; [iii] dedication to the admirers of Wordsworth's poetry; [iv] blank; [v] 'PREFACE.'; [xiii] 'CONTENTS.'; [1] 'SELECTIONS FROM WORDS- WORTH.'; [217] 'MISCELLANEOUS SONNETS.'; 240 'SONNETS DEDICATED TO LIBERTY.'; 254 'ECCLESIASTICAL SKETCHES.'; 266 miscellaneous poems; 273 'THE RIVER DUDDON.'; 280 'THE EXCURSION.'; [327–8] Moxon's advertisements, dated 1 November 1834.

$1, 2 signed, at center of foot. Pagination set in outer margin of headline when running titles are present; otherwise centered at top. Wove paper, without watermark. Sheets bulk $\frac{13}{16}$ in.

Binding. Black, vertically-ribbed cloth; yellow end-papers, renewed in this copy; rebacked. The Dove Cottage copy (formerly William A. Knight's) is in green cloth with a flowered surface, and a copy at Yale is in purple cloth. Both have yellow end-papers and gilt title on spine: [within an ornamental frame] 'SELECTIONS | FROM | WORDSWORTH'.

Second edition (entirely reset). Edited by Joseph Hine.

1835

85 Caption: 'EPITAPH.'.

Imprint. None.

Four unnumbered pages, $10 \times 7\frac{7}{8}$ in., on the first one of which is printed Wordsworth's Epitaph on Charles Lamb, which eventually grew to become the poem now entitled: Written after the Death of Charles Lamb. The version here given consists of thirty-eight lines, beginning 'To the dear memory of a frail good Man' and concluding 'O, he was good, *if e'er* a good Man lived!'. Neither author nor printer is mentioned. The paper bears the watermark 'FELLOWS | 1835'.

A photostatic copy of the unique original in the Ashley Library, British Museum.

86 YARROW REVISITED, | AND | OTHER POEMS. | BY | WILLIAM WORDSWORTH. | [rule] | —"Poets . . . . dwell on earth | To clothe whate'er the soul admires and loves | With language and with numbers." | AKENSIDE. | [rule] | LONDON: | PRINTED FOR | LONGMAN, REES, ORME, BROWN, GREEN, & LONGMAN, | PATERNOSTER-ROW; AND | EDWARD MOXON, DOVER STREET. | 1835.

Special imprints (pp. ii and 350). LONDON: | Printed by A. SPOTTISWOODE, | New-Street-Square.

Collation (6$\frac{13}{16}$ × 4 in.). A⁶ a² B–P¹² Q¹⁰ (–Q10).

Pagination. [i–ix] x–xv [xvi], [1–3] 4–43 [44–6] 47–120 [121–2] 123–58 [159–60] 161–83 [184–6] 187–268 [269–70] 271–93 [294] 295–308 [309–10] 311–22 [323] 324–49 [350–4].

Contents. [i] half title: 'YARROW REVISITED, | AND | 𝔒𝔱𝔥𝔢𝔯 𝔓𝔬𝔢𝔪𝔰.'; [ii] printer's imprint; [iii] title-page; [iv] blank; [v] dedication to Samuel Rogers; [vi] blank; [vii] 'ADVERTISEMENT.'; [viii] blank; [ix] 'CONTENTS.'; [xvi] 'ERRATA AND EMENDATIONS.'; inserted slip: 'ERRATUM.'; [1] fly title: 'YARROW REVISITED, | AND | OTHER POEMS, | COMPOSED (TWO EXCEPTED) DURING A TOUR IN | SCOTLAND, AND ON THE ENGLISH BORDER, | IN THE AUTUMN OF 1831.'; [2] blank; [3] text; 38 'NOTES.'; [44] blank; [45] fly title: 'THE EGYPTIAN MAID; | OR, | THE ROMANCE OF THE WATER LILY.' | [rule] | [eight-line note]; [46] blank; 47 text; 69 text of miscellaneous poems; [121] fly title: 'THE | RUSSIAN FUGITIVE.'; [122] seven-line note; 123 text; 145 text of miscellaneous poems; [159] fly title: 'EVENING VOLUNTARIES.'; [160] blank; 161 text; 178 text of miscellaneous poems; [184] blank; [185] fly title: 'SONNETS | COMPOSED OR SUGGESTED DURING A TOUR IN SCOTLAND, | IN THE SUMMER OF 1833.'; [186] twelve-line note; 187 text; 232 'NOTES.'; 237 text of miscellaneous poems; [269] fly title: 'STANZAS | SUGGESTED | IN A STEAM-BOAT OFF ST. BEES' HEADS, | ON THE COAST OF CUMBERLAND.'; [270] full-page note; 271 text; 280 'NOTE.'; 281 text of miscellaneous poems; [294] blank; 295 text; [309] fly title: 'STANZAS | ON | THE POWER OF SOUND.'; 311 text; [323] 'POSTSCRIPT.'; [350] printer's imprint; [351–4] Longman's advertisements.

$1, 2, 3, 4, 5, 6 signed, at center of foot. Pagination set in outer margin of headline when running titles are present; otherwise centered at top. Wove paper, without watermark. Sheets bulk 1 in.

Binding. Drab boards, backstrip of green cloth with leaf-design surface; white end-papers; uncut. Paper label reads: [thick-and-thin rule] | '*WORDSWORTH'S* | YARROW | REVISITED, | AND | 𝔒𝔱𝔥𝔢𝔯 𝔓𝔬𝔢𝔪𝔰.' | [thin-and-thick rule]. Other copies in original bindings have plain drab boards (Cornell), blue boards with drab paper backstrip (London bookseller), drab boards with purplish cloth backstrip (Dove Cottage); all these have the paper label as above.

First edition. With the errata slip after p. [xvi] and 4 pp. of advertisements at the end.

87 Another copy.

6⅜ × 3¾ in. Green cloth, pebble surface, with plum leather lettering piece. With 4 pp. of advertisements; errata slip absent. Half title inscribed (not in Wordsworth's hand): 'From the Author.'

88 Another copy.

6$\frac{11}{16}$ × 3$\frac{15}{16}$ in. Three-quarter blue calf over marbled boards. With 4 pp. of advertisements and the errata slip.

This copy formerly belonged to J. Dykes Campbell and contains his signature on the title-page and a few notes in the text.

89 Another copy.

6$\frac{13}{16}$ × 4 in. Drab boards with paper label; uncut. With 4 pp. of advertisements; errata slip absent.

90 Another copy.

6½ × 3¾ in. Three-quarter blue morocco over marbled boards. Advertisements, half title, and errata slip lacking.

91 YARROW REVISITED, | AND OTHER | POEMS. | BY | WILLIAM WORDSWORTH. | [rule] | —"Poets .... dwell on earth | To clothe whate'er the soul admires and loves | With language and with numbers." —AKENSIDE. | [rule] | [rule] | BOSTON: | JAMES MUNROE AND CO. | 1835.

Special imprint (p. ii). TUTTLE AND WEEKS, PRINTERS.

Collation (6½ × 4 in.). [1]⁶ 2–15⁸ 16².

Pagination. [i–vii] viii–xii, [17] 18–40 [41] 42–7 [48–9] 50–160 [161] 162–92 [193] 194–220 [221] 222–44. P. 166 misnumbered '116'. The gap between pp. xii and [17] is a discontinuity in pagination only; nothing in the text, apparently, is omitted.

Contents. [i] title-page; [ii] printer's imprint; [iii] dedication to Samuel Rogers; [iv] blank; [v] 'ADVERTISEMENT.'; [vi] blank; [vii] 'CONTENTS.'; [17] 'YARROW REVISITED.'; [41] 'NOTES.'; [48] blank; [49] 'THE EGYPTIAN MAID;'; 63 text of miscellaneous poems; [161] 'NOTES.'; 166 (misnumbered '116') text of miscellaneous poems; [193] 'NOTE.'; 194 text of miscellaneous poems; [221] 'POSTSCRIPT.'.

$1 signed, at left center of foot. Pagination set in outer margin of headline when running titles are present; otherwise centered at top. Wove paper, without watermark. Sheets bulk ⅝ in.

Binding. Blue cloth in a twig-like design; blind-stamped ornamental panel on front and back covers; white end-papers. Binder's stamp on both covers: 'B. BRADLEY'. Gilt title on spine, the author's name set in an arc: 'WORDSWORTH'S | YARROW | REVISITED'. Two copies at Harvard are in green cloth, one with the twig-like design as above, the other with a mosaic-like surface.

First American edition, Boston issue. This issue differs from the New York issue (see below) only in the imprint on the title-page. Except for that imprint, both title-pages are from the same setting of type; in neither issue is the title-page a cancel.

92 YARROW REVISITED, | AND OTHER | POEMS. | BY | WILLIAM WORDSWORTH. | [rule] | "Poets .... dwell on earth | To clothe whate'er the soul admires and loves | With language and with numbers." —AKENSIDE. | [rule] | [rule] | NEW YORK: | R. BARTLETT AND S. RAYNOR. | 1835.

Special imprint (p. ii). TUTTLE AND WEEKS, PRINTERS.

Collation (7 × 4⁷⁄₁₆ in.). [1]⁶ 2–15⁸ 16².

Pagination and *Contents* are the same as those of the Boston issue, described above.

Binding. Drab cloth in a twig-like design; blind-stamped ornamental panel on front and back covers; white end-papers. Binder's stamp on both covers: 'B. BRADLEY'. Gilt title on spine, the author's name set in an arc: 'WORDSWORTH'S | YARROW | REVISITED'.

First American edition, New York issue. This issue differs from the Boston issue (see above) only in the imprint on the title-page. Except for that imprint, both title-pages are from the same setting of type; in neither issue is the title-page a cancel.

93 A | GUIDE | THROUGH THE | DISTRICT OF THE LAKES | IN | 𝕿𝖍𝖊 𝕹𝖔𝖗𝖙𝖍 𝖔𝖋 𝕰𝖓𝖌𝖑𝖆𝖓𝖉, | WITH | A DESCRIPTION OF THE SCENERY, &c. | FOR THE USE OF | TOURISTS AND RESIDENTS. | [rule] | FIFTH EDITION, | WITH CONSIDERABLE ADDITIONS. | [rule] | By WILLIAM WORDSWORTH. | *KENDAL:* | PUBLISHED BY HUDSON AND NICHOLSON, | AND IN LONDON BY | LONGMAN & CO., MOXON, AND WHITTAKER & CO. | 1835.

Special imprints (verso of title-page). KENDAL: | Printed by Hudson and Nicholson.
(On p. 139): [rule] | Kendal: Printed by Hudson and Nicholson.

Collation (6⅝ × 4³⁄₁₆ in.). π² a⁸ b⁴ B–I⁸ K⁴ L².

Pagination. 4 pp. unnumbered, [i] ii–xxiv, [1] 2–139 [140] 2 pp. advertisements.

Contents. Folding map drawn and engraved by Sidney Hall, dated 1822; title-page, with printer's imprint on verso; 'CONTENTS.', continued on verso; [i] 'DIRECTIONS AND INFORMATION |

FOR | THE TOURIST.'; [1] 'DESCRIPTION | OF THE | SCENERY OF THE LAKES.'; 135 an itinerary of the Lakes; [140] 'ERRATA.'; 2 pp. of advertisements of Hudson and Nicholson. $1, 2 signed, at center of foot. Leaf K2 signed on verso (p. 132). Pagination set in outer margin of headline when running titles are present; otherwise centered at top. Wove paper, without watermark. Sheets bulk ½ in.

Binding. Original purple cloth with pebble surface; white end-papers. Label renewed. The Bodleian copy is in plain purple cloth; the Dyce copy (Victoria and Albert Museum) is in purple cloth with a floral surface; the copy at St. John's College, Cambridge, is in purple cloth with 'watered-silk' surface. All have the same label: [thick-and-thin rule] | 'WORDSWORTH'S | GUIDE | through the | *Lake District.* | [rule] | 4*s.*' | [thin-and-thick rule].

Third separate edition. The editions of 1822 and of 1823 were entitled: A Description of the Scenery of the Lakes in the North of England.

94 Another copy.

6⅝ × 3¹⁵⁄₁₆ in. Half brown morocco over marbled boards; green leather lettering-piece.

1836

95 [To the Dear Memory of a Frail Good Man.]

No title-page; no imprint.
Collation (8⅛ × 5¾ in.). Four leaves, quired.
Pagination. [1] 2–7 [8].
Contents. No title. A further development of Wordsworth's Epitaph on Charles Lamb (see No. 85). This version has 132 lines, beginning 'To the dear memory of a frail good Man' and ending 'The sacred tie | Is broken to become more sacred still.'. The text resembles that identified as '1836[1]' in the De Selincourt-Darbishire edition of the *Poetical Works* (IV, 272–6); it differs at four points, in spelling and punctuation. The last page is blank. The four leaves are sewn within fly leaves of a slightly lighter color and gray paper wrappers.

Six other copies only are known to me: two at Dove Cottage; two in the Berg Collection, New York Public Library; one in the Ashley Library, British Museum; and one in the Alexander Turnbull Library, Wellington, New Zealand. See F. M. Todd, 'Wordsworth's Monody on Lamb; Another Copy', *Modern Language Review*, L (1955), 48–50.

96 YARROW REVISITED, | AND | OTHER POEMS. | BY | WILLIAM WORDSWORTH. | [rule] | —"Poets .... dwell on earth | To clothe whate'er the soul admires and loves | With language and with numbers." | AKENSIDE. | [rule] | Second Edition. | LONDON: | PRINTED FOR | LONGMAN, REES, ORME, BROWN, GREEN, & LONGMAN, | PATERNOSTER-ROW; AND | EDWARD MOXON, DOVER STREET, | 1836.

Special imprints (pp. ii and 324). LONDON: | Printed by A. SPOTTISWOODE, | New-Street-Square.
Collation (6¾ × 4 in.). A⁶ B–X⁸ Y².
Pagination. [i–vii] viii–xii, [1–2] 3–45 [46] 47–106 [107–8] 109–38 [139–40] 141–66 [167] 168–227 [228] 229–81 [282–3] 284–323 [324]. Pp. 124, 216, and 287 are defectively paginated in most copies.
Contents. [i] title-page; [ii] printer's imprint; [iii] dedication to Samuel Rogers; [iv] blank; [v] 'ADVERTISEMENT.'; [vi] blank; [vii] 'CONTENTS.'; [1] fly title: 'YARROW REVISITED, | AND | OTHER POEMS, | COMPOSED (TWO EXCEPTED) DURING A TOUR IN | SCOTLAND, AND ON THE ENGLISH BORDER, | IN THE AUTUMN OF 1831.'; [2] blank; 3 text; 38 'NOTES.'; 45 fly title: 'THE EGYPTIAN MAID; | OR, | THE ROMANCE OF THE WATER LILY.' | [rule] | [six-line note]; [46] blank; 47 text; 64 miscellaneous poems; [107] fly title: 'THE | RUSSIAN FUGITIVE.'; [108] seven-line note; 109 text; [139] fly title: 'EVENING VOLUNTARIES.'; [140] blank; 141 text; 161 miscellaneous poems; [167] fly title: 'SONNETS | COM-

POSED OR SUGGESTED DURING A TOUR IN SCOTLAND, | IN THE SUMMER OF 1833.'; 168 twelve-line note; 169 text; 222 'NOTES.'; [228] blank; 229 miscellaneous poems; 247 fly title: 'STANZAS | SUGGESTED | IN A STEAM-BOAT OFF ST. BEES' HEADS, | ON THE COAST OF CUMBERLAND.'; 248 full-page note; 249 text; 256 'NOTE.'; 257 miscellaneous poems; [282] blank; [283] fly title: 'STANZAS | ON | THE POWER OF SOUND.'; 284 'ARGUMENT.'; 285 text; 295 'POSTSCRIPT.'; [324] printer's imprint.

\$1, 2, 3, 4 signed, at foot of center; D1 and Q2 unsigned. Signature of R2 defectively printed in some copies. Pagination set in outer margin of headline when running title is present; otherwise centered at top. Wove paper, without watermark. Sheets bulk $\frac{7}{8}$ in.

Binding. Original drab boards, faded purple cloth backstrip. Paper label: [thick-and-thin rule] | '*WORDSWORTH'S* | YARROW | REVISITED, | AND | 𝔒𝔱𝔥𝔢𝔯 𝔓𝔬𝔢𝔪𝔰.' | [thin-and-thick rule]. Uncut; partly unopened. A copy in the British Museum is in blue vertically ribbed cloth, with label as above.

Second edition.

97 Another copy.

$6\frac{3}{4} \times 4$ in. Half brown morocco over marbled boards by Max Adjarian.

98 YARROW REVISITED, | AND OTHER | POEMS. | BY | WILLIAM WORDSWORTH. | —"Poets....dwell on earth, | To clothe whate'er the soul admires and loves | With language and with numbers." | SECOND EDITION. | BOSTON: | WILLIAM D. TICKNOR. | 1836.

Special imprint (p. ii). Tuttle, Weeks & Dennett.....Printers.....17, School Street.

Collation ($7 \times 4\frac{3}{8}$ in.). $1^6(\pm 1/1)$ 2–15^8 16^2.

Pagination and *Contents* are identical with those of the Boston and of the New York issues of 1835.

Binding. Drab cloth in a twig-like design; blind-stamped ornamental panel on front and back covers; white end-papers. Binder's stamp on both covers: 'B. BRADLEY'. Gilt title on spine, the author's name set in an arc: 'WORDSWORTH'S | YARROW | REVISITED'.

The sheets of the American edition of 1835, with a new title-page.

99 THE | POETICAL WORKS | OF | WILLIAM WORDSWORTH. | [rule] | THE FIRST COMPLETE AMERICAN, | FROM THE LAST LONDON EDITION. | [rule] | IN ONE VOLUME. | [thick-and-thin rule] | NEW-HAVEN: | PRINTED AND PUBLISHED BY PECK & NEWTON. | [rule] | 1836.

Special imprint. None.

Collation ($9\frac{3}{4} \times 6\frac{1}{8}$ in.): [i]^4 ii–iv^4 χ1 1–40^4.

Pagination. [i–iii] iv–xxviii [xxix] xxx–xxxiv, [1] 2–320. P. 285 misnumbered '245'.

Contents. Frontispiece, engraved by Daggett, Hinman & Co., of the Boxall portrait of Wordsworth; [i] title-page; [ii] blank; [iii] dedication to Sir George Beaumont, and Preface; on ix 'ESSAY, | SUPPLEMENTARY TO THE PREFACE.'; on xviii 'PREFACE' [to *Lyrical Ballads*, 1800]; on xxvii 'APPENDIX.'; xxix 'INDEX.'; [1] 'POEMS REFERRING TO THE PERIOD OF CHILD-HOOD.'; on 7 'JUVENILE PIECES.'; on 10 'DESCRIPTIVE SKETCHES'; on 18 'POEMS FOUNDED ON THE AFFECTIONS.'; 40 'THE WAGGONER.'; on 46 'POEMS OF THE FANCY.'; on 56 'POEMS ON THE NAMING OF PLACES.'; on 59 'INSCRIPTIONS.'; on 62 'THE PRIORESS'S TALE.'; on 64 'POEMS OF THE IMAGINATION.'; on 95 'MISCELLA-NEOUS SONNETS.'; on 107 'MEMORIALS OF A TOUR IN SCOTLAND, 1803.'; 115 'MEMORIALS. | OF | A TOUR IN SCOTLAND, 1814.'; 118 'SONNETS DEDICATED TO LIBERTY.'; on 131 'MEMORIALS OF A TOUR ON THE CONTINENT, 1820.'; on 143 'THE RIVER DUDDON. A SERIES OF SONNETS.'; 155 'THE WHITE DOE OF RYL-STONE; OR, THE FATE OF THE NORTONS.'; 171 'ECCLESIASTICAL SKETCHES, IN A SERIES OF SONNETS.'; on 186 'POEMS OF SENTIMENT AND REFLECTION.'; on 202 'POEMS REFERRING TO THE PERIOD OF OLD AGE.'; on 205 'EPITAPHS AND

ELEGIAC POEMS.'; on 210 'THE EXCURSION, BEING A PORTION OF THE RECLUSE.'; on 274 'YARROW REVISITED, AND OTHER POEMS'; 316 'ESSAY UPON EPITAPHS.'.
$1 signed, at left center of foot. Pagination set in outer margin of headline where running titles are present; otherwise centered at top. Wove paper, without watermark. Sheets bulk $\frac{13}{16}$ in.
Binding. Blue cloth in a grape-vine design; blind-stamped panel on front and back covers; white end-papers. Gilt title on spine: 'WORDSWORTH'S | POEMS'.

100 Another copy.

$9\frac{1}{2} \times 6\frac{1}{8}$ in. Half brown morocco over marbled boards, by Max Adjarian.

101 THE | POETICAL WORKS | OF | WILLIAM WORDSWORTH. | [rule] | 𝕬 𝔑𝔢𝔴 𝔈𝔡𝔦𝔱𝔦𝔬𝔫. | IN SIX VOLUMES. | Vol. I [etc.]. | LONDON: | EDWARD MOXON, DOVER STREET. | [rule] | MDCCCXXXVI [–VII].

Special imprints (verso of title-page and end of text in all vols.). LONDON: | BRADBURY AND EVANS, PRINTERS, | WHITEFRIARS.
Collation ($6\frac{3}{4} \times 4\frac{1}{16}$ in.). Vol. 1: [a]⁸ b–c⁸ B–X⁸.
    Vol. 2: [A]⁴ B–Z⁸.
    Vol. 3: [A]⁶ B–Z⁸ 2A².
    Vol. 4: [a]² b⁴ B–Z⁸ 2A⁶.
    Vol. 5: [a]² b⁴ B–2C⁸ 2D⁶.
    Vol. 6: [A]⁸ B–2A⁸ 2B⁴.
Pagination. Vol. 1: [i–v] vi–vii [viii–ix] x–xliii [xliv–xlv] xlvi–xlviii, [1–3] 4–44 [45–6] 47–63 [64–7] 68 [69] 70–105 [106–8] 109–273 [274–6] 277–310 [311] 312–13 [314], [1] 2–6.
    Vol. 2: [i–v] vi–viii, [1–3] 4–76 [77–9] 80–232 [233–5] 236–83 [284–7] 288–302 [303] 304–37 [338–9] 340–5 [346–7] 348–51 [352].
    Vol. 3: [i–v] vi–xii, [1–3] 4–106 [107–9] 110–72 [173–5] 176–203 [204] 205–313 [314–15] 316–52 [353] 354–5 [356].
    Vol. 4: [i–v] vi–xi [xii], [1–3] 4–6 [7] 8–40 [41–2] 43–5 [46] 47–118 [119–20] 121–87 [188–90] 191–310 [311–13] 314 [315] 316–36 [337] 338–64. P. 302 misnumbered '332'.
    Vol. 5: [i–v] vi–xi [xii], [1–3] 4–140 [141–3] 144–78 [179–81] 182–98 [199–201] 202–6 [207–9] 210–53 [254] 255–98 [299–301] 302–45 [346–7] 348–73 [374–5] 376–88 [389] 390–6 [397] 398–412.
    Vol. 6: [i–ix] x–xiv [xv–xvi], [1–3] 4–38 [39–41] 42–73 [74–7] 78–112 [113–15] 116–62 [163–5] 166–201 [202–5] 206–47 [248–51] 252–88 [289–91] 292–312 [313–15] 316–43 [344–5] 346–74, [1] 2.
Contents. Vol. 1: [i] half title: 'THE | POETICAL WORKS | OF | WILLIAM WORDSWORTH.'; [ii] blank; frontispiece, engraved by W. H. Watt from Pickersgill portrait of Wordsworth, dated 1836; [iii] title-page; [iv] printer's imprint; [v] dedication to Sir George Beaumont; [viii] 'ADVERTISEMENT.'; [ix] 'PREFACE | TO THE EDITION OF 1815.'; [xliv] blank; [xlv] 'CONTENTS.'; inserted slip: 'EMENDATIONS AND ERRATA.'; [1] fly title: 'POEMS | REFERRING TO THE PERIOD OF CHILDHOOD.'; [2] blank; [3] text; [45] fly title: 'JUVENILE PIECES.'; [46] thirteen-line note dated 1836; 47 text; [64] blank; [65] fly title: 'DESCRIPTIVE SKETCHES | TAKEN | DURING A PEDESTRIAN TOUR AMONG THE ALPS.'; [66] blank; [67] dedication to Robert Jones; [69] text; [106] blank; [107] fly title: 'POEMS | FOUNDED ON THE AFFECTIONS.'; [108] blank; 109 text; [274] blank; [275] fly title: 'THE WAGGONER.'; [276] dedication to Charles Lamb; 277 text; [311] 'NOTES.'; [314] three-line note; 6 pp. of Moxon's advertisements.
    Vol. 2: [i] half title; [ii] blank; [iii] title-page; [iv] printer's imprint; [v] 'CONTENTS.'; [1] fly title: 'POEMS OF THE FANCY.'; [2] blank; [3] text; [77] fly title: 'POEMS OF THE IMAGINATION.'; [78] blank; [79] text; [233] fly title: 'PETER BELL. | A TALE. | What's in a *Name?* | [row of asterisks] | Brutus will start a Spirit as soon as Cæsar!'; [234] blank; [235] dedication to Southey; 237 text; [284] blank; [285] fly title: 'POEMS | ON THE NAMING OF PLACES.'; [286] 'ADVERTISEMENT.'; [287] text; [303] 'PREFACE' [to *Lyrical Ballads*, 1800]; [338] blank; [339] 'APPENDIX.'; [346] blank; [347] 'NOTES.'; [352] blank.
    Vol. 3: [i] half title; [ii] blank; [iii] title-page; [iv] printer's imprint; [v] 'CONTENTS.'; [1] fly title: 'MISCELLANEOUS SONNETS. | PART I.'; [2] 'DEDICATION.'; [3] text; [107] fly title: 'MEMORIALS | OF | A TOUR IN SCOTLAND.'; [108] blank; [109] text; [173] fly title: 'SONNETS | DEDICATED TO LIBERTY. | PART I.'; [174] blank; [175] text; 255 'THANKSGIVING ODE.'; [274] blank; 275 'INSCRIPTIONS.'; 293 text of miscellaneous poems; [314] blank; [315] 'ESSAY, | SUPPLEMENTARY TO THE PREFACE.'; [353] 'NOTES.'; [356] printer's imprint.

Vol. 4: [i] half title; [ii] blank; [iii] title-page; [iv] printer's imprint; [v] 'CONTENTS.'; [xii] blank; [1] fly title: 'THE RIVER DUDDON. | A SERIES OF SONNETS.'; [2] [five-line note]; [3] dedication to Christopher Wordsworth; [7] text; [41] fly title: 'THE | WHITE DOE OF RYLSTONE; | OR, | THE FATE OF THE NORTONS.'; [42] 'ADVERTISEMENT.'; 43 dedicatory poem to Mary Wordsworth; [46] prefatory poem; 47 text; [119] fly title: 'MEMORIALS | OF | A TOUR ON THE CONTINENT | 1820.'; [120] 'DEDICATION.'; 121 text; [188] blank; [189] fly title: 'ECCLESIASTICAL SONNETS. | IN SERIES. | PART I. | FROM THE INTRO-DUCTION OF CHRISTIANITY INTO BRITAIN, | TO THE CONSUMMATION OF THE PAPAL DOMINION.'; [190] three lines of verse; 191 'ADVERTISEMENT.'; 193 text; [311] fly title: 'POSTSCRIPT, NOTES, &c.'; [312] blank; [313] text.

Vol. 5: [i] half title; [ii] blank; [iii] title-page; [iv] printer's imprint; [v] 'CONTENTS.'; [xii] blank; [1] fly title: 'POEMS | OF | SENTIMENT AND REFLECTION.'; [2] introductory poem; [3] text; [141] fly title: 'YARROW REVISITED, | AND | OTHER POEMS, | COMPOSED (TWO EXCEPTED) DURING A TOUR IN SCOTLAND, AND | ON THE ENGLISH BORDER, IN THE AUTUMN OF 1831.'; [142] dedication to Samuel Rogers; [143] text; [179] fly title: 'THE | RUSSIAN FUGITIVE.'; [180] seven-line note; [181] text; [199] fly title: 'STANZAS | SUG-GESTED | IN A STEAM-BOAT OFF ST. BEES' HEADS, | ON THE COAST OF CUMBER-LAND.'; [200] full-page note; [201] text; [207] fly title: 'SONNETS | COMPOSED OR SUG-GESTED DURING A TOUR IN SCOTLAND, | IN THE SUMMER OF 1833.'; [208] eleven-line note; [209] text; [254] miscellaneous poems; [299] fly title: 'EPITAPHS | AND | ELEGIAC PIECES.'; [300] blank; [301] text; [346] blank; [347] 'POSTSCRIPT.'; [374] blank; [375] 'NOTES.'; [389] 'INDEX TO THE POEMS.'; [397] 'INDEX TO THE FIRST LINES.'.

Vol. 6: [i] half title; [ii] blank; [iii] title-page; [iv] printer's imprint; [v] fly title: 'THE EXCUR-SION.'; [vi] blank; [vii] dedication to the Earl of Lonsdale; [viii] blank; [ix] 'PREFACE,'; [xv] 'CONTENTS.'; [xvi] blank; inserted slip: 'ERRATA.'; [1] fly title: 'THE EXCURSION. | [double rule] | BOOK I. | THE WANDERER.'; [2] 'ARGUMENT.'; [3] text; [39] fly title: 'THE EXCURSION. | [double rule] | BOOK II. | THE SOLITARY.'; [40] 'ARGUMENT.'; [41] text; [74] blank; [75] fly title: 'THE EXCURSION. | [double rule] | BOOK III. | DESPONDENCY.'; [76] 'ARGUMENT.'; [77] text; [113] fly title: 'THE EXCURSION. | [double rule] | BOOK IV. | DESPONDENCY CORRECTED.'; [114] 'ARGUMENT.'; [115] text; [163] fly title: 'THE EXCURSION. | [double rule] | BOOK V. | THE PASTOR.'; [164] 'ARGUMENT.'; [165] text; [202] blank; [203] fly title: 'THE EXCURSION. | [double rule] | BOOK VI. | THE CHURCH-YARD AMONG THE MOUNTAINS.'; [204] 'ARGUMENT.'; [205] text; [248] 'END OF THE SIXTH BOOK.'; [249] fly title: 'THE EXCURSION. | [double rule] | BOOK VII. | THE CHURCH-YARD AMONG THE MOUNTAINS | CONTINUED.'; [250] 'ARGUMENT.'; [251] text; [289] fly title: 'THE EXCURSION. | [double rule] | BOOK VIII. | THE PARSON-AGE.'; [290] 'ARGUMENT.'; [291] text; [313] fly title: 'THE EXCURSION. | [double rule] BOOK IX. | DISCOURSE OF THE WANDERER, &c.'; [314] 'ARGUMENT.'; [315] text; [344] blank; [345] 'NOTES.'; 352 'ESSAY UPON EPITAPHS.'; 2 pp. of Moxon's advertisements.

$1, 2 signed, at center of foot. Pagination set in outer margin of headline where running titles are present; otherwise centered at top. Wove paper without watermark. Vol. 1 sheets bulk 1 in.; vol. 2, 1 in.; vol. 3, 1 in.; vol. 4, 1 in.; vol. 5, $1\frac{3}{16}$ in.; vol. 6, $1\frac{1}{16}$ in. Vols, 1, 2 dated 1836; vols. 3-6, 1837. *Binding.* Green cloth, pebble surface; yellow end-papers. Gilt title on spine: 'WORDSWORTH'S | POETICAL | WORKS | I [etc.]'.

Stereotype edition, re-issued with slight alterations from time to time until superseded by the six-volume edition of 1849-50.

102 Another copy.

$6\frac{3}{4} \times 4\frac{1}{16}$ in. Binding as above. Lacks the errata slip in vol. 1.

103 Another copy.

$6\frac{3}{4} \times 4\frac{1}{8}$ in. Black vertically ribbed cloth; yellow end-papers. Ornamental oval-like design blind-stamped on front and back covers. Title in gilt on spine: 'WORDSWORTH'S | POETICAL | WORKS | [space] | VOL. I [etc.].'.

104 THE | EXCURSION; | 𝔄 𝔓𝔬𝔢𝔪. | BY WILLIAM WORDSWORTH. | A NEW EDITION. | [rule] | LONDON: | EDWARD MOXON, DOVER STREET. | [rule] | MDCCCXXXVI.

Special imprints (pp. iv and 374). LONDON: | BRADBURY AND EVANS, PRINTERS, | WHITE-FRIARS.

Collation (6¹¹⁄₁₆ × 4⅛ in.). [A]⁸(–A₃) B–2A⁸ 2B⁴.

Pagination and *Contents* are the same as those of vol. 6 of the *Poetical Works*, 1836–7, described above.

Binding. Old green cloth, probably not original, with manuscript label. Advertised by Moxon as being in 'boards'.

Except for the alteration of the half title and the title-page, and the removal of A₃ (fly title to *The Excursion*), this volume is made up from the same sheets as is vol. 6 of the edition of 1836–7. In neither volume is the half title or the title-page a cancel. As vol. 6 of the collective edition, the book is common; but as a separate edition of *The Excursion*, with the title-page described above, I know of but one other copy, that at Yale.

1837

105 THE COMPLETE | POETICAL WORKS | OF | WILLIAM WORDS-WORTH: | TOGETHER WITH | A DESCRIPTION OF THE | COUNTRY OF THE LAKES IN THE NORTH OF ENGLAND, | NOW PUBLISHED WITH HIS WORKS. | [rule] | [three lines from Akenside] | [rule] | [eight lines from Daniel] | [rule] | EDITED BY | HENRY REED, | PROFESSOR OF ENGLISH LITERATURE IN THE UNIVERSITY OF PENN-SYLVANIA. | [rule] | PHILADELPHIA: | JAMES KAY, JUN. AND BROTHER, 122 CHESTNUT STREET. | BOSTON: JAMES MUNROE AND COMPANY. | PITTSBURGH: JOHN I. KAY & CO. | [line of dots] | 1837.

Special imprint (on p. ii). STEREOTYPED BY J. FAGAN.....PHILADELPHIA.

Collation (10⅛ × 6¾ in.). [A]⁴ B–U⁴ V–W⁴ X–2U⁴ 2V–2W⁴ 2X–3T⁴.

Pagination. [i–iii] iv [v–ix] x–xvi [xvii] xviii–xxiv, [25–7] 28–37 [38–41] 42–55 [56–9] 60–106 [107–9] 110–25 [126–9] 130–324 [325–7] 328–30 [331] 332–4 [335–7] 338–73 [374–7] 378–80 [381] 382–9 [390–3] 394 [395] 396–412 [413] 414–34 [435] 436–44 [445] 446–82 [483–5] 486–95 [496] 497–507 [508] 509–14 [515] 516–35 [536] 537–42 [543] 544–51 [552].

Contents. Frontispiece, engraved by J. B. Longacre from Boxall's portrait of Wordsworth; [i] title-page; [ii] notice of entry and printer's imprint; [iii] 'PREFACE | BY | THE AMERICAN EDITOR.'; [v] sonnet by Hartley Coleridge; [vi] blank; [vii] dedication to Sir George Beaumont; [viii] blank; [ix] 'PREFACE.'; [xvii] 'CONTENTS'; [25] fly title: 'POEMS | REFERRING TO THE PERIOD OF CHILDHOOD.'; [26] blank; [27] text; [38] blank; [39] fly title: 'JUVENILE PIECES.'; [40] six-line note; [41] text; [56] blank; [57] fly title: 'POEMS | FOUNDED ON THE AFFECTIONS.'; [58] blank; [59] text; [107] fly title: 'POEMS OF THE FANCY.'; [108] blank; [109] text; [126] blank; [127] fly title: 'POEMS OF THE IMAGINATION.'; [128] blank; [129] text; [325] fly title: 'POEMS | ON THE NAMING OF PLACES. | [rule] | INSCRIPTIONS.'; [326] blank; [327] text; [335] fly title: 'POEMS OF SENTIMENT AND REFLECTION.'; [336] blank; [337] text; [374] blank; [375] fly title: 'POEMS | REFERRING TO THE PERIOD OF OLD AGE. | [rule] | EPITAPHS AND ELEGIAC POEMS.'; [376] blank; [377] text; [390] blank; [391] fly title: 'THE EXCURSION, | BEING A PORTION OF | THE RECLUSE.'; [392] dedication to the Earl of Lonsdale; [393] text; [483] fly title: 'APPENDIX'; [484] blank; [485] text; [552] blank.

$1 signed, left of center of foot. Running title on verso: 'WORDSWORTH'S POETICAL WORKS'; on recto: varies with the contents. Pagination set in outer margin of headline. Printed in double column, each page within a border of rules. Wove paper, without watermark. Sheets bulk 1⅝ in.

Binding. Full tan sheep; white end-papers. Black leather label, stamped in gold: 'WORDSWORTH'S | POETICAL | WORKS.'.

1838

106 THE | SONNETS | OF | WILLIAM WORDSWORTH. | COL-
LECTED IN ONE VOLUME, | WITH | A FEW ADDITIONAL ONES,
NOW FIRST PUBLISHED. | LONDON: | EDWARD MOXON, DOVER
STREET. | MDCCCXXXVIII.

Special imprints (pp. ii and 478). LONDON: | BRADBURY AND EVANS, PRINTERS TO THE
QUEEN, | WHITEFRIARS.

Collation (6¾ × 4 in.). [A]² χ⁴ B–2H⁸.

Pagination. [i–v] vi–xi [xii], [1–4] 5–53 [54] 55–115 [116–18] 119–45 [146] 147–87 [188–92] 193–212
[213] 214–36 [237–8] 239–82 [283–5] 286–318 [319–21] 322 [323] 324–61 [362] 363–403 [404]
405–40 [441–42] 443–8 [449] 450–77 [478–80]. P. 345 misnumbered '348'.

Contents. [i] title-page; [ii] printer's imprint; [iii] 'ADVERTISEMENT.'; [iv] blank; [v] 'CON-
TENTS.'; [xii] blank; [1] fly title: 'CLASS FIRST. | [rule] | MISCELLANEOUS SONNETS. |
[rule] | PART I.'; [2] blank; [3] 'DEDICATION.'; [4] blank; 5 text; [54] 'PART II.'; [116]
blank; [117] fly title: 'CLASS SECOND. | [rule] | POLITICAL SONNETS. | [rule] | SERIES I.';
[118] blank; 119 text; [146] 'SERIES II.'; [188] blank; [189] fly title: 'CLASS THIRD. | [rule] |
ITINERARY SONNETS. | [rule] | FIRST SERIES. | SELECTED FROM MEMORIALS OF
A TOUR ON THE CONTINENT, | 1820.'; [190] blank; [191] 'DEDICATION.'; [192] blank;
193 text; [213] 'SECOND SERIES.'; [237] ten-line note; [238] 'THIRD SERIES.'; [283] fly title:
'CLASS FOURTH. | [rule] | THE RIVER DUDDON. | [rule] A SERIES OF SONNETS.'; [284]
five-line note; [285] text; [319] fly title: 'CLASS FIFTH. | [rule] | ECCLESIASTICAL SONNETS. |
IN SERIES. | [rule] | PART I. | FROM THE INTRODUCTION OF CHRISTIANITY INTO
BRITAIN, | TO THE CONSUMMATION OF THE PAPAL | DOMINION.'; [320] three lines
of verse; [321] 'ADVERTISEMENT.'; [323] text; [362] 'PART II.'; [404] 'PART III.'; [441]
'VALEDICTORY SONNET.'; [442] three-line note; 443 text of miscellaneous sonnets; [449]
'NOTES.'; [478] printer's imprint; [479–80] Moxon's advertisements.

$1, 2 signed, at center of foot. Running titles vary with contents. Pagination set in outer margin of
headline. Wove paper, without watermark. Sheets bulk 1⅛ in.

Binding. Dark green cloth with diaper surface; yellow end-papers. Ornamental oval-like design blind-
stamped on front and back covers. Gilt title on spine, within an ornamental frame: 'WORDS-
WORTH'S | SONNETS'. Some copies have dark green cloth with a fine diaper surface (Dyce
Collection, Victoria and Albert Museum), or dark green cloth with a pebble surface (British
Museum), or purple vertically ribbed cloth (St. John's College, Cambridge).

The title-page appears in two states. In one, the word 'LONDON' is followed by a colon, and the
'L' stands directly above the first 'O' in 'MOXON'. In the other, 'LONDON' is followed by no
punctuation, and the 'L' stands above the space between the first 'O' and the 'X' in 'MOXON'.
In the unpunctuated state, the word 'LONDON' is of a very slightly larger type-font.

107 Another copy.

6¼ × 3¹⁵⁄₁₆ in. Full green sheep; yellow end-papers; all edges gilt. With the colon following 'LONDON'
on the title-page. Advertisements lacking.

108 Another copy.

6¹¹⁄₁₆ × 4¹⁄₁₆ in. Half brown morocco over marbled boards, by Max Adjarian. With an additional leaf of
advertisements at the end. Title-page has no colon after 'LONDON'.

1839

109 YARROW REVISITED; | AND | 𝔒𝔱𝔥𝔢𝔯 𝔓𝔬𝔢𝔪𝔰. | BY | WILLIAM WORDSWORTH. | [cut of a cherub with a lyre] | LONDON: | EDWARD MOXON, DOVER STREET. | MDCCCXXXIX.

Special imprints (pp. iv and 250). LONDON: | BRADBURY AND EVANS, PRINTERS, | WHITE-FRIARS. [On p. iv the colon after 'LONDON' is defective.]

Collation (5 9/16 × 3 11/16 in.). [A]⁶ B–Q⁸ R⁴ S².

Pagination. [i–v] vi–xi [xii], [1–3] 4–115 [116–18] 119–66 [167–8] 169–94 [195–6] 197–220 [221] 222–49 [250–2].

Contents. [i] half title: 'YARROW REVISITED; | AND | 𝔒𝔱𝔥𝔢𝔯 𝔓𝔬𝔢𝔪𝔰.'; [ii] blank; [iii] title-page; [iv] printer's imprint; [v] 'CONTENTS.'; [xii] blank; [1] fly title: 'YARROW REVISITED, | AND | OTHER POEMS, | COMPOSED (TWO EXCEPTED) DURING A TOUR IN SCOT-LAND, AND | ON THE ENGLISH BORDER, IN THE AUTUMN OF 1831.'; [2] blank; [3] text; 7 'SONNETS.'; 21 text of miscellaneous poems; 26 'NOTES.'; 31 'THE EGYPTIAN MAID; | OR, | THE ROMANCE OF THE WATER LILY.'; 44 text of miscellaneous poems; 61 'THE ARMENIAN LADY'S LOVE.'; 68 text of miscellaneous poems; 98 'EVENING VOLUNTARIES.'; 111 text of miscellaneous poems; [116] blank; [117] fly title: 'SONNETS | COMPOSED OR SUGGESTED DURING A TOUR IN SCOTLAND, | IN THE SUMMER OF 1833.'; [118] eleven-line note; 119 text; 141 text of miscellaneous poems; 148 'NOTES.'; 153 text of miscellaneous poems; [167] fly title: 'STANZAS | SUGGESTED | IN A STEAM-BOAT OFF ST. BEES' HEADS. | ON THE COAST OF CUMBERLAND.'; [168] full-page note; 169 text; 175 'NOTE.'; 176 text of miscellaneous poems; [195] fly title: 'STANZAS | ON | THE POWER OF SOUND.'; [196] 'ARGUMENT.'; 197 text; 204 text of miscellaneous poems; 212 'EPITAPHS, ETC.'; [221] 'POSTSCRIPT.'; [250] printer's imprint; [251–2] Moxon's advertisement, undated.

$1, 2 signed, at center of foot; R2 unsigned. Pagination set in outer margin of headline when running titles are present; otherwise centered at top. Wove paper, without watermark. Sheets bulk ⅝ in.

Binding. Half brown morocco over marbled boards, by Max Adjarian. The Indiana University copy is in purple cloth with diaper surface and with an elaborate design blind-stamped on front and back covers; yellow end-papers; all edges gilt. On the spine, between two gilt panels, is the title in gilt: 'WORDSWORTH'S | YARROW | REVISITED'. Bound into the Swarthmore College copy is the original cloth binding; unlike the Indiana copy, it is a dark green vertically ribbed cloth.

Third edition. With 'VOL. V.' at the inner margin of the direction line of $1, probably an indication that the volume was designed to be added to the four-volume Longman edition of 1832. For some reason this is an extremely rare book.

110 THE COMPLETE | POETICAL WORKS | OF | WILLIAM WORDS-WORTH: | TOGETHER WITH | A DESCRIPTION OF THE | COUNTRY OF THE LAKES IN THE NORTH OF ENGLAND, | NOW PUBLISHED WITH HIS WORKS. | [rule] | [three lines from Akenside] | [rule] | [eight lines from Daniel] | [rule] | EDITED BY | HENRY REED, | PROFESSOR OF ENGLISH LITERATURE IN THE UNIVERSITY OF PENN-SYLVANIA. | [rule] | PHILADELPHIA: | JAMES KAY, JUN. AND BROTHER, 122 CHESTNUT STREET. | BOSTON: JAMES MUNROE AND COMPANY. | PITTSBURGH:—C. H. KAY & CO. | [line of dots] | 1839.

Except for the imprint and date on the title-page and the better quality of paper, this is identical with the Philadelphia stereotype edition of 1837.

Full tan sheep, with remnants of a black leather label.

1840

111 Caption: 'WE ARE SEVEN.'.

Imprint. None.
Collation (5⅛ × 3⅛ in.). A quire of four leaves.
Pagination. [1] 2–7 [8].
Contents. [1] caption, woodcut of a woman and two men, and text, beginning: 'A simple Child, dear brother Tim'; [8] 'TO A ROBIN REDBREAST.'. Each page contains a woodcut, and the final page is enclosed within a border.

In size and typography, this chapbook closely resembles similar publications bearing the imprint: 'ALNWICK: | PUBLISHED BY W. DAVISON. | [rule] | *One Halfpenny*.'. According to the British Museum Catalogue, the Davison chapbooks appeared about 1840. The poem To a Robin Redbreast is not by Wordsworth. See Helen Hughes, 'Two Wordsworth Chapbooks', *Modern Philology*, xxv (1927), 207–10.

112 Caption (on recto of each leaf): 'ENGLAND IN 1840!'.

Imprint. None.
Collation (7⅝ × 4½ in.). Eight disjunct leaves, unsigned and unpaged, printed on one side only, one poem to the page.
Contents. Fol. [1] 'Another year!—another deadly blow!'; fol. [2] 'England! the time is come when thou should'st wean'; fol. [3] 'This Land we from our fathers had in trust'; fol. [4] 'It was a *moral* end for which they fought'; fol. [5] '[Here pause, the poet] Claims at least this praise.'. [The foregoing words in brackets are omitted; the caption 'England in 1840' is to be read as the subject of 'claims.'. Added to this sonnet are the last four lines of Wordsworth's To Toussaint L'Ouverture.]; fol. [6] 'It is not to be thought of that the Flood'; fol. [7] 'Milton! thou should'st be living at this hour.'; fol. [8] 'There is a bondage worse, far worse to bear.'. Fols. 1, 4, and 5 contain footnotes. At the foot of each page is printed 'WORDSWORTH.'.
Binding. Modern brown morocco; each leaf fastened to a hinge.

The occasion of this publication remains unknown. Only one other copy is known, that at Swarthmore.

113 THE | POETICAL WORKS | OF | WILLIAM WORDSWORTH. | [rule] | A New Edition. | IN SIX VOLUMES. | VOL. I [etc.]. | LONDON: | EDWARD MOXON, DOVER STREET. | [rule] | MDCCCXL.

A re-issue of the stereotype edition of 1836–7 with a few revisions. Bibliographical variations follow.
   Vol. 1: collation is [*a*]⁸ *b*–*c*⁸ B–U⁸ X⁴ Y1.
   Vol. 4: collation is [A]⁶ B–2A⁸ 2B². Pagination unchanged up to p. 319; thereafter, 320–43 [344] 345–71 [372]. Contents unchanged up to p. 320; thereafter, though the text seems to be unchanged, part of it is reset in a larger font.
   Vol. 5: collation is [*a*]⁴ *b*² B–2E⁸ 2F⁶. Pagination unchanged up to p. 388; thereafter, [389–90] 391–402 [403] 404–20 [421] 422–8 [429] 430–44. Contents unchanged up to p. 388; thereafter, [389] fly title: 'APPENDIX.'; [390] 'ADVERTISEMENT.'; 391 text; [403] 'NOTES.'; 405 'EPISTOLA'; [421] 'INDEX TO THE POEMS.'; [429] 'INDEX TO THE FIRST LINES.'.
Binding. Black vertically ribbed cloth with oval-like design blind stamped on front and back covers; yellow end-papers. Gilt title on spine: 'WORDSWORTH'S | POETICAL | WORKS | [space] | VOL. I [etc.].'.

1841

114 THE EXCURSION. | A Poem. | BY | WILLIAM WORDSWORTH. | [rule] | A NEW EDITION. | LONDON: | EDWARD MOXON, DOVER STREET. | [rule] | MDCCCXLI.

A re-issue of the stereotype edition of 1836 and hence presumably identical with vol. 6 of the stereotype collective edition of that year and later.

Binding. Purple cloth with oval-like design blind-stamped on front and back cover; yellow end-papers. Gilt title on spine: 'WORDSWORTH'S | EXCURSION'.

115 THE | POETICAL WORKS | OF | WILLIAM WORDSWORTH. | [rule] | 𝔄 𝔑𝔢𝔴 𝔈𝔡𝔦𝔱𝔦𝔬𝔫. | IN SIX VOLUMES. | VOL. I [etc.]. | LONDON: | EDWARD MOXON, DOVER STREET. | [rule] | MDCCCXLI.

A re-issue of the stereotype edition of 1840, with a few variations, chiefly in vol. 5. In that volume the collation is [A]⁶ B–2C⁸ 2D⁴ 2E². The pagination is unchanged up to p. 388; thereafter, [389] 390–6 [397] 398–412. The contents is unchanged up to p. 388; thereafter, [389] 'INDEX TO THE POEMS.'; [397] 'INDEX TO THE FIRST LINES.'. The Appendix of the volume of 1840 has been omitted.

Binding. As 1840.

116 POEMS | FROM | THE POETICAL WORKS | OF | WILLIAM WORDSWORTH | [rule] | Go forth, my little Book! pursue thy way; | Go forth, and please the gentle and the good. | [rule] | NEW YORK: | GEO. A. LEAVITT, PUBLISHER, | No. 8 HOWARD STREET.

Special imprint. None.
Collation (4½ × 3 in.). [1]⁸ 2–18⁸(–18/8).
Pagination. [i–v] vi–x [xi–xiii] xiv–xvi, 17–281 [282–6]. Numerous defects in pagination.
Contents. [1] half title: 'POMES | OF | WILLIAM WORDSWORTH'; [ii] blank; engraved frontispiece: girl playing a stringed instrument to a group of listeners; [iii] title-page; [iv] notice of entry; [v] 'PREFACE.'; [xi] extract from *The Excursion*; [xii] blank; [xiii] 'CONTENTS.'; 17 text; [282–6] blank.
$1 signed, at center of foot. Sigs. 15 and 16 unsigned. Pagination set in outer margin of headline when running titles are present; otherwise centered at top. Wove paper, without watermark. Sheets bulk 1 in.
Binding. Blue cloth; monogram 'G A L' blind-stamped, within a blind-stamped border, on front and back covers; all edges gilt; yellow end-papers. Spine gilt with gilt title: 'WORDSWORTH'S | POEMS'.

The title-page is without date; the date of entry (p. iv) is 1841.

1842

117 POEMS | ON THE | LOSS AND RE-BUILDING | OF | ST. MARY'S CHURCH, CARDIFF. | BY | WILLIAM WORDSWORTH. | JAMES MONTGOMERY. | THOMAS WILLIAM BOOKER. | JOHN DIX. | [rule] | CARDIFF: W. BIRD. | [rule] | 1842.

Special imprint. None.
Collation (6 × 3¾ in.). One quire, of 12 leaves.
Pagination. [1–7] 8–11 [12–13] 14 [15] 16–19 [20–1] 22–4.
Contents. [1] title-page; [2] blank; [3] note within square brackets: 'The following Poems were written by their respective Authors for the purpose of adding something to the Fund for rebuilding the New Church of Saint Mary, Cardiff. But a limited number were struck off, and numerous applications having been made for them, they are now printed for the first time in a collected form.'; [4] blank; [5] 'SONNET.' [by Wordsworth]; [6] blank; [7] text of another poem; [12] blank; [13] text; [20] blank; [21] text.

A photostat of the only known copy of the original, that in the Ashley Library, British Museum.

118 POEMS, | CHIEFLY OF EARLY AND LATE YEARS; | INCLUDING | THE BORDERERS, | 𝔄 𝔗𝔯𝔞𝔤𝔢𝔡𝔶. | BY WILLIAM WORDSWORTH. | LONDON: | EDWARD MOXON, DOVER STREET. | MDCCCXLII.

Special imprints (pp. ii, 406, 412). LONDON: | BRADBURY AND EVANS, PRINTERS, WHITE-FRIARS.

Collation (6¾ × 4 1/16 in.). [A]⁶ B–2C⁸ 2D⁴ χ².

Pagination. [i–iii] iv–vii [viii–ix] x–xi [xii], [1–3] 4 [5] 6–94 [95–7] 98–146 [147] 148–242 [243–5] 246–397 [398–9] 400–5 [406–12].

Contents. [i] title-page; [ii] printer's imprint; [iii] 'CONTENTS.' [viii] blank; [ix] 'PRELUDE.'; [xii] 'ERRATUM.'; [1] fly title: 'GUILT AND SORROW; | OR, | INCIDENTS UPON SALISBURY PLAIN.'; [2] blank; [3] 'ADVERTISEMENT.'; [5] text; 43 text of miscellaneous poems; [95] fly title: 'MEMORIALS OF A TOUR IN ITALY. | 1837.' | [rule] | TO HENRY CRABBE ROBINSON. | [rule] | [nine lines of verse in italics] | *W. WORDSWORTH.* | RYDAL MOUNT, | *Feb. 14th,* 1842.'; [96] ten-line note; [97] text; [147] 'NOTES.'; 149 text of miscellaneous poems; [243] fly title: 'THE BORDERERS. | 𝔄 𝔗𝔯𝔞𝔤𝔢𝔡𝔶. | (COMPOSED 1795–6.)'; [244] 'DRAMATIS PERSONÆ.'; [245] text; [398] blank; [399] 'NOTES.'; [406] printer's imprint; [407–8] advertisements; [409] a half title: 'THE | POETICAL WORKS | OF | WILLIAM WORDSWORTH.'; [410] blank; [411] a title-page: 'THE | POETICAL WORKS | OF | WILLIAM WORDS-WORTH. | [rule] | VOL. VII. | LONDON: | EDWARD MOXON, DOVER STREET. | [rule] | MDCCCXLII.'; [412] printer's imprint.

$1, 2 signed, at center of foot. Pagination in outer margin of the headline when running titles are present; otherwise centered at top. Wove paper, without watermark. Sheets bulk 1⅛ in.

Binding. Purple cloth with diaper surface; oval-like design blind-stamped on front and back covers; yellow end-papers. Gilt title on spine: 'POEMS | CHIEFLY OF EARLY | AND LATE YEARS | BY | W. WORDSWORTH'. A copy at Yale is in plain-woven purple cloth. The Swarthmore College copy has a variant title on the spine: 'WORDSWORTH'S | POEMS | OF EARLY AND | LATE YEARS'.

First edition. Inserted at the end are a half title and a title-page, the latter designated 'VOL. VII.', for the use of those who wished to consider this vol. 7 of the collective edition. Crabb Robinson's name is misspelled on p. 95.

The title-page bears the following inscription, in the hand of Wordsworth: 'Dorothy Susan Tudor, from her affectionate Aunt Isabella Fenwick, inscribed by Wm Wordsworth, Rydal, July 4th 1842.'

119 THE | POETICAL WORKS | OF | WILLIAM WORDSWORTH. | [rule] | VOL. VII. | LONDON: | EDWARD MOXON, DOVER STREET. | [rule] | MDCCCXLII.

This is *Poems Chiefly of Early and Late Years* with the title-page cancelled and replaced by a half title and a title-page as explained in the note to the previous volume.

Binding. Mottled calf, gilt.

The front fly leaf is inscribed: 'Wm Wordsworth, Rydal Mount, 6th Decʳ 1842.'

120 [Within a frame of rules] POEMS | FROM | THE POETICAL WORKS | OF | WILLIAM WORDSWORTH. | [rule] | Go forth, my little Book! pursue thy way; | Go forth, and please the gentle and the good. | [rule] | *PHILADELPHIA:* | PUBLISHED BY HOOKER & AGNEW, | *Corner of Chestnut and Fifth Streets.* | [row of dots] | 1842.

Special imprint (on p. iv). [wavy rule] | Stereotyped by Murray & Joyce. | [wavy rule] | Printed by T. K. & P. G. Collins. | [wavy rule].

Collation (4 7/16 × 2 13/16 in.). [1]⁸ 2–18⁸.

Pagination and *Contents* are identical with those of the New York edition of [1841] except that leaf 18/1 (pp. 282–3) is present and that the frontispiece differs. The new frontispiece is an engraved title-page illustrating 'THE CUMBERLAND BEGGAR' and misspelling the poet's name 'WARDSWORTH'.

Binding. Brown embossed cloth with a gilt urn on front and back covers. Spine gilt, with title: 'WORDSWORTH'S | POEMS'.

This copy is inscribed: 'Margaret C. Yarnall from her Father, 1873.' It contains a note indicating that this may be the copy Ellis Yarnall showed Wordsworth in 1849 and that Wordsworth (who had not previously seen the edition) signed on a leaf since removed.

1843

121 Caption: 'GRACE DARLING.'.

Imprint (on p. 4). [rule] | Carlisle: Printed at the Office of Charles Thurnam.
Collation (6$\frac{7}{16}$ × 4 in.). A fold of two leaves.
Pagination. [1] 2–4.
Contents. [1] caption and text. Between the last line of verse (p. 4) and the printer's imprint appears the notice: '[*Not published.*]'.
Wove paper, without watermark.

Formerly John Drinkwater's copy, with his signature on p. 1.

122 Another copy.

As above, but with the signature 'Wm Wordsworth' at the foot of p. 4.

123 Another copy.

As above, with the signature 'Wm Wordsworth' at the foot of p. 4.

124 Another copy.

Formerly Joseph Cottle's copy, signed by Wordsworth and inscribed by Cottle: 'By Wordsworth, with his signature, sent by W. W. to J. Cottle.'

125 Caption: 'GRACE DARLING, | BY | WILLIAM WORDSWORTH.'.

Imprint (on p. 3). [rule] | NEWCASTLE: PRINTED BY T. AND J. HODGSON, UNION STREET.
Collation (7$\frac{1}{2}$ × 5 in.). A fold of two leaves.
Pagination. [1] 2–3 [4].
Contents. [1] caption, thin-and-thick rule, text; [4] blank. Laid paper, watermarked '1841'.

126 Caption: 'VERSES | COMPOSED AT THE REQUEST OF JANE WALLAS PENFOLD, | BY WILLIAM WORDSWORTH, ESQ. | POET LAUREATE.'.

Imprint. None.
Collation (12$\frac{1}{2}$ × 9$\frac{15}{16}$ in.). A fold of two leaves. Unpaged.
Contents. [1–2] Wordsworth's poem; [3–4] 'Song of the Madeira Flowers, Composed at the Request of Jane Wallas Penfold, By Mrs. Calverley Bewicke.'. Wordsworth's poem is followed by a facsimile of his signature and a misspelling of his residence: 'Rydul Mount, 1st January, 1843.'.

A facsimile of the only known copy, that in the Ashley Library, British Museum.

127 [Within elaborate decorations] 𝕾𝖊𝖑𝖊𝖈𝖙 𝕻𝖎𝖊𝖈𝖊𝖘 | from the | 𝕻𝖔𝖊𝖒𝖘 | of | 𝖂𝖎𝖑𝖑𝖎𝖆𝖒 𝖂𝖔𝖗𝖉𝖘𝖜𝖔𝖗𝖙𝖍. | [vignette of Rydal Mount] | 𝕷𝖔𝖓𝖉𝖔𝖓. 𝕰𝖉𝖜ᵇ 𝔐𝖔𝖝𝖔𝖓

Special imprints (p. ii). LONDON: | BRADBURY AND EVANS, PRINTERS, WHITEFRIARS. (On p. 264): BRADBURY AND EVANS, PRINTERS, WHITEFRIARS.
Collation (6$\frac{7}{16}$ × 4$\frac{5}{8}$ in.). [A]⁴ χ² B–R⁸ S⁴.
Pagination. [i–xii], [1] 2–263 [264]; many pages are unnumbered.

Contents. [i] half title: [within a frame of rules] '𝔖𝔢𝔩𝔢𝔠𝔱 𝔓𝔦𝔢𝔠𝔢𝔰, | ETC.'; [ii] printer's imprint; [iii] title-page; [iv] blank; [v] dedication to Queen Victoria; [vi] vignette within a border of rules; [vii] 'ADVERTISEMENT.'; [xi] 'CONTENTS.'; [1] text.

$1 signed, in right corner of foot; Sig. K is centered. Each page set in an elaborate ornamental border. Pagination in lower right corner, within the border; pagination omitted when signature is present. No running titles. Wove paper, without watermark. Sheets bulk ¾ in.

Binding. Pale green cloth with a flower-pattern; blind-stamped border on front and back covers; within an elaborate gilt garland on the front cover, in gilt: 'SELECT PIECES | FROM THE POEMS | OF | WORDSWORTH'. Spine decorated in gilt, with gilt title: 'SELECT PIECES | FROM | WORDSWORTH'. Pale yellow end-papers. All edges gilt. Some copies have red cloth.

This copy is inscribed: 'William Wordsworth, Rydal, 21st Augst 1849.'

128 [Within elaborate decorations] 𝔖𝔢𝔩𝔢𝔠𝔱 𝔓𝔦𝔢𝔠𝔢𝔰 | from the | 𝔓𝔬𝔢𝔪𝔰 | of 𝔚𝔦𝔩𝔩𝔦𝔞𝔪 𝔚𝔬𝔯𝔡𝔰𝔴𝔬𝔯𝔱𝔥. | [vignette of Rydal Mount] | 𝔏𝔬𝔫𝔡𝔬𝔫. 𝔍𝔞𝔪𝔢𝔰 𝔅𝔲𝔯𝔫𝔰

Special imprint (p. ii). LONDON: | PRINTED BY ROBSON, LEVEY, AND FRANKLYN, | Great New Street, Fetter Lane.

Collation (6½ × 4¹¹⁄₁₆ in.). [A]⁶ B–Q⁸.

Pagination. [i–xii], [1] 2–240. 4 pp. advertisements. Most of the pages are unnumbered.

Contents. [i] half title: [within a frame of rules] '𝔖𝔢𝔩𝔢𝔠𝔱 𝔓𝔦𝔢𝔠𝔢𝔰, | ETC.'; [ii] printer's imprint; [iii] title-page; [iv] blank; [v] dedication to Queen Victoria; [vi] vignette within a border of rules; [vii] '𝔄𝔡𝔳𝔢𝔯𝔱𝔦𝔰𝔢𝔪𝔢𝔫𝔱.'; [xi] '𝔗𝔬𝔫𝔱𝔢𝔫𝔱𝔰.'; [1] text; [241–4] James Burns's advertisements.

$1 signed, in lower right corner. Each page set in an elaborate ornamental border. Pagination in lower right corner, within the border, but most of the pages are without numbers. No running titles. Wove paper, without watermark. Sheets bulk ¾ in.

Binding. Gray paper; yellow end-papers. Heavily ornamented title on front cover: '𝔖𝔢𝔩𝔢𝔠𝔱 𝔓𝔦𝔢𝔠𝔢𝔰 | from the | 𝔓𝔬𝔢𝔪𝔰 | of | 𝔚𝔦𝔩𝔩𝔦𝔞𝔪 𝔚𝔬𝔯𝔡𝔰𝔴𝔬𝔯𝔱𝔥. | 𝔏𝔬𝔫𝔡𝔬𝔫. | 𝔍𝔞𝔪𝔢𝔰 𝔅𝔲𝔯𝔫𝔰.' On back cover, within an ornamental border, is a vignette of Dungeon-Ghyll Force. Spine flaked away on this copy.

In general appearance this book closely resembles the one preceding, and it contains the same selections, page-borders, and illustrations. The typesetting, however, is different throughout, and the Preface acknowledges Moxon's permission to publish.

129 [Within a frame of rules] POEMS | FROM | THE POETICAL WORKS | OF | WILLIAM WORDSWORTH. | [rule] | Go forth, my little Book! pursue thy way; | Go forth, and please the gentle and the good. | [rule] | 𝔓𝔥𝔦𝔩𝔞𝔡𝔢𝔩𝔭𝔥𝔦𝔞: | PUBLISHED BY JOHN LOCKEN, | *No.* 311 *Market Street.* | [row of dots] | 1843.

Special imprint (on p. iv). GIHON, FAIRCHILD AND CO., PRINTERS, | S. E. Corner of Market and Seventh Sts.

Pagination and *Contents* identical with those of the edition of 1842.

Binding. Green cloth, with a gilt fountain within a blind-stamped border on front and back covers. Spine decorated in gilt, with gilt title: 'WORDSWORTH'S | POEMS'.

130 THE | POETICAL WORKS | OF | WILLIAM WORDSWORTH. | [rule] | 𝔄 𝔑𝔢𝔴 𝔈𝔡𝔦𝔱𝔦𝔬𝔫. | IN SIX VOLUMES. | VOL. I [etc.]. | LONDON: | EDWARD MOXON, DOVER STREET. | [rule] | MDCCCXLIII.

A re-issue of the stereotype edition. Apparently identical with that of 1841.

1844

131 [Within a frame of rules] POEMS | FROM | THE POETICAL WORKS | OF | WILLIAM WORDSWORTH. | [rule] | Go forth, my little Book! pursue thy way; | Go forth, and please the gentle and the good. | [rule] Philadelphia: | PUBLISHED BY JOHN LOCKEN, | *No.* 311 *Market Street.* | [row of dots] | 1844.

Special imprint (on p. iv). [wavy rule] | STEREOTYPED BY C. W. MURRAY & CO. | PRINTED BY BARRINGTON & HASWELL. | [wavy rule].
Pagination and *Contents* identical with those of the 1843 edition, except that the engraved title-page has been re-engraved and the poet's name thereon correctly spelled.
Binding. Brown vertically ribbed cloth with blind-stamped decorations on both covers. Gilt decorations on spine, and title in gilt: 'WORDSWORTH'S | POEMS'.

132 Another copy.

As above, except that the binding is green vertically ribbed cloth.

1845

133 KENDAL AND WINDERMERE | RAILWAY. | [rule] | TWO LETTERS | RE-PRINTED FROM THE MORNING POST. | REVISED, WITH ADDITIONS. | KENDAL: | PRINTED BY R. BRANTHWAITE AND SON.

Special imprint (on p. 23). KENDAL: | PRINTED BY R. BRANTHWAITE AND SON.
Collation ($6\frac{11}{16} \times 4\frac{3}{16}$ in.). A quire of 12 leaves.
Pagination. [1–5] 6–23 [24]. Pagination set at center of top.
Contents. [1] title-page; [2] blank; [3] 'SONNET | ON THE PROJECTED KENDAL AND WINDERMERE RAILWAY.'; [4] blank; [5] text; [24] blank.
Binding. Full green leather.

This copy is twice inscribed by Wordsworth; on the title-page: 'Frederic Westley from Wm Wordsworth, Rydal Mount, 18th Augst –45'; and on the verso of the title-page: 'A Relative of mine, about 30 years older than myself, being congratulated on the great advantage she must have had in being brought up in the romantic County of Cumberland, said dont think about it, when I was young there were *no* Lakes & Mountains. W. W.'

134 Another copy.

KENDAL AND WINDERMERE | RAILWAY. | [rule] | TWO LETTERS | RE-PRINTED FROM THE MORNING POST. | REVISED, WITH ADDITIONS. | LONDON: | WHITTAKER AND CO., AVE MARIA LANE, AND EDWARD | MOXON, DOVER STREET. | R. BRANTH-WAITE AND SON, KENDAL. | [rule] | *Price Four Pence.*

7 × 4¼ in. Stitched, as issued. Title-page varies; otherwise identical with the preceding copy.

135 [Within a frame of rules] THE | POEMS | OF | WILLIAM WORDS-WORTH, D.C.L., | POET LAUREATE, ETC. ETC. | A NEW EDITION. | LONDON: | EDWARD MOXON, DOVER STREET. | [rule] | MDCCCXLV.

Special imprints (pp. ii and 620). LONDON: | BRADBURY AND EVANS, PRINTERS, WHITE-FRIARS.

Collation (9½ × 6¼ in.). [*a*]² *b*⁸ *c*² B–2Q⁸ 2R⁶.

Pagination. [i–v] vi–xxiv, [1] 2–535 [536–7] 538–66 [567] 568–608 [609] 610–12 [613] 614–19 [620].

Contents. Frontispiece, engraved by W. Finden from Chantrey's bust of Wordsworth; engraved title-page with vignette of Rydal Mount, signed G. Howes and W. Finden; [i] title-page; [ii] printer's imprint; [iii] introductory poem; [iv] blank; [v] 'CONTENTS.'; [1] text; [536] blank; [537] 'NOTES.'; [567] 'APPENDIX, PREFACES, | ETC. ETC.'; [609] 'INDEX TO THE POEMS.'; [613] 'INDEX TO THE FIRST LINES.'; [620] printer's imprint.

$1, 2 signed, at foot of right-hand column. Printed in double column, each page enclosed within a frame of rules. Running titles throughout. Pagination in outer margin of headline. Wove paper, without watermark. Sheets bulk 1⅝ in.

Binding. Faded purplish cloth; blind-stamped ornamental panel on front and back covers; pale yellow end-papers. Blind-stamped decoration on spine, with gilt title: 'WORDSWORTH'S | POETICAL | WORKS.'

This edition presents important revisions of the text.

1846

136 [Within a frame of rules] POEMS | FROM | THE POETICAL WORKS | OF | WILLIAM WORDSWORTH. | [rule] | Go forth, my little Book! pursue thy way; | Go forth, and please the gentle and the good. | [rule] | 𝔓𝔥𝔦𝔩𝔞𝔡𝔢𝔩𝔭𝔥𝔦𝔞: | URIAH HUNT & SON, | 44 *North Fourth Street.* | [row of dots] | 1846.

Special imprint. None.

Pagination and *Contents* are identical with those of the edition of 1844.

Binding. Green diagonally ribbed cloth with blind-stamped decorations on both covers. Gilt urn on front cover only. Gilt spine, with gilt title: 'WORDSWORTH'S | POEMS'.

137 Another copy.

Identical with the above except that the binding is yellow cloth with pebble surface.

138 THE | POETICAL WORKS | OF | WILLIAM WORDSWORTH, D.C.L., | POET LAUREATE, HONORARY MEMBER OF THE ROYAL SOCIETY OF EDINBURGH, AND | OF THE ROYAL IRISH ACADEMY, ETC. ETC. | IN SEVEN VOLUMES. | VOL. I [etc.]. | A NEW AND REVISED EDITION. | LONDON: | EDWARD MOXON, DOVER STREET. | MDCCCXLVI.

Special imprints (on both verso of title-page and at end of text in all volumes). LONDON: | BRAD-BURY AND EVANS, PRINTERS, WHITEFRIARS.

Collation (6¾ × 4¹/₁₆ in.). Vol. 1: [*a*]⁸ *b*–*c*⁸ B–X⁸ Y⁸ [–Y8].

Vol. 2: [A]⁴ B–Z⁸.

Vol. 3: [A]⁶ B–Z⁸ 2A².

Vol. 4: [A]⁶ B–2B⁸ 2C1.

Vol. 5: [A]⁶ B–2B⁸ 2C⁴.

Vol. 6: [A]⁸ B–2B⁸.

Vol. 7: [A]⁸ B–2A⁸ 2B⁴.

Pagination: Vol. 1: [i–vii] viii–ix [x–xi] xii–xl [xli] xlii–xliv, [1–3] 4–44 [45–6] 47–63 [64–7] 68 [69] 70–95 [96–9] 100 [101] 102–6 107*–126* [107–8] 109–273 [274–6] 277–310 [311] 312–13 [314].

Vol. 2: [i–v] vi–viii, [1–3] 4–76 [77–9] 80–232 [233–5] 236–83 [284–7] 288–302 302* 303 303* 304–35 [336–7] 338–43 [344–5] 346–9 [350]. No pagination on p. 10.

Vol. 3: [i–v] vi–xii, [1–3] 4–106 [107–9] 110–72 [173–5] 176–203 [204] 205–313 [314–15] 316–52 [353] 354–5 [356].

Vol. 4: [i–v] vi–xii, [1–3] 4–6 [7] 8–40 [41–2] 43–5 [46] 47–118 [119–20] 121–87 [188–90] 191–232 232* 233 233* 234–7 237* 238 238* 239–83 283* 284 284* 285 285* 286 286* 287–94

294* 295 295* 296 296* 297 297* 298 298* 299 299* 300–10 [311–13] 314 [315] 316–43 [344] 345–72.

Vol. 5: [i–v] vi–xi [xii], [1–3] 4–140 [141–3] 144–78 [179–81] 182–98 [199–201] 202–6 206* [207–207*–208–9] 210–98 [299–301] 302–45 [346–7] 348–73 [374–5] 376–88 [389–90]. No pagination on p. 74.

Vol. 6: [i–v] vi–x [xi] xii–xiii [xiv–xvi], [1] 2–49 [50–3] 54–178 [179] 180–217 [218–21] 222–350 [351] 352–9 [360–1] 362–8 [369] 370–84. P. 305 misnumbered '350'.

Vol. 7: [i–ix] x–xiv [xv–xvi], [1–3] 4–38 [39–41] 42–73 [74–7] 78–112 [113–15] 116–62 [163–5] 166–201 [202–5] 206–47 [248–51] 252–88 [289–91] 292–312 [313–15] 316–43 [344–5] 346–74 [375–6].

Contents. Vol. 1: [i] half title: 'THE | POETICAL WORKS | OF | WILLIAM WORDSWORTH.'; [ii] blank; frontispiece, engraved by W. H. Watt from the Pickersgill portrait of Wordsworth, dated 1836; [iii] title-page; [iv] printer's imprint; [v] introductory poem; [vi] blank; [vii] dedication to Sir George Beaumont; [x] blank; [xi] 'PREFACE | TO THE EDITION OF 1815.'; [xli] 'CONTENTS.'; [1] fly title: 'POEMS | REFERRING TO THE PERIOD OF CHILDHOOD.'; [2] blank; [3] text; [45] fly title: 'POEMS WRITTEN IN YOUTH.'; [46] seven lines of notes; 47 text; [64] blank; [65] fly title: 'DESCRIPTIVE SKETCHES | TAKEN | DURING A PEDESTRIAN TOUR AMONG THE ALPS.'; [66] blank; [67] dedication to Robert Jones; [69] text; [96] blank; [97] fly title: 'GUILT AND SORROW; | OR, | INCIDENTS UPON SALISBURY PLAIN.'; [98] blank; [99] 'ADVERTISEMENT,'; [101] text; [107] fly title: 'POEMS | FOUNDED ON THE AFFECTIONS.'; [108] blank; 109 text; [274] blank; [275] fly title: 'THE WAGGONER.' | [rule] | [three lines of verse]; [276] dedication to Charles Lamb; 277 text; [311] 'NOTES.'; [314] printer's imprint. Inserted before the half title are 8 pp. of Moxon's advertisements.

Vol. 2: [i] half title; [ii] blank; [iii] title-page; [iv] printer's imprint; [v] 'CONTENTS.'; [1] fly title: 'POEMS OF THE FANCY.'; [2] blank; [3] text; [77] fly title: 'POEMS OF THE IMAGINATION.'; [78] blank; [79] text; [233] fly title: 'PETER BELL. | A TALE. | What's in a *Name?* | [row of asterisks] | Brutus will start a Spirit as soon as Cæsar!'; [234] blank; [235] dedication to Southey; 237 text; [284] blank; [285] fly title: 'POEMS | ON THE NAMING OF PLACES.'; [286] 'ADVERTISEMENT.'; [287] text; 303* 'PREFACE' [to *Lyrical Ballads*, 1800]; [336] blank; [337] 'APPENDIX.'; [344] blank; [345] 'NOTES.'; [350] blank.

Vol. 3: [i] half title; [ii] blank; [iii] title-page; [iv] printer's imprint; [v] 'CONTENTS.'; [1] fly title: 'MISCELLANEOUS SONNETS. | PART I.'; [2] 'DEDICATION.'; [3] text; [107] fly title: 'MEMORIALS | OF | A TOUR IN SCOTLAND.'; [108] blank; [109] text; [173] fly title: 'SONNETS | DEDICATED TO LIBERTY. | PART I.'; [174] blank; [175] text; [204] 'SONNETS. | PART II.'; [314] blank; [315] 'ESSAY.'; [353] 'NOTES.'; [356] printer's imprint.

Vol. 4: [i] half title; [ii] blank; [iii] title-page; [iv] printer's imprint; [v] 'CONTENTS.'; [1] fly title: 'THE RIVER DUDDON. | A SERIES OF SONNETS.'; [2] five-line note; [3] dedication to Christopher Wordsworth; [7] text; [41] fly title: 'THE | WHITE DOE OF RYLSTONE; | OR, | THE FATE OF THE NORTONS.'; [42] 'ADVERTISEMENT.'; 43 'DEDICATION.'; [46] introductory poem; 47 text; [119] fly title: 'ITINERARY SONNETS. | [rule] | CLASS I. | MEMORIALS OF A TOUR ON THE CONTINENT. | 1820.'; [120] 'DEDICATION.'; 121 text; [188] blank; [189] fly title: 'ECCLESIASTICAL SONNETS. | IN SERIES. | PART I. | FROM THE INTRODUCTION OF CHRISTIANITY INTO BRITAIN, | TO THE CONSUMMATION OF THE PAPAL DOMINION.'; [190] three lines of verse; 191 'ADVERTISEMENT.'; 193 text; [311] fly title: 'POSTSCRIPT, NOTES, &c.'; [312] blank; [313] text.

Vol. 5: [i] half title; [ii] blank; [iii] title-page; [iv] printer's imprint; [v] 'CONTENTS.'; [xii] blank; [1] fly title: 'POEMS | OF | SENTIMENT AND REFLECTION.'; [2] blank; [3] text; [141] fly title: 'YARROW REVISITED, | AND | OTHER POEMS, | COMPOSED (TWO EXCEPTED) DURING A TOUR IN SCOTLAND, AND | ON THE ENGLISH BORDER, IN THE AUTUMN OF 1831.'; [142] dedication to Samuel Rogers; [143] text; [179] fly title: 'THE | RUSSIAN FUGITIVE.'; [180] seven-line note; [181] text; [199] fly title: 'STANZAS | SUGGESTED | IN A STEAM-BOAT OFF ST. BEES' HEADS, | ON THE COAST OF CUMBERLAND.'; [200] full-page note; [201] text; [207] blank; [207*] fly title: 'SONNETS, | COMPOSED OR SUGGESTED DURING A TOUR IN SCOTLAND, | IN THE SUMMER OF 1833.'; [208] eleven-line note; [209] text; [299] fly title: 'EPITAPHS | AND | ELEGIAC PIECES.'; [300] blank; [301] text; [346] blank; [347] 'POSTSCRIPT.'; [374] blank; [375] 'NOTES.'; 2 pp. of Moxon's advertisements.

Vol. 6: [i] half title; [ii] blank; [iii] title-page; [iv] imprint; [v] 'CONTENTS.'; [xi] 'PRELUDE.'; [xiv] blank; [xv] fly title: 'POEMS, | CHIEFLY OF EARLY AND LATE YEARS.'; [xvi] blank; [1] text; [50] blank; [51] fly title: 'MEMORIALS OF A TOUR IN ITALY. | 1837.' | [rule] | [poem to Crabb Robinson]; [52] ten-line note; [53] text; [179] 'MISCELLANEOUS SONNETS.'; [218] blank; [219] fly title: 'THE BORDERERS. | 𝔄 𝔗𝔯𝔞𝔤𝔢𝔡𝔶. | (COMPOSED 1795–6.)'; [220] 'DRAMATIS PERSONÆ.'; [221] text; [351] 'NOTES.'; [360] blank; [361] 'INDEX TO THE POEMS.'; [369] 'INDEX TO THE FIRST LINES.'.

Vol. 7; [i] half title; [ii] blank; [iii] title-page; [iv] printer's imprint; [v] fly title: 'THE EXCUR-SION.'; [vi] blank; [vii] dedication to the Earl of Lonsdale; [viii] blank; [ix] 'PREFACE TO THE EDITION OF 1814.'; [xv] 'CONTENTS.'; [xvi] blank; [1] fly title: 'THE EXCURSION. | [double rule] | BOOK I. | THE WANDERER.'; [2] 'ARGUMENT.'; [3] text; [39] fly title: 'THE EXCURSION. | [double rule] | BOOK II. | THE SOLITARY.'; [40] 'ARGUMENT.'; [41] text; [74] blank; [75] fly title: 'THE EXCURSION. | [double rule] | BOOK III. | DESPONDENCY.'; [76] 'ARGUMENT.'; [77] text; [113] fly title: 'THE EXCURSION. | [double rule] | BOOK IV. | DESPONDENCY CORRECTED.'; [114] 'ARGUMENT.'; [115] text; [163] fly title: 'THE EXCURSION. | [double rule] | BOOK V. | THE PASTOR.'; [164] 'ARGUMENT.'; [165] text; [202] blank; [203] fly title: 'THE EXCURSION. | [double rule] | BOOK VI. | 'THE CHURCH-YARD AMONG THE MOUNTAINS.'; [204] 'ARGUMENT.'; [205] text; [249] fly title: 'THE EXCURSION. | [double rule] | BOOK VII. | THE CHURCH-YARD AMONG THE MOUN-TAINS | CONTINUED.'; [250] 'ARGUMENT.'; [251] text; [289] fly title: 'THE EXCURSION.| [double rule] | BOOK VIII. | THE PARSONAGE'.; [290] 'ARGUMENT.'; [291] text; [313] fly title: 'THE EXCURSION. | [double rule] | BOOK IX. | DISCOURSE OF THE WANDERER. &c.'; [314] 'ARGUMENT.'; [315] text; [344] blank; [345] 'NOTES.'; 352 'ESSAY UPON EPITAPHS.'; [375-6] Moxon's advertisements.

$1, 2, signed, at center of foot. Pagination set in outer margin of headline except where running titles are absent. Wove paper, without watermark. Vol. 1 sheets bulk $\frac{7}{8}$ in.; vol. 2, $\frac{15}{16}$ in.; vol. 3, 1 in.; vol. 4, 1 in.; vol. 5, $1\frac{1}{16}$ in.; vol. 6, $\frac{15}{16}$ in.; vol. 7, 1 in.

Binding. Black, vertically-grained cloth; blind-stamped border on front and back covers; ivory end-papers. Gilt title on spine: 'WORDSWORTH'S | POETICAL | WORKS | VOL. | I [etc].'.

1847

139 THE EXCURSION. | 𝔄 𝔓𝔬𝔢𝔪. | BY | WILLIAM WORDSWORTH. | A NEW EDITION. | LONDON: | EDWARD MOXON, 44, DOVER STREET. | MDCCCXLVII.

Another re-issue of the 1836 (the stereotype) edition.
Binding. Black vertically ribbed cloth with blind-stamped panels on front and back covers. Gilt title on spine: 'WORDSWORTH'S | EXCURSION'.

140 ODE, | PERFORMED IN THE SENATE-HOUSE, CAMBRIDGE, | ON THE SIXTH OF JULY, M.DCCC.XLVII. | AT THE FIRST COM-MENCEMENT | AFTER | THE INSTALLATION | OF | HIS ROYAL HIGHNESS THE PRINCE ALBERT, | 𝔠𝔥𝔞𝔫𝔠𝔢𝔩𝔩𝔬𝔯 𝔬𝔣 𝔱𝔥𝔢 𝔘𝔫𝔦𝔟𝔢𝔯𝔰𝔦𝔱𝔶. | [arms of the University] | CAMBRIDGE: | PRINTED AT THE UNIVERSITY PRESS. | 1847.

Special imprint. None.
Collation (10¾ × 8¼ in.). Four leaves, quired and sewn in wrappers.
Pagination. [1-3] 4-8.
Contents. [1] title-page; [2] blank; [3] text.
Pagination centered at top. No running titles. Wove paper, without watermark. In the original drab wrappers. Title on front cover: 'INSTALLATION ODE. | [rule] | M.DCCC.XLVII.' |[rule].

141 ODE, | PERFORMED IN THE SENATE-HOUSE, CAMBRIDGE, | ON THE SIXTH OF JULY, M.DCCC.XLVII. | AT THE FIRST COM-MENCEMENT | AFTER | THE INSTALLATION | OF | HIS ROYAL HIGHNESS THE PRINCE ALBERT, | 𝔠𝔥𝔞𝔫𝔠𝔢𝔩𝔩𝔬𝔯 𝔬𝔣 𝔱𝔥𝔢 𝔘𝔫𝔦𝔟𝔢𝔯𝔰𝔦𝔱𝔶. | [rule] | WRITTEN BY WILLIAM WORDSWORTH, Esq.; | AND | SET

TO MUSIC BY THOMAS ATTWOOD WALMISLEY, M.A., | MUS. PROF. CANTAB.

Special imprint (on p. 8). [rule] | METCALFE AND PALMER, PRINTERS, CAMBRIDGE.
Collation (11 × 8½ in.). Eight leaves, quired and sewn.
Pagination. [1–3] 4–8.
Contents. [1] title-page; [2] blank; [3] text.
Pagination centered at top. No running titles. Wove paper, without watermark. In blue wrappers.
Title on front cover: 'ODE | ON | THE INSTALLATION | OF | HIS ROYAL HIGHNESS THE PRINCE ALBERT, | 𝔠𝔥𝔞𝔫𝔠𝔢𝔩𝔩𝔬𝔯 𝔬𝔣 𝔱𝔥𝔢 𝔘𝔫𝔦𝔳𝔢𝔯𝔰𝔦𝔱𝔶. | [rule] | 1847.
A photostat from the original owned by Professor C. B. Tinker of Yale.

142 𝔒𝔡𝔢 | 𝔒𝔫 𝔱𝔥𝔢 𝔍𝔫𝔰𝔱𝔞𝔩𝔩𝔞𝔱𝔦𝔬𝔫 | 𝔬𝔣 | 𝔥𝔦𝔰 𝔯𝔬𝔶𝔞𝔩 𝔥𝔦𝔤𝔥𝔫𝔢𝔰𝔰 𝔓𝔯𝔦𝔫𝔠𝔢 𝔄𝔩𝔟𝔢𝔯𝔱 | 𝔞𝔰 | 𝔠𝔥𝔞𝔫𝔠𝔢𝔩𝔩𝔬𝔯 𝔬𝔣 𝔱𝔥𝔢 𝔘𝔫𝔦𝔳𝔢𝔯𝔰𝔦𝔱𝔶 𝔬𝔣 𝔠𝔞𝔪𝔟𝔯𝔦𝔡𝔤𝔢, | 𝔅𝔶 𝔚𝔦𝔩𝔩𝔦𝔞𝔪 𝔚𝔬𝔯𝔡𝔰𝔴𝔬𝔯𝔱𝔥, | 𝔓𝔬𝔢𝔱 𝔏𝔞𝔲𝔯𝔢𝔞𝔱𝔢. | 𝔏𝔬𝔫𝔡𝔬𝔫: 𝔓𝔯𝔦𝔫𝔱𝔢𝔡, 𝔟𝔶 𝔭𝔢𝔯𝔪𝔦𝔰𝔰𝔦𝔬𝔫, 𝔟𝔶 𝔙𝔦𝔷𝔢𝔱𝔢𝔩𝔩𝔶 𝔅𝔯𝔬𝔱𝔥𝔢𝔯𝔰 𝔞𝔫𝔡 𝔠𝔬. | 𝔓𝔲𝔟𝔩𝔦𝔰𝔥𝔢𝔡 𝔟𝔶 𝔊𝔢𝔬𝔯𝔤𝔢 𝔅𝔢𝔩𝔩, 𝔉𝔩𝔢𝔢𝔱 𝔖𝔱𝔯𝔢𝔢𝔱. | [Price 3s. 6d.]

Special imprint. None.
Collation (9¾ × 7¹⁶⁄₁₆ in.). Four leaves, quired and sewn in heavy paper wrappers. 8 pp., without pagination.
Contents. Title as given above is on front cover; verso blank; [1] blank; [2] frontispiece: 'H.R.H. PRINCE ALBERT, | IN HIS ROBES AS CHANCELLOR OF THE UNIVERSITY OF CAMBRIDGE.'; [3] text.
Each page of text is enclosed in an elaborate border of gold, red, and blue. Wove paper, without watermark. Title on front cover is printed in gold, within a gold border. On the back cover, within a similar border, appear the royal arms in gold.

143 [Within a frame of rules] THE | POEMS | OF | WILLIAM WORDS-WORTH, D.C.L., | POET LAUREATE, ETC. ETC., | A NEW EDITION. | LONDON: | EDWARD MOXON, DOVER STREET. | [rule] | MDCCCXLVII.

A re-issue of the edition of 1845. The engraved frontispiece and the engraved title-page differ slightly; otherwise the two issues appear to be alike. Four pp. of Moxon's advertisements are inserted.
Binding. Black vertically ribbed cloth with a blind-stamped decorative panel on both covers. Blind-stamped panels on spine with title in gilt: 'WORDSWORTH'S | POETICAL | WORKS.'.

1849

144 THE EXCURSION: | A POEM. | BY | WILLIAM WORDSWORTH. | [rule] | NEW YORK: | C. S. FRANCIS & CO., 252 BROADWAY. | BOSTON: | J. H. FRANCIS, 128 WASHINGTON STREET. | 1849.

Special imprint. None.
Collation (7⅛ × 4½ in.). [1]⁶ 2–28⁶ 29².
Pagination. [1–6] 7 [8] 9, x–xiv, [15–16] 17–48 [49–50] 51–80 [81–2] 83–114 [115–16] 117–58 [159–60] 161–94 [195–6] 197–235 [236–8] 239–73 [274–6] 277–96 [297–8] 299–340. Pagination of p. 300 defectively printed.
Contents. [1] half title: 'THE EXCURSION.'; [2] publisher's announcements; engraved frontispiece entitled 'THE COTTAGE GIRL'; [3] title-page; [4] blank; [5] 'CONTENTS.'; [6] blank; 7 dedication to the Earl of Lonsdale; [8] blank; 9 'PREFACE'; [15] fly title: 'THE EXCURSION. | [rule] | BOOK FIRST. | [rule] | THE WANDERER.'; [16] blank; 17 text; [49] fly title: 'THE

EXCURSION. | [rule] | BOOK SECOND. | [rule] | THE SOLITARY.'; [50] blank; 51 text; [81] fly title: 'THE EXCURSION. | [rule] | BOOK THIRD. | [rule] DESPONDENCY.'; [82] blank; 83 text; [115] fly title: 'THE EXCURSION. | [rule] | BOOK FOURTH. | [rule] | DESPONDENCY CORRECTED.'; [116] blank; 117 text; [159] fly title: 'THE EXCURSION. | [rule] | BOOK FIFTH. | [rule] THE PASTOR.'; [160] blank; 161 text; [195] fly title: 'THE EXCURSION. | [rule] | BOOK SIXTH. | [rule] | THE CHURCH-YARD AMONG THE | MOUNTAINS.'; [196] blank; 197 text; [236] blank; [237] fly title: 'THE EXCURSION. | [rule] | BOOK SEVENTH. | [rule] | THE CHURCH-YARD AMONG THE | MOUNTAINS.'; [238] blank; 239 text; [274] blank; [275] fly title: 'THE EXCURSION. | [rule] | BOOK EIGHTH. | [rule] | THE PARSONAGE.'; [276] blank; 277 text; [297] fly title: 'THE EXCURSION. | [rule] | BOOK NINTH. | [rule] | DISCOURSE OF THE WANDERER | AND AN | EVENING VISIT TO THE LAKE.'; [298] blank; 299 text; 325 'NOTES.'.

$1, 3 signed, to the left of center of foot; $3 signed with the signature number followed by an asterisk. Running titles throughout. Pagination generally set in outer margin of headline, but set at center of foot on pp. 7 and 9, and on the opening page of each section of the book thereafter. Wove paper, without watermark. Sheets bulk ¾ in.

Binding. Green cloth; front and back covers blind-stamped with monogram 'F & CO' within a border. Corner ornaments blind-stamped: 'COLTON & JENKINS' and 'BINDERS N. YORK'. Blind-stamped decorations on spine, with gilt title: 'THE | EXCURSION | [rule] | WORDSWORTH'; and near the foot: 'FRANCIS & CO.'. Pale yellow end-papers.

First separate American edition.

145 Another copy.

7 × 4¼ in. The fold 1 3/4 is inserted backwards in this copy. Bound in blue-green vertically ribbed cloth with blind-stamped decorations surrounding a large gilt urn on both covers. Spine decorated in gilt with gilt title: 'THE | EXCURSION | [rule] | WORDSWORTH', and toward the foot: 'FRANCIS & CO.'.

146 ODE, | Performed at the Senate House, Cambridge, | *on Tuesday July 6ᵗʰ 1847,* | IN THE PRESENCE OF HER MAJESTY, | AT THE FIRST PUBLIC COMMENCEMENT | *after the* | INSTALLATION | OF | His Royal Highness The Prince Albert, | *Chancellor of the University,* | WRITTEN BY | *William Wordsworth, Esqʳᵉ D.C.L.* | Poet Laureate, | Set to Music by | THOMAS ATTWOOD WALMISLEY, | MUS.DOC. M.A. TRIN:COLL: | *Professor of Music in the University, & Organist of Trinity & Sᵗ. John's Colleges.* | [rule] | *Price 10ˢ/-* | [rule] | *LONDON,* | *Published (for the Author) by CHAPPELL, Music Seller to Her Majesty, 50, New Bond Street.*

Special imprint. None.
Collation (13$\frac{15}{16}$ × 9$\frac{7}{8}$ in.). π² [A]²(–A2) B²+13 unsigned gatherings of 2 leaves each.
Pagination. [i–iv], [1] 2 [5] 6–8; [1] 2–51 [52].
Contents. [i] engraved title-page, lettering of which is approximated in the above transcript; [ii] blank; [iii] engraved dedication to Prince Albert, dated 1 July 1849; [iv] blank; [1] list of subscribers; [5] text, without music; [1] blank; 2 text, with music; [52] blank.

Pagination of the first sequence of numbered pages appears at center of the headline, that of the second sequence at the outer margin of the headline. No running titles. Wove paper, without watermark. In paper wrappers. Front wrapper bears engraved title identical with that of the title-page.

A photostatic copy of the original in the Cambridge University Library.

147 [Within a frame of rules] THE | POEMS | OF | WILLIAM WORDS-WORTH, D.C.L., | POET LAUREATE, ETC. ETC. | A NEW EDITION. | LONDON: | EDWARD MOXON, DOVER STREET. | [rule] | MDCCCXLIX.

A re-issue of the edition of 1847, with which it seems to be identical. With 3 pp. of Moxon's advertisements.

Binding. Purple vertically ribbed cloth with a blind-stamped ornamental border on front and back covers; rebacked.

148 POEMS | BY | WILLIAM WORDSWORTH; | WITH | AN INTRODUCTORY ESSAY ON HIS LIFE AND | WRITINGS.| [rule] | NEW YORK: | C. S. FRANCIS & CO., 252 BROADWAY. | BOSTON: | J. H. FRANCIS, 128 WASHINGTON STREET. | 1849.

Special imprint (p. ii, lower left). [rule] | Printed by | MUNROE AND FRANCIS, | Boston. | [rule].
Collation ($7\frac{1}{16} \times 4\frac{5}{16}$ in.). [1]⁶ 2–29⁶ 30⁴.
Pagination. [i–v] vi–vii [viii] ix–xix [xx], 21–356. P. xvii misnumbered 'xvi'.
Contents. [i] half title: 'POEMS | OF | WILLIAM WORDSWORTH'; [ii] blank; frontispiece, engraved by R. Soper, of Chantrey's bust of Wordsworth; [iii] title-page; [iv] notice of entry and printer's imprint; [v] 'CONTENTS.'; [viii] 'PUBLISHERS' ADVERTISEMENT.'; [ix] essay on Wordsworth by H. T. Tuckerman; [xx] blank; [1] text.
$1, 3 signed, at left center of foot. Running titles throughout, verso: 'WORDSWORTH'S POEMS.'; recto: varying with contents. Pagination in outer margin of headline; pagination of p. ix at foot. Wove paper, without watermark.
Binding. Green cloth; front and back covers blind-stamped with border and monogram 'F & C'; binder's stamp in the corners: 'COLTON & JENKINS' and 'BINDERS | N. YORK'. Blind-stamped decoration on spine, with title in gilt: 'POEMS | OF | WORDSWORTH' and near the foot: 'FRANCIS & CO.'.

Though dated 1849, the book appeared in late 1848.

149 THE | POETICAL WORKS | OF | WILLIAM WORDSWORTH, D.C.L., | POET LAUREATE, HONORARY MEMBER OF THE ROYAL SOCIETY OF EDINBURGH, AND | OF THE ROYAL IRISH ACADEMY, ETC. ETC. | IN SEVEN VOLUMES. | VOL. I [etc.]. | A NEW AND REVISED EDITION. | LONDON: | EDWARD MOXON, DOVER STREET. | MDCCCXLIX.

A re-issue of the seven-volume edition of 1846. Bound in full tan calf with leather lettering-pieces.

150 Another copy.

Bound in full green calf, extra gilt.

151 THE | POETICAL WORKS | OF | WILLIAM WORDSWORTH, D.C.L., | POET LAUREATE, ETC. ETC. | IN SIX VOLUMES. | VOL. I [etc.]. | A NEW EDITION. | LONDON: | EDWARD MOXON, DOVER STREET. | MDCCCXLIX.
[Note: vols. 3, 4, 5, 6 are dated MDCCCL.]

Special imprints (verso of title-page and following the text of each volume). LONDON: | BRADBURY AND EVANS, PRINTERS, WHITEFRIARS.
Collation ($5\frac{5}{16} \times 3\frac{5}{16}$ in.). Vol. 1: [A]⁶ B–N¹² O⁶.
    Vol. 2: [a]⁴ b² B–O¹² P⁸.
    Vol. 3: [A]⁸ B–M¹² N⁴.
    Vol. 4: [A]⁸ B–N¹² O⁴.
    Vol. 5: [A]⁴ B–N¹² O⁸ P².
    Vol. 6: [A]⁴ B–N¹² O⁸.

Pagination. Vol. 1: [i–vii] viii–x [xi–xii], [1] 2–63 [64] 65–297 [298] 299 [300] 4 pp. advertisements.

Vol. 2: [i–v] vi–xii, [1] 2–259 [260] 261–321 [322] 323–7 [328]. P. viii misnumbered 'vii'.

Vol. 3: [i–v] vi–xiv [xv–xvi], [1] 2–39 [40] 41–52 [53] 54–109 [110] 111–51 [152] 153–83 [184] 185–97 [198] 199–217 [218] 219–38 [239] 240–71 [272].

Vol. 4: [i–iv] vi–xvi, [1] 2–56 [57] 58–123 [124] 125–42 [143] 144–78 [179] 180–256 [257] 258–64 [265] 266–72 [273] 274–92 [293–6].

Vol. 5: [i–v] vi–viii, [1] 2–57 [58] 59–71 [72] 73–99 [100] 101–13 [114] 115–54 [155] 156 [157–9] 160–89 [190] 191–5 [196] 197–230 [231] 232 [233] 234–50 [251] 252–79 [280–1] 282–90 [291] 292–307 [308–10]. P. 16 misnumbered '6'.

Vol. 6: [i–viii], [1–3] 4–8 [9–11] 12–38 [39–41] 42–66 [67–9] 70–96 [97–9] 100–35 [136–9] 140–67 [168–71] 172–204 [205–7] 208–36 [237–9] 240–55 [256–9] 260–81 [282–3] 284–301 [302–4].

Contents. Vol. 1: [i] half title: 'THE | POETICAL WORKS | OF | WILLIAM WORDSWORTH.'; [ii] blank; [iii] title-page; [iv] printer's imprint; [v] introductory poem; [vi] blank; [vii] 'CONTENTS.'; [xi] fly title: 'POEMS WRITTEN IN YOUTH.'; [xii] blank; [1] text; 147 'POEMS REFERRING TO THE PERIOD | OF CHILDHOOD.'; 187 'POEMS FOUNDED ON THE AFFECTIONS.'; [298] 'NOTES.'; [300] printer's imprint; 4 pp. Moxon's advertisements dated 1 May 1848.

Vol. 2: [i] half title; [ii] blank; [iii] title-page; [iv] printer's imprint; [v] 'CONTENTS.'; [1] 'POEMS ON THE NAMING OF PLACES.'; 13 'POEMS OF THE FANCY.'; 93 'POEMS OF THE IMAGINATION.'; [260] 'MISCELLANEOUS SONNETS.'; [322] 'NOTES.'; [328] printer's imprint.

Vol. 3: [i] half title; [ii] blank; [iii] title-page; [iv] printer's imprint; [v] 'CONTENTS.'; [xv] fly title: 'MEMORIALS OF A TOUR | IN | SCOTLAND.'; [xvi] blank; [1] text; 40 'MEMORIALS OF A TOUR IN | SCOTLAND. | 1814.'; [53] 'POEMS | DEDICATED TO NATIONAL INDEPENDENCE AND | LIBERTY.'; [110] 'MEMORIALS OF A TOUR ON THE | CONTINENT. | 1820.'; [152] 'MEMORIALS OF A TOUR IN ITALY. | 1837.'; [184] 'THE EGYPTIAN MAID;'; [198] 'THE RIVER DUDDON.'; [218] 'YARROW REVISITED, AND OTHER | POEMS,'; [239] 'NOTES.'; [272] printer's imprint.

Vol. 4: [i] half title; [ii] blank; [iii] title-page; [iv] printer's imprint; [v] 'CONTENTS.'; [1] 'THE WHITE DOE OF RYLSTONE;'; [57] 'ECCLESIASTICAL SONNETS.'; [124] 'EVENING VOLUNTARIES.'; [143] 'POEMS, | COMPOSED OR SUGGESTED DURING A TOUR, IN | THE SUMMER OF 1833.'; [179] 'POEMS OF SENTIMENT AND | REFLECTION.'; [257] 'SONNETS | DEDICATED TO LIBERTY AND ORDER.'; [265] 'SONNETS | UPON THE PUNISHMENT OF DEATH.'; [273] 'NOTES.'; [293] 'BY THE SAME AUTHOR.'; [294–6] blank.

Vol. 5: [i] half title; [ii] blank; [iii] title-page; [iv] printer's imprint; [v] 'CONTENTS.'; [1] 'MISCELLANEOUS POEMS.'; [58] 'INSCRIPTIONS.'; [72] 'SELECTIONS FROM CHAUCER.'; [100] 'POEMS REFERRING TO THE PERIOD | OF OLD AGE.'; [114] 'EPITAPHS AND ELEGIAC PIECES.'; [155] 'NOTES.'; [157] fly title: 'APPENDIX, PREFACES, | ETC. ETC.' | [rule] | seven-line note; [158] blank; [159] 'PREFACE'; [190] 'APPENDIX.'; [196] 'ESSAY, SUPPLEMENTARY TO THE | PREFACE.'; [231] 'DEDICATION. | PREFIXED TO THE EDITION OF 1815.'; [233] 'PREFACE TO THE EDITION OF 1815.'; [251] 'POSTSCRIPT. | 1835.'; [280] blank; [281] 'INDEX TO THE POEMS.'; [291] 'INDEX TO THE FIRST LINES.'; [308] printer's imprint; [309] 'ADDITIONAL NOTE.'; [310] blank.

Vol. 6: [i–ii] blank; [iii] half title; [iv] blank; [v] title-page; [vi] printer's imprint; [vii] 'CONTENTS.'; [viii] blank; [1] fly title: 'THE EXCURSION.'; [2] dedication to the Earl of Lonsdale; [3] 'PREFACE TO THE EDITION OF 1814.'; [9] fly title: 'BOOK FIRST. | THE WANDERER.'; [10] 'ARGUMENT.'; [11] text; [39] fly title: 'BOOK SECOND. | THE SOLITARY.'; [40] 'ARGUMENT.'; [41] text; [67] fly title: 'BOOK THIRD. | DESPONDENCY.'; [68] 'ARGUMENT.'; [69] text; [97] fly title: 'BOOK FOURTH. | DESPONDENCY CORRECTED.'; [98] 'ARGUMENT.'; [99] text; [136] blank; [137] fly title: 'BOOK FIFTH. | THE PASTOR.'; [138] 'ARGUMENT.'; [139] text; [168] blank; [169] fly title: 'BOOK SIXTH. | THE CHURCH-YARD AMONG THE MOUNTAINS.'; [170] 'ARGUMENT.'; [171] text; [205] fly title: 'BOOK SEVENTH. | THE CHURCH-YARD AMONG THE MOUNTAINS | CONTINUED.'; [206] 'ARGUMENT.'; [207] text; [237] fly title: 'BOOK EIGHTH. | THE PARSONAGE.'; [238] 'ARGUMENT.'; [239] text; [256] blank; [257] fly title: 'BOOK NINTH. | DISCOURSE OF THE WANDERER, AND AN | EVENING VISIT TO THE LAKE.'; [258] 'ARGUMENT.'; [259] text; [282] blank; [283] 'NOTES.'; [302] printer's imprint; [303] 'BY THE SAME AUTHOR.'; [304] blank.

\$1, 2, 5 signed, in right-hand margin of foot; \$5 signed '3'. Pagination in outer margin of headline when running titles are present; otherwise centered. Wove paper, without watermark. Sheets of each volume bulk ¾ in.

Binding. Flower-patterned red cloth; blind-stamped decorations on front and back covers; pale yellow end-papers. Spine decorated in gilt, with gilt title: 'WORDSWORTH'S | POEMS | [rule] | VOL. I [etc.].'; all edges gilt. Some sets were bound six volumes in three; that in the British Museum is in blue cloth, that at Harvard in brown.

1850

152 THE PRELUDE, | OR | GROWTH OF A POET'S MIND; | AN AUTOBIOGRAPHICAL POEM; | BY | WILLIAM WORDSWORTH. | LONDON: | EDWARD MOXON, DOVER STREET. | 1850.

Special imprint (p. iv). LONDON: | BRADBURY AND EVANS, PRINTERS, WHITEFRIARS.
Collation ($8\frac{3}{4} \times 5\frac{1}{2}$ in.). [A]⁶ B–2A⁸ 2B² 2C².
Pagination. 2 pp. unnumbered, [i–v] vi–viii [ix] x, [1–3] 4–30 [31–3] 34–52 [53–5] 56–81 [82–5] 86–104 [105–7] 108–32 [133–5] 136–67 [168–71] 172–203 [204–7] 208–35 [236–9] 240–63 [264–7] 268–92 [293–5] 296–314 [315–17] 318–31 [332–5] 336–50 [351–3] 354–72 [373] 374 [375–6].
Contents. 2 blank pages; [i] half title: 'THE PRELUDE, | OR | GROWTH OF A POET'S MIND.'; [ii] blank; [iii] title-page; [iv] printer's imprint; [v] 'ADVERTISEMENT.'; [ix] 'CONTENTS.'; [1] fly title: 'BOOK I. | INTRODUCTION—CHILDHOOD AND SCHOOL-TIME.'; [2] blank; [3] text; [31] fly title: 'BOOK II. | SCHOOL-TIME.—(CONTINUED.)'; [32] blank; [33] text; [53] fly title: 'BOOK III. | RESIDENCE AT CAMBRIDGE.'; [54] blank; [55] text; [82] blank; [83] fly title: 'BOOK IV. | SUMMER VACATION.'; [84] blank; [85] text; [105] fly title: 'BOOK V. | BOOKS.'; [106] blank; [107] text; [133] fly title: 'BOOK VI. | CAMBRIDGE AND THE ALPS.' | [134] blank; [135] text; [168] blank; [169] fly title: 'BOOK VII. | RESIDENCE IN LONDON'; [170] blank; [171] text; [204] blank; [205] fly title: 'BOOK VIII. | RETROSPECT.— LOVE OF NATURE LEADING TO | LOVE OF MAN.'; [206] blank; [207] text; [236] blank; [237] fly title: 'BOOK IX. | RESIDENCE IN FRANCE.'; [238] blank; [239] text; [264] blank; [265] fly title: 'BOOK X. | RESIDENCE IN FRANCE.—(CONTINUED.)'; [266] blank; [267] text; [293] fly title: 'BOOK XI. | FRANCE.—(CONCLUDED.)'; [294] blank; [295] text; [315] fly title: 'BOOK XII. | IMAGINATION AND TASTE, HOW IMPAIRED AND | RESTORED.'; [316] blank; [317] text; [332] blank; [333] fly title: 'BOOK XIII. | IMAGINATION AND TASTE, HOW IMPAIRED AND | RESTORED.—(CONCLUDED.)'; [334] blank; [335] text; [351] fly title: 'BOOK XIV. | CONCLUSION.'; [352] blank; [353] text; [373] 'NOTES.'; [375] Moxon's advertisements; [376] blank. Eight pp. of advertisements, dated July 1850, inserted in front.
$1, 2 signed, at right margin of foot. Running titles throughout, varying with the contents. Pagination set in outer margin of the headline. Wove paper, without watermark. Sheets bulk $1\frac{1}{2}$ in.
Binding. Purple cloth with a grained surface; decorative panel blind-stamped on front and back covers; yellow end-papers. Gilt title on spine: 'THE | PRELUDE | BY | W. WORDSWORTH'.

153 Another copy.

With the advertisements.

154 Another copy.

With the advertisements.
Inscribed by Henry Crabb Robinson: 'Mrs. Pattisson, from her friend H. C. Robinson, 10 Augt 1850.' With marginal notes.

155 Another copy.

Full morocco, extra gilt; inner dentelles; all edges gilt.
Formerly John R. Tutin's copy, with his bookplate and a few pencilled notes.

156 THE PRELUDE; | OR, | GROWTH OF A POET'S MIND. | An Autobiographical Poem. | BY | WILLIAM WORDSWORTH. | NEW-

YORK: | D. APPLETON & COMPANY, 200 BROADWAY. | PHILA-
DELPHIA: | GEO. S. APPLETON, 164 CHESNUT-ST. | 1850.

Special imprint. None.
Collation ($7 \times 4\frac{1}{2}$ in.). π^4 1–15^{12} 16^8.
Pagination. [i–iii] iv–v [vi–vii] viii, [1–3] 4–30 [31–3] 34–52 [53–5] 56–81 [82–5] 86–104 [105–7] 108–32 [133–5] 136–67 [168–71] 172–203 [204–7] 208–35 [236–9] 240–63 [264–7] 268–92 [293–5] 296–314 [315–17] 318–31 [332–5] 336–50 [351–3] 354–72 [373] 374 [375–6].
Contents. [i] title-page; [ii] blank; [iii] 'ADVERTISEMENT.'; [vi] blank; [vii] 'CONTENTS.'; 1–374 a page-for-page reprint of the London edition; [375–6] Appleton's advertisements.
$1, 5 signed, at left center of foot; $5 signed with signature number plus an asterisk. Running titles throughout, varying with contents. Pagination in outer margin of headline. Wove paper, without watermark. Sheets bulk $\frac{15}{16}$ in.
Binding. Purple, vertically-ribbed cloth; blind-stamped panel on front and back covers; buff end-papers. Gilt title on spine: 'THE | PRELUDE' and (near bottom) 'WORDSWORTH'. A copy at Harvard has purple cloth with a plain surface.

157 THE | POETICAL WORKS | OF | WILLIAM WORDSWORTH. | [rule] | A NEW EDITION. | [rule] | BOSTON: | PHILLIPS, SAMPSON AND COMPANY, | 110 WASHINGTON STREET. | 1850.

Special imprint. None.
Collation ($7\frac{7}{16} \times 4\frac{3}{4}$ in.). 1–45^6.
Pagination. [1–5] 6–8 [9–11] 12–16 [17] 18–46 [47] 48–74 [75] 76–104 [105] 106–44 [145] 146–75 [176–7] 178–212 [213] 214–44 [245] 246–63 [264] 265–88 [289–91] 292–330 [331–3] 334–48 [349–51] 352–65 [366–9] 370–82 [383–5] 386–400 [401–3] 404–7 [408–11] 412–539 [540].
Contents. [1] half title: 'WORDSWORTH'S POEMS.'; [2] blank; frontispiece, engraving by O. Pelton of Chantrey's bust of Wordsworth; [3] title-page; [4] blank; [5] 'CONTENTS.'; [9] fly title: 'THE EXCURSION: | BEING A PORTION OF | THE RECLUSE.'; [10] dedication to the Earl of Lonsdale; [11] 'THE EXCURSION. | [rule] | PREFACE.'; [17] text; [289] fly title: 'PETER BELL: | A TALE.'; [290] blank; [291] text; [331] fly title: 'THE IDIOT BOY.'; [332] blank; [333] text; [349] fly title: 'MICHAEL: | A PASTORAL POEM.'; [350] blank; [351] text; [366] blank; [367] fly title: 'THE BROTHERS.'; [368] blank; [369] text; [383] fly title: 'THE RUSSIAN FUGITIVE.'; [384] blank; [385] text; [401] fly title: 'GOODY BLAKE | AND | HARRY GILL.'; [402] blank; [403] text; [408] blank; [409] fly title: 'MISCELLANEOUS POEMS, | SONNETS, &c.'; [410] blank; [411] text; [540] blank.
$1, 3 signed, slightly left of center of foot; $3 signed with the signature number plus an asterisk. Running title throughout: 'WORDSWORTH'S POEMS.'. Pagination set in outer margin of headline. Wove paper, without watermark. Sheets bulk $1\frac{3}{8}$ in.
Binding. Red cloth; spine and both covers elaborately gilt; all edges gilt; yellow end-papers. Title on spine: 'WORDSWORTH'S | POETICAL | WORKS'.

PART II

WRITINGS OF WORDSWORTH
IN BOOK FORM
1851–1955

158 THE PRELUDE, or Growth of a Poet's Mind; an Autobiographical Poem. Second Edition. London: Edward Moxon, 1851.

$6\frac{11}{16} \times 4\frac{1}{16}$ in. x [2] 304 [4] pp.

159 THE POEMS OF WILLIAM WORDSWORTH, D.C.L., Poet Laureate, etc., etc. A New Edition. London: Edward Moxon, 1851.

$9\frac{1}{8} \times 6$ in. xxiv, 619 [1] pp.

160 POEMS OF WILLIAM WORDSWORTH. New York: Leavitt and Co., 1851.

$6\frac{5}{8} \times 4\frac{5}{16}$ in. xvi, 17–281 [1] pp.

161 THE POETICAL WORKS OF WILLIAM WORDSWORTH. A New Edition. Boston: Phillips, Sampson, and Co., 1851.

$7\frac{3}{8} \times 4\frac{5}{8}$ in. 539 [1] pp.

162 THE COMPLETE POETICAL WORKS OF WILLIAM WORDS-WORTH, Poet Laureate, etc., etc. Edited by Henry Reed. Philadelphia: Troutman & Hayes, 1851.

$9\frac{5}{8} \times 6\frac{5}{16}$ in. xxiii [1] 25–728 pp.

1852

163 THE COMPLETE POETICAL WORKS OF WILLIAM WORDS-WORTH, Poet Laureate, etc., etc. Edited by Henry Reed. Philadelphia: Troutman & Hayes, 1852.

$9\frac{5}{8} \times 6\frac{1}{2}$ in. xxiii [1] 25–727 [1] pp.

1853

164 THE EXCURSION. A Poem. A New Edition. London: Edward Moxon, 1853.

$6\frac{3}{4} \times 4\frac{3}{16}$ in. xii [2] 374 [2] pp.

165 A COMPLETE GUIDE TO THE LAKES, Comprising Minute Directions for the Tourist; with Mr. Wordsworth's Description of the Scenery of the Country, etc. and Five Letters on the Geology of the Lake District, by the Rev. Professor Sedgwick. Fourth Edition. Edited by the Publisher. Kendal: John Hudson; London: Longman & Co., and Whittaker and Co.; Liverpool: Webb, Castle-St.; Manchester: Simms and Co., 1853.

$7\frac{1}{8} \times 4\frac{1}{4}$ in. xii, viii, 270 [2] pp.

166 THE POETICAL WORKS OF WILLIAM WORDSWORTH. A New Edition. Boston: Phillips, Sampson, and Co., 1853.

7⅞ × 4¾ in. 539 [1] pp.

167 POEMS FROM THE POETICAL WORKS OF WILLIAM WORDSWORTH. New York: Leavitt & Allen, 1853.

5⅝ × 3¹³⁄₁₆ in. xvi, 17–281 [3] pp.

1854

168 THE POETICAL WORKS OF WILLIAM WORDSWORTH. A New Edition. Boston: Phillips, Sampson, and Co., 1854.

7⅞ × 4¾ in. 539 [1] pp.

169 THE POETICAL WORKS OF WILLIAM WORDSWORTH, D.C.L., Poet Laureate, etc., etc. Boston: Little, Brown, and Co., 1854, 7 vols.

6¹¹⁄₁₆ × 4⅛ in. Vol. 1: xl, 384; vol. 2: x, 406 [4]; vol. 3: x, 342 [4]; vol. 4: xii, 367 [3]; vol. 5: vi, 366 [4]; vol. 6: iv, 371 [3]; vol. 7: [4] 414 pp.

1855

170 THE POETICAL WORKS OF WILLIAM WORDSWORTH. A New Edition. Boston: Phillips, Sampson, and Co.; New York: J. C. Derby, 1855.

7½ × 4¾ in. 539 [3] pp.

1856

171 POEMS FROM THE POETICAL WORKS OF WILLIAM WORDSWORTH. New York: Leavitt & Allen, 1856.

5⅛ × 3¼ in. xvi, 17–281 [5] pp.

172 THE POETICAL WORKS OF WILLIAM WORDSWORTH. A New Edition. Boston: Phillips, Sampson, and Co., 1856.

7½ × 4¾ in. 539 [1] pp.

1857

173 THE EXCURSION. A Poem. A New Edition. London: Edward Moxon, 1857.

6⅛ × 4 in. [4] 301 [3] pp.

174 THE EARLIER POEMS OF WILLIAM WORDSWORTH. Corrected as in the Latest Editions. With Preface, and Notes Showing the Text as It Stood in 1815, by William Johnston. London: Edward Moxon, 1857.

6⅜ × 4 in. xxxvi, 435 [1] pp.

175 THE POETICAL WORKS OF WILLIAM WORDSWORTH. In Six Volumes. A New Edition. London: Edward Moxon, 1857.

6¾ × 4 in. Vol. 1: xii, 362 [2]; vol. 2: xii, 377 [3]; vol. 3: xii, 368; vol. 4: xvi, 395 [1]; vol. 5: viii, 368; vol. 6: vi, 454 [2] pp.

176 THE POETICAL WORKS OF WILLIAM WORDSWORTH. A New Edition. Boston: Phillips, Sampson, and Co., 1857.

6 × 3¾ in. 539 [1] pp.

1858

177 THE POETICAL WORKS OF WILLIAM WORDSWORTH. In Six Volumes. A New Edition. London: Edward Moxon, 1858.

6³⁄₁₆ × 4⅛ in. Vol. 1: x [2] 299 [1]; vol. 2: xii, 327 [1]; vol. 3: xiv [2] 271 [1]; vol. 4: xvi, 292; vol. 5: ix [3] 394 [2]; vol. 6: [8] 453 [3] pp.

178 THE POETICAL WORKS OF WILLIAM WORDSWORTH. A New Edition, Carefully Edited, with a Life. London and New York: G. Routledge & Co., 1858.

6⁵⁄₁₆ × 4 in. xxiii [1] 496 pp. The Life of Wordsworth is signed: W. R.

179 THE POETICAL WORKS OF WILLIAM WORDSWORTH. Boston: Lee and Shepard, [1858].

6⅜ × 3⁵⁄₁₆ in. xxiii [1] 496 pp.

1859

180 THE DESERTED COTTAGE. Illustrated with Twenty-one Designs by Birket Foster, J. Wolf, and John Gilbert, Engraved by the Brothers Dalziel. London and New York: George Routledge & Co., 1859.

7¾ × 5⅝ in. [8] 104 pp.

181 PASSAGES FROM 'THE EXCURSION,' Illustrated with Etchings on Steel by Agnes Fraser. London: Paul and Dominic Colnaghi and Co., 1859.

13⅛ × 19¼ in., oblong. 11 plates, each accompanied by one page of passages from *The Excursion*.

182 THE WHITE DOE OF RYLSTONE; or, the Fate of the Nortons. London: Longman, Brown, Green, Longmans, and Roberts, 1859.

8⁹⁄₁₆ × 6 in. [2] 165 [5] pp.

183 HUDSON'S NEW HAND-BOOK FOR VISITORS TO THE ENGLISH LAKES, with an Introduction by the Late William Wordsworth, Esq., and a New Map of the Lake District; to Which Is Appended a Copious List of Plants Found in the Adjacent Country. Embellished with Steel

Engravings. Kendal: Thomas B. Hudson; London: Longman and Co.; Whittaker and Co.; Hamilton, Adams, and Co., 1859.

$6\frac{3}{8} \times 3\frac{7}{8}$ in. xvi, 80 [8] pp.

184 POEMS OF WILLIAM WORDSWORTH. Selected and Edited by Robert Aris Willmott, Incumbent of Bear Wood. Illustrated with One Hundred Designs by Birket Foster, J. Wolf, and John Gilbert, Engraved by the Brothers Dalziel. London and New York: George Routledge & Co., 1859.

$8\frac{11}{16} \times 6\frac{1}{4}$ in. xiv, 387 [1] pp.

185 THE POETICAL WORKS OF WILLIAM WORDSWORTH. A New Edition. Boston: Phillips, Sampson, and Co., 1859.

$6 \times 3\frac{3}{4}$ in. 539 [3] pp.

1860

186 THE EXCURSION, a Poem. With Topographical Notes. London: Simpkin, Marshall, and Co., [1860].

$6\frac{1}{2} \times 3\frac{7}{8}$ in. [4] v [1] 268 [10] pp.

187 PASTORAL POEMS. Illustrated with Numerous Engravings. London: Sampson, Low, Son, and Co., 1860.

$7\frac{5}{8} \times 5\frac{1}{8}$ in. [2] 55 [3] pp.

188 THE COMPLETE POETICAL WORKS OF WILLIAM WORDS-WORTH, Late Poet Laureate. Edited by Henry Reed. Philadelphia: Porter & Coates, [c. 1860].

$9\frac{5}{8} \times 6\frac{5}{8}$ in. xxiii [1] 728 pp.

1862

189 SELECT POEMS. With Life of the Author. London: Milner and Co., [c. 1862].

$4\frac{5}{8} \times 2\frac{7}{8}$ in. xxxii, 320 pp.

190 THE POETICAL WORKS OF WILLIAM WORDSWORTH. New Edition, Carefully Edited, with a Life. London: Routledge, Warne, and Routledge, 1862.

$6\frac{5}{8} \times 3\frac{7}{8}$ in. xxiii [1] 496 [2] pp.

1863

191 WORDSWORTH'S POEMS FOR THE YOUNG. With Fifty Illustrations by John Macwhirter and John Pettie, and a Vignette by J. E. Millais. Engraved by Dalziel Brothers. London: Alexander Strahan & Co., 1863.

$7\frac{1}{2} \times 5\frac{9}{16}$ in. x [2] 90 [2] pp.

192 THE POETICAL WORKS OF WILLIAM WORDSWORTH. Edinburgh: William P. Nimmo, [*c.* 1863].

6½ × 4⅛ in. xxiv, 574 [10] pp.

1864

193 THE EXCURSION. A Poem. A New Edition. London: Edward Moxon & Co., 1864.

6¾ × 4⅛ in. [6] 332 pp.

194 THE SELECT POETICAL WORKS OF WILLIAM WORDSWORTH. Copyright Edition. In Two Volumes. Leipzig: Bernhard Tauchnitz, 1864.

6½ × 4⅝ in. Vol. 1: xii, 411 [1]; vol. 2: xvi, 400 pp.

195 THE POETICAL WORKS OF WILLIAM WORDSWORTH. A New Edition, Carefully Edited, with a Life. London and New York: Routledge, Warne, and Routledge, 1864.

6½ × 3¹⁵⁄₁₆ in. xxiii [1] 496 pp.

196 THE POETICAL WORKS OF WILLIAM WORDSWORTH. In Six Volumes. New Edition. London: Edward Moxon and Co., 1864.

6¹¹⁄₁₆ × 4⅛ in. Vol. 1: xii, 362 [2]; vol. 2: xii, 377 [3]; vol. 3: xii, 368; vol. 4: xvi, 395 [1]; vol. 5: viii, 368; vol. 6: viii, 454 [2] pp.

197 THE POETICAL WORKS OF WILLIAM WORDSWORTH, D.C.L., Poet Laureate, etc., etc. Boston: Little, Brown, and Co., 1864, 7 vols.

6⅝ × 4¼ in. Vol. 1: xl, 384 [2]; vol. 2: x, 406 [4]; vol. 3: x, 342 [4]; vol. 4: xii, 367 [3]; vol. 5: xi, 366 [4]; vol. 6: [4] 371 [3]; vol. 7: [4] 414 [2] pp.

1865

198 A SELECTION FROM THE WORKS OF WILLIAM WORDSWORTH, Poet Laureate (Moxon's Miniature Poets). Selected and Arranged by Francis Turner Palgrave. London: Edward Moxon & Co., 1865.

6¾ × 5 in. xxviii, 279 [1] pp.

199 POEMS OF NATURE AND SENTIMENT. Elegantly Illustrated. Philadelphia: E. H. Butler & Co., 1865.

7⅝ × 5 in. xii, 13–124 [2] pp.

200 THE POETICAL WORKS OF WILLIAM WORDSWORTH. In Six Volumes. A New and Complete Edition. London: Edward Moxon & Co., 1865.

6¼ × 3⅞ in. Vol. 1: x [2] 299 [1]; vol. 2: xii, 327 [1]; vol. 3: xiv [2] 271 [1]; vol. 4: xvi, 292; vol. 5: ix [3] 394 [2]; vol. 6: [8] 453 [3] pp.

1866

201 OUR ENGLISH LAKES, MOUNTAINS, AND WATERFALLS, as Seen by William Wordsworth. Photographically Illustrated. London: A. W. Bennett, 1866.

$7\frac{1}{2} \times 6$ in. xi [1] 192 pp.

202 POEMS OF WILLIAM WORDSWORTH. Selected and Edited by Robert Aris Willmott. Illustrated with One Hundred Designs by Birket Foster, J. Wolf, and John Gilbert. Engraved by the Brothers Dalziel. London and New York: George Routledge and Sons, 1866.

$8\frac{5}{8} \times 6\frac{5}{16}$ in. [16] 387 [3] pp.

1867

203 THE WHITE DOE OF RYLSTONE; or, the Fate of the Nortons. London: Bell and Daldy, 1867.

$7\frac{1}{8} \times 5\frac{1}{8}$ in. xvi [3] 20–128 pp.

204 THE POETICAL WORKS OF WILLIAM WORDSWORTH. A New Edition. Boston: Crosby & Ainsworth; New York: Oliver S. Felt, 1867.

$6 \times 3\frac{5}{8}$ in. 539 [3] pp.

1869

205 THE POETICAL WORKS OF WILLIAM WORDSWORTH. In Six Volumes. A New Edition. London: E. Moxon, Son, and Co., 1869.

$5\frac{3}{4} \times 3\frac{3}{4}$ in. Vol. 1: x [2] 299 [1]; vol. 2: xii, 327 [3]; vol. 3: xiv [2] 271 [3]; vol. 4: xvi, 292 [2]; vol. 5: ix [3] 394 [2]; vol. 6: [8] 453 [3] pp.

206 THE POETICAL WORKS OF WILLIAM WORDSWORTH (The Only Complete Popular Edition). A New Edition. London: Edward Moxon, Son, and Co., 1869.

$9\frac{3}{8} \times 6\frac{1}{4}$ in. xxiv, 704 pp.

207 POETICAL WORKS OF WILLIAM WORDSWORTH. With a Life of the Author. London, Edinburgh, and New York: T. Nelson and Sons, 1869.

$6\frac{9}{16} \times 4\frac{5}{16}$ in. xxviii, 532 [2] pp.

1870

208 WORDSWORTH'S POEMS FOR THE YOUNG. With Fifty Illustrations by John Macwhirter and John Pettie, and a Vignette by J. E. Millais, R.A. London: Strahan & Co., 1870.

$7\frac{1}{4} \times 5\frac{3}{8}$ in. viii, 91 [1] pp.

209 THE POETICAL WORKS OF WILLIAM WORDSWORTH (The Only Complete Cheap Edition). Edited by William Michael Rossetti. Illustrated by Henry Dell. London: E. Moxon, Son, and Co., [*c.* 1870].

$6\frac{7}{8} \times 4\frac{3}{8}$ in. xiv, 568 [24] pp.

210 THE POETICAL WORKS OF WILLIAM WORDSWORTH. Illustrated by Henry Dell. London: E. Moxon, Son, & Co., [*c.* 1870].

$7 \times 4\frac{1}{2}$ in. xxiv, 568 pp. Prefatory notice by W. M. Rossetti.

211 THE POETICAL WORKS OF WILLIAM WORDSWORTH. Illustrated by Henry Dell. London: E. Moxon, Son, & Co., [*c.* 1870].

$7 \times 4\frac{1}{2}$ in. xiv, 568 [2] pp. The prefatory notice by Rossetti is not present. Cf. the preceding item.

212 THE POETICAL WORKS OF WILLIAM WORDSWORTH (The Centenary Edition). In Six Volumes. A New and Complete Annotated Edition. London: E. Moxon, Son, and Co., 1870.

$6\frac{11}{16} \times 4\frac{1}{8}$ in. Vol. 1: xii, 362 [2]; vol. 2: xii, 377 [3]; vol. 3: xii, 368; vol. 4: xvi, 395 [1]; vol. 5: viii, 368; vol. 6: vi [2] 454 [2] pp.

213 THE POETICAL WORKS OF WILLIAM WORDSWORTH. With Life. Eight Engravings on Steel. Edinburgh: Gall & Inglis, [1870].

$6\frac{1}{2} \times 3\frac{7}{8}$ in. xx, 522 [2] pp.

1871

214 THE POETICAL WORKS OF WILLIAM WORDSWORTH (The Only Cheap Edition). Edited, with a Critical Memoir, by William Michael Rossetti. Illustrated by Artistic Etchings by Edwin Edwards. London: E. Moxon, Son, and Co., 1871.

$8\frac{1}{16} \times 6\frac{1}{8}$ in. xxiv, 568 pp.

215 THE POETICAL WORKS OF WILLIAM WORDSWORTH. With a Memoir. Boston: James R. Osgood and Co., 1871, 7 vols.

$6\frac{1}{8} \times 4\frac{1}{8}$ in. Vol. 1: xi, 384 [2]; vol. 2: x, 406 [4]; vol. 3: x, 342 [2]; vol. 4: xii, 367 [3]; vol. 5: vi, 366 [4]; vol. 6: [4] 371 [3]; vol. 7: [6] 414 [4] pp.

1872

216 THE POETICAL WORKS OF WORDSWORTH (The 'Chandos Classics'). A Reprint of the 1827 Edition, with Memoir, Explanatory Notes, &c. London: Frederick Warne and Co.; New York: Scribner, Welford, and Armstrong, [1872].

$7 \times 4\frac{3}{4}$ in. xxxix [1] 530 [2] pp.

1873

217 THE POETICAL WORKS OF W. WORDSWORTH. Complete, with Numerous Illustrations. London: John Dicks and All Booksellers, 1873.

$7\frac{5}{16} \times 4\frac{7}{8}$ in. [6] 190, iv pp.

1874

218 SELECTIONS FROM THE POETICAL WORKS OF WILLIAM WORDSWORTH (English School-Classics). Edited, with Notes, by H. H. Turner. London, Oxford, and Cambridge: Rivingtons, 1874.

$6\frac{3}{8} \times 4$ in. 87 [1] pp.

219 THE POETICAL WORKS OF WILLIAM WORDSWORTH. A New Edition. London: E. Moxon, Son, & Co., 1874, 6 vols.

$6\frac{1}{8} \times 3\frac{7}{8}$ in. Vol. 1: x [2] 297 [3]; vol. 2: xii, 327 [1]; vol. 3: xiv [2] 271 [1]; vol. 4: xvi, 292; vol. 5: ix [1] 394 [2]; vol. 6: [8] 453 [1] pp.

220 THE POETICAL WORKS OF WILLIAM WORDSWORTH (Centenary Edition). In Six Volumes. A New and Complete Annotated Edition. London: E. Moxon, Son, & Co., 1874.

$6\frac{3}{8} \times 4$ in. Vol. 1: xii, 362 [4]; vol. 2: xii, 377 [5]; vol. 3: xii, 368 [4]; vol. 4: xvi, 395 [5]; vol. 5: viii, 368 [4]; vol. 6: vi [2] 454 [4] pp.

221 THE POETICAL WORKS OF WILLIAM WORDSWORTH. In Six Volumes. A New Edition. London: Ward, Lock, and Co., [1874–8].

$6\frac{1}{8} \times 3\frac{3}{4}$ in. Vol. 1: x [2] 297 [3]; vol. 2: xii, 327 [1]; vol. 3: xiv [2] 271 [1]; vol. 4: xvi, 292; vol. 5: ix [1] 394 [2]; vol. 6: [4] 453 [3] pp.

1876

222 THE PROSE WORKS OF WILLIAM WORDSWORTH. For the First Time Collected, with Additions from Unpublished Manuscripts. Edited, with Preface, Notes, and Illustrations, by the Rev. Alexander B. Grosart, St. George's, Blackburn, Lancashire. In Three Volumes. London: Edward Moxon, Son, and Co., 1876.

$8\frac{5}{8} \times 5\frac{1}{2}$ in. Vol. 1: [4] xxxviii, 360; vol. 2: [4] 347 [1]; vol. 3: xii, 516 [4] pp.

223 Another copy.

1878

224 THE ENGLISH LAKE DISTRICT, as Interpreted in the Poems of Wordsworth. By William Knight. Edinburgh: David Douglas, 1878.

$6\frac{1}{8} \times 3\frac{7}{8}$ in. xxiv, 248 pp.

1879

225 POEMS OF WORDSWORTH, Chosen and Edited by Matthew Arnold. London: Macmillan and Co., 1879.

$7\frac{7}{8} \times 4\frac{3}{4}$ in. xxxi [1] 319 [1] pp.

226 POEMS OF WORDSWORTH, Chosen and Edited by Matthew Arnold. *Franklin Square Library*, 24 October 1879, 60 pp.

227 Another copy.

1880

228 A DESCRIPTION OF THE SCENERY OF THE DISTRICT OF THE LAKES. Windermere: J. Garnett, [*c.* 1880].

$7\frac{7}{16} \times 4\frac{3}{4}$ in. [4] 111 [1] pp.

229 WORDSWORTH'S EXCURSION: THE WANDERER (English School-Classics). Edited, with Life, Introduction, and Notes, by H. H. Turner. New Edition. London, Oxford, and Cambridge: Rivingtons, [*c.* 1880].

$6\frac{3}{8} \times 4$ in. 77 [3] pp.

230 POEMS OF WORDSWORTH, Chosen and Edited by Matthew Arnold. New York: Macmillan and Co., 1880.

$6\frac{1}{8} \times 3\frac{7}{8}$ in. xxxi [1] 325 [1] pp.

231 POEMS OF WORDSWORTH, Selected from the Best Editions. In Two Volumes. London: W. Kent & Co., 1880.

$4\frac{1}{8} \times 2\frac{9}{16}$ in. Vol. 1: xii, 308; vol. 2: viii, 312 pp.

232 THE POETICAL WORKS OF WILLIAM WORDSWORTH, with a Memoir. Seven Volumes in Three. Boston: Houghton, Mifflin, and Co., [*c.* 1880].

$7\frac{1}{2} \times 4\frac{1}{2}$ in. Vol. 1: xl, 406 [2]; vol. 2: xxiii [1] 366 [2]; vol. 3: iv, 414 [4] pp.

233 THE POETICAL WORKS OF WORDSWORTH, with Photographic Illustrations, by Payne Jennings. London: R. & A. Suttaby, [*c.* 1880].

$7\frac{3}{8} \times 4\frac{5}{8}$ in. xiv, 568 [2] pp.

1881

234 THE POETICAL WORKS OF WILLIAM WORDSWORTH. In Six Volumes. Reprinted from the Edition of 1857. London: E. Moxon, Son, & Co., 1881.

$6\frac{11}{16} \times 4$ in. Vol. 1: xii, 362 [2]; vol. 2: xii, 377 [3]; vol. 3: xii, 368 [4]; vol. 4: xvi, 395 [5]; vol. 5: viii, 368 [8]; vol. 6: vi [2] 454 [18] pp.

1882

235 THE POETICAL WORKS OF WILLIAM WORDSWORTH. In Six Volumes. A New Edition. London: E. Moxon, Sons, & Co., 1882.

$7\frac{15}{16} \times 5\frac{1}{8}$ in. Vol. 1: xii, 362 [2]; vol. 2: xii, 377 [3]; vol. 3: xii, 368 [4]; vol. 4: xvi, 395 [5]; vol. 5: viii, 368 [8]; vol. 6: vi [2] 454 [18] pp.

236 THE POETICAL WORKS OF WILLIAM WORDSWORTH. Edited by William Knight, LLD., Professor of Moral Philosophy, St. Andrews. Edinburgh: William Paterson, 1882–9, 11 vols.

$8\frac{13}{16} \times 5\frac{7}{8}$ in. Vol. 1: lxxxiii [1] 313 [1]; vol. 2: viii, 396; vol. 3: vii [1] 424; vol. 4: viii, 387 [1]; vol. 5: [8] 434 [2]; vol. 6: xii, 379 [1]; vol. 7: xvi, 400 [2]; vol. 8: xi [1] 435 [1]; vol. 9: xxiv, 405 [3]; vol. 10: vi, 431 [3]; vol. 11: vii [1] 530 [2] pp.

237 Another copy.

$10\frac{9}{16} \times 7$ in. Limited edition on large paper.

1883

238 READINGS FROM WILLIAM WORDSWORTH (Home College Series No. 36). New York: Hunt & Eaton; Cincinnati: Cranston & Stowe, [*c.* 1883].

$7\frac{1}{8} \times 4\frac{3}{4}$ in. 16 pp.

239 SELECTIONS FROM WORDSWORTH. Edited, with an Introductory Memoir, by J. S. Fletcher. London and Paisley: Alex. Gardner, 1883.

$6\frac{1}{4} \times 3\frac{7}{8}$ in. xii, 13–295 [1] pp.

1884

240 ODE, INTIMATIONS OF IMMORTALITY FROM RECOLLECTIONS OF EARLY CHILDHOOD. Boston: D. Lothrop and Co., 1884.

$8 \times 6\frac{1}{8}$ in. [2] 48 [2] pp.

241 THE RIVER DUDDON, a Series of Sonnets. With Ten Etchings by R. S. Chattock. London: The Fine Art Society, 1884.

$12\frac{7}{8} \times 9\frac{1}{2}$ in. [42] pp.

242 THE SONNETS OF WILLIAM WORDSWORTH, Collected in One Volume, with an Essay on the History of the English Sonnet by Richard Chenevix Trench, D.D. London: Suttaby and Co., 1884.

$6\frac{13}{16} \times 4\frac{1}{2}$ in. xliv, 246 [2] pp.

243 THE WORDSWORTH BIRTHDAY BOOK. Edited by Adelaide and Violet Wordsworth. London: Kegan Paul, Trench, & Co., 1884.

$4\frac{3}{4} \times 3\frac{3}{8}$ in. [4] 277 [7] pp.

244 WORDSWORTH BIRTHDAY BOOK. Compiled and Edited by J. R. Tutin (Member of the Wordsworth Society). London: Hamilton, Adams, and Co., 1884.

4¾ × 3⅜ in. [288] pp.

245 POEMS BY WILLIAM WORDSWORTH. Selected and Prepared for Use in Schools and Classes. From Hudson's Text-Book of Poetry. Selection I. Boston: Ginn, Heath, & Co., 1884.

7¼ × 4½ in. x, 297 [1] pp.

1885

246 ODE ON IMMORTALITY and LINES ON TINTERN ABBEY. Illustrated. London, Paris, New York, and Melbourne: Cassell & Co., 1885.

7⅝ × 6¼ in. 48 [16] pp.

247 POEMS OF WORDSWORTH (Cassell's Miniature Poets). Selected from the Best Editions. In Two Volumes. London, Paris, New York, and Melbourne: Cassell & Co. [1885].

4½ × 2⅞ in. Vol. 1: xii, 308 [16]; vol. 2: viii, 312 pp.

248 THE POETICAL WORKS OF WILLIAM WORDSWORTH (The Canterbury Poets). With a Prefatory Notice, Biographical and Critical, by Andrew James Symington. London and Newcastle-on-Tyne: Walter Scott, 1885.

5¼ × 3¹³⁄₁₆ in. vi, 7–285 [3] pp.

249 THE POETICAL WORKS OF WORDSWORTH (The 'Albion' Edition). With Memoir, Explanatory Notes, etc. London and New York: Frederick Warne and Co., [1885].

7⅜ × 5⅛ in. xliv, 628 [2] pp.

1887

250 MEMORIALS OF COLEORTON, Being Letters from Coleridge, Wordsworth and His Sister, Southey, and Sir Walter Scott to Sir George and Lady Beaumont of Coleorton, Leicestershire, 1803 to 1834. Edited, with Introduction and Notes, by William Knight, University of St. Andrews. Edinburgh: David Douglas, 1887, 2 vols.

7½ × 4⅝ in. Vol. 1: xlvi [2] 227 [1]; vol. 2: vii [1] 294 [2] pp.

1888

251 THE RECLUSE. London and New York: Macmillan and Co., 1888.

6⅞ × 4¼ in. [8] 56 pp.

252 THE PRELUDE, or Growth of a Poet's Mind; an Autobiographical Poem. With Notes by A. J. George. Boston: D. C. Heath & Co., 1888.

$7\frac{3}{16} \times 4\frac{3}{4}$ in. xxxii, 322 [6] pp.

253 SELECTIONS FROM WORDSWORTH by William Knight and Other Members of the Wordsworth Society. With Preface and Notes. London: Kegan Paul, Trench, & Co., 1888.

$7\frac{7}{8} \times 5\frac{1}{8}$ in. xxiv, 309 [3] pp.

254 BITS OF BURNISHED GOLD: WILLIAM WORDSWORTH. Compiled by Rose Porter. New York: Anson D. F. Randolph & Co., [c. 1888].

$3\frac{5}{16} \times 4\frac{3}{16}$ in. [2] 128 [2] pp.

255 THE COMPLETE POETICAL WORKS OF WILLIAM WORDSWORTH (Globe Edition), with an Introduction by John Morley. London and New York: Macmillan and Co., 1888.

$7\frac{1}{2} \times 4\frac{7}{8}$ in. lxv [1] 928 [2] pp.

1889

256 TO THE QUEEN: Dedicatory Verses Addressed to Her Majesty with the Author's Poems, by William Wordsworth, Poet Laureate. Kendal: Printed for the Author by R. Branthwaite and Son, 1846. [Imprint spurious.]

$6\frac{15}{16} \times 4\frac{1}{4}$ in. [8] pp., unopened. A forgery, attributed to T. J. Wise. The date of printing is unknown; the leaflet appeared presumably between 1889 and 1893. See John Carter and Graham Pollard, *An Enquiry into the Nature of Certain Nineteenth Century Pamphlets*, London: Constable; New York: Scribners, 1934, pp. 355-6.

257 EARLY POEMS. London, Glasgow, Manchester, and New York: George Routledge and Sons, 1889.

$5\frac{1}{2} \times 3\frac{3}{4}$ in. xii, 13-256.

258 SELECT POEMS OF WILLIAM WORDSWORTH. Edited, with Notes, by William J. Rolfe, Litt.D., Formerly Head Master of the High School, Cambridge, Mass. With Engravings. New York: Harper & Brothers, 1889.

$6\frac{5}{8} \times 4\frac{7}{8}$ in. vii [2] 10-258 [12] pp.

259 SELECTIONS FROM WORDSWORTH. With Notes by A. J. George, M.A., Editor of Wordsworth's Prelude. Boston: D. C. Heath & Co., 1889.

$7\frac{1}{4} \times 4\frac{5}{8}$ in. xx [2] 434 [2] pp.

260 POEMS BY WILLIAM WORDSWORTH. Selected and Prepared for Use in Schools and Classes. From Hudson's Text-Book of Poetry. Selection II. Boston: Ginn & Co., 1889.

$7\frac{1}{4} \times 4\frac{1}{2}$ in. x, 129-251 [1] pp. For Selection I, see No. 245.

261 THE EXCURSION: BOOK I, THE WANDERER (English School Classics). With Prefatory and Explanatory Notes. New York: Effingham Maynard & Co., 1889.

6⅝ × 4¼ in. 48 pp.

262 SELECTIONS FROM WORDSWORTH, by William Knight and Other Members of the Wordsworth Society. With Preface and Notes. London: Kegan Paul, Trench, & Co., 1889.

7⅜ × 4⅞ in. xxiv, 309 [3] 42 [6] pp. John R. Tutin's copy.

263 LETTERS FROM THE LAKE POETS, Samuel Taylor Coleridge, William Wordsworth, Robert Southey, to Daniel Stuart, Editor of the Morning Post and the Courier, 1800–38. Printed for Private Circulation. London: Printed by West, Newman, and Co., 1889.

8⅝ × 5⅜ in. xv [1] 463 [1] pp.

264 THE POETICAL WORKS OF WILLIAM WORDSWORTH (Complete Copyright Edition). A New Edition. London: E. Moxon, Son, and Co.; Ward, Lock, and Co., 1889.

9⅜ × 6¼ in. xxiv, 704 pp.

265 THE POETICAL WORKS OF WILLIAM WORDSWORTH. In Eight Volumes. Glasgow: David Bryce and Son, [1889].

5 × 3¼ in. Vol. 1: xxii [11] 232; vol. 2: 250 [2]; vol. 3: 256; vol. 4: 256; vol. 5: 256; vol. 6: 254 [2]; vol. 7: 256; vol. 8: 256 pp.

266 Another copy.

267 THE POETICAL WORKS OF WILLIAM WORDSWORTH. In Eight Volumes. New York: A. C. Armstrong and Son, 1889.

4¹¹⁄₁₆ × 3⅛ in. Vol. 1: xxii [4] 232; vol. 2: 250 [2]; vol. 3: 256; vol. 4: 256; vol. 5: 256; vol. 6: 254 [2]; vol. 7: 256; vol. 8: 256 pp.

1890

268 LYRICAL BALLADS, Reprinted from the First Edition of 1798. Edited by Edward Dowden, LL.D., Professor of English Literature in the University of Dublin. London: David Nutt, 1890.

6⅞ × 4⅛ in. xv [3] v [3] 227 [1] 10 pp.

269 PASTORALS, LYRICS, AND SONNETS, from the Poetic Works of William Wordsworth. Boston and New York: Houghton, Mifflin, and Co., 1890.

6½ × 4 in. [2] 212 [2] pp.

270 BIRTHDAY TEXTS FROM WORDSWORTH; Passages for Every Day in the Year from the Poems of William Wordsworth. Edinburgh: W. P. Nimmo, Hay, & Mitchell, [1890].

4⅛ × 3¼ in. [256] pp.

271 SELECT POEMS (The Penny Poets, XXXII). London: W. T. Stead, [*c.* 1890].

7⅛ × 4¾ in. 64 pp.

1891

272 THE RECLUSE. London and New York: Macmillan and Co., 1891.

8¹⁵⁄₁₆ × 5½ in. [8] 56 pp.

273 THE WHITE DOE OF RYLSTONE, with the SONG AT THE FEAST OF BROUGHAM CASTLE, etc. (Clarendon Press Series). Edited, with Introduction and Notes, by William Knight, University of St. Andrews. Oxford: Clarendon Press, 1891.

6⅝ × 4⅜ in. [4] 112 pp.

274 LYRICAL BALLADS, Reprinted from the First Edition (1798). Edited by Edward Dowden, LL.D., Professor of English Literature in the University of Dublin. Second Edition. London: David Nutt, 1891.

6⅞ × 4½ in. xv [3] v [3] 227 [1] pp.

275 A SELECTION FROM THE SONNETS OF WILLIAM WORDS-WORTH, with Numerous Illustrations by Alfred Parsons. New York: Harper & Brothers, 1891.

10½ × 7⅞ in. 86 [6] pp.

276 THE ENGLISH LAKE DISTRICT, as Interpreted in the Poems of Wordsworth. By William Knight. Second Edition, Revised and Enlarged. Edinburgh: David Douglas, 1891.

6⅛ × 3⅞ in. viii, xvi, 270 [2] pp.

277 WORDSWORTH FOR THE YOUNG. Selections, with an Introduction for Parents and Teachers, by Cynthia Morgan St. John. Illustrations Selected and Arranged by the Compiler. Boston: D. Lothrop Co., [1891].

8¾ × 6¾ in. [4] 153 [3] pp.

278 Another copy.

Inscribed: 'To Edwin H. Woodruff, who first conceived the happy thought of the compiler making this selection of the poems, and who gave freely of his assistance and sympathy. With cordial gratitude and regard. Cynthia M. St. John, June 30, 1891.'

1892

279 WORDSWORTH'S PREFACES AND ESSAYS ON POETRY; with
Letter to Lady Beaumont (Heath's English Classics). Edited with Introduction
and Notes by A. J. George, A.M. Boston: D. C. Heath & Co., 1892.

7¼ × 4¾ in. xiv [2] 120 [8] pp.

280 POEMS OF WORDSWORTH, Chosen and Edited by Matthew Arnold.
London: Macmillan and Co., 1892.

8 × 5 in. xxxi [1] 331 [1] pp.

281 LYRICS AND SONNETS OF WORDSWORTH, Selected and Edited
by Clement King Shorter. London: David Stott, 1892.

4⅜ × 2¹⁵⁄₁₆ in. xxxiv, 441 [7] pp.

282 SELECTIONS FROM WORDSWORTH (English Classic Series No. 90).
Edited by James H. Dillard, M.A., Principal of Mary Institute, Washington
University, St. Louis. New York: Effingham Maynard & Co., 1892.

6½ × 4¼ in. 53 [1] pp.

283 SELECTED POEMS FROM WORDSWORTH (Cassell's National
Library). London, Paris, and Melbourne: Cassell & Co., 1892.

5⅝ × 3⅝ in. 191 [5] pp.

284 POEMS OF WORDSWORTH, Chosen and Edited by Matthew Arnold.
Illustrated by Edmund H. Garrett. New York: Thomas Y. Crowell & Co.,
[1892].

7½ × 4⅞ in. xxxiv, 319 [3] pp.

285 THE POETICAL WORKS OF WILLIAM WORDSWORTH. Edited
with a Memoir by Edward Dowden. In Seven Volumes. London and New
York: George Bell & Sons, 1892–3.

6¾ × 4 in. Vol. 1: lxxiv, 408; vol. 2: vii [1] 344; vol. 3: xv [1] 476; vol. 4: xii, 387 [1]; vol. 5: x, 366
[2]; vol. 6: [8] 387 [1]; vol. 7: [8] 402 [2] pp.

1893

286 EVENING VOLUNTARIES by William Wordsworth. Illustrated with
Fifteen Etchings by William Goodrich Beal. Boston: Samuel Edson Cassino,
1893.

8¼ × 6 in. [36] pp.

287 WORDSWORTH FOR THE YOUNG. With Introduction and Notes by J. C. Wright, Author of 'Outline of English Literature,' etc., etc. London: Jarrold & Sons, [1893].

7¾ × 4⅞ in. x, 100 [12] pp.

288 SOME UNPUBLISHED LETTERS OF WILLIAM WORDSWORTH. By James Payn.

The Independent, 2 and 9 March 1893. Clippings.

289 PROSE WRITINGS OF WORDSWORTH; Selected and Edited, with an Introduction, by William Knight, LL.D. London: Walter Scott, [1893].

6⅝ × 4½ in. xxix [3] 198 [16] pp.

290 THE COMPLETE POETICAL WORKS OF WILLIAM WORDS-WORTH, with an Introduction by John Morley. London and New York: Macmillan and Co., 1893.

7 × 4¾ in. lxvii [1] 928 pp.

291 THE POETICAL WORKS OF WILLIAM WORDSWORTH (The Albion Edition). With Memoir, Explanatory Notes, &c. London and New York: Frederick Warne and Co., 1893.

7⅞ × 5¼ in. xliv, 628 pp.

1894

292 THE POETICAL WORKS OF WILLIAM WORDSWORTH (Sir John Lubbock's Hundred Books, 68). With 106 Illustrations by Birket Foster, J. Wolf, and Sir John Gilbert, R.A. London, Manchester, and New York: George Routledge and Sons, 1894.

7½ × 4⅞ in. xii, 564 pp.

293 FAVORITE POEMS BY WILLIAM WORDSWORTH AND SAMUEL TAYLOR COLERIDGE (Modern Classics). Illustrated. Boston: Houghton, Mifflin, & Co., [c. 1894].

5¼ × 3⅜ in. [15] 12–111 [1]; [9] 12–104; [9] 10–82 pp.

1895

294 INTIMATIONS OF IMMORTALITY FROM RECOLLECTIONS OF EARLY CHILDHOOD and Other Poems (The Riverside Literature Series). With Biographical Sketch and Notes. New York: Houghton, Mifflin, and Co., 1895.

6¾ × 4⅜ in. iv, 5–95 [1] pp.

295 SELECT POEMS (The Penny Poets XXXII). London: 'Review of Reviews' Office [*c.* 1895], 2 vols.

7⅛ × 4¾ in. Vol. 1: iv, 5–58, vi; vol. 2: 58, vi pp.

296 THE POETICAL WORKS OF WILLIAM WORDSWORTH (Oxford Edition). With Introductions and Notes. Edited by Thomas Hutchinson, M.A. London: Henry Frowde, 1895.

7¾ × 5 in. xxxii, 976 pp.

297 THE POETICAL WORKS OF WILLIAM WORDSWORTH (Oxford Miniature Wordsworth). With Introductions and Notes. Edited by Thomas Hutchinson, M.A. London: Oxford University Press, 1895, 5 vols.

4¼ × 2⅝ in. Vol. 1: lv [1] 622 [2]; vol. 2: xx, 676; vol. 3: xx, 677 [3]; vol. 4: xi [1] 694 [2]; vol. 5: viii, 652 pp.

1896

298 THE PRELUDE, or Growth of a Poet's Mind (The Temple Classics). London: J. M. Dent and Co., 1896.

5⅞ × 3⅝ in. viii, 264 pp.

299 PROSE WORKS OF WILLIAM WORDSWORTH. Edited by William Knight. London and New York: Macmillan and Co., 1896, 2 vols.

7 × 4⅝ in. Vol. 1: xv [1] 322 [2]; vol. 2: ix [1] 405 [3] pp.

300 QUELQUES POÈMES DE WILLIAM WORDSWORTH, traduits en vers par Émile Legouis, Maître de Conférences à la Faculté des Lettres de Lyon. Paris: Léopold Cerf, 1896.

6⅞ × 4½ in. 156 pp.

301 THE COMPLETE POETICAL WORKS OF WILLIAM WORDS-WORTH, with an Introduction by John Morley. London and New York: Macmillan and Co., 1896.

7⅞ × 5¼ in. lxvii [1] 928 [2] pp.

302 THE POETICAL WORKS OF WILLIAM WORDSWORTH (The Eversley Series). Edited by William Knight. London and New York: Macmillan and Co., 1896, 8 vols.

7 × 4⅝ in. Vol. 1: lxiv, 337 [3]; vol. 2: x, 438 [2]; vol. 3: vi, 406 [2]; vol. 4: ix [1] 283 [3]; vol. 5: [6] 399 [3]; vol. 6: xi [1] 396 [2]; vol. 7: xvii [1] 416 [2]; vol. 8: xxiii [1] 467 [3] pp.

1897

303 POEMS IN TWO VOLUMES by William Wordsworth, Reprinted from the Original Edition of 1807. Edited with a Note on the Wordsworthian Sonnet by Thomas Hutchinson, M.A., Editor of the 'Oxford Wordsworth.' London: David Nutt, 1897, 2 vols.

6¾ × 4⅛ in. Vol. 1: xxxix [9] 226 [2]; vol. 2: [8] 233 [3] pp.

304 THE LYRIC POEMS OF WILLIAM WORDSWORTH, Edited by Ernest Rhys. London: J. M. Dent & Co., [1897].

6 × 3¾ in. xxvi, 344 pp.

305 POEMS DEDICATED TO NATIONAL INDEPENDENCE AND LIBERTY, by William Wordsworth, Reprinted on Behalf of the Greek Struggle for the Independence of Crete, with an Introduction by Stopford Brooke. London: Isbister and Co., 1897.

7⅛ × 4¼ in. vii, 8–96 pp.

306 SELECTIONS FROM WORDSWORTH, Edited with Introduction and Notes by W. T. Webb, M.A., Late Professor of English Literature, Presidency College, Calcutta; Editor of 'Cowper, The Task, Book IV', 'Cowper's Shorter Poems', etc. London and New York: Macmillan and Co., 1897.

6¾ × 4½ in. xlix [3] 215 [1] pp.

307 SELECTIONS FROM THE POETS: WORDSWORTH, by Andrew Lang. Illustrated by Alfred Parsons, A.R.A. London, New York, and Bombay: Longmans, Green, and Co., 1897.

7¼ × 4⅝ in. xxxi [1] 295 [1] pp.

308 THE POETICAL WORKS OF WILLIAM WORDSWORTH (The Apollo Poets). London: Bliss, Sands, & Co., [1897].

8½ × 6 in. xix [1] 688 [4] pp.

1898

309 LYRICAL BALLADS by William Wordsworth and S. T. Coleridge, 1798. Edited with Certain Poems of 1798 and an Introduction and Notes by Thomas Hutchinson. London: Duckworth and Co., 1898.

6⅝ × 4⅛ in. lx [2] v [1] 263 [5] pp.

310 POEMS BY WILLIAM WORDSWORTH (Athenæum Press Series). A Selection Edited by Edward Dowden, Professor of English Literature in the University of Dublin. Boston and London: Ginn and Co., 1898.

7¼ × 4⅝ in. cxvii [1] 522 pp.

311 SELECTIONS FROM THE POEMS OF WILLIAM WORDS-WORTH (Eclectic English Classics). Edited by W. H. Venable, LL.D., of the Walnut Hills High School, Cincinnati. New York, Cincinnati, and Chicago: American Book Co., 1898.

$7 \times 4\frac{1}{2}$ in. 142 [2] pp.

312 POEMS OF WORDSWORTH, Chosen and Edited by Matthew Arnold. London and New York: Macmillan and Co., 1898.

6×4 in. xxxi [1] 331 [1] pp.

1899

313 THE SONNETS OF WILLIAM WORDSWORTH. London: J. M. Dent and Co., 1899.

$5\frac{15}{16} \times 3\frac{11}{16}$ in. [2] vii [1] 285 [1] pp.

314 SELECTIONS FROM THE POETRY OF WILLIAM WORDS-WORTH (New English Series). Edited by E. E. Speight, B.A., with an Introduction by Dr. Edward Caird, Master of Balliol College, Oxford, Late Professor of Moral Philosophy in the University of Glasgow. London: Horace Marshall and Son, 1899.

$7\frac{1}{4} \times 4\frac{3}{4}$ in. viii, 80 [2] pp.

1900

315 THE POETICAL WORKS OF WILLIAM WORDSWORTH. London: Society for Promoting Christian Knowledge, 1900.

$8\frac{1}{2} \times 5\frac{7}{8}$ in. xix [1] 688 pp.

316 WORDSWORTH. London: Henry Frowde, [c. 1900].

$3\frac{3}{4} \times 2\frac{5}{8}$ in. [64] pp.

1901

317 FLOWER POEMS, with Designs by Lona Miller. University of Kansas Fine Arts Department, 1901.

$10 \times 7\frac{5}{8}$ in. Twenty leaves, printed on one side only. No. 45 of fifty-five copies printed.

318 SELECTIONS FROM THE POEMS OF WILLIAM WORDS-WORTH. Edited, with an Introduction and Notes, by Nowell C. Smith, with a Portrait from a Painting by Robert Hancock. London: Methuen & Co., 1901.

$6 \times 3\frac{5}{8}$ in. xliv, 270 [6] pp.

1902

319 SELECTED POEMS OF WILLIAM WORDSWORTH (Silver Series of Classics). Edited, with Introduction and Notes, by Joseph Seabury. New York, Boston, and Chicago: Silver, Burdett, and Co., [1902].

$7\frac{1}{4} \times 4\frac{7}{8}$ in. 136 pp.

320 POEMS FROM WORDSWORTH. Chosen and Edited by T. Sturge Moore & Illustrated by Woodcuts Designed & Engraved by T. S. Moore. Printed at the Ballantyne Press under the Supervision of Charles Ricketts. London: Hacon & Ricketts; New York: John Lane, [*c.* 1902].

$9\frac{1}{8} \times 5\frac{5}{8}$ in. [14] 183 [15] pp.

1903

321 INTIMATIONS OF IMMORTALITY FROM RECOLLECTIONS OF EARLY CHILDHOOD. London: E. Arnold; New York: S. Buckley and Co., 1903.

$7\frac{1}{2} \times 4\frac{3}{4}$ in. [4] 13 [1] pp. Frontispiece by Walter Crane. Printed on vellum, with illuminated initials. Bound in full parchment.

322 THE LYRICAL BALLADS 1798–1805 (Little Library Series). With an Introduction and Notes by George Sampson, with a Frontispiece after Two Portraits by Robert Hancock. London: Methuen & Co., 1903.

$6 \times 3\frac{5}{8}$ in. xxxi [1] 395 [5] pp.

323 A SELECTION OF THE SHORTER POEMS OF WORDSWORTH (Macmillan's Pocket American and English Classics). Edited with Introduction and Notes by Edward Fulton, Ph.D., Assistant Professor of Rhetoric in the University of Illinois. New York and London: Macmillan and Co., 1903.

$5\frac{1}{2} \times 4$ in. lxxviii [2] 181 [3] pp.

324 POEMS BY WILLIAM WORDSWORTH, with an Introduction by Alice Meynell. London: Blackie and Son, 1903.

$6 \times 3\frac{3}{4}$ in. xii, 277 [1] pp.

325 THE COMPLETE POETICAL WORKS OF WILLIAM WORDS-WORTH, with an Introduction by John Morley. London and New York: Macmillan and Co., 1903.

$7\frac{1}{2} \times 5$ in. lxvii [1] 928 pp.

on the other hand I was well aware that by those who should dislike them they would be read with more than common dislike. The result has differed from my expectation in this only, that I have pleased a greater number, than I ventured to hope I should please.

For the sake of variety and from a consciousness of my own weakness I have again requested the assistance of a Friend who contributed largely to the first volume,* and who has now furnished me with the Poem of Christabel, without which I should not yet have ventured to present a second volume to the public. I should not however have requested this assistance, had I not believed that the poems of my Friend would in a great measure have the same tendency as my own, and that,

* The Poems supplied by my Friend, are the ANCIENT MARINER, the FOSTER-MOTHER'S TALE, the NIGHTINGALE, the DUNGEON, and the Poem entitled, LOVE.

---

that they who should be pleased with them would read them with more than common pleasure : and on the other hand I was well aware that by those who should dislike them they would be read with more than common dislike. The result has differed from my expectation in this only, that I have pleased a greater number, than I ventured to hope I should please.

For the sake of variety and from a consciousness of my own weakness I was induced to request the assistance of a Friend, who furnished me with the Poems of the ANCIENT MARINER, the FOSTER-MOTHER'S TALE, the NIGHTINGALE, the DUNGEON, and the Poem entitled LOVE. I should not, however, have requested this assistance, had I not believed that the poems of my Friend would in a great measure have the same tendency as my own, and that,

---

that they who should be pleased with them would read them with more than common pleasure : and on the other hand I was well aware that by those who should dislike them they would be read with more than common dislike. The result has differed from my expectation in this only, that I have pleased a greater number, than I ventured to hope I should please.

For the sake of variety and from a consciousness of my own weakness I was induced to request the assistance of a Friend, who furnished me with the Poems of the ANCIENT MARINER, the FOSTER-MOTHER'S TALE, the NIGHTINGALE, the DUNGEON, and the Poem entitled LOVE. I should not, however, have requested this assistance, had I not believed that the poems of my Friend would in a great measure have the same tendency as my own, and that,

Preface of the Second Edition of *Lyrical Ballads:* Three Settings of page vi.   Nos. 6, 10, and 11

LYRICAL BALLADS,

WITH

OTHER POEMS:

IN TWO VOLUMES.

BY W. WORDSWORTH.

Quam nihil ad genium, Papiniane, tuum!

VOL. I.

FROM THE LONDON SECOND EDITION.

Philadelphia:

PRINTED AND SOLD BY JAMES HUMPHREYS.
At the N.W. Corner of Walnut and Dock-street.
....
1802.

LYRICAL BALLADS,

WITH

OTHER POEMS:

IN TWO VOLUMES.

BY W. WORDSWORTH.

Quam nihil ad genium, Papiniane, tuum!

VOL. I.

FROM THE LONDON SECOND EDITION.

Philadelphia:

PRINTED BY JAMES HUMPHREYS,
FOR JOSEPH GROFF,
At No. 75, South Second-street.
....
1802.

The First American Edition of *Lyrical Ballads:* The Two Imprints.   Nos. 14 and 15

1904

326 LINES WRITTEN AFTER THE DEATH OF CHARLES LAMB. Privately Printed from the Original Edition of 1835, with a Supplementary Note by Cynthia Morgan St. John. Ithaca, 1904.

8 × 5½ in. [4] 7 [2] 14–20 pp. No. 28 of fifty copies printed. The original edition was actually of 1836 (No. 95).

327 Another copy; No. 16 of 50 copies printed.

328 Another copy; proof copy, with corrections in pencil by Cynthia Morgan St. John.

329 LINES COMPOSED A FEW MILES ABOVE TINTERN ABBEY on Revisiting the Banks of the Wye during a Tour, July 13th 1798. With illustrations by Donald Maxwell. London and New York: John Lane, 1904.

5½ × 4¼ in. 37 [7] pp.

330 RESOLUTION AND INDEPENDENCE. With Illustrations by Donald Maxwell. London and New York: John Lane, 1904.

5½ × 4¼ in. 39 [5] pp.

331 THE EXCURSION, Being a Portion of the Recluse (Temple Classics). London: J. M. Dent and Co., 1904.

6 × 4¾ in. [4] ix [3] 350 [2] pp.

332 THE PRELUDE. Edited with Notes and Introduction by Basil Worsfold. London: De la More Press, 1904.

5$\frac{15}{16}$ × 4$\frac{7}{16}$ in. lxxi [3] 429 [3] pp.

333 POEMS OF WORDSWORTH. Selected and Edited by William Knight. London: Simpkin, Marshall, Hamilton, Kent, & Co., [1904].

6½ × 3$\frac{11}{16}$ in. xxii, 639 [1] pp.

334 SELECTIONS FROM WORDSWORTH, Preceded by Lowell's Essay on Wordsworth and Annotated by H. B. Cotterill, M.A. London and New York: Macmillan and Co., 1904.

6⅞ × 4⅜ in. xli [1] 83 [5] pp.

335 THE POETICAL WORKS OF WILLIAM WORDSWORTH (Oxford Edition). With Introductions and Notes. Edited by Thomas Hutchinson, M.A. London, Edinburgh, Glasgow, New York, and Toronto: Henry Frowde, 1904.

7¼ × 4¾ in. xxxii, 976 pp.

336 POEMS OF WILLIAM WORDSWORTH, Selected and Edited by William Knight. London: George Newnes, Ltd.; New York: Charles Scribner's Sons, 1904.

6½ × 3¾ in. xxii, 639 [1] pp.

337 THE COMPLETE POETICAL WORKS OF WILLIAM WORDS-WORTH (Cambridge Edition). Boston and New York: Houghton, Mifflin, and Co., 1904.

8¼ × 5½ in. xlii [2] 937 [3] pp. Edited by Andrew J. George.

1905

338 WORDSWORTH'S LITERARY CRITICISM, Edited with an Introduction by Nowell C. Smith, Late Fellow of New College, Oxford. London: Henry Frowde, 1905.

6¾ × 4½ in. xxi [1] 260 pp.

339 THE COMPLETE POETICAL WORKS OF WILLIAM WORDS-WORTH. With an Introduction by John Morley. London and New York: Macmillan and Co., 1905.

7¼ × 4¾ in. lxvii [1] 928 [2] pp.

1906

340 WORDSWORTH'S GUIDE TO THE LAKES, Fifth Edition (1835), with an Introduction, Appendices, and Notes Textual and Illustrative by Ernest de Selincourt, with a Map and Eight Illustrations. London: Henry Frowde, 1906.

6⅝ × 4½ in. xxxii, 203 [1] pp.

1907

341 THE PRELUDE. Edited with Notes and Introduction by Basil Worsfold. London: Chatto & Windus; Boston: John W. Luce and Co., 1907.

6 × 4½ in. lxxi [3] 429 [3] pp.

342 WITH WORDSWORTH IN ENGLAND, Being a Selection of the Poems and Letters of William Wordsworth Which Have to Do with English Scenery and English Life. Selected and Arranged by Anna Benneson McMahan. With over Sixty Illustrations from Photographs. Chicago: A. C. McClurg & Co., 1907.

7⅜ × 5 in. xxvi, 352 [6] pp.

343 LETTERS OF THE WORDSWORTH FAMILY from 1787 to 1855. Collected and Edited by William Knight. In Three Volumes. Boston and London: Ginn and Co., 1907.

7 × 4⅝ in. Vol. 1: xxxiii [1] 542; vol. 2: xxix [1] 509 [3]; vol. 3: xxxi [1] 498 pp.

344 THE SHORTER POEMS OF WILLIAM WORDSWORTH (Everyman's Library). London: J. M. Dent & Co.; New York: E. P. Dutton & Co., [1907].

6¾ × 4⅛ in. xxxiv, 696 pp.

345 POEMS BY WILLIAM WORDSWORTH. Selected with an Introduction by Stopford A. Brooke. Illustrated by Edmund H. New. New York: McClure Phillips & Co.; London: Methuen & Co., 1907.

8⅝ × 5½ in. [4] xliv [4] 327 [1] pp.

346 THE COMPLETE POETICAL WORKS OF WILLIAM WORDSWORTH, with an Introduction by John Morley. New York: Thomas Y. Crowell & Co., [1907].

8⅛ × 5½ in. iv, 951 [1] pp.

1908

347 INTIMATIONS OF IMMORTALITY, an Ode by William Wordsworth. Portland, Maine: Thomas B. Mosher, 1908.

5⅝ × 5½ in. vii [1] 13 [9] pp.

348 THE LONGER POEMS OF WILLIAM WORDSWORTH (Everyman's Library). London: J. M. Dent & Co.; New York: E. P. Dutton & Co., [1908].

6¾ × 4⅛ in. ix [1] 688 pp.

349 THE POEMS OF WILLIAM WORDSWORTH, Edited with an Introduction and Notes by Nowell Charles Smith, M.A., Late Fellow of New College, and Formerly Fellow of Magdalen College, Oxford. In Three Volumes, with a Frontispiece. London: Methuen & Co., 1908.

8½ × 5¾ in. Vol. 1: lxx [2] 547 [3]; vol. 2: xix [1] 551 [1]; vol. 3: viii, 616 pp.

1909

350 A WORDSWORTH CALENDAR, Edited by Albert E. Sims. New York: Thomas Y. Crowell & Co., [*c*. 1909].

7⅜ × 4¾ in. [4] 162 pp.

351 WORDSWORTH DAY BY DAY, Edited by Albert E. Sims. New York: Thomas Y. Crowell & Co., [*c*. 1909].

7⅜ × 5 in. [8] 162 [4] pp.

352 THE LAKES in Wordsworth and Some Early Tourists. Selected by J.H.W. Ambleside: George Middleton, Printer, 1909.

6⅜ × 4¾ in. [2] 58 pp.

353 GEMS FROM WORDSWORTH. London: Ernest Nister; New York: E. P. Dutton & Co., [1909].

4⅞ × 6¼ in., oblong. [32] pp. Printed in Bavaria.

354 A DAY WITH THE POET WORDSWORTH (Days with the Poets). New York: Hodder & Stoughton, [c. 1909].

8 × 5¹¹⁄₁₆ in. 48 pp.

355 IV SONNETS. n.p., Xmas, 1909.

8½ × 6⅜ in. Eight leaves, printed on one side only. Colophon: 'CXLIII copies printed by Bruce Rogers.' With a presentation inscription by the printer.

1910

356 LXXV SONNETS. n.p., Riverside Press, [1910].

8⅜ × 6¼ in. [14], [154] pp. Printed on one side only. No. 435 of 440 copies printed.

357 THE SOLITARY REAPER, MDCCCIII: MDCCCCX. London: Printed at the L.C.C. Central School of Arts and Crafts: Day Technical School of Book Production: by F. R. Beckett, [1910].

8¾ × 6¾ in. 3 [1] pp.

358 THE POETICAL WORKS OF WILLIAM WORDSWORTH (Oxford Edition). Edited by Thomas Hutchinson. London, New York, Toronto, and Melbourne: Oxford University Press, 1910.

7¼ × 4½ in. xxxii, 986 [2] pp.

359 THE COMPLETE POETICAL WORKS OF WILLIAM WORDS-WORTH. Boston and New York: Houghton, Mifflin, & Co., 1910–11, 10 vols.

8⅝ × 5¾ in. Vol. 1: xxxviii [2] 221 [1]; vol. 2: xi [3] 353 [3]; vol. 3: vii [1] 325 [5]; vol. 4: xiv [2] 318 [2]; vol. 5: xv [1] 310 [4]; vol. 6: vii [1] 386 [4]; vol. 7: xxiii [1] 385 [3]; vol. 8: xvii [1] 355 [3]; vol. 9: xvii [1] 270 [2]; vol. 10: vii [1] 340 [4] pp.

1911

360 A DECADE OF YEARS; Poems by William Wordsworth, 1798–1807. [Hammersmith: Doves Press], 1911.

9¼ × 6½ in. [10] 230 [12] pp. 212 copies printed. With autograph presentation inscription from the printer, T. J. Cobden-Sanderson.

361 TO A PICTURE BY LUCA GIORDANO, in the Museo Barbonica, at Naples. Ithaca: Privately Printed, 1911.

7⅞ × 4⅞ in. Folder of two leaves. Printed for Cynthia Morgan St. John and given to guests assembled at her home on 7 April 1911 to commemorate the poet's birthday.

362 Another copy.

363 LYRICAL BALLADS, 1798, Edited by Harold Littledale. London: Henry Frowde, 1911.

6⅛ × 4½ in. v [3] 210 [2] pp.

364 WORDSWORTH (The Regent Library). By E. Hallam Moorhouse. London: Herbert & Daniel, 1911.

6⅜ × 4½ in. xxii [2] 437 [1] pp.

365 THE COMPLETE POETICAL WORKS OF WILLIAM WORDS-WORTH (Grasmere Edition). Boston and New York: Houghton, Mifflin, & Co., 1911, 10 vols.

7½ × 4⅞ in. Vol. 1: xxxviii [2] 221 [3]; vol. 2: xi [1] 353 [3]; vol. 3: vii [1] 325 [1]; vol. 4: xiv [2] 318 [2]; vol. 5: xv [1] 310 [4]; vol. 6: vii [1] 386 [2]; vol. 7: xxiii [1] 385 [3]; vol. 8: xvii [1] 355 [3]; vol. 9: xvii [1] 270 [4]; vol. 10: vii [1] 400 [4] pp.

366 Another copy.

1913

367 INTIMATIONS OF IMMORTALITY FROM RECOLLECTIONS OF EARLY CHILDHOOD. With Twelve Illustrations in Colour by Norah Neilson Gray. London: J. M. Dent and Sons, 1913.

9½ × 7⅞ in. [20] pp.

368 THE COMPLETE POETICAL WORKS OF WILLIAM WORDS-WORTH. With an Introduction by John Morley. London: Macmillan and Co., 1913.

7⅜ × 5 in. lxvii [1] 928 pp.

1914

369 DAYS WITH WORDSWORTH. Calendar—1914. Selected and Illuminated by Edith A. Ibbs. London: Ernest Nister; New York: E. P. Dutton & Co., 1914.

4⅜ × 5⅞ in. [28] pp.

370 POEMS IN TWO VOLUMES, 1807, Edited by Helen Darbishire, Tutor in English, Somerville College, Oxford. Oxford: Clarendon Press, 1914.

7 × 4½ in. lii, 470 [6] pp.

1915

371 WORDSWORTH'S TRACT ON THE CONVENTION OF CINTRA, Published 1809, with Two Letters of Wordsworth Written in the Year 1811, Now Republished with an Introduction by A. V. Dicey. London: Humphrey Milford, 1915.

6⅛ × 4½ in. xl, 244 pp.

372 THE PRELUDE; an Autobiographical Poem by William Wordsworth, 1799–1805. [Hammersmith: Doves Press], 1915.

9¼ × 6½ in. [10] 301 [11] pp. With autograph presentation inscription by the printer, T. J. Cobden-Sanderson.

373 THE PATRIOTIC POETRY OF WILLIAM WORDSWORTH, a Selection with Introduction and Notes by Right Hon. Arthur H. D. Acland, Honorary Fellow of Balliol College, Oxford. Oxford: Clarendon Press, 1915.

6 × 3¾ in. 143 [1] pp.

374 THE HAPPY WARRIOR and Other Poems by William Wordsworth. London: For the Medici Society by Philip Lee Warner, 1915.

5¾ × 4¼ in. 36 [4] pp.

1916

375 THE LAW OF COPYRIGHT, by William Wordsworth. London: Printed for Private Circulation, 1916.

9 × 7½ in. 10 [2] pp. Presentation copy, autographed twice by the editor, Thomas J. Wise.

376 WORDSWORTH'S SHORTER POEMS. Illustrated by H. K. Elcock. London and Glasgow: Collins' Clear-Type Press, [*c*. 1916].

6 × 3¾ in. 383 [1] pp.

1918

377 SELECT POEMS, Chosen and Edited by S. G. Dunn, M.A. London: Oxford University Press, 1918.

6½ × 4¼ in. 128 pp.

1919

378 THE COMPLETE POETICAL WORKS OF WILLIAM WORDS-WORTH. Boston and New York: Houghton, Mifflin, & Co., 1919, 10 vols.

6⅞ × 4½ in. Vol. 1: viii, 221 [1]; vol. 2: ix [1] 353 [1]; vol. 3: [6] 324 [2]; vol. 4: xi [1] 318 [2]; vol. 5: xiii [1] 310 [2]; vol. 6: [4] 386 [2]; vol. 7: xxi [1] 385 [1]; vol. 8: xv [1] 355 [1]; vol. 9: xv [1] 255 [1]; vol. 10: vi, 339 [3] pp.

1920

379 LYRICAL BALLADS. Edited with Certain Poems of 1798 and an Introduction and Notes by Thomas Hutchinson. Third Edition. London: Duckworth and Co., 1920.

6½ × 4 in. lix [3] v [1] 263 [1] pp.

380 WORDSWORTH: AN ANTHOLOGY. Thavies Inn: Richard Cobden-Sanderson, 1920.

8¾ × 5⅝ in. 254 [2] pp.

381 COLERIDGE, BIOGRAPHIA LITERARIA CHAPTERS I–IV, XIV–XXII; WORDSWORTH, PREFACES AND ESSAYS ON POETRY 1800–1815. Edited by George Sampson, with an Introductory Essay by Sir Arthur Quiller-Couch. Cambridge: Cambridge University Press, 1920.

7¾ × 5⅝ in. xxxix [1] 327 [1] pp.

1922

382 THE ECCLESIASTICAL SONNETS, a Critical Edition (Cornell Studies in English), by Abbie Findlay Potts. New Haven: Yale University Press, 1922.

8½ × 5½ in. x, 316 pp.

383 POEMS OF WILLIAM WORDSWORTH, Selected and Edited by Clara L. Thomson. Cambridge: Cambridge University Press, 1922.

6¾ × 4¼ in. xxviii, 144 pp.

1923

384 SELECTED POEMS OF WILLIAM WORDSWORTH (Riverside College Classics). Edited by Solomon Francis Gingerich. Boston: Houghton Mifflin Co., [c. 1923].

6⅞ × 4¼ in. xxii, 319 [1] pp.

1924

385 THE PRELUDE, or, Growth of a Poet's Mind, an Autobiographical Poem by William Wordsworth. Selections Arranged and Edited by Bernard Groom, M.A. London: Macmillan and Co., 1924.

6⅝ × 4⁵⁄₁₆ in. xv [1] 108 [4] pp.

386 WILLIAM WORDSWORTH (Nelson's Poets). With an Introduction by Viscount Grey of Fallodon. London and Edinburgh: Thomas Nelson & Sons, [1924].

6⅛ × 4 in. xxii, 438 [2] pp.

387 WORDSWORTH: POETRY & PROSE, with Essays by Coleridge, Hazlitt, De Quincey; with an Introduction by David Nichol Smith, and Notes. Oxford: Clarendon Press, 1924.

7¼ × 4¾ in. xx, 212 pp.

1925

388 THE GRASMERE WORDSWORTH, a Redaction (in One Volume) (Five Years in Preparation) as Suggested by Matthew Arnold, and Approved by Lord Morley of Blackburn. Edited by John Hawke, Editor of 'Poems and Songs.'. London: Selwyn and Blount, 1925.

$6\frac{1}{2} \times 4$ in. xx, 396 pp.

1926

389 LYRICAL BALLADS, 1798 (The Noel Douglas Replicas). London: Noel Douglas, 1926.

$8\frac{7}{8} \times 5\frac{1}{2}$ in. [12] v [3] 210 [6] pp. Charles Whibley's copy.

390 THE PRELUDE, or Growth of a Poet's Mind. Edited from the Manuscripts, with Introduction, Textual and Critical Notes, by Ernest de Selincourt. Oxford: Clarendon Press, 1926.

$8\frac{3}{4} \times 5\frac{5}{8}$ in. lxii [2] 614 [2] pp.

391 POEMS OF WORDSWORTH, Chosen by Matthew Arnold (Modern Readers' Series). Edited by Ashley H. Thorndike. New York: Macmillan Co., 1926.

$7\frac{1}{8} \times 4\frac{5}{8}$ in. xxxviii, 301 [3] pp.

1927

392 LYRICAL BALLADS, Edited by Harold Littledale. London: Oxford University Press, 1927.

$6\frac{1}{2} \times 4\frac{1}{4}$ in. [6] v [3] 210 [6] pp.

1928

393 THE PRELUDE, Books I, II, and Parts of V and XII. Edited by Helen Darbishire. Oxford: Clarendon Press, 1928.

$6\frac{5}{8} \times 4\frac{3}{8}$ in. 63 [1] pp.

394 WORDSWORTH: POETRY & PROSE, with Essays by Coleridge, Hazlitt, De Quincey; with an Introduction by David Nichol Smith, and Notes. Oxford: Clarendon Press, 1928.

$7\frac{1}{8} \times 4\frac{5}{8}$ in. xx, 212, 23 [1] pp.

395 A SELECTION OF SHORTER POEMS (The Ormond Poets). Edited by G. D. H. & M. I. Cole. London: Noel Douglas, 1928.

$6\frac{1}{2} \times 4$ in. 61 [3] pp.

396 WILLIAM WORDSWORTH (The Augustan Books of English Poetry, Second Series, No. 19). London: Ernest Benn, [1928].

$8\frac{3}{4} \times 5\frac{1}{2}$ in. v [1] 7–31 [1] pp.

1929

397 SELECTED POEMS OF WILLIAM WORDSWORTH. London: Oxford University Press, 1929.

$5\frac{7}{8} \times 3\frac{1}{2}$ in. xviii, 569 [1] 16 pp.

1931

398 WAYSIDE FLOWERS, Poems of the Out-of-Doors by William Wordsworth. Selected and Introduced by Edna Turpin. Illustrated by Helene Carter. New York: Macmillan Co., 1931.

$8\frac{1}{2} \times 5\frac{1}{2}$ in. viii, 76 [4] pp.

1932

399 THE PRELUDE, or Growth of a Poet's Mind. Edited from the Manuscripts, with Introduction, Textual and Critical Notes, by Ernest de Selincourt. Oxford: Clarendon Press, 1932.

$8\frac{3}{4} \times 5\frac{5}{8}$ in. lxii [2] 614 pp.

400 WORDSWORTH, Extracts from The Prelude, with Other Poems. Edited with Introduction and Notes by George Mallaby, B.A. Cambridge: Cambridge University Press, 1932.

$7\frac{1}{4} \times 4\frac{7}{8}$ in. xxiv, 139 [1] pp.

401 SELECTIONS FROM WORDSWORTH, Edited with Notes and an Introduction by Philip Wayne, M.A., Headmaster of St Marylebone Grammar School. London: Ginn and Co., [1932].

$6\frac{1}{2} \times 4\frac{1}{2}$ in. xxxix [1] 200 pp.

1933

402 WORDSWORTH & REED; the Poet's Correspondence with His American Editor, 1836–1850, and Henry Reed's Account of His Reception at Rydal Mount, London, and Elsewhere in 1854. Edited by Leslie Nathan Broughton, Professor of English in Cornell University. Ithaca: Cornell University Press, 1933.

$8\frac{1}{2} \times 5\frac{7}{8}$ in. xviii [2] 288 [4] pp.

403 THE PRELUDE, or Growth of a Poet's Mind (Text of 1805). Edited from the Manuscripts with Introduction and Notes by Ernest de Selincourt. London: Oxford University Press, 1933.

$7\frac{1}{8} \times 4\frac{13}{16}$ in. xxxix [1] 327 [1] pp.

404 THE POETICAL WORKS OF WORDSWORTH (Oxford Standard Edition). Edited by Thomas Hutchinson, and with Introduction and Notes by George McLean Harper. New York: Oxford University Press, 1933.

7¼ × 4¾ in. [2] li [1] 992 [4] pp.

1934

405 THE SHORTER POEMS OF WILLIAM WORDSWORTH (Everyman's Library). London and Toronto: J. M. Dent & Sons; New York: E. P. Dutton & Co., 1934.

6¾ × 4 in. xxxiv, 696 pp.

1935

406 THE EARLY LETTERS OF WILLIAM AND DOROTHY WORDSWORTH (1787–1805). Arranged and Edited by Ernest de Selincourt. Oxford: Clarendon Press, 1935.

8⅝ × 5⅝ in. xviii, 578 [4] pp. For the later volumes, see Nos. 409, 411.

407 THE EXCURSION, Preceded by Book I of The Recluse. Edited by E. E. Reynolds. London: Macmillan and Co., 1935.

6 × 3¾ in. xii, 292 pp.

1936

408 LONGER POEMS (Everyman's Library). London: J. M. Dent & Sons; New York: E. P. Dutton & Co., 1936.

6¾ × 4 in. ix [1] 688 pp.

409 THE LETTERS OF WILLIAM AND DOROTHY WORDSWORTH: the Middle Years. Arranged and Edited by Ernest de Selincourt. Vol. 1: 1806–June 1811. Vol. 2: August 1811–1820. Oxford: Clarendon Press, 1937.

8¾ × 5⅝ in. Vol. 1: xx, 458f; vol. 2: xi [1] 459–932 [2] pp. For the earlier and later volumes see Nos. 406, 411.

410 REPRESENTATIVE POEMS, Selected and Edited by Arthur Beatty, Professor of English, University of Wisconsin. Garden City, New York: Doubleday, Doran, & Co., 1937.

7 × 4½ in. lxxi [1] 741 [3] pp.

1939

411 THE LETTERS OF WILLIAM AND DOROTHY WORDSWORTH: the Later Years. Arranged and Edited by Ernest de Selincourt. Vol. 1: 1821–1830; vol. 2: 1831–1840; vol. 3: 1841–1850. Oxford: Clarendon Press, 1939.

8¾ × 5½ in. Vol. 1: xxxviii, 543 [1]; vol. 2: xiv, 545–1059 [1]; vol. 3: xii, 1061–1407 [1] pp. For the earlier volumes, see Nos. 406, 409.

1940

412 THE WHITE DOE OF RYLSTONE: a Critical Edition (Cornell Studies in English No. 29). By Alice Pattee Comparetti, Instructor in English in Colby College. Ithaca: Cornell University Press, 1940.

8½ × 5⅞ in. [12] 311 [5] pp.

413 THE POETICAL WORKS OF WILLIAM WORDSWORTH: Poems Written in Youth; Poems Referring to the Period of Childhood. Edited from the Manuscripts, with Textual and Critical Notes, by E. de Selincourt. Oxford: Clarendon Press, 1940.

8⅝ × 5⅝ in. xv [1] 379 [1] pp. For the other volumes in this edition see Nos. 417 and 431, 420 and 435, 421, 424.

1941

414 SOME LETTERS OF THE WORDSWORTH FAMILY, Now First Published, with a Few Unpublished Letters of Coleridge and Southey and Others. Edited by Leslie Nathan Broughton, Professor of English and Curator of the Wordsworth Collection at Cornell University. Ithaca: Cornell University Press, 1942.

9 × 6 in. x [2] 131 [5] pp.

415 WORDSWORTH, with Four Colour Plates & Seventeen Black and White Illustrations (Britain in Pictures). Edited by Dorothy Wellesley. London: William Collins, 1942.

7 × 4¼ in. [2] 79 [1] pp.

1943

416 AN EDITION OF WORDSWORTH'S PRELUDE, BOOK III (Cornell University Ph.D. Thesis). By Russell Fessenden. Ithaca: Typescript, 1943.

10¼ × 7¾ in. [10] 347 [3] pp.

1944

417 THE POETICAL WORKS OF WILLIAM WORDSWORTH: Poems Founded on the Affections; Poems on the Naming of Places; Poems of the Fancy; Poems of the Imagination. Edited from the Manuscripts, with Textual and Critical Notes, by E. de Selincourt. Oxford: Clarendon Press, 1944.

8⅝ × 5⅝ in. xi [1] 537 [1] pp. For the other volumes in this edition see Nos. 413, 420 and 435, 421, 424. For the second edition of this volume, see No. 431.

1946

418 POEMS: Lyrics and Sonnets. Mount Vernon, New York: Peter Pauper Press, [1946].

9 × 5½ in. [2] 92 [2] pp.

419 A WORDSWORTH ANTHOLOGY, Selected with an Introduction by Laurence Housman. New York: Charles Scribner's Sons, 1946.

7¼ × 5 in. vi [2] 151 [1] pp.

420 THE POETICAL WORKS OF WILLIAM WORDSWORTH: Miscellaneous Sonnets; Memorials of Various Tours; Poems Dedicated to National Independence and Liberty; The Egyptian Maid; The River Duddon Series; The White Doe and Other Narrative Poems; Ecclesiastical Sonnets. Edited from the Manuscripts, with Textual and Critical Notes, by E. de Selincourt and Helen Darbishire. Oxford: Clarendon Press, 1946.

8⅝ × 5⅝ in. xxiii [1] 596 pp. For the other volumes in this edition see Nos. 413, 417 and 431, 421, 424. For the second edition of this volume, see No. 435.

1947

421 THE POETICAL WORKS OF WILLIAM WORDSWORTH: Evening Voluntaries; Itinerary Poems of 1833; Poems of Sentiment and Reflection; Sonnets Dedicated to Liberty and Order; Miscellaneous Poems; Inscriptions; Selections from Chaucer; Poems Referring to the Period of Old Age; Epitaphs and Elegiac Poems; Ode: Intimations of Immortality. Edited from the Manuscripts, with Textual and Critical Notes, by E. de Selincourt and Helen Darbishire. Oxford: Clarendon Press, 1947.

8⅝ × 5⅝ in. xvi, 490 [2] pp. For the other volumes in this edition see Nos. 413, 417 and 431, 420 and 435, 424.

1948

422 A GUIDE THROUGH THE DISTRICT OF THE LAKES in the North of England, with a Description of the Scenery &c. For the Use of Tourists and Residents. Facsimile of the Definitive Fifth Edition of 1835. By William Wordsworth. Malvern: Tantivy Press, [1948].

7⅞ × 4⅞ in. xxiv, 131 [5] pp.

1949

423 WORDSWORTH, an Introduction and a Selection, by Norman Nicholson. London: Phoenix House, [1949].

7¼ × 4¾ in. xxvi, 238 pp.

424 THE POETICAL WORKS OF WILLIAM WORDSWORTH: The Excursion; The Recluse, Part I, Book I. Edited from the Manuscripts, with Textual and Critical Notes, by E. de Selincourt and Helen Darbishire. Oxford: Clarendon Press, 1939.

$8\frac{5}{8} \times 5\frac{5}{8}$ in. vii [1] 498 [2] pp. For the other volumes in this edition see Nos. 413, 417 and 431, 420 and 435, 421.

1950

425 WORDSWORTH; a Selection by W. E. Williams. Revised Edition. Harmondsworth: Penguin Books, [1950].

7×4 in. 192 pp.

426 SELECTED POETRY (Modern Library). Edited, with an Introduction, by Mark Van Doren. New York: Modern Library, [1950].

$7 \times 4\frac{1}{2}$ in. xxii, 714 pp.

427 THE POETICAL WORKS OF WORDSWORTH, with Introduction and Notes, Edited by Thomas Hutchinson. A New Edition, Revised by Ernest de Selincourt. London, New York, Toronto: Oxford University Press, [1950].

$7\frac{1}{8} \times 4\frac{5}{8}$ in. xxx, 779 [3] pp.

1951

428 A GUIDE THROUGH THE DISTRICT OF THE LAKES in the North of England, with a Description of the Scenery &c. For the Use of Tourists and Residents. By William Wordsworth. With Illustrations by John Piper, and an Introduction by W. M. Merchant. London: Rupert Hart-Davis, 1951.

$7\frac{1}{4} \times 4\frac{3}{4}$ in. 174 [2] pp.

1952

429 A GUIDE THROUGH THE DISTRICT OF THE LAKES in the North of England, with a Description of the Scenery &c. For the Use of Tourists and Residents. By William Wordsworth. With Illustrations by John Piper, and an Introduction by W. M. Merchant. Bloomington: Indiana University Press, 1952.

$7\frac{1}{4} \times 4\frac{11}{16}$ in. 174 [2] pp.

430 LYRICAL BALLADS (1798). Historisch-kritisch herausgegeben mit Einleitung und Anmerkungen von F. W. Schulze. Halle/Saale: Max Niemeyer, 1952.

$8 \times 5\frac{1}{2}$ in. x, 199 [1] pp.

431 THE POETICAL WORKS OF WILLIAM WORDSWORTH: Poems Founded on the Affections; Poems on the Naming of Places; Poems of the Fancy; Poems of the Imagination. Edited from the Manuscripts, with Textual and Critical Notes, by E. de Selincourt. Second Edition. Oxford: Clarendon Press, 1952.

$8\frac{5}{8} \times 5\frac{5}{8}$ in. xi [1] 548 pp. Revised edition.

1953

432 POLITICAL TRACTS OF WORDSWORTH, COLERIDGE, AND SHELLEY, Edited with an Introduction by R. J. White. Cambridge: Cambridge University Press, 1953.

$8\frac{7}{8} \times 5\frac{1}{2}$ in. xliv, 303 [1] pp.

1954

433 THE PRELUDE; with a Selection from the Shorter Poems, the Sonnets, The Recluse, The Excursion, and Three Essays on the Art of Poetry (Rinehart Editions). Edited with an Introduction by Carlos Baker. New York: Rinehart, [1954].

$7\frac{1}{8} \times 4\frac{3}{4}$ in. xxix [1] 480 pp.

434 THE LETTERS OF WILLIAM WORDSWORTH (World's Classics), Selected, and with an Introduction, by Philip Wayne, [1954].

$5\frac{7}{8} \times 3\frac{1}{2}$ in. xxiv [2] 295 [1] pp.

435 THE POETICAL WORKS OF WILLIAM WORDSWORTH: Miscellaneous Sonnets; Memorials of Various Tours; Poems Dedicated to National Independence and Liberty; The Egyptian Maid; The River Duddon Series; The White Doe and Other Narrative Poems; Ecclesiastical Sonnets. Edited from the Manuscripts, with Textual and Critical Notes, by E. de Selincourt and Helen Darbishire. Second Edition. Oxford: Clarendon Press, 1954.

$8\frac{5}{8} \times 5\frac{5}{8}$ in. xxiii [1] 596 pp. Revised edition.

1955

436 WORDSWORTH'S POEMS, in Three Volumes (Everyman's Library). Edited with an Introduction by Philip Wayne, M.A. London: J. M. Dent & Sons; New York: E. P. Dutton & Co., 1955.

$7\frac{1}{16} \times 4\frac{1}{2}$ in. Vol. 1: xxxii, 412 [4]; vol. 2: xxii, 542 [10]; vol. 3: [6] 419 [5] pp.

437 WORDSWORTH: POETRY & PROSE. Selected by W. M. Merchant. London: Rupert Hart-Davis, 1955.

$7\frac{7}{8} \times 5$ in. 883 [1] pp.

UNDATED

438 THE BOOKLOVER'S LIBRARY OF POETICAL LITERATURE, in Twenty-five Volumes. Vols. 1, 2, 3: William Wordsworth. With a Critical and Biographical Introduction by Edwin Markham, and a Frontispiece in Color by A. E. Becher. New York and London: Co-operative Publication Society.

$7\frac{7}{8} \times 5\frac{3}{8}$ in. Vol. 1: [2] 575 [1]; vol. 2: [4] 577–1208 [2]; vol. 3: [2] 1209–782 pp.

439 THE COMPLETE POETICAL WORKS OF WILLIAM WORDS-WORTH, with an Introduction by John Morley and Explanatory Notes by the Author. New York: A. L. Burt.

$7\frac{1}{4} \times 4\frac{3}{4}$ in. xxii, 786 pp.

440 THE COMPLETE POETICAL WORKS OF WILLIAM WORDS-WORTH ('Edina' Edition). With Biographical Introduction and Notes by Charles Kennett Burrow. London, Edinburgh and New York: Eyre and Spottiswoode.

$7\frac{1}{4} \times 5$ in. xxx [2] 977 [3] pp.

441 THE COMPLETE WORKS OF WILLIAM WORDSWORTH, with Introduction and Notes by Charles Kennett Burrow, with Numerous Illustrations. London and Glasgow: Collins' Clear-Type Press.

$7\frac{1}{4} \times 5\frac{1}{8}$ in. xxviii, 977 [7] pp.

442 GLEANINGS FROM WORDSWORTH, Edited by J. Robertson. New York: White, Stokes, and Allen.

$3\frac{3}{4} \times 2\frac{5}{8}$ in. xxvii [2] 30–128 [2] pp.

443 ODE ON INTIMATIONS OF IMMORTALITY from Recollections of Early Childhood. Philadelphia: George W. Jacobs & Co.

$5\frac{1}{2} \times 3\frac{1}{2}$ in. [2] 26 [4] pp.

444 POEMS OF WORDSWORTH, Chosen and Edited by Matthew Arnold. New York: Harper and Brothers.

$4\frac{5}{8} \times 3$ in. viii [2] 407 [1] pp.

445 POEMS OF WORDSWORTH (The Golden Poets). Selected and with an Introduction by Professor W. MacNeile Dixon, M.A. Edinburgh: T. C. & E. C. Jack.

$6\frac{3}{4} \times 4\frac{5}{8}$ in. lvi, 260 pp.

446 THE POETICAL WORKS OF WILLIAM WORDSWORTH. London: Ward, Lock, & Co.

$7 \times 4\frac{1}{2}$ in. xiv, 497 [19] pp. With six pages of manuscript notes on *The Excursion* bound in.

447 THE POETICAL WORKS OF WILLIAM WORDSWORTH, with 106 Illustrations by Birket Foster, J. Wolf, and Sir John Gilbert, R.A. London and New York: George Routledge and Sons.

7 × 4¾ in. xii, 564 pp.

448 THE POETICAL WORKS OF WORDSWORTH (The Lansdowne Poets). With Memoir, Explanatory Notes, etc., Portrait and Original Illustrations. London: Frederick Warne and Co.

7 × 4¾ in. xxxix [1] 600 [2] pp.

449 THE POETICAL WORKS OF WILLIAM WORDSWORTH (Savoy Edition). With Introduction by Edward Dowden. London, Edinburgh, and New York: Eyre & Spottiswoode.

7¼ × 4⅝ in. xxxix [1] 744 pp.

450 POETICAL WORKS OF WILLIAM WORDSWORTH. Chicago: Henneberry Co.

7¼ × 4⅝ in. xliv [2] 628 [4] pp.

451 SELECTED POEMS OF WORDSWORTH (King's Treasury of Literary Masterpieces). London: William Robertson; George G. Harrap & Co.

5⅝ × 3⅝ in. [4] 192 pp.

452 Two Poems of Wordsworth in Dutch.

Two extracts from an unidentified source published by Stangen, and Arme Geerte.

453 WE ARE SEVEN, with Drawings by Mary L. Gow. New York: E. P. Dutton.

9⅛ × 7¼ in. [20] pp.

454 WE ARE SEVEN, and Other Poems. Illustrated with Numerous Engravings. Philadelphia: J. B. Lippincott Co.

8 × 6⅛ in. 39 [1] pp.

455 WE ARE SEVEN, and Other Poems. Illustrated with Numerous Engravings. Philadelphia: J. B. Lippincott Co.

8 × 6⅛ in. [2] 47 [1] pp.

456 WORDSWORTH THOUGHTS, Selected by Louey Chisholm. Philadelphia: George W. Jacobs & Co.

3⅞ × 2¼ in. [4] 58 [6] pp.

457 WORDSWORTH'S EARLIEST SONNET: On Seeing Miss Helen Maria Williams Weep at a Tale of Distress.

A single page. Presentation copy to Cynthia Morgan St. John from J. R. Tutin.

POEMS,

IN

TWO VOLUMES,

BY

WILLIAM WORDSWORTH,

AUTHOR OF

THE LYRICAL BALLADS.

Posterius graviore sono tibi Musa loquetur
Nostra: dabunt cum securos mihi tempora fructus.

VOL. I.

LONDON:

PRINTED FOR LONGMAN, HURST, REES, AND ORME,
PATERNOSTER-ROW.

1807.

Robert Southey from William Wordsworth

CONCERNING

THE RELATIONS

OF

GREAT BRITAIN, SPAIN, AND PORTUGAL,

TO EACH OTHER, AND TO THE COMMON ENEMY,

AT THIS CRISIS;

AND SPECIFICALLY AS AFFECTED BY

THE

CONVENTION OF CINTRA:

The whole brought to the test of those Principles, by which
alone the Independence and Freedom of Nations
can be Preserved or Recovered.

Qui didicit patriæ quid debeat ;————
Quod sit conscripti, quod judicis officium ; quæ
Partes in bellum missi ducis.

BY WILLIAM WORDSWORTH.

London:

PRINTED FOR LONGMAN, HURST, REES, AND ORME,
PATERNOSTER-ROW.

1809.

Southey's Copy of *The Convention of Cintra*, the Gift of Wordsworth. No. 22

PART III

WRITINGS OF WORDSWORTH
IN EARLY PERIODICALS

HWC

1787

458 *The European Magazine, and London Review*, xi (March 1787).

Sonnet, on Seeing Miss Helen Maria Williams Weep at a Tale of Distress, p. 202. This sonnet, signed 'Axiologus' and hence attributed to Wordsworth, is the earliest of his work to appear in print.

1800

459 *The Morning Post and Gazetteer*, 2 April 1800.

The Mad Mother.

1801

460 *The Charms of Melody, or Siren Medley*, No. 94, Dublin, *c*. 1801.

Lucy Gray; We are Seven.

461 *The Port Folio*, Philadelphia, i (1801).

Simon Lee, p. 24; The Last of the Flock, p. 48; The Thorn, pp. 94–5; Anecdote for Fathers, p. 232; Ellen Irwin, pp. 391–2; Strange Fits of Passion, p. 392; The Waterfall and the Eglantine, p. 403; Lucy Gray, p. 403; Andrew Jones, p. 403.

1803

462 *The Port Folio*, Philadelphia, iii (1803).

The Fountain, p. 288; 'A whirl-blast from behind the hill', p. 320.

1804

463 *The Port Folio*, Philadelphia, iv (1804).

The Oak and the Broom, p. 96; Written in Germany, on One of the Coldest Days of the Century, p. 342.

1805

464 *The Balance and Columbian Repository*, Hudson, New York, iv (1805).

We are Seven, p. 144.

1807

465 *The Balance and Columbian Repository*, Hudson, New York, vi (1807).

Alice Fell, p. 328.

1812

466 *The Friend, a Series of Essays.* London: Gale and Curtis, 1812.

'Another year!—another deadly blow!', p. 88; 'Oh! pleasant exercise of hope and joy' (lines from The Prelude), p. 163; 'Of mortal Parents is the Hero born'; 'Advance—come forth from thy Tyrolean ground', p. 171; 'Alas! what boots the long laborious quest', p. 208; 'Two Voices are there; one is of the Sea'; 'The Land we from our Fathers had in trust'; 'And is it among rude untutor'd vales'; 'O'er the wide earth, on mountain and on plain'; 'It was a *moral* end for which they fought', pp. 273–4; 'There never breath'd a man who, when his life'; 'Destined to war from very infancy', pp. 289–90; 'Wisdom and Spirit of the Universe!', pp. 303–4; A Reply to 'Mathetes', pp. 268–72, 305–18; 'Not without heavy grief of heart did He'; 'Pause, courteous Spirit!—Balbi supplicates', pp. 319–20; 'Perhaps some needful service of the State'; 'O Thou who movest onward with a mind', pp. 401–2; Essay upon Epitaphs, pp. 402–16. See also No. 1735.

1816

467 *The Examiner*, 28 January 1816.

'How clear, how keen, how marvellously bright', p. 57.

468 *The Examiner*, 11 February 1816.

'While not a leaf seems faded, while the fields', p. 92.

469 *The Examiner*, 31 March 1816.

To B. R. Haydon, p. 203.

1819

470 *Blackwood's Edinburgh Magazine*, IV (January 1819).

'Pure element of waters! whereso'er'; 'Was the aim frustrated by force or guile'; 'At early dawn, or when the warmer air', p. 471.

1824

471 *The Wesleyan-Methodist Magazine for the Year 1824 (an Abridged Edition, Containing Selections from the Larger Work), Being a Continuation of the Arminian or Methodist Magazine*, III 3S (1824).

Inscription in a Hermit's Cell, p. 80.

1831

472 *The New Monthly Magazine and Literary Journal* (*Original Papers*), XXXIII (July 1831).

To B. R. Haydon, on Seeing His Picture of Napoleon Buonaparte on the Island of St. Helena, p. 26.

1832

473 *The Penny Magazine of the Society for the Diffusion of Useful Knowledge*, 1832.

'I grieved for Buonaparte, with a vain', p. 79; Fidelity, p. 320.

1833

474 *The Penny Magazine of the Society for the Diffusion of Useful Knowledge*, 1833.

To My Sister, p. 104; Lines Composed above Tintern Abbey, pp. 285–6.

475 *Greenbank's Periodical Library*, Philadelphia, II (1833).

Fourteen poems by Wordsworth, pp. 186–202.

1835

476 *The Athenaeum*, 12 December 1835.

Extempore Effusion, upon Reading, in the Newcastle Journal, the Notice of the Death of the Poet, James Hogg, pp. 930–1.

1836

477 *The Gentleman's Magazine*, v, n.s. (January 1836).

Extempore Effusion upon the Death of James Hogg, p. 98.

1839

478 *Tait's Edinburgh Magazine*, VI (September 1839).

George and Sarah Green, p. 573.

1841

479 *The Quarterly Review*, LXIX (December 1841).

Sonnets upon the Punishment of Death, pp. 42–9. Fourteen sonnets.

1842

480 *The New World, a Weekly Journal of Popular Literature, Science, Music, and the Arts. Containing the Latest Works by Distinguished Authors, Sermons by Eminent Divines, Original and Selected Tales and Poetry*, &c., &c., January–July 1842.

To the Clouds; Suggested by a Picture of a Bird of Paradise; Maternal Grief, p. 245; Guilt and Sorrow, pp. 291–3; Chaucer and Windsor [an erroneous attribution to Wordsworth], p. 294.

1847

481 *The Home Journal*, 2 October 1847.

A clipping, containing a sonnet, at the end of which is printed: 'William Wordsworth. Rydal Mount, Westmoreland, Oct. 22, 1839.' The introductory note reads: 'A valuable correspondent sends us the following exquisite sonnet, to a picture by Luca Giordano, in the Museo Borbonico, at Naples, which he says he has reason to believe was never before published.' The sonnet begins: 'A sad and lovely face, with upturn'd eyes'.

PART IV

WRITINGS OF WORDSWORTH
IN EARLY ANTHOLOGIES
AND OTHER BOOKS

482 WRANGHAM, FRANCIS. *Poems* by Francis Wrangham, M.A., Member of Trinity College, Cambridge. London: Sold by J. Mawman, 1795.

6⅞ × 4⅜ in. vii [1] 111 [1] pp. La Naissance de l'Amour, translated by Wordsworth, pp. 106–11.

1802

483 *The Beauties of Modern Literature, in Prose and Verse.* Richmond: Printed and Sold by T. Bowman, 1802.

7¼ × 4¼ in. xii, 13–180. The Pet Lamb, pp. 159–61.

1803

484 MELMOTH, SIDNEY (ED.). *Beauties of British Poetry.* Second Edition. Huddersfield: Printed and Sold by Brook and Lancashire. Sold also by T. Hurst, Crosby & Co. and T. Ostell, London, 1803.

6¾ × 4 in. [12] 448 pp. Goody Blake and Harry Gill, p. 306.

1804

485 *The Anti-Gallican; or Standard of British Loyalty, Religion, and Liberty; Including a Collection of the Principal Papers, Tracts, Speeches, Poems, and Songs, That Have Been Published on the Threatened Invasion: together with Many Original Pieces on the Same Subject.* London: Vernor and Hood, and J. Asperne, 1804.

8⅝ × 5⅜ in. 496 [4] pp. Anticipation, p. 426.

1805

486 *The Poetical Register, and Repository of Fugitive Poetry for 1803.* Second Edition. London, 1805.

7½ × 4⅞ in. xi [1] 468 pp. Anticipation, p. 340.

1807

487 *The Parnassian Garland; or, Beauties of Modern Poetry: Consisting of Upwards of Two Hundred Pieces, Selected from the Works of the Most Distinguished Poets of the Present Age, with Introductory Lines to Each Article. Designed for the Use of Schools and the Admirers of Poetry in General.* London: James Cundee, 1807.

4½ × 2⅝ in. xxii, 264 [2] pp. Song for the Wandering Jew, pp. 80–1.

1809

488 MURRAY, LINDLEY. *Introduction to the English Reader: or, a Selection of Pieces in Prose and Poetry; Calculated to Improve the Younger Classes of Learners in Reading, and to Imbue Their Minds with the Love of Virtue. With Rules and Observations for Assisting Children to Read with Propriety.* The Fifth Philadelphia Edition. Philadelphia: Johnson and Warner, 1809.

6¾ × 4 in. iv, 225 [5] pp. The Pet Lamb, p. 160.

1810

489 WILKINSON, JOSEPH. *Select Views in Cumberland, Westmoreland, and Lancashire.* By the Rev. Joseph Wilkinson, Rector of East and West Wretham, in the County of Norfolk, and Chaplain to the Marquis of Huntly. London: Published, for the Rev. Joseph Wilkinson, by R. Ackermann, at His Repository of Arts, 1810.

19½ × 12⅝ in. xxxiv [1] 36–46 pp. + 48 full-page plates. The Introduction is by Wordsworth and was later published separately as *A Description of the Scenery of the Lakes* (No. 65).

1818

490 *Annals of the Fine Arts, for 1817.* London: Sherwood, Neely, and Jones, ... 1818.

8½ × 5¼ in. [4] v [3] 602 [16] pp. Upon the Sight of a Beautiful Picture, p. 561; To B. R. Haydon, p. 561.

1821

491 WILKINSON, JOSEPH. *Select Views in Cumberland, Westmoreland, and Lancashire.* By the Rev. Joseph Wilkinson, Rector of East and West Wretham, in the County of Norfolk, and Chaplain to the Marquis of Huntley. London: Published for the Rev. Joseph Wilkinson by R. Ackermann, at His Repository of Arts, 1821.

20 × 13½ in. xxxiv [1] 36–46 pp. + 48 full-page plates. Introduction by Wordsworth.

1823

492 BAILLIE, JOANNA (ED.). *A Collection of Poems, Chiefly Manuscript, and from Living Authors.* Edited for the Benefit of a Friend, by Joanna Baillie. London: Longman, Hurst, Rees, Orme, and Brown, 1823.

8¼ × 5¼ in. xliv, 330 pp. 'Not Love, not War, nor the tumultuous swell'; 'A volant Tribe of Bards on earth are found', pp. 52–3.

493 SCOTT, ELIZABETH (ED.). *Specimens of British Poetry: Chiefly Selected from Authors of High Celebrity, and Interspersed with Original Writings.* Edinburgh: James Ballantyne, 1823.

8¼ × 5¼ in. [4] 395 [1] pp. September 1819, p. 260.

1826

494 KNOX, VICESIMUS. *Elegant Extracts, or Useful and Entertaining Passages, from the Best English Authors and Translations; Principally Designed for the Use of Young Persons.* Originally Compiled by the Rev. Vicesimus Knox, D.D. A New Edition, Embellished with Elegant Engravings. Prepared by James G. Percival. Boston: Samuel Walker, 1826.

8¾ × 5⅛ in. Vol. 1: xvi, 416; vol. 2: v [1] 408 [2]; vol. 3: [4] xv [1] 384; vol. 4: [2] v [3] 384; vol. 5: [4] xii, 388; vol. 6: [2] viii, 372 [2] pp. Contributions by Wordsworth: vol. 5, pp. 360–6; vol. 6, pp. 205, 209–10, 253–5.

1828

495 CROLY, GEORGE (ED.). *The Beauties of the British Poets, with a Few Introductory Observations.* London: Seeley and Burnside, 1828.

6⅞ × 4¼ in. xxiii [3] 367 [3] pp. Wordsworth, pp. 231–42.

496 JOHNSTONE, JOHN. *Specimens of the Lyrical, Descriptive, and Narrative Poets of Great Britain, from Chaucer to the Present Day: with a Preliminary Sketch of the History of Early English Poetry, and Biographical and Critical Notices.* Edinburgh: Oliver and Boyd, 1828.

5 × 3 in. [4] xv [1] 560 [4] pp. Wordsworth, pp. 447–65.

1829

497 *The Casket, a Miscellany, Consisting of Unpublished Poems.* London: John Murray, 1829.

8¾ × 5½ in. xxi [1] 451 [1] pp. The Peat Stack (i.e. 'Untouched through all severity of cold'), p. 259.

498 Another copy.

499 [DIX, DOROTHEA LYND (ED.)]. *The Garland of Flora.* London: R. J. Kennett; Boston: S. G. Goodrich & Co., and Carter & Hendee, 1829.

8½ × 5¼ in. [4] 188 pp. Brief passages from Wordsworth, pp. 126, 137, 161–2, 171, 175–6.

500 [REYNOLDS, FRANCIS MANSEL (ED.)]. *The Keepsake for MDCCCXXIX.* London: Published for the Proprietor, by Hurst, Chance, and Co., and R. Jennings, [1829].

7⅜ × 4¾ in. vii [1] 360 pp. The Country Girl (i.e. The Gleaner), pp. 50–1; The Triad, pp. 72–9; The Wishing Gate, pp. 108–10; A Gravestone upon the Floor of Worcester Cathedral, p. 156; A Tradition of Darley Dale, p. 183.

1830

501 *The Casket: or Youth's Pocket Library.* Third Edition, Improved. Boston: George Davidson, 1830.

$4\frac{15}{16} \times 3\frac{1}{4}$ in. vi [1] 8–254 [4] pp. To a Skylark ('Ethereal minstrel!'), p. 116.

502 *The Laurel: Fugitive Poetry of the XIX Century.* London: John Sharpe, 1830.

$5\frac{1}{2} \times 3\frac{1}{2}$ in. xii, 368 pp. The Wishing Gate, p. 57; To a Highland Girl, p. 220.

1831

503 PIERPONT, JOHN (ED.). *The American First Class Book; or, Exercises in Reading and Recitation: Selected Principally from Modern Authors of Great Britain and America; and Designed for the Use of the Highest Class in Publick and Private Schools.* Boston: Hilliard, Gray, Little, and Wilkins; and Richardson, Lord, and Holbrook, 1831.

$7 \times 4\frac{1}{4}$ in. 480 pp. Wordsworth, pp. 146–50, 267–8, 306–8, 317–19, 333–7.

1832

504 *The Philosophical Museum.* Cambridge, 1832, 2 vols.

$8\frac{3}{4} \times 5\frac{1}{2}$ in. Vol. 1: iv, 706; vol. 2: iv, 706 pp. Translation of Part of the First Book of the *Aeneid*, vol. 1, pp. 383–6.

1833

505 DYCE, ALEXANDER (ED.). *Specimens of English Sonnets.* London: William Pickering, 1833.

$5\frac{1}{2} \times 4\frac{3}{8}$ in. viii, 224 pp. Wordsworth, pp. 190–204.

506 *The Naturalist's Poetical Companion; with Notes.* London: Hamilton, Adams, and Co.; Leeds: J. Y. Knight, 1833.

$6\frac{3}{4} \times 4\frac{1}{8}$ in. xv [1] 352 [4] pp. To the Cuckoo, p. 34; Fidelity, p. 60; To the Small Celandine, p. 85; The Sky-lark, p. 122; The Green Linnet, p. 303.

507 WATTS, ALARIC A. (ED.). *The Literary Souvenir.* London: Longman, Rees, Orme, Brown, Green, and Longman, 1833.

$5\frac{7}{8} \times 3\frac{3}{4}$ in. xiv, 306 [2] pp. On Sir Walter Scott's Quitting Abbotsford for Naples, p. 1.

508 WHITELAW, ALEX. (ED.). *The Casquet of Literary Gems*. Glasgow: Blackie and Son; Dublin: W. Curry, Jun. and Son; London: Simpkin and Marshall, 1833, 2 vols.

7⅞ × 4¾ in. Vol. 1: xii, 396; vol. 2: x, 362 pp. Vol. 1: The Italian Itinerant, pp. 8–9; To a Highland Girl, p. 123; The Seven Sisters, pp. 143–4; 'She dwelt among the untrodden ways', p. 179; 'The world is too much with us', p. 276; The Fountain, p. 298. Vol. 2: The Three Cottage Girls, p. 129; Glen Almain, p. 134; 'Earth has not anything to show more fair', p. 190; 'Where lies the land to which yon ship must go?', p. 270.

1834

509 *The Bard: a Selection of Poetry*. London: Hamilton, Adams, and Co.; York: J. Shillito, 1834.

4½ × 2¾ in. xv [1] 335 [1] pp. To a Skylark ('Ethereal minstrel!'), p. 154; Composed upon Westminster Bridge, p. 240; The Swan (i.e. Dion), p. 272.

510 HOUSMAN, R. F. (ED.). *A Collection of English Sonnets*. London: Whittaker and Co., 1835.

7¼ × 4⅝ in. xxiii [2] 358 pp. Wordsworth, pp. 119–75.

1837

511 NORTHAMPTON, LORD. *The Tribute: a Collection of Miscellaneous Unpublished Poems*, by Various Authors. London: John Murray, 1837.

8⅞ × 5½ in. xiv [2] 422 pp. Stanzas (i.e. A Night Thought), p. 3.

1838

512 FROST, JOHN (ED.). *Select Works of the British Poets, in a Chronological Series from Falconer to Sir Walter Scott*. With Biographical and Critical Notices. Designed as a Continuation of Dr. Aikin's British Poets. Philadelphia: Thomas Wardle, 1838.

9⅜ × 5½ in. [4] 732 [2] pp. Wordsworth, pp. 417–90.

513 HALL, SAMUEL CARTER. *The Book of Gems: the Modern Poets and Artists of Great Britain*. London: Whittaker and Co., 1838.

8½ × 5¼ in. xvi, 304 [4] pp. Wordsworth, pp. 2–13.

514 MURRAY, LINDLEY. *Introduction to the English Reader, or, a Selection of Pieces, in Prose and Poetry, Calculated to Improve the Younger Classes of Learners in Reading, and to Imbue Their Minds with a Love of Virtue, to Which Are Added, Rules and Observations for Assisting Children to Read with Propriety*. Philadelphia: G. W. Mentz & Son, 1838.

5¾ × 3¹¹⁄₁₆ in. x, 11–162 [2] pp. The Pet Lamb, p. 124.

1839

515 *The Lily, a Holiday Present, with Steel Embellishments.* New York: E. Sands, [*c.* 1839].

5⅝ × 3½ in. [10] vi [3] 8–232 [8] pp. The Cottage Girl (i.e. The Gleaner), pp. 49–50.

516 *The Poetic Wreath: Consisting of Select Passages from the Works of English Poets, from Chaucer to Wordsworth. Alphabetically Arranged.* Philadelphia: Lea & Blanchard, 1839.

6 × 3⅞ in. [4] vii [2] 14–370 [10] pp. Wordsworth, pp. 26, 34, 56, 58, 64, 75–6, 91, 144–5, 150, 152–4, 160, 190, 195–6, 210–11, 218, 220, 222, 251–2, 275, 294–5, 308–9, 319–20, 321–2, 326–7, 365–8.

517 *Il Trifoglio; ovvero Scherzi Metrici d'un'Inglese, non pubblicati, ma presentati a quei pochi amici, cui piacque 'meas esse putare nugas.'* Seconda impressione. Londra: Wertheimer e cia, 1839.

8¼ × 5¼ in. [2] 89 [1] pp. To a Skylark (in Italian), pp. 32–3.

1840

518 *Selections from the British Poets.* New York: Harper and Brothers, 1840–1, 2 vols.

6 × 3¾ in. Vol. 1: ix [4] 14–359 [3]; vol. 2: x [3] 14–360 pp. Wordsworth, vol. 2, pp. 306–27.

1841

519 HORNE, RICHARD HENGIST (ED.). *The Poems of Geoffrey Chaucer, Modernized.* London: Whittaker and Co., 1841.

6⅝ × 4 in. cxlvii [3] 331 [1] pp. The Cuckoo and the Nightingale, pp. 35–53; Extract from *Troilus and Cresida*, pp. 125–35.

1842

520 *Book of the Poets; the Modern Poets of the Nineteenth Century.* London: Scott, Webster, and Geary, 1842.

8¼ × 5 in. [6] 490 [4] pp. Wordsworth, pp. 102–21.

521 HALL, SAMUEL CARTER. *Gems of the Modern Poets, with Biographical Notices.* Philadelphia: Carey and Hart, 1842.

7⅝ × 4⅝ in. xi [4] 14–408 [6] pp. Wordsworth, pp. 13–27.

522 SEDGWICK, ADAM. *A Complete Guide to the Lakes, Comprising Minute Directions for the Tourist, with Mr. Wordsworth's Description of the Scenery of the*

Country, &c., and Three Letters upon the Geology of the Lake District, by the Rev. Professor Sedgwick. Edited by the Publishers. Kendal: Hudson and Nicholson; London: Longman and Co., and Whittaker and Co.; Liverpool: Webb; Manchester: Simms and Co., 1842.

7 × 4¼ in. vii [1] viii, 82, 55 [1] pp. With a folding map, colored.

523 RIO, ALEXIS FRANÇOIS. *La Petite Chouannerie ou Histoire d'un Collège Breton sous l'Empire*. Paris: Olivier Fulgence, 1842.

8¼ × 5 in. [4] 598 pp. The Eagle and the Dove, pp. 31–5.

1844

524 GRISWOLD, RUFUS WILMOT (ED.). *The Poetry of Love*. Boston: Gould, Kendall, & Lincoln, 1844.

4⅜ × 2⅝ in. viii, 9–128 [2] pp. 'She was a phantom of delight', p. 34; 'She dwelt among the untrodden ways', pp. 120 and 113.

525 GRISWOLD, RUFUS WILMOT (ED.). *The Poetry of Love, from the Most Celebrated Authors, with Several Original Pieces*. Philadelphia: Thomas Wardle, 1844.

4⅛ × 2⅝ in. [6] 224 [2] pp. 'She dwelt among the untrodden ways', p. 21; 'Look at the fate of summer flowers', pp. 44–5; 'Let other bards of angels sing', pp. 139–40; 'As often as I murmur here', p. 149.

1845

526 [ALBIN, THOMAS (ED.)]. *A Token of Friendship*. A New Edition. Edited by the Author of 'Affection's Keepsake.' New-York: D. Appleton & Co., [c. 1845].

4 × 2½ in. x, 128 pp. Conversation with a Friend (i.e. The Fountain), pp. 55–8.

527 GRISWOLD, RUFUS WILMOT (ED.). *Poets and Poetry of England in the Nineteenth Century*. Philadelphia: Carey and Hart, 1845.

9¼ × 5⅞ in. [10] 504 [6] pp. Wordsworth, pp. 48–63.

528 *Spencer Farm, with Some Account of Its Owners*. Sudbury: George Williams Fulcher; London: Longman, Brown, Green, and Longmans, 1845.

6¼ × 4 in. viii, 160 [2] pp. Preface by Wordsworth.

1846

529 HARVEY, THOMAS. *The Poetical Reader; a Selection from the Eminent Poets of the Last Period of English Literature, with a Preliminary Essay, Biographical Introductions, and Notes in French and German, for the Use of Young People of Both Nations.* By Thomas Harvey, Teacher at the College of Geneva. Geneva: J. Kessmann; Paris: A. Derache, 1846.

6⅞ × 4 in. xxxii, 518 pp. Wordsworth, pp. 148–93.

530 LINWOOD, WILLIAM. *Anthologia Oxoniensis*, Decerpsit Gulielmus Linwood, M.A., Aedis Christi Alumnus. Londini: Impensis Longman, Brown, Green, et Longman, MDCCCXLVI.

8¼ × 5⅜ in. xxi [3] 306 [2] [64] pp. Contains the following poems, in both English and Latin: 'She dwelt among the untrodden ways', p. 30; 'My heart leaps up', p. 60; ''Tis sung in ancient minstrelsy', p. 68; 'Not seldom, cloth'd in saffron vest', p. 142.

531 M'KIM, JAMES MILLER. *Voices of the True-Hearted.* Philadelphia: J. Miller M'Kim, 1846.

9¾ × 6⅛ in. iii [1] 288 [4] pp.; 3–16 missing. Wordsworth, pp. 164–5, 200–1, 207–10, 218–19, 288.

532 SEDGWICK, ADAM. *A Complete Guide to the Lakes, Comprising Minute Directions for the Tourist, with Mr. Wordsworth's Description of the Scenery of the Country, &c. and Four Letters on the Geology of the Lake District,* by the Rev. Professor Sedgwick. Third Edition, Edited by the Publisher. Kendal: J. Hudson; London: Longman and Co., and Whittaker and Co.; Liverpool: Webb; Manchester: Simms and Co., 1846.

7 × 4¼ in. ix [1] vi, 245 [1] pp. With folding map.

1847

533 *The Glasgow University Album for 1847.* Edited by Students of the University. Glasgow: George Richardson, 1847.

7 × 4⅛ in. 287 [1] pp. On the Banks of a Rocky Stream, p. 99.

534 LUNT, MRS. J. S. F. (ED.). *Forget-me-not; or the Philipena.* Lowell, Massachusetts: N. L. Dayton, 1847.

4¼ × 2⅝ in. [2] vi, 7–128 [2] pp. 'A pen—to register; a key—', p. 19; '"Beloved Vale!" I said, "when shall I con"', p. 74.

1848

535 GRIFFITH, MARY LOUISA (ED.). *Literary Extracts, in Prose and Verse; with a Few Original Pieces.* Bath: E. Collings, 1848.

6½ × 4 in. iv, 221 [3] pp. Final stanza of Hymn for the Boatmen, as They Approach the Rapids under the Castle of Heidelberg, p. 176.

1849

536 CROLY, GEORGE (ED.). *The Beauties of the British Poets, with a Few Introductory Observations.* Boston: Phillips, Sampson, & Co., 1849.

7½ × 4¾ in. xxiii [3] 26–395 [3] pp. Wordsworth, pp. 256–67.

537 *Evenings at Derley Manor. Pencillings and Sketches of the English Poets and Their Favourite Scenes.* London: Thomas Nelson, 1849.

6⅜ × 3¹⁵⁄₁₆ in. [15] 14–256 pp. Virtue (i.e. *The Excursion*, IV, 1062–77), p. 247.

538 GRISWOLD, RUFUS WILMOT (ED.). *The Sacred Poets of England and America, for Three Centuries. Illustrated with Steel Engravings.* New York: D. Appleton & Co.; Philadelphia: Geo. S. Appleton, 1849.

9⅛ × 6 in. [6] 552 [2] pp. Wordsworth, pp. 356–69.

1850

539 *Sabrinae Corolla in Hortulis Regiae Scholae Salopiensis Contexuerunt Tres Viri Floribus Legendis.* Londini: Impensis Georgii Bell. MDCCCL.

8¼ × 5½ in. xxii [2] 328 pp. Contains two poems of Wordsworth, in both English and Latin: Lines in a Lady's Album ('Small service is true service while it lasts'), pp. 198–9; Milton, pp. 200–1.

540 SCRYMGEOUR, DANIEL (ED.). *The Poetry and Poets of Britain, from Chaucer to Tennyson, with Biographical Sketches, and a Rapid View of the Characteristic Attributes of Each. Preceded by an Introductory Essay on the Origin and Progress of English Poetical Literature.* Edinburgh: Adam and Charles Black, 1850.

7¼ × 4½ in. xxx, 544 [4] pp. Wordsworth, pp. 368–76.

1851

541 *Christmas with the Poets: a Collection of Songs, Carols, and Descriptive Verses, Relating to the Festival of Christmas, from the Anglo-Norman Period to the Present Time. Embellished with Fifty Tinted Illustrations by Birket Foster, and with Initial Letters and Other Ornaments.* London: David Bogue; New York: D. Appleton & Co., 1851.

9½ × 6½ in. x [2] 189 [1] pp. Christmas Minstrelsy (i.e. To the Rev. Dr. Wordsworth), pp. 144–7; Church Decking at Christmas (i.e. Regrets), p. 176.

1853

542 FOSTER, H. C. (ED.). *An Excursion among the Poets.* Richmond, Virginia: H. C. Foster, [*c.* 1853].

7¾ × 5 in. 360 pp. Wordsworth, pp. 79–88.

543 GRISWOLD, RUFUS WILMOT (ED.). *Gift of Affection: a Souvenir for 1853*. New York: Leavitt and Allen, 1853.

6⅝ × 4¼ in. x [2] 11–288 pp. 'She dwelt among the untrodden ways', p. 74; The Deserted Wife (i.e. *The Excursion*, I, 791–816), p. 111; The Reproach ('Why art thou silent! Is thy love a plant'), p. 114.

1855

544 GOODRICH, SAMUEL GRISWOLD (ED.). *A Gem Book of British Poetry: with Biographical Sketches*. Elegantly Illustrated. Philadelphia: E. H. Butler & Co., 1855.

8 × 6¼ in. x, 11–362 [8] pp. Wordsworth, pp. 222–31.

545 SCRYMGEOUR, DANIEL (ED.). *The Poetry and Poets of Britain, from Chaucer to Tennyson; with Biographical Sketches of Each, and an Introductory Essay on the Origin and Progress of English Poetical Literature*. Fifth Edition. Edinburgh: Adam and Charles Black, 1855.

7¼ × 4½ in. xxx, 544 pp. Wordsworth, pp. 368–76.

1856

546 [COOPER, SUSAN FENIMORE (ED.)]. *The Rhyme and Reason of Country Life: or, Selections from Fields Old and New*. By the Author of 'Rural Hours,' etc., etc. New York: G. P. Putnam & Co., 1856.

7⅜ × 4¾ in. xii [3] 14–428 [2] pp. Wordsworth, pp. 109, 130, 156, 201, 286, 288, 377, 390.

1858

547 PAYNE, JOSEPH (ED.). *Select Poetry for Children: with Brief Explanatory Notes. Arranged for the Use of Schools and Families*. Thirteenth Edition. London: Arthur Hall, Virtue & Co., 1858.

5½ × 3⅜ in. [2] xii, 310 [2] pp. Wordsworth, pp. 30–2, 72–4, 105–7, 149, 152–4, 171–3, 248–9, 283–5.

1860

548 *Our Life, Illustrated by Pen and Pencil, the Designs by Noel Humphreys, J. D. Watson, C. H. Selous, Du Maurier, Barnes, Wimperis, Green, Pinwell, Sulman, Lee, and Other Eminent Artists*. Engraved by Butterworth and Heath. London: Religious Tract Society, [c. 1860].

8½ × 5⅞ in. xvi [1] 18–224 pp. Wordsworth, pp. 28–9, 35, 73–4, 115, 127.

1861

549 PALGRAVE, FRANCIS TURNER (ED.). *The Golden Treasury of the Best Songs and Lyrical Poems in the English Language.* Cambridge and London: Macmillan and Co., 1861.

6¼ × 4 in. [12] 332 pp. Contains forty-one poems by Wordsworth.

1864

550 SIMON, HERMANN. *Selection of English Poems*, Translated from the English into German by Hermann Simon. With the English Text. Leipzig: Arnold, 1864.

6 × 4⅛ in. vi, 367 [1] pp. Wordsworth, pp. 308–18.

1865

551 ALEXANDER, MRS. CECIL FRANCES (ED.). *The Sunday Book of Poetry*, Selected and Arranged by C. F. Alexander, Author of 'Hymns for Little Children,' etc. London and Cambridge: Macmillan and Co., 1865.

6 × 4 in. viii, 318 [2] pp. Wordsworth, pp. 14–16, 19, 259, 260, 298–300.

1866

552 GILPIN, SIDNEY (ED.). *The Songs and Ballads of Cumberland, to Which Are Added Dialect and Other Poems; with Biographical Sketches, Notes, and Glossary.* London: Geo. Routledge and Sons; Edinburgh: John Menzies; Carlisle: Geo. Coward, 1866.

6¾ × 4⅜ in. [2] xiv, 556 [2] pp. Wordsworth, pp. 445–60.

553 WILLMOTT, ROBERT ARIS (ED.). *The Poets of the Nineteenth Century.* Selected and Edited by the Rev. Robert Aris Willmott. Illustrated with One Hundred Engravings, Drawn by Eminent Artists, and Engraved by the Brothers Dalziel. New Edition. London: Frederick Warne and Co., 1866.

8 × 5⅝ in. xvi, 384 [2] pp. Wordsworth, pp. 141–51.

1867

554 HUNT, LEIGH, AND LEE, SAMUEL ADAMS (EDS.). *The Book of the Sonnet.* Boston: Roberts Brothers, 1867, 2 vols.

7 × 4½ in. Vol. 1: xiv, 340; vol. 2: vi, 343 [3] pp. Wordsworth, vol. 1, pp. 226–42.

1868

555 TRENCH, RICHARD CHENEVIX. *A Household Book of English Poetry*, Selected and Arranged, with Notes, by Richard Chenevix Trench, D.D., Archbishop of Dublin. London: Macmillan and Co., 1868.

6⅜ × 4¼ in. xii, 430 [2] pp.

1872

556 HALES, JOHN WESLEY (ED.). *Longer English Poems, with Notes Philological and Explanatory, and an Introduction on the Teaching of English. Chiefly for Use in Schools*. London: Macmillan and Co., 1872.

6¾ × 4⅜ in. xxxviii [3] 427 [73] pp. Wordsworth, pp. 154–64.

1880

557 VALENTINE, LAURA JEURY (ED.). *Gems of National Poetry* (Chandos Classics). London: Frederick Warne, [*c.* 1880].

7¼ × 4¾ in. xiv, 533 [1] pp. Numerous poems by Wordsworth.

1881

558 DENNIS, JOHN (ED.). *English Sonnets: a Selection*. Second Edition. London: C. Kegan Paul & Co., 1881.

6¾ × 4³⁄₁₆ in. xii, 238 [2] pp. Wordsworth, pp. 94–119.

559 EMERSON, RALPH WALDO (ED.). *Parnassus*. Boston: Houghton, Mifflin and Co., 1881.

7⅜ × 4¾ in. xxxiv, 534 [4] pp. Numerous poems by Wordsworth. Edward Dowden's copy.

560 GOSSE, EDMUND W. (ED.). *English Odes*. London: C. Kegan Paul & Co., 1881.

6¼ × 3¾ in. vi, 259 [5] pp. Wordsworth, pp. 147–61.

1883

561 FARRAR, EREDERIC WILLIAM. *With the Poets: a Selection of English Poetry*. New York: Funk & Wagnalls, 1883.

7¼ × 4¾ in. xxviii [1] 30–290 pp. Wordsworth, pp. 171–88.

1884

562 LINTON, WILLIAM JAMES, AND STODDARD, RICHARD HENRY (EDS.). *English Verse Lyrics of the XIXth Century.* London: Kegan Paul, Trench, & Co., 1884.

7¼ × 4¾ in. xliv [2] 336 pp. Wordsworth, pp. 1–19.

1889

563 MAIN, DAVID M. (ED.). *A Treasury of English Sonnets, Edited from the Original Sources with Notes and Illustrations.* New York: Worthington Co., 1889.

9³⁄₁₆ × 5¾ in. viii, 470 [2] pp. Wordsworth, pp. 90–120.

1890

564 BORLAND, ROBERT (ED.). *Yarrow: Its Poets and Poetry.* With Introduction and Notes by R. Borland, Minister of Yarrow. Dalbeattie: Thomas Fraser, 1890.

8⅝ × 5½ in. viii, 239 [1] pp. Contains forty-seven poems about Yarrow, three of them by Wordsworth.

1892

565 PALGRAVE, FRANCIS TURNER (ED.). *The Golden Treasury of the Best Songs and Lyrical Poems in the English Language.* New York: Frederick A. Stokes Company, 1892.

6 × 3⅞ in. xiii [1] 405 [1] pp. Contains forty-one poems by Wordsworth.

1893

566 DE VERE, AUBREY (ED.). *The Household Poetry Book: an Anthology of English-speaking Poets from Chaucer to Faber.* With Biographical and Critical Notes. London: Burns & Oates, 1893.

6½ × 4 in. xii, 308 pp. Wordsworth, pp. 191–204.

1895

567 SYKES, FREDERICK HENRY (ED.). *Select Poems of Coleridge, Wordsworth, Campbell, Longfellow.* Edited from Authors' Editions, with Introductions and Annotations by Frederick Henry Sykes, A.M., Ph.D., Sometime Fellow of the Johns Hopkins University. Toronto: W. J. Gage Company, 1895.

6¾ × 4½ in. xxxviii, 360 [2] pp. Wordsworth, pp. xx–xxvi, 31–41, 217–36, 336, 345, 347–8, 351, 355, 356.

1896

568 ELLIS, ADELE (ED.). *Chosen English: Selections from Wordsworth, Byron, Shelley, Lamb, Scott, Prepared with Short Biographies and Notes for the Use of Schools.* London and New York: Macmillan and Co., 1896.

6¾ × 4½ in. 205 [3] pp. Wordsworth, pp. 31–42, 106–24.

1897

569 CRAWFURD, OSWALD JOHN FREDERICK (ED.). *Four Poets: Poems from Wordsworth, Coleridge, Shelley, and Keats.* London: Chapman and Hall, 1897.

6⅜ × 4⅛ in. viii, 479 [1] pp. Wordsworth, pp. 1–133.

570 M'DONNELL, A. C. (ED.). *XIX-Century Poetry* (Literary Epoch Series). London: Adam and Charles Black, 1897.

6¾ × 4½ in. vi [2] 120 [8] pp. Wordsworth, pp. 12–31.

571 RHYS, ERNEST (ED.). *Literary Pamphlets, Chiefly Relating to Poetry from Sidney to Byron, Selected and Arranged with an Introduction and Notes.* London: Kegan Paul, Trench, Trübner & Co., 1897, 2 vols.

7⅝ × 5 in. Vol. 1: 278 [2]; vol. 2: 273 [3] pp. A Letter to a Friend of Robert Burns, by Wordsworth, vol. 2, pp. 220–50.

1900

572 HENLEY, WILLIAM ERNEST (ED.). *English Lyrics, Chaucer to Poe.* London: Methuen and Co., 1900.

7½ × 5 in. xiv [2] 412 [40] pp. Wordsworth, pp. 334–7.

1901

573 ARBER, EDWARD (ED.). *The Cowper Anthology, 1775–1800 A.D.* London: Henry Frowde, 1901.

7⅜ × 4¾ in. vi, 336 [8] pp. Wordsworth, pp. 165–83.

1902

574 EDGAR, PELHAM (ED.). *Coleridge and Wordsworth: Select Poems Prescribed for the Matriculation and Departmental Examinations for 1903* (Morang's Educational Series). Toronto: George N. Morang & Company, 1902.

7⅜ × 5 in. [8] 244 [6] pp.

575 LUCAS, EDWARD VERRAL (ED.). *The Open Road: a Little Book for Wayfarers.* London: Grant Richards, 1902.

6⅝ × 3⅞ in. xiv, 311 [1] pp. Wordsworth, pp. 53, 107, 114, 117, 191, 214, 248, 257, 294.

576 QUILLER-COUCH, ARTHUR THOMAS (ED.). *The Oxford Book of English Verse, 1250–1900.* Oxford: Clarendon Press, 1902.

7⅜ × 4¾ in. xii, 1084 pp. Wordsworth, pp. 515–41.

577 WARD, THOMAS HUMPHRY (ED.). *The English Poets: Selections with Critical Introductions by Various Writers and a General Introduction by Matthew Arnold.* Vol. 4: Wordsworth to Tennyson. New York: Macmillan Company, 1902.

7¾ × 4⅞ in. xvi, 828 pp. Wordsworth, pp. 1–88.

1904

578 PAGE, CURTIS HIDDEN (ED.). *British Poets of the Nineteenth Century.* Boston: Benjamin H. Sanborn & Co., [*c.* 1904].

8⅝ × 6 in. xviii, 923 [1] pp. Wordsworth, pp. 1–63.

1905

579 MARSHALL, JOHN, AND STEVENSON, ORLANDO JOHN (EDS.). *Select Poems; Being the Literature Prescribed for the Junior Matriculation and Junior Leaving Examinations, 1905, . . .* with Introduction, Notes, and an Appendix. Toronto: Copp, Clark Company, 1905.

7⅜ × 4⅞ in. xix [1] 239 [5] pp. Wordsworth, pp. 85–93, 150–84, 199–214, 217, 228–9, 232–9.

1907

580 BRONSON, WALTER COCHRANE (ED.). *English Poems, Selected and Edited, with Illustrative and Explanatory Notes and Bibliographies,* by Walter C. Bronson. Chicago: University of Chicago Press, 1907.

7¾ × 5 in. xv [1] 619 [1] pp. Wordsworth, pp. 3–53.

1909

581 *English Poets of the Romantic School.* University of Peking, [*c.* 1909].

9⅝ × 6¾ in. 166 fols., printed on one side only. Selections from Wordsworth and Shelley, in English.

PART V

WORDSWORTHIANA

582 [FINCH, ANNE, COUNTESS OF WINCHILSEA]. *Miscellany Poems, on Several Occasions. Written by a Lady.* London: Printed for J. B. and Sold by Benj. Tooke, William Taylor, and James Round, 1713.

7½ × 4⅝ in. [10] 390 [2] pp. Poems admired by Wordsworth.

583 SHELVOCKE, GEORGE. *A Voyage Round the World by the Way of the Great South Sea, Perform'd in the Years 1719, 20, 21, 22, in the Speedwell of London, of 24 Guns and 100 Men,* ... London: Printed for J. Senex, W. and J. Innys, and J. Osborn and T. Longman, 1726.

7¾ × 4¾ in. [8] xxxii [4] 468 pp. Four plates and folding map. Source of one of Wordsworth's contributions to The Rime of the Ancient Mariner. Listed in the Sale Catalogue of the St. John Collection as from Wordsworth's library; no other evidence of his ownership.

584 HARTLEY, DAVID. *Observations on Man, His Frame, His Duty, and His Expectations.* London: Printed by S. Richardson for James Leake and Wm. Frederick, and Sold by Charles Hitch and Stephen Austen, 1749, 2 vols.

8¼ × 4⅞ in. Vol. 1: xix [1] iv [1] 6–512 [4]; vol. 2: xv [1] iv [1] 6–455 [13] pp. An important influence on the young Wordsworth.

585 Another copy.

586 [WOLCOT, JOHN]. *A Commiserating Epistle to James Lowther, Earl of Lonsdale and Lowther, Lord Lieut. and Cust. Rot. of the Counties of Cumberland and Westmorland.* By Peter Pindar, Esq. London: Printed for J. Evans, 1791.

10 × 7⅝ in. [6] 23 [1] pp. A satire. Lowther had employed Wordsworth's father but refused to pay him or his children.

587 WILLIAMS, HELEN MARIA. *Letters Written in France, in the Summer 1790, to a Friend in England; Containing Various Anecdotes Relative to the French Revolution; and Memoirs of Mons. and Madame du F——.* Second Edition. London: Printed for Cadell, 1791.

6⅝ × 3⅞ in. [8] 223 [3] pp. See No. 458.

1793

588 Review of *An Evening Walk*.

European Magazine and London Review, XXIV (September 1793), 192–3.

589 Review of *Descriptive Sketches* and *An Evening Walk*.

Monthly Review, XII (October 1793), 216–18.

1794

590 Review of *An Evening Walk*.

Gentleman's Magazine, LXIV (March 1794), 252–3.

1795

591 BRYDGES, SAMUEL EGERTON. *Sonnets and Other Poems.* New Edition. London: Printed for B. and J. White, 1795.

$6\frac{1}{2} \times 4$ in. xii, 113 [5] pp. Brydges and Wordsworth held somewhat similar theories of poetry.

592 FAWCET, JOSEPH. *The Art of War: a Poem.* London: Printed for J. Johnson, 1795.

$9\frac{5}{8} \times 7\frac{3}{8}$ in. 52 pp. A poem admired by Wordsworth. Fawcet (or Fawcett) is a prototype of the Solitary in *The Excursion*. See No. 1384.

593 HEARNE, SAMUEL. *A Journey from Prince of Wales's Fort in Hudson's Bay, to the Northern Ocean. Undertaken by Order of the Hudson's Bay Company, for the Discovery of Copper Mines, a North West Passage, &c., in the Years 1769, 1770, 1771 & 1772.* London: Printed for A. Strahan and T. Cadell, 1795.

$11\frac{1}{2} \times 9\frac{1}{4}$ in. [3] iv–xliv, 458 [2] pp. Chapter 7 is the source for The Complaint of a Forsaken Indian Woman.

1796

594 GILBERT, WILLIAM. *The Hurricane: a Theosophical and Western Eclogue. To Which Is Subjoined a Solitary Effusion in a Summer's Evening.* Bristol: Printed and Sold for the Author by R. Edwards, 1796.

$7\frac{1}{4} \times 4\frac{5}{8}$ in. vii [2] 104 [2] pp. Edward Dowden's copy. Gilbert was a friend of Coleridge and Southey. Wordsworth knew this book and quoted from p. 69 in his preface to *The Excursion*.

1798

595 LLOYD, CHARLES. *Edmund Oliver.* Bristol: Printed by Bulgin and Rosser for Joseph Cottle, and sold in London by Messrs. Lee and Hurst, 1798, 2 vols.

$6\frac{3}{4} \times 4\frac{1}{8}$ in. Vol. 1: [i–vii] viii–xii, 252; vol. 2: [iv] 294+1 pp. A novel containing references to Coleridge. Lloyd was an early associate of the Wordsworth-Coleridge group and later a neighbor of Wordsworth's in Westmorland.

596 LLOYD, CHARLES, AND LAMB, CHARLES. *Blank Verse*, by Charles Lloyd and Charles Lamb. London: Printed by T. Bensley; for John and Arthur Arch, 1798.

$6\frac{5}{8} \times 4\frac{1}{4}$ in. 96 pp.

1799

597 SOUTHEY, ROBERT (ED.). *The Annual Anthology.* Bristol: Printed by Biggs and Co., for T. N. Longman and O. Rees, London, 1799–1800, 2 vols.

$6\frac{1}{2} \times 4$ in. Vol. 1: [8] 300; vol. 2: [6] 299 [1] pp. Poems by Wordsworth's associates Coleridge, Lloyd, Lovell, Lamb, Dyer, and Southey.

598 [BURNEY, CHARLES]. Review of *Lyrical Ballads.*

Monthly Review, xxix (June 1799), 202–10.

599 [WRANGHAM, FRANCIS]. Review of *Lyrical Ballads.*

British Critic, xiv (October 1799), 364–9.

1801

600 *The Port Folio*, Philadelphia, 1 (1801).

Reprint of a review of *Lyrical Ballads*, 1800, from the *British Critic*, pp. 188–9; praise for *Lyrical Ballads*, p. 191; announcement of forthcoming Philadelphia edition, p. 407.

601 [WRANGHAM, FRANCIS]. Review of *Lyrical Ballads*, 1800.

British Critic, xvii (February 1801), 125–31.

1802

602 Brief review of vol. 2, *Lyrical Ballads*, 1800.

Monthly Review, xxxviii (June 1802), 209. A clipping.

603 *The Port Folio*, ii (1802).

Note on the popularity of *Lyrical Ballads*, p. 62.

1803

604 BAYLEY, PETER, JR. *Poems*. London: Printed for William Miller, 1803.

$7\frac{5}{8} \times 4\frac{7}{8}$ in. [10] 209 [3] pp. In a letter to De Quincey, of 8 March 1804, Wordsworth complained of the parodies and plagiarisms in this work.

605 COTTLE, JOSEPH, AND SOUTHEY, ROBERT (EDS.). *The Works of Thomas Chatterton*. London: Printed by Biggs and Cottle, for T. N. Longman and O. Rees, 1803, 3 vols.

$8\frac{3}{8} \times 4\frac{7}{8}$ in. Vol. 1: [22] clx, 361 [1]; vol. 2: [8] 536; vol. 3: [8] 537 [7] pp.

606 *The Port Folio*, iii (1803).

Love, by Coleridge, reprinted and attributed to Wordsworth, p. 210.

607 Review of *Poems* by Peter Bayley. *Monthly Review*, xlii (September 1803), 157–63.

1804

608 BAYLEY, PETER. *Poems*. Philadelphia: Printed by T. and G. Palmer, 1804.

$6 \times 3\frac{3}{4}$ in. [11] 12–231 [1] pp. See No. 604.

609 *The Port Folio*, iv (1804).

Request for a copy of *Descriptive Sketches*, p. 87; parodies of Wordsworth by R. H. Rose, pp. 257–8, 342–3.

1805

610 WHITAKER, THOMAS DUNHAM. *The History and Antiquities of the Deanery of Craven, in the County of York*. London: Printed by Nichols and Son, 1805.

$13\frac{1}{2} \times 9\frac{1}{2}$ in. xii, 437 [1] 16 pp. Source of *The White Doe of Rylstone*.

1807

611 *The Athenaeum*, a Magazine of Literary and Miscellaneous Information.

Vols. i–v, 1 January 1807 to 1 June 1809. The complete run.

612 [JEFFREY, FRANCIS]. Review of *Poems in Two Volumes*, 1807.

Edinburgh Review, xi (October 1807), 214–31.

613 Review of *Poems in Two Volumes*, 1807.

The Satirist, or Monthly Meteor, 1 (November 1807), 188–91.

1808

614 *The Simpliciad; a Satirico-Didactic Poem. Containing Hints for the Scholars of the New School, Suggested by Horace's Art of Poetry, and Improved by a Contemplation of the Works of the First Masters.* London: Printed for John Joseph Stockdale, 1808.

$6\frac{3}{16} \times 3\frac{3}{8}$ in. [4] vi [1] 8–51 [5] pp. A satire, by an unidentified author, against Wordsworth, Coleridge, and Southey.

1809

615 The Bards of the Lakes.

The Satirist, or Monthly Meteor, v (December 1809), 548–56.

616 BYRON, LORD. *English Bards and Scotch Reviewers. A Satire.* London: James Cawthorn, [1809].

$6\frac{1}{2} \times 4$ in. [iii]–vi, 54 pp.

617 Review of *Poems in Two Volumes*, 1807.

British Critic, xxxiii (March 1809), 298–9.

618 Review of *The Convention of Cintra*.

British Critic, xxxiv (September 1809), 305–6.

1810

619 BYRON, LORD. *English Bards and Scotch Reviewers; a Satire.*
Fourth Edition. London: James Cawthorn, 1810.

$8\frac{3}{4} \times 5\frac{5}{8}$ in. vii [1] 85 [3] pp.

620 [ROSE, ROBERT HUTCHINSON]. *Sketches in Verse.* Philadelphia: C. & A. Conrad & Co., 1810.

$9\frac{5}{8} \times 5\frac{7}{8}$ in. viii [1] 8–184 [4] pp. Parody of Wordsworth, pp. 58–73.

1811

621 SEWARD, ANNA. *Letters of Anna Seward: Written between the
Years 1784 and 1807.* Edinburgh: Archibald Constable & Co.; London:
Longman, Hurst, Rees, Orme, and Brown; William Miller; and
John Murray, 1811, 6 vols.

$7\frac{1}{8} \times 4\frac{3}{4}$ in. Vol. 1: xv [3] 399 [3]; vol. 2: viii, 399 [3]; vol. 3: viii, 397 [5];
vol. 4: vii [1] 397 [5]; vol. 5: vii [1] 432 [2]; vol. 6: vii [1] 490, xiv [2] pp.
References to Wordsworth, vol. 6, pp. 31, 258, 366–7.

1812

622 [SMITH, JAMES AND HORACE]. *Rejected Addresses: or the New
Theatrum Poetarum.* Sixth Edition. London: John Miller; Edinburgh:
John Ballantyne and Co., 1812.

$6\frac{1}{4} \times 3\frac{5}{8}$ in. xiii [3] 127 [1] pp. Parody of Wordsworth, pp. 5–10.

1813

623 FROME, SAMUEL BLAKE. *Poems, with a Letter to the Subscribers
and a Critique on the Work.* London: Printed for the Author, 1813.

$6\frac{7}{8} \times 4$ in. 47 [1] 135 [1] pp. Wordsworth subscribed (p. 21) and received the
author's thanks (p. 45).

624 W., W. AND Q., Q. (EDS.). *Leaves of Laurel, or New Probationary
Odes for the Vacant Laureatship.* London: T. Becket and J. Porter, 1813.

$8\frac{3}{8} \times 5$ in. [4] 24 [4] pp. Parody of Wordsworth (p. 14) and of Coleridge
(p. 15).

1814

625 BRYDGES, SIR EGERTON. *Select Poems, with a Preface.* Printed at the Private Press of the Priory; by Johnson and Warwick, 1814.

12⅛ × 9½ in. [6] 40 pp. See No. 591.

626 HAZLITT, WILLIAM. Review of *The Excursion.*

The Examiner (21, 28 August, 2 October 1814), pp. 541–2, 555–8, 636–8.

627 HUNT, LEIGH. *The Feast of the Poets, with Notes, and Other Pieces in Verse,* by the Editor of *The Examiner.* London: James Cawthorn, 1814.

6⅜ × 4 in. xiv [2] 157 [3] pp. Wordsworth, pp. 12–14, 78, 81–2, 87–109.

628 [JEFFREY, FRANCIS]. Review of *The Excursion.*

Edinburgh Review, xxix (November 1814), 1–30. 'This will never do!'

629 [LAMB, CHARLES]. Review of *The Excursion.*

Quarterly Review, xii (October 1814), 100–11.

630 [LAMB, CHARLES]. Review of *The Excursion.*

Reprinted in an unidentified periodical from the *Quarterly Review.*

631 LICKBARROW, ISABELLA. *Poetical Effusions.* Kendal: Printed for the Authoress by M. Branthwaite & Co.; Sold by J. Richardson, London, 1814.

8⅜ × 5¼ in. xii, 131 [1] pp. With the list of subscribers, among whom are Southey and Wordsworth.

1815

632 [GIFFORD, WILLIAM]. Reviews of *Poems,* 2 vols., 1815; and of *The White Doe of Rylstone.*

Quarterly Review, xiv (October 1815), 201–25.

633 HUNT, LEIGH. *The Feast of the Poets, with Other Pieces in Verse.* Second Edition. London: Gale and Fenner, 1815.

6¾ × 4 in. x [2] 177, [15] pp.

634 [JEFFREY, FRANCIS]. Review of *The White Doe of Rylstone.*

Edinburgh Review, xxv (October 1815), 355–63.

635 QUILLINAN, EDWARD. *Monthermer: a Poem.* London: Longman, Hurst, Rees, Orme, and Brown, 1815.

9 × 5½ in. [2] 177 [5] pp. The author later became Wordsworth's son-in-law.

636 Review of *The Excursion.*

Monthly Review, LXXVI (February 1815), 123–36.

637 Review of *The Excursion.*

British Critic, III, n.s. (May 1815), 449–67.

638 Review of *The Excursion.*

Analectic Magazine, VI (October 1815), 273–91. Reprinted from the *British Critic.*

639 Review of *The White Doe of Rylstone.*

Monthly Review, LXXVIII (November 1815), 235–8.

640 Review of *The White Doe of Rylstone.*

Gentleman's Magazine, LXXXV (December 1815), 524–5.

641 Review of *Poems,* 2 vols., 1815.

Monthly Review, LXXVIII (November 1815), 225–34.

1816

642 *The Amusing Chronicle, a Weekly Repository for Miscellaneous Literature, Consisting of Interesting Essays in Prose and Verse.* Vol. I. From September 19, to December 25 Inclusive. With Ten Outline Plates. London: Printed by George Stobb, 1816.

8¾ × 5 in. [4] 236 [4] pp. A re-telling in prose of Wordsworth's *White Doe of Rylstone,* pp. 44–6, 54–6, 67–9.

643 [HOGG, JAMES]. *The Poetic Mirror, or the Living Bards of Britain.* London: Longman, Hurst, Rees, Orme, and Brown; and John Ballantyne, Edinburgh, 1816.

6½ × 3¾ in. iv [2] 275 [3] pp. Parodies of Wordsworth, pp. 131–53, 155–70, 171–87.

644 [JEFFREY, FRANCIS]. Review of *Poems in Two Volumes*, 1807.

A reprint of the *Edinburgh Review* for October 1807. New York: Eastburn, Kirk, & Co., 1816.

645 Review of *Thanksgiving Ode, 1816*.

British Critic, VI, n.s. (September 1816), 313–15.

1817

646 COLERIDGE, SAMUEL TAYLOR. *Biographia Literaria; or Biographical Sketches of My Literary Life and Opinions*. London: Rest Fenner, 1817, 2 vols.

$8\frac{1}{4} \times 5$ in. Vol. 1: [2] 296; vol. 2: [2] 309 [1] pp.

647 HAZLITT, WILLIAM. *The Round Table; a Collection of Essays on Literature, Men, and Manners*. Edinburgh: Archibald Constable and Co.; London: Longman, Hurst, Rees, Orme, and Brown, 1817.

$6\frac{1}{16} \times 3\frac{11}{16}$ in. Vol. 1: viii, 238; vol. 2: vi, 261 [3] pp. Wordsworth, vol. 2, pp. 95–122.

648 On the Cockney School of Poetry, No. I.

Blackwood's Edinburgh Magazine, II (October 1817), 38–41.

649 On the Cockney School of Poetry, No. II.

Blackwood's Edinburgh Magazine, II (November 1817), 194–201.

650 PEACOCK, THOMAS LOVE. *Melincourt*. London: T. Hookham, Jun. & Co., and Baldwin, Cradock, & Joy, 1817.

$6\frac{1}{2} \times 3\frac{3}{4}$ in. Vol. 1: [6] 224 [2]; vol. 2: [6] 216; vol. 3: [6] 208 [2] pp. Peacock's 'Mr. Paperstamp' is Wordsworth.

651 Review of *Thanksgiving Ode, 1816*.

Monthly Review, LXXXII (January 1817), 98–100.

652 [WILSON, JOHN]. Observations on Mr. Wordsworth's Letter Relative to a New Edition of Burns' Works.

Blackwood's Edinburgh Magazine, I (June 1817), 261–6.

653 [WILSON, JOHN]. Vindication of Mr. Wordsworth's Letter to Mr. Gray, on a New Edition of Burns.

Blackwood's Edinburgh Magazine, II (October 1817), 65–73.

654 [WILSON, JOHN]. Letter Occasioned by N's Vindication of Mr. Wordsworth in Last Number.

Blackwood's Edinburgh Magazine, II (November 1817), 201–4.

1818

655 Two Sonnets to Wordsworth.

Blackwood's Edinburgh Magazine, II (February 1818), 512–13.

656 The Cockney School of Poetry, No. III.

Blackwood's Edinburgh Magazine, III (July 1818), 453–6.

657 The Cockney School of Poetry, No. IV.

Blackwood's Edinburgh Magazine, III (August 1818), 519–24.

658 [DE QUINCEY, THOMAS]. *Close Comments upon a Straggling Speech.* Kendal: Airey and Bellingham, Printers, 1818.

$8\frac{5}{8} \times 5\frac{1}{4}$ in. 16 pp. On the Westmorland election. See Nos. 42, 43, and 663–8.

659 Essays on the Lake School of Poetry No. I: Wordsworth's *White Doe of Rylstone*.

Blackwood's Edinburgh Magazine, III (July 1818), 367–81.

660 Essays on the Lake School of Poetry: On the Habits of Thought Inculcated by Wordsworth.

Blackwood's Edinburgh Magazine, IV (December 1818), 257–63.

661 HAZLITT, WILLIAM. *Lectures on the English Poets.* Delivered at the Surrey Institution. London: Taylor and Hessey, 1818.

$8\frac{1}{4} \times 5$ in. [6] 331 [1] pp. Wordsworth, pp. 309–31.

662 Remarks on Mr. Hazlitt's Lectures on the English Poets.

Edinburgh Magazine and Literary Miscellany, III (July 1818), 3–12.

663 *Westmorland Election, 1818.* An Account of the Proceedings at Appleby, from Saturday, the 27th of June, to the Final Close of the Poll. Kendal: Printed by Richard Lough, [1818].

$7\frac{5}{8} \times 4\frac{1}{4}$ in. 47 [1] pp. See Nos. 42, 43, and 664–8.

664 *An Address to the Yeomanry of the Counties of Westmorland & Cumberland, on the Present State of Their Representation in Parliament.* Kendal: Printed by Richard Lough, [1818].

$8\frac{5}{8} \times 5\frac{3}{8}$ in. 16 pp.

665 *An Address to the Yeomanry in the Counties of Westmorland and Cumberland, on the Present State of Their Representation in Parliament.* By a Westmorland Yeoman. London: Printed by F. Jollie, Jun., and Sold by the Booksellers of Westmorland and Cumberland, 1818.

$8\frac{5}{8} \times 5\frac{1}{2}$ in. 16 pp.

666 *To the Freeholders of Westmorland.* Kendal: Airey and Bellingham, Printers, [1818].

$13 \times 8\frac{1}{4}$ in. Single sheet. From the *Carlyle Patriot.* Not the same as No. 43.

667 *The Poll for the Knights of the Shire, to Represent the County of Westmorland,* Taken at Appleby, on Tuesday, the 30th June; Wednesday, the 1st, Thursday, the 2d, and Friday, the 3d Days of July, 1818. Kendal: Airey and Bellingham, and M. and R. Branthwaite, 1818.

$7\frac{7}{8} \times 4\frac{7}{8}$ in. [2] 79 [1] pp.

668 *Correct Edition. The Poll for the Knights of the Shire to Represent the County of Westmorland,* Taken at Appleby, by Thomas Briggs, Esquire, Under-Sheriff, on Tuesday, Wednesday, Thursday, and Friday, the 30th of June, and 1st, 2d, & 3d of July, 1818. Printed and Sold by R. Lough; Sold Also by B. Dowson, Kendal, F. Jollie, Jun., London, and the Agents of the Kendal Chronicle.

$6\frac{1}{4} \times 4$ in. vii [1] 67 [1] pp.

1819

669 *The Dead Asses. A Lyrical Ballad.* London: Smith and Elder, 1819.

$8\frac{3}{16} \times 5\frac{1}{8}$ in. 24 pp. A parody of Wordsworth. Edward Dowden's copy.

670 Memoir of Wordsworth.

Analectic Magazine, XIII (June 1819), 487–91. Reprinted from the *Monthly Magazine.*

671 On the Cockney School of Poetry No. V.

Blackwood's Edinburgh Magazine, v (April 1819), 97–100.

672 Review of *Peter Bell*.

Blackwood's Edinburgh Magazine, v (May 1819), 130–6.

673 Reviews of *Peter Bell* and of Reynolds's parody, *Peter Bell, a Lyrical Ballad*.

Gentleman's Magazine, LXXXIX (May 1819), 441–2.

674 Review of *Peter Bell*.

British Critic, XI, n.s. (June 1819), 584–603.

675 Review of *Peter Bell*.

The Athenaeum; or Spirit of the English Magazines, Boston, v (June 1819), 272–8. Reprinted from the *Literary Gazette*.

676 Review of *Peter Bell*.

Analectic Magazine, XIV (1819), 304–11. Reprinted from the *Journal of Belles Lettres*.

677 Review of *Peter Bell*.

Monthly Review, LXXXIX (August 1819), 419–22.

678 Review of *The Waggoner*.

Blackwood's Edinburgh Magazine, v (June 1819), 332–4.

679 Review of *The Waggoner*.

General Review, or Weekly Literary Epitome, I (June 1819), 36–46.

680 Reviews of *The Waggoner*, and of the parody, *Benjamin the Waggoner, a Ryghte Merrie and Conceitede Tale in Verse*.

Gentleman's Magazine, LXXXIX (August 1819), 143–4.

681 Reviews of *The Waggoner*, and of the parody, *Benjamin the Waggoner, a Ryghte Merrie and Conceitede Tale in Verse*.

Monthly Review, XC (September 1819), 36–42.

682 [REYNOLDS, JOHN HAMILTON]. *Benjamin the Waggoner, a Ryghte Merrie and Conceitede Tale in Verse.* A Fragment. London: Baldwin, Cradock, and Joy, 1819.

$8\frac{1}{4} \times 5$ in. xxiii [2] 26–96 [2] pp. A parody. Edward Dowden's copy.

683 [REYNOLDS, JOHN HAMILTON]. *Peter Bell. A Lyrical Ballad.* London: Taylor and Hessey, 1819.

$8\frac{3}{4} \times 5\frac{1}{2}$ in. viii, 29 [3] pp. A parody.

684 [REYNOLDS, JOHN HAMILTON]. *Peter Bell. A Lyrical Ballad.* Third Edition. London: Taylor and Hessey, 1819.

$7\frac{1}{2} \times 4\frac{7}{8}$ in. vii [1] 9–30 pp.

685 Another copy.

686 [REYNOLDS, JOHN HAMILTON]. Peter Bell. A Lyrical Ballad.

The Athenaeum, or the Spirit of the English Magazines, Boston, v (June 1819), 277–8. The introductory paragraph wrongly attributes the parody to 'H. Smith.'

687 STANLEY, GEORGE. On Seeing the Portrait of Wordsworth by Haydon.

Annals of the Fine Arts for MDCCCXVIII, iii (1819), 331.

688 Yarrow Unvisited.

Blackwood's Edinburgh Magazine, vi (November 1819), 194–5. A parody.

1820

689 *The Battered Tar, or, the Waggoner's Companion. A Poem, with Sonnets, &c.* London: J. Johnston, [c. 1820].

$8\frac{3}{8} \times 5\frac{1}{8}$ in. vii [1] 39 [1] pp. Parodies of Wordsworth.

690 MOORE, JOHN. *A Journal during a Residence in France, from the Beginning of August to the Middle of December 1792: to Which Is Added, an Account of the Most Remarkable Events That Happened at Paris from That Time to the Death of the Late King of France* (vol. 3 of *The Works of John Moore*, Edinburgh: Stirling and Slade, ... 1820, 7 vols.).

$8\frac{3}{8} \times 5\frac{1}{8}$ in. [6] 501 [1] pp. The France known to Wordsworth during his visit of 1792.

691 Review of *The River Duddon*, 1820.

Blackwood's Edinburgh Magazine, VII (May 1820), 206–13.

692 Review of *The River Duddon*.

Monthly Review, XCIII (October 1820), 132–43.

693 The Sable School of Pugilism.

Blackwood's Edinburgh Magazine, VIII (October 1820), 60–7. Contains a parody of Wordsworth.

694 WIFFEN, JEREMIAH HOLMES. *Julia Alpinula; with the Captive of Stamboul and Other Poems*. Second Edition. London: John Warner, 1820.

$7\frac{1}{8} \times 4\frac{1}{8}$ in. x [4] 237 [3] pp. Sonnet to Wordsworth, p. 233.

1821

695 [BAYLEY, PETER]. *Sketches from St. George's Fields*. By Giorgione Di Castel Chiuso. Second Edition. London: R. and M. Stodart, 1821.

$6\frac{5}{8} \times 4$ in. viii, 287 [3] pp. Reference to Wordsworth, p. 6.

696 *Lost Valentines Found; with Other Trifles in Rhyme*. London: T. and J. Allman, 1821.

$6\frac{5}{8} \times 4$ in. x [2] 96 pp. To Mrs. Hannah More from W— W—ds—th, a parody, 44–53.

697 A Parody of Wordsworth.

Two leaves excerpted from an unidentified periodical, printed perhaps in Philadelphia and perhaps about 1821. The text, pp. 249–50, begins: 'The book's half ended and I am well pleas'd.' It is incomplete.

698 Review of *The River Duddon*.

British Critic, xv (February 1821), 113–35.

699 *The Salt-Bearer: a Periodical Work*. By an Etonian. From May 1820 to April 1821. London: B. E. Lloyd and Son, 1821.

$8\frac{1}{4} \times 5$ in. vii [1] 380, 36 pp. Wordsworth, pp. 278–83.

700 Sonnet to Wordsworth.

Blackwood's Edinburgh Magazine, VIII (February 1821), 542.

701 SOUTHEY, ROBERT. *A Vision of Judgement.* London: Longman, Hurst, Rees, Orme, and Brown, 1821.

$8\frac{1}{2} \times 5\frac{1}{4}$ in. xxvii [5] 79 [1] pp. Bound in are *The Liberal*, 1 (1822), 1–[40], containing Byron's Vision of Judgment, and also thirty pages of newspaper clippings giving an account of the trial of John Hunt, 15 January 1824. Added is another clipping containing a long parody of Southey's *Vision of Judgement*.

1822

702 *The Argo* (25 November 1822).

An attack on Wordsworth and Southey, signed 'I,' pp. 6–7.

703 The Cursed Tree.

Brighton Magazine, 1 (May 1822), 483–4. A parody, with a preface signed 'W.W.'.

704 *The Green Book; or Register of the Order of the Emerald Star.* n.p., n.d.

$16 \times 9\frac{3}{4}$ in. 18 pp. The opening sentence: 'A certain number of Literary Persons, not exceeding twenty-five, formed the society, out of which this Chapteral Order arose. It was necessary not to divulge their own names in the first instance. And their Book of Proceedings shews that the election, by which they made the first addition to their members, passed *sub silentio*.' There follows a list of names, among which are Byron, Southey, and Wordsworth. A satire.

705 [HARLEY, JAMES]. *The Press, or Literary Chit-chat.* A Satire. London: Printed for Lupton Relfe, 1822.

$6\frac{1}{2} \times 4$ in. 132 pp. 'In yonder modest mansion Wordsworth dwells', a satire, p. 24.

706 [MONTGOMERY, GERALD]. *On Wordsworth's Poetry.* The Etonian. Second Edition. London: Henry Colburn and Co.; Windsor: Knight and Dredge, 1822, 2 vols, vol. 1, pp. 99–104.

$8\frac{1}{4} \times 5$ in. Vol. 1: 412; vol. 2: 488 pp.

707 MS Notes on the Last Number of the *Edinburgh Review*.

Blackwood's Edinburgh Magazine, XII (December 1822), 785–90.

708 Reviews of *Ecclesiastical Sketches*, and of *Memorials of a Tour on the Continent*.

British Critic, XVIII (November 1822), 522–31.

709 Review of *Memorials of a Tour on the Continent*.

Edinburgh Review, XXXVII (November 1822), 449–56.

710 Wordsworth's *Sonnets* and *Memorials*.

Blackwood's Edinburgh Magazine, XII (August 1822), 175–91.

1823

711 BARNES, ROBERT. *The Poetical Works of Robert Barnes. To Which Is Prefixed a Sketch of the Life of the Author*. Cockermouth: Printed for the Author by Thomas Bailey, 1823.

$6\frac{3}{16} \times 3\frac{5}{8}$ in. 102 pp. A Cockermouth poet.

712 GRISCOM, JOHN. *A Year in Europe. Comprising a Journal of Observations in England, Scotland, Ireland, France, Switzerland, the North of Italy, and Holland*. New York: Collins & Co., and E. Bliss & E. White; Philadelphia: H. C. Carey and J. Lea; Boston: Wells & Lilly, 1823, 2 vols.

$8\frac{3}{8} \times 5\frac{1}{8}$ in. Vol. 1: viii [5] 10–520 [4]; vol. 2: [8] 562 [4] pp. Wordsworth and the Lake Country, vol. 2, pp. 497–522. John Gough, the blind scientist described in *The Excursion*, vol. 2, pp. 518–21.

713 JOHNSTON, CHARLES. *Sonnets, Original and Translated*. London: John Murray, 1823.

$7\frac{3}{4} \times 4\frac{7}{8}$ in. [12] 173 [7] pp. Sonnet to Wordsworth, p. 53.

714 LANDOR, WALTER SAVAGE. Imaginary Conversation between Mr. Southey and Professor Porson.

London Magazine, VIII (July 1823), 5–9.

715 LLOYD, CHARLES. *Poems*. London: Longman, Hurst, Rees, Orme, and Brown; and C. and H. Baldwin; Birmingham: Beilby and Knotts, 1823.

$6\frac{5}{8} \times 4\frac{1}{8}$ in. [2] 96 [2] pp. By the early friend of Coleridge and Wordsworth.

716 Obituary of Peter Bayley, Jun.

Gentleman's Magazine, XCIII (May 1823). A clipping.

717 *Time's Telescope for 1823;* or, a Complete Guide to the Almanac: Containing an Explanation of Saints' Days and Holidays; with Illustrations of British History and Antiquities, Notices of Obsolete Rites and Customs, Sketches of Comparative Chronology, and Contemporary Biography. Astronomical Occurrences in Every Month; Comprising Remarks on the Phenomena of the Celestial Bodies, with an Account of Indispensable Astronomical Instruments; and the Naturalist's Diary; Explaining the Various Appearances in the Vegetable and Animal Kingdoms. To Which Are Prefixed an Introduction on the Habits, Economy, and Uses of British Insects; and an Ode to Time by Bernard Barton. London: Sherwood, Neely, and Jones, 1823.

$7\frac{3}{4} \times 4\frac{3}{8}$ in. lxxi [1] 359 [13] pp. Contains quotations from Wordsworth.

1824

718 [DEACON, WILLIAM FREDERICK]. *Warreniana; with Notes, Critical and Explanatory*, by the Editor of the *Quarterly Review*. Boston: Wells and Lilly, 1824.

$7\frac{7}{8} \times 4\frac{1}{8}$ in. iv [4] 9–162 [2] pp. Parody of Wordsworth, pp. 20–5.

719 Good Versification Essential to Good Poetry.

American Monthly Magazine, 1 (February 1824), 97–113. Adverse criticism of Wordsworth, especially pp. 102–5.

720 LANDOR, WALTER SAVAGE. *Imaginary Conversations of Literary Men and Statesmen.* Second Series. London: Taylor and Hessey, 1824–28, 3 vols.

$8\frac{3}{8} \times 5\frac{3}{8}$ in. Vol. 1: [5] vi–xvi, 363 [4]; vol. 2: [5] vi–xiv, 399 [1]; vol. 3: [5] vi–xvi, 546 [2] pp. Southey and Porson, vol. i, pp. 51–95.

1825

721 HAZLITT, WILLIAM. *The Spirit of the Age: or Contemporary Portraits.* London: Henry Colburn, 1825.

$9 \times 5\frac{1}{4}$ in. [4] 424 pp. Wordsworth, pp. 229–50.

722 JEWSBURY, MARIA JANE. *Phantasmagoria, or Sketches of Life and Literature.* London: Hurst, Robinson, & Co.; Edinburgh: Archibald Constable & Co., 1825, 2 vols.

$7\frac{1}{4} \times 4\frac{1}{2}$ in. Vol. 1: [4] 309 [1]; vol. 2: [6] 309 [3] pp. Dedicated to Wordsworth.

723 On the Genius and Poetry of Wordsworth.

Literary Magnet, III (1825–6?), 67–72.

724 HEMANS, FELICIA. To the Author of *The Excursion* and the *Lyrical Ballads*.

Literary Magnet, I, n.s. (April 1826), 169–70. Other references to Wordsworth, pp. 17–22, 68–76.

725 LANDOR, WALTER SAVAGE. *Imaginary Conversations of Literary Men and Statesmen*. Second Edition. London: Henry Colburn, 1826–8, 3 vols.

$8\frac{3}{4} \times 5\frac{1}{2}$ in. Vol. 1: xvi, 512; vol. 2: xii, 632; vol. 3: xvi, 546 [2] pp. Southey and Porson, vol. i, pp. 51–95.

726 Another copy.

1827

727 E., A.S. Remarks upon Wordsworth's Poetry.

Christian Spectator, I, n.s. (May 1827), 244–7.

728 HONE, WILLIAM. *The Table Book*. With Engravings. London: Published for William Hone by Hunt and Clarke, 1827.

$9 \times 5\frac{3}{4}$ in. Account of a personal interview with Wordsworth, pp. 550–6.

729 TAYLOR, JOHN. *Poems on Various Subjects*. London: Payne and Foss; Longman, Rees, Orme, & Co.; J. Richardson; J. Murray, 1827, 2 vols.

$7\frac{3}{8} \times 4\frac{3}{4}$ in. Vol. 1: xxxii, 316 [2]; vol. 2: xv [1] 308 pp. Sonnet to Wordsworth, vol. 1, p. 191.

730 WORDSWORTH, CHARLES. *Mexica. Poema Cancellarii Praemio Donatum et in Theatro Sheldoniano Recitatum*. Sext. Cal. Jun. MDCCCXXVII. Oxford, 1827.

$8\frac{1}{8} \times 5\frac{3}{16}$ in. 18 pp.

1828

731 BYRON, LORD. *Don Juan*. London: Thomas Davison, 1828, 2 vols.

$6\frac{1}{2} \times 3\frac{3}{4}$ in. Vol. 1: [2] 343 [1]; vol. 2: [2] 371 [1] pp.

1829

732 An Essay on the Theory and the Writings of Wordsworth.

Blackwood's Edinburgh Magazine, XXVI (September, October, November, December 1829), 453–63, 593–609, 774–88, 894–910.

733 GODWIN, CATHARINE GRACE. *The Wanderer's Legacy; a Collection of Poems, on Various Subjects.* London: Samuel Maunder, 1829.

$7\frac{7}{8} \times 4\frac{7}{8}$ in. [8] 227 [3] pp. Dedicatory letter to Wordsworth, p. [v].

1831

734 HARDAKER, JOSEPH. *The Bridal of Tomar; and Other Poems.* Keighley: Charles Crabtree; London: Simpkin and Marshall, 1831.

$7 \times 4\frac{1}{8}$ in. viii, 114. Wordsworth, p. 114.

735 LEWIS, ALONZO. *Poems.* Boston: John H. Eastburn, 1831.

$7\frac{3}{8} \times 4\frac{3}{4}$ in. [4] 208 pp. Poem on Wordsworth, p. 117.

736 PUNGENT, PIERCE. Mr. Wordsworth.

Fraser's Magazine, III (June 1831), 557-66.

737 Review of *Selections from the Poems of W. Wordsworth for the Use of Schools and Young Persons.*

New Monthly Magazine and Literary Journal: Historical Register, XXXIII (July 1831), 304.

738 Sonnets on the Coronation, by a Lyrist from the Lakes.

New Monthly Magazine and Literary Journal: Original Papers, XXXII (October 1831), 331–2. A parody.

739 WORDSWORTH, CHARLES. *Oratio Cancellarii Praemio Donata, et in Theatro Sheldoniano habita Die Junii XVto*, A.D. MDCCCXXXI. Oxford: D. A. Talboys, 1831.

$8\frac{1}{8} \times 5\frac{3}{16}$ in. 41 [1] pp. Signed, 'Carolus Wordsworth.'

1832

740 SOUTHEY, ROBERT. *Essays, Moral and Political*, by Robert Southey, Esq., LL.D., Poet Laureate, &c., Now First Collected. London: John Murray, 1832, 2 vols.

$6\frac{1}{4} \times 3\frac{3}{4}$ in. Vol. 1: viii, 442; vol. 2: [2] 443 [1] pp.

741 Wordsworth's Poetry, Its Excellence and Beauty.

National Omnibus; and General Advertiser, II (June 1832), 193–4.

1833

742 DANA, RICHARD HENRY. *Poems and Prose Writings*. Boston: Russell, Odiorne, and Co., 1833.

$6\frac{5}{8} \times 4\frac{1}{4}$ in. ix [3] 450 [6] pp. Wordsworth, pp. 148–9.

743 LYTTON, EDWARD, LORD. *England and the English*. New York: J. and J. Harper, 1833, 2 vols.

$7\frac{1}{4} \times 4\frac{5}{8}$ in. Vol. 1: [2] 243 [11]; vol. 2: [2] 220 [10] pp. Wordsworth and Shelley, vol. 2, pp. 67–71.

744 [MERRYWEATHER, I. A.]. *The Hermit of Eskdaleside, with Other Poems*. Whitby: R. Kirby, 1833.

$7\frac{1}{4} \times 4\frac{1}{4}$ in. [8] 136 [2] pp. Poem to Wordsworth, p. 117.

745 [REYNOLDS, FREDERIC MANSEL]. '*Miserrimus*.' London: Thomas Hookham, 1833.

$6\frac{5}{8} \times 4\frac{1}{8}$ in. 208 pp. Wordsworth, pp. 12–13.

746 Sketch of the Genius and Character of William Wordsworth, with Selections from His *Lyrical Ballads*.

Greenbank's Periodical Library, Philadelphia, II (1833), 181–202. The sketch is by Hazlitt, reprinted from his Spirit of the Age.

1834

747 DE VERE, AUBREY. On a Visit to Wordsworth, after a Mountain Excursion.

The Literary Souvenir (ed. Alaric A. Watts). London: Longman, Rees, Orme, Brown, Green, & Longman; Philadelphia: Wardle; Berlin: Asher, 1834, p. 178. $5\frac{3}{4} \times 3\frac{3}{4}$ in. xiv, 306 [4] pp.

748 DOYLE, FRANCIS HASTINGS. *Miscellaneous Verses.* London: John Taylor, 1834.

6⅝ × 4 in. iv, 83 [1] pp. Sonnet Written in the First Page of Wordsworth's *Poems*, p. 59.

749 *The Oxford University Magazine:* Volume the First. Oxford: D. A. Talboys; London: Whittaker and Co., 1834.

8½ × 5⅛ in. [4] 498 pp. Wordsworth, pp. 10, 12, 93–4.

750 [TAYLOR, HENRY]. Reviews of *The Poetical Works of William Wordsworth*, 4 Vols., 1832; and of *Selections from the Poems of William Wordsworth*, 1834.

Quarterly Review, LII (November 1834), 317–58.

1835

751 BELL, GEORGE. *Descriptive and Other Miscellaneous Pieces, in Verse.* Penrith: Printed for the Author by J. Brown, 1835.

4 × 6½ in. viii [2] 205 [3] pp. Poem entitled Rydal Mount, p. 112.

752 MEREDITH, LOUISA ANNE (TWAMLEY). *Poems of Louisa Anne Twamley.* With Original Illustrations, Drawn and Etched by the Authoress. London: Charles Tilt, 1835.

7⅛ × 4½ in. ix [1] 182 [2]. By an admirer of Wordsworth. See No. 762.

753 *The New-York Mirror:* Devoted to Literature and the Fine Arts, XII (June 1835), 388.

Wordsworth, p. 388.

754 Review of *Yarrow Revisited.*

Fraser's Magazine, XI (June 1835), 689–707.

755 Review of *Yarrow Revisited.*

Quarterly Review, LIV (July 1835), 181–5.

756 [WORDSWORTH, CHRISTOPHER]. *Ode Performed in the Senate House, Cambridge, on the Seventh of July, M.DCCC.XXXV. At the First Commencement after the Installation, and in the Presence, of the Most Noble John Jeffreys, Marquess Camden, K.G., Chancellor of the University.* Cambridge: Printed at the Pitt Press, 1835.

8¼ × 5¼ in. 7 [1] pp.

1836

757 *Attempts at Verse.* London: George Mann, 1836.

$6\frac{5}{8} \times 3\frac{7}{8}$ in. vii [1] 147 [1] pp. Dedicated to Wordsworth.

758 The Poets of Our Age Considered as to Their Philosophic Tendencies.

London and Westminster Review, III and XXV (April 1836), 60–71.

759 DEWEY, ORVILLE. *The Old World and the New; or a Journal of Reflections and Observations Made on a Tour in Europe.* New-York: Harper & Brothers, 1836, 2 vols.

$7\frac{5}{16} \times 5\frac{5}{16}$ in. Vol. 1: xii [1] 14–262 [6]; vol. 2: viii [1] 10–330 [4] pp. Wordsworth, vol. 1, pp. 89–96.

760 [FELTON, C. C.]. Review of *Yarrow Revisited.*

Christian Examiner, XIX (January 1836), 375–83.

761 LANDOR, WALTER SAVAGE. *A Satire on Satirists, and Admonition to Detractors.* London: Saunders and Otley, 1836.

$7\frac{7}{8} \times 4\frac{7}{8}$ in. 38 [4] pp. Wordsworth, p. 30.

762 MEREDITH, LOUISA ANNE (TWAMLEY). *The Romance of Nature; or, the Flower Seasons Illustrated.* The Plates Engraved after Original Drawings from Nature by the Author. London: Charles Tilt, 1836.

$8\frac{3}{8} \times 5\frac{1}{4}$ in. xviii [2] 253 [3] pp. Dedicated to Wordsworth.

763 MONTGOMERY, JAMES. *Lectures on General Literature, Poetry, &c.,* Delivered at the Royal Institution in 1830 and 1831. New York: Harper & Brothers, 1836.

$6 \times 3\frac{3}{4}$ in. 324 [2] pp. Wordsworth, pp. 99–101, 118–24.

764 English Sonnets (a review of Wordsworth's sonnets).

American Quarterly Review, XIX (June 1836), 420–42.

765 Review of *Yarrow Revisited.*

American Quarterly Review, XX (September 1836), 66–88.

766 [PORTER, NOAH]. Wordsworth and His Poetry.

Quarterly Christian Spectator, VIII (March 1836), 127–51.

767 PRAY, ISAAC CLARKE, JR. *Prose and Poetry from the Port Folio of an Editor*. Boston: Russell, Shattuck, and Co., 1836.

$7\frac{1}{8} \times 4\frac{1}{2}$ in. 186 [2] pp. Wordsworth, pp. 56–9.

768 SMITH, SAMUEL J. *Miscellaneous Writings of the Late Samuel J. Smith, of Burlington, N.J., Collected and Arranged by One of the Family, with a Notice Illustrative of His Life and Character*. Philadelphia: Henry Perkins; Boston: Perkins & Marvin, 1836.

$9\frac{1}{2} \times 5\frac{11}{16}$ in. [3] 4–222 [4] pp. Wordsworth, pp. 180–6.

769 [WILLMOTT, ROBERT ARIS]. *Conversations at Cambridge*. London: John W. Parker, 1836.

$6\frac{3}{4} \times 4$ in. vi [2] 292 [2] pp. The Poet Wordsworth and Professor Smythe, pp. 235–52.

1837

770 CROSSLEY, THOMAS. *Flowers of Ebor*. London: Longman, Rees, Orme, Brown, Green, and Longman, 1837.

$8\frac{3}{4} \times 5\frac{1}{2}$ in. xi [1] 198 [2] pp. Sonnet to Wordsworth, p. 176.

771 HERAUD, JOHN ABRAHAM. *Substance of a Lecture on Poetic Genius as a Moral Power:* Delivered 2nd October, 1837, at the Milton Institution, to Which Is Added an Ode; by John A. Heraud, Esq., Author of *The Oration on Coleridge*, etc., etc. London: James Fraser, 1837.

$8\frac{1}{2} \times 5\frac{1}{4}$ in. [3] 36–55 [1] pp. Wordsworth, pp. 44–8.

772 LOCKHART, JOHN GIBSON. *Memoirs of the Life of Sir Walter Scott, Bart*. Edinburgh: R. Cadell, 1837–8.

$7\frac{7}{8} \times 4\frac{7}{8}$ in. Vol 1: [6] viii, 417 [5]; vol. 2: [8] iv, 407 [1]; vol. 3: [8] iv, 414; vol. 4: [8] iv, 383 [1]; vol. 5: [8] viii, 418; vol. 6: [4] x, 393 [1]; vol. 7: [8] xvi, 478 [2] pp. Wordsworth *passim*; see Index.

773 TALFOURD, THOMAS NOON. *Ion; a Tragedy, in Five Acts*. Fourth Edition; to Which Are Added Sonnets. London: Edward Moxon, 1837.

$8\frac{1}{2} \times 5\frac{1}{4}$ in. xxii, 128 [2] pp. Wordsworth, p. xii.

774 TALFOURD, THOMAS NOON. *A Speech Delivered...in the House of Commons, on Thursday, 18th May, 1837, on Moving for Leave to Bring in a Bill to Consolidate the Law Relating to Copyright, and to Extend the Term of Its Duration.* London: Edward Moxon, 1837.

8 × 5 in. vi, 16 pp. Talfourd's Copyright Bill was a major interest of Wordsworth's.

775 [WALKER, JAMES]. Review of the *Poetical Works*, Philadelphia, 1837.

Christian Examiner, XXII (March 1837), 132.

1838

776 CHORLEY, HENRY F. William Wordsworth.

Museum of Foreign Literature, Science, and Art, Philadelphia, IV, n.s. (January 1838), 110–13. Reprinted from *The Authors of England*; see below.

777 COLLAS, ACHILLE. *The Authors of England.* A Series of Medallion Portraits of Modern Literary Characters, Engraved from the Works of British Artists, by Achille Collas. With Illustrative Notices by Henry F. Chorley. London: Charles Tilt, 1838.

12⅛ × 9½ in. vi [4] 93 [19] pp. Wordsworth, pp. 87–93.

778 HARE, AUGUSTUS WILLIAM AND JULIUS CHARLES. *Guesses at Truth by Two Brothers.* Second Edition. First Series. London: Taylor and Walton, 1838.

6¾ × 4⅛ in. xiv [2] 370 pp. Dedicated to Wordsworth.

779 HEMANS, FELICIA. *The Poetical Works of Mrs. Felicia Hemans;* Complete in One Volume. New Edition with a Critical Preface, and a Bibliographical Memoir. Philadelphia: Grigg & Elliot, 1838.

8⅝ × 5⅛ in. [16] xvi, 479 [5] pp. To the Poet Wordsworth, p. 281.

780 JAMES, ROBERT. *Poems.* Cambridge: Printed by Glover and Foister, 1838.

8¼ × 5¼ in. 20 pp. Parodies of Wordsworth, pp. 8–9.

781 OSBORN, LAUGHTON. *The Vision of Rubeta, an Epic Story of the Island of Manhattan.* With Illustrations Done on Stone. Boston: Weeks, Jordan, and Co., 1838.

9 × 5⅝ in. xviii [2] 424 pp. Wordsworth, pp. ix–x, 186, 187, 284, 391–411.

782 [WALLACE, HORACE BINNEY]. *Stanley; or the Recollections of a Man of the World*. Vol. II. Philadelphia: Lea & Blanchard, 1838.

$7\frac{1}{2} \times 4\frac{1}{2}$ in. [11]–256 pp.; introductory pages missing. Chapter 3, pp. 70–97, concerns Coleridge, Davy, Southey, and Wordsworth.

1839

783 [DE QUINCEY, THOMAS]. Lake Reminiscences, from 1807 to 1830.

Tait's Edinburgh Magazine, VI (January, February, April 1839), 1–12, 90–103, 246–54.

784 DE QUINCEY, THOMAS. Recollections of Grasmere.

Tait's Edinburgh Magazine, VI (September 1839), 569–81.

785 ELLISON, HENRY. *Madmoments: or First Verseattempts*. By a Bornnatural. Addressed to the Lightheaded of Society at Large. London: Painter, 1839, 2 vols.

$6\frac{1}{4} \times 3\frac{3}{4}$ in. Vol. 1: [2] ii, 484; vol. 2: [2] 482 [2] pp. Wordsworth and Byron, vol. 2, p. 399.

786 HUGHES, MRS. *Memoir of the Life and Writings of Mrs. Hemans*. By Her Sister. Philadelphia: Lea and Blanchard, 1839.

$7\frac{3}{8} \times 4\frac{3}{8}$ in. [4] 29–336 [6] pp. Numerous references to Wordsworth.

787 *Now Exhibiting at the Egyptian Hall, Piccadilly, an Extremely Interesting Pictorial and Mechanical Exhibition, Embracing Every Minute Particular of the Terrific Storm at Sea! in Which Grace Darling and Her Father Rescued the Sufferers from the Wreck of the Forfarshire Steamer, and Landed Them at the Fern Lighthouse*. London: Printed by T. Goode, 1839.

$6\frac{3}{4} \times 4$ in. [7] 8–21 [3] pp. See Nos. 121, 125.

788 Reviews of *The Complete Poetical Works of William Wordsworth*, Philadelphia, 1837; and of *The Poetical Works of William Wordsworth*, London, 1836, 6 vols.

New York Review, IV (January 1839), 1–70.

789 WORDSWORTH, CHRISTOPHER. *Ecclesiastical Biography; or, Lives of Eminent Men, Connected with the History of Religion in England; from the Commencement of the Reformation to the Revolution;* ... Third Edition, with a Large Introduction, Some New Lives, and Many Additional Notes. London: J. G. & F. Rivington, 1839, 4 vols.

$8\frac{3}{8} \times 5\frac{1}{4}$ in. Vol. 1: xxviii, 646 [6]; vol. 2: [10] 679 [5]; vol. 3: [10], 675 [7]; vol. 4: [10] 719 [7] pp.

1840

790 *The Cambridge University Magazine.* Vol. I. Cambridge: W. P. Grant, 1840.

$8\frac{3}{8} \times 5\frac{3}{8}$ in. vi, 508 pp. To the Poet Wordsworth (a sonnet), p. 69; Lines in Imitation of Wordsworth (signed B.R.J.), pp. 197–8.

791 HUNT, LEIGH. *The Indicator, and the Companion; a Miscellany for the Fields and the Fire-side.* In Two Parts. *The Seer; or, Common-places Refreshed.* In Two Parts. London: Edward Moxon, 1840.

$9\frac{1}{2} \times 6$ in. Contents as follows: The Indicator, Part 1, [4] 84; Part 2, [4] 60 pp. The Companion, pp. 61–93 + [3]. The Seer, Part 1, [8] 87 [1]; Part 2, [4] 79 [1] pp. Wordsworth and Milton, in The Seer, Part 1, pp. 53–5.

792 BENNOCH, FRANCIS. *The Storm, and Other Poems.* London: William Smith, 1841.

$6\frac{3}{4} \times 4\frac{3}{8}$ in. ix [3] 136 pp. Dedicated to Wordsworth. Sonnet to Wordsworth, p. 130.

793 DOYLE, FRANCIS HASTINGS. *Miscellaneous Verses.* Second Edition. London: Saunders and Otley, 1841.

$6\frac{3}{4} \times 4\frac{1}{4}$ in. vii [1] 283 [1] pp. Sonnet Written in the First Page of Wordsworth's *Poems*, p. 155.

794 QUILLINAN, EDWARD. *The Conspirators, or the Romance of Military Life.* London: Henry Colburn, 1841, 3 vols.

$8 \times 4\frac{3}{4}$ in. Vol. 1: [4] 311 [1]; vol. 2: [2] 320; vol. 3: 315 [1] pp. By Wordsworth's son-in-law.

795 Review of *The Sonnets of William Wordsworth Collected in One Volume.*

Quarterly Review, LXIX (December 1841), 1–51.

1842

796 HARCOURT, MAURICE. Windermere and Wordsworth.

Bradshaw's Journal, IV (December 1842), 1–6.

797 LANDOR, WALTER SAVAGE. Southey and Porson.

Blackwood's Edinburgh Magazine, LII (December 1842), 687–715.

798 *The New World*, IV (April, May 1842).

Wordsworth references, pp. 240, 244–5, 254, 291–2, 294, 321.

799 POWELL, THOMAS. *Poems*. London: Effingham Wilson, 1842.

$6\frac{5}{8} \times 4\frac{1}{4}$ in. vii [1] 338 pp. Poem to Wordsworth, p. 177.

800 Review of Wordsworth's Sonnets on the Punishment of Death.

United States Magazine, and Democratic Review, x (March 1842), 272–88.

801 RIO, ALEXIS FRANÇOIS. *La Petite Chouannerie, ou, Histoire d'un Collège Breton sous l'Empire*. Paris: Olivier Fulgence, 1842.

$8\frac{1}{4} \times 5$ in. [4] 598 pp. Wordsworth, pp. 31–5.

802 STORY, ROBERT. *Love and Literature; Being the Reminiscences, Literary Opinions, and Fugitive Pieces, of a Poet in Humble Life*. London: Longman, Brown, Green, and Longmans, 1842.

$7\frac{3}{8} \times 4\frac{3}{8}$ in. viii [1] 10–264 [2] pp. The Poets Moore, Wordsworth, and Southey, pp. 180–91.

803 WILSON, JOHN. *The Recreations of Christopher North*. Edinburgh and London: William Blackwood and Sons, 1842.

$7\frac{7}{8} \times 4\frac{3}{4}$ in. Vol. 1: [8] 388; vol. 2: [6] 403 [3]; vol. 3: [6] 416 pp. An Hour's Talk about Poetry, vol. 1, pp. 267–342; Stroll to Grasmere, vol. 3, pp. 336–97.

1843

804 ROBBERDS, JOHN W. *A Memoir of the Life and Writings of the Late William Taylor of Norwich, ... Containing His Correspondence of Many Years with the Late Robert Southey, Esq., and Original Letters from Sir Walter Scott, and Other Eminent Literary Men*. London: John Murray, 1843, 2 vols.

$8\frac{3}{4} \times 5\frac{1}{2}$ in. Vol. 1: viii, 523 [1]; vol. 2: iv, 576 [8] pp.

805 SHELDON, FREDERICK. *Mieldenvold, the Student; or, the Pilgrimage through Berwickshire, Northumberland, Durham, and Adjacent Counties.* Berwick-upon-Tweed: Published at the Warder Office, 1843.

$8\frac{3}{4} \times 5\frac{3}{8}$ in. xiv [1] 176. Wordsworth, p. ix.

806 Wordsworth's Sonnets to Liberty.

United States Magazine, and Democratic Review, XII (February 1843), 158–63.

1844

807 DEARDEN, WILLIAM. *The Vale of Caldene; or, the Past and the Present: a Poem, in Six Books.* London: Longman & Co., ... 1844.

$6\frac{3}{4} \times 4$ in. xv [1] 254 [6] pp. Wordsworth, pp. 249–50.

808 ELLIS, SARAH. *Irish Girl: and Other Poems.* By Sarah Ellis, Author of *Women of England, Poetry of Life, Brother and Sister*, &c., &c. New York: James Langley; Philadelphia: Thomas Cowperthwait and Co.; Boston: Tappan and Dennet, 1844.

$7\frac{3}{8} \times 4\frac{1}{4}$ in. vii [1] 263 [25] pp. To the Poet Wordsworth (a poem), pp. 107–9.

809 William Wordsworth.

The Evergreen, or Church-Offering for All Seasons; a Repository of Religious, Literary, and Entertaining Knowledge, for the Christian Family, 1 (October 1844), 289–93.

810 GRANT, JOHN PETER. *Memoir and Correspondence of Mrs. Grant of Laggan*, Author of *Letters from the Mountains, Memoirs of an American Lady*, etc. London: Longman, Brown, Green, and Longmans, 1844. 3 vols.

$7\frac{5}{8} \times 4\frac{3}{4}$ in. Vol. 1: xvi, 312 [32]; vol. 2: xv [1] 335 [1]; vol. 3: xvi, 325 [3] pp. Wordsworth, vol. 2, pp. 59, 224–5, 281–2, 308, and elsewhere.

811 HORNE, RICHARD HENGIST. *A New Spirit of the Age.* London: Smith, Elder and Co., 1844, 2 vols.

$8 \times 4\frac{3}{4}$ in. Vol. 1: ix [3] 332; vol. 2: [6] 310 [50] pp. William Wordsworth and Leigh Hunt, vol. 1, pp. 305–32.

812 KEBLE, JOHN. *De Poeticæ Vi Medica. Prælectiones Academicæ Oxonii Habitæ*, Annis MDCCCXXXII ... MDCCCXLI, a Joanne Keble, A.M. Poeticæ Publico Prælectore, Collegii Orielensis Nuper Socio. Oxonii: J. H. Parker, M.DCCC.XLIV.

$8\frac{1}{2} \times 5$ in. [6] 853 [3] pp. Dedicated to Wordsworth. References, pp. 615, 789.

813 [LORDAN, CHRISTOPHER LEGGE]. *Colloquies, Desultory, but Chiefly upon Poetry and Poets; between an Elder, Enthusiastic, and an Apostle of the Law.* London: Orr and Co.; and Houlston & Stoneman; Romsey: Lordan, 1844.

8¼ × 5¼ in. [10] iv [2] 268 pp. Chapter on Wordsworth, pp. 59–86. (The author of this book, a printer, wrote no manuscript but put his thoughts directly into type as he went.)

814 Signs of Hope.

Christian Remembrancer, June 1844, pp. 163–83. Includes a commentary on an article published in the *Leeds Christian Miscellany* entitled Testimonies of W. Wordsworth and of S. T. Coleridge to Catholic Truth.

815 WORDSWORTH, CHRISTOPHER. *Theocritus.* Codicum Manuscriptorum Ope Recensuit et Emendavit Christophorus Wordsworth, S.T.P., Scholæ Harroviensis Magister: Nuper Coll. S.S. Trin. Cant. Socius et Academiæ Orator Publicus. Cantabrigiæ: Typis academicis excudit Joannes G. Parker. Veneunt Londini apud Joannes Gul. Parker; Cantabrigiæ apud J. et J. J. Deightonos, M.DCCC.XLIV.

8¾ × 5¼ in. xxxviii [2] 410 [10] pp.

1845

816 [BROWNING], ELIZABETH BARRETT. *A Drama of Exile: and Other Poems.* By Elizabeth Barrett Barrett, Author of *The Seraphim: and Other Poems.* New-York: Henry G. Langley, 1845, 2 vols.

6⅞ × 4⅜ in. Vol. 1: xii [3] 16–264 [2]; vol. 2: iv [3] 8–279 [11] pp. Sonnet, On a Portrait of Wordsworth by B. R. Haydon, vol. 1, p. 137.

817 DE QUINCEY, THOMAS. On Wordsworth's Poetry.

Tait's Edinburgh Magazine, xii (September 1845), 545–54.

818 FERRETT, E. Byron and Wordsworth.

Arthur's Ladies' Magazine of Elegant Literature and the Fine Arts, Philadelphia, iii (June 1845), 284–6.

819 Mrs. Hemans.

Smith's Weekly Volume for Town and Country, Philadelphia, i (April 1845), 227–31. Contains references to Wordsworth.

820 STANLEY, ARTHUR PENRHYN. *The Life and Correspondence of Thomas Arnold, D.D.* Fourth Edition. London: B. Fellowes, 1845, 2 vols.

$8\frac{3}{4} \times 5\frac{1}{2}$ in. Vol. 1: xxiii [3] 440; vol. 2: xvi [2] 448 pp. Contains references to Wordsworth; see Index.

821 WORDSWORTH, CHRISTOPHER. *Diary in France, Mainly on Topics concerning Education and the Church.* London: Francis and John Rivington, 1845.

$7\frac{7}{8} \times 4\frac{3}{4}$ in. viii, 234 [2] pp.

1846

822 FULLER, SARAH MARGARET. *Papers on Literature and Art.* New York: Wiley and Putnam, 1846, 2 vols.

$7 \times 4\frac{1}{2}$ in. Vol. 1: [2] viii, 164; vol. 2: [6] 183 [5] pp. Modern British Poets (including Wordsworth), vol. 1, pp. 58–99.

823 GILFILLAN, GEORGE. *Sketches of Modern Literature, and Eminent Literary Men.* New York: D. Appleton & Co.; Philadelphia: Geo. S. Appleton, 1846, 2 vols.

$7\frac{1}{2} \times 4\frac{7}{8}$ in. Vol. 1: xii [1] 14–261 [11]; vol. 2: [3] 268–492 pp. William Wordsworth, vol. 2, pp. 347–60.

824 TUCKERMAN, HENRY THEODORE. *Thoughts on the Poets.* New York: C. S. Francis & Co.; Boston: J. H. Francis, 1846.

$6\frac{1}{2} \times 4\frac{1}{8}$ in. [3]–318 [8] pp. Wordsworth, pp. 214–25.

1847

825 Poets of the Age.

Eton School Magazine, No. 2 [c. 1847], pp. 41–6. Contains references to Wordsworth and the Lake Poets.

826 HEATON, WILLIAM. *The Flowers of Calder Dale: Poems.* London: Longman & Co.; Halifax: Leyland & Son, 1847.

$7\frac{1}{2} \times 4\frac{1}{4}$ in. xi [1] 140 pp. Wordsworth subscribed to the book. Stanzas to William Wordsworth, Esq., pp. 19–20; To William Wordsworth, p. 84.

827 HOWITT, WILLIAM. *Homes and Haunts of the Most Eminent British Poets.* The Illustrations Engraved by M. W. Mewet. New York: Harper & Brothers, 1847, 2 vols.

$7\frac{7}{8} \times 4\frac{3}{4}$ in. Vol. 1: [8] 566 [6]; vol. 2: [6] 536 [12] pp. William Wordsworth, vol. 2, pp. 295–333.

828 *The Literary World, a Gazette for Authors, Readers, and Publishers*, 1 (1847).

References to Wordsworth, pp. 5, 34, 132, 470, 515.

829 QUILLINAN, DORA (WORDSWORTH). *Journal of a Few Months' Residence in Portugal, and Glimpses of the South of Spain.* London: Edward Moxon, 1847, 2 vols.

8 × 4¾ in. Vol. 1: xv [1] 242 [2]; vol. 2: [4] 247 [1] pp.

830 SOUTHEY, ROBERT AND CAROLINE. *Robin Hood: a Fragment.* Edinburgh and London: William Blackwood and Sons, 1847.

7⅜ × 4½ in. xx, 248 pp.

831 TAYLOR, HENRY. *Notes from Life, in Six Essays.* London: John Murray, 1847.

8 × 4⅞ in. ix [3] 192 [6] pp. By a friend and admirer of Wordsworth.

1848

832 BRYDGES, SAMUEL EGERTON. *Human Fate, and an Address to the Poets Wordsworth and Southey: Poems.* By the Late Sir Egerton Brydges, Bart. Now First Printed .... Totham: Printed by Charles Clark (an Amateur) at his Private Press, 1848.

8¾ × 5¼ in. 24 fols. With the volume is a manuscript copy of E. J. Hytche's sonnet, William Wordsworth, from *Stray Thoughts in Prose and Verse*, London, 1845, p. 17.

833 FRY, HENRIETTA JOAN. *Portraits in Miniature; or, Tableaux du Cœur.* London: Charles Gilpin, 1848.

8¾ × 5½ in. xxiv, 204 [4] pp. Wordsworth, pp. 29–31.

834 GRANT, JAMES GREGOR. *Madonna Pia, and Other Poems.* London: Smith, Elder, and Co., 1848, 2 vols.

7¼ × 4¾ in. Vol. 1: x [2] 320; vol. 2: xiii [1] 359 [1] pp. Dedicated to Wordsworth. On the First Perusal and Study of Wordsworth's Poetry (a sonnet), vol. 1, p. 204; Memorials of an English Lake Tour (sonnets), vol. 2, pp. 47–92.

835 *The Literary World, a Journal of American and Foreign Literature, Science, and Art*, III (1848).

A Visit to the Poet Wordsworth, pp. 879–80; a review of *Poems by William Wordsworth*, New York, 1849 [for 1848], pp. 896–7.

836 LOWELL, JAMES RUSSELL. *A Fable for Critics*. Second Edition. New York: G. P. Putnam, 1848.

$7\frac{1}{2} \times 4\frac{3}{4}$ in. v [8] 8–80 [10] pp. Contains a comparison of Bryant and Wordsworth, pp. 210–29.

837 [SMITH, JAMES AND HORACE]. *Rejected Addresses: or the New Theatrum Poetarum*. From the Last London Edition, Carefully Revised, with an Original Preface and Notes. Fourth American Edition. Boston: William D. Ticknor & Co., 1848.

$7 \times 4\frac{3}{8}$ in. xxx [2] 159 [1] pp. Parody of Wordsworth, pp. 6–12.

838 WALLACE, WILLIAM. Wordsworth (a poem).

Home Journal, June 1848. A clipping.

1849

839 GRAHAM, G. F. *English Synonymes Classified and Explained; with Practical Exercises*, Designed for Schools and Private Tuition. Edited, with an Introduction and Illustrative Authorities, by Henry Reed. New York: D. Appleton, 1849.

$7\frac{1}{4} \times 4\frac{1}{2}$ in. xiv [2] 344 [24] pp. Over 400 quotations from Wordsworth.

840 HOWE, JULIA WARD. Wordsworth (a poem).

Literary World, a Journal of American and Foreign Literature, Science, and Art, IV (January 1849), 4–5. Other references to Wordsworth, pp. 1, 169.

841 POWELL, THOMAS. *The Living Authors of England*. New York: D. Appleton & Co.; Philadelphia: Geo. S. Appleton, 1849.

$7\frac{1}{4} \times 4\frac{3}{4}$ in. [2] 316 [2] pp. Wordsworth, pp. 25–30.

842 Review of *The Excursion*, New York, 1849.

Literary World, a Journal of American and Foreign Literature, Science, and Art, V (December 1849), 463–4.

843 SOUTHEY, CHARLES CUTHBERT. *The Life and Correspondence of Robert Southey*, Edited by His Son, the Rev. Charles Cuthbert Southey. London: Longman, Brown, Green, and Longmans, 1849–50, 6 vols.

$7\frac{3}{4} \times 4\frac{3}{4}$ in. Vol. 1: xii [2] 352 [32]; vol. 2: vii [3] 360 [32]; vol. 3: viii [2] 352; vol. 4: viii [2] 390 [2]; vol. 5: viii [2] 368; vol. 6: viii [2] 408 pp.

844 TAYLOR, HENRY. *Notes from Books, in Four Essays.* London: John Murray, 1849.

7⅞ × 4¾ in. xviii [2] 295 [5] pp. The Poetical Works of Mr. Wordsworth (from the *Quarterly Review*, November 1834), pp. 1–90; Mr. Wordsworth's *Sonnets* (from the *Quarterly Review*, December 1841), pp. 91–186.

845 Peter Brown and Dolly Cross.

Yale Literary Magazine, Conducted by the Students of Yale College, xiv (July 1849), 356–61. A parody of Wordsworth.

1850

846 *The Christian Parlor Book: Devoted to Science, Literature, and Religion.* New York: George Pratt, 1850.

9⅝ × 6¼ in. A made-up volume of several paginations. Wordsworth's Ode on Immortality, pp. 298–301 (first pagination); William Wordsworth, pp. 58–60 (second pagination).

847 FIELDS, JAMES THOMAS. Wordsworth (a poem).

Graham's Magazine, October 1850, p. 237. A clipping.

848 *Harper's New Monthly Magazine*, Vol. 1, June to November 1850. New York, 1850.

William Wordsworth (from the *London Athenaeum*), pp. 103–5; Lord Byron, Wordsworth, and Charles Lamb (from the *Autobiography of Leigh Hunt*), pp. 272–4; Wordsworth's Posthumous Poem (from the *London Examiner*), pp. 546–8; Wordsworth's prose writings, p. 559; Wordsworth—His Character and Genius, by George Gilfillan (from the *Eclectic Review*), pp. 577–84.

849 HUNT, LEIGH. *The Autobiography of Leigh Hunt, with Reminiscences of Friends and Contemporaries.* New York: Harper & Brothers, 1850, 2 vols.

7⅝ × 5 in. Vol. 1: xii [1] 14–299 [11]; vol. 2: viii [1] 10–332 [8] pp. Wordsworth, vol. 1, pp. 41, 265; vol. 2, pp. 11, 40, 239.

850 HUNTER, JOSEPH. The Old Genealogical Oak Chest in the Possession of the Poet Wordsworth.

Gentleman's Magazine, xxxiv, n.s. (July 1850), 43–4.

851 *The Literary World, a Journal of American and Foreign Literature, Science, and Art,* VI (1850).

William Wordsworth (obituary), p. 485; Wordsworth's Unpublished Poem (from De Quincey's account of *The Prelude*), pp. 565–6; Wordsworth, by Henry Reed, pp. 581–2.

852 *The Literary World, a Journal of American and Foreign Literature, Science, and Art,* VII (1850).

Passages in Advance (of *The Prelude*), pp. 167–8; Visit to Wordsworth's Grave, p. 255; Wordsworth (a poem), by E.A.W., p. 255; A Visit to Wordsworth, by J. A. Spencer, pp. 406–7; other references, pp. 237–8, 388.

853 [MUZZEY, A. B.]. Wordsworth the Christian Poet.

Christian Examiner, Boston, XLIX (July 1850), 100–10.

854 *Chambers's Edinburgh Journal,* XIII (1850).

Wordsworth the Poet (his lack of a sense of smell), p. 96; Wordsworth and His Poetry, pp. 363–6.

855 Review of *The Prelude*.

Westminster and Foreign Quarterly Review, LIV (October 1850), 271–7.

856 Review of *The Prelude*.

The Knickerbocker, XXXVI (October 1850), 373.

857 TALFOURD, THOMAS NOON. *Tragedies; to Which Are Added a Few Sonnets and Verses.* Tenth Edition. London: Edward Moxon, 1850.

$6 \times 3\frac{5}{8}$ in. xii, 276 [2] pp. On the Reception of the Poet Wordsworth at Oxford (a poem), p. 246.

858 William Wordsworth. *Chambers's Papers for the People.* Vol. 5. Edinburgh: William and Robert Chambers, 1850.

$7\frac{3}{4} \times 5$ in. 8 sections of 32 pages each, the last of which contains the article on Wordsworth.

859 William Wordsworth.

Household Words: a Weekly Journal Conducted by Charles Dickens, I (May 1850), 210–13.

860 WILLIS, NATHANIEL PARKER. *The Prose Works of N. P. Willis.* New Edition in One Volume. Philadelphia: Henry C. Baird, 1850.

10½ × 6½ in. xv [1] 798 [4] pp. Wordsworth, pp. 198–200, 729–30.

861 Review of *The Prelude.*

Gentleman's Magazine, XXXIV, n.s. (November 1850), 459–68.

1851

862 CLEVELAND, CHARLES DEXTER. *English Literature of the Nineteenth Century: on the Plan of the Author's 'Compendium of English Literature,' and Supplementary to It.* Designed for Colleges and Advanced Classes in Schools, as Well as for Private Reading. Philadelphia: E. C. & J. Biddle ..., 1851.

7½ × 4⅝ in. xvi [1] 18–746 [8] pp. Wordsworth, 549–64, 744. A parody of Wordsworth by Horace Smith, pp. 510–12.

863 [DEACON, WILLIAM FREDERICK]. *Warreniana: with Notes Critical and Explanatory*, by the Editor of the *Quarterly Review.* Boston: Ticknor, Reed, and Fields, 1851.

7⅛ × 4⅜ in. vi [3] 10–191 [3] pp. Parody of Wordsworth, pp. 24–30.

864 GILLIES, R. P. *Memoirs of a Literary Veteran; Including Sketches and Anecdotes of the Most Distinguished Literary Characters from 1794 to 1849.* London: Richard Bentley, 1851, 3 vols.

7¾ × 4⅞ in. Vol. 1: xii, 344; vol. 2: vi, 340; vol. 3: vi, 339 [1] pp. Wordsworth, vol. 2, pp. 136–73.

865 *Harper's New Monthly Magazine*, III (July 1851).

Review of Christopher Wordsworth's *Memoirs of William Wordsworth*, p. 280; Wordsworth, Byron, Scott, and Shelley, pp. 502–5.

866 *The Literary World, a Journal of American and Foreign Literature, Science, and Art*, VIII (1851).

Excerpt from the forthcoming Boston edition of Christopher Wordsworth's *Memoirs of William Wordsworth*, pp. 411–13; review of the *Memoirs*, pp. 471–3.

867 *The Literary World, a Journal of American and Foreign Literature, Science, and Art*, IX (1851).

Review (continued from vol. viii) of the *Memoirs of William Wordsworth*, pp. 24–6, 83–5; Paris Unvisited, by Carl Benson (a parody), p. 501.

868 *The Poetic Companion, for the Fireside, the Fields, the Woods, and the Streams.* Vol. 1. London: J. Passmore Edwards, 1851.

$7\frac{1}{2} \times 4\frac{7}{8}$ in. viii [1] 4–488 [10] pp. Wordsworth, pp. 168–73.

869 Review of Christopher Wordsworth's *Memoirs of William Wordsworth.*

Christian Examiner, LI (September 1851), 275–98.

870 Review of Christopher Wordsworth's *Memoirs of William Wordsworth.*

The Knickerbocker, XXXVIII (August 1851), 161.

871 Reviews of Christopher Wordsworth's *Memoirs of William Wordsworth,* and of the *Poetical Works of Wordsworth,* 1851, 6 vols.

Dublin Review, XXXI (December 1851), 312–65.

872 Review of Christopher Wordsworth's *Memoirs of William Wordsworth.*

International Monthly Magazine of Literature, Art, and Science, III (June 1851), 322.

873 W., O. W. William Wordsworth.

American Whig Review, XIV (July 1851), 68–80.

874 WALLACE, WILLIAM ROSS. *Meditations in America, and Other Poems.* New York: Charles Scribner, 1851.

$7\frac{1}{8} \times 4\frac{1}{2}$ in. vi [1] 10–143 [1] pp. Wordsworth (a poem), pp. 81–8.

875 WORDSWORTH, CHRISTOPHER. *Memoirs of William Wordsworth,* Poet-Laureate, D.C.L. London: Edward Moxon, 1851, 2 vols.

$8\frac{3}{4} \times 5\frac{1}{2}$ in. Vol. 1: xii [8] 457 [5]; vol. 2: viii, 524 [4] pp.

876 WORDSWORTH, CHRISTOPHER. *Memoirs of William Wordsworth,* Poet-Laureate, D.C.L. Edited by Henry Reed. Boston: Ticknor, Reed, and Fields, 1851, 2 vols.

$7\frac{1}{8} \times 4\frac{3}{8}$ in. Vol. 1: xvi, 472 [4]; vol. 2: viii, 518 [2] pp.

1852

877 BELFAST, FREDERICK CHICHESTER, EARL OF. *Poets and Poetry of the XIXth Century:* a Course of Lectures by the Earl of Belfast. London: Longman, Brown, Green, and Longmans, 1852.

6¾ × 4 in. xii, 283 [33] pp. Wordsworth, pp. 35–56.

878 CHEEVER, GEORGE BARRELL. *Voices of Nature to Her Foster-Child, the Soul of Man: a Series of Analogies between the Natural and the Spiritual Worlds.* Glasgow and London: William Collins, [*c.* 1852].

7¼ × 4¼ in. 343 [1] pp. Numerous references to Wordsworth. Pasted opposite the title-page is the following note: 'Given to me, when a boy of 16, (Feb. 1852). The book which started me on a study of Wordsworth. William Knight, 1876.'

879 DALLAS, ENEAS SWEETLAND. *Poetics: an Essay on Poetry.* London: Smith, Elder, and Co., 1852.

7½ × 4⅞ in. viii, 294 [18] pp. Numerous references to Wordsworth.

880 FIELDS, JAMES THOMAS. *Verdicts.* London: Effingham Wilson, 1852.

7½ × 4⅞ in. iv, 70 [2] pp. Wordsworth, pp. 43–51.

881 MITFORD, MARY RUSSELL. *Recollection of a Literary Life; or, Books, Places, and People.* London: Richard Bentley, 1852, 3 vols.

7¾ × 4¾ in. Vol. 1: xi [1] 323 [1]; vol. 2: v [1] 302; vol. 3: vii [1] 296 pp. Wordsworth, vol. 3, pp. 1–20.

882 MOIR, DAVID MACBETH. *Sketches of the Poetical Literature of the Past Half-Century,* in Six Lectures, Delivered at the Edinburgh Philosophical Association. Second Edition. Edinburgh and London: William Blackwood, 1852.

6¾ × 4⅛ in. xii, 335 [5] pp. Wordsworth, pp. 60–83.

883 [PHILLIPS, GEORGE SEARLE]. *Memoirs of William Wordsworth, Compiled from Authentic Sources; with Numerous Quotations from His Poems, Illustrative of His Life and Character.* By January Searle. London: Partridge & Oakey, 1852.

7¼ × 4¾ in. [13]–312 pp.

884 TAYLOR, BAYARD. *A Book of Romances, Lyrics, and Songs.* Boston: Ticknor, Reed, and Fields, 1852.

7 × 4⅜ in. iv, 153 [5] pp. Wordsworth (a poem), p. 152.

885 Thomas De Quincey and His Depreciation of Wordsworth.

Literary World, a Journal of American and Foreign Literature, Science, and Art, XI (November 1852), 311–12.

1853

886 AUSTIN, WILTSHIRE STANTON, AND RALPH, JOHN. *The Lives of the Poets-Laureate, with an Introductory Essay on the Title and Office.* London: Richard Bentley, 1853.

8⅜ × 5¼ in. vi [2] 428 [2] pp. Wordsworth, pp. 396–428.

887 *An Essay on the Poetry of Wordsworth.*

Reprinted from the *Wesleyan Methodist Magazine.* 6½ × 4⅛ in. 72 pp.

888 HENRY, JAMES. *My Book, Containing Minor Poems and Six Photographs of the Heroic Times, Being a Metrical Translation of the First Six Books of the Eneis.* Dresden, 1853.

8⅞ × 5½ in. [220] 313 [1] pp. Poems ridiculing Wordsworth, pp. [157–60] of the first part, which is without pagination.

889 HOLT, DAVID. *Janus, Lake Sonnets, etc., and Other Poems.* London: William Pickering, 1853.

6⅝ × 4 in. vii [1] 207 [1] pp. A Pathway at Rydal, p. 32; At the Grave of Wordsworth, p. 35.

890 LANDOR, WALTER SAVAGE. *The Last Fruit off an Old Tree.* London: Edward Moxon, 1853.

7½ × 4⅝ in. x [2] 520 [2] pp. Wordsworth, pp. 332 ff. and 450.

891 *The Literary World,* XII (1853).

A Memorial of Wordsworth, by Henry Reed, pp. 512–13; other references, pp. 208–9.

892 *The Literary World,* XIII (1853).

Wordsworth, Keats, and Charles Lamb after Dinner at Haydon's, pp. 26–7; Dr. Holmes' Lecture on Wordsworth, pp. 233–4; The Lake District in England, pp. 331–2.

SONNET, on seeing Miss HELEN MARIA WILLIAMS weep at a Tale of Distress.

SHE wept.——Life's purple tide began to
   flow
In languid streams through every thrilling
   vein;
Dim were my swimming eyes—my pulse
   beat slow,
And my full heart was swell'd to dear deli-
   cious pain.

Life left my loaded heart, and closing eye;
A sigh recall'd the wanderer to my breast;
Dear was the pause of life, and dear the
   sigh
That call'd the wanderer home, and home
   to rest.

That tear proclaims——in thee each virtue
   dwells,
And bright will shine in misery's midnight
   hour;
As the soft star of dewy evening tells
What radiant fires were drown'd by day's
   malignant pow'r,
That only wait the darkness of the night
To chear the wand'ring wretch with hospi-
   table light.

                AXIOLOGUS.

WOMAN: an EFFUSION.

THO' each gift the learned prize,
   At my wish were bade to rise;
Tho' Peru her treasures pour'd;
Tho' Great Britain hail'd me lord;
'Midst them all my soul, forlorn,
Justly would the baubles scorn,
If not woman's kisses, sighs,
Fir'd my breast, and clos'd my eyes;
Clos'd them to the paltry things,
Fit for wretches——fit for kings.
Years by countless thousands told,
'Midst ambition, pow'r, and gold,
Not one pleasure could excite,
Woman only gives delight!
O the music of her voice,
How it makes one's soul rejoice!
O the bliss her eyes inspire,
Melting sweet with soft desire!
O the joys her lips impart,
Thrilling rapture to the heart!
Woman! source of every joy,
Every moment should employ!
Life without thee were no more
Than a far and desert shore
Is to the wretch the waves have left,
Of joy, peace, comfort, hope bereft!

                RUSTICUS.

SONNET, written in WALDERSHARE WILDERNESS.

MY Daphne's lovely image here
   In Fancy's eye each scene shall chear;

Improve the flowret's glossy hues,
And people all the lawny views;
And steal into the woodland's gloom,
And all its mazy walks illume!
The liquid notes that float around,
Shall breathe the most enchanting sound:
And if a captive bird I see,
Be mine to set the trembler free.
No branch shall fade—no flowret die,
But this touch'd bosom heaves a sigh;
And all this tenderness of soul
Shall owe its source to love's controul;
To her who every thought employs,
To Daphne! mistress of my joys!
Tho' not a human voice be near,
Her image shall each scene endear.

                RUSTICUS.

LINES written on a Retired COTTAGE.

THOU Genius of this vale serene,
   Who dwell'st amidst its shades, unseen,
Shall care this beauteous seat annoy,
And damp the reign of tranquil joy?
No!—Peace, sweet nymph! inhabits here,
And leads around the happy year;
And Health, too, is a constant guest,
Delighted with the frugal feast.
O surely this retreat was giv'n,
To bless below, and lead to Heav'n!
   Thus reader, as thou wander'st here,
Will Fancy whisper to thy ear.
Ah heed not what the syren says—
Step in, and round the cottage gaze.
Well, thou hast seen the tenant's nose,
How large 'tis grown, how fierce it glows!
Its spots inlaid of various hue,
Like Parian marble to the view:
And thou hast seen his deaden'd eyes,
Whence rheums in gummy streamlets rise;
And thou hast seen the palsied hand,
The faltering voice, the soul unman'd,
These thou hast seen—and now declare,
If peace or health inhabits here?
Alas! alas! that Holland's gin
Should flow into so fair a scene.
Dover.
                RUSTICUS.

TRANSLATION of the ODE

Diffugere nives redeunt jam gramina campis.
              HOR. Lib. IV.

By Dr. JOHNSON, in Nov. 1784.

THE snow, dissolv'd, no more is seen;
   The fields and woods, behold, are
   green;
The changing year renews the plain;
The rivers know their banks again;
The sprightly nymph and naked grace
The mazy dance together trace:
The changing year's successive plan
Proclaims mortality to Man.

                   Rough

Wordsworth's First Appearance in Print, 1787.   No. 458

I think how Headley, wanderer here no more!
With eagle eye was wont thy fancls to tread,
By soft compaffion and the Mufes led,
To weave new garlands for the bards of yore,
Sorrow for him her tender tear fhall fhed,
Long as the furges lave thy pebbled fhore.

HYMN TO HEALTH
TRANSLATED.
See RAMBLER, No. XLVIII.

HEALTH, of all the heavenly powers
Faireft Goddefs, ever bleft!
Long as I count life's circling hours,
O live with me a welcome gueft!

The Monarch's crown, the golden pile,
Or joys which happy parents prove
From tender babes or wanton wile,
That baits the filken fnare of love;

Or if new blifs be fent by Heaven
To cheer the heart of man below—
If the fair fmiles of Hope be given,
All, all to thee their beauties owe!

Thy prefence pours a brighter ray
O'er every fcene—thy charms divine
Give luftre to the vernal day,
And perfeĉt happinefs is thine.

An Evening Walk. An Epiftle in Verfe, addreffed to a Young Lady from the Lakes of the North of England. By W. Wordfworth, B. A. of St. John's Cambridge. 4to. 2s. Johnfon. 1793.

A LIVING poetical writer has ob-
ferved,
" That which was formed to captivate the
eye,
" The ear muft coldly tafte; defcription's
weak,
" And the Mufe falters in the vain attempt."

To the truth of this remark we cannot refufe our affent, after comparing
fome of the beft defcriptions given by
our greateft writers with the objeĉts
defcribed. Perhaps of all the fcenes
which Great Britain can boaft as pof-
feffing fuperior beauty and grandeur,
none exceed the Englifh Alps in the
northern parts of this ifland; but of
the various defcriptions which have
been from time to time given of them,
how inadequate have the beft of them
been, and how little fatisfaĉtion have
they afforded to the reader, when com-
pared with the fenfations produced by
the beautiful originals. Mr. Wordfworth's paintings, however, do not
want force or effeĉt, and read on the
fpot, we are convinced would receive
additional advantages from the minute-
nefs and accuracy of his pencil. His
defcription of the fate of the Beggar
and her Children is very pathetically
delineated, and other parts of the poem
are intitled to praife. As a fpecimen
we fhall feleĉt the following lines:

Now while the folemn evening fhadows
fail
On red flow waving pinions down the vale,
And fronting the bright Weft in ftronger lines,
The oak its dark'ning boughs and foliage
twines,

I love befide the glowing lake to ftray,
Where winds the road along the fecret bay,
By rills that tumble down the woody fteeps,
And run in tranfport to the dimpling deeps
Along the " wild meand'ring fhore;" to view
Obfequious grace the winding fwan purfue;
He fwells his lifted cheft, and backward flings
His bridling neck between his tow'ring
wings;
Stately, and burning in his pride, divides,
And glorying looks around the filent tides;
On as he floats, the filver'd waters glow,
Proud of the varying arch and movelefs form
of fnow.
While tender cares and mild domeftic loves
With furtive watch purfue her as fhe moves,
The female with a meeker charm fucceeds,
And her brown little ones around her leads,
Nibbling the water lilies as they pafs,
Or playing wanton with the floating grafs:
She in a mother's care her beauty's pride
Forgets; unweary'd watching every fide,
She calls them near, and with affeĉtion fweet
Alternately relieves their weary feet;
Alternately * they mount her back and reft,
Clofe by her mantling wings embraces preft.

Long may ye roam thefe hermit waves
that fleep
In birch-befprinkled cliffs embofom'd deep;
Thefe fairy holms untrodden ftill and green,
Whofe fhades proteĉt the hidden wave ferene;
Whence fragrance fcents the water's defart
gale,
The violet and the lily † of the vale;
Where, tho' her far off twilight ditty fteal,
They not the trip of harmlefs milkmaid feel.

Yon tuft conceals your home, your cottage
bow'r,
Frefh-water rufhes ftrew the verdant floor,

* This is a faĉt of which I have been an eye-witnefs.
† The lily of the valley is found in great abundance in the fmaller iflands of Winan-
dermere.

Long

An Early Review of Wordsworth's First Book, 1793.　No. 588

893 *The National Magazine: Devoted to Literature, Art, and Religion*, II (January–June 1853).

A proposal to erect a memorial to Wordsworth, p. 92.

894 *The National Magazine: Devoted to Literature, Art, and Religion*, III (July–December 1853).

An Estimate of Wordsworth's Poetry, pp. 36–40.

895 QUILLINAN, EDWARD. *Poems, with a Memoir by William Johnston*. London: Edward Moxon, 1853.

Wordsworth's Home (a poem), p. 71; To the Poet (a poem), p. 101; many references in the Memoir.

896 [RICHARDSON, LADY]. William Wordsworth.

Sharpe's London Magazine, XVII (1853), 148–55.

897 ROBERTSON, FREDERICK WILLIAM. *Wordsworth: a Criticism*. London: H. R. Allenson, [*c.* 1853].

$6\frac{3}{4} \times 4\frac{1}{4}$ in. 58 [6] pp.

898 TERRINGTON, THOMAS JOHN. *Christmas at the Hall, the Hero's Grave, Night Musings, and Other Poems*. London: Longman, Green, and Longman, [*c.* 1853].

$7\frac{3}{8} \times 4\frac{3}{4}$ in. xiii [1] 196 pp. Rydal Water: Addressed to Wordsworth, p. 122.

899 TILLOTSON, JOHN. *Lives of Eminent Men: or, Biographical Treasury. Containing Memoirs of the Most Celebrated British Characters of the Past and Present Day*. Illustrated with Numerous Fine Steel Plate Portraits. London: Thomas Holmes, [*c.* 1853].

$7\frac{3}{4} \times 4\frac{1}{2}$ in. viii, 304 pp. Wordsworth, pp. 252–63.

900 WRIGHT, JOHN. *The Genius of Wordsworth Harmonized with the Wisdom and Integrity of His Reviewers*. By the Late John Wright, Author of *Poetry Sacred and Profane*. London: Longman, Brown, Green, and Longmans, 1853.

$8\frac{3}{4} \times 5\frac{3}{8}$ in. iv, 130 [2] pp.

1854

901 DIX, JOHN ROSS. *Lions: Living and Dead; or, Personal Recollections of the 'Great and Gifted.'* Second Edition. London: W. Tweedie, 1854.

6¾ × 4⅛ in. xii [1] 14–360 pp. Wordsworth, pp. 13–20.

902 GILES, HENRY. *Illustrations of Genius, in Some of Its Relations to Culture and Society.* Boston: Ticknor and Fields, 1854.

7 × 4⅜ in. 362 [12] pp. Wordsworth, pp. 239–66.

903 HOLLAND, JOHN, AND EVERETT, JAMES. *Memoirs of the Life and Writings of James Montgomery, Including Selections from His Correspondence, Remains in Prose and Verse, and Conversations on Various Subjects.* London: Longman, Brown, Green, and Longmans, 1854–6, 7 vols.

7⅝ × 4⅝ in. Vol. 1: xvi, 330 [6]; vol. 2: viii, 366 [2]; vol. 3: viii, 390 [2]; vol. 4: viii, 392; vol. 5: viii, 439 [1]; vol. 6: vii [1] 232; vol. 7: xv [1] 307 [1] pp. Several references to Wordsworth; see Index.

904 KEATS, JOHN. *The Poetical Works of John Keats, with a Memoir by James Russell Lowell.* New York: James Miller, [1854].

6¾ × 4⅜ in. v [2] 8–340 [2] pp. References to Wordsworth in Lowell's Memoir.

905 TALFOURD, THOMAS NOON. *Critical and Miscellaneous Writings of T. Noon Talfourd,* Author of *Ion.* Third American Edition. With Additional Articles Never Before Published in This Country. Boston: Phillips, Sampson, and Co., 1854.

9⅜ × 5⅝ in. iv [1] 6–176 pp. On the Genius and Writings of Wordsworth, pp. 47–59.

906 [QUINCY, EDMUND]. *Wensley: a Story without a Moral.* Boston: Ticknor and Fields, 1854.

7 × 4¼ in. [4] 302 [12] pp. Wordsworth, pp. 105–6.

1855

907 MAGINN, WILLIAM. *The Odoherty Papers, by the Late William Maginn, LL.D.* Annotated by Dr. Shelton Mackenzie. Vol. II. New York: Redfield, 1855.

7¼ × 4⅞ in. vi [1] 8–383 [15] pp. Parodies of Wordsworth, pp. 55–9, 263.

908 REED, HENRY. *Lectures on English Literature, from Chaucer to Tennyson*. Third Edition, Revised and Corrected. Philadelphia: Parry and McMillan, 1855.

7 × 4¼ in. xxiii [2] 26–411 [3] pp. Numerous references to Wordsworth throughout.

909 Review of the *Poetical Works of Wordsworth*, Boston, 1854.

Christian Examiner, LVIII (January 1855), 154.

910 WILSON, JOHN (CHRISTOPHER NORTH). *The Works of Professor Wilson of the University of Edinburgh*, Edited by His Son-in-Law Professor Ferrier. Edinburgh and London: William Blackwood and Sons, 1855–8, 12 vols.

7½ × 4⅞ in. Vol. 1: xxviii, 384 [16]; vol. 2: xiv, 428 [4]; vol. 3: xii [1] 382 [2]; vol. 4: xi [1] 368; vol. 5: vi [2] 408 [16]; vol. 6: [6] 397 [1]; vol. 7: [8] 431 [1]; vol. 8: [8] 459 [1]; vol. 9: [8] 440; vol. 10: iv, 433 [9]; vol. 11: [10] 557 [1]; vol. 12: vii [1] 560 [8] pp. Numerous references to Wordsworth. See especially vol. 5, pp. 387–403; vol. 10, pp. 53–74; vol. 4, Index.

1856

911 EMERSON, RALPH WALDO. *English Traits*. Boston: Phillips, Sampson and Co., 1856.

7⅜ × 4½ in. 312 [2] pp. Wordsworth, pp. 256, 293–7.

912 HOOD, EDWIN PAXTON. *William Wordsworth; a Biography*. London: W. and F. G. Cash; Edinburgh: John Menzies; Dublin: Hodges & Smith, 1856.

7½ × 4½ in. ix [3] 508 [2] pp.

913 LEE, SAMUEL ADAMS. Wordsworth's and Tennyson's Portraiture of Woman.

Illustrated Waverley Magazine and Literary Repository, XII (May 1856), 340–1.

914 WALLACE, HORACE BINNEY. *Literary Criticisms and Other Papers*. By the Late Horace Binney Wallace. Philadelphia: Parry & McMillan, 1856.

7¾ × 5 in. vi, 460 [2] pp. Coleridge, Davy, Southey, and Wordsworth, pp. 330–55.

1857

915 ABELL, MRS. L. G. *The Young Ladies' Reticule; or, Gems by the Way-side. An Offering of Purity and Truth.* Boston: Higgins, Bradley & Dayton, 1857.

$6\frac{3}{4} \times 4\frac{3}{8}$ in. vii [2] 10–256. Personal reminiscence of Wordsworth, pp. 39–41.

916 GASKELL, MRS. ELIZABETH CLEGHORN. *The Life of Charlotte Brontë.* New York: D. Appleton and Co., 1857, 2 vols.

$7\frac{1}{4} \times 4\frac{1}{2}$ in. Vol. 1: viii, 285 [9]; vol. 2: viii, 269 [13] pp. Branwell Brontë's letter to Wordsworth, vol. 1, pp. 133–5.

917 GOODRICH, SAMUEL GRISWOLD. *Recollections of a Lifetime, or Men and Things I Have Seen: in a Series of Familiar Letters to a Friend, Historical, Biographical, Anecdotal, and Descriptive.* New York and Auburn: Miller, Orton, and Mulligan, 1857, 2 vols.

$7\frac{7}{8} \times 4\frac{7}{8}$ in. Vol. 1: 542 [2]; vol. 2: 563 [5] pp. Wordsworth, vol. 2, pp. 102–3.

918 KNIGHT, HELEN CROSS. *Life of James Montgomery.* Boston: Gould and Lincoln, 1857.

$7\frac{5}{8} \times 4\frac{5}{8}$ in. x [1] 12–416 [16] pp. References to Wordsworth, pp. 128–30, 297–300, 349–51, 365–6.

919 Notes on Note-Worthies of Divers Orders, Either Sex, and Every Age, by Sir Nathaniel: VI. William Wordsworth.

Colburn's New Monthly Magazine, CIX (April 1857), 379–92.

920 REED, HENRY. *Lectures on the British Poets.* London: Sampson, Low, Son, and Co.; Philadelphia: Parry & McMillan, 1857, 2 vols.

$7\frac{1}{4} \times 4\frac{1}{2}$ in. Vol. 1: 328; vol. 2: 312 [24] pp. Wordsworth, vol. 2, pp. 199–231.

921 REED, HENRY. *Lectures on the British Poets.* London: John Farquhar Shaw, 1857.

$7\frac{3}{8} \times 4\frac{3}{4}$ in. viii, 408 pp. Wordsworth, pp. 335–56.

1858

922 TRELAWNY, EDWARD JOHN. *Recollections of the Last Days of Shelley and Byron.* London: Edward Moxon, 1858.

$7\frac{1}{2} \times 4\frac{1}{2}$ in. viii, 304 pp.

1859

923 *Catalogue of the Varied and Valuable Historical, Poetical, Theological, and Miscellaneous Library, of the Late Venerated Poet-Laureate, William Wordsworth, Esquire, D.C.L.,* Last, not Least, of the Line of Lake Minstrels; Comprising Works of Ancient and Modern Continental Authors & Commentators; Curious and Rare Editions of Old English Worthies, in Black Letter and Other Early Typography; and an Extensive Aggregation of Later Lucubrations and the Productions of Contemporary Celebrities; Numbering Together Nearly Three Thousand Volumes: Also a Fine Gallery Picture, by L. Giordano: Which Will Be Sold by Auction, by Mr. John Burton (of Preston) at That Haunt of Hallowed Memories, Rydal Mount, Near Ambleside, Windermere, on Tuesday the 19th, Wednesday the 20th, and Thursday the 21st days of July 1859; at Eleven O'Clock 'Fore Noon Each Day;— in Pursuance of Instructions from the Executors.... Preston: Printed by Charles Ambler, [1859].

$8\frac{1}{2} \times 5\frac{1}{4}$ in. [4] 59 [1] pp.

924 HEY, REBECCA. *Holy Places, and Other Poems.* London: Hatchard and Co., 1859.

$6\frac{5}{8} \times 4\frac{1}{8}$ in. xii, 163 [1] 4, 32 pp. On Visiting Wordsworth's Grave in Grasmere Churchyard, 1850, pp. 105-7.

925 PARKER, THEODORE. *Theodore Parker's Experience as a Minister, with Some Account of His Early Life, and Education for the Ministry; Contained in a Letter from Him to the Members of the Twenty-eighth Congregational Society of Boston.* Boston: Rufus Leighton, Jr., 1859.

$8 \times 4\frac{7}{8}$ in. v [2] 8-182 [6] pp. Wordsworth, p. 52.

1861

926 CHURTON, EDWARD. *Memoir of Joshua Watson.* Oxford and London: J. H. and Jas. Parker, 1861, 2 vols.

$7\frac{3}{4} \times 4\frac{7}{8}$ in. Vol. 1: xii, 333 [3]; vol. 2: vi, 327 [17] pp. Several references to Wordsworth; see Index.

927 CRAIK, GEORGE LILLIE. *A Compendious History of English Literature, and of the English Language, from the Norman Conquest. With Numerous Specimens.* London: Griffin, Bohn, and Co., 1861, 2 vols.

$8\frac{5}{8} \times 5\frac{1}{2}$ in. Vol. 1: xvii [3] 593 [3]; vol. 2: x [2] 556 [4] pp. Wordsworth, vol. 2, pp. 435-56.

928 LANDRETH, P. *Studies and Sketches in Modern Literature: Periodical Contributions.* Edinburgh: William Oliphant and Co.; London: Hamilton, Adams, and Co., 1861.

7½ × 5 in. vi [2] 433 [7] pp. Wordsworth's *Peter Bell*, pp. 135–43.

1862

929 GORDON, MARY WILSON. *'Christopher North,' a Memoir of John Wilson. Compiled from Family Papers and Other Sources by His Daughter Mrs. Gordon.* Edinburgh: Edmonston and Douglas, 1862.

7⅝ × 5 in. Vol. 1: xii [4] 335 [25]; vol. 2: ix [3] 399 [1] pp. Several references Wordsworth; see Index.

930 KENT, W. CHARLES. *Dreamland, with Other Poems.* London: Longman, Green, Longman, and Roberts, 1862.

6¾ × 4 in. xvii [1] 244 p. Wordsworth at Rydal (a poem), pp. 97–100.

1863

931 BROWNING, ELIZABETH BARRETT. *Essays on the Greek Christian Poets and the English Poets.* New York: James Miller, 1863.

6⅝ × 4⅛ in. 233 [7] pp. Wordsworth, pp. 214–33.

932 DE QUINCEY, THOMAS. *Recollections of the Lakes and the Lake Poets, Coleridge, Wordsworth, and Southey.* Edinburgh: Adam and Charles Black, 1863.

7⅜ × 4⅞ in. vi [2] 244 pp.

933 RUSHTON, WILLIAM. *On the Classical and Romantic Schools of English Literature as Represented by Spenser, Dryden, Pope, Scott, and Wordsworth.* The Afternoon Lectures on English Literature, Delivered in the Theatre of the Museum of Industry, S. Stephen's Green, Dublin, in May and June, 1863. London: Bell and Daldy, ... 1863.

6⅝ × 4 in. xi [1] 252 pp.

934 WHEWELL, WILLIAM. *The Elements of Morality, Including Polity.* New York: Harper & Brothers, 1863, 2 vols.

6½ × 4⅛ in. Vol. 1: xxvi [1] 28–401 [7]; vol. 2: xxi [2] 26–424 [4] pp. This work was dedicated to Wordsworth, 14 April 1845.

935 WORDSWORTH, CHRISTOPHER. *Journal of a Tour in Italy, with Reflections on the Present Condition and Prospects of Religion in That Country.* Second Edition. London: Rivingtons, 1863, 2 vols.

$7\frac{3}{4} \times 4\frac{3}{4}$ in. Vol. 1: cxvi [2] 309 [3]; vol. 2: xii, 353 [3] pp.

1864

936 KNIGHT, CHARLES. *Passages of a Working Life During Half a Century: with a Prelude of Early Reminiscences.* London: Bradbury & Evans, 1864–5, 3 vols.

$7\frac{3}{4} \times 4\frac{3}{4}$ in. Vol. 1: xi [6] 18–346; vol. 2: [4] 336; vol. 3: [4] 344 pp. Wordsworth, vol. 1, 206, 221; vol. 3, 27–9.

937 Wordsworth: the Man and the Poet.

Living Age, LXXXIII (October 1864), 51–80. Reprinted from the *North British Review,* XLI (August 1864), 1–54.

1865

938 *The Home of William Wordsworth.* London: John Walker, [c. 1865].

$6 \times 7\frac{1}{4}$ in., oblong. [14] pp.

939 Review of the *Works of Wordsworth,* Boston, 1864, 7 vols.

North American Review, CCVI (April 1865), 508–21.

940 ROBERTSON, FREDERICK WILLIAM. *Life, Letters, Lectures, and Addresses of Fredk. W. Robertson.* New York: Harper & Brothers, [c. 1865].

$7\frac{1}{2} \times 4\frac{3}{4}$ in. xxiii [2] 26–840 [2] pp. Wordsworth, pp. 805–35.

941 Two Poets of England [Wordsworth and Landor].

Temple Bar, XVI (December 1865), 106–16.

1866

942 CALVERT, GEORGE HENRY. *First Years in Europe.* Boston: William V. Spencer, 1866.

$7 \times 4\frac{1}{2}$ in. vi [3] 10–303 [9] pp. A few references to Wordsworth, *passim.*

943 JERDAN, WILLIAM. *Men I Have Known.* Illustrated with Facsimile Autographs. London and New York: George Routledge and Sons, 1866.

7¾ × 4¾ in. [2] ix [1] 490 [2] pp. Wordsworth, pp. 474–86.

1867

944 ALGER, WILLIAM ROUNSEVILLE. *The Solitudes of Nature and of Man; or, the Loneliness of Human Life.* Boston: Roberts Brothers, 1867.

7 × 4½ in. xii [3] 20–412 [2] pp. Wordsworth, pp. 277–89.

945 '*Bibliomania.*' Edinburgh: Edmonston and Douglas, 1867.

6⅝ × 4½ in. Reprinted from the *North British Review.* Contains an account of Wordsworth's copy of *Scriptores de Re Rustica*, Paris, 1543, now a part of this Collection (No. 2226).

946 MILL, JOHN STUART. *Dissertations and Discussions: Political, Philosophical, and Historical.* Boston: William V. Spencer, 1867–8, 4 vols.

7⅞ × 5⅛ in. Vol. 1: viii [2] 425 [5]; vol. 2: [2] 415 [3]; vol. 3: [2] 391 [3]; vol. 4: [2] 460 [4] pp. Thoughts on Poetry and Its Varieties, vol. 1, pp. 89–120.

947 SOUTHEY, CAROLINE BOWLES. *The Poetical Works. Collected Edition.* Edinburgh and London: William Blackwood and Sons, 1867.

6¼ × 4 in. vii [1] 304 [16] pp.

1868

948 BUCHANAN, ROBERT. *David Gray, and Other Essays, Chiefly on Poetry.* London: Sampson, Low, Son, and Marston, 1868.

7 × 4¾ in. vi [2] 318 [28] pp. References to Wordsworth in the first and last essays.

949 *Catalogue of the Third and Concluding Exhibition of National Portraits Commencing with the Fortieth Year of the Reign of George the Third and Ending with the Year MDCCCLXVII, on Loan to the South Kensington Museum.* London: Printed by Strangeways and Walden, 1868.

9⅞ × 7¼ in. [10] 209 [1] pp. Contains descriptions of paintings of Wordsworth and Coleridge.

950 CHANNING, WILLIAM ELLERY. *Memoir of William Ellery Channing, with Extracts from His Correspondence and Manuscripts.* Ninth Edition. Boston: American Unitarian Association, 1868, 3 vols.

$7\frac{1}{2} \times 4\frac{1}{2}$ in. Vol. 1: xiii [1] 427 [3]; vol. 2: vi, 459 [3]; vol. 3: vi, 494 [4] pp. Wordsworth, vol. 2, pp. 95–7, 207–20.

1869

951 CLOUGH, ARTHUR HUGH. *The Poems and Prose Remains of Arthur Hugh Clough, with a Selection from His Letters and a Memoir Edited by His Wife.* Vol. I: Life, Letters, Prose Remains. London: Macmillan and Co., 1869.

$7\frac{1}{4} \times 4\frac{7}{8}$ in. [8] 426 [2] pp. Wordsworth, pp. 307–25.

952 FORSTER, JOHN. *Walter Savage Landor; a Biography.* Boston: Fields, Osgood, & Co., 1869.

$7\frac{7}{8} \times 5\frac{1}{4}$ in. v [3] 693 [5] pp. Numerous references to Wordsworth; see Index.

953 GRAVES, ROBERT PERCEVAL. *Recollections of Wordsworth and the Lake Country.* Lectures on Literature and Art. Delivered in the Theatre of the Royal College of Science, S. Stephen's Green, Dublin. Dublin: William McGee; London: Simpkin, Marshall, and Co., [1869].

$6\frac{1}{2} \times 4$ in. [4] 348 pp.

954 LEIGH, HENRY SAMBROOKE. *Carols of Cockayne.* With Numerous Illustrations by Alfred Concanen and the Late John Leech. London: John Camden Hotten, 1869.

$7\frac{1}{4} \times 5\frac{1}{4}$ in. xiii [2] 10–207 [9] pp. Only Seven: a Pastoral Story after Wordsworth, pp. 47–8.

955 MACDONALD, GEORGE. *England's Antiphon.* n.p.: J. B. Lippincott & Co., and Macmillan & Co., [1869].

$7\frac{1}{4} \times 4\frac{3}{4}$ in. viii, 332 pp. Wordsworth, pp. 255–6.

956 MARTINEAU, HARRIET. *Biographical Sketches.* London: Macmillan and Co., 1869.

$7\frac{3}{8} \times 4\frac{3}{4}$ in. ix [3] 445 [97] pp. Mrs. Wordsworth, pp. 402–8.

957 *The Old College, Being the Glasgow University Album for MDCCCLXIX.*
Edited by Students. Glasgow: James Maclehose, 1869.

8⅝ × 6⅝ in. [10] 360 pp. William Wordsworth, pp. 243–59; Notes on a
Lecture by George MacDonald, pp. 290–305.

958 WELLS, THORNTON. *Poems.* London: Longman, Green, and
Co., 1869.

7⅝ × 4⅛ in. viii, 131 [1] pp. Wordsworth, p. 45.

1870

959 ARNOLD, THOMAS. *Chaucer to Wordsworth: a Short History of
English Literature, from the Earliest Times to the Present Day.* London:
Thomas Murby, [1870].

6¼ × 3⅞ in. xv [1] 454 [2] pp. Wordsworth, pp. 396–403.

960 *Chambers's Papers for the People.* London and Edinburgh: William
and Robert Chambers, 1870.

7⅝ × 4⅞ in. 16 separate paginations of 32 pages each. The eighth article,
Paper No. 40, is on Wordsworth.

961 MACKENZIE, ROBERT SHELTON. *Life of Charles Dickens.
With Personal Recollections and Anecdotes, Letters by 'Boz,' Never Before
Published, and Uncollected Papers in Prose and Verse. With Portrait and
Autograph.* Philadelphia: T. B. Peterson & Brothers, [1870].

7¼ × 4¾ in. 479 [31] pp. Wordsworth, pp. 243–4.

962 MASSON, ROSALINE. *Wordsworth* (The People's Books).
London: T. C. & E. C. Jack, ... [c. 1870].

6⅜ × 4¼ in. iii [1] 5–94 pp.

963 REED, HENRY. *Lectures on the British Poets.* Philadelphia:
Claxton, Remsen, & Haffelfinger, 1870, 2 vols.

6⅝ × 4¼ in. Vol. 1: 328 [2]; vol. 2: 312 [2] pp. Wordsworth, vol. 2, pp. 197–
228.

964 WHITTIER, JOHN GREENLEAF. *The Poetical Works.* Complete Edition. Boston: Fields, Osgood, & Co., 1870.

5⅜ × 3⅞ in. xi [1] 430 [4] pp. Wordsworth: Written on a Blank Leaf of His
Memoirs (a poem), pp. 198–9.

1871

965 A Century of Great Poets from 1750 Downwards. No. III: William Wordsworth.

Blackwood's Edinburgh Magazine, cx (September 1871), 299–326.

966 *Cues from All Quarters; or, the Literary Musings of a Clerical Recluse.* Boston: Roberts Brothers, 1871.

6¾ × 4½ in. [6] 340 [2] pp. Wordsworth, pp. 296–309 and elsewhere.

967 METEYARD, ELIZA. *A Group of Englishmen (1795 to 1815), Being Records of the Younger Wedgwoods and Their Friends, Embracing the History of the Discovery of Photography, and a Facsimile of the First Photograph.* London: Longmans, Green, and Co., 1871.

8¾ × 5½ in. xxii, 416 [24] pp. Several references to Wordsworth; see Index.

968 PALGRAVE, FRANCIS TURNER. *Lyrical Poems.* London and New York: Macmillan and Co., 1871.

6¾ × 4½ in. William Wordsworth (a poem), pp. 127–9.

969 PORTER, NOAH. *Books and Reading; or, What Books Shall I Read and How Shall I Read Them?* New York: Charles Scribner & Co., 1871.

7¾ × 5 in. viii, 378 [8] pp. Wordsworth, *passim*.

970 REID, WILLIAM B. *Among My Books.* Second Edition. New York: E. J. Hale & Son, 1871.

6½ × 4¼ in. 270 [6] pp. Henry Reed, pp. 256–70.

971 ROBINSON, HENRY CRABB. *Diary, Reminiscences, and Correspondence.* Selected and Edited by Thomas Sadler. Boston: James R. Osgood and Co., 1871, 2 vols.

7½ × 4¾ in. Vol. 1: xxiii [1] 496 [2]; vol. 2: vi, 555 [3] pp. Numerous references to Wordsworth; see Index.

972 WORDSWORTH, CHRISTOPHER. *The Maccabees and the Church, or the History of the Maccabees Considered with Reference to the Present Condition and Prospects of the Church.* Two Sermons Preached before the University of Cambridge. By Chr. Wordsworth, D.D., Bishop of Lincoln. London, Oxford, and Cambridge: Rivingtons, 1871.

6¾ × 4⅝ in. [6] 85 [37] pp.

973 YOUNG, JULIAN CHARLES. *A Memoir of Charles Mayne Young, Tragedian, with Extracts from His Son's Journal.* London and New York: Macmillan and Co., 1871, 2 vols.

$7\frac{3}{8} \times 4\frac{3}{4}$ in. Vol. 1: xviii [2] 374 [2]; vol. 2: ix [3] 368 pp. Wordsworth and Coleridge, vol. 1, pp. 171–85.

974 YOUNG, JULIAN CHARLES. *A Memoir of Charles Mayne Young, Tragedian, with Extracts from His Son's Journal.* Second Edition. London and New York: Macmillan and Co., 1871.

$7\frac{1}{8} \times 4\frac{3}{4}$ in. xvi, 476 pp. Wordsworth and Coleridge, pp. 117–24.

1872

975 COOPER, THOMAS. *The Life of Thomas Cooper, Written by Himself.* Third Thousand. London: Hodder and Stoughton, 1872.

$7\frac{1}{8} \times 5\frac{1}{4}$ in. viii, 400 pp. Interview with Wordsworth in 1846, pp. 285–95.

976 DE MORGAN, AUGUSTUS. *A Budget of Paradoxes.* London: Longmans, Green, and Co., 1872.

$8\frac{3}{4} \times 5\frac{1}{2}$ in. vii [1] 511 [49] pp. Wordsworth and Byron, p. 435.

977 FIELDS, JAMES THOMAS. *Yesterdays with Authors.* London: Sampson, Low, Marston, Low, and Searle, 1872.

$7\frac{3}{8} \times 4\frac{3}{4}$ in. [8] 352 [2] pp. Wordsworth, pp. 253–60.

978 ROBERTS, LOUIS A. *High Art: Pictures from the Poets, and Other Notions.* Springfield, Mass.: D. E. Fisk & Co., 1872.

$8\frac{3}{8} \times 5\frac{1}{2}$ in. 65 leaves, foliated. Wordsworth, p. 58.

979 Wordsworth Impartially Weighed.

Temple Bar, xxxiv (February 1872), 310–30.

980 YOUNGE, CHARLES DUKE. *Three Centuries of English Literature.* New York: D. Appleton and Co., 1872.

$7\frac{1}{4} \times 4\frac{7}{8}$ in. xxi [1] 649 [3] pp. Wordsworth, pp. 251–67.

1873

981 COLERIDGE, SIR JOHN DUKE. Wordsworth.

Macmillan's Magazine, xxviii (August 1873), 289–302.

982 DEVEY, JOSEPH. *A Comparative Estimate of Modern English Poets.* London: E. Moxon, Son, and Co., 1873.

7½ × 5 in. vii [1] 421 [1] pp. Wordsworth, pp. 87–103.

983 HAMERTON, PHILIP GILBERT. *The Intellectual Life.* Boston: Roberts Brothers, 1873.

7⅞ × 4⅞ in. xix [1] 455 [3] pp. Several references to Wordsworth; see Index.

984 MILL, JOHN STUART. *Autobiography.* London: Longmans, Green, Reader, and Dyer, 1873.

8¼ × 5 in. vi, 313 [3] pp. Wordsworth, pp. 146–50.

985 MORLEY, HENRY. *A First Sketch of English Literature.* Fourth Edition. London, Paris, and New York: Cassell Petter & Galpin, [1873].

7 × 4½ in. viii, 914 [10] pp. Wordsworth, pp. 866, 867, 870–3, 876, 878–81, 885–8, 890, 892.

986 SHERWEN, JOHN, AND COGAN, THOMAS. *Old Age in Bath: Recollections of Two Retired Physicians, Dr. John Sherwen and Dr. Thomas Cogan; to Which Are Added a Few Unpublished Remains of William Wordsworth, the Poet, and Joseph Hunter, F.S.A., by Dr. Henry Julian Hunter.* Bath: William Lewis, 1873.

6 × 3¾ in. viii, 75 [3] pp. Wordsworth, pp. 57–75.

987 TAINE, HIPPOLYTE ADOLPHE. *History of English Literature.* Translated from the French by H. Van Laun. Complete in One Volume. New York: John Wurtele Lovell, 1873.

7¼ × 4¾ in. 722 [2] pp. Wordsworth, pp. 523, 532–5.

1874

988 BACKUS, TRUMAN JAY. *Shaw's New History of English Literature.* Prepared on the Basis of *Shaw's Manual.* New York: Sheldon and Co., [1874].

7¼ × 4¾ in. xv [2] 6–404 [6] pp. Wordsworth, pp. 318–22.

989 [CHAMBERS, WILLIAM]. William and Dorothy Wordsworth.

Chambers's Journal of Popular Literature, Science, and Art, 15 August 1874, pp. 514–16.

990 LAMB, MARY AND CHARLES. *Mary and Charles Lamb: Poems, Letters, and Remains: Now First Collected, with Reminiscences and Notes,* by W. Carew Hazlitt. With Portrait, and Numerous Facsimiles and Illustrations of Their Favourite Haunts in London and the Suburbs. London: Chatto and Windus, 1874.

$7\frac{1}{2} \times 4\frac{3}{4}$ in. 307 [1] 31 [49] pp. Numerous references to Wordsworth, *passim.*

991 MASSON, DAVID. *Wordsworth, Shelley, Keats, and Other Essays.* London: Macmillan and Co., 1874.

$7\frac{1}{4} \times 5$ in. 305 [1] pp.

992 PATER, WALTER HORATIO. On Wordsworth.

Fortnightly Review, xv, n.s. (April 1874), 455–65.

993 WORDSWORTH, DOROTHY. *Recollections of a Tour Made in Scotland A.D. 1803.* Edited by J. C. Shairp. Second Edition. Edinburgh: Edmonston and Douglas, 1874.

$7\frac{3}{8} \times 4\frac{7}{8}$ in. 1, 316 [6] pp. Inlaid is an undated letter from J. C. Shairp concerning his article on Coleridge.

994 WORDSWORTH, DOROTHY. *Recollections of a Tour Made in Scotland A.D. 1803.* Edited by J. C. Shairp. Second Edition. New York: G. P. Putnam's Sons, 1874.

$7 \times 4\frac{1}{2}$ in. xlviii, 316 [6] pp.

See also Sara Coleridge, *Memoir and Letters* (No. 1805).

1875

995 BROOKE, STOPFORD AUGUSTUS. *Theology in the English Poets: Cowper, Coleridge, Wordsworth, and Burns.* New York: D. Appleton and Co., 1875.

$7\frac{3}{4} \times 4\frac{7}{8}$ in. vii [3] 339 [13] pp. Wordsworth, pp. 93–286.

996 DE VERE, SIR AUBREY. *Sonnets.* A New Edition. London: Basil Montagu Pickering, 1875.

$6\frac{3}{4} \times 4\frac{1}{8}$ in. xix [1] 104 pp. Dedicated to Wordsworth. Rydal with Wordsworth (a poem), p. 37.

997 FLETCHER, ELIZA. *Autobiography of Mrs. Fletcher, with Letters and Other Family Memorials.* Edited by the Survivor of Her Family. Edinburgh: Edmonston and Douglas, 1875.

7½ × 5 in. xi [1] 377 [3] pp. Wordsworth, pp. 78–9, 213–14, 227–9, 243–9, 264–5, 282–5.

998 GOSTWICK, JOSEPH. *English Poets: Twelve Essays.* With Twelve Portraits. New York: Stroefer & Kirchner, 1875.

8½ × 6⅜ in. [6] 229 [5] pp. Wordsworth, pp. 137–56.

999 MACBETH, JOHN WALKER VILANT. *The Might and Mirth of Literature: a Treatise on Figurative Language, in Which Upwards of Six Hundred Writers Are Referred to, and Two Hundred and Twenty Figures Illustrated.* New York: Harper and Brothers, 1875.

7¾ × 5 in. liv, 542 [4] pp.

1000 MARTIN, THEODORE. *The Life of His Royal Highness the Prince Consort.* New York: D. Appleton and Co., 1875–82, 5 vols.

7⅝ × 4⅞ in. Vol. 1: [4] 420 [14]; vol. 2: [4] 464 [6]; vol. 3: [4] 432 [2]; vol. 4: [4] 424 [10]; vol. 5: [4] 433 [11] pp. Wordsworth's Installation Ode, vol. 1, pp. 319–22.

1876

1001 FANSHAWE, CATHERINE MARIA. *The Literary Remains of Catherine Maria Fanshawe, with Notes by the Late Rev. William Harkness.* London: Basil Montagu Pickering, 1876.

6¾ × 4¼ in. viii, 79 [1] pp. Imitation of Wordsworth, pp. 69–71.

1002 *The Girlhood of Celebrated Women, Women of Worth, and the Mothers of the Bible.* Two Volumes in One, Illustrated. New York: World Publishing House, 1876.

6¾ × 4⅜ in. Vol. 1: viii [1] 10–302; vol. 2: [10] 335 [9] pp. Mrs. Wordsworth, vol. 1, pp. 267–71.

1003 GOSTWICK, JOSEPH. *English Poets: Twelve Essays.* London: Frederick Bruckmann, 1876.

8½ × 6⅜ in. [6] 229 [3] pp. Wordsworth, pp. 135–56.

1004 [HARE, AUGUSTUS WILLIAM AND JULIUS CHARLES]. *Guesses at Truth, by Two Brothers.* New Edition. London: Macmillan and Co., 1876.

$6\frac{1}{8} \times 4$ in. [5] x–liv [2] 576 pp. This book, first published in 1826, is dedicated to Wordsworth and contains many brief references to him.

1005 HAYDON, BENJAMIN ROBERT. *The Life, Letters, and Table Talk of Benjamin Robert Haydon* (Sans-Souci Series). Edited by Richard Henry Stoddard. New York: Scribner, Armstrong, and Co., 1876.

$6\frac{5}{8} \times 4\frac{5}{8}$ in. xxxiii [5] 311 [5] pp. Wordsworth, pp. 189–202.

1006 HAYDON, BENJAMIN ROBERT. *Benjamin Robert Haydon: Correspondence and Table-talk.* With a Memoir by His Son, Frederic Wordsworth Haydon. With Facsimile Illustrations from His Journals. London: Chatto and Windus, 1876, 2 vols.

$8\frac{3}{4} \times 5\frac{3}{8}$ in. Vol. 1: xix [5] 469 [1]; vol. 2: [8] 484 [24] pp. Correspondence with Wordsworth, vol. 2, pp. 18–59.

1007 HUTTON, RICHARD HOLT. *Essays in Literary Criticism.* Philadelphia: Porter & Coates, 1876.

$7\frac{1}{8} \times 4\frac{5}{8}$ in. xi [1] 355 [3] pp. Wordsworth, pp. 180–226.

1008 JENKINS, OLIVER LOUIS. *The Student's Handbook of British and American Literature, Containing Sketches Biographical and Critical of the Most Distinguished English Authors, from the Earliest Times to the Present Day, with Selections from Their Writings, and Questions Adapted to the Use of Schools.* Baltimore: John Murphy & Co., 1876.

$7\frac{1}{4} \times 4\frac{1}{2}$ in. xxiii [2] 26–564 [2] pp. Wordsworth, pp. 346–50.

1009 PAUL, C. KEGAN. *William Godwin: His Friends and Contemporaries,* by C. Kegan Paul, with Portraits and Illustrations. London: Henry S. King & Co., 1876, 2 vols.

$7\frac{3}{4} \times 5\frac{3}{8}$ in. Vol. 1: viii, 387 [1]; vol. 2: viii, 340. Wordsworth, vol. 2, pp. 8, 78–9, 218–20.

1010 Review of *The Prose Works of William Wordsworth,* ed. Alexander Grosart, 1876, 3 vols.

Quarterly Review, CXLI (January 1876), 104–36.

1011 STEPHEN, LESLIE. *Hours in a Library* (Second Series). London: Smith, Elder, & Co., 1876.

$7\frac{5}{8} \times 4\frac{3}{4}$ in. [6] 393 [1] pp. A few slight references to Wordsworth.

WE ARE SEVEN.

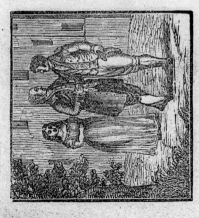

A simple Child, dear brother Tim,
That lightly draws its breath,
And feels its life in every limb,
What should it know of death?

FRONTISPIECE.

Whene'er I take my walks abroad,
How many poor I see!
What shall I render to my God
For all his gifts to me?

THE

LITTLE MAID

AND

The Gentleman;

OR,

WE ARE SEVEN.

EMBELLISHED WITH ENGRAVINGS.

YORK:

Printed by J. Kendrew, 23, Colliergate.

Chapbook Versions of *We Are Seven*. Nos. 57 and 111

S. Hutchinson

𝔓𝔬𝔢𝔪𝔰,

BY

S. T. COLERIDGE.

Felix curarum, cui non Heliconia cordi
Serta, nec imbelles Parnassi e vertice laurus!
Sed viget ingenium, et magnos accinctus in usus
Fert animus quascunque vices.——Nos tristia vitæ
Solamur cantu.

STAT. SILV. Lib. iv. 4.

THIRD EDITION.

LONDON:
Printed by N. Biggs, Crane-court, Fleet-street,
FOR T. N. LONGMAN AND O. REES, PATER-
NOSTER-ROW.

1803.

Sara Hutchinson's Copy of Coleridge's *Poems.*   No. 1722

1012 STODDARD, RICHARD HENRY (ED.). *Personal Reminiscences by Constable and Gillies* (Bric-a-Brac Series). New York: Scribner, Armstrong, and Co., 1876.

$6\frac{5}{8} \times 4\frac{3}{4}$ in. xxx [3] 34–336 [10] pp. Slight references to Wordsworth, pp. 229, 295–6, and elsewhere.

1013 Wordsworth's Ethics.

Cornhill Magazine, xxxiv (August 1876), 206–26.

1877

1014 BENNOCH, FRANCIS. *Poems, Lyrics, Songs, and Sonnets.* London: Hardwicke and Bogue, 1877.

$6\frac{1}{4} \times 3\frac{7}{8}$ in. xx [4] 400 [2] pp. To Wordsworth (a poem), p. 331, and a reference to Wordsworth, pp. vii–viii.

1015 BOWRING, SIR JOHN. *Autobiographical Recollections of Sir John Bowring, with a Brief Memoir by Lewin B. Bowring.* London: Henry S. King & Co., 1877.

$8\frac{3}{4} \times 5\frac{5}{8}$ in. viii, 401 [7] pp. Wordsworth, pp. 60, 356.

1016 BRADFORD, JOHN STRICKER. *Autumn Winds, and Other Poems.* New York: Robert M. Malcolm, 1877.

$7\frac{3}{8} \times 4\frac{1}{2}$ in. [2] 132 [4] pp. Charade (Words-worth), pp. 81–2.

1017 BROWNING, ELIZABETH BARRETT. *Letters of Elizabeth Barrett Browning Addressed to Richard Hengist Horne, with Comments on Contemporaries*, ed. S. R. Townshend Mayer. London: Richard Bentley and Son, 1877, 2 vols.

8×5 in. Vol. 1: viii [2] 272; vol. 2: [6] 296 pp. Wordsworth, vol. 2, pp. 35–42.

1018 COAN, TITUS MUNSON. Wordsworth's Corrections.

The Galaxy, xxiii (March 1877), 322–36.

1019 DOYLE, SIR FRANCIS HASTINGS. *Lectures on Poetry, Delivered at Oxford.* Second Series. London: Smith, Elder, & Co., 1877.

$7\frac{3}{4} \times 5\frac{1}{4}$ in. xiv, 292 pp. Wordsworth, pp. 1–77.

1020 *Every Man His Own Poet; or, the Inspired Singer's Recipe Book. By a Newdigate Prizeman.* Third Edition, Enlarged. London: Simpkin, Marshall, & Co.; Oxford: Thos. Shrimpton & Son, 1877.

$6\frac{3}{8} \times 4\frac{1}{8}$ in. 31 [1] pp. Wordsworth satirized, pp. 8–9.

1021 HALL, SAMUEL CARTER. *A Book of Memories of Great Men and Women of the Age, from Personal Acquaintance.* Second Edition. London: Virtue and Co., 1877.

$9 \times 6\frac{1}{2}$ in. xiv [2] 495 [1] pp. Wordsworth, pp. 289–319.

1022 [JAPP, ALEXANDER HAY]. *Thomas De Quincey: His Life and Writings, with Unpublished Correspondence.* By H. A. Page. New York: Scribner, Armstrong, & Co., 1877, 2 vols.

$7\frac{1}{4} \times 4\frac{3}{4}$ in. Vol. 1: viii, 398 [4]; vol. 2: vi, 362 [2] pp. Many references to Wordsworth; see Index.

1023 MASON, JAMES. *The Great Triumphs of Great Men.* London and Edinburgh: William P. Nimmo, 1877.

$7\frac{1}{8} \times 4\frac{5}{8}$ in. [4] 608 pp. Wordsworth, pp. 194–7.

1024 PROCTER, BRYAN WALLER. *Bryan Waller Procter (Barry Cornwall): an Autobiographical Fragment and Biographical Notes, with Personal Sketches of Contemporaries, Unpublished Lyrics, and Letters of Literary Friends.* Boston: Roberts Brothers, 1877.

$7\frac{1}{8} \times 4\frac{3}{4}$ in. xiv, 306 [2] pp. Wordsworth, pp. 137–44.

1025 SHAIRP, JOHN CAMPBELL. *On Poetic Interpretation of Nature.* New York: Hurd and Houghton, 1877.

$7 \times 4\frac{1}{2}$ in. x, 279 [1] pp. Wordsworth, pp. 235–79.

1026 TICKNOR, GEORGE. *Life, Letters, and Journals of George Ticknor.* Sixth Edition. Boston: James R. Osgood and Co., 1877, 2 vols.

$8\frac{3}{4} \times 5\frac{3}{4}$ in. Vol. 1: viii, 524 [2]; vol. 2: vi, 533 [3] pp. Numerous references to Wordsworth; see Index.

1878

1027 CALVERT, GEORGE HENRY. *Wordsworth: a Biographic Aesthetic Study.* Boston: Lee and Shepard; New York: Charles T. Dillingham, 1878.

$6\frac{5}{8} \times 4\frac{3}{8}$ in. [4] 232 [2] pp.

1028 CLARKE, CHARLES AND MARY COWDEN. *Recollections of Writers. With Letters of Charles Lamb, Leigh Hunt, Douglas Jerrold, and Charles Dickens; and a Preface by Mary Cowden Clarke.* New York: Charles Scribner's Sons, [1878].

$7\frac{1}{4} \times 4\frac{5}{8}$ in. viii, 347 [7] pp. Wordsworth, pp. 149–50.

1029 DOWDEN, EDWARD. The Text of Wordsworth's Poems.

Contemporary Review, xxxiii (November 1878), 734–57.

1030 EDMONDS, HERBERT. *Well-Spent Lives: a Series of Modern Biographies.* London: C. Kegan Paul & Co., 1878.

$7\frac{3}{8} \times 4\frac{7}{8}$ in. vi [2] 398 [66] pp. Wordsworth, pp. 1–29.

1031 FLEMING, CHARLES. *Poems, Songs, and Essays, by the Late Charles Fleming, Weaver in Paisley, with Memoir and Notes, by Robert Brown, of Underwood Park.* Paisley: J. & J. Cook, 1878.

$8\frac{1}{2} \times 5\frac{3}{8}$ in. xxviii [1] 10–327 [1] pp. To Wordsworth on His Being Appointed Poet Laureate, p. 78.

1032 REED, HENRY. *Lectures on English Literature, from Chaucer to Tennyson.* Sixth Edition, Revised and Corrected. Philadelphia: Claxton, Remsen, & Haffelfinger, 1878.

$6\frac{3}{4} \times 4\frac{5}{8}$ in. xxiii [2] 411 [1] pp. Numerous references to Wordsworth throughout.

1033 ROSSETTI, WILLIAM MICHAEL. *Lives of Famous Poets.* A Companion Volume to the Series, Moxon's Popular Poets. London: E. Moxon, Son, & Co., 1878.

$7\frac{1}{2} \times 4\frac{7}{8}$ in. xii [2] 406 [2] pp. Wordsworth, pp. 203–18 and elsewhere.

1879

1034 ADAMS, WILLIAM DAVENPORT. *Dictionary of English Literature, Being a Comprehensive Guide to English Authors and Their Works.* New and Revised Edition. London, Paris, and New York: Cassell Petter & Galpin, [c. 1879].

$8\frac{1}{2} \times 6\frac{1}{8}$ in. iv, 708 pp. Wordsworth, p. 700.

1035 BAGEHOT, WALTER. *Literary Studies*. London: Longmans, Green, and Co., 1879.

8½ × 5¼ in. Vol. 1: lxvii [1] 406; vol. 2: [4] 444 pp. Wordsworth, Tennyson, and Browning, vol. 1, pp. 338–90.

1036 DESHLER, CHARLES D. *Afternoons with the Poets*. New York: Harper & Brothers, 1879.

7⅜ × 5⅝ in. [2] vi [3] 8–320 [4] pp. Several references to Wordsworth; see Index.

1037 GODWIN, MARY WOLLSTONECRAFT. *Letters to Gilbert Imlay, with a Prefatory Memoir by C. K. Paul*. Boston: Roberts Brothers, 1879.

7¼ × 4¾ in. lxiii [1] 207 [1] pp. Indirect light on Wordsworth without specific mention of him.

1038 HAMILTON, WALTER. *The Poets Laureate of England, Being a History of the Office of Poet Laureate, Biographical Notices of Its Holders, and a Collection of the Satires, Epigrams, and Lampoons Directed against Them*. London: Elliot Stock, 1879.

7⅜ × 4⅞ in. xxv [3] 308 pp. Wordsworth, pp. 243–62.

1039 JEFFREY, FRANCIS. *Contributions to the Edinburgh Review, by Francis Jeffrey, Now One of the Judges of the Court of Session in Scotland*. Four Volumes in One. New York: D. Appleton and Co., 1879.

9¼ × 5¾ in. xii [1] 14–762 [8] pp. Wordsworth, pp. 457–72.

1040 KNIGHT, WILLIAM ANGUS. *Studies in Philosophy and Literature*. London: C. Kegan Paul & Co., 1879.

7½ × 5 in. xx, 426 pp. Wordsworth, pp. 283–317, 405–26.

1041 Richard Henry Dana.

Harper's New Monthly Magazine, LVIII (April 1879), 769–76. Discusses Wordsworth and his influence on Bryant.

1042 MARTINEAU, HARRIET. *Harriet Martineau's Autobiography*. Edited by Maria Weston Chapman. Fourth Edition. Boston: Houghton, Osgood, and Co., 1879, 2 vols.

8⅝ × 5⅝ in. Vol. 1: x [2] 594 [4]; vol. 2: vi [2] 596 [2] pp. Wordsworth, vol. 1, pp. 502–12.

1043 STEPHEN, LESLIE. *Hours in a Library* (Third Series). London: Smith, Elder, & Co., 1879.

$7\frac{3}{8} \times 4\frac{7}{8}$ in. viii, 408 pp. Wordsworth, pp. 178–229.

1044 SYMONDS, JOHN ADDINGTON. Matthew Arnold's Selections from Wordsworth.

Fortnightly Review, XXVI, n.s. (November 1879), 686–701.

1045 WORDSWORTH, CHRISTOPHER. *Ten Addresses at the Triennial Visitation of the Cathedral Church and Diocese of Lincoln in October 1879*, by Christopher Wordsworth, D.D., Bishop of Lincoln. Lincoln: James Williamson; London, Oxford, and Cambridge: Rivingtons, 1879.

$7\frac{1}{4} \times 4\frac{7}{8}$ in. xvi, 167 [1] lvi [2] pp.

1046 WORDSWORTH, CHRISTOPHER. *Miscellanies Literary and Religious.* London, Oxford, and Cambridge: Rivingtons, 1879.

$8\frac{5}{8} \times 5\frac{1}{2}$ in. Vol. 1: xvi, 493 [3]; vol. 2: xii, 433 [3]; vol. 3: xvi, 483 [1] pp. Presentation copy signed, 'C. Lincoln.' Inserted is a letter of 7 February 1882 to Mrs. Gainsford from Susanna H. Wordsworth, wife of Christopher.

1880

1047 CAIRD, EDWARD. Wordsworth.

Fraser's Magazine, CXXII, n.s. (February 1880), 205–21.

1048 CAIRD, EDWARD. Wordsworth.

Littell's Living Age, XXX (April 1880), 88–98.

1049 CLAPP, WILLIAM W. *Joseph Dennie: Editor of the Port Folio and Author of The Lay Preacher.* Not Published. Cambridge: John Wilson and Son, 1880.

$9 \times 5\frac{3}{4}$ in. 41 [1] pp. Dennie, who died in 1812, first publicized Wordsworth in America.

1050 CORKRAN, ALICE. *The Poet's Corner, or Haunts and Homes of the Poets.* Illustrated by Allan Barraud, with Introduction by Fred E. Weatherly. London: Ernest Nister; New York: E. P. Dutton, [*c.* 1880].

$7\frac{1}{2} \times 6\frac{1}{2}$ in. [64] pp. Printed in Nuremberg.

1051 *Grace Darling; Her True Story.* From Unpublished Papers in Possession of Her Family. London: Hamilton, Adams, & Co., 1880.

7 × 2⅜ in. [2] 74 [6] pp. See Nos. 121, 125.

1052 Milton and Wordsworth.

Temple Bar, LX (September 1880), 106–15.

1053 Milton and Wordsworth.

Library Magazine of Select Foreign Literature, Vol. V. New York: American Book Exchange, ... 1880, pp. 356–63. 6¼ × 4⅜ in. vii [1] 401 [3] pp. The article cited is reprinted from *Temple Bar.*

1054 SWINTON, WILLIAM. *Studies in English Literature, Being Typical Selections of British and American Authorship, from Shakespeare to the Present Time, together with Definitions, Notes, Analyses, and Glossary as an Aid to Systematic Literary Study.* For Use in High and Normal Schools, Academies, Seminaries, &c. New York: Harper & Brothers, 1880.

7⅞ × 5⅝ in. xxxiii [1] 638 [4] pp. Wordsworth, pp. 289–301.

1055 WEBSTER, E. HEDGE. *Clover Blossoms.* Engravings by E. Hedge Webster. Boston: Printed by W. G. Crawford, [*c.* 1880].

7¾ × 5 in. vii [2] 10–224 [2] pp. An Evening with Wordsworth, pp. 177–8.

1056 WORDSWORTH, BARBARA. *Jacob's Ladder.* With Musical Illustrations by Arthur Henry Brown. London: Wyman & Sons, 1880.

8¼ × 6½ in. [4] 173 [3] pp.

1881

1057 BAYNE, PETER. *Two Great Englishwomen: Mrs. Browning & Charlotte Brontë; with an Essay on Poetry, Illustrated from Wordsworth, Burns, and Byron.* London: James Clarke & Co., 1881.

7⅜ × 4⅞ in. lxxviii [2] 340 pp.

1058 BEDFORD, EDWIN JACKSON. *Genealogical Memoranda Relating to the Family of Wordsworth.* London: Privately Printed, 1881.

10¾ × 8¼ in. 27 [1] pp. Limited to fifty copies.

1059 CARLYLE, THOMAS. *Reminiscences.* Edited by James Anthony Froude. New York: Charles Scribner's Sons, 1881.

7¾ × 5 in. x [2] 536 [6] pp. Wordsworth, pp. 513–36.

1060 FIELDS, JAMES THOMAS. *Ballads and Other Verses*. Boston: Houghton, Mifflin, and Co., 1881.

$6\frac{7}{8} \times 4\frac{1}{8}$ in. vi [1] 133 [9] in. With Wordsworth at Rydal, pp. 66-7.

1061 MYERS, FREDERIC WILLIAM HENRY. *Wordsworth* (English Men of Letters). New York: John Wurtele Lovell, 1881.

$7\frac{1}{2} \times 4\frac{3}{4}$ in. 120 pp.

1062 SHAIRP, JOHN CAMPBELL. *Aspects of Poetry*. Oxford: Clarendon Press, 1881.

8×5 in. xi [1] 464 pp. The Three Yarrows, pp. 316-44; The White Doe of Rylstone, pp. 345-76.

1063 SOUTHEY, ROBERT. *The Correspondence of Robert Southey with Caroline Bowles. To Which Are Added: Correspondence with Shelley, and Southey's Dreams*. Edited, with an Introduction, by Edward Dowden. Dublin: Hodges, Figgis, & Co.; London: Longmans, Green, & Co., 1881.

$9 \times 5\frac{1}{2}$ in. xxxii, 388 [24] pp. Numerous references to Wordsworth; see Index.

1064 SYMINGTON, ANDREW JAMES. *William Wordsworth: a Biographical Sketch, with Selections from His Writings in Poetry and Prose*. Boston: Roberts Brothers, [*c.* 1881], 2 vols.

$6\frac{1}{2} \times 4\frac{1}{4}$ in. Vol. 1: xii [1] 14-256 [2]; vol. 2: x [1] 12-256 [2] pp.

1882

1065 BRIMLEY, GEORGE. *Essays*. Edited by William George Clark. Third Edition. London: Macmillan and Co., 1882.

$7 \times 4\frac{5}{8}$ in. xiv [4] 327 [1] pp. Wordsworth, pp. 102-83.

10 6 CAINE, THOMAS HENRY HALL. *Recollections of Dante Gabriel Rossetti*. London: Elliot Stock, 1882.

8×5 in. xiii [1] 297 [3] pp. Wordsworth, pp. 146-53. Inserted is a manuscript poem to Rossetti, signed, 'T. H. Hall Caine, May 12, 1880.'

1067 FOX, CAROLINE. *Memories of Old Friends, Being Extracts from the Journals and Letters of Caroline Fox of Penjerrick, Cornwall, from 1835 to 1871*. Edited by Horace N. Pym. London: Smith, Elder, & Co., 1882.

$10\frac{3}{8} \times 7$ in. xxvii [1] 355 [1] pp. Several references to Wordsworth; see Index.

1068 GRAVES, ROBERT PERCEVAL. *Life of Sir William Rowan Hamilton ... Including Selections from His Poems, Correspondence, and Miscellaneous Writings.* Dublin: Hodges, Figgis, & Co.; London: Longmans, Green, & Co., 1882–9, 3 vols.

$8\frac{7}{8} \times 5\frac{1}{2}$ in. Vol. 1: xviii [2] 698 [50]; vol. 2: xv [1] 719 [3]; vol. 3: xxxv [1] 673 [3] pp. Numerous references to Wordsworth; see Indexes.

1069 MACDONALD, GEORGE. *Orts.* London: Sampson, Low, Marston, Searle, Rivington, 1882.

$6\frac{7}{8} \times 4\frac{1}{2}$ in. vi [2] 312 [64]. Wordsworth, pp. 245–63.

1070 MATHESON, A. Sonnets after Coppée: To William Wordsworth.

Journal of Education, London, IV, n.s. (April 1882), 126.

1071 OLIPHANT, MRS. MARGARET. *The Literary History of England in the End of the Eighteenth and Beginning of the Nineteenth Century.* London: Macmillan and Co., 1882, 3 vols.

$8\frac{5}{8} \times 5\frac{1}{2}$ in. Vol. 1: viii, 395 [1]; vol. 2: vi, 405 [3]; vol. 3: [4] 392 pp. Numerous references to Wordsworth; see Index.

1072 PHELPS, AUSTIN. *Men and Books, or Studies in Homiletics, Lectures Introductory to the Theory of Preaching.* New York: Charles Scribner's Sons, 1882.

$8 \times 4\frac{7}{8}$ in. xi [1] 354 [8] pp. Several references to Wordsworth; see Index.

1073 Reviews of *Poems of Wordsworth Chosen and Edited by Matthew Arnold*, 1880; and of *Wordsworth et La Poésie Moderne d'Angleterre, par Ed. Scherer*, 1881.

Quarterly Review, CLIV (July 1882), 53–82.

1074 SHAIRP, JOHN CAMPBELL. *Aspects of Poetry, Being Lectures Delivered at Oxford.* Boston: Houghton, Mifflin, and Co., 1882.

$7 \times 4\frac{1}{2}$ in. x, 401 [5] pp. Wordsworth, pp. 270–322.

1075 SHAIRP, JOHN CAMPBELL. *Studies in Poetry and Philosophy.* Fifth Edition. Boston: Houghton, Mifflin, and Co., 1882.

$7 \times 4\frac{1}{2}$ in. xvii [3] 340 [2] pp. Wordsworth, pp. 1–89.

1076 SHAIRP, JOHN CAMPBELL. *On Poetic Interpretation of Nature.* Boston: Houghton, Mifflin, and Co., 1882.

7 × 4½ in. x [1] 12–279 [3] pp. Wordsworth, pp. 235–79.

1077 *Transactions of the Wordsworth Society*, No. 1. n.p., [1882].
8¾ × 5¼ in. 16 pp.

1078 *Transactions of the Wordsworth Society*, No. 2. n.p., [c. 1882].
8¾ × 5⅜ in. 44 pp.

1079 *Transactions of the Wordsworth Society*, No. 3. n.p., [c. 1882].
8¾ × 5¼ in. 76 pp.

1079a *Transactions of the Wordsworth Society*, No. 4. n.p., [c. 1882].
8½ × 5 in. 77–91 [1] pp.

1883

1080 CAINE, THOMAS HENRY HALL. *Cobwebs of Criticism: a Review of the First Reviewers of the ' Lake,' ' Satanic,' and ' Cockney' Schools.* London: Elliot Stock, 1883.

8 × 5⅛ in. xxiv, 266 [6] pp. Wordsworth, pp. 3–29.

1081 CARLYLE, THOMAS, AND EMERSON, RALPH WALDO. *The Correspondence of Thomas Carlyle and Ralph Waldo Emerson 1834–1872.* Boston and New York: Houghton, Mifflin, and Co., [1883–4], 2 vols.

7¾ × 4⅞ in. Vol. 1: xv [3] 399 [3]; vol. 2: xiii [3] 422 [2] pp. Wordsworth, vol. 2, p. 190.

1082 COTTERILL, HENRY BERNARD, AND ROLLESTON, THOMAS WILLIAM. *Ueber Wordsworth und Walt Whitman.* Zwei Vorträge gehalten vor dem Literarischen Verein zu Dresden. Dresden: Carl Tittmann, 1883.

9⅛ × 5¾ in. 68 [2] pp.

1083 DE QUINCEY, THOMAS. *Literary Reminiscences; from the Autobiography of an English Opium-Eater.* Boston: Houghton, Mifflin, and Co., [c. 1883].

7¼ × 4¾ in. 712 [2] pp. Vol. 3 of the Riverside Edition of De Quincey's *Works.* Numerous references to Wordsworth, throughout.

1084 GILCHRIST, ANNE. *Mary Lamb*. London: W. H. Allen & Co., 1883.

7¼ × 4¾ in. xii, 255 [1] pp. Several references to Wordsworth, *passim*.

1085 HALL, SAMUEL CARTER. *Retrospect of a Long Life: from 1815 to 1883*. New York: D. Appleton and Co., 1883.

8 × 5¼ in. v [1] 612 [6] pp. Wordsworth, pp. 324–8.

1086 MACDONALD, GEORGE. *The Imagination, and Other Essays*. Chicago: Interstate Publishing Co. 1883.

7¼ × 4¾ in. 6, 312 pp. Wordsworth, pp. 245–63.

1087 MALLESON, FREDERICK AMADEUS. Wordsworth and the Duddon: a Holiday Study.

Good Words, 1883, pp. 573–81.

1088 MALLESON, FREDERICK AMADEUS. Wordsworth and the Duddon.

Choice Literature, a Monthly Magazine, ii (November 1883), 418–32.

1089 PEDDER, HENRY C. Wordsworth and the Modern Age.

The Manhattan, an Illustrated Monthly Magazine, ii (December 1883), 270–5.

1090 PIÑEYRO, ENRIQUE. *Poetas Famosos del Siglo XIX Sus Vidas y Sus Obras*. Madrid, Libreria Gutenberg, 1883.

9 × 5⅜ in. [10] 366 [2] pp. Wordsworth, pp. 114–22.

1091 ST. JOHN, CYNTHIA MORGAN. Scrapbook entitled: *Wordsworth Floral Album*.

13½ × 11 in. A collection of flowers, ferns, and grasses, collected in the Lake District in the summer of 1883, with photographs of the places where they were gathered.

1092 THWING, CHARLES FRANKLIN. *The Reading of Books, Its Pleasures, Profits, and Perils*. Boston: Lee and Shepard; New York: Charles T. Dillingham, 1883.

6¾ × 4½ in. [3] 170 [4] pp. Wordsworth, p. 79.

1093 *Transactions of the Wordsworth Society*, No. 5. Edited by the Hon. Secretary. n.p., [*c.* 1883].

9 × 5½ in. [4] 132 [8] pp.

1094 WELLINGTON, CARRIE L. FISHER. *Leaflets along the Pathway of Life*. Collected and Dedicated to Her Friends as a Tribute of Sisterly Affection by Sarah C. Fisher. For Private Distribution. Boston: Copyrighted by Austin C. Wellington, 1883.

$6\frac{3}{4} \times 4\frac{3}{4}$ in. xi [1] 274 [2] pp. Wordsworth (a sonnet), p. 40.

1095 WELSH, ALFRED HIX. *Development of English Literature and Language*. Third Edition. Chicago: S. C. Griggs and Co., 1883.

$8\frac{1}{4} \times 5\frac{1}{2}$ in. xx, 560 [2] pp. Wordsworth, vol. 2, pp. 330–8.

1884

1096 BREWER, EBENEZER COBHAM. *Authors and Their Works, with Dates, Being the Three Appendices to 'The Reader's Handbook,'* by the Rev. E. Cobham Brewer. London: Chatto and Windus, 1884.

$7\frac{1}{4} \times 4\frac{7}{8}$ in. [4] [1133]–1399. Wordsworth, p. 1357.

1097 BRUNSWICK, ALFRED. *Wordsworth's Theorie der poetischen Kunst*. Inaugural-Dissertation zur Erlangung der Philosophischen Doktorwürde genehmigt von der Philosophischen Fakultät der Vereinigten Friedrichs-Universität Halle-Wittenberg. Halle, 1884.

$7\frac{7}{8} \times 4\frac{1}{2}$ in. 34 [2] pp.

1098 *Constitution of the Wordsworth Society*. n.p., [c. 1884].

$9\frac{1}{8} \times 5\frac{1}{2}$ in. 4 pp. Accompanying the leaflet is an eight-page List of Members.

1099 COURTHOPE, WILLIAM JOHN. Wordsworth's Theory of Poetry.

National Review, IV (December 1884), 512–27.

1100 CROSS, JOHN WALTER. *George Eliot's Life as Related in Her Letters and Journals*, Arranged and Edited by Her Husband J. W. Cross, with Illustrations. New York: Harper & Brothers, 1884.

$7\frac{1}{4} \times 4\frac{1}{2}$ in. Vol. 1: ix [5] 366 [4]; vol. 2: [12] 324 [2]; vol. 3: [12] 340 [6] pp. Wordsworth, vol. 3, p. 280.

1101 DURFEE, CHARLES AUGUSTUS. *A Concise Poetical Concordance to the Principal Poets of the World, Embracing Titles, First Lines, Characters, Subjects, and Quotations*. New York: John B. Alden, 1884.

$7\frac{1}{4} \times 4\frac{3}{4}$ in. [2] 639 [3] pp.

1102 HUDSON, HENRY NORMAN. *Studies in Wordsworth; Culture and Acquirement; Ethics of Tragedy; and Other Papers.* Boston: Little, Brown, and Co., 1884.

$7\frac{5}{8} \times 4\frac{7}{8}$ in. vii [1] 351 [3] pp.

1103 LOWELL, JAMES RUSSELL. *Among My Books.* Second Series. Ninth Edition. Boston: Houghton, Mifflin, and Co., 1884.

$7\frac{1}{2} \times 4\frac{3}{4}$ in. [8] 327 [3] pp. Wordsworth, pp. 201–51.

1104 SHAIRP, JOHN CAMPBELL. Wordsworth and Natural Religion.

Good Words, 1884, pp. 307–13.

1105 SWINBURNE, ALGERNON CHARLES. Wordsworth and Byron.

Nineteenth Century, xv (April 1884), 582–609.

1106 *Transactions of the Wordsworth Society,* No. 6. Edited by the Hon. Secretary. n.p., [c. 1884].

$8\frac{7}{8} \times 5\frac{1}{2}$ in. iv [5] 10–257 [5] pp.

1107 WATTS, ALARIC ALFRED. *Alaric Watts; a Narrative of His Life, by His Son, Alaric Alfred Watts, with Portraits.* London: Richard Bentley and Son, 1884, 2 vols.

$7\frac{1}{2} \times 4\frac{7}{8}$ in. Vol. 1: viii, 349 [1]; vol. 2: vi, 342 [6] pp. Wordsworth and Coleridge, vol. 1, pp. 235–47, 281–93.

1885

1108 CARNE, JOHN. *John Carne Letters 1813–1837.* Privately Printed, 1885.

$7 \times 4\frac{3}{4}$ in. xxiv, 286 [2] pp. Wordsworth, pp. 133–8. J. Dykes Campbell's copy.

1109 COURTHOPE, WILLIAM JOHN. *The Liberal Movement in English Literature.* London: John Murray, 1885.

$7 \times 4\frac{5}{8}$ in. xiv [2] 240 [32] pp. Wordsworth's Theory of Poetry, pp. 71–108.

1110 MAGINN, WILLIAM. *Miscellanies: Prose and Verse.* Edited by R. W. Montagu. London: Sampson, Low, Marston, Searle, & Rivington, 1885, 2 vols.

$7\frac{1}{2} \times 4\frac{5}{8}$ in. Vol. 1: xix [1] 373 [3]; vol. 2: vi, 384 pp. Wordsworth, vol. 1, pp. 89–91, 140–3.

1111 MASON, EDWARD TUCKERMAN. *Personal Traits of British Authors: Wordsworth, Coleridge, Lamb, Hazlitt, Leigh Hunt, Procter.* With Portraits. New York: Charles Scribner's Sons, 1885.

$7\frac{3}{8} \times 4\frac{3}{4}$ in. xi [1] 295 [3] pp. Wordsworth, pp. 9–54.

1112 TAYLOR, HENRY. *Autobiography of Henry Taylor 1800–1875.* New York: Harper & Brothers, 1885, 2 vols.

$7\frac{3}{8} \times 4\frac{3}{4}$ in. Vol. 1: ix [1] 307 [1]; vol. 2: vii [1] 287 [3] pp. Wordsworth, vol. 1, pp. 147–50, 156–8, 275–9; vol. 2, pp. 47–53.

1113 *Transactions of the Wordsworth Society*, No. 7. Edited by the Hon. Secretary. n.p., [*c.* 1885].

$8\frac{3}{4} \times 5\frac{1}{2}$ in. [2] iv [5] 10–129 [5] pp.

1114 TUTIN, JOHN RAMSDEN. *Wordsworth in Yorkshire.* n.p., 1885.

$6\frac{3}{4} \times 4\frac{1}{4}$ in. A home-made book consisting of a printed title-page followed by six pages of mounted clippings from the Wakefield Free Press for 25 April and 2 May 1885.

1886

1115 [CALVERLEY, C. S.]. *Fly Leaves, with Additions from the Author's Earlier Volume of 'Verses and Translations'* (Leisure Hour Series). Fourth Edition. New York: Henry Holt and Co., 1886.

$6\frac{1}{2} \times 4\frac{1}{4}$ in. iv [2] 249 [1] pp. Slight references to Wordsworth, pp. 121–33.

1116 CHAMPLIN, EDWIN ROSS. *Heart's Own Verses.* Chicago: Charles H. Kerr & Co., 1886.

$6\frac{7}{8} \times 4\frac{5}{8}$ in. v [6] 12–69 [1] pp. Wordsworth (a poem), p. 53.

1117 COAN, TITUS MUNSON. Wordsworth's Passion.

New Princeton Review, 1 (May 1886), 297–319.

1118 JOHNSON, CHARLES FREDERICK. Wordsworth.

Temple Bar, LXXVII (July 1886), 336–55.

1119 LEE, EDMUND. *Dorothy Wordsworth: the Story of a Sister's Love.* London: James Clarke & Co., 1886.

$7\frac{1}{2} \times 4\frac{3}{4}$ in. xi [3] 214 [2] pp.

1120 NICHOLSON, CORNELIUS. *Wordsworth and Coleridge: Two Parallel Sketches.* A Lecture, Delivered at Ambleside, June, 1886. Published by Special Request of the Audience, 1886.

$8\frac{1}{2} \times 5\frac{1}{2}$ in. 28 pp.

1121 CARLYLE, THOMAS. *Early Letters of Thomas Carlyle.* Edited by Charles Eliot Norton. London and New York: Macmillan and Co., 1886.

$7\frac{1}{4} \times 4\frac{5}{8}$ in. viii [2] 363 [1] pp. Wordsworth, pp. 267, 294.

1122 NOEL, RODEN. *Essays on Poetry and Poets.* London: Kegan Paul, Trench, & Co., 1886.

$8\frac{5}{8} \times 5\frac{1}{2}$ in. viii [2] 356 [16] pp. Wordsworth, pp. 132–49, and elsewhere.

1123 RUSSELL, ADDISON PEALE. *Library Notes.* New Edition, Revised and Enlarged. Eighth Edition. Boston: Houghton, Mifflin, and Co., 1886.

$7\frac{1}{2} \times 4\frac{3}{4}$ in. [6] 402 [2] pp. Numerous references to Wordsworth; see Index.

1124 RUSSELL, PERCY. *The Literary Manual; or, a Complete Guide to Authorship.* London: London Literary Society, 1886.

$7\frac{1}{8} \times 4\frac{3}{4}$ in. viii, 234 [10] pp. Wordsworth mentioned, pp. 57–8.

1125 SANBORN, KATHERINE ABBOTT. *The Vanity and Insanity of Genius.* New York: George J. Coombes, 1886.

$6\frac{7}{8} \times 4\frac{1}{2}$ in. xiv [4] 198 [6] pp. Several references to Wordsworth; see Index.

1126 SWINBURNE, ALGERNON CHARLES. *Miscellanies.* New York: Worthington Co., 1886.

$7\frac{1}{4} \times 4\frac{3}{4}$ in. x [2] 390 [4] pp. Wordsworth and Byron, pp. 63–156.

1127 *Transactions of the Wordsworth Society*, No. 8. Edited by the Hon. Secretary. n.p., [c. 1886].

$8\frac{3}{4} \times 5\frac{5}{8}$ in. [2] vi [3] 10–202 [2] pp.

1887

1128 AINGER, ALFRED. Coleridge's Ode to Wordsworth.

Macmillan's Magazine, LVI (June 1887), 81–7.

1129 AXON, WILLIAM E. A. Wordsworth in London.

Manchester Quarterly, VI (October 1887), 310–13.

1130 BURROUGHS, JOHN. *Birds and Poets, with Other Papers.* Eighth Edition. Boston: Houghton, Mifflin, and Co., 1887.

6⅝ × 4¾ in. iv [5]–263 [29] pp. Wordsworth mentioned and quoted, *passim*.

1131 BYRON, LORD. *The Letters of Lord Byron.* Edited, with Introduction, by Mathilde Blind. London: Walter Scott, 1887.

6¾ × 4¾ in. xvi, 346 [3] pp. Wordsworth, pp. 112, 115, 129, 176, 185, 216, 244, and elsewhere.

1132 DE VERE, AUBREY. *Essays, Chiefly on Poetry.* London and New York: Macmillan and Co., 1887, 2 vols.

7 × 4⅝ in. Vol. 1: [12] 314 [2]; vol. 2: [8] 295 [3] pp. The Genius and Passion of Wordsworth, vol. 1, pp. 101–73; The Wisdom and Truth of Wordsworth's Poetry, vol. 1, pp. 174–264; Recollections of Wordsworth, vol. 2, 275–95.

1133 DOWDEN, EDWARD. *Studies in Literature 1789–1877.* Fourth Edition. London: Kegan Paul, Trench, & Co., 1887.

7⅞ × 5 in. xii, 523 [1] pp. Wordsworth, pp. 10–15, 65–9, 122–58. Tipped in is a letter from Dowden to Cynthia Morgan St. John, dated from Dublin, 21 June 1890.

1134 *The Eagle*, a Magazine Supported by Members of St. John's College, Vol. XIV. Cambridge: E. Johnson, 1887.

Wordsworth, pp. 244, 252.

1135 HALE, EDWARD EVERETT. *Standard Biographies: Lights of Two Centuries.* Illustrated with Fifty Portraits. New York, Cincinnati, and Chicago: American Book Co., [1887].

8 × 5½ in. [4] iv, 603 [5] pp. Wordsworth, pp. 449–60.

1136 KNIGHT, WILLIAM ANGUS (ED.). *Memorials of Coleorton, Being Letters from Coleridge, Wordsworth and His Sister, Southey, and Sir Walter Scott to Sir George and Lady Beaumont of Coleorton, Leicestershire,*

1803 to 1834. Edited, with Introduction and Notes, by William Knight. Edinburgh: David Douglas, 1887, 2 vols.

7½ × 4⅝ in. Vol. 1: xlvi [2] 227 [1]; vol. 2: vii [1] 294 pp.

1137 KNIGHT, WILLIAM ANGUS (ED.). *Memorials of Coleorton, Being Letters from Coleridge, Wordsworth and His Sister, Southey, and Sir Walter Scott to Sir George and Lady Beaumont of Coleorton, Leicestershire, 1803 to 1834.* Edited, with Introduction and Notes, by William Knight. Boston and New York: Houghton, Mifflin, and Co., 1887, 2 vols.

7⅝ × 4¾ in. Vol. 1: xlvi [2] 227 [1]; vol. 2: vii [1] 294 pp.

1138 LINDSAY, LADY CAROLINE BLANCHE. Some Recollections of Miss Margaret Gillies.

Temple Bar, LXXXI (October 1887), 265–73. Miss Gillies painted both Wordsworth and his wife.

1139 LOWELL, JAMES RUSSELL. *Democracy, and Other Addresses.* Boston and New York: Houghton, Mifflin, and Co., 1887.

7 × 4⅝ in. vi, 245 [29] pp. Address as president of the Wordsworth Society, pp. 135–56.

1140 MATHEWS, WILLIAM. *Men, Places, and Things.* Chicago: S. C. Griggs and Co., 1887.

7⅞ × 4⅞ in. viii, 386 [2] pp. Wordsworth, p. 91.

1141 MORTIMER, JOHN. Wordsworth on Beggars.

Manchester Quarterly, VI (October 1887), 314–23.

1142 MYERS, FREDERIC WILLIAM HENRY. *Wordsworth* (English Men of Letters). New York: Harper & Brothers, [1887].

7⅜ × 4¾ in. vi, 182 [6] pp.

1143 NOBLE, JAMES ASHCROFT. *Verses of a Prose Writer.* Edinburgh: David Douglas, 1887.

7 × 4¾ in. xii [2] 141 [9] pp. Couplet to Wordsworth, p. [115].

1144 NODAL, JOHN H. Recent Work on Wordsworth.

Manchester Quarterly, VI (October 1887), 297–309.

1145 OWEN, FRANCES MARY. *Essays and Poems*. London: John Bumpus, 1887.

7⅞ × 4⅞ in. [8] 252 [4] pp. Wordsworth, pp. 44–60, 132–62.

1146 PARK, JOHN. *A Greenockian's Visit to Wordsworth*. From Journals of Late Reverend Dr Park of St. Andrews. Greenock, 1887.

8⅛ × 5 in. 18 [2] pp.

1147 SUTHERLAND, JAMES MIDDLETON. *William Wordsworth: the Story of His Life, with Critical Remarks on His Writings*. London: Elliot Stock, 1887.

7⅛ × 4¾ in. xiv, 225 [1] pp.

1148 TROLLOPE, THOMAS ADOLPHUS. *What I Remember*. Second Edition. London: Richard Bentley, 1887, 2 vols.

8¾ × 5½ in. Vol. 1: viii, 407 [1]; vol. 2: vii [1] 404 [4] pp. Wordsworth, vol. 2, pp. 15–17.

1888

1149 BESANT, WALTER. *Fifty Years Ago*. With One Hundred and Thirty-seven Plates and Woodcuts. London: Chatto & Windus, 1888.

8¾ × 5½ in. xvi [2] 268 [64] pp. The London of Wordsworth's later visits.

1150 CATTY, CHARLES. *Poems in the Modern Spirit*. London: Walter Scott, 1888.

6⅝ × 4⅛ in. viii [5] 14–135 [1]. Dedicated to the memory of Wordsworth, Coleridge, Keats, and Shelley.

1151 HOUGHTON, RICHARD MONCKTON MILNES, LORD. *Some Writings and Speeches of Richard Monckton Milnes, Lord Houghton, in the Last Year of His Life, with a Notice in Memoriam by George Stovin Venables*. London: Privately Printed at the Chiswick Press, 1888.

8¼ × 6 in. [8] 136 [2] pp. Wordsworth Society, pp. 105–32.

1152 KNIGHT, WILLIAM ANGUS. *Principal Shairp and His Friends*. London: John Murray, 1888.

8¾ × 5½ in. xix [1] 457 [67] pp. Numerous references to Wordsworth; see Index.

1153 OVERTON, JOHN HENRY, AND WORDSWORTH, ELIZABETH. *Christopher Wordsworth, Bishop of Lincoln, 1807–1885.* London: Rivingtons, 1888

$8\frac{3}{4} \times 5\frac{1}{2}$ in. xvi, 542 [38] pp.

1154 SANDFORD, MRS. HENRY. *Thomas Poole and His Friends.* London and New York: Macmillan and Co., 1888, 2 vols.

$7\frac{1}{2} \times 5$ in. Vol. 1: xi [1] 307 [1]; vol. 2: [4] 330 [2] pp. Numerous references to Wordsworth; see Index.

1155 SAUNDERS, FREDERICK. *The Story of Some Famous Books.* Second Edition. London: Elliot Stock, 1888.

$6\frac{3}{4} \times 4\frac{1}{8}$ in. xii, 208 [4] pp. Wordsworth, pp. 125–8.

1889

1156 ARNOLD, MATTHEW. *Selected Poems of Matthew Arnold.* London and New York: Macmillan and Co., 1889.

$6\frac{1}{8} \times 4$ in. vii [1] 235 [1] pp. Memorial Verses, pp. 203–6.

1157 CLAYDEN, P. W. *Rogers and His Contemporaries.* London: Smith, Elder, & Co., 1889, 2 vols.

$7\frac{3}{4} \times 5$ in. Vol. 1: xviii, 456; vol. 2: ix [1] 466 [6] pp. Numerous references to Wordsworth; see Index.

1158 KNIGHT, WILLIAM ANGUS (ED.). *Wordsworthiana: a Selection from Papers Read to the Wordsworth Society.* London and New York: Macmillan and Co., 1889.

$7\frac{3}{8} \times 5$ in. xxiv, 352 pp.

1159 PATER, WALTER. *Appreciations, with an Essay on Style.* London and New York: Macmillan and Co., 1889.

$7 \times 4\frac{5}{8}$ in. [8] 264 pp. Wordsworth, pp. 37–63.

1160 Review of *The Recluse,* 1888; *Complete Poetical Works,* ed. John Morley, 1888; *Wordsworthiana,* ed. William Knight, 1889.

Edinburgh Review, CLXIX (April 1889), 415–47.

1161 S., G.C.M. Review of *The Recluse,* 1888.

The Eagle, a Magazine Supported by Members of St. John's College, xv (1889), 461–8.

1162 STEDMAN, EDMUND CLARENCE. *Poets of America.* Boston and New York: Houghton, Mifflin, and Co., 1889.

7¾ × 4⅞ in. xviii [2] 516 [8] pp. Several references to Wordsworth; see Index.

1163 STEDMAN, EDMUND CLARENCE. *Victorian Poets. Revised and Extended, by a Supplementary Chapter, to the Fiftieth Year of the Period under Review.* Boston and New York: Houghton, Mifflin, and Co., 1889.

7⅝ × 5 in. xxiv [2] 521 [5] pp. Numerous references to Wordsworth; see Index.

1890

1164 *Book Catalogue No. 184,* William George's Sons. Bristol, 1890.

Offers for sale the Shuter portrait of Wordsworth now in this Collection.

1165 BROOKS, SARAH WARNER. *English Poetry and Poets.* Boston: Estes and Lauriat, 1890.

7⅞ × 5⅜ in. x [1] 12–506 [2] pp. Wordsworth and the Lake School, pp. 298–317.

1166 DAVEY, SIR HORACE. *Wordsworth: an Address ... Read to the Stockton Literary and Philosophical Society, on January 8th, 1890.* Stockton-on-Tees: Printed by John Sharp, 1890.

8½ × 5¾ in. 24 pp.

1167 DAWSON, WILLIAM JAMES. *The Makers of Modern English: a Popular Handbook to the Greater Poets of the Century.* New York: Thomas Whittaker, 1890.

7⅝ × 5 in. viii, 375 [3] pp. Wordsworth, pp. 91–154.

1168 DENNIS, JOHN. Dorothy Wordsworth.

Leisure Hour, xxxix (February 1890), 121–5.

1169 *De Quincey's Editorship of the Westmorland Gazette, with Selections from His Work on That Journal, from July, 1818, to November, 1819.* Kendal: Atkinson and Pollitt; London: Simpkin, Marshall, Hamilton, Kent, & Co., 1890.

8¼ × 5¼ in. [2] 79 [1] pp. Introduction signed Charles Pollitt. Wordsworth, pp. 25–7.

1170 PATTISON, THOMAS HARWOOD. The Religious Influence of Wordsworth.

Baptist Quarterly Review, xii (July 1890), 265–83.

1171 WATSON, SIR WILLIAM. *Wordsworth's Grave, and Other Poems* (Cameo Series). London: T. Fisher Unwin, 1890.

$7\frac{3}{8} \times 4\frac{1}{2}$ in. [2] 76 pp.

1891

1172 BUSSIÈRE, GEORGES, AND LEGOUIS, ÉMILE. *Le Général Michel Beaupuy (1755–1796), avec un portrait original; la famille de Beaupuy; les relations de Beaupuy avec le poète Wordsworth; son journal inédit du siège de Mayence; ses campagnes en Vendée et à l'armée de Rhin-et-Moselle.* Paris: Félix Alcan, 1891.

$8\frac{1}{4} \times 5\frac{1}{4}$ in. viii, 246 [4] pp.

1173 DE QUINCEY, THOMAS. *De Quincey Memorials, Being Letters and Other Records, Here First Published, with Communications from Coleridge, the Wordsworths, Hannah More, Professor Wilson, and Others.* Edited, with Introduction, Notes, and Narrative, by Alexander H. Japp. New York: United States Book Co., 1891, 2 vols.

$8\frac{3}{4} \times 5\frac{1}{2}$ in. Vol. 1: viii, 298 [3]; vol. 2: viii, 274 [4] pp. Wordsworth, vol. 1: pp. 119–26, 148–219.

1174 GOSSE, EDMUND W. *Gossip in a Library.* London: William Heinemann, 1891.

$7\frac{3}{8} \times 5$ in. viii, 338 pp. Peter Bell and His Tormentors, pp. 251–67.

1175 GRAHAM, PETER ANDERSON. *Nature in Books: Some Studies in Biography.* London: Methuen and Co., 1891.

$7\frac{1}{2} \times 5$ in. xx, 194 [2] pp. Wordsworth, pp. 174–94.

1176 INGRAM, JOHN H. *Edgar Allan Poe, His Life, Letters, and Opinions.* London, New York, and Melbourne: Ward, Lock, Bowden, & Co., 1891.

$7\frac{1}{8} \times 4\frac{3}{4}$ in. xii, 490 [10] pp. Wordsworth, pp. 78–81, 389.

1177 [JAPP, ALEXANDER HAY]. Early Intercourse of the Wordsworths and De Quincey. By De Quincey's Biographer. With Hitherto Unpublished Letters.

Century Magazine, xix, n.s. (April 1891), 853–64.

1178 *Portraits of English Poets, from Drawings Made for Joseph Cottle of Bristol. Reproduced in Photogravure from the Originals: Charles Lamb, Samuel Taylor Coleridge, William Wordsworth, Robert Southey, Walter Savage Landor.* Bristol: William George's Sons, 1891.

10½ × 7¼ in. A folder containing 5 plates.

1179 QUICK, ROBERT HEBERT. *Essays on Educational Reformers. Only Authorized Edition of the Work as Rewritten in 1890.* New York: D. Appleton and Co., 1891.

7 × 4¾ in. xxxiv, 560 [14] pp. Several references to Wordsworth; see Index.

1180 SCHERER, EDMOND. *Essays on English Literature,* trans. George Saintsbury. New York: Charles Scribner's Sons, 1891.

7⅛ × 4¾ in. xl, 309 [3] pp. Wordsworth and Modern Poetry in England, pp. 174–225.

1181 TUCKWELL, WILLIAM. *Tongues in Trees and Sermons in Stones.* London and Orpington: George Allen, 1891.

7⅜ × 5¼ in. [14] 151 [1] pp. Wordsworth and Ruskin, pp. 117–23.

1182 TUTIN, JOHN RAMSDEN. *The Wordsworth Dictionary of Persons and Places, with the Familiar Quotations from His Works (Including Full Index) and a Chronologically-arranged List of His Best Poems.* Hull: J. R. Tutin, 1891.

7¾ × 5⅛ in. 216 pp.

1183 WILDE, LADY JANE FRANCESCA. *Notes on Men, Women, and Books: Selected Essays.* First Series. London: Ward & Downey, 1891.

7½ × 5⅛ in. [8] 352 pp. Wordsworth, pp. 247–60.

1184 WORDSWORTH, CHARLES. *Annals of My Early Life 1806– 46, with Occasional Compositions in Latin and English Verse.* By Charles Wordsworth, D.D., D.C.L., Bishop of St Andrews and Fellow of Winchester College. London: Longmans, Green, and Co., 1891.

8¾ × 5½ in. xvi, 420 [48] pp.

1185 WORDSWORTH, ELIZABETH. *William Wordsworth.* By Elizabeth Wordsworth, Principal of Lady Margaret Hall, Oxford. London: Percival and Co., 1891.

7½ × 5 in. x [2] 232 pp.

1892

1186 COCHRANE, ROBERT. *The Treasury of Modern Biography: a Gallery of Literary Sketches of Eminent Men and Women of the Nineteenth Century.* Edinburgh: W. P. Nimmo, Hay, and Mitchell, 1892.

9⅛ × 6 in. 544 pp. Wordsworth, pp. 98–116.

1187 DAWSON, WILLIAM JAMES. *Quest and Vision, Essays in Life and Literature.* New York: Hunt & Eaton; Cincinnati: Cranston & Curts, 1892.

7⅛ × 4¾ in. [4] 233 [3] pp. Wordsworth, pp. 41–72.

1188 FLAGG, JARED BRADLEY. *The Life and Letters of Washington Allston, with Reproductions from Allston's Pictures.* New York: Charles Scribner's Sons, 1892.

9½ × 6¾ in. xvii [1] 435 [1] pp. Numerous references to Wordsworth; see Index.

1189 HALES, JOHN WESLEY. The Last Decade of the Last Century.

Contemporary Review Advertiser, LXII (September 1892), 422–41. Contains many references to Wordsworth.

1190 MABIE, HAMILTON WRIGHT. *Short Studies in Literature.* New York: Dodd, Mead, & Co., 1892.

6¾ × 4⅜ in. vi, 201 [1]. Wordsworth, pp. 101–3 and elsewhere.

1191 SMYTH, ALBERT HENRY. *The Philadelphia Magazines and Their Contributors 1741–1850.* Philadelphia: Robert M. Lindsay, 1892.

7 × 5⅛ in. [2] 264 [2] pp. Wordsworth, pp. 109–10, 163.

1192 STEDMAN, EDMUND CLARENCE. *The Nature and Elements of Poetry.* Boston and New York: Houghton, Mifflin, and Co., 1892.

7½ × 4⅞ in. xx, 338 [8] pp. Many references to Wordsworth; see Index.

1193 SUTHERLAND, JAMES MIDDLETON. *William Wordsworth: the Story of His Life, with Critical Remarks on His Writings.* Second Edition, Revised and Enlarged. London: Elliot Stock, 1892.

7 × 4¾ in. xvi, 242 [2] pp.

1194 TUTIN, JOHN RAMSDEN. *An Index to the Animal and Vegetable Kingdoms of Wordsworth*. Hull: J. R. Tutin, 1892.

$8\frac{3}{4} \times 5\frac{3}{4}$ in. 20 pp.

1195 WINTRINGHAM, WILLIAM H. *The Birds of Wordsworth, Poetically, Mythologically, and Comparatively Examined*, by William H. Wintringham, Compiler of 'British Birds: Key to the Present Classification, 1890.' London: Hutchinson & Co., 1892.

$8\frac{5}{8} \times 5\frac{1}{2}$ in. [8] 426 pp. Inserted opposite p. 142 is a photograph of Dickens's raven, 'Grip.'

1893

1196 BAMBURGH, WILLIAM CUSHING. *The Echo and the Poet, with Other Poems*. New York: Privately Printed for the Author, 1893.

$8\frac{7}{8} \times 5\frac{7}{8}$ in. x, 62 [2] pp. To Wordsworth (a poem), pp. 45–6.

1197 EWART, HENRY C. Wordsworth.

In the Footsteps of the Poets, by Professor David Masson and Others, with Numerous Illustrations. London: Isbister & Co., [1893,] pp. 203–33. $7 \times 4\frac{5}{8}$ in. [2] 381 [3] pp.

1198 GOTHEIN, MARIE. *William Wordsworth, sein Leben, seine Werke, seine Zeitgenossen*. Halle: Max Niemeyer, 1893, 2 vols.

$7\frac{5}{8} \times 4\frac{3}{4}$ in. Vol. 1: xii, 374; vol. 2: vi, 178 pp.

1199 HALES, JOHN WESLEY. *Folia Litteraria: Essays and Notes on English Literature*. London: Seeley and Co., 1893.

$7\frac{1}{2} \times 4\frac{3}{4}$ in. xi [1] 367 [5] pp. Numerous references to Wordsworth; see Index.

1200 JAPP, ALEXANDER HAY. *The Circle of the Year, a Sonnet-Sequence with Proem and Envoi*. Printed for the Author, 1893.

$6\frac{3}{4} \times 4\frac{1}{4}$ in. In three parts; 1: 116, 2: 125 [1], 3: 77 [1] pp. Wordsworth (a sonnet), Part 2, p. 94. Presentation copy from the author to Richard Le Gallienne.

1201 LITHGOW, ROBERT ALEXANDER DOUGLAS. *The Lake School and Its Influence on English Poetry*. n.p., [c. 1893].

$8\frac{1}{2} \times 5\frac{1}{4}$ in. 36 pp.

1202 THOMPSON, MAURICE. *The Ethics of Literary Art: the Carew Lectures for 1893.* Hartford, Conn.: Hartford Seminary Press, 1893.

$7\frac{3}{8} \times 5$ in. [2] 89 [3] pp. Slight references to Wordsworth, *passim.*

1203 WORDSWORTH, CHARLES. *Annals of My Life 1847–1856.* By Charles Wordsworth, D.D., D.C.L., Bishop of St. Andrews and Fellow of Winchester College. Edited by W. Earl Hodgson. London: Longmans, Green, and Co., 1893.

$8\frac{3}{4} \times 5\frac{1}{2}$ in. xxxvi, 230 [50] pp. A continuation of No. 1184.

1894

1204 LITHGOW, R. A. DOUGLAS. On the Lake School and Its Influence on English Poetry.

Royal Society of Literature: Afternoon Lectures on English Literature, Delivered by Members of the Council from January to June, 1893. London: Asher and Co., [1894].

1205 MINTO, WILLIAM. *The Literature of the Georgian Era.* Edited, with a Biographical Introduction, by William Knight. Edinburgh and London: William Blackwood and Sons, 1894.

$7\frac{1}{2} \times 4\frac{7}{8}$ in. I, 315 [1] pp. Wordsworth, pp. 140–84.

1206 ROBBINS, SIR ALFRED FARTHING. *The Early Public Life of William Ewart Gladstone, Four Times Prime Minister, with Three Portraits.* New York: Dodd, Mead, & Co., 1894.

$7\frac{3}{8} \times 4\frac{7}{8}$ in. xv [3] 464 pp. Several references to Wordsworth; see Index.

1207 SCUDDER, HORACE ELISHA. *Childhood in Literature and Art, with Some Observations on Literature for Children: a Study.* Boston and New York: Houghton, Mifflin, and Co., 1894.

$7\frac{5}{8} \times 4\frac{3}{4}$ in. [8] 253 [3] pp. Numerous references to Wordsworth; see Index.

1208 TALFOURD, THOMAS NOON. *Memoirs of Charles Lamb.* Edited and Annotated by Percy Fitzgerald. London: Gibbings & Co., 1894.

$7\frac{3}{8} \times 4\frac{7}{8}$ in. xviii, 291 [1] pp. A few references to Wordsworth; see Index.

1209 Unpublished Letters of Wordsworth and Coleridge.

The Athenaeum, 8 December 1894, p. 791.

1895

1210 CHENEY, JOHN VANCE. *That Dome in Air: Thoughts on Poetry and the Poets.* Chicago: A. C. McClurg and Co., 1895.

7 × 4½ in. 236 [4] pp. Wordsworth, pp. 207–17.

1211 FITZGERALD, PERCY. *Memoirs of an Author.* London: Richard Bentley and Son, 1895, 2 vols.

8¾ × 5½ in. Vol. 1: xv [3] 395 [1]; vol. 2: x, 408 pp. Wordsworth, vol. 1, p. 193; vol. 2, pp. 146–7.

1212 HUBBARD, ELBERT. *Little Journeys to the Homes of Good Men and Great: William Wordsworth.* New York and London: G. P. Putnam's Sons, 1895.

6⅞ × 4¼ in. Pp. 205–29.

1213 MEDBOROUGH, JAMES. *Some Wordsworth Finds?* Arranged and Introduced by James Medborough. London: At the University Press, 1895.

7½ × 5 in. xxiii [1] 24 [4] pp.

1214 QUILLINAN, DORA WORDSWORTH. *Journal of a Few Months' Residence in Portugal and Glimpses of the South of Spain.* New Edition, Edited, with Memoir, by Edmund Lee, Author of 'Dorothy Wordsworth,' etc. With Portrait. London: Longmans, Green, and Co., 1895.

7¾ × 5 in. xlvii [1] 288 pp.

1215 SCUDDER, VIDA DUTTON. *The Life of the Spirit in the Modern English Poets.* Boston and New York: Houghton, Mifflin, and Co., 1895.

7⅝ × 4⅞ in. v [1] 349 [3] pp. Numerous references to Wordsworth; see Index.

1896

1216 ANDERSON, MELVILLE BEST. *Some Representative Poets of the Nineteenth Century: a Syllabus of University Extension Lectures.* San Francisco: William Doxey, 1896.

8 × 5½ in. [2] 76 [4] pp. Wordsworth, pp. 3–7.

1217 *A Catalogue of Old and Rare Books, Being a Portion of the Stock of, and Offered for Sale by, Pickering and Chatto,* 1896.

7⅜ × 5 in. [2] 518 [2] pp. Many Wordsworth items.

1218 DARMESTETER, JAMES. *English Studies*, trans. Mary Darmesteter. London: T. Fisher Unwin, 1896.

7½ × 5 in. xix [1] 311 [1] pp. The French Revolution and Wordsworth, pp. 73–95.

1219 FIELD, EUGENE. *The Love Affairs of a Bibliomaniac*. London: John Lane, 1896.

7⅛ × 4⅝ in. xiii [1] 252 [3] pp. Wordsworth, pp. 239–40.

1220 KNIGHT, WILLIAM ANGUS. *Memoir of John Nichol, Professor of English Literature in the University of Glasgow*. Glasgow: James MacLehose and Sons, 1896.

9 × 5½ in. xxiv, 315 [1] pp. Wordsworth, pp. xvi, 8, 42, 67, 229, 303.

1221 LAUSCHE, RICHARD. *Über den epischen und dramatischen Blankvers bei William Wordsworth*. Inaugural-Dissertation zur Erlangung der Doktorwürde der Hohen Philosophischen Fakultät der Vereinigten Friedrichs-Universität Halle-Wittenberg. Halle: C. A. Kaemmerer, 1896.

8⅛ × 5¼ in. 47 [1] pp.

1222 LE GALLIENNE, RICHARD. *Retrospective Reviews: a Literary Log*. London: John Lane; New York: Dodd, Mead, and Co., 1896, 2 vols.

7⅝ × 4⅝ in. Vol. 1: xix [1] 281 [3]; vol. 2: [4] 281 [23] pp. Wordsworth, vol. 1, pp. 39–48.

1223 LEGOUIS, ÉMILE. *La Jeunesse de William Wordsworth 1770–98: Étude sur le 'Prelude.'* Paris: G. Masson, 1896.

10 × 6¼ in. viii, 495 [1] pp.

1224 LOCKER-LAMPSON, FREDERICK. *My Confidences, an Autobiographical Sketch Addressed to My Descendants*. London: Smith, Elder, & Co., 1896.

8¾ × 5½ in. x [2] 440 pp. A few references to Wordsworth, *passim*.

1225 MARTIN, ARTHUR SHADWELL. *On Parody*. New York: Henry Holt and Co., 1896.

7 × 5 in. iii [1] 280 [4] pp. Wordsworth, pp. 95–100, 130, 144–5, 173–4.

1226 RAWNSLEY, HARDWICKE DRUMMOND. *A Reminiscence of Wordsworth Day*, Cockermouth, April 7th, 1896. Edited by the Rev. H. D. Rawnsley, M.A., Hon. Canon of Carlisle, with Prefatory Notes on Cockermouth by the Rev. H. J. Palmer, M.A., Vicar of Christ Church, Cockermouth, and an Essay on Wordsworth by the Rev. J. Llewelyn Davies, D.D. Illustrated by Views of the Memorial Fountain, the Birth Place and Terrace Walk of the Poet, and the Grave of the Poet's Father. Cockermouth: Brash Brothers, 1896.

$7\frac{1}{8} \times 4\frac{3}{4}$ in. [2] 88 [6] pp.

1227 REYNOLDS, MYRA. *The Treatment of Nature in English Poetry between Pope and Wordsworth.* Chicago: University of Chicago Press, 1896.

$10\frac{11}{16} \times 7$ in. x, 290 [2] pp. A dissertation.

1228 STEPHEN, JAMES KENNETH. *Lapsus Calami, and Other Verses.* Cambridge: Macmillan and Bowes, 1896.

$6\frac{3}{4} \times 4\frac{1}{4}$ in. xix [3] 202 [4] pp. Parody of Wordsworth, pp. 32–3.

1897

1229 ADAMS, MARY M. Wordsworth (a sonnet).

The Aegis, a Monthly Magazine, Madison, Wisconsin, xi (February 1897), 129.

1230 BAUMGARTNER, ANDREAS. *William Wordsworth, nach seiner gemeinverständlichen Seite dargestellt.* Mit Bild, zwölf Originalgedichten und Übersetzungen. Zürich: Art. Institut Orell Füssli, 1897.

$8\frac{1}{8} \times 5\frac{5}{8}$ in. 119 [1] pp.

1231 DE VERE, AUBREY. *Recollections of Aubrey de Vere.* Second Edition. London and New York: Edward Arnold, 1897.

$8\frac{7}{8} \times 5\frac{1}{2}$ in. vi [2] 374 [18] pp. Wordsworth, pp. 40–2, 50, 59–60, 121–34, 185–7, 202–5, and elsewhere.

1232 DOWDEN, EDWARD. *The French Revolution and English Literature, Lectures Delivered in Connection with the Sesquicentennial Celebration of Princeton University.* London: Kegan Paul, Trench, Trübner, & Co., 1897.

$7\frac{1}{2} \times 5$ in. vi [2] 285 [99] pp. Wordsworth, pp. 195–239.

1233 LEGOUIS, ÉMILE. *The Early Life of William Wordsworth 1770–98: a Study of ' The Prelude.'* Translated by J. W. Matthews, with a Prefatory Note by Leslie Stephen. New York: Charles Scribner's Sons, 1897.

$8\frac{1}{2} \times 5\frac{1}{2}$ in. xvi, 477 [3] pp.

1234 MAGNUS, LAURIE. *A Primer of Wordsworth, with a Critical Essay.* London: Methuen & Co., 1897.

$7\frac{1}{2} \times 4\frac{7}{8}$ in. viii, 227 [49] pp.

1235 PALGRAVE, FRANCIS TURNER. *Landscape in Poetry from Homer to Tennyson, with Many Illustrative Examples.* London and New York: Macmillan and Co., 1897.

$7\frac{5}{8} \times 5$ in. xi [1] 302 [4] pp. Wordsworth, pp. 232–56.

1236 PEABODY, ANDREW PRESTON. William Wordsworth.

The Forum, XXIII (July 1897), 622–8.

1237 PRATT, TINSLEY. *Wordsworth at Rydal, and Other Poems.* Manchester and London: John Heywood, 1897.

$7\frac{1}{2} \times 4\frac{1}{4}$ in. 70 [2] pp. Thomas Hutchinson's copy, with eight lines of verse in the author's hand. Inserted is a letter from Pratt to Hutchinson expressing the wish that the book might be suppressed.

1238 WHITE, WILLIAM HALE. *A Description of the Wordsworth & Coleridge Manuscripts in the Possession of T. Norton Longman*, with Three Facsimile Reproductions. London, New York, and Bombay: Longmans, Green, and Co., 1897.

$11\frac{5}{8} \times 9$ in. vi, 72 pp.

1239 WORDSWORTH, DOROTHY. *Journals of Dorothy Wordsworth*, Edited by William Knight. London and New York: Macmillan and Co., 1897.

$7\frac{1}{4} \times 4\frac{3}{4}$ in. Vol. 1: xvii [1] 255 [1]; vol. 2: [8] 292 pp.

1898

1240 BATES, WILLIAM. *The Maclise Portrait Gallery of Illustrious Literary Characters, with Memoirs Biographical, Critical, Bibliographical, and Anecdotal Illustrative of the Literature of the Former Half of the Present Century.* New Edition with Eighty-five Portraits. London: Chatto & Windus, 1898.

$7\frac{3}{8} \times 4\frac{7}{8}$ in. xv [3] 540 [32] pp. Wordsworth, pp. 138–43.

1241 BROWNING, ELIZABETH BARRETT. *The Letters of Elizabeth Barrett Browning.* Edited with Biographical Additions by Frederic G. Kenyon, with Portraits. Third Edition. London: Smith, Elder, & Co., 1898, 2 vols.

$7\frac{1}{2} \times 4\frac{7}{8}$ in. Vol. 1: xiv, 478 [2]; vol. 2: vi, 464 [8] pp. Numerous references to Wordsworth; see Index.

1242 GEIKIE, SIR ARCHIBALD. *Types of Scenery and Their Influence on Literature* (The Romanes Lecture, 1898). London and New York: Macmillan and Co., 1898.

$8\frac{1}{2} \times 5\frac{3}{4}$ in. [7] 6–59 [7] pp. Several references to Wordsworth, *passim.*

1243 HALL, RICHARD. An Unpublished Poem of William Wordsworth.

Seminary Magazine, Louisville, Kentucky, XII (December 1898), 113–17.

1244 HODGKINS, LOUISE MANNING. *A Guide to the Study of Nineteenth Century Authors.* Boston: D. C. Heath, 1898.

$7\frac{1}{4} \times 5$ in. vi [4] 56 pp. Wordsworth, pp. 11–16.

1245 LUCAS, E. V. (ED.). *Charles Lamb and the Lloyds.* London: Smith, Elder, & Co., 1898.

$7 \times 4\frac{5}{8}$ in. ix [5] 297 [7] pp. Wordsworth, pp. 274–5.

1246 MABIE, HAMILTON WRIGHT. The Background of Wordsworth's Poetry.

The Outlook, 5 March 1898, pp. 591–606.

1247 Peter Bell.

The Speaker, 5 February 1898, Supplement. The article is signed 'Gideon Goslowly.'

1248 SPEIGHT, ERNEST E. On Literary Introductions, with Especial Reference to Wordsworth.

Parents' Review, IX (1898), 171–7.

1249 STEPHEN, LESLIE. *Studies of a Biographer.* New York: G. P. Putnam's Sons; London: Duckworth & Co., 1898, 2 vols.

$8 \times 5\frac{1}{8}$ in. Vol. 1: [8] 267 [1]; vol. 2: [8] 284 pp. Wordsworth's Youth, vol. 1, pp. 227–67.

1250 WHITE, WILLIAM HALE. *An Examination of the Charge of Apostasy against Wordsworth.* London, New York, and Bombay: Longmans, Green, and Co., 1898.

7⅞ × 5 in. [8] 63 [1] pp.

1251 WORDSWORTH, CHRISTOPHER. *Notes on Mediaeval Services in England, with an Index of Lincoln Ceremonies:* By Chr. Wordsworth, M.A., Rector of St. Peter and St. Paul's, Marlborough, Prebendary of Lincoln, and Co-editor of 'Breviarium ad usum Sarum,' &c. London: Thomas Baker, 1898.

8⅝ × 5⅝ in. xiii [1] 313 [1] pp.

1899

1252 BEERS, HENRY AUGUSTIN. *From Chaucer to Tennyson, with Twenty-nine Portraits, and Selections from Thirty Authors.* New York: The Macmillan Co., 1899.

7½ × 5⅛ in. [2] 325 [1] pp. Wordsworth, pp. 191–7.

1253 BROWNING, ROBERT AND ELIZABETH BARRETT. *The Letters of Robert Browning and Elizabeth Barrett Barrett 1845–1846, with Portraits and Facsimiles.* New York and London: Harper & Brothers, 1899, 2 vols.

8¼ × 5¼ in. Vol. 1: [12] 574 [2]; vol. 2: [8] 571 [5] pp. Several references to Wordsworth; see Index.

1254 FOTHERINGHAM, JAMES. *Wordsworth's 'Prelude' as a Study of Education.* London: Horace Marshall & Son, 1899.

6½ × 4 in. 73 [1] pp.

1255 HANCOCK, ALBERT ELMER. *The French Revolution and the English Poets: a Study in Historical Criticism.* New York: Henry Holt and Co., 1899.

7¼ × 4⅞ in. xvi, 197 [11] pp. Wordsworth, pp. 119–56.

1256 HERFORD, CHARLES HAROLD. *The Age of Wordsworth.* London: George Bell and Sons, 1899.

6¾ × 4⅜ in. xxix [1] 315 [5] pp.

1257 POLLOCK, SIR FREDERICK. *Spinoza, His Life and Philosophy.* Second Edition. London: Duckworth and Co.; New York: Macmillan Co., 1899.

8⅝ × 5½ in. xxiv, 427 [1] pp. Coleridge and Wordsworth, pp. 374–7.

1258 SAINTSBURY, GEORGE. *A History of Nineteenth Century Literature (1780–1895)*. New York and London: Macmillan and Co., 1899.

7½ × 5 in. xii, 477 [7] pp. Wordsworth, pp. 49–56.

1259 STRONG, AUGUSTUS HOPKINS. *The Great Poets and Their Theology*. Philadelphia: American Baptist Publication Society, 1899.

8⅝ × 5⅝ in. xvii [1] 531 [1] pp. Wordsworth, pp. 333–72.

1260 THOMPSON, ALEXANDER HAMILTON. *Cambridge and Its Colleges*. Illustrated by Edmund H. New. Boston: L. C. Page & Co.; London: Methuen & Co., 1899.

6 × 3¹¹⁄₁₆ in. xvi, 315 [1] pp.

1261 WINCHESTER, CALEB THOMAS. *Some Principles of Literary Criticism*. New York: Macmillan Co., ... 1899.

6⅞ × 4⅝ in. xii, 352 [4] pp.

1262 WORDSWORTH, JOHN, Bishop of Salisbury. *The Episcopate of Charles Wordsworth, Bishop of St Andrews, Dunkeld, and Dunblane, 1853–1892: a Memoir together with Some Materials for Forming a Judgment on the Great Questions in the Discussion of Which He Was Concerned*. London: Longmans, Green, and Co., 1899.

8¾ × 5½ in. xxv [1] 402 [2] pp.

1263 YARNALL, ELLIS. *Wordsworth and the Coleridges, with Other Memories Literary and Political*. New York: Macmillan Co., 1899.

8¾ × 5¾ in. ix [1] 331 [3] pp.

1900

1264 CLARK, JOHN SCOTT. *A Study of English and American Poets; a Laboratory Method*. New York: Charles Scribner's Sons, 1900.

7¾ × 4⅞ in. xiv, 859 [5] pp. Wordsworth, pp. 452–96.

1265 HARRIS, A. M. *Rustic Figures in Wordsworth's Poetry*, n.p., [*c.* 1900].

8¹¹⁄₁₆ × 5⅝ in. [4] pp.

1266 KNIGHT, WILLIAM ANGUS. A Literary Shrine: Dove Cottage, the Home of Wordsworth and De Quincey.

Century Magazine, LX (May 1900), 53–62.

1267 MELLOWS, EMMA SALISBURY. *The Story of English Litera-ture.* London: Methuen and Co., 1900.

$7\frac{3}{16} \times 4\frac{3}{4}$ in. xi [1] 292 [40]. Wordsworth, pp. 242–5.

1268 SCHUMAN, A. T. When Wordsworth Walked (a poem).

The Optimist: a Little Journal of Criticism, Review, and Inspiration, Boone, Iowa, 1 (September 1900), 33.

1269 SHARP, ROBERT FARQUHARSON. *Architects of English Literature: Biographical Sketches of Great Writers from Shakespeare to Tennyson.* Illustrated with Facsimiles from Autograph MSS. London: Swan Sonnenschein & Co., 1900.

$8 \times 5\frac{1}{8}$ in. [10] 326 [2] pp. Wordsworth, pp. 146–55.

1270 SHORTER, CLEMENT. *Victorian Literature: Sixty Years of Books and Bookmen.* London: James Bowden, 1900.

$7 \times 4\frac{3}{4}$ in. [10] 227 [1] pp. Several references to Wordsworth; see Index.

1271 WOODBERRY, GEORGE EDWARD. *Makers of Literature.* New York and London: Macmillan and Co., 1900.

$7 \times 4\frac{3}{4}$ in. viii [2] 440 [2] pp. Sir George Beaumont, Coleridge, and Wordsworth, pp. 250–70.

1901

1272 CHURCH, RICHARD WILLIAM. *Dante and Other Essays.* London: Macmillan and Co., 1901.

$7 \times 4\frac{5}{8}$ in. [8] 260 [4] pp. Wordsworth, pp. 193–219.

1273 DOWDEN, EDWARD. *The French Revolution and English Litera-ture, Lectures Delivered in Connection with the Sesquicentennial of Princeton University.* New York: Charles Scribner's Sons, 1901.

$7\frac{1}{4} \times 4\frac{3}{4}$ in. vi [2] 285 [3] pp. Wordsworth, pp. 195–239. The English edition was 1897.

1274 The Inman Portrait of Wordsworth.

Alumni Register, University of Pennsylvania, v (May 1901), 264–5.

1275 LAMB, CHARLES. *The Complete Works of Charles Lamb in Prose and Verse, Including 'Poetry for Children' and 'Prince Dorus.'* A New

Edition, with Two Portraits and a Facsimile. London: Chatto and Windus, 1901.

$7\frac{1}{2} \times 5$ in. xxv [3] 856 [32] pp. Wordsworth, pp. 60, 313–24.

1276 OEFTERING, WILLIAM E. *Wordsworth's und Byron's Natur-Dichtung.* Karlsruhe: Ferd. Thiergarten, 1901.

$8\frac{5}{8} \times 5\frac{1}{2}$ in. 198 pp.

1277 TUCKWELL, WILLIAM. *The Poet Wordsworth:* a Lecture Delivered at the House of Education, Ambleside, on Thursday, June 20th, 1901. Reprinted from the *Parents' Review.* Grasmere: Sam Read, 1901.

1278 WORDSWORTH, JOHN, Bishop of Salisbury. *The Ministry of Grace: Studies in Early Church History with Reference to Present Problems.* London, New York, and Bombay: Longmans, Green, and Co., 1901.

$8\frac{3}{4} \times 5\frac{5}{8}$ in. xxiv, 488 [4] pp.

1279 YARNALL, ELLIS. Henry Reed.

Alumni Register, University of Pennsylvania, v (May 1901), 257–64. Sketch of Wordsworth's American editor.

1902

1280 BURROUGHS, JOHN. *Literary Values, and Other Papers.* Boston and New York: Houghton, Mifflin, and Co., 1902.

$6\frac{5}{8} \times 4\frac{3}{4}$ in. [10] 264 [4] pp. Many references to Wordsworth, *passim.*

1281 CORSON, HIRAM. *A Primer of English Verse, Chiefly in Its Aesthetic and Organic Character.* Boston: Ginn & Co., 1902.

$7\frac{1}{4} \times 4\frac{5}{8}$ in. iv, 232 [4] pp. Many references to Wordsworth, *passim.* Presentation copy from Corson to Cynthia Morgan St. John.

1282 CUYLER, THEODORE LEDYARD. *Recollections of a Long Life: an Autobiography.* New York: Baker & Taylor, 1902.

$7\frac{1}{2} \times 5\frac{1}{8}$ in. viii [2] 356 [4] pp. Wordsworth, pp. 13–16.

1283 DAWSON, WILLIAM JAMES. *Literary Leaders of Modern England: Selected Chapters from 'The Makers of Modern Poetry,' and 'The Makers of Modern Prose,'* by Permission of the Publisher, Thos. Whittaker, New York. New York, Chautauqua, Springfield, Chicago, 1902.

$7\frac{1}{4} \times 4\frac{3}{8}$ in. [8] 275 [3] pp. Wordsworth, pp. 1–60, 251–6.

1284 DOWDEN, EDWARD. *Southey* (English Men of Letters). London: Macmillan and Co., 1902.

7¼ × 4⅝ in. [8] 205 [3] pp.

1285 GRISWOLD, HATTIE TYNG. *Home Life of Great Authors.* Seventh Edition. Chicago: A. C. McClurg & Co., 1902.

7¼ × 4¾ in. 385 [3] pp. Wordsworth, pp. 45–53.

1286 KNIGHT, WILLIAM ANGUS. *A Catalogue of Portraits of Philosophers, Poets, and Others.* Presented to the United College of St. Andrews, by Professor Knight in the Year 1902, and Hung in the Moral Philosophy Classroom for the Use of Students. St. Andrews: Printed by W. C. Henderson & Son, 1902.

6¼ × 4½ in. 27 [1] pp. Wordsworth, pp. 25–6.

1287 MATTHES, OTTO. *Naturbeschreibung bei Wordsworth.* Inaugural-Dissertation der Hohen Philosophischen Fakultät der Universität Leipzig. Leipzig: Emil Glausch, 1902.

8½ × 6¼ in. 85 [3] pp.

1288 MENGIN, URBAIN. *L'Italie des Romantiques.* Paris: Librairie Plon, 1902.

9$\frac{3}{16}$ × 5⅞ in. [8] xxiv, 394 [4] pp.

1289 MOULTON, CHARLES WELLS. *The Library of Literary Criticism of English and American Authors.* Vol. V, 1825–54. Buffalo: Moulton Publishing Co., 1902.

10 × 6¾ in. [2] 768 [2] pp. Wordsworth, pp. 605–47.

1290 PANCOAST, HENRY SPACKMAN. *An Introduction to English Literature.* New York: Henry Holt and Co., 1902.

6½ × 4¾ in. xiv [2] 556 [4] pp. Wordsworth, pp. 308–24.

1291 PUGHE, FRANCIS HEVENINGHAM. *Studien über Byron und Wordsworth.* Heidelberg: C. Winter, 1902.

9 × 6 in. viii, 167 [1] pp.

1292 ST. JOHN, CYNTHIA MORGAN. A Curious Bibliographical Mystery Detected and Explained.

Publishers' Weekly, LXI (February 1902), 439–40.

1293 SMART, GEORGE THOMAS. *Wordsworth: a Lecture.* Boston: Samuel Usher, 1902.

$7\frac{3}{4} \times 5\frac{1}{4}$ in. 30 pp.

1294 WORSFOLD, WILLIAM BASIL. *The Principles of Criticism: an Introduction to the Study of Literature.* New Edition. London: George Allen, 1902.

$7\frac{1}{2} \times 4\frac{7}{8}$ in. viii, 256 [4] pp. Numerous references to Wordsworth; see Index.

1903

1295 ARNOLD, MATTHEW. *Essays in Criticism:* Second Series. London and New York: Macmillan, 1903.

$7\frac{1}{8} \times 4\frac{5}{8}$ in. vii [3] 331 [3] pp. Wordsworth, pp. 122–62.

1296 COLERIDGE, HARTLEY. *Poems.* Edited, with a Preface, by W. Bailey-Kempling. Ulverston: W. Holmes, 1903.

$6 \times 4\frac{3}{4}$ in. xx, 76 pp. To William Wordsworth, p. 40.

1297 O'REILLY, ELIZABETH BOYLE. *My Candles, and Other Poems.* Boston: Lee and Shepard, 1903.

$7\frac{1}{2} \times 5\frac{1}{4}$ in. [2] 122 pp. Wordsworth (a poem), p. 56.

1298 RALEIGH, WALTER ALEXANDER. *Wordsworth.* Second Impression. London: Edward Arnold, 1903.

$7\frac{1}{2} \times 5$ in. [8] 232 pp.

1299 RAWNSLEY, HARDWICKE DRUMMOND. *Lake Country Sketches.* Glasgow: James MacLehose, 1903.

$7\frac{3}{8} \times 5$ in. x [2] 241 [3] pp. Reminiscences of Wordsworth among the Peasantry of Westmorland, pp. 1–58.

1300 WINCHILSEA, ANNE, COUNTESS OF. *The Poems of Anne Countess of Winchilsea, from the Original Edition of 1713 and from Unpublished Manuscripts.* Edited with an Introduction and Notes by Myra Reynolds. Chicago: University of Chicago Press, 1903.

$8\frac{5}{8} \times 5\frac{3}{4}$ in. cxxxiv, 436 [6] pp. See No. 582.

1904

1301 BANFIELD, EDITH COLBY. *The Place of My Desire, and Other Poems*. Boston: Little, Brown, and Co., 1904.

$7\frac{1}{2} \times 5$ in. xiii [3] 154 [2] pp. Wordsworth (a poem), p. 20.

1302 BEERBOHM, MAX. *The Poet's Corner*. London: Heinemann, 1904.

$14\frac{3}{4} \times 10\frac{1}{4}$ in. [2] pp., 20 plates, including one of Wordsworth.

1303 COLERIDGE, ERNEST HARTLEY. *Life & Correspondence of John Duke Lord Coleridge, Lord Chief Justice of England*. New York: D. Appleton and Co., 1904, 2 vols.

$8\frac{5}{8} \times 5\frac{5}{8}$ in. Vol. 1: ix [5] 306 [2]; vol. 2: [10] 451 [1] pp. Numerous references to Wordsworth; see Index.

1304 GWYNN, STEPHEN. *The Masters of English Literature*. New York and London: Macmillan & Co., 1904.

$6\frac{3}{4} \times 4\frac{1}{2}$ in. xiii [3] 423 [1] pp. The Lake School, pp. 329–55.

1305 HANEY, JOHN LOUIS (ED.). *Early Reviews of English Poets*. Edited with an Introduction. Philadelphia: Egerton Press, 1904.

$8\frac{1}{2} \times 6$ in. lix [1] 227 [1] pp. Wordsworth, pp. 16–46.

1306 HERING, MAURICE G. Studies in Wordsworth: Ode to Duty.

Round-About, the Monthly Post-Bag of the Members of the English-Speakers' Link and the Correspondence Club, New Edition, 1 (July 1904), 5–11.

1307 LOCKWOOD, FRANK C. The Critical Doctrines of Wordsworth and Coleridge.

Methodist Review, LXXXVI (March 1904), 187–98.

1308 MUIRHEAD, JOHN HENRY. Wordsworth's Ideal of Early Education.

International Journal of Ethics, XIV (April 1904), 339–52.

1309 PLUMMER, HENRY. *The 'Lucy' Poems of Wordsworth*, by Henry Plummer, Reprinted from the *Manchester Quarterly*, January 1904. London and Manchester: Sherratt & Hughes, 1904.

$8 \times 5\frac{1}{4}$ in. 12 pp.

1310 POE, EDGAR ALLAN. *The Works of Edgar Allan Poe*, with an Introduction by Edwin Markham. Vol. I: Introductions and Poems. New York and London: Funk & Wagnalls Co., 1904.

6⅛ × 4 in. xxxix [1] 208 pp. Wordsworth, pp. 58–61.

1311 WATSON, SIR WILLIAM. *Wordsworth's Grave*. With Illustrations by Donald Maxwell. London and New York: John Lane, 1904.

5½ × 4⅜ in. 44 [6] pp. A poem.

1312 WORDSWORTH, CHRISTOPHER, AND LITTLEHALES, HENRY. *The Old Service-Books of the English Church*. London: Methuen & Co., 1904.

8¾ × 5½ in. xv [1] 319 [1] pp.

1905

1313 BRANDES, GEORGE. *Main Currents in Nineteenth Century Literature*. Vol. IV: Naturalism in England (1875). New York: Macmillan Co., 1905.

8⅝ × 5⅝ in. viii, 366 [2] pp. Numerous references to Wordsworth, *passim*.

1314 KENT, ARMINE THOMAS. *Otia: Poems, Essays, and Reviews*. Edited by Harold Hodge, with a Memoir by Arthur A. Baumann. London and New York: John Lane, 1905.

7½ × 5 in. vii [5] 271 [5] pp. Wordsworth, pp. 84–91.

1315 LUCAS, EDWARD VERRALL. *The Life of Charles Lamb*. New York and London: G. P. Putnam, 1905, 2 vols.

8⅞ × 6 in. Vol. 1: xv [1] 550; vol. 2: viii [2] 550 [6] pp. Numerous references to Wordsworth; see Index.

1316 *Poems and Extracts Chosen by William Wordsworth for an Album Presented to Lady Mary Lowther*, Christmas, 1819. Printed Literally from the Original Album, with Facsimiles. London: Henry Frowde, 1905.

6¾ × 4½ in. xvii [7] 106 [2] pp. Preface by J. Rogers Rees; Introduction by Harold Littledale.

1317 SEAMAN, SIR OWEN. *A Harvest of Chaff*. New York: Henry Holt and Co., 1905.

6¾ × 4¼ in. [12] 147 [3] pp. Parodies of Wordsworth, pp. 1–4, 75–7.

1318 SESSIONS, FREDERICK. *Literary Celebrities of the English Lake-District.* London: Elliot Stock, 1905.

7⅝ × 5 in. vii [3] 238 [2] pp. Wordsworth, pp. 113–20.

1319 TOMLINSON, MAY. *Sound and Motion in Wordsworth's Poetry* (Poet Lore Brochures). Boston: Poet Lore Co., 1905.

7½ × 4¼ in. [2] 31 [3] pp.

1906

1320 BÖMIG, KARL. *William Wordsworth im Urteile seiner Zeit.* Inaugural-Dissertation zur Erlangung der Doktorwürde der Philosophischen Fakultät der Universität Leipzig. Borna-Leipzig: Robert Noske, 1906.

8¾ × 5⅜ in. viii, 88 [2] pp.

1321 CESTRE, CHARLES. *John Thelwall, a Pioneer of Democracy and Social Reform in England during the French Revolution.* London: Swan Sonnenschein & Co.; New York: Charles Scribner's Sons, 1906.

7¼ × 4⅞ in. 204 [8] pp. Wordsworth, pp. 27–9.

1322 CESTRE, CHARLES. *La Révolution Française et les Poètes Anglais (1789–1809).* Paris: Hachette & Cie., 1906.

9½ × 6 in. [4] 570 pp. A few references to Wordsworth; see Index.

1323 DOBELL, BERTRAM. *Catalogue of Books Printed for Private Circulation. Collected by Bertram Dobell, and Now Described and Annotated by Him.* London: Published by the Author, 1906.

8⅞ × 5½ in. 238 [2] pp. Wordsworth, pp. 25, 105, 233, and elsewhere.

1324 INGE, WILLIAM RALPH. *Studies of English Mystics: St. Margaret's Lectures 1905.* London: John Murray, 1906.

7⅞ × 5⅛ in. vi [2] 239 [1] pp. Wordsworth, pp. 173–206.

1325 JENKS, TUDOR. *In the Days of Scott.* New York: A. S. Barnes & Co., 1906.

6¾ × 4⅛ in. x, 279 [1] pp. Wordsworth, pp. 79, 197, 223.

1326 UPTON, GEORGE PUTNAM. *Tales from Foreign Lands: Memories, from the German of Max Müller.* Chicago: A. C. McClurg, 1906.

6⅜ × 4⅛ in. 173 [3] pp. Wordsworth, pp. 124–38.

1327 WOODBERRY, GEORGE EDWARD. *The Torch: Eight Lectures on Race Power in Literature Delivered before the Lowell Institute of Boston MCMIII.* New York: McClure, Phillips, & Co., 1906.

7 × 4⅝ in. vi, 217 [1] pp. Wordsworth, pp. 165–90.

1907

1328 ALLINGHAM, WILLIAM. *A Diary.* Edited by H. Allingham and D. Radford. London: Macmillan and Co., 1907.

8¾ × 5½ in. ix [1] 404 pp. Wordsworth, pp. 293–5.

1329 BROWN, JOHN. *Letters of Dr. John Brown, with Letters from Ruskin, Thackeray, and Others.* Edited by His Son and D. W. Forrest, D.D., with Biographical Introductions by Elizabeth T. M'Laren. London: Adam and Charles Black, 1907.

8⅝ × 5¾ in. xi [3] 367 [1] pp. Several references to Wordsworth; see Index.

1330 COOPER, LANE. A Glance at Wordsworth's Reading.

Modern Language Notes, XXII (March and April 1907), 83–98, 110–17.

1331 COOPER, LANE. Some Wordsworthian Similes.

Journal of English and Germanic Philology, VI (January 1907), 179–89.

1332 GUNSAULUS, FRANK WAKELEY. *The Higher Ministries of Recent English Poetry.* New York, Toronto, Chicago, London, and Edinburgh: Fleming H. Revell Co., 1907.

7⅛ × 4¾ in. 233 [7] pp. Many references to Wordsworth, *passim.*

1333 LANG, ANDREW (ED.). *Poet's Country.* Contributors, Prof. J. Churton Collins, W. J. Loftie, F.S.A., E. Hartley Coleridge, Michael Macmillan, Andrew Lang. With Fifty Illustrations in Colour by Francis S. Walker. London and Edinburgh: T. C. & E. C. Jack, 1907.

9 × 6⅜ in. xiv, 363 [1] pp. Several references to Wordsworth; see Index.

1334 PAYNE, WILLIAM MORTON. *The Greater English Poets of the Nineteenth Century.* New York: Henry Holt and Co., 1907.

7½ × 5⅛ in. vi [2] 388 [4] pp. Wordsworth, pp. 128–58.

1335 PUNCH, CATHARINE. *Wordsworth, an Introduction to His Life & Works.* London: Allman & Son, [*c.* 1907].

7⅛ × 4¾ in. vi [2] 120 pp.

1336 RANNIE, DAVID WATSON. *Wordsworth and His Circle*. With Twenty Illustrations. New York: G. P. Putnam's Sons; London: Methuen & Co., 1907.

$8\frac{3}{4} \times 5\frac{5}{8}$ in. xii, 360 pp.

1337 SANFTLEBEN, PAUL. *Wordsworth's 'Borderers' und die Entwicklung der nationalen Tragödie in England im 18. Jhd.* Inaugural-Dissertation zur Erlangung der Doktorwürde der Hohen Philosophischen Fakultät der Universität Rostock. Rostock: Adlers Erben, 1907.

$8\frac{3}{8} \times 5\frac{1}{4}$ in. 56 [4] pp.

1338 SYMONDS, JOHN ADDINGTON. *Essays Speculative and Suggestive*. Third Edition. London: Smith, Elder, & Co.; London: Charles Scribner's Sons, 1907.

$7\frac{3}{4} \times 5\frac{1}{4}$ in. xviii, 431 [1] pp. Wordsworth, pp. 315–34.

1339 VAN DYKE, HENRY. *Four Sonnets, Dedicated to the Class of 1907, Princeton University*. Privately Printed, 1907.

$7\frac{1}{2} \times 5$ in. [4] pp. The sonnets are entitled Shelley; Keats; Wordsworth; and Browning.

1340 VAUGHAN, CHARLES EDWYN. *The Romantic Revolt*. New York: Charles Scribner's Sons, 1907.

$7\frac{5}{8} \times 5$ in. vii [3] 507 [3] pp. Wordsworth, pp. 53–75.

1341 WOODBERRY, GEORGE EDWARD. *The Appreciation of Literature*. New York: Baker & Taylor Co., 1907.

$9\frac{3}{8} \times 6\frac{1}{4}$ in. [12] 195 [1] pp. Numerous references to Wordsworth, *passim*.

1908

1342 CLARKE, WILLIAM. *William Clarke: a Collection of His Writings, with a Biographical Sketch*. London: Swan Sonnenschein & Co., 1908.

$8\frac{3}{8} \times 5\frac{1}{4}$ in. xxix [1] 420 pp. Wordsworth, pp. 393–6.

1343 COOPER, LANE. A Survey of the Literature on Wordsworth.

Publications of the Modern Language Association of America, XXIII (March 1908), 119–27.

1344 GINGERICH, SOLOMON FRANCIS. *Wordsworth, a Study in Memory and Mysticism.* Elkhart, Indiana: Mennonite Publishing Co., 1908.

$6\frac{3}{4} \times 4\frac{3}{4}$ in. 207 [1] pp.

1345 LIENEMANN, KURT. *Die Belesenheit von William Wordsworth.* Berlin: Mayer & Müller, 1908.

$8\frac{5}{8} \times 5\frac{3}{8}$ in. [2] 259 [1] pp.

1346 WILSON, JAMES GRANT. The Footprints of Wordsworth.

Putnam's Monthly, III (January 1908), 459–64.

1909

1347 BRADLEY, ARTHUR CECIL. *Oxford Lectures on Poetry.* London: Macmillan and Co., 1909.

$8\frac{3}{4} \times 5\frac{1}{2}$ in. viii [2] 395 [1] pp. Wordsworth, pp. 97–145.

1348 DUNBAR, ALICE RUTH. Wordsworth's Use of Milton's Description of the Building of Pandemonium.

Modern Language Notes, XXIV (April 1909), 124–5.

1910

1349 COOPER, LANE. On Wordsworth's 'To Joanna.'

The Academy, 29 January 1910, pp. 108–10.

1350 COOPER, LANE. Wordsworth: Variant Readings.

Notes and Queries, XXXVIII (September 1910), 222–3.

1351 JEFFREY, FRANCIS. *Jeffrey's Literary Criticism.* Edited by D. Nichol Smith. London: Henry Frowde, 1910.

$6\frac{1}{2} \times 4\frac{1}{4}$ in. xxiv, 216 pp. Wordsworth, pp. 107–39.

1352 STRONG, ARCHIBALD THOMAS. *Nature in Meredith and Wordsworth, Being the Presidential Address to the Literature Society of Melbourne for 1910.* Melbourne: Advocate Printing and Publishing Co., 1910.

$7\frac{1}{2} \times 4\frac{5}{8}$ in. 58 [4] pp.

1911

1353 COOPER, LANE. *A Concordance to the Poems of William Words-worth*. New York: E. P. Dutton & Co., 1911.

10¾ × 8¼ in. xiii [1] 1136 pp.

1354 GINGERICH, SOLOMON FRANCIS. *Wordsworth, Tennyson, and Browning, a Study in Human Freedom*. Ann Arbor, Michigan: George Wahr, 1911.

7⅜ × 5⅛ in. 263 [1] pp.

1355 WORDSWORTH, JOHN. *The National Church of Sweden*, by John Wordsworth, D.D., Bishop of Salisbury ..., Delivered in St. James' Church, Chicago, 24–29th October, 1910 (the Hale Lectures, 1910). London and Oxford: A. R. Mowbray & Co.; Milwaukee: Young Churchman Co., 1911.

8¼ × 5¼ in. xix [1] 459 [1] pp.

1912

1356 HARPER, GEORGE McLEAN. Rousseau, Godwin, and Wordsworth.

Atlantic Monthly, cix (May 1912), 639–50.

1357 SNEATH, ELIAS HERSHEY. *Wordsworth, Poet of Nature and Poet of Man*. Boston and London: Ginn and Co., 1912.

8⅛ × 5⅜ in. viii [2] 320 [4] pp.

1358 WATT, LAUCHLAN MACLEAN. *Literature and Life*. London: A. & C. Black; Edinburgh: R. & R. Clark, 1912.

7⅜ × 4⅝ in. [6] x, 136 pp. Several references to Wordsworth; see Index.

1359 WORDSWORTH, ELIZABETH. *Glimpses of the Past*, by Elizabeth Wordsworth, Late Principal of Lady Margaret Hall, Oxford. With Eight Illustrations. London: A. R. Mowbray; ... 1912.

8¾ × 5½ in. viii, 218 pp. References to Wordsworth in Chapters 1 and 2.

1913

1360 FRYE, PROSSER HALL. The Terms 'Classic' and 'Romantic.'

Mid-West Quarterly, 1 (October 1913), 1–24.

1361 KIMPTON, EDITH. *Book Ways: an Introduction to the Study of English Literature*. London: Ralph, Holland, & Co., 1913.

$7\frac{1}{2} \times 4\frac{3}{4}$ in. [4] 292 pp. *Lyrical Ballads*, pp. 176–91.

1362 KNIGHT, WILLIAM ANGUS. *Coleridge and Wordsworth in the West Country, Their Friendship, Work, and Surroundings*. Illustrated by Edmund H. New. London: Elkin Mathews, 1913.

$8\frac{1}{2} \times 5\frac{1}{2}$ in. xvi, 237 [3] pp.

1363 RICE, RICHARD ASHLEY. Wordsworth's Mind.

Indiana University Studies, XI (July 1913), 1–45.

1364 STEBBING, WILLIAM. *Five Centuries of English Verse*. London: Oxford University Press, 1913, 2 vols.

$7\frac{1}{2} \times 5$ in. Vol. 1: iv, 412; vol. 2: vi, 429 [1] pp. Wordsworth, vol. 2, pp. 1–16. The printer's copy, consisting of two volumes of the work in its earlier form (*The Poets, Geoffrey Chaucer to Alfred Tennyson, 1340–1892*, London, ... 1907), with corrections, alterations, and additions in the hand of the author.

1914

1365 BOAS, FREDERICK S. *Wordsworth's Patriotic Poems and Their Significance Today* (English Association Pamphlet No. 30). London, 1914.

$9\frac{1}{4} \times 6$ in. 18 [2] pp.

1366 GÜTTLER, FELIX. *Wordsworth's politische Entwicklung*. Inaugural-Dissertation zur Erlangung der Doktorwürde der Hohen Philosophischen Fakultät der Schlesischen Friedrich-Wilhelms-Universität zu Breslau. Stuttgart: J. B. Metzlersche.

$8\frac{3}{4} \times 5\frac{1}{4}$ in. viii, 39 [1] pp.

1367 HUDSON, WILLIAM HENRY. *Wordsworth & His Poetry*. London: George C. Harrap & Co., 1914.

$6\frac{3}{4} \times 4\frac{1}{2}$ in. [2] 197 [3] pp.

1368 STORK, CHARLES WHARTON. The Influence of the Popular Ballad on Wordsworth and Coleridge.

PMLA, xxix (September 1914), 299–326.

1369 STRUNK, WILLIAM, JR. Some Related Poems of Wordsworth and Coleridge.

Modern Language Notes, xxix (November 1914), 201–5.

1915

1370 ACLAND, ARTHUR HERBERT DYKE. Wordsworth's Patriotic Poetry.

Littell's Living Age, lxvi (February 1915), 502–6. Reprinted from the *Westminster Gazette*.

1371 COBDEN-SANDERSON, THOMAS JAMES. *Wordsworth's Cosmic Poetry*. Hammersmith: Doves Press, [*c.* 1915].

$9\frac{3}{16} \times 6\frac{1}{2}$ in. [4] pp. Reprinted from the *Westminster Gazette* for 28 December 1914.

1372 COOPER, LANE. Review of *The Cambridge History of English Literature*, Vol. 9.

The Dial, 18 March 1915, pp. 205–8. Many references to Wordsworth.

1373 DE SELINCOURT, ERNEST. *English Poets and the National Ideal: Four Lectures*. London: Oxford University Press, 1915.

$8\frac{5}{8} \times 5\frac{1}{2}$ in. 119 [1] pp. Wordsworth, pp. 61–88.

1374 ELLIS, HAROLD MILTON. *Joseph Dennie and His Circle: a Study in American Literature from 1792 to 1812*. Austin: University of Texas, 1915.

$9\frac{1}{8} \times 5\frac{3}{4}$ in. vii [2] 10–285 [3] pp. Numerous references to Wordsworth; see Index.

1375 WATSON, E. W. *Life of Bishop John Wordsworth*. London and New York: Longmans, Green, and Co., 1915.

$8\frac{7}{8} \times 5\frac{1}{2}$ in. vi [2] 409 [3] pp.

1916

1376 GREENER, AMY. *A Lover of Books: the Life and Literary Papers of Lucy Harrison*, Written and Arranged by Amy Greener, with Portraits & Illustrations. London, Paris, and Toronto: J. M. Dent & Co.; New York: E. P. Dutton & Co., 1916.

7¾ × 5¼ in. xi [3] 318 [2] pp. Wordsworth, pp. 161–82.

1377 HARPER, GEORGE McLEAN. *William Wordsworth, His Life, Works, and Influence.* London: John Murray, 1916, 2 vols.

8¾ × 5½ in. Vol. 1: xv [3] 441 [3]; vol. 2: vii [1] 451 [1] pp.

1378 HERFORD, CHARLES HAROLD. *The Age of Wordsworth.* London: G. Bell and Sons, 1916.

6¾ × 4½ in. xxix [1] 315 [5] pp. Wordsworth, pp. 147–68.

1379 THAYER, MARY REBECCA. *The Influence of Horace on the Chief English Poets of the Nineteenth Century.* New Haven: Yale University Press, 1916.

9¼ × 5⅞ in. 117 [3] pp. Cornell dissertation. Wordsworth, pp. 53–64.

1380 WINCHESTER, CALEB THOMAS. *William Wordsworth: How to Know Him.* Indianapolis: Bobbs-Merrill Co., 1916.

7½ × 5 in. [18] 296 [8] pp.

1381 WISE, THOMAS JAMES. *A Bibliography of the Writings in Prose and Verse of William Wordsworth.* London: Printed for Private Circulation Only, 1916.

8½ × 6⅞ in. xv [1] 268 [4]. Presentation copy to Cynthia Morgan St. John from T. J. Wise.

1917

1382 BARSTOW, MARJORIE LATTA. *Wordsworth's Theory of Poetic Diction: a Study of the Historical and Personal Background of the* Lyrical Ballads (Yale Studies in English, LVII). New Haven: Yale University Press, 1917.

8⅝ × 5⅝ in. xv [1] 191 [1] pp. Yale dissertation.

1383 DICEY, ALBERT VENN. *The Statesmanship of Wordsworth: an Essay.* Oxford: Clarendon Press, 1917.

8⅝ × 5½ in. viii, 134 [2] pp.

1918

1384 BEATTY, ARTHUR. *Joseph Fawcett: The Art of War; Its Relation to the Early Development of William Wordsworth.* Madison, Wisconsin: University of Wisconsin, 1918.

9⅛ × 6 in. Pp. 225–70. Reprinted from *University of Wisconsin Studies in Language and Literature*, No. 2, 1918.

1919

1385 BROWNING, ELIZABETH BARRETT. *A Note on William Wordsworth with a Statement of Her Views on Spiritualism.* London: Printed for Private Circulation Only, 1919.

7½ × 5 in. 17 [3] pp. Printed for T. J. Wise.

1920

1386 BROOKE, STOPFORD. *Naturalism in English Poetry.* New York: E. P. Dutton, [1920].

8⅛ × 5¼ in. vii [3] 289 [5] pp. Wordsworth, pp. 135–87.

1387 BROUGHTON, LESLIE NATHAN. *The Theocritean Element in the Works of William Wordsworth.* Halle: Max Niemeyer, 1920.

8¾ × 5½ in. [8] 193 [1] pp.

1388 CAMPBELL, OSCAR JAMES. Sentimental Morality in Wordsworth's Narrative Poetry.

University of Wisconsin Studies in Language and Literature, No. 11. Madison: University of Wisconsin Press, 1920, pp. 21–57.

1389 *Collection of Wordsworthiana Made by the Late Mrs. Cynthia Morgan St. John, of Ithaca, N.Y., the Most Complete Collection of This Poet Ever Gathered.* n.p., [c. 1920].

9 × 6 in. 30 pp. Sale Catalogue of the St. John Collection.

1390 DUNN, ESTHER CLOUDMAN. Inman's Portrait of Wordsworth.

Scribner's Magazine, LXVII (February 1920), 251–6.

1391 HARPER, GEORGE McLEAN. *John Morley, and Other Essays.* Princeton: Princeton University Press, 1920.

8 × 5⅜ in. viii, 162 [2] pp. Wordsworth at Blois, pp. 111–24; Wordsworth's Love Poetry, pp. 125–33.

1392 KNOWLTON, E. C. The Novelty of Wordsworth's 'Michael' as a Pastoral.

PMLA, xxxv (December 1920), 432–46.

1393 MADARIAGA, SALVADOR DE. *Shelley & Calderón, and Other Essays on English and Spanish Poetry.* London: Constable & Co., 1920.

9¾ × 5½ in. xii, 98 [2] pp. The Case of Wordsworth, pp. 125–90.

1394 POTTS, ABBIE FINDLAY. Wordsworth and the Bramble.

Journal of English and Germanic Philology, xix (July 1920), 340–9.

1921

1395 BASSI, EMILIA. *William Wordsworth e la sua Poesia.* Bologna: Nicola Zanichelli, 1921.

9½ × 6⅜ in. 160 pp.

1396 DUNN, ESTHER CLOUDMAN. A Retrospect of Rydal Mount.

Scribner's Magazine, lxix (May 1921), 549–55.

1397 HARPER, GEORGE McLEAN. *Wordsworth's French Daughter: the Story of Her Birth, with the Certificates of Her Baptism and Marriage.* Princeton: Princeton University Press, 1921.

6¾ × 5 in. 41 [3] pp.

1398 WELLS, JOHN EDWIN. The Story of Wordsworth's Cintra.

Studies in Philology, xviii (January 1921), 15–77.

1922

1399 ANDERTON, BASIL. *Sketches from a Library Window.* Cambridge: W. Heffer & Sons, 1922.

8⅝ × 5½ in. [8] 182 [2] pp. Wordsworth, pp. 110–34.

1400 BABENROTH, ADOLPH CHARLES. *English Childhood: Wordsworth's Treatment of Childhood in the Light of English Poetry from Prior to Crabbe.* New York: Columbia University Press, 1922.

$7\frac{15}{16} \times 5\frac{1}{2}$ in. vii [3] 401 [1] pp.

1401 BEATTY, ARTHUR. *William Wordsworth, His Doctrine and Art in Their Historical Relations* (University of Wisconsin Studies in Language and Literature, No. 17). Madison, 1922.

$9\frac{1}{4} \times 6$ in. 284 [4] pp.

1402 BIRRELL, AUGUSTINE. *Collected Essays and Addresses, 1880–1920.* London and Toronto: 1922, 3 vols.

$8 \times 5\frac{1}{2}$ in. Vol. 1: xii, 408; vol. 2: vi, 390; vol. 3: vi, 382 pp. Peter Bell (1898), vol. 3, pp. 71–5.

1403 GUTHRIE, ANNA MARIA BRUCE. *Wordsworth and Tolstoi, and Other Papers.* With Preface by H. J. C. Grierson. Edinburgh: Privately Printed by T. and A. Constable at the University Press, 1922.

$8\frac{5}{8} \times 5\frac{1}{2}$ in. xviii [2] 124 pp.

1404 LEGOUIS, ÉMILE. *William Wordsworth and Annette Vallon.* London and Toronto: J. M. Dent & Sons; New York: E. P. Dutton & Co., 1922.

$7\frac{1}{4} \times 4\frac{3}{4}$ in. xiv, 146 pp.

1405 MERRILL, L. R. Vaughan's Influence upon Wordsworth's Poetry.

Modern Language Notes, xxxvii (February 1922), 91–6.

1406 ROBINSON, HENRY CRABB. *Blake, Coleridge, Wordsworth, Lamb, etc., Being Selections from the Remains of Henry Crabb Robinson.* Edited by Edith J. Morley. Manchester: Manchester University Press; London: Longmans, Green, and Co., 1922.

$7\frac{1}{4} \times 4\frac{3}{4}$ in. xxii [2] 175 [1] pp.

1923

1407 GARROD, HEATHCOTE WILLIAM. *Wordsworth: Lectures and Essays.* Oxford: Clarendon Press, 1923.

$7\frac{5}{8} \times 5$ in. [4] 211 [1] pp.

1408 FARINGTON, JOSEPH. *Diary, 1793–1821.* Edited by James Greig. Third Edition. New York: George H. Doran Co., 1923, 8 vols.

9 × 6 in. Vol. 1: xx, 398 [2]; vol. 2: xxi [3] 332; vol. 3: xvii [3] 346 [2]; vol. 4: xiv [2] 291 [1]; vol. 5: xxii [2] 335 [1]; vol. 6: xviii [2] 296; vol. 7: xxii [2] 299 [1]; vol. 8: xxi [3] 311 [1] pp. A few references to Wordsworth; see Index.

1409 HARPER, GEORGE McLEAN. Review of *William Words- worth: His Doctrine and Art in Their Historical Relations,* by Arthur Beatty, 1922.

Journal of English and Germanic Philology, XXII (October 1923), 566–9.

1410 LEGOUIS, ÉMILE. Quelques mots encore sur la fille française de Wordsworth.

Revue Anglo-Américaine, 1 (October 1923), 66–73.

1411 LEGOUIS, ÉMILE. *Wordsworth in a New Light.* Cambridge: Harvard University Press, 1923.

$7\frac{3}{4} \times 4\frac{7}{8}$ in. [2] 44 [2] pp.

1412 ORVIETO, ANGIOLO. *Poesie di Amore e d'Incanto, Versioni dall'Inglese,* con Prefazione di L. E. Marshall. Firenze: Felice le Monnier, 1923.

$7\frac{1}{4} \times 4\frac{3}{8}$ in. xii, 216 [8] pp. Translations from Wordsworth, pp. 13–29.

1413 SHACKFORD, MARTHA HALE. Wordsworth's Italy.

PMLA, XXXVIII (June 1923), 236–52.

1414 SHACKFORD, MARTHA HALE. Wordsworth's 'Michael.'

Sewanee Review, XXXI (July 1923), 275–80.

1415 TURNER, ALBERT MORTON. Wordsworth and Hartley Coleridge.

Journal of English and Germanic Philology, XXII (October 1923), 538–57.

1416 WOODS, MARGARET LOUISA. *A Poet's Youth.* New York: Boni and Liveright, [c. 1923].

$7\frac{1}{2} \times 5\frac{1}{2}$ in. 340 pp. The early life of Wordsworth in the form of a novel.

1924

1417 GINGERICH, SOLOMON FRANCIS. *Essays in the Romantic Poets*. New York: Macmillan Co., 1924.

8½ × 5⅝ in. [8] 276 pp. Wordsworth, pp. 91–191.

1418 MORLEY, F. V. *Dora Wordsworth, Her Book*. With Portraits and Facsimiles. London: Selwyn and Blount, 1924.

7½ × 5 in. [14] 175 [1] pp. Clement Shorter's copy.

1419 RICE, RICHARD ASHLEY. Wordsworth since 1916.

Smith College Studies in Modern Languages, v (January 1924), 27–66.

1925

1420 BEACH, JOSEPH WARREN. Expostulation and Reply.

PMLA, xl (June 1925), 346–61.

1421 HERZBERG, MAX JOHN. William Wordsworth and German Literature.

PMLA, xl (June 1925), 302–45.

1422 KAUFMAN, PAUL. Defining Romanticism, a Survey and a Program.

Modern Language Notes, xl (April 1925), 193–204.

1423 MOORE, JOHN ROBERT. Wordsworth's Unacknowledged Debt to Macpherson's *Ossian*.

PMLA, xl (June 1925), 362–78.

1424 MORLEY, F. V. *Dora Wordsworth, Her Book*. With Portraits and Facsimiles. Boston and New York: Houghton Mifflin Co., 1925.

7⅜ × 4⅞ in. [14] 175 [1] pp.

1425 RICE, RICHARD ASHLEY. Rousseau and the Poetry of Nature in Eighteenth Century France.

Smith College Studies in Modern Languages, vi (April and July 1925), [10] 96 [2] pp.

1426 WHITEHEAD, ALFRED NORTH. *Science and the Modern World.* Cambridge: Cambridge University Press, [1925].

$8\frac{3}{8} \times 5\frac{1}{4}$ in. xi [1] 296 [4] pp. The Romantic Reaction, pp. 105–33.

1926

1427 DARBISHIRE, HELEN. Wordsworth's 'Prelude.'

Nineteenth Century and After, xcix (May 1926), 718–31.

1428 GREEVER, GARLAND (ED.). *A Wiltshire Parson and His Friends: the Correspondence of William Lisle Bowles Together with Four Hitherto Unidentified Reviews by Coleridge.* London: Constable and Co., 1926.

$8\frac{3}{4} \times 5\frac{5}{8}$ in. xiv [2] 207 [1] pp. Several references to Wordsworth; see Index.

1429 HAYDON, BENJAMIN ROBERT. *The Autobiography and Memoirs of Benjamin Robert Haydon (1786–1846).* Edited from His Journals by Tom Taylor. A New Edition with an Introduction by Aldous Huxley, Illustrated. London: Peter Davies, 1926, 2 vols.

$8\frac{1}{4} \times 5\frac{1}{8}$ in. Vol. 1: xxxi [1] 427 [1]; vol. 2: x [429]–875 [1] pp. Numerous references to Wordsworth; see Index.

1430 DE SELINCOURT, ERNEST. The Hitherto Unpublished Preface to Wordsworth's 'Borderers.'

Nineteenth Century and After, c (November 1926), 723–41.

1927

1431 BEATTY, ARTHUR. *William Wordsworth; His Doctrine and Art in Their Historical Relations* (University of Wisconsin Studies in Language and Literature, No. 24). Second Edition. Madison, 1927.

$9\frac{1}{8} \times 6$ in. 310 [2] pp.

1432 BROUGHTON, LESLIE NATHAN. Review of *The Prelude,* ed. Ernest de Selincourt, 1926.

Journal of English and Germanic Philology, xxvi (July 1927), 427–32.

1433 GARROD, HEATHCOTE WILLIAM. *Wordsworth: Lectures and Essays.* Second Edition. Oxford: Clarendon Press, 1927.

$7\frac{5}{8} \times 5$ in. [4] 231 [1] pp.

1434 HALL, RICHARD. Items Hitherto Unpublished from a Note-book of William Wordsworth.

The Chimes, Rome, Georgia, XL (December 1927), 5–9.

1435 HAVENS, RAYMOND D. Review of *The Prelude*, ed. Ernest de Selincourt, 1926.

Modern Language Notes, XLII (April 1927), 256–8.

1436 KNAPLUND, PAUL. Correspondence Relating to the Grant of a Civil List Pension to William Wordsworth, 1842.

Modern Language Notes, XLII (June 1927), 385–9.

1437 MACLEAN, CATHERINE MACDONALD. *Dorothy and William Wordsworth*. Cambridge: Cambridge University Press, 1927.

$7\frac{3}{8} \times 4\frac{3}{4}$ in. [12] 129 [3] pp.

1438 PATTON, CORNELIUS H. The Increasing Interest in the Poet of the Lakes and His Influence during the Great War.

Boston Evening Transcript, 11 June 1927, Part 6.

1439 ROBINSON, HENRY CRABB. *The Correspondence of Henry Crabb Robinson with the Wordsworth Circle (1808–1866)*, the Greater Part Now for the First Time Printed from the Originals in Dr Williams's Library, London. Chronologically Arranged and Edited with Introduction, Notes, and Index by Edith J. Morley, ... with Portraits and Facsimiles. Oxford: Clarendon Press, 1927, 2 vols.

$8\frac{3}{4} \times 5\frac{5}{8}$ in. Vol. 1: xii, 537 [3]; vol. 2: [8] 903 [3] pp.

1440 ROWLEY, JAMES. *Wordsworth, and Other Essays*. Bristol: J. W. Arrowsmith, [1927].

$7\frac{1}{2} \times 5$ in. 206 [2] pp.

1441 WISE, THOMAS JAMES. *Two Lake Poets: a Catalogue of Printed Books, Manuscripts, and Autograph Letters by William Wordsworth and Samuel Taylor Coleridge*, Collected by Thomas J. Wise. London: Printed for Private Circulation Only, 1927.

$10 \times 7\frac{1}{2}$ in. xxxi [5] 135 [1] pp.

1442 Another copy.

1928

1443 COOPER, LANE. Coleridge, Wordsworth, and Mr. Lowes.

PMLA, XLIII (June 1928), 582–92.

1444 GARNIER, CHARLES-MARIE. *Édouard Dowden. Extrait de la* Revue Anglo-Américaine, Décembre 1928–Février 1929.

$9\frac{1}{4} \times 6\frac{1}{8}$ in. 36 pp. Many references to Wordsworth.

1445 HARPER, GEORGE McLEAN. *Spirit of Delight.* New York: Henry Holt and Co., 1928.

$8 \times 5\frac{1}{4}$ in. xi [1] 198 [2] pp. The first three essays are on Coleridge, Dorothy Wordsworth, and William Wordsworth.

1446 JOHNSON, REGINALD BRIMLEY (ED.). *The Undergraduate, from Dr. Christopher Wordsworth's 'Social Life at the English Universities in the Eighteenth Century,'* Revised, Abridged, and Re-arranged with an Introduction by R. Brimley Johnson. Sixteen Full-page Illustrations; Ten Line Blocks in Text. London: Stanley Paul & Co., 1928.

$8\frac{1}{2} \times 5\frac{1}{8}$ in. 335 [1] pp.

1447 NEWTON, ANNABEL. *Wordsworth in Early American Criticism.* Chicago: University of Chicago Press, 1928.

$7\frac{5}{8} \times 5$ in. ix [1] 210 pp.

1929

1448 BERNBAUM, ERNEST. The Romantic Movement.

English Journal, XVIII (March 1929), 221–30.

1449 BIGHAM, HELEN RUTHERFORD. *Wordsworth as a Metrist* (Cornell M.A. Thesis). Ithaca: Typescript, 1929.

$10\frac{3}{8} \times 7\frac{1}{2}$ in. 4, iii, 66 [10] pp.

1450 BROWN, EMILIE MATHILDE. *Folklore in the Poems of William Wordsworth* (Cornell Ph.D. Thesis). Ithaca: Typescript, 1929.

$10\frac{1}{8} \times 7\frac{3}{8}$ in. [5] 224 pp.

1451 CHAPMAN, JOHN ALEXANDER. *Papers on Shelley, Wordsworth, & Others.* London: Oxford University Press, 1929.

$7\frac{1}{2} \times 5$ in. [8] 171 [1] pp.

1452 COBBAN, ALFRED. *Edmund Burke and the Revolt against the Eighteenth Century: a Study of the Political and Social Thinking of Burke, Wordsworth, Coleridge, and Southey*. London: George Allen & Unwin, 1929.

$7\frac{5}{8} \times 5\frac{1}{8}$ in. 280 pp.

1453 COOPER, LANE. Matthew Arnold's Essay on Wordsworth.

The Bookman, N.Y., LXIX (July 1929), 479–84.

1454 DINGLE, HERBERT. The Analytical Approach to Wordsworth.

The Realist, I (June 1929), 142–59.

1455 FOERSTER, NORMAN. Wordsworth in America.

Studies in Philology, XXVI (January 1929), 85–95. A review of *Wordsworth in Early American Criticism*, by Annabel Newton, 1928.

1456 GARSTANG, W. Wordsworth's Green Linnet.

Nineteenth Century and After, CVI (September 1929), 375–82.

1457 GINGERICH, SOLOMON FRANCIS. *Essays in the Romantic Poets*. New York: Macmillan Co., 1929.

$8\frac{1}{2} \times 5\frac{3}{4}$ in. [8] 276 [4] pp. Wordsworth, pp. 91–191.

1458 GRIGGS, EARL LESLIE. *Hartley Coleridge, His Life and Work*. Thesis Approved for the Degree of Doctor of Philosophy in the University of London. London: University of London Press, 1929.

$7\frac{1}{4} \times 4\frac{3}{4}$ in. xi [1] 255 [1] pp. Numerous references to Wordsworth; see Index.

1459 HARPER, GEORGE McLEAN. *William Wordsworth, His Life, Works, and Influence*. London: John Murray, 1929.

$8\frac{1}{2} \times 5\frac{1}{2}$ in. xi [1] 621 [7] pp. Third edition.

1460 HARRINGTON, JANETTE. Wordsworth's *Descriptive Sketches* and *The Prelude*, Book VI.

PMLA, XLIV (December 1929), 1144–58.

1461 HAVENS, RAYMOND DEXTER. A Project of Wordsworth's.

Review of English Studies, V (July 1929), 320–2.

1462 HERFORD, CHARLES HAROLD. Goethe and Wordsworth.

Contemporary Review, cxxxvi (October 1929), 465–75.

1463 HUXLEY, ALDOUS. Wordsworth in the Tropics.

Yale Review, xviii (Summer 1929), 672–83.

1464 KESSEL, MARCEL. *A Comparative Study of Blake and Words-worth as Mystical Writers:* an Abstract of a Thesis Presented to the Faculty of the Graduate School of Cornell University for the Degree of Doctor of Philosophy. Ithaca, 1929.

$9 \times 5\frac{7}{8}$ in. [4] pp.

1465 KING, R. W. *England from Wordsworth to Dickens.* New York: Harcourt, Brace, & Co., [*c.* 1929].

$7\frac{3}{8} \times 4\frac{3}{4}$ in. xv [1] 238 [2] pp.

1466 MEAD, MARIAN. *Four Studies in Wordsworth.* Menasha, Wisconsin: George Banta, 1929.

$7\frac{5}{8} \times 5$ in. vi [2] 274 pp.

1467 POTTS, ABBIE FINDLAY. The Date of Wordsworth's First Meeting with Hazlitt.

Modern Language Notes, xliv (May 1929), 296–9.

1468 POTTS, ABBIE FINDLAY. Wordsworth and William Fleet-wood's Sermons.

Studies in Philology, xxvi (October 1929), 444–56.

1469 STALLKNECHT, NEWTON P. Wordsworth and Philosophy.

PMLA, xliv (December 1929), 1116–43.

1470 WORDSWORTH, GORDON GRAHAM. *Some Notes on the Wordsworths of Peniston and Their Aumbry.* Ambleside: Printed for Private Circulation by George Middleton, 1929.

$8\frac{3}{8} \times 6\frac{1}{2}$ in. [12] 34 [4] pp.

1930

1471 BERNBAUM, ERNEST. *Anthology of Romanticism and Guide through the Romantic Movement.* New York: Thomas Nelson and Sons, 1930, 5 vols.

6⅛ × 4 in. Vol. 1: ix [1] 11–480; vol. 2: 470 [2]; vol. 3: 410 [6]; vol. 4: 392; vol. 5: 415 [1] pp. Wordsworth, vol. 1, pp. 117–62; vol. 3, pp. 109–251.

1472 BROUGHTON, LESLIE NATHAN. W. A. Knight's First Interest in Wordsworth.

Philological Quarterly, ix (October 1930), 402–3.

1473 BUSTICO, ISA. *Il Sentimento della Natura in William Wordsworth.* Vercelli: Pei Tipi Gallardi, 1930.

8⅝ × 5¼ in. [6] 84 [4] pp.

1474 DIXON, WILLIAM MacNEILE. *Chatterton* (Warton Lecture on English Poetry, British Academy, 1930). London: Humphrey Milford, [1930].

9¾ × 6⅛ in. 22 [2] pp. Discusses the Romantic Movement.

1475 HARTMAN, HERBERT. The 'Intimations' of Wordsworth's Ode.

Review of English Studies, vi (April 1930), 129–48.

1476 HENSEL, GERHARD. *Das Optische bei Wordsworth: Ein Beitrag zur Psychologie des dichterischen Schaffens.* Inaugural-Dissertation zur Erlangung der Doktorwürde der Hohen Philosophischen Fakultät der Philipps-Universität zu Marburg. Marburg, 1930.

8¾ × 5⅝ in. [5] 84–192 [2] pp.

1477 HERFORD, CHARLES HAROLD. *Wordsworth. With a Portrait.* London: George Routledge & Sons, 1930.

7¼ × 4¾ in. [10] 255 [1] pp.

1478 HOOKER, EDWARD NILES. *Descriptive Sketches* and *The Prelude,* Book VI.

PMLA, xlv (June 1930), 619–23.

1479 LOWES, JOHN LIVINGSTON. *Convention and Revolt in Poetry.* Boston and New York: Houghton Mifflin Co., 1930.

7⅞ × 5 in. viii [2] 346 pp. Several references to Wordsworth, *passim.*

1480 POTTS, ABBIE FINDLAY. A Letter from Wordsworth to Thomas Powell.

Modern Language Notes, xLV (April 1930), 215–18.

1481 READ, HERBERT. *Wordsworth* (The Clark Lectures, 1929–30). London and Toronto: Jonathan Cape, 1930.

$7\frac{7}{8} \times 5\frac{1}{4}$ in. [2] 271 [1] pp.

1482 ROBERTSON, W. B. *Relation of Wordsworth to Science* (Cornell University M.A. Thesis). Ithaca: Typescript, 1930.

$10\frac{3}{8} \times 7\frac{5}{8}$ in. [4] 176 [2] pp.

1483 SCHUMACHER, ELISABETH. *Einheit und Totalität bei Wordsworth (unter dem Gesichtspunkt psychologischer Strukturtypologie)*. Inaugural-Dissertation zur Erlangung der Doktorwürde der Hohen Philosophischen Fakultät der Universität Marburg. Marburg, 1930.

$8\frac{5}{8} \times 5\frac{7}{8}$ in. [2] 88 [2] pp.

1484 THOMAS, VIRGINIA EVELYN. *Wordsworth's Acquaintance with Rustic Characters* (Cornell University M.A. Thesis). Ithaca: Typescript, 1930.

$10\frac{3}{8} \times 7\frac{1}{2}$ in. [5] 82 pp.

1485 TUCKERMAN, UNA VENABLE. Wordsworth's Plan for His Imitation of Juvenal.

Modern Language Notes, xLV (April 1930), 209–15.

1486 WORDSWORTH, DOROTHY. *Journals of Dorothy Wordsworth*. Edited by William Knight. London: Macmillan and Co., 1930.

$7\frac{1}{2} \times 5$ in. xvii [1] 544 pp.

1931

1487 BABBITT, IRVING. The Primitivism of Wordsworth.

The Bookman, N.Y., LXXIV (September 1931), 1–10.

1488 BANERJEE, SRIKUMAR. *Critical Theories and Poetic Practice in the 'Lyrical Ballads.'* London: Williams & Norgate, 1931.

$8\frac{5}{8} \times 5\frac{5}{8}$ in. [4] 205 [3] pp.

1489 BEATY, JOHN O., AND BOWYER, JOHN W. (EDS.). *Famous Editions of English Poets.* New York: Richard R. Smith, 1931.

$10\frac{1}{8} \times 6\frac{1}{8}$ in. xxi [1] 1312 pp. Reprints *Lyrical Ballads*, 1798, and *Poems in Two Volumes*, 1807.

1490 BREDE, ALEXANDER. Theories of Poetic Diction in Wordsworth and Others and in Contemporary Poetry.

Papers of the Michigan Academy of Science, Arts, and Letters, XIV, 1930. Ann Arbor: University of Michigan, 1931, pp. 537–65.

1491 BROUGHTON, LESLIE NATHAN. *The Wordsworth Collection Formed by Cynthia Morgan St. John and Given to Cornell University by Victor Emanuel.* Ithaca: Cornell University Library, 1931.

9×6 in. xii [2] 124.

1492 Another copy.

1493 CIESIELSKI, ELISABET. *Vergleich und Metapher bei W. Wordsworth: Eine stilistiche Studie nach Wordsworth's 'Poems of the Imagination.'* Inaugural-Dissertation zur Erlangung der Doktorwürde der Hohen Philosophischen Fakultät der Philipps-Universität zu Marburg. Marburg: Franz Fischer, 1931.

$8\frac{1}{4} \times 5\frac{3}{8}$ in. 93 [3] pp.

1494 CORBIN, MARIAN. *Wordsworth: Travel Poet* (Cornell University Ph.D. Thesis). Ithaca: Typescript, 1931.

$10\frac{1}{2} \times 7\frac{5}{8}$ in. [3] 179 pp.

1495 DE SELINCOURT, ERNEST. Early Readings in *The Prelude.*

Times Literary Supplement, 12 November 1931, p. 886. A clipping.

1496 FAIRCHILD, HOXIE NEALE. *The Romantic Quest.* New York: Columbia University Press, 1931.

$8\frac{1}{8} \times 5\frac{1}{2}$ in. viii [2] 444 [6] pp.

1497 RADER, MELVIN MILLER. Presiding Ideas in Wordsworth's Poetry.

University of Washington Publications in Language and Literature, Vol. 8, No. 2. Seattle: University of Washington Press, 1931, pp. 121–215.

1498 REA, JOHN D. Hartley Coleridge and Wordsworth's Lucy.

Studies in Philology, xxviii (January 1931), 118–35.

1499 RIMMER, CLARA. *Wordsworth's Tragedy The Borderers* (Cornell University M.A. Thesis). Ithaca: Typescript, 1931.

$10\frac{3}{8} \times 7\frac{5}{8}$ in. [5] 157 [2] pp.

1500 *The International Aspect of the Debts of the State of Mississippi Repudiated before the Civil War.* Extracted from the 57th Annual Report of the Council of Foreign Bondholders. London: Council House, 1931.

$8\frac{1}{2} \times 5\frac{1}{2}$ in. 20 pp. Wordsworth, pp. 14, 19–20.

1932

1501 ANDERS, HERMANN. *Die Bedeutung Wordsworthscher Gedankengänge für das Denken und Dichten von John Keats.* Breslau: Trewendt & Granier, 1932.

$7\frac{3}{8} \times 5\frac{1}{2}$ in. viii, 65 [1] pp.

1502 BABBITT, IRVING. *On Being Creative, and Other Essays.* London: Constable and Co., 1932.

$7\frac{1}{4} \times 4\frac{3}{4}$ in. xliii [3] 265 [1] pp. Several references to Wordsworth; see Index.

1503 BALD, ROBERT CECIL (ED.). *Literary Friendships in the Age of Wordsworth.* Cambridge: Cambridge University Press, 1932.

$7\frac{1}{2} \times 5$ in. xxiv, 283 [1] pp.

1504 CHAPMAN, JOHN ALEXANDER. *Wordsworth and Literary Criticism* (The Russell Lecture, 1931). London: Oxford University Press, 1932.

$8\frac{1}{2} \times 5\frac{1}{4}$ in. [6] 28 pp.

1505 EVANS, BERGEN, AND PINNEY, HESTER. Racedown and the Wordsworths.

Review of English Studies, viii (January 1932), 1–18.

1506 FAUSSET, HUGH I'ANSON. Wordsworth's Mysticism.

Aryan Path, iii (October 1932), 654–9.

1507 JEWSBURY, MARIA JANE. *Occasional Papers. Selected, with a Memoir,* by Eric Gillett. London: Oxford University Press, 1932.

$8\frac{3}{8} \times 5\frac{3}{8}$ in. lxvii [1] 107 [1] pp. Occasional mention of Wordsworth, *passim.*

1508 LEGOUIS, ÉMILE. Review of *The Wordsworth Collection at Cornell University,* by L. N. Broughton, 1931.

Revue Anglo-Américaine, x (October 1932), 58.

1509 McCABE, JOSEPH. *Edward Clodd: a Memoir.* London: John Lane, 1932.

$7\frac{1}{4} \times 4\frac{3}{4}$ in. vii [5] 219 [1] pp. Wordsworth, p. 105.

1510 MACLEAN, CATHERINE MACDONALD. *Dorothy Wordsworth: the Early Years.* London: Chatto and Windus, 1932.

$9\frac{5}{8} \times 6$ in. xiii [1] 439 [1] pp.

1511 *On Wordsworth's Birthday.* Waterville, Maine: Colby College Chapter of Phi Beta Kappa, 1932.

$8 \times 5\frac{3}{8}$ in. 32 pp.

1512 POTTS, ABBIE FINDLAY. The Spenserian and Miltonic Influence in Wordsworth's Ode and Rainbow.

Studies in Philology, XXIX (October 1932), 607–16.

1513 REA, JOHN D. Intimations of Immortality Again.

Philological Quarterly, XI (October 1932), 396–400.

1514 ROBERTS, CHARLES WALTER. The Influence of Godwin on Wordsworth's Letter to the Bishop of Llandaff.

Studies in Philology, XXIX (October 1932), 588–606.

1515 ROBERTSON, WILLIAM BRUNNER. *The Relation of Wordsworth to Science* (Cornell University Ph.D. Thesis). Ithaca: Typescript, 1932.

$10\frac{1}{4} \times 7\frac{5}{8}$ in. [6] 320 pp.

1516 SMITH, ELSIE. *An Estimate of William Wordsworth by His Contemporaries 1793–1822.* Oxford: Basil Blackwell, 1932.

$8\frac{1}{2} \times 5\frac{3}{8}$ in. viii, 371 [1] pp.

1517 WILLIAM, CHARLES. *The English Poetic Mind*. Oxford: Clarendon Press, 1932.

$7\frac{1}{8} \times 4\frac{5}{8}$ in. vii [1] 213 [3] pp. Wordsworth, pp. 153–71.

1933

1518 ARNOLD, FREDERICK S. William Wordsworth the Churchman.

American Church Monthly, xxiv (October 1933), 174–7.

1519 BATHO, EDITH CLARA. *The Later Wordsworth*. Cambridge: Cambridge University Press, 1933.

$8\frac{5}{8} \times 5\frac{1}{2}$ in. [2] 417 [1] pp.

1520 DE SELINCOURT, ERNEST. *Dorothy Wordsworth: a Biography*. Oxford: Clarendon Press, 1933.

$8\frac{5}{8} \times 5\frac{1}{4}$ in. xii [2] 428 [2] pp.

1521 FAGIN, NATHAN BRYLLION. *William Bartram, Interpreter of the American Landscape*. Baltimore, Maryland: Johns Hopkins Press, 1933.

9×6 in. ix [3] 229 [1] pp. Numerous references to Wordsworth; see Index.

1522 FAUSSET, HUGH I'ANSON. *The Lost Leader: a Study of Wordsworth*. London: Jonathan Cape, 1933.

$7\frac{7}{8} \times 5\frac{1}{2}$ in. 447 [1] pp.

1523 RABINOW, KENNETH. *Friends of Wordsworth* (Cornell University M.A. Thesis). Ithaca: Typescript, 1933.

$10\frac{1}{2} \times 7\frac{1}{2}$ in. [4] 310 pp.

1524 REUL, PAUL DE. *La Poésie Anglaise de Wordsworth à Keats*. Paris: Éditions Albert, 1933.

$7 \times 4\frac{3}{8}$ in. 266 [6] pp.

1525 W., J. P. Wordsworth's Soul-struggle.

Aryan Path, iv (June 1933), 421–4. Review of *The Lost Leader*, by Hugh I'Anson Fausset.

1526 WEBER, CARL JEFFERSON. *Thanks to the Censor*. Waterville, Maine: Colby College Chapter of Phi Beta Kappa, [*c.* 1933].

8 × 5¼ in. [3] 10–28 [2] pp. On two letters from Annette Vallon to Wordsworth.

1934

1527 BROUGHTON, LESLIE NATHAN. Reviews of *Dorothy Wordsworth: a Biography*, by Ernest de Selincourt; and *The Later Wordsworth*, by Edith C. Batho.

Yale Review, XXIII (Spring 1934), 638–40.

1528 BROWN, EDITH MORROW. *The Influence of the Bible on Wordsworth's Diction* (Cornell University Ph.D. Thesis). Ithaca: Typescript, 1934.

10¼ × 7½ in. [7] 345 pp.

1529 BURTON, MARY ELIZABETH. *Wordsworth's Revision of The Prelude* (Cornell University Ph.D. Thesis). Ithaca: Typescript, 1934.

10 × 7⅝ in. [4] 292 pp.

1530 COLLIS, JOHN STUART. Wordsworthian Pantheism.

Aryan Path, V (November 1934), 716–20.

1531 DE SELINCOURT, ERNEST. *Oxford Lectures on Poetry*. Oxford: Clarendon Press, 1934.

8⅝ × 5⅜ in. [8] 256 pp. Wordsworth's Preface to 'The Borderers,' pp. 157–79.

1532 GRAY, CHARLES HAROLD. Wordsworth's First Visit to Tintern Abbey.

PMLA, XLIX (March 1934), 123–33.

1533 HARTMAN, HERBERT. Wordsworth's 'Lucy' Poems.

PMLA, XLIX (March 1934), 134–42.

1534 HAVENS, RAYMOND DEXTER. *Descriptive Sketches* and *The Prelude*.

ELH, I (September 1934), 122–5.

1535 HAVENS, RAYMOND DEXTER. Wordsworth's Shipwrecked Geometrician.

ELH, i (September 1934), 120–1.

1536 MUESCHKE, PAUL, AND GRIGGS, EARL LESLIE. Wordsworth as the Prototype of the Poet in Shelley's Alastor.

PMLA, xlix (March 1934), 229–45.

1537 ROBERTS, CHARLES WALTER. Wordsworth, *The Philanthropist*, and *Political Justice*.

Studies in Philology, xxxi (January 1934), 84–91.

1538 SHERWOOD, MARGARET. *Undercurrents of Influence in English Romantic Poetry*. Cambridge, Massachusetts: Harvard University Press.

$8\frac{1}{2} \times 5\frac{3}{4}$ in. ix [1] 365 [3] pp. Numerous references to Wordsworth; see Index.

1539 SMITH, JOHN HARRINGTON. Genesis of The Borderers.

PMLA, xlix (September 1934), 922–30.

1540 STALLKNECHT, NEWTON PHELPS. The Doctrine of Coleridge's 'Dejection' and Its Relation to Wordsworth's Philosophy.

PMLA, xlix (March 1934), 196–207.

1541 STROUT, ALAN LANG. William Wordsworth and John Wilson; a Review of Their Relations between 1802 and 1817.

PMLA, xlix (March 1934), 143–83.

1935

1542 BISHOP, DAVID HORACE. Wordsworth's 'Hermitage': Racedown or Grasmere?

Studies in Philology, xxxii (July 1935), 483–507.

1543 CELAURO, PIETRO. *William Wordsworth*. Palermo: Vincent Belotti, 1935.

$9\frac{1}{2} \times 6\frac{3}{4}$ in. [3] 189 [5] pp.

1544 GILKYSON, CLAUDE. Henry Reed, 1825: Wordsworth's American Editor.

General Magazine and Historical Chronicle, Philadelphia, xxxviii (1935–6), 84–90, 163–72, 318–32, 333–71.

1545 HARRIS, RENDEL. *Wordsworth's Lucy* (The After-Glow Essays, No. 8). London: University of London Press, 1935.

$8\frac{3}{16} \times 6\frac{5}{8}$ in. 24 pp.

1546 LAMB, CHARLES. *The Letters of Charles Lamb, to Which Are Added Those of His Sister, Mary Lamb.* Edited by E. V. Lucas. London: J. M. Dent & Sons; and Methuen & Co., [1935], 3 vols.

$8\frac{1}{2} \times 5\frac{1}{2}$ in. Vol. 1: xliv, 431 [1]; vol. 2: [4] 467 [1]; vol. 3: [4] 467 [1] pp. Numerous references to Wordsworth; see Index.

1547 PATTON, CORNELIUS HOWARD. *The Rediscovery of Wordsworth.* Boston: Stratford Co., 1935.

$8\frac{1}{2} \times 5\frac{1}{2}$ in. vii [1] 258 pp.

1548 SPERRY, WILLARD LEAROYD. *Wordsworth's Anti-Climax.* Cambridge, Massachusetts: Harvard University Press.

$8\frac{1}{8} \times 5\frac{3}{8}$ in. vii [3] 228 [2] pp.

1936

1549 BURRA, PETER. *Wordsworth* (Great Lives). London: Duckworth, 1936.

$7\frac{1}{4} \times 4\frac{1}{4}$ in. 160 pp.

1550 DAVIS, PAULINE ALEXANDRA. *A Study of Fancy in Wordsworth's Poetry* (Cornell University M.A. Thesis). Ithaca: Typescript, 1936.

$10\frac{1}{4} \times 7\frac{3}{4}$ in. xvi, 101 pp.

1551 DE SELINCOURT, ERNEST. *The Early Wordsworth* (The English Association Presidential Address, 1936). n.p., 1936.

$9\frac{5}{8} \times 5\frac{3}{4}$ in. 28 pp.

1552 EATON, HORACE AINSWORTH. The Letters of De Quincey to Wordsworth, 1803–7.

ELH, iii (March 1936), 15–30.

(1)

Dear Sir,

I have not for some time been
more flattered then by the highly accepta
:ble present of the Southey's Joan of
Arc, with which you honoured me by
the hands of Mr Pinney. I should
have returned you my acknowledgements
immediatly, had I not imagined that
they would be more acceptable if accom
panied with an MSS copy of my Salisbury
plain, which I have been prevented
from transmitting you by unforeseen
engagements. I am now at leisure
and promise myself, in a few days,
that pleasure. In the mean while
I am [with respect to] I remain your very obliged
Coleridge and
say I wish [] W. Wordsworth
to hear from him

Early Handwriting of Wordsworth: Letter to Joseph Cottle, 1796.   No. 2298

Saturday Paris

Twelve o'clock
at night

My dearest Dora

You must have thought we
were lost! I would now merely to tell
you, we start to morrow for Fontainebleau
on our way to Lyons, & that I have written
at great length that you will receive
from your Mother, through Mr. Stephen-
son got her on Wednesday; and I have
never slept since." To morrow in the
Carriage we shall be quiet; as we mean
to leave this place about 12 or one o'clock
— I hope you take care of your health I
am well. And love to Mrs & Miss
Nash, and god almighty bless you
and grant us all to happy meeting.
Mr Thoson came with us to Paris
and will be the bearer of this & also
one other Letters. — farewell again & again
farewell. —

your most affectionate
Father W Wordsworth

Pray beg of Mr Nash to thank he
son for the invaluable book he
sent us. —

Later Handwriting of Wordsworth: Letter to Dora Wordsworth, 1837.   No. 2419

1553 HAVENS, RAYMOND DEXTER. Wordsworth's Adolescence.

Modern Language Notes, LI (March 1936), 137–42.

1554 LEAVIS, FRANK RAYMOND. *Revaluation: Tradition and Development in English Poetry*. London: Chatto & Windus, [1936].

$8\frac{1}{8} \times 5$ in. viii [2] 275 [1] pp. Wordsworth, pp. 154–202, and elsewhere.

1555 MARTIN, ARTHUR DAVIS. *The Religion of Wordsworth*. London: George Allen & Unwin, 1936.

$7\frac{1}{4} \times 4\frac{3}{4}$ in. [2] 100 [4] pp.

1556 PATTON, CORNELIUS HOWARD. *The Amherst Wordsworth Collection: a Descriptive Bibliography*. Amherst, Massachusetts: Trustees of Amherst College, 1936.

$9\frac{1}{4} \times 6$ in. xi [5] 304 [2] pp. With the addenda entitled: The Amherst Wordsworth Collection, Section III, Autograph Letters and Manuscripts, 8 pp.

1557 WORDSWORTH, DOROTHY. *George & Sarah Green, a Narrative, by Dorothy Wordsworth*. Edited from the Original Manuscript, with a Preface, by Ernest de Selincourt. Oxford: Clarendon Press, 1936.

$7\frac{3}{8} \times 4\frac{7}{8}$ in. 91 [1] pp.

1937

1558 ASHTON, HELEN, AND DAVIES, KATHARINE. *I Had a Sister: a Study of Mary Lamb, Dorothy Wordsworth, Caroline Herschel, Cassandra Austen*, with Illustrations by William Townsend. London: Lovat Dickson, 1937.

$8\frac{1}{2} \times 5\frac{1}{2}$ in. xv [3] 19–286 [2] pp.

1559 BAKER, JOHN MILTON. *Henry Crabb Robinson of Bury, Jena, The Times, and Russell Square*. London: George Allen & Unwin, 1937.

$8\frac{1}{2} \times 5\frac{1}{4}$ in. [2] 256 pp. A few references to Wordsworth; see Index.

1560 BRAHMSTAEDT, HERBERT. *William Wordsworths politisches Denken im Zusammenhang mit seiner Weltanschauung von 1790 bis 1814*. Dissertation zur Erlangung der Doktorwürde der Philosophischen Fakultät der Hansischen Universität Hamburg. Hamburg, 1937.

$8\frac{3}{4} \times 5\frac{7}{8}$ in. 80 [2] pp.

1561 CARRITT, EDGAR FREDERICK. Addison, Kant, and Wordsworth.

Essays and Studies by Members of the English Association, XXII (1937), 26–36.

1562 GILL, FREDERICK CYRIL. *The Romantic Movement and Methodism: a Study of English Romanticism and the Evangelical Revival.* London: Epworth Press, 1937.

$8\frac{1}{2} \times 5\frac{1}{4}$ in. 189 [3] pp. Numerous references to Wordsworth; see Index.

1563 GRIERSON, HERBERT JOHN CLIFFORD. *Milton & Wordsworth, Poets and Prophets: a Study of Their Reactions to Political Events.* New York: Macmillan Co.; Cambridge: Cambridge University Press, 1937.

$8 \times 5\frac{1}{4}$ in. x, 185 [1] pp.

1564 HAMILTON, MARIE PADGETT. Wordsworth's Relation to Coleridge's Osorio.

Studies in Philology, XXXIV (July 1937), 429–37.

1565 HARPER, GEORGE McLEAN. *Literary Appreciations.* Indianapolis, Indiana: Bobbs-Merrill Co., 1937.

$7\frac{7}{8} \times 5\frac{1}{4}$ in. xiii [5] 19–240 pp. Wordsworth's Poetical Technique, pp. 152–89.

1566 LINDSAY, JULIAN IRA. A Note on the Marginalia (see below).

Huntington Library Quarterly, 1 (October 1937), 95–9.

1567 SHEARER, EDNA ASHTON. Wordsworth and Coleridge Marginalia in a Copy of Richard Payne Knight's *Analytical Inquiry into the Principles of Taste.*

Huntington Library Quarterly, 1 (October 1937), 63–94.

1568 VIEBROCK, HELMUT. *Erlebnis und Gestaltung des Schönen in der Dichtung von Wordsworth (1798–1808).* Inaugural-Dissertation zur Erlangung der Doktorwürde der Philosophischen Fakultät der Phillips-Universität zu Marburg. Marburg-Lahn: Hermann Bauer, 1937.

$9\frac{1}{8} \times 6$ in. viii, 67 [1] pp.

1569 WHICHER, GEORGE F. Notes on a Wordsworth Collection.

The Colophon, II, n.s. (Summer 1937), 367–80. The subject is the Amherst Wordsworth Collection.

1938

1570 ASHTON, HELEN (PSEUD.). *William and Dorothy.* New York: Macmillan Co., 1938.

8 × 5¼ in. [2] 414 pp. A novel. Helen Ashton is the pseudonym of Mrs. Helen Rosalie Jordan.

1571 *An Exhibition of First and Other Early Editions of the Works of William Wordsworth (1770–1850) with a Few Autographs and Manuscripts,* Lent from the Personal Library of Professor John Edwin Wells, of Connecticut College for Women. New London, Connecticut: Mimeographed sheets, 1938.

11 × 8½ in. 8 pp.

1572 *An Exhibition of Paintings and Drawings by Sir George Beaumont,* Seventh Baronet, 1753–1827, Leicester Art Gallery, June 29th to August 7th, 1938. n.p., [1938].

8½ × 5¼ in. [2] 23 [1] pp. Peel Castle, facing p. 10.

1573 GOHLINGHORST, EDNA. *Unity of Thought in Wordsworth's Poetry* (Cornell University M.A. Thesis). Ithaca: Typescript, 1938.

10¼ × 7⅝ in. [3] 178 [1] pp.

1574 MORLEY, CHRISTOPHER. '*No Crabb, No Christmas.*' Chicago: Black Cat Press, 1938.

5½ × 4 in. 20 [4] pp. Crabb Robinson's Christmases.

1575 WELLS, JOHN EDWIN. *Lyrical Ballads,* 1800: Cancel Leaves.

PMLA, LIII (March 1938), 207–29.

1576 WELLS, JOHN EDWIN. Wordsworth's *Lyrical Ballads,* 1820.

Philological Quarterly, XVII (October 1938), 398–402.

1577 WINWAR, FRANCES. *Farewell the Banner: Coleridge, Wordsworth, and Dorothy.* New York: Doubleday, Doran, & Co., 1938.

8⅜ × 5½ in. xi [1] 348 pp.

16-2

1939

1578 BARRETT, ELIZABETH. *Letters from Elizabeth Barrett to B. R. Haydon.* Edited by Martha Hale Shackford. New York, London, and Toronto: Oxford University Press, 1939.

$8\frac{1}{2} \times 5\frac{3}{8}$ in. lxxii, 78 [8] pp. Several references to Wordsworth; see Index.

1579 BEATTY, FREDERIKA. *William Wordsworth of Rydal Mount, an Account of the Poet and His Friends in the Last Decade.* New York: E. P. Dutton & Co., 1939.

$8\frac{1}{2} \times 5\frac{1}{2}$ in. xi [1] 307 [1] pp.

1580 BRONOWSKI, JACOB. *The Poet's Defence.* Cambridge: Cambridge University Press, 1939.

$7\frac{7}{8} \times 4\frac{7}{8}$ in. [8] 258 [2] pp. Wordsworth and Coleridge, pp. 127–84.

1581 BROWNE, HELEN BIGHAM. *Walter Savage Landor as a Literary Critic* (Cornell University Ph.D. Thesis). Ithaca: Typescript, 1939.

$10\frac{1}{2} \times 7\frac{3}{4}$ in. [4] iii, 155 pp. Many references to Wordsworth, *passim*.

1582 GRIGGS, EARL LESLIE (ED.). *Wordsworth and Coleridge Studies in Honor of George McLean Harper.* Edited by Earl Leslie Griggs; Essays by Émile Legouis, Raymond D. Havens, Oscar James Campbell, Newton P. Stallknecht, Ernest de Selincourt, Leslie Nathan Broughton, M. Ray Adams, Samuel H. Monk, Gerard Hartley Buchan Coleridge, B. R. McElderry, Jr., Earl Leslie Griggs, Clarence DeWitt Thorpe, Edith J. Morley; an Appreciation by J. Duncan Spaeth; a Bibliography by Evelyn Griggs. Princeton: Princeton University Press, 1939.

$9 \times 5\frac{7}{8}$ in. viii, 254 [2] pp.

1583 Another copy.

With an inserted letter from G. M. Harper to L. N. Broughton thanking Professor Broughton for his contribution to the volume.

1584 MERRIAM, HAROLD GUY. *Edward Moxon, Publisher of Poets.* New York: Columbia University Press, 1939.

9×6 in. vii [3] 222 [6] pp. Many references to Wordsworth; see Index.

1585 *The Renowned Library of the Late John A. Spoor.* Public Sale April 26, 27, 28 [May 3, 4, 5] at the Parke-Bernet Galleries. Inc. New York, 1939, 2 vols.

$10\frac{1}{4} \times 6\frac{7}{8}$ in. Vol. 1: [14] 202 [4]; vol. 2: [8] 201 [5] pp. Wordsworth, vol. 2, pp. 192–9.

1586 THORNTON-COOK, ELSIE. *Justly Dear: Charles and Mary Lamb, a Biographical Novel.* New York: Charles Scribner's Sons, 1939.

$7\frac{3}{8} \times 5\frac{1}{8}$ in. 351 [1] pp. Many references to Wordsworth.

1587 THORPE, CLARENCE DeWITT. The Imagination: Coleridge vs. Wordsworth.

Philological Quarterly, XVIII (January 1939), 1–18.

1588 WILSON, JOHN DOVER. *Leslie Stephen and Matthew Arnold as Critics of Wordsworth.* The Leslie Stephen Lecture Delivered before the University of Cambridge on 2 May 1939. Cambridge: Cambridge University Press, 1939.

$7\frac{1}{4} \times 4\frac{7}{8}$ in. [2] 58 [4] pp.

1940

1589 BEACH, JOSEPH WARREN. Reason and Nature in Wordsworth.

Journal of the History of Ideas, 1 (June 1940), 335–51.

1590 BERNBAUM, ERNEST. Is Wordsworth's Nature-Poetry Antiquated?

ELH, VII (December 1940), 333–40.

1591 CROFTS, J. *Wordsworth and the Seventeenth Century* (Warton Lecture in English Poetry). London: Humphrey Milford, 1940.

$10 \times 6\frac{1}{8}$ in. 20 pp.

1592 DAVIS, HERBERT, DEVANE, WILLIAM C., AND BALD, R. C. (EDS.). *Nineteenth-Century Studies.* Ithaca: Cornell University Press, 1940.

$9 \times 5\frac{7}{8}$ in. [10] 303 [3] pp. Wordsworth, pp. 84–8.

1593 EIGERMAN, HYMAN. *The Poetry of Dorothy Wordsworth.* Edited from the Journals by Hyman Eigerman. New York: Columbia University Press, 1940.

$7\frac{3}{4} \times 5\frac{1}{8}$ in. [64] pp. Passages from the Journal arranged as verse.

1594 GRIERSON, SIR HERBERT. *Essays and Addresses.* London: Chatto & Windus, 1940.

$8\frac{3}{4} \times 5\frac{3}{8}$ in. x, 274 [2] pp. Wordsworth, pp. 261–75.

1595 KNIGHT, GEORGE WILSON. *The Starlit Dome: Studies in the Poetry of Vision.* London: Oxford University Press, 1940.

$8\frac{1}{4} \times 5\frac{1}{2}$ in. [viii] 314 pp. The Wordsworthian Profundity, pp. 1–82.

1596 WELLS, JOHN EDWIN. Wordsworth and De Quincey in Westmorland Politics, 1818.

PMLA, LV (December 1940), 1080–128.

1597 WILLEY, BASIL. *The Eighteenth Century Background.* London: Chatto & Windus, 1940.

$8\frac{5}{8} \times 5\frac{1}{4}$ in. viii, 315 [1] pp. Numerous references to Wordsworth; see Index.

1941

1598 BISHOP, DAVID HORACE. The Origin of *The Prelude*, and the Composition of Books I and II.

Studies in Philology, XXXVIII (July 1941), 494–520.

1599 HANKINS, EVERETT MORRISON. *Literary Criticism by William Wordsworth* (Cornell University Ph.D. Thesis). Ithaca: Typescript, 1941, 2 vols.

$10\frac{1}{4} \times 7\frac{3}{4}$ in. Vol. 1: lx [2] 460; vol. 2: 461–819 pp.

1600 HAVENS, RAYMOND DEXTER. *The Mind of a Poet: a Study of Wordsworth's Thought, with Particular Reference to The Prelude.* Baltimore: Johns Hopkins Press, 1941.

9×6 in. xviii, 670 [2] pp.

1601 Another copy.

1602 NOYES, RUSSELL. *Wordsworth and Jeffrey in Controversy* (Indiana University Publications, Humanities Series No. 5). Bloomington: Indiana University, 1941.

$9\frac{3}{4} \times 6\frac{5}{8}$ in. 54 [2] pp.

1603 PARKER, W. M. Letter, Wordsworth to John Scott, 11 June 1816.

Times Literary Supplement, 27 December 1941, p. 660.

1604 PFEIFFER, KARL G. The Prototype of the Poet in 'The Great Stone Face'.

Research Studies of the State College of Washington, IX (June 1941), 100–8.

1605 POPE-HENNESSY, UNA. *Durham Company*. London: Chatto & Windus, 1941.

$8\frac{1}{8} \times 5\frac{1}{4}$ in. 223 [1] pp. Wordsworth, pp. 83–144.

1606 POTTLE, FREDERICK ALBERT. *The Idiom of Poetry*. Ithaca: Cornell University Press, 1941.

$7\frac{3}{4} \times 5\frac{1}{8}$ in. ix [5] 139 [3] pp. Many references to Wordsworth, *passim*.

1607 WELLS, JOHN EDWIN. De Quincey and *The Prelude* in 1839.

Philological Quarterly, XX (January 1941), 24.

1608 WIEST, REX M. *A Dictionary of Proper Names in the Poetry of Wordsworth* (Cornell University M.A. Thesis). Ithaca: Typescript, 1941.

$10\frac{1}{4} \times 7\frac{1}{2}$ in. [3] 774 pp.

1609 WORDSWORTH, DOROTHY. *Journals of Dorothy Wordsworth*. Edited by Ernest de Selincourt. New York: Macmillan Co., 1941, 2 vols.

$8\frac{1}{2} \times 5\frac{5}{8}$ in. Vol. 1: xxv, [1] 443 [1]; vol. 2: vii [1] 433 [3] pp.

1942

1610 BROUGHTON, LESLIE NATHAN. *The Wordsworth Collection Formed by Cynthia Morgan St. John and Given to Cornell University by Victor Emanuel: a Supplement to the Catalogue*. Ithaca: Cornell University Press, 1942.

$9 \times 5\frac{7}{8}$ in. viii, 81 [1] pp.

1611 BURTON, MARY E. *The One Wordsworth.* Chapel Hill: University of North Carolina Press, [1942].

8¼ × 5½ in. x [4] 237 [1] pp.

1612 CAMERON, KENNETH WALTER. Wordsworth, Bishop Doane, and the Sonnets on the American Church.

Historical Magazine of the Protestant Episcopal Church, XI (March 1942), 83–91.

1613 HEALEY, GEORGE HARRIS. *Wordsworth's Pocket Notebook.* Ithaca: Cornell University Press, 1942.

8½ × 5⅜ in. [12] 106 [2] pp.

1614 JORDAN, JOHN E. Wordsworth and the Witch of Atlas.

ELH, IX (December 1942), 320–5.

1615 MILES, JOSEPHINE. *Wordsworth and the Vocabulary of Emotion.* Berkeley and Los Angeles: University of California Press, 1942.

9 × 5⅞ in. [10] 181 [1] pp.

1943

1616 BARZUN, JACQUES. *Romanticism and the Modern Ego.* Boston: Little, Brown, & Co., 1943.

7⅞ × 5⅜ in. viii [2] 359 [3] pp. Several references to Wordsworth; see Index.

1617 MEYER, GEORGE WILBUR. *Wordsworth's Formative Years* (University of Michigan Publications, Language and Literature, Vol. XX). Ann Arbor: University of Michigan Press, 1943.

9⅛ × 5⅞ in. vii [1] 265 [5] pp.

1618 PEEK, KATHERINE MAY. *Wordsworth in England: Studies in the History of His Fame.* Bryn Mawr, Pennsylvania, 1943.

8¹³⁄₁₆ × 5¾ in. 276 pp.

1944

1619 BEACH, JOSEPH WARREN. *A Romantic Review of Poetry, Being Lectures Given at the Johns Hopkins University on the Percy Turnbull Memorial Foundation in November 1941.* Minneapolis: University of Minnesota Press, 1944.

8½ × 5⅜ in. [4] 133 [3] pp.

1620 COMPARETTI, ALICE PATTEE. Two Wordsworth Letters.

Colby Library Quarterly, I (January 1944), 80–2.

1621 DOCKHORN, KLAUS. *Wordsworth und die rhetorische Tradition in England* (Nachrichten der Akademie der Wissenschaften in Göttingen philologisch-historische Klasse, Nr. 11). Göttingen: Vanderhoeck & Ruprecht, 1944.

$9\frac{1}{2} \times 6\frac{5}{8}$ in. 255–92 pp.

1622 HOUSMAN, LAURENCE. What Happened to Wordsworth?

Atlantic Monthly, CLXXIV (November 1944), 66–71.

1623 LEHMANN, JOHN. Wordsworth's Journey through France.

Geographical Magazine, XVII (August 1944), 170–81.

1624 METZDORF, ROBERT F. A New Wordsworth Letter.

Modern Language Notes, LIX (March 1944), 168–70.

1625 NOYES, RUSSELL. Wordsworth and Burns.

PMLA, LIX (September 1944), 813–32.

1626 PFEIFFER, KARL G. The Theme of Desertion in Wordsworth.

Research Studies of the State College of Washington, XII (June 1944), 122–8.

1627 SMITH, J. C. *A Study of Wordsworth*. Edinburgh: Oliver and Boyd, 1944.

$7\frac{1}{4} \times 4\frac{3}{4}$ in. vii [1] 103 [1] pp.

1628 WORDSWORTH, DORA. *The Letters of Dora Wordsworth*. Edited, with an Introduction, by Howard P. Vincent. Chicago: Packard & Co., 1944.

$8\frac{3}{8} \times 4\frac{5}{8}$ in. ix [1] 98 [2] pp.

1945

1629 SHACKFORD, MARTHA HALE. *Wordsworth's Interest in Painters and Pictures*. Wellesley, Massachusetts: Wellesley Press, 1945.

9×6 in. 90 pp.

1630 STALLKNECHT, NEWTON P. *Strange Seas of Thought: Studies in William Wordsworth's Philosophy of Man and Nature.* Durham, North Carolina: Duke University Press, 1945.

9 × 6 in. ix [1] 284 [2] pp.

1631 WARD, WILLIAM SMITH. Wordsworth, the 'Lake' Poets, and Contemporary Magazine Critics, 1798–1820.

Studies in Philology, XLII (January 1945), 87–113.

1946

1632 CHRISTENSEN, FRANCIS. Creative Sensibility in Wordsworth.

Journal of English and Germanic Philology, XLV (October 1946), 361–8.

1633 GRIERSON, H. J. C., AND SMITH, J. C. *Critical History of English Poetry.* New York: Oxford University Press, 1946.

8¼ × 5½ in. viii, 593 [3] pp. Wordsworth, pp. 335–60.

1634 LAIRD, JOHN. *Philosophical Incursions into English Literature.* Cambridge: Cambridge University Press, 1946.

8½ × 5⅜ in. [8] 223 [1] pp. Wordsworth and 'Natural Piety', pp. 92–115.

1635 TAPIONLINNA, TELLERVO. *Järvikoulun runotar. Dorothy Wordsworth ja hänen vaikutuksensa William Wordsworthiin ja S. T. Coleridgeen.* Porvoo, Finland: W. Söderström, [1946].

7⅝ × 5 in. 430 pp. A dissertation, Helsingfors University.

1636 WORTHINGTON, JANE. *Wordsworth's Reading of Roman Prose.* New Haven: Yale University Press, 1946.

9¼ × 5⅞ in. xi [3] 84 pp.

1947

1637 BROOKS, CLEANTH. *The Well Wrought Urn: Studies in the Structure of Poetry.* New York: Reynal & Hitchcock, [1947].

7⅞ × 5⅜ in. xi [1] 270 [4] pp. Wordsworth and the Paradox of the Imagination, pp. 114–38.

1638 DE SELINCOURT, ERNEST. *Wordsworthian and Other Studies.* Oxford: Clarendon Press, 1947.

8⅝ × 5½ in. [8] 206 [2] pp.

1639 DUFFIN, HENRY CHARLES. *The Way of Happiness, a Reading of Wordsworth.* London: Sidgwick and Jackson, [1947].

7 × 4⅝ in. viii, 128 pp.

1640 LOGAN, JAMES VENABLE. *Wordsworthian Criticism, a Guide and Bibliography.* Columbus: Ohio State University Press, 1947.

8⅞ × 5⅞ in. xii, 304 [4] pp.

1641 *William Wordsworth 1770–1850.* Rockford, Illinois: Rockford College, 1947.

8½ × 5½ in. [2] 26 [2] pp. Catalogue of an exhibition.

1948

1642 CHEW, SAMUEL CLAGGETT. *The Nineteenth Century and After (1789–1939).* New York: Appleton-Century-Crofts, [1948].

9⅜ × 6¼ in. viii, 1111–605 pp. Vol. 4 of *A Literary History of England*, by Albert C. Baugh and others. Wordsworth, pp. 1136–48, and elsewhere.

1643 DOUGLAS, WALLACE WARNER. Wordsworth as a Business Man.

PMLA, LXIII (June 1948), 625–41.

1644 ELWIN, MALCOLM. *The First Romantics.* New York: Longmans, Green, & Co., 1948.

8¼ × 5⅜ in. viii, 280 pp. Numerous references to Wordsworth; see Index.

1645 GEORGE, ERIC. *The Life and Death of Benjamin Robert Haydon, 1786–1846.* London: Oxford University Press, 1948.

8⅜ × 5⅜ in. vi [4] 314 + 16 pp. of plates. Several references to Wordsworth; see Index.

1646 GREIG, JAMES A. *Francis Jeffrey of the Edinburgh Review.* Edinburgh: Oliver and Boyd, 1948.

8½ × 5¼ in. xii, 326 pp. Numerous references to Wordsworth; see Index.

1647 JAMES, DAVID GWILYM. *The Romantic Comedy*. London: Oxford University Press, 1948.

$8\frac{3}{8} \times 5\frac{1}{4}$ in. xi [1] 275 [1] pp. Numerous references to Wordsworth; see Index.

1648 LACEY, NORMAN. *Wordsworth's View of Nature and Its Ethical Consequences*. Cambridge: Cambridge University Press, 1948.

8×5 in. viii, 128 pp.

1649 OLNEY, CLARKE. Wordsworth and Haydon.

Notes and Queries, 12 June and 24 July, 1948, pp. 250–3, 314–17.

1949

1650 BOWERS, ROBERT HOOD. Wordsworthian Solitude.

Modern Language Quarterly, x (September 1949), 389–99.

1651 DARBISHIRE, HELEN. *Some Variants in Wordsworth's Text in the Volumes of 1836–7 in the King's Library*. Oxford: Printed for Presentation to Members of the Roxburghe Club, 1949.

$10\frac{1}{2} \times 8$ in. xiii [1] 58 [4] pp.

1652 FAIRCHILD, HOXIE NEALE. *Religious Trends in English Poetry*. Vol. III: 1780–1830, Romantic Faith. New York: Columbia University Press, 1949.

9×6 in. xii, 550 pp. Wordsworth, pp. 138–262, and elsewhere.

1653 *Wordsworth Centenary*, Grasmere, 1950 (published 1949).

The Programme; and a circular with an application for tickets for the celebration. Two sheets.

1950

1654 [BALD, ROBERT CECIL]. *The Cornell Wordsworth Collection. A Brief Account together with a Catalogue of the Exhibition Held in the University Library on the Occasion of the Centenary of Wordsworth's Death*. Ithaca: Cornell University Press, 1950.

9×5 in. [6] 42 [2] pp.

1655 BONNER, FRANCIS W. Wordsworth's Philosophy of Education.

Furman Studies: Bulletin of Furman University, xxxiii (Spring 1950), 1–26.

1656 Centenary of a Poet: Friendly Wordsworth Walks from Musty Diary.

Christian Science Monitor, 20 April 1950. In an envelope with views of the Lake District excerpted from the issue of 15 April 1950.

1657 CRAIG, HARDIN. *A History of English Literature*. New York: Oxford University Press, 1950.

9 × 5¾ in. xii, 697 [1] pp. Wordsworth, pp. 469–74, and elsewhere; see Index.

1658 DARBISHIRE, HELEN. *The Poet Wordsworth*. Oxford: Clarendon Press, 1950.

7⅜ × 4¾ in. vi [2] 182 pp.

1659 FIELDING, GEORGE. *William Wordsworth Centenary, 1850–1950: the Wordsworth Memorial Chapel in St. Mary's Church, Ambleside*. Ambleside, 1950.

8¾ × 5⅝ in. 19 [1] pp.

1660 GORDAN, JOHN D. *William Wordsworth, 1770–1850: an Exhibition*. New York: New York Public Library, 1950.

10 × 7 in. 31 [1] pp.

1661 JAMES, DAVID GWILYM. *Wordsworth and Tennyson* (The Warton Lecture on English Poetry, 1950). London: Geoffrey Cumberlege, [1950].

10⅜ × 6½ in. 113–29 pp.

1662 LYON, JUDSON STANLEY. *The Excursion, a Study*. New Haven: Yale University Press, 1950.

9¼ × 6 in. x, 154 pp.

1663 MacLEAN, KENNETH. *Agrarian Age: a Background for Wordsworth*. New Haven: Yale University Press, 1950.

9¼ × 6 in. xiii [1] 110 [2] pp.

1664 MALLABY, GEORGE. *Wordsworth: a Tribute.* Oxford: Blackwell, 1950.

$7\frac{3}{4} \times 5\frac{1}{4}$ in. xii, 108 pp.

1665 NOYCE, WILFRED. *Scholar Mountaineers: Pioneers of Parnassus.* With Wood-engravings by R. Taylor. London: Dennis Dobson, [1950].

$8\frac{1}{2} \times 5\frac{1}{4}$ in. 164 pp. The Wordsworths, pp. 81–92.

1666 PEACOCK, MARKHAM L., JR. (ED.). *The Critical Opinions of William Wordsworth.* Baltimore: Johns Hopkins Press, 1950.

$9\frac{1}{4} \times 6$ in. xxvi, 469 [1] pp.

1667 PITTMAN, CHARLES LEONARD. An Introduction to a Study of Wordsworth's Reading in Science.

Furman Studies: Bulletin of Furman University, xxxiii (Spring 1950), 27–60.

1668 POLICARDI, SILVIO. *William Wordsworth, Anno Academico 1949–1950.* Venezia: La Goliardica, [1950].

$9\frac{1}{4} \times 6$ in. [4] 242 [2] pp.

1669 POTTLE, FREDERICK ALBERT. The Eye and the Object in the Poetry of Wordsworth.

Yale Review, xl (September 1950), 27–42.

1670 RANSOM, JOHN CROWE. William Wordsworth: Notes toward an Understanding of His Poetry.

Kenyon Review, xii (Summer 1950), 498–519.

1671 RAYSOR, THOMAS MIDDLETON (ED.). *The English Romantic Poets,* a Review of Research, by Ernest Bernbaum, Samuel C. Chew, Thomas M. Raysor, Clarence D. Thorpe, Bennett Weaver, René Wellek. New York: Modern Language Association of America, 1950.

$5\frac{1}{2} \times 8$ in. [10] 241 [5] pp.

1672 SERGEANT, HOWARD. *The Cumberland Wordsworth.* London: Williams & Norgate, [1950].

$7\frac{1}{4} \times 4\frac{5}{8}$ in. 120 pp.

1673 SPARK, MURIEL, AND STANFORD, DEREK, (EDS.). *Tribute to Wordsworth: a Miscellany of Opinion for the Centenary of the Poet's Death.* Foreword by Herbert Read. Edited with Introductions by Muriel Spark & Derek Stanford. London and New York: Wingate, [1950].

$8\frac{1}{2} \times 5\frac{1}{4}$ in. 232 pp.

1674 TRILLING, LIONEL. Wordsworth and the Iron Time.

Kenyon Review, XII (Summer 1950), 477–97.

1675 *Wordsworth at Cambridge:* a Record of the Commemoration Held at St. John's College, Cambridge, in April 1950. Cambridge: Cambridge University Press, [1950].

$8\frac{1}{2} \times 5\frac{1}{2}$ in. 71 [13] pp.

1676 *Wordsworth Centenary Program*, Cornell University, 1950.

Preserved with the program are two lecture posters and three photographs, one of Robert Frost, one of the other speakers, and one of the exhibition in the University Library. Also Greetings to the Convocation at Cornell from Princeton University and a copy of the reply from Cornell.

1677 *Wordsworth Commemoration*, 22 April 1950. St. John's College, Cambridge, [1950].

$8\frac{3}{4} \times 6$ in. [12] pp.

1678 The World of William Wordsworth.

Life, XXIX (17 July 1950), 82–90.

1951

1679 DUNKLIN, GILBERT T. (ED.). *Wordsworth Centenary Studies at Cornell and Princeton Universities* by Douglas Bush, Frederick A. Pottle, Earl Leslie Griggs, John Crowe Ransom, B. Ifor Evans, Lionel Trilling, Willard L. Sperry. Princeton: Princeton University Press, 1951.

$8\frac{1}{2} \times 5\frac{3}{8}$ in. xii [4] 169 [7] pp.

1680 FLEISHER, DAVID. *William Godwin; a Study in Liberalism.* New York: A. M. Kelly, [1951].

$8\frac{1}{2} \times 5\frac{1}{2}$ in. 154 pp. Wordsworth, pp. 19, 24, 38.

1681 HAYDEN, DONALD E. *After Conflict, Quiet: a Study of Words-worth's Poetry in Relation to His Life and Letters.* New York: Exposition Press, [1951].

$8\frac{3}{8} \times 5\frac{1}{2}$ in. xvii [1] 230 pp.

1682 RAND, FRANK PRENTICE. *Not without Hope.* Mimeo-graphed, n.p., n.d.

44 p. A play is six Episodes, with historical notes; the principal characters are the Wordsworths and their friends.

1952

1683 ABERCROMBIE, LASCELLES. *The Art of Wordsworth.* Lon-don: Oxford University Press, 1952.

$7\frac{1}{2} \times 4\frac{3}{4}$ in. vi [2] 157 [3] pp.

1684 COOPER, LANE. *Late Harvest: Sketches of Cook, Adams, and Kleist; the College President; with Philosophical Reviews, and Papers on Coleridge, Wordsworth, and Byron.* Ithaca: Cornell University Press, 1952.

9×6 in. xii, 228 pp.

1685 MARSH, FLORENCE. *Wordsworth's Imagery: a Study in Poetic Vision.* New Haven: Yale University Press, 1952.

1953

1686 ABRAMS, MEYER HOWARD. *The Mirror and the Lamp: Romantic Theory and the Critical Tradition.* New York: Oxford University Press, 1953.

$9\frac{3}{16} \times 6\frac{1}{16}$ in. xiii [1] 406 pp. Numerous references to Wordsworth; see Index.

1687 COE, CHARLES NORTON. *Wordsworth and the Literature of Travel.* New York: Bookman Associates, [1953].

$8\frac{1}{4} \times 5\frac{3}{8}$ in. 122 [6] pp.

1688 DARBISHIRE, HELEN. *Wordsworth.* London, New York, and Toronto: Published for the British Council and the National Book League by Longmans, Green, & Co., 1953.

$8\frac{1}{2} \times 5\frac{3}{8}$ in. [2] 48 pp.

Sir

Rydal Mount 4th September
1818

I know you will excuse the liberty
I am going to take, in requesting that
you will take the trouble to inquire at
the Coach office at Whitehaven if an
Umbrella is lying there, which was
left at the Top of the Coach on
Monday morning, by a little Boy
who got on to the Coach at Ry-
-dal & went as far as Wythebum,
& when he dismounted forgot his Umbrel-
-la ... If the Umbrella is found, pray
desire that it may be brought by the
Coach, directed for Wm Wilberforce Esqr
Rydal, near Ambleside.. If you hear
nothing of it you need not trouble your-
-self to write. I am, Sir
turn over   yours respectfully
Dorothy Wordsworth

Handwriting of Dorothy Wordsworth.   No. 2572

4.

Rydal Mount,
July 16th

Dear Sir

Without your sanction
I continue to forward letters to
William thro' your medium. If
I do wrong I trust to your telling
me so, & that you will keep for
us an account of Postage should
it not be in your power to
send letters, to William's altered
address, without expence.

Mr W. would have written to
you had he not been particularly
engaged—he deputes me to convey
his kindest regards. Believe me
Dr Sir to be your obliged M. Wordsworth

Handwriting of Mary Wordsworth.   No. 2591

1689 HOUGH, GRAHAM GOULDEN. *The Romantic Poets.* London: Hutchinson's University Library, [1953].

$7\frac{1}{4} \times 4\frac{5}{8}$ in. vii [1] 9–200 pp. Wordsworth and Coleridge, pp. 27–96.

1690 JORDAN, JOHN EMORY. De Quincey on Wordsworth's Theory of Diction.

PMLA, LXVIII (September 1953), 764–78.

1691 MARGOLIOUTH, HERSCHEL MAURICE. *Wordsworth and Coleridge, 1795–1834.* London: Oxford University Press, 1953.

$6\frac{1}{2} \times 4\frac{1}{8}$ in. vii [1] 206 pp.

1692 POTTS, ABBIE FINDLAY. *Wordsworth's Prelude; a Study of Its Literary Form.* Ithaca: Cornell University Press, 1953.

$9 \times 5\frac{7}{8}$ in. xii [2] 392 [2] pp.

1693 READ, HERBERT EDWARD. *The True Voice of Feeling: Studies in English Romantic Poetry.* London: Faber and Faber, [1953].

$8\frac{1}{2} \times 5\frac{3}{8}$ in. 382 [2] pp. A Complex Delight: Wordsworth, pp. 38–54; Wordsworth's Philosophical Faith, pp. 189–211; for other references, see Index.

1694 ROGERS, SAMUEL. *Recollections of the Table-talk of Samuel Rogers, First Collected by the Revd. Alexander Dyce.* Edited, with an Introduction, by Morchard Bishop. Lawrence: University of Kansas Press, 1953.

$7\frac{1}{2} \times 4\frac{3}{4}$ in. xxv [1] 248 [2] pp. Several references to Wordsworth; see Index.

1695 WAIN, JOHN (ED.). *Contemporary Reviews of Romantic Poetry* (Life, Literature, and Thought Library). London: G. G. Harrap & Co., 1953.

$7\frac{3}{16} \times 4\frac{3}{4}$ in. 240 pp. Wordsworth, pp. 51–85.

1696 WARD, WILLIAM SMITH. An Early Champion of Wordsworth: Thomas Noon Talfourd.

PMLA, LXVIII (December 1953), 992–1000.

1697 WORDSWORTH, DOROTHY. *Dorothy Wordsworth's Journals.* Edited with Notes by R. H. Blyth. [Tokyo]: Hokuseido, [*c.* 1953].

7×5 in. xv, 157 pp.

1954

1698 BATESON, FREDERICK WILSE. *Wordsworth: a Re-interpretation.* London: Longmans, Green, & Co., 1954.

$8\frac{1}{2} \times 5\frac{1}{4}$ in. ix [1] 227 [1] pp.

1699 FOXON, D. F. *The Printing of Lyrical Ballads, 1798.* London: Bibliographical Society, 1954.

$9\frac{1}{2} \times 6\frac{1}{2}$ in. Reprinted from *The Library*, 5S, ix (December 1954), 221–41.

1700 HARTMAN, GEOFFREY H. *The Unmediated Vision: an Interpretation of Wordsworth, Hopkins, Rilke, and Valéry.* New Haven: Yale University Press, 1954.

$9\frac{1}{4} \times 6$ in. xii, 206 pp.

1701 HUTCHINSON, SARA. *The Letters of Sara Hutchinson from 1800 to 1835.* Edited by Kathleen Coburn. London: Routledge & Kegan Paul, [1954].

$8\frac{1}{2} \times 5\frac{3}{8}$ in. xxxviii, 474 pp. Numerous references to Wordsworth; see Index.

1702 JONES, JOHN. *The Egotistical Sublime: a History of Wordsworth's Imagination.* London: Chatto & Windus, 1954.

$7\frac{7}{8} \times 5$ in. ix, 212 pp.

1703 MAYO, ROBERT. The Contemporaneity of the *Lyrical Ballads.*

PMLA, LXIX (June 1954), 486–522.

1955

1704 TRILLING, LIONEL. *The Opposing Self: Nine Essays in Criticism.* New York: Viking Press, 1955.

$8\frac{3}{4} \times 5\frac{1}{2}$ in. 232 pp. Wordsworth and the Rabbis, pp. 118–50.

1705 WAIN, JOHN (ED.). *Interpretations; Essays on Twelve English Poets.* London: Routledge and Kegan Paul, 1955.

$8\frac{1}{2} \times 5\frac{3}{8}$ in. xv [1] 237 [1] pp. William Wordsworth: Resolution and Independence (by W. W. Robson), pp. 113–28.

1706 ZALL, PAUL M. Wordsworth and the Copyright Act of 1842.

PMLA, LXX (March 1955), 132–44.

UNDATED

1707 BAYLDON, ARTHUR A. D. Wordsworth.

A sonnet, in manuscript.

1708 PAYN, JAMES. *Some Literary Recollections by James Payn.* New York: Harper & Brothers.

$7\frac{1}{4} \times 4\frac{3}{4}$ in. 205 [11] pp. A few references to Wordsworth, *passim.*

1709 ST. JOHN, CYNTHIA MORGAN. *A Wordsworth Scrap-Book.*

$10\frac{3}{4} \times 14$ in. (oblong). 17 leaves, containing maps, pictures, woodcuts, and miscellaneous illustrations.

1710 SHERARD, ROBERT HARBOROUGH. *Modern Paris, Some Sidelights on Its Inner Life.* London: T. Werner Laurie.

$8\frac{5}{8} \times 5\frac{3}{8}$ in. [10] 300 pp. Wordsworth, pp. 64–5, 89. The author was a great-grandson of Wordsworth.

1711 TRELAWNY, EDWARD JOHN. *Records of Shelley, Byron, and the Author* (New Universal Library). London: George Routledge & Sons.

$6 \times 3\frac{5}{8}$ in. xxiv, 264 pp. A few references to Wordsworth, *passim.*

1712 TUTIN, JOHN RAMSDEN. *The Wordsworth Year-Book: a Double Calendar; Being a Collection of Poems and Passages, Personal, Philosophical, Seasonal, etc., from the Works in Verse and Prose of William Wordsworth.* Compiled by J. R. Tutin, Compiler of the *Wordsworth Birthday Book, The Wordsworth Dictionary,* etc., etc.

The compiler's manuscript, unbound. Apparently unpublished.

PART VI

COLERIDGE AND HIS FAMILY

1713 COLERIDGE, SAMUEL TAYLOR, AND SOUTHEY, ROBERT. *The Fall of Robespierre. An Historic Drama.* Cambridge: Printed by Benjamin Flower, for W. H. Lunn, and J. and J. Merrill; and Sold by J. March, Norwich, 1794.

7¾ × 5 in. [5] 6–37 [1] pp.

1714 WRANGHAM, FRANCIS. *Poems by Francis Wrangham*, M.A., Member of Trinity College, Cambridge. London: J. Mawman, 1795.

6⅞ × 4½ in. viii [6] 6–111 [1] pp. Coleridge's translation of Hendecasyllabi ad Brutonam, pp. 79–83.

1715 COLERIDGE, SAMUEL TAYLOR. *Conciones ad Populum. Or Addresses to the People.* n.p., 1796.

6⅛ × 3¾ in. 69 [1] pp.

1716 COLERIDGE, SAMUEL TAYLOR. *Poems on Various Subjects.* London: Printed for G. G. and J. Robinsons, and J. Cottle, Bookseller, Bristol, 1796.

6⅛ × 3⅝ in. xvi, 188 [4] pp. Written on the fly-leaf in Coleridge's hand: 'Mrs. Evans from the Author.'

1717 COLERIDGE, SAMUEL TAYLOR. *The Watchman*, Nos. 1–10 (1 March–13 May 1796).

9 × 5½ in. The original parts. Uncut.

1718 COLERIDGE, SAMUEL TAYLOR. *Poems by S. T. Coleridge, Second Edition. To Which Are Now Added Poems by Charles Lamb and Charles Lloyd.* Printed by N. Biggs, for J. Cottle, Bristol, and Messrs. Robinsons, London, 1797.

6⅛ × 3¾ in. xx, 278. Formerly owned by Augusta, Duchess of Sussex, daughter-in-law of George III. Title-page signed 'The Duchess of Sussex'; p. vii signed 'Augusta.'

1798

1719 *Flowers of Poesy, Consisting of Elegies, Songs, Sonnets, Etc.* Carlisle: Printed by and for J. Mitchell; and Sold by T. N. Longman, London, 1798.

$7\frac{5}{8} \times 4\frac{3}{8}$ in. 72 pp. Contains 'Thou gentle Look, that didst my soul beguile', by Coleridge.

See also *Lyrical Ballads* (No. 3) and *Annual Anthology* (No. 597).

1800

1720 COLERIDGE, SAMUEL TAYLOR. *The Piccolomini, or the First Part of Wallenstein, a Drama in Five Acts.* Translated from the German of Frederick Schiller by S. T. Coleridge. London: Printed for T. N. Longman and O. Rees, 1800. *Separate title-page, Part 2:* The Death of Wallenstein. A Tragedy in Five Acts. Translated from the German of Frederick Schiller by S. T. Coleridge. London: Printed for T. N. Longman and O. Rees, 1800.

$8\frac{1}{4} \times 5\frac{1}{8}$ in. [10] ii [2] 214 [2]; [6] 157 [7] pp. Lacks the general title-page. From the library of Coleridge's friend Sir George Beaumont, with a one-page manuscript commentary on the two plays in the hand of Coleridge.

See also *Lyrical Ballads* (No. 6).

1802

See *Lyrical Ballads* (No. 12).

1803

1721 COLERIDGE, SAMUEL TAYLOR. *Poems.* Third Edition. London: Printed by N. Biggs, for T. N. Longman and O. Rees, 1803.

$6\frac{1}{4} \times 3\frac{3}{4}$ in. xi [1] 202 pp.

1722 Another copy.

$6\frac{1}{8} \times 3\frac{7}{8}$ in. Sara Hutchinson's copy with an annotation by Coleridge. Title-page signed 'S. Hutchinson.' On p. 103 Coleridge has vigorously crossed out his sonnet, 'Not Stanhope! with the Patriot's doubtful name', and in the lower margin has written: 'infamous Insertion! It was written in ridicule of Jacobinical Bombast put into the first Edition by a blunder of Cottle's, rejected indignantly from the second & here maliciously reprinted in my Absence. S. T. Coleridge.' On a blank page is the following note: 'This Book was given me by Mrs. Wordsworth, in remembrance of her Sister, Sarah Hutchinson, whose dying eyes I closed. Thomas Carr, Hill Top, Ambleside, 1835.'

1804

1723 ROBINSON, M. E. *The Wild Wreath.* [London]: Richard
Phillips, 1804.

6⅞ × 4¼ in. viii, 228 [6] pp. Contains Coleridge's Mad Monk.

1805

See *Lyrical Ballads* (No. 17).

1812

1724 COLERIDGE, SAMUEL TAYLOR, AND SOUTHEY,
ROBERT. *Omniana, or Horæ Otiosiores.* London: Printed for Longman,
Hurst, Rees, Orme, and Brown, 1812, 2 vols.

6¼ × 3¾ in. Vol. 1: ix [1] 336; vol. 2: vi, 330 pp.
See also *The Friend* (No. 466).

1813

1725 COLERIDGE, SAMUEL TAYLOR. *Remorse.* A Tragedy, in
Five Acts. London: Printed for W. Pople, 1813.

7¹⁵⁄₁₆ × 5 in. viii [4] 72 pp.

1816

1726 COLERIDGE, SAMUEL TAYLOR. *Christabel; Kubla Khan,
a Vision; the Pains of Sleep.* London: Printed for John Murray, 1816.

8½ × 5⅛ in. vii [1] 64 [4] pp.

1727 COLERIDGE, SAMUEL TAYLOR. *The Statesman's Manual;
or the Bible the Best Guide to Political Skill and Foresight: a Lay Sermon
Addressed to the Higher Classes of Society, with an Appendix Containing
Comments and Essays Connected with the Study of the Inspired Writings.*
London: Printed for Gale and Fenner; J. M. Richardson; and
Hatchard, 1816.

8⅛ × 5 in. 65 [3] xlvii [1] pp.

1817

1728 COLERIDGE, SAMUEL TAYLOR (TRANSLATOR). *A
Hebrew Dirge, Chaunted in the Great Synagogue, St. James's Place, Aldgate,
on the Day of the Funeral of Her Royal Highness the Princess Charlotte.* By
Hyman Hurwitz. London: T. Boosey; Lackington, Allen & Co.;
Briggs and Burton; H. Barnett, 1817.

8½ × 5½ in. 13 [1] pp.

1729 COLERIDGE, SAMUEL TAYLOR. *A Lay Sermon, Addressed to the Higher and Middle Classes, on the Existing Distresses and Discontents.* London: Printed for Gale and Fenner; J. M. Richardson; J. Hatchard, 1817.

$8\frac{1}{8} \times 4\frac{7}{8}$ in. xxxi [1] 134 pp.

1730 [COLERIDGE, SAMUEL TAYLOR?]. [*Prospectus to the Encyclopaedia Metropolitana.* Camberwell: Printed for Rest Fenner by S. Curtis, 1817?].

$8\frac{1}{4} \times 5\frac{3}{16}$ in. 8 pp.

1731 Another copy.

1732 Another copy.

1733 COLERIDGE, SAMUEL TAYLOR. *Sibylline Leaves: a Collection of Poems.* London: Rest Fenner, 1817.

$8\frac{3}{4} \times 5\frac{3}{8}$ in. [4] x, 303 [3] pp. Contains corrections and alterations in Coleridge's hand. The fly-leaf is inscribed: 'John Wordsworth from his affectionate Uncle William Wordsworth.' The half-title is signed, perhaps in the poet's hand, 'Wm Wordsworth.'

1734 COLERIDGE, SAMUEL TAYLOR. *Zapolya: a Christmas Tale, in Two Parts: the Prelude Entitled 'The Usurper's Fortune'; and the Sequel Entitled 'The Usurper's Fate.'* London: Printed for Rest Fenner, 1817.

$8\frac{7}{8} \times 5\frac{3}{8}$ in. [10] 128 [10] pp.
See also *Biographia Literaria* (No. 646).

1818

1735 COLERIDGE, SAMUEL TAYLOR. *The Friend: a Series of Essays, in Three Volumes, to Aid in the Formation of Fixed Principles in Politics, Morals, and Religion, with Literary Amusements Interspersed.* A New Edition. London: Printed for Rest Fenner, 1818.

$7\frac{3}{8} \times 4\frac{1}{2}$ in. Vol. 1: ix [3] 356; vol. 2: [4] 336; vol. 3: [4] 375 [1] pp.

1819

1736 *Poetry of the College Magazine.* Windsor: Knight and Son, 1819.

$8\frac{1}{4} \times 4\frac{7}{8}$ in. [2] 104 [4] pp. Contains the Bride of the Cave, by Henry Nelson Coleridge, pp. 5–16.

1737 COLERIDGE, SAMUEL TAYLOR. Fancy in Nubibus, a Sonnet, Composed on the Sea Coast.

Blackwood's Edinburgh Magazine, VI (November 1819), 196.

1738 Essays on the Lake School of Poetry: No. 3, Coleridge.

Blackwood's Edinburgh Magazine, VI (October 1819), 3–12.

1739 HAZLITT, WILLIAM. *Political Essays, with Sketches of Public Characters.* London: Printed for William Hone, 1819.

$8\frac{1}{8} \times 5\frac{1}{8}$ in. xxxvi, 439 [3] pp. Contains four articles by Coleridge.

1825

1740 COLERIDGE, SAMUEL TAYLOR. *Aids to Reflection in the Formation of a Manly Character on the Several Grounds of Prudence, Morality, and Religion:* Illustrated by Select Passages from Our Elder Divines, Especially from Archbishop Leighton. London: Printed for Taylor and Hessey, 1825.

$7\frac{1}{2} \times 4\frac{5}{8}$ in. xii [4] 404 [4] pp.

1826

1741 *The Wasp. A Literary Satire. Containing an Expose of Some of the Most Notorious Literary and Theatrical Quacks of the Day. An Abundance of Every Sort and Manner of Facetiæ, in the Shape of Puns, Epigrams, Bon Mots, Epitaphs, Parodies, Impromptus, Declarations of Inefficiency, by Several Eminent Professors, Authors, Actors, and Others, Aphorisms of Notorious and Celebrated Characters, and Every Other Description of Witticism, Perfectly Original.* London: W. Adams.

Vol. I (30 September–16 December 1826), Nos. 1–12. Introductory Essay to a Course of Facetiæ, a parody, pp. 86–8.

1828

1742 *The Amulet; or Christian and Literary Remembrancer.* London: W. Baynes & Son, and Wightman & Cramp. 1828.

$5\frac{3}{8} \times 3\frac{3}{8}$ in. [4] 426 [6] pp. Coleridge's New Thoughts on Old Subjects, pp. 37–47.

1829

1743 COLERIDGE, SAMUEL TAYLOR. *The Poetical Works of S. T. Coleridge, Including the Dramas of Wallenstein, Remorse, and Zapolya.* London: William Pickering, 1829, 3 vols.

7¼ × 4¼ in. Vol. 1: x, 353 [1]; vol. 2: [2] 394; vol. 3: [2] 428 pp.

1830

1744 [COLERIDGE, SAMUEL TAYLOR]. *The Devil's Walk; a Poem.* By Professor Porson. Edited with a Bibliographical Memoir and Notes, by H. W. Montagu. London: Marsh and Miller, [1830].

6⅜ × 4 in. viii [1] 10–33 [3] pp. With wood engravings after Cruikshank. First issue, with pp. 21–2 omitted in paging.

1745 [COLERIDGE, SAMUEL TAYLOR]. *The Devil's Walk; a Poem.* By Professor Porson. Edited with a Bibliographical Memoir and Notes by H. W. Montagu. London: Marsh and Miller, [1830].

6 × 3¾ in. viii [1] 10–31 [1] pp. Has the correct pagination at pp. 20–1. Bound with the following:
The Devil's Progress. A Poem by the Editor of the Court Journal. Second Edition. London: L. Relfe, 1830. 67 [1] pp.
The Devil's Visit; a Poem, from the Original Manuscript. With Notes by a Barrister. London: W. Kidd, 1830. 35 [1] pp.
The Blue Devils; or New Police, a Poem: in Three Cantos, by a Hypochondriac. London: G. Henderson, 1830. 34 pp.
Old Booty! A Serio-comic Sailor's Tale. By W. T. Moncrieff, Esq. London: W. Kidd, 1830. 36 pp.
The Real Devil's Walk. Not by Professor Porson ... with Notes, and Extracts from the Devil's Diary. London: E. Wilson, 1830. 34 pp.

1746 MACRAY, J. (ED.). *The Golden Lyre.* Second Series. Specimens of the Poets of England, France, Germany, Italy, and Spain. London: J. D. Haas, 1830.

5¾ × 3¾ in. No pagination; 42 leaves. Printed in gold. Contains Coleridge's Lines to Beautiful Spring.

1747 Review of the *Poetical Works of S. T. Coleridge, Esq.*, 3 vols., 1829.

Westminster Review, XII (January 1830), 1–31.

1832

1748 Coleridge and His Philosophy. Professor Wilson and the Lake School.

National Omnibus: and General Advertiser, II (June 1832), 201–2.

1833

1749 COLERIDGE, HARTLEY. *Poems by Hartley Coleridge.* Leeds: F. E. Bingley; and Baldwin and Cradock, London, 1833.

8¾ × 5⅜ in. viii, 157 [5] pp. J. Dykes Campbell's copy with his autograph.

1834

1750 COLERIDGE, SAMUEL TAYLOR. *The Poetical Works of S. T. Coleridge.* London: William Pickering, 1834, 3 vols.

6⅝ × 4⅛ in. Vol. 1: xiv, 288; vol. 2: vi, 338; vol. 3: [4] 331 [1] pp.

1751 *Friendship's Offering; and Winter's Wreath:* a Christmas and New Year's Present for MDCCCXXXIV. London: Smith, Elder, and Co., 1834.

6⅛ × 3¾ in. xii, 384 [2] pp. Ten poems by Coleridge here first published.

1752 A Note on Coleridge's Death.

Quarterly Review, LII (November 1834), 291–2.

1753 OLDCASTLE, GEOFFREY. The Late S. T. Coleridge, Esq.

Canterbury Magazine, I (September 1834), 121–31.

1754 Review of *The Poetical Works of S. T. Coleridge*, London, 1834, 3 vols.

Quarterly Review, LII (August 1834), 1–38.

1835

1755 COLERIDGE, SAMUEL TAYLOR. *The Poetical Works of S. T. Coleridge.* London: William Pickering, 1835, 3 vols.

6⅝ × 4 in. Vol. 1: xiv, 288 [2]; vol. 2: vi, 338 [2]; vol. 3: [4] 331 [1] pp.

1756 COLERIDGE, SAMUEL TAYLOR. *Specimens of the Table Talk of the Late Samuel Taylor Coleridge.* London: John Murray, 1835, 2 vols.

5¾ × 3¾ in. Vol. 1: lxxvii [3] 267 [1]; vol. 2: xi [1] 364 [4] pp.

1757 COLERIDGE, SAMUEL TAYLOR. *Specimens of the Table Talk of the Late Samuel Taylor Coleridge.* New York: Harper and Brothers, 1835, 2 vols.

7¾ × 4¾ in. Vol. 1: xxxii [1] 168; vol. 2: 183 [7] pp.

1758 Coleridgeiana.

Fraser's Magazine, XI (January 1835), 50–8.

1759 OLDCASTLE, GEOFFREY. Unpublished Letters of the Late S. T. Coleridge.

Canterbury Magazine, II (January 1835), 31–5.

1760 Review of *Specimens of the Table Talk of the Late S. T. Coleridge.*

Quarterly Review, LIII (February 1835), 79–103.

1761 Review of *Specimens of the Table Talk of the Late S. T. Coleridge.*

Edinburgh Review, LXI (April 1835), 129–53.

1836

1762 COLERIDGE, SAMUEL TAYLOR. *Aids to Reflection in the Formation of a Manly Character on the Several Grounds of Prudence, Morality, and Religion,* Illustrated by Extracts from Our Elder Divines, Especially from Archbishop Leighton. London: William Pickering, 1836.

8 × 4⅞ in. xv [1] 407 [1] pp.

1763 COLERIDGE, SAMUEL TAYLOR. *Letters, Conversations, and Recollections of S. T. Coleridge.* London: Edward Moxon, 1836, 2 vols.

7¼ × 4⅜ in. Vol. 1: xii, 234; vol. 2: [2] 240 pp.

1764 COLERIDGE, SAMUEL TAYLOR. *Specimens of the Table Talk of Samuel Taylor Coleridge.* Second Edition. London: John Murray, 1836.

6⅞ × 4¼ in. xxviii, 326 [2] pp.

1765 Review of *Poems by Hartley Coleridge*.

American Quarterly Review, xx (December 1836), 478–504.

1766 Review of *Specimens of the Table Talk of the Late Samuel Taylor Coleridge*, New York, 1835.

American Quarterly Review, xix (March 1836), 1–28.

1837

1767 COLERIDGE, SAMUEL TAYLOR. *Letters, Conversations, and Recollections of S. T. Coleridge*, ed. Thomas Allsop. New York: Harper & Brothers, 1836.

$7\frac{3}{8} \times 4\frac{3}{8}$ in. xii [1] 14–266 [2] pp.

1768 COTTLE, JOSEPH. *Early Recollections; Chiefly Relating to the Late Samuel Taylor Coleridge, during His Long Residence in Bristol*. London: Longman, Rees & Company, and Hamilton, Adams & Co., 1837, 2 vols.

$7\frac{3}{4} \times 4\frac{3}{4}$ in. Vol. 1: xxxviii, 325; vol. 2: [6] 346 [2] pp.

1769 Reviews of the *Literary Remains of Samuel Taylor Coleridge*, 1836, and of Joseph Cottle, *Early Recollections, Chiefly Relating to the Late S. T. Coleridge*, 1837.

Quarterly Review, lix (July 1837), 1–32.

1770 Review of the *Literary Remains of Samuel Taylor Coleridge*, 1836.

Church of England Quarterly Review, ii (July 1837), 24–56.

1838

1771 COLERIDGE, HARTLEY. *God Save the Queen, a New National Song, for the Coronation of Queen Victoria*, June 28th, 1838.

Broadsheet. On the margin are alterations in pencil in the hand of the author, followed by this note: 'The above is Hartley Coleridge's writing with my pencil, E. C---.' The sheet was found in a copy of Hartley Coleridge's *Poems*, 1833, that was once the property of J. Dykes Campbell (No. 1749).

1839

1772 [TREVENEN, EMILY]. *Little Derwent's Breakfast, by a Lady.* London: Smith, Elder, and Co., 1839.

$6\frac{3}{4} \times 4\frac{1}{8}$ in. viii, 84 [4] pp. Poems written for the amusement of Derwent, the seven-year-old grandson of S. T. Coleridge. See also No. 3186.

1840

1773 COLERIDGE, SAMUEL TAYLOR. *Confessions of an Inquiring Spirit.* Edited from the Author's MS by Henry Nelson Coleridge. London: William Pickering, 1840.

$6\frac{3}{4} \times 4\frac{1}{8}$ in. [4] x [2] 95 [1] pp.

1841

1774 CHILCOTT, J. E. *Chilcott's Clevedon New Guide, with Historical Notices of Clevedon Court, Walton Castle,* &c. &c. &c. Also, a Description of Coleridge's Cottage, and of the Principal Attractions of the Neighbourhood. Embellished with Copper Plates. Third Edition, Enlarged and Greatly Improved. Bristol: J. Chilcott..., [*c.* 1841].

$7\frac{1}{8} \times 4\frac{1}{4}$ in. 60 [6] pp.

1843

1775 COLERIDGE, SAMUEL TAYLOR. *The Poetical Works of S. T. Coleridge.* Edited by Herman Hooker. Philadelphia: John Locken, 1843.

$4\frac{5}{16} \times 2\frac{3}{4}$ in. xiv [3] 18–256 [4] pp.

1844

1776 COLERIDGE, SAMUEL TAYLOR. *The Poetical and Dramatic Works of S. T. Coleridge.* London: William Pickering, 1844, 3 vols.

$6\frac{1}{2} \times 3\frac{7}{8}$ in. Vol. 1: xiv, 288 [2]; vol. 2: vi, 338 [2]; vol. 3: [4] 331 [1] pp.

1777 COLERIDGE, SAMUEL TAYLOR. *The Poetical Works of S. T. Coleridge.* Edited by Herman Hooker. Philadelphia: John Locken, 1844.

$4\frac{1}{8} \times 2\frac{5}{8}$ in. xiv [3] 18–256 [2] pp.

1778 SCOTT, WILLIAM. Manuscript Fragments of S. T. Coleridge.

Christian Remembrancer, xxxviii, n.s. (June 1844), 250–5.

1847

1779 COTTLE, JOSEPH. *Reminiscences of Samuel Taylor Coleridge and Robert Southey.* London: Houlston and Stoneman, 1847.

7¾ × 4⅝ in. xx, 516 [2] pp.

1848

1780 COLERIDGE, SAMUEL TAYLOR. *Aids to Reflection*, Edited by H. N. Coleridge. London: William Pickering, 1848, 2 vols.

6¾ × 4⅛ in. Vol. 1: xx, 338; vol. 2: lxvi, 322 pp.

1781 COLERIDGE, SAMUEL TAYLOR. *Hints toward the Formation of a More Comprehensive Theory of Life*, Edited by Seth B. Watson. London: John Churchill, 1848.

7⅞ × 4⅞ in. 94 [10] pp.

1782 COLERIDGE, SAMUEL TAYLOR. *The Poems of S. T. Coleridge.* London: William Pickering, 1848.

6⅜ × 4 in. xvi, 372 pp.

1783 COTTLE, JOSEPH. *Reminiscences of Samuel Taylor Coleridge and Robert Southey.* New York: Wiley and Putnam, 1848.

7⅜ × 5 in. xvi, 378 [4] pp.

1849

1784 COLERIDGE, SAMUEL TAYLOR. *Confessions of an Inquiring Spirit, and Some Miscellaneous Pieces by Samuel Taylor Coleridge*, Edited from the Author's MS. by Henry Nelson Coleridge. London: William Pickering, 1849.

6¾ × 3⅞ in. xlii [6] 289 [1] pp.

1850

1785 *Sabrinae Corolla in Hortulis Regiae Scholae Salopiensis contexuerunt Tres Viri Floribus Legendis.* Londini: Impensis Georgii Bell, MDCCCL.

8¼ × 5½ in. xxii [2] 328 pp. Two poems of Coleridge with translations, one into Greek, the other into Latin.

1851

1786 COLERIDGE, HARTLEY. *Poems by Hartley Coleridge, with a Memoir of His Life by His Brother.* Second Edition. London: Edward Moxon, 1851, 2 vols.

6⅝ × 4³⁄₁₆ in. Vol. 1: ccxxxii, iv, 168; vol. 2: xii, 367 [1] pp.

1787 Hartley Coleridge as Man, Poet, Essayist.

Fraser's Magazine, XLIII (June 1851), 603–15.

1852

1788 COLERIDGE, SAMUEL TAYLOR. *The Dramatic Works of Samuel Taylor Coleridge*, Edited by Derwent Coleridge. A New Edition. London: Edward Moxon, 1852.

6¾ × 4⅛ in. xiv [2] 427 [1] pp.

1789 COLERIDGE, SAMUEL TAYLOR. *The Poems of Samuel Taylor Coleridge*. Edited by Derwent and Sara Coleridge. A New Edition. London: Edward Moxon, 1852.

6¼ × 4 in. xxvii [1] 388 pp.

1853

1790 COLERIDGE, SAMUEL TAYLOR. *Notes, Theological, Political, and Miscellaneous*, by Samuel Taylor Coleridge. Edited by the Rev. Derwent Coleridge. London: Edward Moxon, 1853.

6¾ × 4⅛ in. xii, 415 [1] pp.

1854

1791 COLERIDGE, SAMUEL TAYLOR. *The Poetical and Dramatic Works of S. T. Coleridge*. With a Memoir. Boston: Little, Brown, and Co.; New York: Evans and Dickerson; Philadelphia: Lippincott, Grambo and Co., 1854, 2 vols.

6⅝ × 4 in. Vol. 1: ciii [1] 322 [2]; vol. 2: vi, 370 [2] pp.

1857

1792 COLERIDGE, HARTLEY. The Tea-Table: an Unpublished Poem.

Fraser's Magazine, LV (January 1857), 113–17.

1860

1793 COLERIDGE, HERBERT. English Etymology.

Macmillan's Magazine, I (March 1860), 347–53.

1864

1794 COLERIDGE, SAMUEL TAYLOR. *The Poems of S. T. Coleridge.* London: Bell and Daldy; and Sampson, Low, Son, and Co., 1864.

5¼ × 3³⁄₁₆ in. xiii [3] 299 [3] pp. Arthur Symon's copy, with his autograph signature and the following note: 'In the life and art of Coleridge the hours of sleep seem to have been almost more important than the waking hours.'

1795 COLERIDGE, SAMUEL TAYLOR. *The Political and Dramatic Works,* with a Life of the Author, by Charles E. Norton. Boston; Little, Brown & Co., 1864, 3 vols.

6⅝ × 4⅛ in. Vol. 1: ciii [1] 325 [5]; vol. 2: vi, 372 [2]; vol. 3: 331 [1] pp.

1796 Letters from Coleridge to William Godwin.

Macmillan's Magazine, IX (April 1864), 524–36.

1865

1797 Reminiscences of Hartley Coleridge.

Littell's Living Age, XXXI, 3S. (December 1865), 433–6. Reprinted from *Macmillan's Magazine,* November 1865.

1866

1798 COLERIDGE, SAMUEL TAYLOR. *Biographia Literaria; or, Biographical Sketches of My Literary Life and Opinions; and Two Lay Sermons* .... London: Bell and Daldy, [1866?].

7¼ × 4½ in. [2] v [3] 440 [4] pp.

1799 COLERIDGE, SAMUEL TAYLOR. *The Friend: a Series of Essays. To Aid in the Formation of Fixed Principles in Politics, Morals, and Religion. With Literary Amusements Interspersed.* London: Bell and Daldy, 1866.

7⅛ × 4½ in. [12] 389 [1] pp.

1800 [SHAIRP, JOHN CAMPBELL]. Samuel Taylor Coleridge.

Littell's Living Age, XXXI, 3S. (13 and 20 January 1866), 81–99; 161–82. Reprinted from the *North British Review,* December 1865.

1867

1801 COLERIDGE, SAMUEL TAYLOR. *The Friend: a Series of Essays. To Aid in the Formation of Fixed Principles in Politics, Morals, and Religion. With Literary Amusements Interspersed.* London: Bell and Daldy, 1867.

$7\frac{1}{4} \times 4\frac{5}{8}$ in. [12] 389 [5] pp.

1868

1802 Coleridge as a Poet.

Living Age, XCVIII (29 August 1868), 515–29. Reprinted from the *Quarterly Review*, CXXV (July 1868), 78–106. Appears also in the *American Presbyterian Review*, IV, 80 ff.

1871

1803 PHILLIPS, SAMUEL. *Essays from 'The Times.' Being a Selection from the Literary Papers Which Have Appeared in That Journal.* New Edition, with a Portrait. London: John Murray, 1871, 2 vols.

$6\frac{3}{8} \times 4$ in. Vol. 1: vi [1] 325 [1]; vol. 2: [4] 338 [2] pp. Reminiscences of Coleridge and Southey by Cottle, I, 237–54.

1873

1804 COLERIDGE, SAMUEL TAYLOR. *Christabel and the Lyrical and Imaginative Poems ...* Arranged and Introduced by Algernon Charles Swinburne. London: Sampson, Low, Marston, Low, and Searle, 1873.

$5\frac{3}{4} \times 4\frac{1}{4}$ in. xxvii [1] 150 [2] pp.

1874

1805 COLERIDGE, SARA. *Memoir and Letters of Sara Coleridge.* Edited by Her Daughter. New York: Harper & Brothers, 1874.

$8 \times 5\frac{1}{4}$ in. xxxi [2] 34–528 [8] pp.

1806 COLERIDGE, SARA. *Phantasmion, a Fairy Tale.* With an Introductory Preface by Lord Coleridge. London: Henry S. King & Co., 1874.

$7\frac{3}{8} \times 4\frac{7}{8}$ in. xvi, 348 [4] pp. Inscribed on fly-leaf: 'Caroline Coleridge, with best love, from Edith Coleridge.'

1875

1807 COLERIDGE, SARA. *Pretty Lessons in Verse for Good Children.* With Some Lessons in Latin, in Easy Rhyme. A New Edition. London: Henry S. King & Co., 1875.

$6\frac{7}{8} \times 4\frac{1}{2}$ in. vii [1] 185 [3] pp.

1877

1808 COLERIDGE, SAMUEL TAYLOR. *The Poetical and Dramatic Works of Samuel Taylor Coleridge, Founded on the Author's Latest Edition of 1834, with Many Additional Pieces Now First Included, and with a Collection of Various Readings.* London: Basil Montagu Pickering, 1877, 4 vols.

$6\frac{5}{8} \times 4$ in. Vol. 1: cxviii, 224; vol. 2: xii, 381 [1]; vol. 3: [4] 413 [3]; vol. 4: [6] 290 [14] pp. Edward Dowden's copy, with manuscript notes by him.

1880

1809 CALVERT, GEORGE HENRY. *Coleridge, Shelley, Goethe: Biographic Aesthetic Studies.* Boston: Lee and Shepard; New York: C. T. Dillingham, [1880].

$6\frac{3}{4} \times 4\frac{3}{8}$ in. 298 pp.

1810 COLERIDGE, SAMUEL TAYLOR. *The Poetical and Dramatic Works of Samuel Taylor Coleridge, Founded on the Author's Latest Edition of 1834, with Many Additional Pieces Now First Included, and with a Collection of Various Readings.* London: Macmillan and Co., 1880, 4 vols.

$6\frac{3}{4} \times 4\frac{1}{8}$ in. Vol. 1: cxviii, 224; vol. 2: xii, 381 [1]; vol. 3: [6] 413 [3]; vol. 4: [6] 290 pp. Nowell C. Smith's copy, with his autograph in each volume.

1885

1811 COLERIDGE, SAMUEL TAYLOR. *Miscellanies, Aesthetic and Literary: to Which Is Added the Theory of Life* ... Collected and Arranged by T. Ashe. London: George Bell and Sons, 1885.

$7\frac{1}{4} \times 4\frac{1}{2}$ in. ix [1] 442 [24] pp.

1886

1812 JOHNSON, CHARLES F. Coleridge.

Temple Bar, LXXVIII (September 1886), 35–54.

1887

1813 CAINE, SIR THOMAS HENRY HALL. *Life of Samuel Taylor Coleridge*. London: Walter Scott, 1887.

$8\frac{3}{8} \times 5\frac{3}{8}$ in. 154, xxi [9] pp.

1814 KNIGHT, WILLIAM (ED.). *Memorials of Coleorton, Being Letters from Coleridge, Wordsworth and His Sister, Southey, and Sir Walter Scott to Sir George Beaumont and Lady Beaumont of Coleorton*. Edinburgh: David Douglas, 1887, 2 vols.

$7\frac{1}{2} \times 4\frac{5}{8}$ in. Vol. 1: xlvi [2] 227 [1]; vol. 2: vii [1] 294 [2] pp.

1889

1815 TAYLOR, WILLIAM F. (ED.). *Critical Annotations by S. T. Coleridge*, Being Marginal Notes Inscribed in Volumes Formerly in the Possession of Coleridge. Harrow: William F. Taylor, 1889.

$9\frac{5}{8} \times 7\frac{3}{4}$ in. [14] 48 [2] pp. With the editor's autograph.

1890

1816 COLERIDGE, SAMUEL TAYLOR. *The Friend: a Series of Essays. To Aid in the Formation of Fixed Principles in Politics, Morals, and Religion. With Literary Amusements Interspersed*. London: George Bell and Sons, 1890.

$7 \times 4\frac{1}{2}$ in. [12] 389 [25] pp.

1817 JAMES, IVOR. *The Source of 'The Ancient Mariner.'* Cardiff: Daniel Owen and Co., 1890.

$6\frac{1}{4} \times 4\frac{1}{2}$ in. [4] 88 pp.

1893

1818 COLERIDGE, SAMUEL TAYLOR. *The Poetical Works of Samuel Taylor Coleridge*. Edited with a Biographical Introduction by James Dykes Campbell. London and New York: Macmillan and Co., 1893.

$7\frac{1}{2} \times 4\frac{7}{8}$ in. cxxiv, 667 [1] pp.

1895

1819 COLERIDGE, SAMUEL TAYLOR. *Coleridge's Principles of Criticism:* Chapters i, iii, iv, xiv–xxii of 'Biographia Literaria,' with Introduction and Notes by Andrew J. George (Heath's English Classics). Boston: D. C. Heath & Co., 1895.

$7\frac{1}{8} \times 4\frac{3}{4}$ in. xxix [1] 226 pp.

1820 COLERIDGE, SAMUEL TAYLOR. *The Golden Book of Coleridge*, Edited by Stopford A. Brooke. London: J. M. Dent, 1895.

$6\frac{7}{8} \times 4\frac{1}{2}$ in. xii, 298 [3] pp.

1821 COLERIDGE, SAMUEL TAYLOR. *Letters of Samuel Taylor Coleridge*, Edited by Ernest Hartley Coleridge. Boston and New York: Houghton, Mifflin and Co., 1895, 2 vols.

$8\frac{5}{8} \times 5\frac{3}{4}$ in. Vol. 1: xix [3] 444 [2]; vol. 2: vii [6] 448–813 [5] pp.

1896

1822 CAMPBELL, JAMES DYKES. *Samuel Taylor Coleridge: a Narrative of the Events of His Life.* Second Edition, with a Memoir of the Author by Leslie Stephen. London and New York: Macmillan and Co., 1896.

$8\frac{7}{8} \times 5\frac{1}{2}$ in. xlviii, 319 [5] pp.

1898

1823 COLERIDGE, ERNEST HARTLEY. *Poems by Ernest Hartley Coleridge....* London and New York: John Lane, 1898.

$7\frac{5}{8} \times 4\frac{1}{4}$ in. 107 [1] pp.

1899

1824 COLERIDGE, SAMUEL TAYLOR. *Coleridge's Poems; a Facsimile Reproduction of the Proofs and MSS. of Some of the Poems.* Edited by the Late James Dykes Campbell ... with a Preface and Notes by W. Hale White. Westminster: A. Constable and Co., 1899.

$6\frac{7}{8} \times 4\frac{1}{4}$ in. xii, 134 pp.

1900

1825 COLERIDGE, SAMUEL TAYLOR. *Lectures and Notes on Shakespeare and Other English Poets* .... Now First Collected by T. Ashe. London: George Bell and Sons, 1900.

$7 \times 4\frac{1}{2}$ in. xi [1] 552 [32] pp.

1901

1826 COLERIDGE, SAMUEL TAYLOR. *The Poetical Works of Samuel Taylor Coleridge*, Edited with a Biographical Introduction by James Dykes Campbell. London and New York: Macmillan, 1901.

$7\frac{3}{8} \times 5$ in. cxxiv, 667 [1] pp.

1902

1827 HANEY, JOHN LOUIS. *The German Influence on Samuel Taylor Coleridge:* an Abridgement of a Thesis Presented to the Faculty of the Department of Philosophy of the University of Pennsylvania .... Philadelphia, 1902.

$8\frac{3}{4} \times 5\frac{1}{2}$ in. iii [1] 44 pp.

1828 TRAILL, HENRY DUFF. *Coleridge* (English Men of Letters). New York: Harper and Brothers, 1902.

$7\frac{3}{8} \times 4\frac{3}{4}$ in. x, 199 [7] pp.

1903

1829 COOPER, LANE. Review of *Select Poems of Samuel Taylor Coleridge*, Edited by A. J. George, Boston, 1902.

Journal of English and Germanic Philology, v (December 1903), 194-7.

1830 HANEY, JOHN LOUIS. *A Bibliography of Samuel Taylor Coleridge*. Philadelphia: Printed for Private Circulation, 1903.

$9\frac{3}{8} \times 6\frac{1}{4}$ in. xiv [2] 144 pp.

1906

1831 COOPER, LANE. Review of *The German Influence on Samuel Taylor Coleridge* by John Louis Haney, Philadelphia, 1902.

Journal of English and Germanic Philology, vi (October 1906), 141-6.

1907

1832 COLERIDGE, SAMUEL TAYLOR. *The Ancient Mariner und Christabel, mit literarhistorischer Einleitung und Kommentar*, hrsg. von Albert Eichler. Wien und Leipzig: W. Braumüller, 1907.

$9 \times 5\frac{7}{8}$ in. xi [1] 133 [1] pp.

1833 COLERIDGE, SAMUEL TAYLOR. *Biographia Literaria by S. T. Coleridge*, Edited with His Aesthetical Essays by J. Shawcross. Oxford: Clarendon Press, 1907, 2 vols.

$7\frac{1}{2} \times 5$ in. Vol. 1: xcvii [7] 272; vol. 2: 334 [2] pp.

1834 COLERIDGE, SAMUEL TAYLOR. *Christabel, Illustrated by a Facsimile of the Manuscript and by Textual and Other Notes by Ernest Hartley Coleridge*. London: Henry Frowde, 1907.

$10\frac{3}{4} \times 7\frac{3}{4}$ in. ix [3] 113 [3] pp.

1835 COOPER, LANE. Review of *A Bibliography of Samuel Taylor Coleridge* by John Louis Haney, Philadelphia, 1903.

Journal of English and Germanic Philology, vi (April 1907), 478–91.

1836 HELMHOLTZ, ANNA AUGUSTA. The Indebtedness of Samuel Taylor Coleridge to August Wilhelm von Schlegel.

Bulletin of the University of Wisconsin, No. 163. Philology and Literature Series, Vol. 3, No. 4, 1907, pp. 273–370.

1910

1837 COOPER, LANE. The Power of the Eye in Coleridge.

Reprinted from *Studies in Honor of James Morgan Hart*, New York: Henry Holt, [1910], pp. 78–121.

1912

1838 COLERIDGE, SAMUEL TAYLOR. *The Complete Poetical Works of Samuel Taylor Coleridge, Including Poems and Versions of Poems Now Published for the First Time*. Edited with Textual and Bibliographical Notes by Ernest Hartley Coleridge. Oxford: Clarendon Press, 1912, 2 vols.

$8\frac{7}{8} \times 5\frac{1}{2}$ in. Vol. 1: xxvi [2] 492; vol. 2: viii [3] 496–1198 [2] pp.

1916

1839 COLERIDGE, STEPHEN. An Evening in My Library among the English Poets. London: John Lane, 1916.

$7\frac{3}{8} \times 5$ in. ix, 217 [3] pp. Title-page inscribed: 'Doris Toge from Stephen Coleridge. The 14 of April 1919.'

1918

1840 SNYDER, ALICE DOROTHEA. *The Critical Principle of the Reconciliation of Opposites as Employed by Coleridge.* Ann Arbor: University of Michigan, 1918.

$9\frac{1}{2} \times 6$ in. [6] 59 [1] pp.

1919

1841 COLERIDGE, SAMUEL TAYLOR. *Marriage.* London: Printed for Private Circulation, 1919.

$7\frac{1}{4} \times 4\frac{7}{8}$ in. 22 [2] pp. Printed for Thomas J. Wise.

1920

1842 COLERIDGE, SAMUEL TAYLOR. *Biographia Literaria* (Everyman's Library). London: J. M. Dent; New York: E. P. Dutton, [1920].

$6\frac{7}{8} \times 4\frac{1}{4}$ in. xv [1] 334 [2] pp.

1843 SAMPSON, GEORGE (ED.). *Coleridge, Biographia Literaria Chapters i–iv, xiv–xxii; Wordsworth, Prefaces and Essays on Poetry 1800–1815;* with an Introductory Essay by Sir Arthur Quiller-Couch. Cambridge: at the University Press, 1920.

$7\frac{3}{4} \times 5\frac{3}{8}$ in. xxxix [1] 327 [1] pp.

1923

1844 COLERIDGE, SAMUEL TAYLOR. *Poems of Nature and Romance 1794–1807*, Edited by Margaret A. Keeling. Oxford: Clarendon Press, 1923.

$7 \times 4\frac{5}{8}$ in. 246 [2] pp.

1845 ORVIETO, ANGIOLO. *Poesie di Amore e d'Incanto.* Versioni dall'Inglese, con Prefazione di L. E. Marshall. Firenze: Felice le Monnier Editore, 1923.

$7\frac{1}{4} \times 4\frac{3}{8}$ in. xii, 216 [6] pp.

1924

1846 COLERIDGE, SAMUEL TAYLOR. *Select Poems*, Chosen and Edited by S. G. Dunn. London: Oxford University Press, 1924.

$6\frac{3}{8} \times 4\frac{1}{8}$ in. [2] 127 [1] pp.

1847 SNYDER, ALICE DOROTHEA. Coleridge's Cosmogony: a Note on the Poetic 'World View.'

Studies in Philology, XXI (October 1924), 616–25.

1848 [STUTTAFORD, CHARLES]. *Coleridge at Stowey*. London: National Trust for Places of Historic Interest or Natural Beauty, [1924].

$7\frac{1}{8} \times 4\frac{3}{4}$ in. 31 [1] pp.

1925

1849 GREENLAW, EDWIN. Modern English Romanticism.

Studies in Philology, XXII (October 1925), 538–50.

1850 POTTER, GEORGE REUBEN. Coleridge and the Idea of Evolution.

PMLA, XL (June 1925), 379–97.

1851 RAYSOR, THOMAS M. Unpublished Fragments on Aesthetics by S. T. Coleridge.

Studies in Philology, XXII (October 1925), 529–37.

1926

1852 THOMPSON, FRANK T. Emerson's Indebtedness to Coleridge.

Studies in Philology, XXIII (January 1926), 55–76.

1853 WRIGHT, HERBERT. The Tour of Coleridge and His Friend Hucks in Wales in 1794.

Nineteenth Century and After, XCIX (May 1926), 732–44.

1928

1854 *S. T. Coleridge* (the Augustan Books of English Poetry, Second Series, No. 23). London: Ernest Benn, [1928].

$8\frac{3}{8} \times 5\frac{1}{4}$ in. iv, 5–31 [1] pp.

1855 BROUGHTON, LESLIE NATHAN. Review of *The Road to Xanadu* by John Livingston Lowes.

Journal of English and Germanic Philology, XXVII (July 1928), 429–34.

1929

1856 BABBITT, IRVING. Coleridge and the Imagination.

Nineteenth Century and After, cvi (September 1929), 383–98.

1857 CHARPENTIER, JOHN. *Coleridge the Sublime Somnambulist*, trans. M. V. Nugent. New York: Dodd, Mead and Co., 1929.

$8\frac{1}{2} \times 5\frac{5}{8}$ in. x, 332 [2] pp.

1858 RAYSOR, THOMAS M. Coleridge and 'Asra.'

Studies in Philology, xxvi (July 1929), 305–24.

1930

1859 COLERIDGE, SAMUEL TAYLOR. *Coleridge's Shakespearean Criticism.* Edited by Thomas Middleton Raysor. London: Constable and Co., 1930, 2 vols.

$8\frac{5}{8} \times 5\frac{5}{8}$ in. Vol. 1: lxi [1] 256; vol. 2: vi, 375 [1] pp.

1860 GRIGGS, EARL LESLIE. Coleridge and the Wedgwood Annuity.

Review of English Studies, vi (January 1930), 63–72.

1861 LOWES, JOHN LIVINGSTON. *The Road to Xanadu: a Study in the Ways of the Imagination.* Boston and New York: Houghton Mifflin Co., 1930.

$9\frac{1}{8} \times 6\frac{1}{4}$ in. xx, 639 [1] pp.

1862 MUIRHEAD, JOHN. *Coleridge as Philosopher.* London: Allen and Unwin; New York: Macmillan Co., 1930.

$8\frac{3}{8} \times 5\frac{1}{2}$ in. 287 [1] pp.

1931

1863 HARTMAN, HERBERT. *Hartley Coleridge, Poet's Son and Poet.* London: Oxford University Press, 1931.

$8\frac{5}{8} \times 5\frac{3}{8}$ in. ix [5] 205 [1] pp.

1864 WELLEK, RENÉ. *Immanuel Kant in England 1793–1838.* Princeton: Princeton University Press, 1931.

$9 \times 5\frac{3}{4}$ in. vii [1] 317 [7] pp.

1932

1865 COLERIDGE, SAMUEL TAYLOR. *Unpublished Letters of Samuel Taylor Coleridge, Including Certain Letters Republished from Original Sources*, Edited by Earl Leslie Griggs. London: Constable and Co., 1932, 2 vols.

$8\frac{3}{4} \times 5\frac{1}{2}$ in. Vol. 1: xxii [2] 460; vol. 2: [4] 476 pp.

1866 HOSCH, MARGARETE. *Das Naturgefühl bei S. T. Coleridge.* Inaugural-Dissertation ... der Philipps-Universität zu Marburg. Marburg: Heinr. Pöppinghaus, 1932.

$8 \times 5\frac{1}{2}$ in. vii [1] 112 pp.

1933

1867 MÖLLER, MARIA. *S. T. Coleridge, seine künstlerische Persönlichkeit und ihre Entwicklung.* Inaugural-Dissertation ... der Philipps-Universität zu Marburg. Marburg: F. W. Kalbfleisch, 1933.

1934

1868 BLUNDEN, EDMUND, AND GRIGGS, EARL LESLIE (EDS.). *Coleridge, Studies by Several Hands on the Anniversary of His Death.* London: Constable and Co., 1934.

$8\frac{5}{8} \times 5\frac{1}{2}$ in. viii, 243 [1] pp.

1869 COLERIDGE, SAMUEL TAYLOR. *S. T. Coleridge's Treatise on Method as Published in the Encyclopaedia Metropolitana.* Edited with Introduction, Manuscript Fragments, and Notes for a Complete Collation with the Essays on Method in 'The Friend,' by Alice D. Snyder. London: Constable and Co., 1934.

$8\frac{5}{8} \times 5\frac{3}{8}$ in. xxviii, 92 pp.

1870 GIBBS, WARREN E. Unpublished Letters concerning Cottle's Coleridge.

PMLA, xlix (March 1934), 208–28.

1871 LINDSAY, JULIAN. Coleridge Marginalia in a Volume of Descartes.

PMLA, xlix (March 1934), 184–95.

1872 POTTER, STEPHEN. *Minnow among Tritons: Mrs. S. T. Coleridge's Letters to Thomas Poole, 1799–1834.* London: Nonesuch Press, 1934.

9 × 5¼ in. xxxvi [2] 185 [3] pp.

1935

1873 BLIESENER, IRMGARD. *Bild-Erlebnisse Coleridge's und ihre Einwerkung auf sein künstlerisches Schaffen.* Inaugural-Dissertation ... der Georg-August-Universität zu Göttingen. Göttingen: R. Erbs und K. Meisel, 1935.

1874 GERDT, GEORG. *Coleridge's Verhältnis zur Logik.* Inaugural-Dissertation ... der Friedrich-Wilhelms-Universität zu Berlin. Berlin: Triltsch & Huther, 1935.

8 × 5½ in. 55 [1] pp.

1937

1875 BROUGHTON, LESLIE NATHAN. *Sara Coleridge and Henry Reed.* Ithaca, N.Y.: Cornell University Press, 1937.

8½ × 5¾ in. 137 [3] pp.

1876 DE SELINCOURT, ERNEST. Coleridge's Dejection: an Ode.

Essays and Studies by Members of the English Association, XXII (1937), 7–25.

1877 McELDERRY, BRUCE. Walton's *Lives* and Gillman's *Life of Coleridge.*

PMLA, LII (June 1937), 412–22.

See also Edna Aston Shearer, *Wordsworth and Coleridge Marginalia* (No. 1567).

1938

1878 CHAMBERS, SIR EDMUND KERCHEVER. *Samuel Taylor Coleridge, a Biographical Study.* Oxford: Clarendon Press, 1938.

8⅝ × 5⅜ in. xvi, 373 [3] pp.

1879 HANSON, LAWRENCE. *The Life of S. T. Coleridge: the Early Years.* London: Allen and Unwin, 1938.

8½ × 5¾ in. [8] 575 [3] pp.

1880 WAGNER, LYDIA ELIZABETH. Coleridge's Use of Laudanum and Opium as Connected with His Interest in Contemporary Investigations concerning Stimulation and Sensation.

Psychoanalytic Review, xxv (July 1938), 309–34.

1881 COLERIDGE, SAMUEL TAYLOR. *The Political Thought of Samuel Taylor Coleridge*, a Selection, by R. J. White. London: Jonathan Cape, 1938.

$7\frac{7}{8} \times 5\frac{1}{4}$ in. 272 pp.

1939

1882 NETHERCOT, ARTHUR HOBART. *The Road to Tryermaine, a Study of the History, Background, and Purposes of Coleridge's 'Christabel.'* Chicago: University of Chicago Press, 1939.

9×6 in. ix [1] 230 pp.

1883 RAYSOR, THOMAS MIDDLETON. Coleridge's Criticism of Wordsworth.

PMLA, LIV (June 1939), 496–510.

1884 WHEELER, CHARLES BENJAMIN. *Coleridge on Imagination, with a Consideration of the Theories of I. A. Richards* (Cornell University M.A. Thesis). Ithaca, N.Y.: Typescript, 1939.

$10\frac{1}{4} \times 7\frac{1}{2}$ in.

1940

1885 ARMOUR, RICHARD WILLARD, AND HOWES, RAYMOND F. *Coleridge the Talker; a Series of Contemporary Descriptions and Comments, with a Critical Introduction.* Ithaca, N.Y.: Cornell University Press, 1940.

$9\frac{1}{4} \times 6$ in. xvi, 480 pp.

1886 BROUGHTON, LESLIE NATHAN. Some Early Nineteenth-Century Letters Hitherto Unpublished.

$8\frac{3}{4} \times 5\frac{5}{8}$ in. Pp. 47–88. An offprint from *Nineteenth-Century Studies* (No. 1592).

1887 GRIGGS, EARL LESLIE. *Coleridge Fille: a Biography of Sara Coleridge.* London: Oxford University Press, 1940.

$8\frac{1}{2} \times 5\frac{1}{4}$ in. xiii [1] 259 [1] pp.

1942

1888 ALLEN, NED B. A Note on Coleridge's 'Kubla Khan.'

Modern Language Notes, LVII (February 1942), 108–13.

1889 COLERIDGE, SAMUEL TAYLOR. *Coleridge: with Four Colour Plates & Seventeen Black and White Illustrations*, Edited by Dorothy Wellesley (Britain in Pictures). London: Collins, 1942.

$6\frac{7}{8} \times 4\frac{1}{4}$ in. [2] 80 pp.

1890 SANDERS, CHARLES RICHARD. *Coleridge and the Broad Church Movement*. Durham, N.C.: Duke University Press, 1942.

9×6 in. viii, 307 [5] pp.

1943

1891 JOUGHIN, GEORGE LOUIS. Coleridge's 'Lewti', the Biography of a Poem.

Reprinted from *Studies in English*, University of Texas, Austin, 1943, pp. 66–93.

1946

1892 COLERIDGE, SAMUEL TAYLOR. *Rime of the Ancient Mariner, Illustrated by Alexander Calder, with an Essay by Robert Penn Warren.* New York: Reynal and Hitchcock, [1946].

$10 \times 7\frac{1}{4}$ in. [4] 148 [4] pp.

1951

1893 COLERIDGE, SAMUEL TAYLOR. *Selected Poetry and Prose*, Edited, with an Introduction, by Donald A. Stauffer (Modern Library), New York: Random House, [1951].

$6\frac{7}{8} \times 4\frac{5}{8}$ in. xxviii, 608 [4] pp.

1953

1894 COLERIDGE, SAMUEL TAYLOR. *Christobel [sic], Parts I and II by Samuel Taylor Coleridge, Parts III and IV Mainly by Dean B. Lyman, Jr.* [Amherst, Mass.] 1953.

$9 \times 5\frac{7}{8}$ in. 39 [1] pp.

1895 HOUSE, HUMPHRY. *Coleridge* (the Clark Lectures, 1951–2). London: Rupert Hart-Davis, 1953.

$7\frac{1}{4} \times 4\frac{3}{8}$ in. 167 [1] pp.

1896 RAINE, KATHLEEN J. *Coleridge.* Published for the British Council by Longmans, Green, [1953].

$8\frac{3}{8} \times 5\frac{3}{8}$ in. 44 pp.

1897 SCHNEIDER, ELISABETH. *Coleridge, Opium, and Kubla Khan.* Chicago: University of Chicago Press, [1953].

9⅛ × 6 in. xi [1] 377 [3] pp.

1954

1898 CARPENTER, MAURICE. *The Indifferent Horseman; the Divine Comedy of Samuel Taylor Coleridge.* London: Elek Books, [1954].

8½ × 5⅜ in. [14] 368 [4] pp.

1955

1899 WHALLEY, GEORGE. *Coleridge and Sara Hutchinson and the Asra Poems.* London: Routledge & Kegan Paul, [1955].

8½ × 5¼ in. xxii, 188 pp.

PART VII

THE LAKE DISTRICT

1900 *A Description of the Lake at Keswick (and the Adjacent Country) in Cumberland.* Communicated in a Letter to a Friend, by a Late Popular Writer. Kendal: Printed by W. Pennington. Sold by J. Hodgson at the Queen's Head in Keswick, 1771.

$6\frac{7}{8}$ in. 8 pp.

1901 HUTCHINSON, WILLIAM. *An Excursion to the Lakes in Westmoreland and Cumberland; with a Tour through Part of the Northern Counties, in the Years 1773 and 1774.* London: Printed for J. Wilkie, and W. Charnley, in Newcastle, 1776.

$8\frac{3}{8} \times 5\frac{1}{8}$ in. [4] 382 [4] pp. 19 plates.

1902 NICOLSON, JOSEPH, AND BURN, RICHARD. *The History and Antiquities of the Counties of Westmorland and Cumberland.* London: Printed for W. Strahan and T. Cadell, 1777, 2 vols.

$10\frac{3}{4} \times 8\frac{5}{8}$ in. Vol. 1: cxxxiv, 630; vol. 2: [2] 615 [9]. Maps. This book is the source of several characters and incidents in Wordsworth's poetry.

1903 GRAHAM, CHARLES. *Miscellaneous Pieces, in Prose and Verse.* Kendal: Printed by W. Pennington, 1778.

$6\frac{1}{2} \times 4$ in. xii 203 [3] pp. Richard Wordsworth and three of the Cooksons were subscribers.

1904 [WEST, THOMAS]. *A Guide to the Lakes, In Cumberland, Westmorland, and Lancashire.* By the Author of the Antiquities of Furness. The Second Edition, Revised Throughout and Greatly Enlarged. London: Printed for Richardson and Urquhart; J. Robson; and W. Pennington, Kendal, 1780.

$7\frac{1}{4} \times 4\frac{1}{2}$ in. viii, 291 [1] pp.

1782

1905 GILPIN, WILLIAM. *Observations on the River Wye, and Several Parts of South Wales, &c. Relative Chiefly to Picturesque Beauty; Made in the Summer of the Year 1770.* London: Printed for R. Blamire. Sold by B. Law and R. Faulder, 1782.

8⅝ × 5⅜ in. vii [5] 99 [1] pp. Plates.

1784

1906 [WEST, THOMAS]. *A Guide to the Lakes, In Cumberland, Westmorland, and Lancashire.* By the Author of the Antiquities of Furness. The Third Edition, Revised Throughout and Greatly Enlarged. London: Printed for B. Law; Richardson and Urquhart; J. Robson; and W. Pennington, Kendal, 1784.

8 × 4⅞ in. xii, 306 [2] pp. Map.

1786

1907 GILPIN, WILLIAM. *Observations, Relative Chiefly to Picturesque Beauty, Made in the Year 1772, on Several Parts of England; Particularly the Mountains, and Lakes, of Cumberland, and Westmoreland.* London: Printed for R. Blamire, 1786, 2 vols.

8½ × 5⅜ in. Vol. 1: xxxi [1] xiv, 230; vol. 2: 268, xvi pp. A source for the geography and scenery of The Borderers.

1787

1908 CLARKE, JAMES. *A Survey of the Lakes of Cumberland, Westmorland, and Lancashire; together with an Account, Historical, Topographical, and Descriptive, of the Adjacent Country. To Which Is Added, a Sketch of the Border Laws and Customs.* London: Printed for the Author, 1787.

17 × 10¼ in. xliii, 193 [1]. 10 maps. The story told on pp. 55–6 was used by Wordsworth in *An Evening Walk*.

1788

1909 Keswick and Cumberland Lakes (untitled).

Six maps of the district, four of them published in 1783, one in 1785, and one in 1788.

1910 GILPIN, WILLIAM. *Observations on Several Parts of England, Particularly the Mountains and Lakes of Cumberland and Westmoreland, Relative Chiefly to Picturesque Beauty, Made in the Year 1772.* Second Edition. Vol. 2. London: Printed for R. Blamire, 1788.

8⅝ × 5⅜ in. [4] 268, xiv pp. Accompanied by the third edition of vol. 1, 1808 (No. 1937) in uniform binding. This work was a source for the geography and scenery of The Borderers.

1792

1911 GILPIN, WILLIAM. *Observations on the River Wye, and Several Parts of South Wales, &c. Relative Chiefly to Picturesque Beauty; Made in the Summer of the Year 1770.* Third Edition. London: Printed for R. Blamire, 1792.

8¾ × 5½ in. xvi, 152 [4] pp. 17 aquatint plates.

1912 GILPIN, WILLIAM. *Observations, Relative Chiefly to Picturesque Beauty, Made in the Year 1776, on Several Parts of Great Britain; Particularly the High-Lands of Scotland.* London: R. Blamire, 1792, 2 vols.

9¼ × 5½ in. Vol. 1: xi [1] 221 [3]; vol. 2: [1] 195 [1] xvi.

1913 WALKER, ADAM. *Remarks Made in a Tour from London to the Lakes of Westmoreland and Cumberland, in the Summer of 1791. Originally Published in the Whitehall Evening Post, and Now Reprinted with Additions and Corrections. To Which Is Annexed, a Sketch of the Police, Religion, Arts, and Agriculture of France, Made in an Excursion to Paris in 1785.* London: Printed for G. Nicol and C. Dilly, 1792.

8⅛ × 4⅞ in. [8] 251 [1] pp.

1914 *A Tour from London to the Lakes: Containing Natural, Oeconomical, and Literary Observations, Made in the Summer of 1791.* By a Gentleman. London: Printed and Sold by John Abraham, 1792.

6⅜ × 3⅜ in. [2] 117 [3] pp.

1793

1915 [WEST, THOMAS]. *A Guide to the Lakes, in Cumberland, Westmorland, and Lancashire.* By the Author of the Antiquities of Furness. Fifth Edition. London: Printed for W. Richardson; J. Robson and W. Clarke; and W. Pennington, Kendal, 1793.

8¼ × 4⅞ in. xii, 311 [7] pp. Map and plates.

1794

1916 HUTCHINSON, WILLIAM. *The History of the County of Cumberland, and Some Places Adjacent, from the Earliest Accounts to the Present Time: Comprehending the Local History of the County; Its Antiquities, the Origin, Genealogy, and Present State of the Principal Families, with Biographical Notes; Its Mines, Minerals, and Plants, with Other Curiosities, Either of Nature or of Art. Particular Attention Is Paid to, and a Just Account Given of Every Improvement in Agriculture, Manufactures, &c. &c.* Carlisle: Printed by F. Jollie; and Sold by B. Law and Son, W. Clarke, and T. Taylor, London, 1794, 2 vols.

$10\frac{7}{8} \times 8\frac{3}{8}$ in. Vol. 1: [12] 600; vol. 2: [2] 688 [22] pp.

1917 Keswick and the Cumberland Lakes (untitled).

Seven maps of the district, four published in 1783, one in 1785, one in 1788, one in 1794. With the bookplate of John Ruskin.

1795

1918 [BUDWORTH, JOSEPH]. *A Fortnight's Ramble to the Lakes in Westmoreland, Lancashire, and Cumberland.* By a Rambler. Second Edition. London: Printed for J. Nichols, 1795.

$8\frac{1}{4} \times 5$ in. xxxii, 292 pp.

1919 *An Account of an Extraordinary Phenomenon Said to Have Happened at Southerfell, in Cumberland, in the Year 1744.*

An excerpt from an unidentified periodical, xviii (May 1795), 244–5, recounting a story from James Clarke's *Survey of the Lakes,* 1787 (No. 1908), and used by Wordsworth in *An Evening Walk.*

1920 Views of the English Lakes (untitled).

Sixteen plates in monotint, most of them drawn by John Smith and engraved by S. Alken. Published by W. Clarke, London, 1794 and 1795.

1796

1921 [WEST, THOMAS]. *A Guide to the Lakes, in Cumberland, Westmorland, and Lancashire.* By the Author of the Antiquities of Furness. Sixth Edition. London: Printed for W. Richardson [etc.], 1796.

$8\frac{1}{4} \times 5$ in. xii, 313 [3] pp. Plates and map.

1798

1922 BUDWORTH, JOSEPH. *Windermere, a Poem.* London: Printed for T. Cadell, Jr., and W. Davies, 1798.

$8\frac{7}{8} \times 5\frac{1}{2}$ in. [2] 28 pp.

1923 *The Satellite, or, Repository of Literature; Consisting of Miscellaneous Essays (Chiefly Original) Intended for the Diffusion of Useful and Polite Knowledge.* No. 1, 10 Nov. 1798. Carlisle: Printed by and for J. Mitchell.

$7\frac{3}{4} \times 4\frac{3}{4}$ in. 28 pp. First issue of a North Country periodical.

1800

1924 HOUSMAN, JOHN. *A Topographical Description of Cumberland, Westmoreland, Lancashire, and Parts of the West Riding of Yorkshire; Comprehending, First, a General Introductory View; Secondly, a More Detailed Account of Each County ...; Thirdly, a Tour through the Most Interesting Parts of the District ...;* Illustrated with Various Maps, Plans, Views, and Other Useful Appendages. Carlisle: Printed by Francis Jollie, and Sold by C. Law, and W. Clarke, London, 1800.

$8\frac{1}{4} \times 5$ in. xi [1] 536 [4] pp.

1925 HOUSMAN, JOHN. *A Descriptive Tour, and Guide to the Lakes, Caves, Mountains, and Other Natural Curiosities, in Cumberland, Westmoreland, Lancashire, and a Part of the West Riding of Yorkshire.* Carlisle: Printed by F. Jollie; and Sold by C. Law, London, 1800.

$8\frac{1}{4} \times 5\frac{1}{4}$ in. iv [2] 226 [2] pp. Map. With the bookplate of John Ruskin.

1926 SANDERSON, THOMAS. *Original Poems.* Carlisle: Printed by F. Jollie; London: W. Clarke, J. Robson, and R. Paudler, 1800.

7×4 in. xxiii [1] 238 pp. With 15 pp. of subscribers.

1801

1927 PENNANT, THOMAS. *A Tour from Downing to Alston-Moor.* London: Printed by Wilson & Co. for E. Harding, 1801.

$11\frac{1}{4} \times 8\frac{7}{8}$ in. viii, 195 [1] pp.

1802

1928 HOUSMAN, JOHN. *A Descriptive Tour, and Guide to the Lakes, Caves, Mountains, and Other Natural Curiosities, in Cumberland, Westmoreland, Lancashire, and a Part of the West Riding of Yorkshire.* Second Edition,

Embellished with Several Additional Plates. Carlisle: Printed by F. Jollie; and Sold by C. Law, London, 1802.

$8\frac{3}{4} \times 5\frac{3}{8}$ in. iv [4] 226 [2] pp. Maps and plates.

1929 WHEELER, ANN. *The Westmorland Dialect, in Four Familiar Dialogues: in Which an Attempt Is Made to Illustrate the Provincial Idiom.* Second Edition, to Which Is Added a Dialogue Never Before Published. London: Printed for W. J. and J. Richardson [etc.] by M. Branthwaite, Kendal, 1802.

$6\frac{3}{4} \times 4$ in. ix [1] 11–121 [11] pp. Printed on blue paper.

1930 *The Names of Parishes and Other Divisions Maintaining Their Poor Separately in the County of Westmorland: with the Population of Each: on a Plan Which May Facilitate the Execution of the Poor Laws, and the Ascertainment of the Number of Inhabitants in England.* By a Justice of the Peace for the Counties of Westmorland and Lancashire. Kendal: Printed by W. Pennington; and Sold by W. J. and J. Richardson [etc.], London, 1802.

$6\frac{1}{4} \times 4$ in. xii, 17 [1] pp.

1804

1931 DENHOLM, JAMES. *A Tour to the Principal Scotch and English Lakes.* Glasgow: Printed by R. Chapman for A. Macgoun, 1804.

8×5 in. vi [1] 10–306 pp.

1932 STAGG, JOHN. *Miscellaneous Poems.* Carlisle: Printed by B. Scott, 1804.

$7\frac{1}{8} \times 4\frac{1}{4}$ in. xii, 204 pp. A Cumberland poet.

1805

1933 COCKIN, WILLIAM. *The Rural Sabbath, a Poem, in Four Books; and Other Poems.* London: Printed by W. Bulmer and Co., for G. and W. Nicol, and J. Asperne, 1805.

$6\frac{1}{2} \times 4$ in. viii, 184 pp. Lakes poetry.

1934 MAWMAN, JOSEPH. *An Excursion to the Highlands of Scotland and the English Lakes, with Recollections, Descriptions, and References to Historical Facts.* London: Printed for J. Mawman by T. Gillet, 1805.

$8\frac{1}{4} \times 5$ in. xv [2] 6–291 [1] pp. Map.

1806

1935 [TRAVERS, BENJAMIN]. *A Descriptive Tour to the Lakes of Cumberland and Westmoreland, in the Autumn of 1804.* London: Printed for T. Ostell by W. Pople, 1806.

6⅞ × 4¼ in. viii, 164 pp.

1807

1936 PALMER, SAMUEL. *The General Union of Believers at the Coming of Christ.* A Sermon Preached at Hackney, August 23, 1807, on the Death of the Rev. Daniel Fisher, D.D. London: Printed for the Author, by S. Couchman, 1807.

8¾ × 5⅜ in. 32 pp. Bound in a volume of Lakes pamphlets.

1808

1937 GILPIN, WILLIAM. *Observations on Several Parts of England, Particularly the Mountains and Lakes of Cumberland and Westmoreland, Relative Chiefly to Picturesque Beauty, Made in the Year 1772.* Third Edition. Vol. 1. London: Printed for T. Cadell and W. Davies, 1808.

8⅝ × 5⅛ in. xlvii [1] 283 [4] pp. Accompanied by the second edition of vol. 2, 1788 (No. 1910) in uniform binding. This work was a source for the geography and scenery of The Borderers.

1809

1938 [WEST, THOMAS]. *The Descriptive Part of Mr. West's Guide to the Lakes in Cumberland, Westmorland, and Lancashire.* Kendal: Printed by W. Pennington; and Sold by J. Richardson and W. Clarke, London, 1809.

6½ × 4 in. [4] 149 [1] pp.

1939 The Floating Island in Derwentwater.

The Athenaeum, a Magazine of Literary and Miscellaneous Information, v (March 1809), 246–7.

1810

1940 GREEN, WILLIAM. *A Description of Sixty Studies from Nature; Etched in the Soft Ground, by William Green, of Ambleside; after Drawings Made by Himself in Cumberland, Westmorland, and Lancashire. Comprising a*

General Guide to the Beauties of the North of England. London: Printed for the Author by J. Barfield, and Published for Longman, Hurst, Rees, and Orme; Mr. Mann; and W. Green, Ambleside, 1810.

$7\frac{3}{8} \times 4\frac{1}{2}$ in. x, 122 pp. Presentation copy from the author.

1941 COOKE, GEORGE ALEXANDER. *A Topographical and Statistical Description of the County of Cumberland: Containing an Account of Its Situation, Minerals, Agriculture, Extent, Fisheries, Curiosities, Towns, Manufactures, Antiquities, Roads, Trade, Natural Rivers, Commerce, History, Civil and Ecclesiastical Jurisdiction, &c. to Which Are Prefixed the Direct and Principal Cross Roads, Distances of Stages, Inns, and Noblemen and Gentlemen's Seats. Also a List of the Markets and Fairs, and an Index Table.* Second Edition. Illustrated with a Map of the County, and a Copious Description of the Lakes &c. London: Sherwood, Jones & Co., [c. 1810].

$5\frac{3}{4} \times 3\frac{3}{8}$ in. [2] 136 pp. With the bookplate of John Ruskin.

1811

1942 JOLLIE, F. *Jollie's Cumberland Guide and Directory.* Part the First. Containing a List of All the Parishes, Chapelries, Townships, Principal Villages, Gentlemen's Seats, and Biography of Eminent Men, Natives of the County, or Who Have Been Nearly Connected with It. Antiquities, &c. A Concise Account of the Ancient and Present State of Carlisle; an Account of the Market Towns of Longtown, Brampton, Kirkoswald, Alston, and Penrith: with a Tour through the Most Interesting Parts of That District, Describing Whatever Objects Are Most Worthy of Notice. And a List of Principal Persons and Those in Trade and Public Situations, in Carlisle and the Market Towns Above Mentioned. Illustrated and Imbellished with a Map of the County, Plans of the City and Cathedral, and a Number of Other Useful Appendages. Carlisle: Printed by F. Jollie and Sons, 1811.

$8\frac{7}{8} \times 5\frac{1}{4}$ in. viii, 84, xxxix [3]. Presentation copy from the author to the Duke of Norfolk.

1943 JOLLIE, F. *Jollie's Sketch of the Cumberland Manners and Customs: Partly in the Provincial Dialect, In Prose and Verse.* With a Glossary. Carlisle: Printed by F. Jollie & Sons for Longman & Co. and W. Clarke, London, 1811.

$6\frac{7}{8} \times 3\frac{7}{8}$ in. [2] iv [1] 6–48 pp.

1812

1944 HARGROVE, ELY. *The Yorkshire Gazetteer, or, a Dictionary of the Towns, Villages, and Hamlets; Monasteries and Castles; Principal Mountains, Rivers, &c.; in the County of York, and Ainsty, or the County of the City of York: Describing the Situation of Each, and the Various Events by Which Some of Them Have Been Distinguished.* Second Edition, with a Neat Map of the County. Knaresbrough: Printed by Hargrove and Sons ..., 1812.

6¾ × 3⅞ in. 375 [1] pp.

1945 [WEST, THOMAS]. *A Guide to the Lakes in Cumberland, Westmorland, and Lancashire.* By the Author of the Antiquities of Furness. Tenth Edition. Kendal: Printed by W. Pennington, and Sold by J. Richardson, and W. Clarke, 1812.

8⅜ × 4⅞ in. vi [2] 311 [3] pp. Map.

1946 WHITAKER, THOMAS DUNHAM. *The History and Antiquities of the Deanery of Craven, in the County of York.* Second Edition, with Many Additions, Corrections, Map, and Views of Gentlemen's Seats, Antiquities, &c. London: Printed by J. Nichols and Son, for W. Edwards and Son, Hallifax, 1812.

12½ × 9⅞ in. [4] vii [1] 530 pp.

1947 WILKINSON, THOMAS. *Thoughts on Inclosing Yanwath Moor, and Round Table.* Addressed to the Claimants Thereon. Penrith: Printed by J. Brown, 1812.

8⅛ × 5⅛ in. [2] 38 pp.

1813

1948 *Observations on a Pamphlet, Written by a Clergyman of the Church of England, Entitled 'An Account of the Happy Death of William Grierson, Who Was Executed at Appleby, on Tuesday, September 21st 1813, for Robbery and an Attempt to Commit Murder.'* By a Cumberland Vicar. Penrith: Printed and Sold by F. Jollie ..., [c. 1813].

7½ × 4½ in. 22 pp. Bound in a volume of Lakes pamphlets.

1814

1949 GREEN, WILLIAM. *A Description of a Series of Sixty Small Prints, Etched by William Green ... from Drawings Made by Himself.* London: Printed for the Author, by J. Tyler, and Published by W. Green, Ambleside, 1814.

7 × 9 in. [2] 34 + 60 plates [2] pp.

1815

1950 [GREEN, WILLIAM]. Views of the Lakes (untitled).

Thirty colored aquatint plates, $8\frac{3}{4} \times 12$ in., published at Ambleside, [1815].

1816

1951 HORNE, THOMAS HARTWELL. *The Lakes of Lancashire, Westmoreland, and Cumberland; Delineated in Forty-three Engravings, from Drawings by Joseph Farington, R.A., with Descriptions Historical, Topographical, and Picturesque; the Result of a Tour Made in the Summer of the Year 1816.* London: Printed for T. Cadell and W. Davies, 1816.

$15\frac{3}{8} \times 11$ in. iv [8] 96 pp.

1817

1952 MARSHALL, JOHN. *The Village Paedagogue, a Poem, and Other Lesser Pieces; Together with a Walk from Newcastle to Keswick.* The Second Edition, with Additions and Improvements. Printed for the Author by Preston & Heaton, 1817.

$6\frac{3}{4} \times 4$ in. 122 pp.

1818

1953 BRIGGS, JOHN. *Poems, on Various Subjects.* Ulverston: Printed for the Author by J. Soulby, 1818.

$7 \times 4\frac{1}{4}$ in. viii, 142 pp. A Lakes author.

1819

1954 GREEN, WILLIAM. *The Tourist's New Guide, Containing a Description of the Lakes, Mountains, and Scenery, in Cumberland, Westmorland, and Lancashire, with Some Account of Their Bordering Towns and Villages. Being the Result of Observations Made During a Residence of Eighteen Years in Ambleside and Keswick.* Kendal: R. Lough and Co., ... 1819, 2 vols.

$8\frac{3}{8} \times 5$ in. Vol. 1: viii [2] 461 [5]; vol. 2: viii [2] 507 [1] lv [5] pp.

1955 ROBINSON, JOHN. *A Guide to the Lakes, In Cumberland, Westmorland, and Lancashire, Illustrated with Twenty Views of Local Scenery, and a Travelling Map of the Adjacent Country.* London: Lackington, Hughes, Harding, Mavor, and Jones, 1819.

$7\frac{1}{2} \times 4\frac{5}{8}$ in. viii [2] 328 [2] pp.

1956 Keswick and Cumberland Lakes (untitled).

Six maps of the district; a reprint of No. 1909 (1788).

1821

1957 ACKERMANN, RUDOLPH. *A Picturesque Tour of the English Lakes, Containing a Description of the Most Romantic Scenery of Cumberland, Westmoreland, and Lancashire, with Accounts of Antient and Modern Manners and Customs, and Elucidations of the History and Antiquities of That Part of the Country, &c. &c. Illustrated with Forty-eight Coloured Views, Drawn by Messrs. T. H. Fielding, and J. Walton, During a Two Years' Residence among the Lakes.* London: R. Ackermann, 1821.

$10\frac{1}{16} \times 7\frac{7}{8}$ in. vi [2] 288 pp. Colored plates.

1958 [WEST, THOMAS]. *A Guide to the Lakes, in Cumberland, West-morland, and Lancashire.* By the Author of the Antiquities of Furness. Eleventh Edition. Kendal: Printed for W. Pennington, and Sold by J. Richardson, London, 1821.

$8\frac{3}{4} \times 5\frac{3}{8}$ in. v [3] 312 pp. Map.

1959 [GREEN, WILLIAM]. Views of Ambleside (untitled).

Thirty-six etchings ($13\frac{1}{8} \times 17$ in.) of Ambleside and vicinity, published at Ambleside, 1809–21.

1822

1960 FIELDING, THEODORE HENRY ADOLPHUS. *Cumberland, Westmorland, and Lancashire Illustrated, in a Series of Forty-four Engravings, Exhibiting the Scenery of the Lakes, Antiquities, and Other Picturesque Objects.* London: Printed for Thomas M'Lean, by Howlett and Brimmer, 1822.

$17 \times 11\frac{3}{8}$ in. Unpaged. Large-paper copy. Proofs on India paper.

1961 WILKINSON, THOMAS. *Tours to the British Mountains, with the Descriptive Poems of Lowther, and Emont Vale.* London: Taylor and Hessey, 1824.

$7\frac{1}{8} \times 4\frac{3}{8}$ in. vii [1] 320 [2] pp.

1825

1962 BRIGGS, JOHN. *Letters from the Lakes: to Which Are Added, an Excursion over Harter-Fell to Longsleddale; and the Farewell to the Lakes.* Kirkby Lonsdale: Arthur Foster, 1825.

$7 \times 4\frac{1}{4}$ in. vi [1] 8–198 [2] pp.

1963 BRIGGS, JOHN. *The Remains of John Briggs: Late Editor of 'The Lonsdale Magazine,' and of 'The Westmorland Gazette': Containing Letters from the Lakes; Westmorland as It Was; Theological Essays; Tales; Remarks on the Newtonian Theory of Light; and Fugitive Pieces. To Which Is Added a Sketch of His Life.* Published for the Benefit of His Widow and Children. Kirkby Lonsdale: Arthur Foster, 1825.

7 × 4⅜ in. vi [1] 8–408 pp. Among the subscribers are Hartley Coleridge, Southey, and Wordsworth.

1964 OTLEY, JONATHAN. *A Concise Description of the English Lakes, and Adjacent Mountains, with General Directions to Tourists; and Observations on the Mineralogy and Geology of the District; on Meteorology; the Floating Island in Derwent Lake; and the Black-lead Mine in Borrowdale.* Second Edition. Keswick: Published by the Author.... 1825.

7 × 4¾ in. [2] vi [1] 8–141 [1] pp. Map.

1826

1965 *The Poll for the Knights of the Shire, to Represent the County of Westmorland in Parliament*, Taken at Appleby, on Thursday, Friday, Saturday, Monday, Tuesday, Wednesday, Thursday, and Friday, the 22nd, 23rd, 24th, 26th, 27th, 28th, 29th, and 30th days of June, and Saturday, the First of July, 1826; with the State of the Poll at the Close of Each Day, and the Majorities of the Two Members Returned over the Defeated Candidate; also a Table, Shewing According to the Returns of the Deputy Sheriff, the Number of Votes Polled in Each Ward Every Day during the Contest. Kendal: Tyras Redhead, 1826.

8 × 5 in. [6] 34 pp. Interleaved are MS. pages containing the names and Westmorland addresses of hundreds of persons.

1827

1966 CARTER, NATHANIEL HAZELTINE. *Letters from Europe, Comprising the Journal of a Tour through Ireland, England, Scotland, France, Italy, and Switzerland, in the Years 1825, '26, and '27.* New-York: B. & C. Carvill, 1827, 2 vols.

8⅝ × 5³⁄₁₆ in. Vol. 1: [17] 10–528 [4]; vol. 2: [4] 571 [5] pp. The account of a personal visit to Wordsworth appears on pp. 196–8.

1967 OTLEY, JONATHAN. *A Concise Description of the English Lakes, and Adjacent Mountains: with General Directions to Tourists; Observations on the Mineralogy and Geology of the District; on Meteorology; the Floating Island* *in Derwent Lake; and the Black-lead Mine in Borrowdale; and an Account of an Excursion to the Top of Skiddaw.* Third Edition. Keswick: Published by the Author, . . . 1827.

$7\frac{3}{8} \times 4\frac{3}{8}$ in. [2] vi [1] 8–150 pp. Map.

1828

1968 HODGSON, THOMAS. *Plan of the County of Westmorland, Describing Minutely the Boundaries of Wards, Parishes, & Townships, the Courses of Rivers and Brooks, Turnpike, Carriage, Bridle, and Roman Roads, also the Positions of Towns, Villages, Seats & Farm Houses, Commons, Parks, Woods, Lakes, Mountains, &c. &c. From an Actual Personal Survey, Taken during the Years 1823, 4 & 5.* London: Engraved and Printed by W. R. Gardner, 1828.

Two maps; scale, 1 mile = $1\frac{1}{16}$ in. With the bookplate of John Ruskin.

1829

1969 BAINES, EDWARD. *A Companion to the Lakes of Cumberland, Westmoreland, and Lancashire; in a Descriptive Account of a Family Tour, and an Excursion on Horseback; Comprising a Visit to Lancaster Assizes. With a New, Copious, and Correct Itinerary.* London: Hurst, Chance and Co., 1829.

$7\frac{3}{8} \times 4\frac{3}{8}$ in. xii, 48 pp.

1970 DAVIS, J. SCARLETT. *Fourteen Views in Lithography, of Bolton Abbey, Wharfedale, Yorkshire, from Drawings of This Beautiful Ruin, and the Adjoining Scenery, Taken on the Spot, by J. Scarlett Davis, Under the Immediate Approval of the Rev. W. Carr, B.D., to Which Is Added a Description of Each View.* Second Edition. London: Charles Frederick Cock, 1829.

$11\frac{5}{8} \times 18\frac{5}{8}$ in. [4] 5 [1] pp. + 14 plates.

1971 PARSON, WILLIAM, AND WHITE, WILLIAM. *History, Directory, and Gazetteer, of the Counties of Cumberland and Westmorland, with That Part of the Lake District in Lancashire, Forming the Lordships of Furness and Cartmel: Illustrated by Maps and Tables. And Containing a Descriptive and Geological View of the Lakes, Tarns, Cataracts, Rivers, Mountains, Fells, Rocks, Caverns, Mines, Quarries, Antiquities, Curiosities, Scenery, &c. Including Lists of the Seats of the Nobility, Gentry, and Clergy, with a Variety of Commercial, Agricultural, and Statistical Information, and a History of the Diocese of Carlisle.* Leeds: W. White and Co., 1829.

7×4 in. 732, xxxiv [6] pp.

1972 SANDERSON, THOMAS. *The Life and Literary Remains of Thomas Sanderson.* The Life by the Rev. J. Lowthian, A.M., Vicar of Kellington, and Late Fellow of Trinity College, Cambridge. Embellished with a Portrait of Mr. Sanderson. Carlisle: B. Scott, 1829.

$6\frac{1}{8} \times 3\frac{13}{16}$ in. lxxxix [1] 303 [3] pp.

1830

1973 BAINES, EDWARD, JR. *A Companion to the Lakes of Cumberland, Westmoreland, and Lancashire; in a Descriptive Account of a Family Tour and Excursions on Horseback and on Foot. With a New, Copious, and Correct Itinerary.* Second Edition. London: Hurst, Chance and Co., 1830.

$7\frac{1}{2} \times 4\frac{1}{4}$ in. viii, 312 pp.

1974 *Leigh's Guide to the Lakes and Mountains of Cumberland, Westmoreland, and Lancashire.* London: S. Leigh, [1830].

$6\frac{7}{8} \times 4\frac{1}{4}$ in. viii, 136 [2] pp. Maps.

1832

1975 BREE, JOHN. *St. Herbert's Isle: a Legendary Poem; in Five Cantos. With Some Smaller Pieces.* By the Late John Bree, Esq. of Emerald, Near Keswick. London: Longman, Rees, Orme, Brown, Green, and Longman, 1832.

$7\frac{3}{4} \times 4\frac{3}{4}$ in. xv [1] 175 [1] pp. A Lakes poet.

1976 PEARSON, GEORGE. *Evenings by Eden-side, or Essays and Poems.* Kendal: Printed for the Author by M. and R. Branthwaite, 1832.

$6\frac{3}{4} \times 4$ in. xl [3] 137 [1] pp. A Westmorland poet.

1833

1977 ROSE, THOMAS. *Westmorland, Cumberland, Durham, and North-umberland, Illustrated. From Original Drawings by Thomas Allom, George Pickering, &c. With Descriptions by T. Rose.* London: H. Fisher, R. Fisher, & P. Jackson, 1833.

$10\frac{3}{4} \times 8\frac{1}{8}$ in. [4] 220 [2] pp. 215 plates.

1978 SOPWITH, THOMAS. *An Account of the Mining Districts of Alston Moor, Weardale, and Teesdale, in Cumberland and Durham; Comprising Descrip-*

tive Sketches of the Scenery, Antiquities, Geology, and Mining Operations, in the Upper Dales of the Rivers Tyne, Wear, and Tees. Alnwick: W. Davison, 1833.

7⅛ × 4⅜ in. viii, 183 [1] pp. Map.

1834

1979 OTLEY, JONATHAN. *A Concise Description of the English Lakes, and Adjacent Mountains: with General Directions to Tourists; Notices of the Botany, Mineralogy, and Geology of the District; Observations on Meteorology; the Floating Island in Derwent Lake; and the Black-lead Mine in Borrowdale.* Fifth Edition. Keswick: Published by the Author;... 1834.

7 × 4⅛ in. viii, 184 pp.

1835

1980 BRISTOW, JOHN CHARLES. *Ullsmere, a Poem.* London: Samuel Hodgson, 1835.

7⅞ × 4¾ in. xv [3] 271 [1] pp.

1981 *Leigh's Guide to the Lakes and Mountains of Cumberland, Westmorland, and Lancashire; Illustrated with a Map of the Country, and Maps of Windermere, Derwent Water, Borrowdale, Ullswater, Grasmere, Rydal Water, and Langdale.* Third Edition, Carefully Revised and Corrected. London: Leigh and Son, 1835.

7 × 4⅛ in. viii, 160 [4] pp.

1836

1982 [TATTERSALL, GEORGE]. *The Lakes of England.* London: Sherwood and Co.; and Hudson & Nicholson, Kendal, 1836.

7¾ × 4¾ in. xii, 165 [51] pp. Map and plates.

1837

1983 DEANS, CHARLOTTE. *Memoirs of the Life of Mrs. Charlotte Deans, from Her Earliest Infancy, Comprising the Periods When She Was Miss Charlotte Lowes, Mrs. Johnson, and Mrs. Deans; Being a Journal of a Seventy Years Pilgrimage, with Anecdotes of Many with Whom It Has Been Her Good and Bad Fortune to Associate.* Arranged by Herself. Wigton: Printed by H. Hoodless, 1837.

6½ × 4 in. 111 [1] pp. An actress in the Lake District.

1984 HETHERINGTON, WILLIAM. *Branthwaite Hall, and Other Poems.* Carlisle: Printed for the Author by Charles Thurnam, 1837.

8 × 5 in. xii, 192 pp. A Cockermouth poet.

1838

1985 OTLEY, JONATHAN. *A Concise Description of the English Lakes and Adjacent Mountains: with General Directions to Tourists; Notices of the Botany, Mineralogy, and Geology of the District; Observations on Meteorology; the Floating Island in Derwent Lake; and the Black-lead Mine in Borrowdale.* Sixth Edition. Keswick: Published by the Author; by Simpkin and Marshall, London; and Arthur Foster, Kirkby Lonsdale, 1838.

7 × 4 in. vii [1] 184 pp. Map.

1986 Another copy.

1839

1987 LANDON, LETITIA ELIZABETH. *The Poetical Works of Miss Landon. Comprising the Improvisatrice, Golden Violet, the Troubadour, Vow of the Peacock, Venetian Bracelet, the Easter Gift, etc. etc. etc.* Philadelphia: E. L. Carey and A. Hart, 1839.

$9\frac{1}{8}$ × $5\frac{5}{8}$ in. [6] 348 [2] pp. Several poems describing the Lake Country, one of which is entitled: Rydal Water and Grasmere Lake, the Residence of Wordsworth, pp. 340–1.

1988 *Westmoreland and Cumberland Dialects. Dialogues, Poems, Songs, and Ballads, by Various Writers, in the Westmoreland and Cumberland Dialects, Now First Collected: with a Copious Glossary of Words Peculiar to Those Counties.* London: John Russell Smith, 1839.

$7\frac{5}{8}$ × $4\frac{3}{4}$ in. xii [5] 14–403 [25] pp.

1840

1989 WHEELER, ANN. *The Westmoreland Dialect in Four Familiar Dialogues, in Which an Attempt Is Made to Illustrate the Provincial Idiom. A New Edition. To Which Is Added a Copious Glossary of Westmoreland and Cumberland Words.* London: John Russell Smith, 1840.

$7\frac{5}{8}$ × $4\frac{3}{4}$ in. xii [1] 14–175 [1] pp.

1990 *Specimens of the Yorkshire Dialect, in Various Dialogues, Tales, and Songs. To Which Is Added, a Glossary of Such of the Yorkshire Words As Are Not Likely to Be Generally Understood.* Otley: Printed by William Walker, [1840?].

$7\frac{1}{2}$ × $4\frac{1}{4}$ in. 34 pp.

1841

1991 [HEY, REBECCA]. *Recollections of the Lakes, and Other Poems*, by the Author of the Moral of Flowers and the Spirit of the Woods. London: Tilt and Bogue, 1841.

6¾ × 4⅛ in. xvi, 284 [4] pp.

1992 RITCHIE, LEITCH. *The Wye and Its Associations, a Picturesque Ramble.* London: Longman, Orme, Brown, Green, and Longmans, 1841.

7¾ × 4¾ in. vii [1] 211 [17] pp. Plates.

1842

1993 CLOSE, JOHN. *The Book of the Chronicles: or, Winter Evening Tales of Westmorland. With an Account of Its Antiquities, Romantic and Picturesque Scenery, Manners, Customs, &c., &c., according to the Best Authorities.* Appleby: Printed for the Author by Jonathan Barnes, 1842.

7⅛ × 4⅜ in. xii, 254 [2] pp.

1994 JEFFERSON, SAMUEL. *The History and Antiquities of Allerdale Ward, above Derwent, in the County of Cumberland: with Biographical Notices and Memoirs.* Carlisle: S. Jefferson, 1842.

8¾ × 5½ in. xiii [7] 462 [2] pp. Plates.

1995 OTLEY, JONATHAN. *A Descriptive Guide to the English Lakes, and Adjacent Mountains: with Notices of the Botany, Mineralogy, and Geology of the District. Seventh Edition. To Which Is Added, an Excursion through Lonsdale to the Caves.* Keswick: Published by the Author; by Simkin and Marshall, London; and Arthur Foster, Kirkby Lonsdale, 1842.

7 × 4$\frac{3}{16}$ in. vii [1] 220 pp. Map.

1996 *A Guide to the Lakes of Cumberland, Westmorland, & Lancashire, with a Sketch of Carlisle, Storrs Hall, Windermere Lake, Westmorland.* Carlisle: Hudson Scott ..., [1842].

6⅜ × 3⅞ in. viii, 164 [4] iv pp. From the library of John Ruskin.

1846

1997 *A Guide through the Ruins of Furness Abbey, with a Brief Account of Pile Fouldrey.* Ulverston: David Atkinson, 1846.

6¼ × 3¾ in. 22 pp.

1998 MACKAY, CHARLES. *The Scenery and Poetry of the English Lakes. A Summer Ramble.* With Illustrations from Original Sketches; Drawn on Wood by W. Harvey, J. Gilbert, D. H. M'Kewan, D. Cox, Jun., W. C. Smith, G. Fennel, W. Dickes, W. P. Smith, and E. Gilks. Engraved by Thomas Gilks. London: Longman, Brown, Green, and Longmans, 1846.

$7\frac{7}{8} \times 5$ in. xvi, 234 [5] pp.

1848

1999 TUDOR, HENRY. *Domestic Memoirs of a Christian Family Resident in the County of Cumberland. With Descriptive Sketches of the Scenery of the British Lakes.* London: J. Hatchard and Son, 1848.

$8\frac{3}{4} \times 5\frac{1}{2}$ in. vii [1] 416 [20] pp.

1849

2000 ATKINSON, GEORGE. *The Worthies of Westmorland: or, Notable Persons Born in That County since the Reformation.* London: J. Robinson, 1849, 2 vols.

$8 \times 4\frac{3}{4}$ in. Vol. 1: [6] 319 [1]; vol. 2: [4] 360 pp.

2001 [GIBSON, ALEXANDER CRAIG]. *The Old Man; or, Ravings and Ramblings round Conistone.* London: Whittaker and Co.; Kendal: J. Hudson, 1849.

$6\frac{3}{4} \times 4$ in. vi, 142 [2] pp. A few references to Wordsworth.

2002 OTLEY, JONATHAN. *A Descriptive Guide to the English Lakes, and Adjacent Mountains: with Notices of the Botany, Mineralogy, and Geology of the District. Eighth Edition. To Which Is Added, an Excursion through Lonsdale to the Caves.* Keswick: Published by the Author; Simpkin, Marshall, and Co., London; and John Foster, Kirkby Lonsdale, 1849.

7×4 in. vii [1] 215 [5] pp. Map.

2003 ROSE, THOMAS. *Cumberland, Its Lake and Mountain Scenery etc., etc.* Illustrated from Drawings on the Spot by Thomas Allom. With Descriptions by Thomas Rose. London: Peter Jackson, [1849].

$10\frac{1}{2} \times 8\frac{1}{4}$ in. [2] 72 pp. 62 plates.

2004 *The Life of John Hatfield Commonly Called the Keswick Impostor, with an Account of His Trial and Execution for Forgery, Also His Marriage with 'Mary of Buttermere.' To Which Is Added a Pastoral Dialogue, and the Celebrated Borrowdale Letter, Shewing the Native Dialect of This District.* Keswick: James Ivison, [c. 1849].

$6\frac{5}{8} \times 4$ in. iv, 32, 12 pp.

1850

2005 HETHERINGTON, WILLIAM. *A Third and Concluding Canto of the Poem of Branthwaite Hall, Descriptive of the Feudal Times, in Cumberland and the Borders; with Other Poems.* Cockermouth: Printed for the Author by Daniel Fidler, 1850.

$8\frac{1}{4} \times 5$ in. xii, 193 [1] pp. A Cockermouth poet.

1852

2006 CLARKE, JAMES FREEMAN. *Eleven Weeks in Europe; and What May Be Seen in That Time.* Boston: Ticknor, Reed, and Fields, 1852.

$7\frac{1}{8} \times 4\frac{1}{4}$ in. xv [1] 328 pp. The English Lake Country, pp. 46–51.

2007 TUVAR, LORENZO. *Tales & Legends of the English Lakes and Mountains.* Collected from the Best and Most Authentic Sources. London: Longmans & Co., [1852].

$7\frac{1}{4} \times 4\frac{1}{4}$ in. [4] 312 pp.

2008 *Furness Abbey; and the Best Way to See the Lakes.* London: Whittaker and Co.; Ulverston: Stephen Soulby, 1853.

$7\frac{1}{8} \times 4$ in. 54 pp.

2009 *The History of the Church of Crosthwaite, Cumberland.* London: John Bowyer Nichols, 1853.

$8\frac{3}{4} \times 5\frac{3}{8}$ in. viii, 146 [2] pp. Presentation copy.

1854

2010 *Esthwaite Water: a Poem, in Three Parts, Including an Episode to Nature, with Explanatory Notes for the Young,* by a Lady. London: Whittaker and Co.; Kendal: J. Hudson, 1854.

$8\frac{1}{4} \times 5\frac{1}{4}$ in. 44 pp.

2011 *A Guide through the Ruins of Furness Abbey, with a Brief Account of Dalton and Pile Castle.* Ulverston: D. Atkinson, 1854.

$7\frac{1}{4} \times 4\frac{1}{2}$ in. 32 pp.

2012 NEWBY, GEORGE. *Henllywarc; or, ' The Druid's Temple,' Near Keswick: a Poem.* London: Longman, Brown, Green, and Longmans; Keswick: James Ivison, 1854.

$6\frac{1}{2} \times 4$ in. [6] 72 pp. With the bookplate of John Ruskin.

1855

2013 MARTINEAU, HARRIET. *A Complete Guide to the English Lakes. Illustrated from Drawings by T. L. Aspland and W. Banks, and a Map Coloured Geologically by John Ruthven. To Which Are Added an Account of the Flowering Plants, Ferns, and Mosses of the District, and a Complete Directory.* Windermere: John Garnett; London: Whittaker and Co., 1855.

$6\frac{1}{2} \times 4$ in. [16] 233 [27] pp.

1856

2014 COXE, ARTHUR CLEVELAND. *Impressions of England; or, Sketches of English Scenery and Society.* New-York: Dana and Co., 1856.

$7\frac{1}{4} \times 4\frac{7}{8}$ in. xix [1] 321 [5] pp. The Lakes and the Lakers, pp. 295–303.

1857

2015 *English Lakes.* Black's Guide Books for Tourists. [Edinburgh: A. and C. Black, *c.* 1857].

$7\frac{1}{8} \times 4\frac{1}{2}$ in. iv, 75 [3] 64 pp. Map.

2016 DAVY, JOHN. *The Angler in the Lake District; or, Piscatory Colloquies and Fishing Excursions in Westmoreland and Cumberland.* London: Longman, Brown, Green, Longmans, and Roberts, 1857.

$6\frac{3}{4} \times 4$ in. viii, 352 [64] pp.

2017 SULLIVAN, JEREMIAH. *Cumberland & Westmorland, Ancient and Modern: the People, Dialect, Superstitions and Customs.* London: Whittaker and Co.; Kendal: John Hudson, Jos. Dawson, and Jas. Robinson, 1857.

$8\frac{3}{4} \times 5\frac{1}{2}$ in. [4] 111 [1] 171 [1] pp.

1859

2018 DICKINSON, WILLIAM. *A Glossary of the Words and Phrases of Cumberland.* Whitehaven: Callander & Dixon; London: John Russell Smith, 1859.

$6\frac{3}{8} \times 4$ in. xii [4] 138 [2] pp.

2019 *Old Abbeys and Castles of England.* London: Nelson and Sons, 1859.

$5\frac{3}{4} \times 3\frac{5}{8}$ in. 63 [1] pp., and a supplement of ten colored plates.

2020 PYNE, JAMES BAKER. *Lake Scenery of England,* Drawn on Stone by T. Picken. London: Day & Son, [1859].

$11\frac{1}{4} \times 8$ in. [4] vii [97] pp. Twenty-five aquatint plates.

1860

2021 FOSTER, BIRKET. *Views of the English Lakes.* Edinburgh: A. and C. Black, [*c.* 1860].

$4\frac{7}{8} \times 7\frac{3}{8}$ in. 50 pp. Twenty-four views.

2022 MORRISON, WILLIAM. *Border Sketches, Ancient and Modern. A Glance at the History of Gretna Green, and the Law and Practice of Clandestine Marriages Explained. Also a Description of the Roman Wall and the Debateable Lands, and the Law of the Border.* Longtown: Published and Sold by the Author, [*c.* 1860].

$7\frac{1}{8} \times 4\frac{1}{4}$ in. [6] vi, 48 pp.

2023 WAUGH, EDWIN. *Chapel Island; or, an Adventure on Ulverstone Sands.* Manchester: A. Ireland and Co., [*c.* 1860].

$7 \times 4\frac{3}{8}$ in. 16 pp.

2024 WAUGH, EDWIN. *Over Sands to the Lakes.* Manchester: A. Ireland & Co., 1860.

$7\frac{1}{2} \times 4\frac{3}{4}$ in. 49 [1] pp.

2025 WHELLAN, WILLIAM. *The History and Topography of the Counties of Cumberland and Westmoreland, Comprising Their Ancient and Modern History, a General View of Their Physical Character, Trade, Commerce, Manufactures, Agricultural Condition, Statistics, etc., etc.* Pontefract: W. Whellan and Co. . . . 1860.

$11\frac{1}{8} \times 8\frac{1}{2}$ in. vi, 396, viii pp.

1861

2026 NICHOLSON, CORNELIUS. *The Annals of Kendal: Being a Historical and Descriptive Account of Kendal and the Neighbourhood: with Biographical Sketches of Many Eminent Personages Connected with the Town.* Second Edition. London: Whitaker & Co.; Kendal: T. Wilson, T. Atkinson, W. Fisher, and J. Robinson, 1861.

$8\frac{7}{8} \times 5\frac{1}{2}$ in. xii, 412 pp. Presentation copy from the author.

2027 *Rambling Notes of a Rambling Tour through Some of the English Lake Scenery.* By a Volunteer Rifleman. Sunderland: Wm. Henry Hills; Windermere: J. Garnett, 1861.

$6\frac{3}{8} \times 4\frac{1}{8}$ in. [4] 108 pp.

1864

2028 LINTON, ELIZABETH LYNN. *The Lake Country.* With a Map and One Hundred Illustrations Drawn and Engraved by W. J. Linton. London: Smith, Elder, and Co., 1864.

$9\frac{1}{4} \times 6\frac{3}{4}$ in. xxxix [1] 350 [2] pp.

1865

2029 CLARKE, THOMAS, AND SOUTHEY, ROBERT. *Specimens of the Westmorland Dialect; Consisting of T' Reysh Bearin, and Jonny Shippard's Journa to Lunnan. Reprinted from 'The Westmorland Gazette.' Also, T' Terrible Knitters E' Dent.* By Robert Southey. Reprinted by Permission from 'The Doctor.' Kendal: Printed by Thomas Atkinson, 1865.

$6\frac{7}{8} \times 4\frac{1}{4}$ in. 24 pp.

2030 HAY, ROBERT. *Redstan: a Tale of the Welsh Border, and Other Sketches, Biographical and Descriptive.* London: Wm. Tweedie; Manchester: John Heywood, 1865.

$7\frac{5}{8} \times 4\frac{3}{4}$ in. iv [1] 6–100 pp. Includes sketches of the Lake District.

2031 MARTINEAU, HARRIET. *A Complete Guide to the English Lakes, Illustrated from Drawings by T. L. Aspland and W. Banks.* Third Edition. Edited and Enlarged by Maria Martineau. Windermere: John Garnett; ... [c. 1865].

$6\frac{3}{8} \times 4$ in. [12] 281 [27] pp. Maps and plates.

2032 PRIOR, HERMAN. *Ascents and Passes in the Lake District of England; Being a New Pedestrian and General Guide to the District.* London: Simpkin, Marshall, & Co.; Windermere: J. Garnett, 1865.

$6\frac{1}{2} \times 4$ in. ix [1] v [1] 269 [1] v [1] xv [1] pp.

2033 WEBB, MARIA. *The Fells of Swarthmoor Hall and Their Friends, with an Account of Their Ancestor Anne Askew, the Martyr. A Portraiture of Religious and Family Life in the 17th Century,* Compiled Chiefly from Original Letters and Other Documents, Never Before Published. London: Alfred W. Bennett; Dublin: J. Robertson, 1865.

$7\frac{1}{8} \times 4\frac{1}{2}$ in. x [2] 434 pp. The famous Lancashire family.

2034 A review of ten books about Westmorland.

Quarterly Review, CXII (April 1867), 347–81.

1868

2035 LONSDALE, HENRY. *The Worthies of Cumberland: the Right Honourable Sir J. R. G. Graham, Bart., of Netherby.* London: George Routledge & Sons, 1868.

$7\frac{1}{2} \times 4\frac{7}{8}$ in. xii, 304 [4] pp.

2036 PEABODY, ANDREW PRESTON. *Reminiscences of European Travel.* New York: Hurd and Houghton, 1868.

$6\frac{7}{8} \times 4\frac{3}{8}$ in. viii, 316 [4] pp. References to Wordsworth and the Lakes, pp. 60–2.

2037 GIBSON, ALEXANDER CRAIG. *The Folk-Speech of Cumberland and Some Districts Adjacent; Being Short Stories and Rhymes in the Dialects of the West Border Counties.* London: John Russell Smith; Carlisle: Geo. Coward, 1869.

$6\frac{7}{8} \times 4\frac{1}{2}$ in. viii, 232 [8] pp.

2038 GIBSON, ALEXANDER CRAIG. *The Last Popular Risings in the Lancashire Lake Country.* Liverpool, 1869.

$8\frac{1}{8} \times 5\frac{1}{2}$ in. 12 pp. Bound with the above are four pamphlets, variously paged: 1. Hawkshead Town, Church, and School, pp. 139–60; 2. Hawkshead Parish, pp. 153–74; 3. The Two Conistons, pp. 111–30; Yewdale, Tilberthwaite, Little Langdale, Seathwaite, pp. 47–66.

2039 MORRIS, J. P. *A Glossary of the Words and Phrases of Furness (North Lancashire) with Illustrative Quotations, Principally from the Old Northern Writers.* London: J. Russell Smith; Carlisle: Geo. Coward, 1869.

$6\frac{5}{8} \times 4\frac{1}{2}$ in. xvi, 114 [6] pp.

2040 PAYN, JAMES. *Furness Abbey and Its Neighbourhood.* Windermere: J. Garnett; London: Simpkin, Marshall, and Co., [1869].

$6\frac{1}{2} \times 4$ in. [6] 68 [12] pp. Map.

1870

2041 *The Echoes of the Lakes and Mountains: or Wonderful Things in the Lake District.* (Being a Companion to the Guides.) Embracing: Antiquities—Romantic Legends—Phenomenal Marvels—Graves and Epitaphs—Optical Illusions and Marvellous Echoes—Picturesque Spots and Places—Eccentric Characters—New and Old Records and Anecdotes of the Illustrious Men and Women Who Have Made It Their Home, with Portrait of 'Mary of Buttermere' and View of the 'Fish' Inn, Buttermere, by an 'Antiquarian, Guide, Philosopher and Friend.' London: James Ivison, [c. 1870].

$6\frac{3}{8} \times 4$ in. vii [1] 144 pp.

2042 *Stories of Home Life in the North and South of England.* Adapted for Short Readings at the Sea Side and by the Winter Fire. London: William Freeman; Kendal: Edward Gill, 1870.

$7\frac{1}{4} \times 4\frac{3}{4}$ in. [4] 135 [1] pp.

1871

2043 GOUGH, THOMAS. *Personal Reminiscences of the Habits of Animals.* Kendal: Printed by Atkinson and Pollitt, 1872.

$8 \times 5\frac{1}{4}$ in. [8] 49 [3] pp.

2044 HALL, SPENCER T. *Biographical Sketches of Remarkable People, Chiefly from Personal Recollection; with Miscellaneous Papers and Poems.* London: Simpkin, Marshall and Co., 1873.

$8\frac{1}{4} \times 5\frac{1}{4}$ in. ix [3] 450 pp. Presentation copy from the author. Includes Lake District material.

2045 LONSDALE, HENRY. *The Worthies of Cumberland: the Howards, Rev. R. Matthews, John Rooke, Captain Joseph Huddart.* London: George Routledge and Sons, 1872.

$7\frac{3}{8} \times 4\frac{7}{8}$ in. vii [1] 311 [1] pp.

2046 NICHOLS, W. L. *Quantocks and Their Associations.* A Paper Read before the Members of the Bath Literary Club on the 11th December, 1871. Bath: Printed for Private Circulation, 1873.

$8\frac{3}{8} \times 5\frac{1}{4}$ in. [11] 10–41 [1] xxxiii [3] pp.

2047 PAYN, JAMES. *The Lakes in Sunshine: Being Photographic and Other Pictures of the Lake District, with Descriptive Letterpress* by James Payn. London: Simpkin, Marshall & Co.; Windermere: J. Garnett, 1873.

$11\frac{1}{8} \times 8\frac{1}{4}$ in. [10] 99 [1] 92 pp.

2048 RICHARDSON, JOHN. *'Cumberland Talk,' Being Short Tales and Rhymes in the Dialect of That County together with a Few Miscellaneous Pieces of Verse.* London: John Russell Smith; Carlisle: Geo. Coward, 1871.

$6\frac{3}{4} \times 4\frac{3}{8}$ in. viii, 199 [13] pp.

2049 *The Tourist's Picturesque Guide to Furness Abbey and Windermere District.* With Twelve Tinted Illustrations, and a Map of the District. Second Edition. London: Graphotyping Company; Simpkin, Marshall, and Co.; Ulverston: D. Atkinson, [*c.* 1872].

$6\frac{3}{8} \times 4\frac{1}{4}$ in. viii, 56 [2] pp.

2050 WHITE, JOHN PAGEN. *Lays and Legends of the English Lake Country, with Copious Notes.* London: John Russell Smith; Carlisle: G. & T. Coward, 1873.

$6\frac{7}{8} \times 4\frac{3}{8}$ in. xvi, 334 [10] pp.

1874

2051 *Legends of Westmorland and the Lake District.* Second Edition. London: Hamilton, Adams, and Co.; Kendal: Rawdon B. Lee, 1874.

$6\frac{1}{4} \times 4$ in. [2] 179 [1] pp.

1875

2052 BONNEY, THOMAS GEORGE. *Welsh Scenery (Chiefly in Snowdonia).* By Elijah Walton, F.G.S. With Descriptive Text, by T. G. Bonney. London: W. M. Thompson, 1875.

$12\frac{7}{8} \times 9\frac{1}{2}$ in. Unpaged; twenty colored plates, each followed by a page of description.

2053 LOFTIE, WILLIAM JOHN. *Gems of Home Scenery. Views in the English Lake District from Original Drawings* by T. L. Rowbotham,

Member of the Society of Painters in Water-Colors, with Descriptive Notes Compiled by the Rev. W. J. Loftie. Second Edition. London: Marcus Ward & Co., 1875.

$8\frac{1}{2} \times 6\frac{1}{2}$ in. 114 pp. Five chromographs and five woodcuts.

1876

2054 BONNEY, THOMAS GEORGE. *English Lake Scenery.* By Elijah Walton, F.G.S., Author of 'Flowers from the Upper Alps,' 'The Coast of Norway,' 'Vignettes: Alpine and Eastern,' 'The Bernese Oberland,' 'Welsh Scenery,' etc., etc. With Descriptive Text, by T. G. Bonney, M.A., F.S.A., F.G.S., Fellow and Tutor of St. John's College, Cambridge, Author of 'The Alpine Regions,' etc., etc. London: W. M. Thompson, 1876.

$13\frac{7}{8} \times 9\frac{1}{4}$ in. [2] 9 [3] pp. + 22 plates, each followed by a one-page description.

2055 MARTINEAU, HARRIETT. *The English Lake District.* With Maps, Plans of Towns, and Illustrations. Fifth Edition. Edited, with the Approval of the Authoress, by the Printer and Publisher. Windermere: J. Garnett; London: Simpkin, Marshall & Co., 1876.

$6\frac{7}{8} \times 4\frac{1}{2}$ in. xiv, 367 [21] pp.

2056 *Troutbeck: Its Scenery, Old Architecture, Noted Characters, and Folklore.* With Illustrative Folklore, Especially from Scandinavia. By a Member of the Scandinavian Society, &c. &c. Kendal: Atkinson and Pollitt, 1876.

$6\frac{1}{2} \times 4$ in. 139 [1] pp.

2057 YARNALL, ELLIS. Walks and Visits in Wordsworth's Country.

Lippincott's Magazine, XVIII (November 1876), 543–54, and XVIII (December 1876), 669–82.

1877

2058 BELL, CHARLES DENT. *Voices from the Lakes, and Other Poems.* London: James Nisbet & Co., 1877.

$6\frac{7}{8} \times 4\frac{1}{2}$ in. viii [1] 4–362 [2] pp.

2059 BRATHWAITE, RICHARD. *Natures Embassie, Divine and Morall Satyres: Shepheards Tales, Both Parts: Omphale: Odes, or Philomels Tears, &c.* Boston (Lincs): Printed by Robert Roberts, 1877.

$7\frac{5}{8} \times 4\frac{7}{8}$ in. xliii [1] 312 pp. Brathwaite (or Braithwaite) was a seventeenth-century poet of the Lake District.

2060 JACKSON, WILLIAM. *The Orfeurs of Highclose*. Kendal: T. Wilson, 1877.

$8\frac{1}{2} \times 5\frac{1}{4}$ in. 30 pp. History of a Cumberland family. Presentation copy from the author.

1879

2061 *Our Lake and Mountain Scenery*. Barrow-in-Furness: J. Richardson, 1879.

$4\frac{1}{4} \times 6\frac{3}{4}$ in. [2] pp. + 12 plates.

1880

2062 DOVER, W. KINSEY. *Pre-historic Remains in the Lake District*. A Paper Read before the Keswick Literary and Scientific Society, January 6th, 1879. Keswick: Printed at the 'Visitor and Guardian' Office, 1880.

$8\frac{1}{2} \times 5\frac{1}{4}$ in. [4] 33 [1] pp.

2063 GOUGH, THOMAS. *Observations on the Heron and the Heronry at Dallam Tower, Westmorland*. Kendal: Printed by Atkinson and Pollitt, 1880.

$8\frac{1}{4} \times 5\frac{3}{8}$ in. 23 [1] pp.

2064 *Handy Guide to the English Lakes, and Shap Spa*. With Map and Views. London: Bemrose and Sons; Carlisle: A. B. Moss; Kendal: T. Wilson, [*c.* 1880].

$7\frac{1}{4} \times 4\frac{5}{8}$ in. [20] 134, xiii pp.

1881

2065 JENKINSON, HENRY IRWIN. *Practical Guide to the English Lake District*. With Maps and Views. Seventh Edition. London: Edward Stanford, 1881.

$6\frac{1}{2} \times 4$ in. xciii [3] 364 [48] pp.

2066 RAWNSLEY, HARDWICKE DRUMMOND. *Sonnets at the English Lakes*. London: Longmans, Green & Co., 1881.

$6\frac{1}{2} \times 4\frac{1}{8}$ in. xi [1] 124 pp. Contains a sonnet on Wordsworth's tomb and other tributes to the poet.

2067 The English Lakes and Their Genii.

Harper's New Monthly Magazine, LXII (January 1881), 161–77.

2068 *High House, Ings, the Property of Mr. J. J. Addison.* Kendal: Printed by T. Wilson, 1881.

$8\frac{1}{2} \times 5\frac{1}{4}$ in. Contents: T. Wilson, 'Remains at Hugill, Near Windermere,' pp. 1–5; J. Holme Nicholson, 'Notes on High House in Hugill,' pp. 6–9.

1882

2069 BIRTLES, WILLIAM. *Musings o'er Flood and Fell.* Manchester and London: John Heywood, 1882.

$6\frac{1}{2} \times 4$ in. viii, 106 [4] pp.

2070 FERGUSON, RICHARD SAUL. *Hand-Book to the Principal Places to Be Visited by the Royal Archaeological Institute of Great Britain and Ireland in the Vicinity of Carlisle.* Carlisle: Chas. Thurnam & Sons, 1882.

$7 \times 4\frac{5}{8}$ in. [4] 176 pp.

2071 FLEMING, SIR DANIEL. *Description of the County of Westmoreland,* by Sir Daniel Fleming of Rydal, A.D. 1671. Ed. for the Cumberland and Westmorland Antiquarian and Archaeological Society, from the Original MS. in the Bodleian Library, by Sir G. F. Duckett, Bart. (Cumberland and Westmorland Antiquarian and Archaeological Society Tract Series No. 1). London: B. Quaritch, 1882.

$9 \times 5\frac{5}{8}$ in. [4] 41 [3] pp.

2072 GRINDON, LEOPOLD HARTLEY. *Lancashire: Brief Historical and Descriptive Notes* by Leo H. Grindon. With Fourteen Etchings and Numerous Vignettes. London: Seeley, Jackson, and Halliday, 1882.

$13\frac{1}{2} \times 9\frac{1}{2}$ in. [10] 84 pp.

2073 *The Prince of Wales Lake Hotel Guide. And Hand Book to Grasmere and Its Neighbourhood.* Grasmere: Printed for Edward Brown, 1882.

$4\frac{5}{8} \times 3\frac{1}{2}$ in. 16 [2] pp.

2074 Another copy.

2075 *Thompson's Guide to Ullswater and Its Vicinity, with Map.* Second Edition. Penrith: R. Scott, Printer, 1882.

$5\frac{3}{8} \times 4\frac{1}{8}$ in. 20 [6] pp.

& he brought so bad a cold
home with him that had not
the today [rain] prevented our getting
to you I think that would, &
fearing the like causes may
prevent us tomorrow as well
you are plagued with this long
history but pray dont think it
necessary to send me a written
answer, a verbal one will be
brought to me safely by the
Bearer — With kind love
to Mrs Jackson Believe me
        Your's sincerely
        Dora Wordsworth

Mill Grove
Wednesday Evening

Handwriting of Dora Wordsworth.   No. 2562

Epitaph

In Grasmere Church to the memory
of Mrs Quillinan
(by her Husband)

gloom
These vales were saddened with no common
When good Jemima perished in her bloom;
When (such the awful will of Heaven) she died
By flames breathed on her from her own fire side
On earth we dimly see, & but in part
                                        heart.
We know, yet Faith sustains the sorrowing
And She, the pure the patient & the meek,
Might have fit Epitaph could feelings speak;
If words could tell & monuments record,
How treasures lost are by the heart deplored,
No name of grief's fond eloquence adorned
More than Jemima's would be praised & mourned.
The tender virtues of her blameless life
Bright in the Daughter, brighter in the wife,
And in the cheerful Mother brighter shone:
That Light is passed away — the will of God be
                                        done!

Sarah Hutchinson
    Rydal Mount
        Sepr 27th 1829

Handwriting of Sara Hutchinson. No. 3186

1883

2076 KUPER, M. E. *Seven Volumes of the Dalston Parish Registers.* Communicated at a Meeting of the Cumberland and Westmorland Archaeological and Antiquarian Society, Aug. 22, 1883. Kendal: Printed by T. Wilson, 1883.

$8\frac{3}{4} \times 5\frac{1}{4}$ in. Pp. 156–220. Presentation copy from the author.

1884

2077 BRAITHWAITE, GEORGE FOSTER. *The Salmonidae of Westmorland, Angling Reminiscences, and Leaves from an Angler's Note Book.* London: Hamilton, Adams, and Co.; Kendal: Printed by Atkinson and Pollitt, 1884.

$7\frac{1}{8} \times 4\frac{3}{4}$ in. xiv, 188 pp.

2078 BRUCE, JOHN COLLINGWOOD. *The Hand-Book to the Roman Wall: a Guide to Tourists Traversing the Barrier of the Lower Isthmus.* Second Edition. London: Alfred Russell Smith; Newcastle-upon-Tyne: Andrew Reid, 1884.

$7\frac{1}{4} \times 4\frac{3}{4}$ in. [4] iv [2] 251 [3] pp.

2079 CLOSE, JOHN. *Poet Close's Fifteenth Christmas Book, Containing New Poems on the Great Men of the Age, ... the Enchanted Isle, a Grand Epic Poem, and Other Poems and Sketches,* with Plates and Portraits. Kirkby Stephen: Published and Sold by Poet Close, at Poet's Hall, at the Railway Station, and at the Lakes, Windermere (in Summer Only), 1884.

$8\frac{1}{4} \times 5\frac{1}{4}$ in. [2] 116 pp. Bound with: General Post-Office Information for 1885, 24 pp.

2080 ROSCOE, E. The Industries of the English Lake District.

English Illustrated Magazine, May 1884, pp. 480–8.

1885

2081 *Archbishop Sandys' Endowed School, Hawkshead, Near Ambleside.* Tercentenary Commemoration, Thursday, September 17th, 1885. Kendal: Printed by Atkinson and Pollitt, [1885].

$5\frac{5}{16} \times 8\frac{1}{4}$ in. 26 [2] pp.

2082 BURROUGHS, JOHN. *Fresh Fields.* Second Edition. Boston: Houghton, Mifflin and Co., 1885.

6⅝ × 4¾ in. [8] 298 [2] pp. In Wordsworth's Country, pp. 161–72.

1886

2083 GAGE, WILLIAM LEONARD. *A Leisurely Journey.* Boston: D. Lothrop and Co., 1886.

6⅝ × 4⅜ in. x, 168 pp.

2084 LAW, DAVID. *Wordsworth's Country: a Series of Five Etchings of the English Lake District.* London: Robert Dunthorne, 1886.

5 × 3⅝ in. [12] pp. Apparently a prospectus; no plates are included.

1887

2085 DENTON, JOHN. *An Accompt of the Most Considerable Estates and Families in the County of Cumberland, from the Conquest unto the Beginning of the Reign of K. James.* Edited by R. S. Ferguson (Cumberland and Westmoreland Antiquarian and Archaeological Society Tract Series, No. 2). Kendal: T. Wilson, 1887.

8½ × 5⅛ in. [6] vii [1] 214 [2] pp.

2086 GIBSON, THOMAS. *Legends and Historical Notes of North Westmoreland.* Chilworth and London: Unwin Brothers, 1887.

7⅜ × 4¾ in. xv [1] 308 pp.

2087 GOODWIN, HARRY, AND KNIGHT, WILLIAM ANGUS. *Through the Wordsworth Country.* London: Swan Sonnenschein, 1887.

11¾ × 7¾ in. xix [1] 268 [2] pp. Fifty-six full-page illustrations; the text is largely from Wordsworth's prose and poetry.

1888

2088 BELLASIS, EDWARD. *Westmorland Church Notes, Being the Heraldry, Epitaphs, and Other Inscriptions in the Thirty-two Ancient Parish Churches and Churchyards of That County.* Kendal: T. Wilson, 1888, 1889, 2 vols.

9⅝ × 6 in. Vol. 1: xi [1] 281 [1]; vol. 2: [4] 340 [2] pp.

2089 ELLWOOD, THOMAS. *Leaves from the Annals of a Mountain Parish in Lakeland: Being a Sketch of the History of the Church and Benefice of Torver, together with Its School Endowments, Charities, and Other Trust Funds.* Ulverston: Printed by James Atkinson, 1888.

$7\frac{1}{8} \times 4\frac{1}{2}$ in. iv, 70 pp.

2090 FORSHAW, CHARLES FREDERICK (ED.). *Yorkshire Poets, Past & Present, Illustrated. With Selections from Their Writings and Short Biographical Sketches of Their Lives.* No. 4, June 1888. Bradford: T. Brown, 1888.

$7\frac{1}{8} \times 4\frac{3}{4}$ in. Pp. 50–80.

2091 HOPE, ROBERT DIXON. *Poems, Including Some in Scottish and Westmorland Dialects.* Kendal: Printed by T. Wilson, 1888.

$6\frac{3}{4} \times 4\frac{1}{8}$ in. vii [1] vii [1] 83 [1] pp.

2092 WIPER, WILLIAM. *The Layburnes of Cunswick.* Read at Kendal, July 11, 1888.

$8\frac{3}{4} \times 5\frac{3}{8}$ in. Pp. 124–57, excerpted from an unidentified publication.

1889

2093 RAWNSLEY, HARDWICKE DRUMMOND. *Five Addresses on the Lives and Work of St. Kentigern and St. Herbert,* Delivered in St. Kentigern's Church, Crosthwaite. Second Edition. Carlisle: Chas. Thurnam and Sons; London: George Bell and Sons, 1889.

$10 \times 7\frac{5}{8}$ in. vii [3] 54 [2] pp.

1890

2094 BROOKE, STOPFORD AUGUSTUS. *Dove Cottage, Words-worth's Home from 1800–1808, December 21, 1799 to May —, 1808.* London: Macmillan and Co., 1890.

$7 \times 4\frac{7}{8}$ in. 75 [1] pp. Later editions appeared in 1894 and 1902.

2095 FERGUSON, RICHARD S. *A History of Cumberland* (Popular County Histories). London: Elliot Stock, 1890.

$8\frac{7}{8} \times 5\frac{1}{2}$ in. [8] 312 pp.

2096 KNIGHT, WILLIAM ANGUS. *Through the Wordsworth Country: a Companion to the Lake District.* With 56 Plates and a Frontispiece after the Statue in Westminster Abbey, by Harry Goodwin. Second Edition. London: Swan Sonnenschein & Co., 1890.

$7\frac{3}{8} \times 4\frac{3}{4}$ in. xix [1] 268 [2] pp.

2097 MALLESON, FREDERICK AUGUSTUS. *Holiday Studies of Wordsworth by Rivers, Woods, and Alps. The Wharfe, the Duddon, and the Stelvio Pass.* London, Paris, and Melbourne: Cassell and Co., 1890.

$8\frac{7}{8} \times 6\frac{3}{4}$ in. x [3] 14–115 [17] pp.

2098 SANDFORD, EDMUND. *A Cursory Relation of All the Antiquities and Familyes in Cumberland.* By Edmund Sandford. Circa 1675. Edited, for the Cumberland and Westmorland Antiquarian and Archaeological Society, by the Worshipful Chancellor Ferguson, M.A., LL.M., F.S.A., President of the Society (Cumberland and Westmorland Antiquarian and Archaeological Society Tract Series, No. 4). Kendal: Printed by T. Wilson, 1890.

$8\frac{1}{2} \times 5\frac{3}{8}$ in. [8] 54 [2] pp.

2099 TODD, HUGH. *Account of the City and Diocese of Carlisle.* By Hugh Todd, D.D. Edited, for the Cumberland and Westmorland Antiquarian and Archaeological Society, by the Worshipful Chancellor Ferguson, M.A., LL.M., F.S.A., President of the Society (Cumberland and Westmorland Antiquarian and Archaeological Society Tract Series, No. 5). Kendal: Printed by T. Wilson, 1890.

$8\frac{3}{4} \times 5\frac{1}{2}$ in. 54 pp.

2100 TUTIN, JOHN RAMSDEN. Wordsworth in Yorkshire.

$8\frac{1}{2} \times 5\frac{1}{2}$ in. From *Yorkshire Notes and Queries* [1890]. Loose leaves, [16] pp.

1891

2101 ARMISTEAD, WILSON. *Tales and Legends of the English Lakes.* London: Simpkin, Marshall, and Co.; Glasgow: Thomas D. Morison, 1891.

$7\frac{7}{8} \times 5\frac{1}{4}$ in. xii [1] 289 [3] pp.

2102 GIBSON, ALEXANDER CRAIG. *The Folk-Speech of Cumberland and Some Districts Adjacent; Being Short Stories and Rhymes in the Dialects of the West Border Countries.* Fourth Edition. London: Bemrose & Sons; Carlisle: G. & T. Coward, the Wordsworth Press, 1891.

$6\frac{7}{8} \times 4\frac{1}{2}$ in. viii, 208 pp.

2103 *The Skiddaw Hermit.* Ambleside: George Middleton, 1891.

7½ × 4¾ in. [2] 26 [2] pp. Sketch of George Smith, a Lake District eccentric.

2104 NICHOLS, WILLIAM LUKE. *The Quantocks and Their Associations. With an Account of Dodington, Holford, and St. Audries.* Second Edition, Revised and Enlarged, with Map and Eleven Illustrations. London: Sampson, Low, Marston, and Co.; Bath: G. A. Mundy, 1891.

7½ × 4⅞ in. [16] 109 [11] pp.

2105 RAWNSLEY, HARDWICKE DRUMMOND. *A Coach-Drive at the Lakes: Windermere to Keswick.* Second Edition. Keswick: T. Blakewell, 1891.

6⅝ × 4 in. [viii] 96 [2] pp.

1892

2106 COWPER, HENRY SWAINSON. *The Monumental Inscriptions in the Parish Church and Churchyard of Hawkshead, Lancashire, and in the Burial Grounds of Satterthwaite, the Baptists at Hawkshead Hill, and the Quakers at Colthouse.* Kendal: T. Wilson, 1892.

7⅛ × 4⅞ in. vi [2] 84 pp.

2107 JACKSON, WILLIAM. *Papers and Pedigrees, Mainly Relating to Cumberland and Westmorland.* Reprinted from Various Local and Other Publications, and Edited by Mrs. Jackson. London: Bemrose & Sons; Carlisle: Charles Thurname & Sons; Kendal: T. Wilson, 1892, 2 vols.

8¾ × 5½ in. Vol. 1: [14] 370; vol. 2: [8] 369 [1] pp.

2108 MACPHERSON, H. A. *A Vertebrate Fauna of Lakeland, Including Cumberland and Westmorland with Lancashire North of the Sands.* With a Preface by R. S. Ferguson. Edinburgh: David Douglas, 1892.

9 × 5½ in. civ, 552 [20] pp.

2109 WALKER, JOHN. *A Spring Day at Keswick.* Manchester: John Heywood, 1892.

8½ × 5⅜ in. 24 pp.

2110 WAUGH, EDWIN. *Rambles in the Lake Country and Other Travel Sketches.* Edited by George Milner. Manchester: John Heywood, [1892].

7⅜ × 4⅞ in. ix [3] 290 pp. Map.

2111 WINTER, WILLIAM. *Gray Days and Gold in England and Scotland*. New Edition. New York: Macmillan and Co., 1892.

5$\frac{3}{16}$ × 3$\frac{5}{8}$ in. 334 [10] pp. The Land of Wordsworth, pp. 80–97.

1893

2112 NEASHAM, GEORGE. *North-Country Sketches, Notes, Essays and Reviews*. With 13 Full-page Illustrations, and 47 Woodcuts by Thomas and John Bewick and Their Pupils. Durham: Printed for the Author by Thos. Caldcleugh, 1893.

8$\frac{5}{8}$ × 5$\frac{1}{2}$ in. vi [2] 400 pp.

2113 ROBINSON, JACOB, AND GILPIN, SIDNEY. *North Country Sports and Pastimes*. Wrestling and Wrestlers: Biographical Sketches of Celebrated Athletes of the Northern Ring; to Which Is Added Notes on Bull and Badger Baiting. London: Bemrose and Sons; Carlisle: the Wordsworth Press, 1893.

6$\frac{3}{4}$ × 4$\frac{1}{2}$ in. xlvii [1] 251 [1] pp.

1894

2114 BROOKE, STOPFORD AUGUSTUS. *Dove Cottage, Wordsworth's Home from 1800–1808, December 21, 1799 to May —, 1808*. London: Macmillan and Co., 1894.

7 × 4$\frac{3}{4}$ in. 75 [1] pp.

2115 FERGUSON, RICHARD SAUL. *A History of Westmorland* (Popular County Histories). London: Elliot Stock, 1894.

8$\frac{7}{8}$ × 5$\frac{1}{2}$ in. viii, 312 pp.

2116 LEACH, R. E. *Benefactors to the Library, Appleby Grammar School*. Kendal: Printed by T. Wilson, 1894.

8$\frac{7}{8}$ × 5$\frac{1}{4}$ in. Pp. 20–36. Reprinted from *Transactions of the Cumberland and Westmorland Antiquarian and Archaeological Society*.

2117 *Middleton's Illustrated Handbook to Grasmere*. Ambleside: George Middleton, 1894.

6$\frac{1}{2}$ × 4$\frac{1}{4}$ in. [4] 48 [4] pp.

1895

2118 HARWOOD, JOHN JAMES. *History and Description of the Thirlmere Water Scheme*. Manchester: Henry Blacklock and Co., 1895.

8$\frac{5}{8}$ × 5$\frac{1}{2}$ in. xv [1] 277 [3] pp.

2119 HUSON, THOMAS. *Round about Helvellyn:* Twenty-four Plates by Thomas Huson, R.I., R.P.E. With Notes by the Artist and Descriptive Passages from Wordsworth's Poems. London: Seeley and Co., 1895.

12½ × 8½ in. [8] 51 [5] pp.

2120 ROGERS, SHOWELL. *A Bank Holiday on Blencathara.* August 5th, 1895.

3 pp. A typewritten poem in four parts, 21 quatrains, with notes.

1896

2121 ROPER, WILLIAM OLIVER. *Borwick Hall.* A Paper Read before the Historic Society of Lancashire and Cheshire, 21st February, 1895. Liverpool: Printed by Thomas Brakell, 1896.

8½ × 5¼ in. 6 pp.

1897

2122 COWPER, HENRY SWAINSON. *The Oldest Register Book in the Parish of Hawkshead in Lancashire, 1568–1704.* With Introductory Chapters and Four Illustrations. London: Bemrose and Sons, 1897.

9¼ × 6 in. civ, 451 [5] pp.

2123 CREIGHTON, MANDELL. *The Story of Some English Shires.* With a Photogravure Frontispiece after an Unpublished Drawing by Thomas Hearne, and Ninety-eight Engravings. London: the Religious Tract Society, 1897.

11¼ × 8⅞ in. 312 pp.

2124 LLOYD, ELEANOR. *Notes on a Sun-dial at Patrington* ... and a Note by the Rev. Canon Maddock, M.A. Hull: William Andrews & Co., 1897.

8⅜ × 5½ in. 14 pp.

1898

2125 BOGG, EDMUND. *A Thousand Miles of Wandering along the Roman Wall, the Old Border Region, Lakeland, and Ribblesdale.* One Hundred and Eighty Illustrations. Leeds: Edmund Bogg and James Miles, 1898.

9⅝ × 7⅛ in. xi [1] 256 pp.

2126 FERGUSON, RICHARD SAUL. *A History of Cumberland.* London: E. Stock, 1898.

9 × 5½ in. 312 pp.

2127 KIRKBY, B. *Lakeland Words: a Collection of Dialect Words and Phrases as Used in Cumberland and Westmorland, with Illustrative Sentences in the North Westmorland Dialect.* With Preface by Joseph Wright. Kendal: T. Wilson, 1898.

7⅛ × 4¾ in. xiv [2] 168 pp.

2128 Another copy.

1899

2129 COWPER, HENRY SWAINSON. *Hawkshead: Its History, Archaeology, Industries, Folklore, Dialect, etc., etc.* London: Bemrose and Sons, 1899.

9¾ × 6 in. xvi, 580 pp.

2130 RAWNSLEY, HARDWICKE DRUMMOND. *Life and Nature at the English Lakes.* Glasgow: MacLehose and Sons, 1899.

7½ × 4⅞ in. viii, 192 [52] pp.

2131 SCOTT, DANIEL. *Bygone Cumberland and Westmorland.* London: W. Andrews & Co., 1899.

8½ × 5¼ in. 262 pp.

1900

2132 JONES, OWEN GLYNNE. *Rock-Climbing in the English Lake District.* Second Edition, with a Memoir and Portrait of the Author, Thirty-one Full Page Illustrations in Collotype, Nine Outline Plates of the Chief Routes, and an Appendix by George and Ashley Abraham. Keswick: G. P. Abraham and Sons, 1900.

9 × 5⅞ in. lxiv, 322 [10] pp.

2133 KIRKBY, B. *Granite Chips and Clints: or Westmorland in Words.* Kendal: T. Wilson, 1900.

7⅛ × 4⅝ in. xii [2] 130 pp.

2134 RAWNSLEY, HARDWICKE DRUMMOND. *The Story of Gough and His Dog.* n.p., [c. 1900].

8½ × 5¼ in. 30 pp. An account of the death of Charles Gough in 1805. Wordsworth tells the story in the poem Fidelity.

1901

2135 RAWNSLEY, HARDWICKE DRUMMOND. *Literary Associations of the English Lakes, in Two Volumes.* Volume 1. Cumberland, Keswick, and Southey's Country, with Fifteen Illustrations. [Volume 2. Westmoreland, Windermere, and the Haunts of Wordsworth, with Seventeen Illustrations.] Glasgow: James MacLehose and Sons, 1901.

$7\frac{5}{8} \times 5$ in. Vol. 1: xi [3] 236 [4]; vol. 2: vii [3] 251 [1] pp.

1902

2136 BENSON, CLAUDE ERNEST. *Crag and Hound in Lakeland.* London: Hurst and Blackett.

$8\frac{1}{2} \times 5\frac{1}{2}$ in. xvi, 313 [7] pp.

2137 BROOKE, STOPFORD AUGUSTUS. *Dove Cottage, Wordsworth's Home from 1800–1808, December 21: 1799 to May —, 1808.* London: Macmillan and Co., 1902.

$6\frac{7}{8} \times 4\frac{5}{8}$ in. 75 [3] pp.

2138 COLLINGWOOD, WILLIAM GERSHON. *The Ancient Ironworks of Coniston Lake.* A Paper Read before the Historic Society of Lancashire and Cheshire, 14th February, 1901. Liverpool: Printed by Thomas Brakell, 1902.

$8\frac{1}{4} \times 5\frac{3}{8}$ in. 22 [2] pp.

2139 HOPE, WILLIAM HENRY ST. JOHN. *The Abbey of St. Mary in Furness, Lancashire.* Kendal: T. Wilson, 1902.

$12\frac{1}{8} \times 9\frac{3}{8}$ in. [12] 82 [2] pp. Steel engravings, collotypes, and plans.

2140 *The Official Catalogue of the Contents of Dove Cottage, Grasmere, Wordsworth's Home from 1799 to 1808, and Afterwards De Quincey's Residence.* Ambleside: George Middleton, 1902.

$6\frac{1}{2} \times 4\frac{1}{4}$ in. 33 [1] pp.

2141 PALMER, WILLIAM THOMAS. *Lake Country Rambles ....* London: Chatto & Windus, 1902.

$7\frac{3}{8} \times 5$ in. viii, 334 pp.

2142 RAWNSLEY, HARDWICKE DRUMMOND. *A Rambler's Note-Book at the English Lakes.* Glasgow: James MacLehose and Sons, 1902.

$7\frac{1}{2} \times 5$ in. viii [2] 258 [2] pp. Plates.

1903

2143 GAYTHORPE, HARPER. *Neolithic Man in Low Furness, with Notes on the Geological Strata.* Barrow-in-Furness: G. M. Carruthers, 1903.

$8\frac{3}{8} \times 5$ in. Pp. 47–51. Reprinted from *Barrow Naturalists' Field Club's Annual Report, Proceedings, &c.*, vol. XVI.

2144 PALMER, WILLIAM THOMAS. *In Lakeland Dells and Fells.* London: Chatto & Windus, 1903.

$7\frac{1}{2} \times 5$ in. vi, 352 pp.

1904

2145 MORTIMER, JOHN. *Shap Fells.* London and Manchester: Sherratt and Hughes, 1904.

$8\frac{3}{4} \times 5\frac{1}{4}$ in. 8 pp. Reprinted from the *Manchester Quarterly*, April 1904.

2146 SCOTT, SAMUEL HASLAM. *A Westmorland Village, the Story of the Old Homesteads and 'Statesman' Families of Troutbeck by Windermere.* With Illustrations by the Author. Westminster: Archibald Constable & Co., 1904.

$7\frac{1}{2} \times 5$ in. [8] 269 [3] pp.

2147 SHARP, WILLIAM. *Literary Geography.* London: Offices of the 'Pall Mall Publications,' 1904.

$9\frac{7}{8} \times 7\frac{3}{8}$ in. xvi [2] 248 pp.

1905

2148 GRAHAM, JOHN. *Conditions of the Border at the Union: Destruction of the Graham Clan.* Glasgow: MacLehose and Sons, 1905.

$7\frac{1}{2} \times 5$ in. xvi [2] 307 [1] pp. Presentation copy from the author.

1906

2149 GAYTHORPE, HARPER. *Pre-historic Implements in Furness.* Kendal: Titus Wilson, 1906.

$8\frac{3}{4} \times 5\frac{1}{2}$ in. Pp. 143–8. Reprinted from the Cumberland and Westmorland Antiquarian and Archaeological Society's *Transactions*, vol. 6.

2150 HIRST, TOM OAKES. *A Grammar of the Dialect of Kendal (Westmoreland), Descriptive and Historical, with Specimens and a Glossary.* Heidelberg: C. Winter, 1906.

9×6 in. iv [4] 170 pp.

1908

2151 BRADLEY, ARTHUR GRANVILLE. *Highways and Byways in the Lake District.* With Illustrations by Joseph Pennell. London: Macmillan and Co., 1908.

$7\frac{3}{4} \times 5\frac{1}{8}$ in. xii, 332 [2] pp.

2152 CAINE, CAESAR. *Capella de Gerardegile, or, the Story of a Cumberland Chapelry (Garrigill).* Haltwhistle: R. M. Saint, 1908.

$8\frac{7}{8} \times 5\frac{5}{8}$ in. xxv [1] 248 pp.

2153 NURSE, EUSTON JOHN. *History of the Parish Church, Windermere (Sometimes Erroneously Called Bowness Parish Church).* n.p., 1908.

$6\frac{1}{2} \times 4$ in. [12] 83 [5] pp.

1909

2154 NOBLE, S. C. *The Kendal Newsroom.* n.p., Printed for Private Circulation, 1909.

$8\frac{1}{2} \times 5\frac{1}{2}$ in. 16 pp.

2155 WAKEFIELD, A. M. *Cartmel Priory and Sketches of North Lonsdale.* Grange-over-Sands: H. T. Mason, 1909.

$7\frac{3}{8} \times 4\frac{7}{8}$ in. [16] 81 [3] pp.

1910

2156 BRADLEY, ARTHUR GRANVILLE. *The English Lakes.* Pictured by E. W. Haslehurst. London, Glasgow, and Bombay: Blackie and Son, 1910.

$9 \times 6\frac{1}{2}$ in. [2] 56 pp.

2157 GAYTHORPE, HARPER. *Swarthmoor Meeting-house, Ulverston: a Quaker Stronghold*. Kendal: Printed by Titus Wilson, 1910.

8⅜ × 5¼ in. 48 pp. Reprinted from the *Transactions* of the Cumberland and Westmorland Antiquarian and Archaeological Society, vol. 6. With a four-page letter from the author tipped in.

2158 PHILLIMORE, W. P. W., AND RUSTON-HARRISON, C. W. *Cumberland Parish Registers: Marriages*. London: Phillimore and Co., 1910, 2 vols.

8¾ × 5¼ in. Vol. 1: [8] 192; vol. 2: [8] 157 [3] pp.

1911

2159 BRYDSON, A. P. *Sidelights on Mediaeval Windermere*. Kendal: Titus Wilson, 1911.

8¾ × 5⅝ in. [4] 107 [1] pp.

2160 RAWNSLEY, HARDWICKE DRUMMOND. *The Book of the Coronation Bonfires*. Carlisle: Charles Thurnam and Sons, 1911.

9¾ × 7⅜ in. [2] 85 [3] pp. + 24 plates.

2161 ROBERTSON, ERIC. *Wordsworthshire: an Introduction to a Poet's Country*. Illustrated with Forty-seven Drawings by Arthur Tucker, R.B.A., and Maps. London: Chatto and Windus, 1911.

8¾ × 5½ in. xii, 351 [1] pp.

1912

2162 ARMITT, MARY L. *The Church of Grasmere: a History*. With Illustrations by Margaret L. Sumner. Kendal: Titus Wilson, 1912.

8⅞ × 5½ in. [14] 227 [1] pp.

2163 BROWN, JAMES WALTER. *Carlisle in Ballad and Story*. A Lecture Delivered before the Carlisle Scientific and Literary Society, on October 31st, 1911; and, by Request, to the Cumberland and Westmorland Association of London, on February 21st, 1912. Carlisle: Chas. Thurnam and Sons, 1912.

8½ × 5½ in. [2] 40 [6] pp.

1913

2164 ABRAHAM, GEORGE DIXON. *Motor Ways in Lakeland*. With Twenty-four Illustrations and a Map. London: Methuen & Co., 1913.

8¾ × 5½ in. xi [1] 307 [63] pp.

2165 PALMER, WILLIAM THOMAS. *Odd Corners in English Lakeland: Rambles, Scrambles, Climbs, and Sport*. With Fifteen Illustrations. London: Skeffington & Sons, 1913.

$7\frac{5}{8} \times 5$ in. viii, 186 [2] pp.

2166 PAPE, THOMAS. *Warton and George Washington's Ancestors*. Morecambe: Visitor Printing Works, 1913.

$7\frac{1}{4} \times 4\frac{3}{4}$ in. 46 [4] pp.

2167 RAWNSLEY, HARDWICKE DRUMMOND. *Chapters at the English Lakes*. Glasgow: James MacLehose and Sons, 1913.

$7\frac{3}{8} \times 5$ in. 252 pp.

1914

2168 FALCONER, HUGH. *Merrie Carlisle, and Poems of Tradition*. Second Edition, Revised. Carlisle: Chas. Thurnam, 1914.

$7\frac{1}{4} \times 4\frac{7}{8}$ in. [2] 127 [1] pp.

2169 JENKINSON, EMILY. *Barbara Lynn: a Tale of the Dales and Fells*. London: Edward Arnold, 1914.

$7\frac{3}{8} \times 4\frac{3}{4}$ in. iv, 314 [2] pp.

2170 NICHOLSON, JOSIAH WALKER. *Crosby Garrett, Westmorland: a History of the Manor of Crosby Garrett in Westmorland, with Local Customs and Legends*. Kirkby Stephen: J. W. Braithwaite & Sons, 1914.

$7\frac{1}{4} \times 4\frac{3}{4}$ in. xv [1] 136 pp.

2171 WITHERS, PERCY. *In a Cumberland Dale*. London: Grant Richards, 1914.

$7\frac{1}{4} \times 5$ in. ix [1] 296 pp.

1915

2172 NICHOLSON, FRANCIS, AND AXON, ERNEST. *The Older Nonconformity in Kendal: a History of the Unitarian Chapel in the Market Place with Transcripts of Registers and Notices of the Nonconformist Academies of Richard Frankland, M.A., and Caleb Rotheram, D.D. Kendal:* Titus Wilson, 1915.

$8\frac{7}{8} \times 5\frac{1}{2}$ in. x, 677 [3] pp. References to Wordsworth on pp. 374, 375, 496, 522, 523.

333

1916

2173 RAWNSLEY, WILLINGHAM FRANKLIN (ED.). *Rydal, by the Late Miss Armitt,* Author of the 'Church at Grasmere.' Kendal: Titus Wilson, 1916.

8¾ × 5½ in. xv [1] 727 [1] pp. References to Wordsworth on pp. 673–7, 684.

1920

2174 CLAPHAM, RICHARD. *Foxhunting on the Lakeland Fells.* With an Introduction by the Right Hon. J. W. Lowther, Speaker of the House of Commons. With 43 Illustrations from Photographs by the Author. London: Longmans, Green, and Co., 1920.

8½ × 5½ in. xvi, 113 [3] pp.

1922

2175 ABRAHAM, ASHLEY PERRY. *The English Lakeland; 52 Views in De Luxe Photogravure, Comprising All the Lakes.* 22 Prize Medals Awarded. Keswick: G. P. Abraham, [*c.* 1922].

7½ × 10½ in. 56 pp.

2176 SALT, HENRY STEPHENS. *On Cambrian and Cumbrian Hills: Pilgrimages to Snowdon and Scafell* (Revised Edition). London: C. W. Daniel, 1922.

6⅝ × 4 in. 124 [4] pp. Pencil corrections, pp. 119–23.

2177 *The Official Catalogue of the Contents of Dove Cottage, Grasmere, the Home of Wordsworth (1799–1808) and of De Quincey (1808–1809 circ.).* Ambleside: George Middleton, 1922.

6¼ × 3⅞ in. 44 [4] pp.

1925

2178 COLLINGWOOD, WILLIAM GERSHON. *Lake District History.* Kendal: Titus Wilson & Son, 1925.

7½ × 5 in. viii, 176 pp.

2179 WATSON, JOHN. *The English Lake District Fisheries.* With a Foreword by Sir Herbert Maxwell, Bart., Illustrated. London and Edinburgh: T. N. Foulis, 1925.

8¼ × 5½ in. xv [1] 271 [1] pp.

1926

2180 ABRAHAM, ASHLEY PERRY. *Beautiful Lakeland.* With 32 Full-page Monogravure Illustrations by G. P. Abraham, F.R.P.S. & Sons. Keswick: G. P. Abraham, 1926.

9⅝ × 7⅛ in. [2] 52 [8] pp.

1927

2181 REYNOLDS, JOAN BERENICE. *The English Lake District* (Quotation and Picture Series). London: A. & C. Black, 1927.

8⅝ × 6 in. 34 [2] pp.

1928

2182 ABRAHAM, ASHLEY PERRY. *Some Portraits of the Lake Poets and Their Homes.* With 29 Full-page Monogravure Illustrations, by G. P. Abraham, F.R.P.S., & Sons. Keswick: G. P. Abraham, 1928.

8½ × 6⅛ in. [2] 56 [4] pp.

2183 MacBRIDE, MACKENZIE. *Wild Lakeland*, with Illustrations by A. Heaton Cooper. London: A. & C. Black, 1928.

8 × 5⅜ in. viii, 229 [3] pp. Thirty-two colored illustrations.

1929

2184 GRAVES, RALPH A. Through the English Lake District Afoot and Awheel.

National Geographic Magazine, LV (May 1929), 577–603.

2185 PALMER, WILLIAM THOMAS. *The English Lakes*, with Illustrations by A. Heaton Cooper. London: A. & C. Black, 1929.

8 × 5⅜ in. [2] 191 [5] pp.

1930

2186 FLETCHER, E. G. *Grasmere's Saint: Verses and Poems. A Reply to ' Wild Lakeland.'* Oxford: 1930.

7¼ × 4¾ in. [8] pp.

2187 SIZE, NICHOLAS. *The Secret Valley: the Real Romance of Unconquered Lakeland.* With a Foreword by Hugh Walpole. (Third Edition.) London and New York: Frederick Warne, 1930.

7½ × 5 in. ix [1] 86 pp.

2188 WILSON, JOHN. *Letters from the Lakes* by Professor Wilson. Fourth Edition. Ambleside: George Middleton, 1930.

$6\frac{1}{2} \times 4\frac{1}{8}$ in. 76 [2] pp. Wordsworth, pp. 55–76.

2189 *A souvenir of the Rushbearing Service held at Grasmere*, 9 August 1930.

$8\frac{3}{4} \times 5\frac{1}{2}$ in. [12] pp. No title. Eight pp. of hymns followed by a four-page description of Grasmere Church and Churchyard.

1931

2190 *The Rushbearing in Grasmere and Ambleside.* n.p., 1931.

$7\frac{1}{8} \times 4\frac{7}{8}$ in. 32 pp.

1932

2191 COLLINGWOOD, WILLIAM GERSHON. *The Lake Counties.* With Special Articles on Birds, Butterflies and Moths, Flora, Geology, Fox-Hunting, Mountaineering, Yachting, Motor-Boating, Fishing, Shooting, and Cycling, and Including a Full Gazetteer and Map, with Sixteen Plates in Colour, and Seventy-two Line Illustrations by A. Reginald Smith, R.W.S. London and New York: Frederick Warne and Co., 1932.

$9\frac{1}{2} \times 7$ in. xv [1] 367 [1] pp.

2192 SIZE, NICHOLAS. *Shelagh of Eskdale, or the Stone of Shame.* Founded on 'The Story of Shelagh' by Dr. C. A. Parker. London and New York: Frederick Warne and Co., 1932.

$7\frac{1}{2} \times 5$ in. xiii [1] 82 pp.

1937

2193 MEE, ARTHUR. *The Lake Counties: Cumberland, Westmorland* (The King's England). With 217 Places and 124 Pictures. London: Hodder and Stoughton, 1937.

$7\frac{3}{4} \times 5\frac{1}{4}$ in. viii [2] 289 [3] pp.

1938

2194 YEE, CHIANG. *The Silent Traveller: a Chinese Artist in Lakeland.* With a Preface by Herbert Read. London: Country Life Ltd.; New York: Charles Scribner's Sons, 1938.

$8\frac{3}{4} \times 5\frac{1}{2}$ in. [14] 65 [3] pp. Numerous illustrations by the author.

My very dear Cottle

The moment I received
Mr Wedgewood's letter, I accepted his
offer — how a contrary report could
arise, I cannot guess —/— I hope to see you
at the close of next week — I have been
respectfully & kindly treated at Shrewsbury,
& am well, & now & ever

Your grateful & affectionate
Friend

S. T. Coleridge

— Send the inclosed as soon as possible
to Mr Wade. ———

Handwriting of Coleridge: Letter to Joseph Cottle, 1798.   No. 2647

Sonnet by a young old Man. 1829.

Youth, thou art fled — but where are all the joys
That though with thee they come, & with thee fly
Should leave a perfume and sweet memory —
A pleasing sadness which no fear annoys.
No wish disquiets, no possession cloys?
Methinks in all the volume of my brain
I find no hour that I would bring again
From the abyss of time which age destroys
The momentary births of mortal being.
Could one short word restore my boyish years,
My hopes, my loves, my smiles and rapt'rous tears.
Yes And p my strong Faith to own ours Truth decreeing.
That little word my lips should never say —
Thank heaven, my youth is past, my head is grey.

                              Transcribed by S. C.

Handwriting of Sara Coleridge.   No. 3186

1940

2195 POUCHER, W. A. *Lakeland through the Lens: a Ramble over Fell and Dale.* With One Hundred and Twenty-two Photographs by the Author. London: Chapman and Hall, 1940.

11 × 8 in. 151 [1] pp.

1947

2196 CLAY, NOEL I. *Together Met; the Story of Ambleside Church and Some of Its Associations.* Gloucester: British Publishing Co., 1947.

$7\frac{3}{16}$ × $4\frac{3}{4}$ in. xii, 116 pp. Presentation copy from the author.

1948

2197 WARD, E. M. *Days in Lakeland, Past and Present.* Third Edition, Revised. London: Methuen, [1948].

$7\frac{1}{4}$ × $4\frac{3}{4}$ in. viii, 255 [1] pp.

1949

2198 NICHOLSON, NORMAN. *Cumberland and Westmorland.* London: Robert Hale, 1949.

$8\frac{1}{2}$ × $5\frac{1}{2}$ in. x, 259 [1] pp. Map.

2199 PALMER, WILLIAM THOMAS. *The Lake District* (The Penguin Guides). Harmondsworth: Penguin, 1949.

$7\frac{1}{8}$ × $4\frac{1}{4}$ in. 173 [3] pp.

1950

2200 TAYLOR, ROLAND. *The Homeland Guide to the Lake District.* Second Edition. London: Homeland Association, [c. 1950].

$7\frac{1}{4}$ × $4\frac{5}{8}$ in. 128 pp.

1952

2201 PALMER, J. H. *Historic Farmhouses in and around Westmorland.* Revised and Edited by W. T. McIntyre. Kendal: Westmorland Gazette, 1952.

$9\frac{5}{8}$ × $7\frac{1}{8}$ in. [2] 124 [4].

1954

2202 LOFTHOUSE, JESSICA. *The Curious Traveller through Lakeland; Historic Ways North from Kendal and Cartmel to Keswick and Penrith.* Illus. by the Author. London: R. Hale, [1954].

$8\frac{1}{2} \times 5\frac{3}{8}$ in. 199 [1] pp.

2203 SINGLETON, FRANK. *The English Lakes.* Illustrated from Colour Photographs by Wilfred Elms. London: Batsford, [1954].

$8\frac{3}{8} \times 5\frac{3}{8}$ in. 208 pp.

UNDATED

2204 BADDELEY, MOUNTFORD JOHN BADDELEY. *The English Lake District.* Originally Compiled by M. J. B. Baddeley, B.A. With 15 Coloured Contour Maps (Mostly on the Scale of One Inch to the Mile). Fifteenth Edition, Revised. London: Ward, Lock & Co.

$6\frac{1}{2} \times 4\frac{1}{4}$ in. 320 pp.

2205 BARTHOLOMEW, JOHN. *Bartholomew's Revised One Inch to Mile Lake District, Coloured, for Motorists and Cyclists.* Grasmere: Sam Read.

$7\frac{1}{2} \times 4\frac{1}{4}$ in., folded: a map.

2206 BRYDSON, A. P. *Some Records of Two Lakeland Townships* (Blawith and Nibthwaite). London: Elliot Stock.

$8\frac{1}{2} \times 5\frac{1}{4}$ in. 204 pp.

2207 JOHNSTON, W. AND A. K. *Views of the English Lakes with Map by W. and A. K. Johnston and Descriptive Letterpress.* London, Edinburgh, and New York: T. Nelson and Sons.

$5\frac{3}{8} \times 3\frac{5}{8}$ in. 32 pp. + 12 colored plates.

2208 [MOGRIDGE, GEORGE]. *Loiterings among the Lakes of Cumberland and Westmoreland,* by Old Humphrey. A New Edition. London: Religious Tract Society.

$5\frac{1}{4} \times 4$ in. vii [1] 208 [4] pp. References to Wordsworth, pp. 26–37, 45–8, and elsewhere.

2209 *One Hundred and Fifty Views: the English Lakes.* London: Rock Brothers.

11 $\times 8\frac{1}{2}$ in. [24] pp.

2210 *Ordnance Survey Tourist Map of the Lake District.* Scale: 1 Inch to 1 Mile.

2211 OUSELEY, F. A. GORE, AND MONK, EDWIN GEORGE.
The Canticles and Hymns of the Church Pointed for Chanting, and Set to Appropriate Chants. London.

$7\frac{1}{8} \times 4\frac{1}{4}$ in. 12 pp. This book came from Wythburn Church.

2212 *Round and about Ambleside.* Kendal: Atkinson and Pollitt.

$8\frac{3}{8} \times 5\frac{1}{2}$ in. [6] 55 [13] pp. Map.

2213 *The Rushbearing.* Leeds: Printed at the 'Weekly Churchman' Press, Bramley.

$8\frac{1}{2} \times 5\frac{1}{2}$ in. 43 [1] pp. Cover inscribed: 'Martin Sampson, Grasmere 1896.'

2214 *W. H. Smith and Son's Reduced Ordnance Map of the Lake District & Windermere.* Scale 4 Miles to an Inch. London: W. H. Smith and Son.

PART VIII

BOOKS OF ASSOCIATIVE INTEREST

2215 ALFORD, HENRY. *The School of the Heart and Other Poems.* Cambridge: Printed at the Pitt Press, by John Smith, Printer to the University, for Longman and Co., London, and J. and J. J. Deighton, Cambridge, 1835, 2 vols.

$7\frac{3}{4} \times 4\frac{3}{4}$ in. Vol. 1: viii, 169 [1]; vol. 2: [4] 129 [1] pp. Vol. 1 signed 'Wm Wordsworth, Rydal Mount' and inscribed 'W. Wordsworth Esqr, a small tribute of Admiration and gratitude from the Author.' Vol. 2 signed 'Wm Wordsworth, Rydal.'

2216 ALLSTON, WASHINGTON. *Monaldi: a Tale.* London: Moxon, 1842.

$7\frac{3}{4} \times 4\frac{3}{4}$ in. xx, 253 [3] pp. Signed on half-title 'Wm Wordsworth, Rydal Mount,' and on title-page 'W Wordsworth.'

2217 ATTERBURY, FRANCIS. *Fourteen Sermons Preach'd on Several Occasions, together with a Large Vindication of the Doctrine Contain'd in the Sermon Preach'd at the Funeral of Mr Thomas Bennet.* London: Printed by E. P. for Jonah Bowyer, 1708.

$7\frac{1}{2} \times 4\frac{1}{2}$ in. [36] lxix [3] 456 pp. Title-page signed 'Wm Wordsworth.'

2218 BARTRAM, WILLIAM. *Travels through North and South Carolina, Georgia, East and West Florida, the Cherokee Country, the Extensive Territories of the Muscogulges or Creek Confederacy, and the Country of the Chactaws. Containing an Account of the Soil and Natural Productions of Those Regions; together with Observations on the Manners of the Indians.* Embellished with Copperplates. The Second Edition in London. Philadelphia: Printed by James and Johnson; London: Reprinted for J. Johnson, 1794.

$8\frac{5}{8} \times 5\frac{1}{4}$ in. xxiv, 520 [14] pp. Bookplate of Richard Ellsworth Gall. Listed in the Sale Catalogue of the St. John Collection as from Wordsworth's library. No autograph.

2219 *The Holy Byble, Conteining the Olde Testament and the Newe.* Authorised and Appointed to Be Read in Churches. London: Christopher Barker, 1585.

$16 \times 10\frac{1}{4}$ in. [17] 135 fols. Title-page signed 'Wm Wordsworth, Rydal Mount 1845.' Pasted inside the front cover is a slip inscribed 'To Mr. Wordsworth from his obliged and sincere friend John Elliot.' The missing final leaf is supplied in manuscript by Mary Wordsworth and bears the following note: 'This manuscript addition,—completing this copy of the Holy Bible,—is in the hand-writing of Mary Wordsworth, wife of William Wordsworth, of Rydal

Mount; to whom this book belonged as may be seen by his autograph on the Title page; after whose death it came into my possession.—Cloister, West-minster Abbey, Good Friday, 1861, Chr. Wordsworth.'

2220 BLAKESLEY, JOSEPH WILLIAMS. *A Life of Aristotle, Includ-ing a Critical Discussion of Some Questions of Literary History Connected with His Works.* Cambridge: J. and J. J. Deighton; London: John W. Parker, 1839.

$8\frac{5}{8} \times 5\frac{3}{8}$ in. [6] 181 [35] pp. Presentation copy from the author to Words-worth. Autograph on fly-leaf: 'Wm Wordsworth, Rydal Mount.'

2221 BRYDGES, SIR SAMUEL EGERTON. *The Ruminator: Con-taining a Series of Moral, Critical, and Sentimental Essays.* London: Printed for Longman, Hurst, Rees, Orme, and Brown, 1813. 2 vols.

$7 \times 4\frac{1}{4}$ in. Vol. 1: viii [2] 302; vol. 2: xi [1] 327 [1] pp. Wordsworth's copy presented by R. R. Gillies. Autograph on title-page: 'W Wordsworth.' In a 'petticoat' binding, presumably by Mrs. Southey, of the same fabric used in the cover of James Burgh's *Political Disquisitions* (No. 2223).

2222 BRYDGES, SIR SAMUEL EGERTON. *Sonnets and Other Poems.* First Published in 1785. London: Printed for G. and T. Wilkie, 1789.

8×5 in. [6] 70 pp. Wordsworth's manuscript note on Sonnet V (p. 5): 'I cannot resist an impulse to record my admiration for this Sonnet. In *creative* imagination it is not surpassed by any composition, of the kind, in our Language. The *feelings* of melancholy and joyousness are most happily contrasted; and the intermediate line that describes the evanescence of Silence, is sublime.— Wm Wordsworth.' At the bottom of that page is the following note: 'The above note was written by Mr. Wordsworth at Lee Priory, May 16, 1823.' The book later became the property of Jemima and Rotha Quillinan, stepdaughters of Dora Wordsworth.

2223 [BURGH, JAMES]. *Political Disquisitions: or, an Enquiry into Public Errors, Defects, and Abuses.* Illustrated by, and Established upon Facts and Remarks Extracted from a Variety of Authors, Ancient and Modern. Calculated to Draw the Timely Attention of Government and People to a Due Consideration of the Necessity, and the Means, of Reforming Those Errors, Defects, and Abuses; of Restoring the Constitution, and Saving the State. London: Printed for Edward and Charles Dilly, 1774, 3 vols.

$8\frac{7}{8} \times 5\frac{1}{2}$ in. Vol. 1: xxiii [9] 486; vol. 2: vii [9] 477 [1]; vol. 3: [8] 460 [44] pp. Inscription on fly-leaf: 'From Thomas de Quincey to William Wordsworth, Grasmere, Friday, June 22—1810.' Below is De Quincey's autograph, pasted in. The half-title of vol. 1 is signed 'W Wordsworth' and 'W W,' that of vol. 2, 'W W.' No. 59 in the Sale Catalogue of Wordsworth's library. All three volumes are in 'petticoat' bindings, presumably by Mrs. Southey, of fabric similar to that used for Brydges's *Ruminator* (No. 2221).

2224 BURNS, ROBERT. *Poems of Robert Burns, with His Life and Character.* Dundee: Printed by F. Ray, 1802.

$5\frac{1}{2} \times 3\frac{3}{8}$ in. xxiv, 227 [1] pp. Inscribed on title-page by Dorothy Wordsworth: 'D. Wordsworth, Lady Beaumont, September 10, 1807.'

2225 *The Case of the Orphan, and Creditors, of John Ayliffe, Esq; for the Opinion of the Public: with an Addenda of Interesting Queries for the Answer of Those It Concerns. The Whole Fairly Stated and Indisputably Authenticated from Originals.* London: Printed for the Author, 1761.

$9\frac{3}{8} \times 7\frac{1}{16}$ in. 36 pp. Autograph on title-page: 'W Wordsworth.'

2226 CATO, MARCUS PORCIUS, AND OTHERS. *Scriptores de Re Rustica.* Paris: Ex Officina Roberti Stephani, 1543, 2 vols.

$6\frac{1}{2} \times 4\frac{1}{4}$ in. Vol. 1: 118 fols. + 400 pp.; vol. 2: pp. 402–98 [20]; [170]; pp. 3–186 [6]; 72 fols. Blank leaf in vol. 1 signed 'Wm Wordsworth.' Many manuscript annotations, some by Coleridge, others perhaps by him; none, apparently, by Wordsworth.

2227 CHARRON, PETER. *Of Wisdome, Three Bookes Written in French by Peter Charron,* Doctor of Lawe in Paris. Translated by Samson Lennard. London: Printed for Luke Fawne, [1651].

$7\frac{3}{8} \times 5\frac{1}{2}$ in. [28] 524 [20] pp. Wordsworth's copy, with notes in his hand. Title-page signed 'W Wordsworth.' No. 209 in the Sale Catalogue of Wordsworth's library.

2228 CLAPPERTON, HUGH. *Journal of a Second Expedition into the Interior of Africa from the Bite of Benin to Soccatoo by the Late Commander Clapperton of the Royal Navy. To Which Is Added the Journal of Richard Lander from Kano to the Sea-Coast, Partly by a More Eastern Route ...* London: John Murray, 1829.

$11\frac{1}{4} \times 5\frac{5}{8}$ in. xxiii [5] 355 [3] pp. Inside the front cover, in Wordsworth's hand, is written: 'Mr Southey's, bought at Greta Hall June 1843.' Pasted on the title-page is a slip upon which appears, in Southey's hand: 'God bless you R S.' On the title-page Mary Wordsworth has written: 'This Book, bought at Greta Hall June 1843—is given to Charles Wordsworth, as a memorial of Robt Southey, by his Grandmother, Mary Wordsworth. Rydal Mount. June 29th 1843.' Inserted in the book is Alfred Hart's typewritten account of the book and of its unfortunate owner, Charles Wordsworth, grandson of the poet.

2229 CLARKE, SAMUEL. *A Letter to Mr. Dodwell; Wherein All the Arguments in His Epistolary Discourse against the Immortality of the Soul Are Particularly Answered, and the Judgement of the Fathers Concerning That Matter Truly Represented.* The Third Edition. London: Printed by W. Botham for James Knapton, 1708. Bound with the preceding are four other pamphlets by Clarke on the same subject, and also William Higden, *A Defence of the View of the English Constitution with Respect to the Sovereign Authority of the Prince, and the Allegiance of the Subject.* London: S. Keble and R. Gosling, 1710.

$7\frac{1}{2} \times 4\frac{1}{2}$ in. Title-page signed 'W Wordsworth.'

2230 COSTANZO, TORQUATO. *Bernardo Tasso e Poetesse del Secolo XVI.* Venezia: Presso Antonio Zatta e Figli, 1787.

$6\frac{1}{2} \times 4$ in. [8] 280 pp. Half-title is signed 'W Wordsworth'; title-page is initialed 'W W.'

2231 DOBSON, SUSANNAH DAWSON. *The Literary History of the Troubadours. Containing Their Lives, Extracts from Their Works, and Many Particulars Relative to the Customs, Morals, and History of the Twelfth and Thirteenth Centuries.* Collected and Abridged from the French of Mr. de Saint-Palaye. London: Vernor, Hood, and Sharpe; Longman, Hurst, Rees, and Orme; and J. Walker, 1807.

$6\frac{3}{4} \times 4\frac{1}{8}$ in. xvi, 223 [1] pp. Title-page signed 'W Wordsworth.'

2232 DUBOIS, JEAN ANTOINE. *Description of the Character, Manners, and Customs of the People of India; and of Their Institutions, Religious and Civil.* London: Longman, Hurst, Rees, Orme, and Brown, 1817.

$11\frac{1}{4} \times 8\frac{5}{8}$ in. xxvi [1] 565 [3] pp. Fly-leaf inscribed: 'With Messrs Longman & Co's Compliments.' Title-page signed 'W Wordsworth.' In a 'petticoat' binding, presumably by Mrs. Southey, with a hand-written paper label.

2233 FEATLEY, DANIEL. *The Dippers Dipt, or, the Anabaptists Duck'd and Plung'd over Head and Ears, at a Disputation in Southwark* . . . London: Printed for N. B. and Richard Royston, 1647.

$7\frac{1}{4} \times 5\frac{1}{4}$ in. [14] 258 pp. Title-page signed 'W Wordsworth.' No. 231 in the Sale Catalogue of Wordsworth's library.

2234 FENTON, SIR GEOFFRAIE. [*Certaine Tragicall Discourses Written Oute of Frenche and Latin*, by G. F., No Lesse Profitable then Pleasant, and of Like Necessitye to Al Degrees That Take Pleasure in Antiquityes or Foreine Reapports. London: T. Marshe, 1567.]

$6\frac{3}{4} \times 4\frac{7}{8}$ in. About 270 leaves. Title and some preliminary leaves missing. Blank page signed 'W Wordsworth.' No. 528 in Sale Catalogue of Wordsworth's library.

2235 FIORENTINO, LORENZO FRANCIOSCINI. *Vocabolario Italiano, e Spagnolo Non Piu Dato in Luce.* Geneva: Appresso Pietro Margello, 1636.

6½ × 4 in. [8] 668; [8] 784 pp. Fly-leaf signed 'Wordsworth,' and 'Wm Wordsworth, Rydal Mount.'

2236 FORSYTH, JOSEPH. *Remarks on Antiquities, Arts, and Letters During an Excursion in Italy, in the Years 1802 and 1803.* Second Edition. London: John Murray, 1816.

8⅞ × 5¼ in. viii, 479 [1] pp. Fly-leaf inscribed: 'From Saml Rogers to William Wordsworth, March 18, 1837.' No. 535 in the Sale Catalogue of Wordsworth's library.

2237 FROME, SAMUEL BLAKE. *The Songs, Odes, Ballads, Duets, and Glees, in an Opera Entitled Sketches from Life; or, the Wandering Bard.* London: Printed for the Author by J. Dennett. Sold by R. Dutton; R. Huntley; and C. Chapple, 1809.

8⅜ × 4¾ in. vi [2] 22 pp. Blank page inscribed: 'Mr. Wordsworth from his friend the Author.'

2238 *A Glossary of Terms Used in Grecian, Roman, Italian, and Gothic Architecture.* The Fourth Edition, Enlarged. Exemplified by Eleven Hundred Woodcuts. Oxford: John Henry Parker; David Bogue, London, 1845, 2 vols.; and *A Companion to the Fourth Edition of a Glossary of Terms Used in Grecian, Roman, Italian, and Gothic Architecture,* Containing Four Hundred Additional Examples, a Chronological Table, and a General Index. Oxford: John Henry Parker; David Bogue, London, 1846.

8¾ × 5½ in. Vol. 1: ix [1] 416 [4]; vol. 2: [4] 23 [1] 164 plates; vol. 3: [14] 154 [38] 40 plates, [42] pp. Pasted to a blank leaf in vol. 1 is a slip bearing two inscriptions: 'H. R. C. [Henry Crabb Robinson] to W. W. 7th May 1845' and '—This Book will not be less acceptable to Mr. Reed for having belonged to me, Wm Wordsworth.' Another blank page is inscribed: 'Presented to Henry Reed by Isabella Fenwick, Rydal Mount, Augst 1st—1845.'

2239 GREATREX, CHARLES BUTLER. *Leisure Hours, a Series of Early Poems, Revised, with Additions.* Second Edition. London: Tilt and Bogue; Liverpool: W. Grapel, 1843.

7¼ × 4¼ in. [2] 109 [1] pp. Title-page inscribed: 'Willm Wordsworth Esq. with the Authors Compts.' With a long manuscript poem from the author to Wordsworth.

2240 GRIFFIN, GREGORY. *The Microcosm, a Periodical Work*. The Third Edition. Windsor: C. Knight, 1790, 1793, 2 vols.

$7\frac{3}{8} \times 4\frac{1}{4}$ in. Vol. 1: ix [1] 242 [4]; vol. 2: x, 228 pp. Title-page of each volume signed 'W Wordsworth.' No. 400 in the Sale Catalogue of Wordsworth's library.

2241 HAINING, SAMUEL. *A Historical Sketch and Descriptive View of the Isle of Man; Designed as a Companion to Those Who Visit and Make the Tour of It*. Douglas: G. Jefferson, 1822.

$6\frac{1}{4} \times 3\frac{5}{8}$ in. viii, 192 [4] pp. Wordsworth's copy. The fly-leaf is inscribed: 'H Hutchinson, Douglas, Isle of Man, Octr 3d 1824'; the half-title is inscribed: 'Henry Hutchinson to his respected Friend Miss Wordsworth'; and the title-page is signed 'Wm Wordsworth, Rydal Mount.'

2242 HAMMOND, HENRY. *A Practical Catechism, 13th Ed., Whereunto Is Added the Reasonableness of Christian Religion by the Same Authour*. London: Printed by M. Clarke for Henry Dickenson and Richard Green, 1691.

$6\frac{3}{4} \times 4\frac{1}{4}$ in. [12] 482 [4] pp. Title-page signed 'Wm Wordsworth.'

2243 HARE, JULIUS CHARLES AND AUGUSTUS WILLIAM. *Guesses at Truth*. Second Edition, Second Series. London: Taylor and Walton; Cambridge: Macmillan, 1848.

$6\frac{3}{4} \times 4$ in. [6] 383 [41] pp. Inscribed on title-page: 'To William Wordsworth with the Younger Brother's affectionate regards.'

2244 HAYNES, HENRY W. *The Pleasures of Poesy*. A Poem in Two Cantos . . . . London: Edwin Yates, 1846.

$6\frac{3}{4} \times 4\frac{1}{8}$ in. ix [2] 14–96 [2] pp. Title-page inscribed: 'William Wordsworth Esqr With the Author's Compliments.' Fly-leaf signed 'W Wordsworth'; verso signed 'Wm Wordsworth, Rydal Mount.' The book is dedicated to Wordsworth.

2245 HOMERUS. *Homeri Hymni et Epigrammata*, edidit Godofredus Hermannus. Lipsiæ, in Libraria Weidmannia, 1806.

$8\frac{1}{4} \times 5$ in. cxxii, 206 pp. Annotations in Latin and Greek by Samuel Taylor Coleridge on pp. vi–vii; transcribed and translated in an inserted note signed by E. H. Coleridge, 24 March 1894. The book bears the bookplate of Derwent Coleridge and the shelf-number of Helston Grammar School Library, of which he was Headmaster.

2246 HOOTEN, HENRY. *A Bridle for the Tongue: or, Some Practical Discourses under These Following Heads, Viz. Of Profane, or Atheistical Discourse. Of Blasphemy. Of Rash and Vain Swearing. Of Calumny, or Slander* [etc.]. London: W. Taylor, 1709.

$7\frac{1}{4} \times 4\frac{3}{8}$ in. [4] 244 pp. Inscribed in Wordsworth's hand: 'John Carter from W. Wordsworth—bought at Workington July 26th 1835.'

2247 JUVENALIS, DECIMUS JUNIUS, AND PERSIUS FLACCUS, AULUS. *D. Iun. Iuvenalis et Auli Persii Flacci Satyrae, ex Doct: Virorum Emendatione.* Hagae-Comitum et Roterodami apud Arnoldum et Regnerum Leers, 1683.

$4\frac{1}{2} \times 2\frac{3}{8}$ in. 119 [1] pp. On the fly-leaf is written: 'W. Mathews to W. Wordsworth,' beneath which Wordsworth has written: 'This friend of mine was the elder son of Mr Mathews, Bookseller near Northumberland House, Strand. He went to practise as a Barrister in the West Indies, and died almost immediately on his arrival there. W. Wordsworth.'

2248 LAING, MALCOLM. *The History of Scotland, from the Union of the Crowns ... to the Union of the Kingdoms in the Reign of Queen Anne.* Second Edition. London: J. Mawman, 1804. Vol. 3.

$8 \times 5\frac{1}{4}$ in. [4] 551 [1] pp. Contains one page of manuscript notes signed 'S. T. C.'; the handwriting may not be that of Coleridge.

2249 MONTAGU, BASIL. *Female Affection.* London: J. Bohn, 1845.

$6\frac{1}{4} \times 3\frac{7}{8}$ in. vi [1] 4–52 pp. Fly-leaf inscribed: 'To W. Wordsworth with the regards and respects of his old friend Basil Montagu.'

2250 MOULTRIE, JOHN. *The Dream of Life, Lays of the English Church, and Other Poems.* London: William Pickering, 1843.

$6\frac{3}{4} \times 3\frac{3}{4}$ in. vii [1] 368 [2] pp. Inscribed: 'Mary Caroline Coleridge, with her husband's love.' Signed in two places 'Edward Coleridge, 1866.' Written in is a key to characters described in the book, including Derwent Coleridge, Henry Nelson Coleridge, Sara Coleridge, and T. B. Macaulay.

2251 MURPHY, JAMES CAVANAH. *Travels in Portugal; through the Provinces of Entre Douro e Minho, Beira, Estremadura, and Alem-tetjo, in the Years 1789 and 1790, Consisting of Observations on the Manners, Customs, Trade, Public Buildings, Arts, Antiquities, &c. of That Kingdom.* London: A. Strahan, and T. Cadell Jun. and W. Davies, 1795.

$11\frac{3}{4} \times 9\frac{1}{8}$ in. xii, 311 [1] pp. 24 plates. Title-page signed 'W Wordsworth, Rydal Mount.'

2252 *Novum Testamentum Graece*. Londini: Impensis J. Mackinlay, et Cuthell et Martin, 1809–10, 2 vols. .

$8\frac{1}{4} \times 5\frac{1}{8}$ in. Vol. 1: [4] cxxiii [1] 554; vol. 2: [4] xlvii [1] 709 [1] pp. Upper right corner of fly-leaf signed 'H N C. King's Coll. 1818.' Below is written: 'Johanni Wordsworth hos libellos benevolentiae ejus et officii memores gratis animis dant Henricus Nelson et Sara Coleridge, Sept. Kal. Novembris. MDCCCXXIX.'

2253 [PEACE, JOHN]. *A Descant upon Railroads*. By X. A. P. London: John Bohn, 1842.

$7\frac{3}{4} \times 5$ in. 42 pp. Inscribed: 'To William Wordsworth with the author's profound respect.'

2254 [PEACE, JOHN]. *A Descant upon Weather-Wisdom*. By ——. London: Longman, Brown, Green, and Longmans, 1845.

$7\frac{7}{8} \times 5$ in. 32 pp. Inscribed: 'To William Wordsworth Esqre with profound respect.'

2255 PROCOPIUS. *Procopii Caesariensis de Rebus Gothorum, Persarum ac Vandalorum libri vii, una cum aliis mediorum temporum historicis, quorum catalogum sequens indicabit pagina. His omnibus accessit rerum copiosissimus index.* Basileae: ex Officina Ioannis Hervagii Mense Septembri, Anno M.D.XXXI.

$13\frac{1}{4} \times 8\frac{1}{4}$ in. [48] 690 [2] 46 [2] 194 [2] pp. Signed 'Wm Wordsworth.' No. 62 in the Sale Catalogue of Wordsworth's library.

2256 READE, JOHN EDMUND. *Italy: a Poem, in Six Parts, with Historical and Classical Notes*. London: Saunders and Otley, 1838.

$8\frac{5}{8} \times 5\frac{1}{2}$ in. xviii [4] 550 [2] pp. Inscribed: 'May 25th 1838 To William Wordsworth Esq. This Volume is offered with the highest Sentiments of respect from the Author. Dover St. 21 Piccadilly.' Below, in pencil, but hardly in Wordsworth's hand, comes: 'Acknowledged—but yet must write when read.' And finally: 'Bought at Rydal Mount Sale July 1859.' No. 631 in the Sale Catalogue.

2257 RICHARDSON, GEORGE. *The Outlaw, a Poem in Five Cantos*. Carlisle: E. Thurnam, 1819.

$6\frac{3}{4} \times 4$ in. 6, 120 pp. Inscription pencilled on front end-paper: 'From Wordsworth's Library.' Other evidence is lacking.

2258 ROGERS, SAMUEL, AND OTHERS. Nine items bound together in one volume, assembled by Henry Crabb Robinson with a manuscript table of contents in his hand.

$9\frac{1}{8} \times 5\frac{7}{8}$ in. Contents as follows:

1. Samuel Rogers. *Poems*. London: Moxon, 1839. [4] iv, 48 pp. Inscribed: 'To H. C. Robinson Esq. from the Author.'

2. Samuel Rogers, *Italy, a Poem*. London: Moxon, 1840. iv, 56 pp. Inscribed: 'To H. C. Robinson Esq. from the Author.'

3. Charles Lamb. *The Adventures of Ulysses*. London: Moxon, 1840. [4] 71 [1] pp.

4. Charles Lamb. *Tales from Shakespeare*. London: Moxon, 1841. [4] 104 pp.

5. Dante Alighieri. *Lyrical Poems*, trans. Charles Lyell. London: William Smith, 1840. xvi, 48 pp.

6. Copy of the Carruthers portrait of Wordsworth, and two engravings: The Poet's Dream, and St. Michael's Mount.

7. [Lady Richardson]. 'William Wordsworth', *Sharpe's London Magazine*, XVII (1853), 148–55.

8. *Chambers' Edinburgh Journal* for 17 July 1852. 16 pp.

9. William Howitt. 'William Wordsworth', *People's Journal*, 1 (1846), 43–5.

2259 RYVES, BROWNE. *Mercurius Rusticus: or, the Countries Complaint of the Barbarous Outrages Committed by the Sectaries of This Late Flourishing Kingdom. Together with a Brief Chronology of the Battels, Sieges, Conflicts, and Other Most Remarkable Passages, from the Beginnings of This Unnatural War, to the 25th of March, 1646*. London: Printed for R. Royston ..., 1685.

$7 \times 4\frac{1}{2}$ in. [8] 216 pp. On the title-page Wordsworth has written: 'Curious and rare, Wm Wordsworth,' and also 'W W.'

2260 SCOTT, JOHN. *The Christian Life, from Its Beginning to Its Consummation in Glory*. With Proper and Useful Indexes. The Ninth Edition. London: Printed for James and John Knapton ..., 1729.

$13\frac{1}{2} \times 8\frac{5}{8}$ in. [16] 700 [12] pp. Two pages of manuscript annotations in the hand of Samuel Taylor Coleridge.

2261 SENECA. *L. Annæi Senecæ Philosophi, et M. Annæi Senecæ Rhetoris quæ extant opera*. Raphelengii: ex Officina Plantiniana, 1609.

$4\frac{3}{4} \times 2\frac{7}{8}$ in. [4] 980 [4] pp. Blank leaf signed 'W Wordsworth'; title-page signed 'S. T. Coleridge.'

2262 SHELLEY, MARY. *Rambles in Germany and Italy, in 1840, 1842, and 1843*. London: Edward Moxon, 1844, 2 vols.

$7\frac{1}{2} \times 4\frac{1}{2}$ in. Vol. 1: xx, 280 [2]; vol. 2: vii [1] 296 [2] pp. Vol. 1, title-page signed 'Wm Wordsworth.' Vol. 2, half-title signed 'W Wordsworth,' and fly-leaf signed 'Wm Wordsworth, Rydal Mount.' Note on inside back cover of vol. 2: 'Bought by Mrs. Clayton at Rydal Mount 1860.'

2263 SHUTTLEWORTH, PHILIP NICHOLAS. *Consistency of the Whole Scheme of Revelation, with Itself and with Human Reason.* London: for J. G. and F. Rivington, 1832.

$6\frac{3}{4} \times 4\frac{1}{8}$ in. xv [1] 369 [9] pp. Fly-leaf inscribed: 'John Wordsworth from his affect. cousin Charles Wordsworth May, 1832.'

2264 SNOW, ROBERT. *Memorials of a Tour on the Continent to Which Are Added Miscellaneous Poems.* London: William Pickering, 1845.

$7\frac{5}{8} \times 4\frac{5}{8}$ in. vii [1] 311 [1] pp. The title-page is inscribed: 'With the Authors compliments,' above which appear the autograph of the poet, 'Wm Wordsworth, Rydal Mount,' and also that of his son, 'W Wordsworth.'

2265 SPENSER, EDMUND. *A View of the State of Ireland as It Was in the Reign of Queen Elizabeth. Written by Way of Dialogue between Eudoxus and Ireneus . . . to Which Is Prefix'd the Author's Life, and an Index Added to the Work.* Dublin: Printed for Laurence Flin and Ann Watts, 1763.

$6\frac{7}{16} \times 3\frac{3}{4}$ in. xxii, 258 [20] pp. Wordsworth's copy, the title-page inscribed: 'Wm Wordsworth, Rydal Mount, Janry 1841.'

2266 THOMSON, JAMES. *The Castle of Indolence, an Allegoricall Poem Written in Imitation of Spenser.* London: A. Millar, 1747.

$9\frac{1}{2} \times 7\frac{1}{2}$ in. [2] 81 [3] pp. Bound with eight other pieces in one volume. A blank leaf bears the signature: 'William Wordsworth, Rydal Mount, 20 Septr 1846.' Inside the back cover is the bookplate of Wordsworth's friend John Peace, of Bristol. Titles of the other pieces follow:

Gilbert West. *Education, a Poem.* London: R. Dodsley, 1751.

Joseph Warton. *Odes on Various Subjects.* London: R. Dodsley, 1747.

W. Whitehead. *An Hymn to the Nymph of Bristol Spring.* London: R. Dodsley, 1751. 37 [3] pp.

The Rosciad, a Poem. London: J. Robinson, 1750. 24 pp.

[William Mason]. *Musaeus: a Monody to the Memory of Mr. Pope, in Imitation of Milton's Lycidas.* London: R. Dodsley, 1747. 24 pp.

[T. Tyrwhitt]. *Mr. Pope's Messiah, Mr. Philips's Splendid Shilling, in Latin; the Eighth Isthmian of Pindar in English.* Oxford: James Fletcher, 1752. 21 pp.

The Triumph of Isis. London: W. Owen, 1750. 15 pp.

[Thomas Gray]. *An Elegy Written in a Country Churchyard.* Seventh Edition, Corrected. London: R. Dodsley, 1752. 11 pp.

2267 VIRGIL. [*Eclogues, Georgics, and Aeneid.* Title-page missing.]

$6\frac{3}{8} \times 3\frac{3}{4}$ in. [12] 427 [17] pp. First page is signed 'Wm Wordsworth, Rydal.' No. 347 in the Sale Catalogue. Wordsworth is said to have used this book in preparing his son for the University.

2268 WADE, THOMAS. *Mundi et Cordis: de Rebus Sempiternis et Temporariis: Carmina. Poems and Sonnets.* London: John Miller, 1835.

8 × 5⅛ in. xvi, 285 [5] pp. Inscribed: 'For William Wordsworth, Esq. With the Author's innermost heart-respects.' On a blank page appears the signature 'Wm Wordsworth, Rydal Mount.'

2269 WHITE, HENRY KIRKE. *The Remains of Henry Kirke White, of Nottingham, Late of St. John's College, Cambridge: with an Account of His Life, by Robert Southey.* Twelfth Edition. London: Longman, Rees, Orme, Brown, and Green, 1830.

5⅜ × 2⅞ in. lxiii [1] 493 [3] pp. Inscribed: 'Rotha Quillinan from Dora Wordsworth, August 1838.'

2270 WHITE, HENRY KIRKE. *The Poetical Works of Henry Kirke White.* London: William Pickering, 1830.

6¼ × 3⅞ in. lviii, 252 [2] pp. The fly-leaf bears two inscriptions: 'John Wordsworth to his dear Cousin Dora Wordsworth, Jany 1838,' and, lower on the page, 'To Henry Wordsworth from Rotha Quillinan in remembrance of his dear Aunt Dora. Loughrigg Holme, February 5 1853.'

2271 WORDSWORTH, CHRISTOPHER. *Documentary Supplement to 'Who Wrote Εἰκὼν Βασιλική?' Including Recently Discovered Letters and Papers of Lord Chancellor Hyde, and of the Gauden Family.* London: John Murray, 1825.

8¾ × 4¼ in. [4] 50 pp. Inscribed: 'From the Author.'

2272 WORDSWORTH, CHRISTOPHER. *King Charles the First, the Author of Icôn Basilikè, Further Proved, in a Letter to His Grace, the Archbishop of Canterbury, in Reply to the Objections of Dr. Lingard, Mr. Todd, Mr. Broughton, the Edinburgh Review, and Mr. Hallam.* London: John Murray, 1828.

8¾ × 4½ in. [4] 256 [2] pp. The title-page is signed 'Wm Wordsworth's.' Another leaf bears three inscriptions: 'Chr: Wordsworth,' and then 'Wm Wordsworth, Rydal Mount,' and finally 'Fras Merewether, Bought at the Sale at Rydal Mount July 19, 1859.'

2273 WORDSWORTH, CHRISTOPHER, BISHOP OF LINCOLN. *Notes at Paris, Particularly on the State and Prospects of Religion.* London: Rivington, 1854.

7¾ × 5 in. viii, 152 pp. Mary Wordsworth's copy. Title-page signed 'M. Wordsworth, Rydal Mount, 1854,' and a question written in her hand on back fly-leaf.

PART IX

MANUSCRIPTS

WORDSWORTH AND HIS FAMILY

WILLIAM WORDSWORTH

2274 Poem now entitled: Remembrance of Collins, Composed upon the Thames near Richmond ('How rich the wave in *front*, impress'd'). Signed and dated 29 March 1797. Written in the Joseph Cottle Album. 1 p., folio.

2275 Poem now entitled: Composed on the Eve of the Marriage of a Friend in the Vale of Grasmere. Endorsed by Robert Southey: 'On Miss Monkhouse, by Mr. Wordsworth.' Undated, but probably of 1812. 1 p., quarto.

2276 Transcript, in the hand of Mary Wordsworth, of the poem now entitled: Composed upon an Evening of Extraordinary Splendour and Beauty. With a note in the hand of Wordsworth, part of which reads: 'Transcribed by Mrs. Wordsworth for Mr. Alston, in gratitude for the pleasure she received from the sight of his Pictures.' Undated, but probably of 1818. The recipient was Washington Allston, the American painter. 3 pp., folio.

2277 The opening stanza of The Cuckoo and the Nightingale. Signed and dated from London, 1820. $\frac{1}{2}$ p., quarto.

2278 Notebook, in the hand of Dorothy (and perhaps William) Wordsworth, containing early versions of thirty-eight poems of Wordsworth, thirty-two of them later published as *Ecclesiastical Sketches* (1822 and later), the others else-where. Six of the poems appear in two versions each; two of them appear in three versions each. In addition, the book contains a half-dozen fragments of verse. The following poems are present: Introduction (to *Ecclesiastical Sketches*); Conjectures (two versions); Uncertainty; Persecution; The Fall of the Aar—Handec; Persuasion (two versions); Reflections; Archbishop Chicheley to Henry V; Decay of Piety; The Jung-Frau; Troubles of Charles I; Wicliffe; Eminent Reformers (two versions); 'Down a swift stream, thus far, a bold design'; Sky-prospect—from the Plain of France (three versions); Papal Abuses; An Interdict; Papal Dominion; Scene in Venice (two versions); Pastoral Character; 'Not Love, not War, nor the tumultuous swell'; Charles the Second; English Reformers in Exile; The Liturgy; Crusades (two versions); Gunpowder Plot; Waldenses (three versions); Recovery; General View of the Troubles of the Reformation; Elizabeth; Eminent Reformers II; The Monument Commonly Called Long Meg (two versions); Old Abbeys; Cranmer; Inside of King's College Chapel II; A Parsonage in Oxfordshire; New Churchyard; Mutability. The notebook contains 58 pp. and measures $8\frac{1}{2} \times 6\frac{3}{4}$ in.

2279 Poem entitled: To the Lady le Fleming—Composed upon Seeing the Foundation Preparing for the Erection of a Chapel in the Village of Rydal. The manuscript is in the hand of Sara Hutchinson and is dated January 1823. $3\frac{1}{2}$ pp., folio.

2280 Poem, in the hand of Dora Wordsworth, entitled: A Grave Stone on the Floor of the Cloisters of Worcester Cathedral. Dated January 1825. Inserted in the Joseph Cottle Album. 1 p., octavo.

2281 Poem, in the hand of Dora Wordsworth, entitled: On Seeing a Needle-case in the Form of a Harp, the Work of Edith Southey ('Frowns are on every Muse's face'), [1827]. 3 pp., octavo.

2282 One of the Ecclesiastical Sonnets, entitled: Sponsors ('Father—to God himself we cannot give'). Signed and dated at Coleorton Hall, 7 December 1827. 1 p., quarto.

2283 Opening stanzas, in the hand of Dorothy Wordsworth, of the poem entitled: On the Power of Sound; *c.* 1828. Three lines added by Wordsworth. 2 pp., quarto. With a letter of 15 November 1922, commenting on the manuscript, by Gordon Wordsworth.

2284 Fifteen lines from *The Excursion* ('As the ample Moon'). Signed and dated at Rydal Mount, 23 April 1832. 1 p., quarto.

2285 Notebook written in the hands of both William and Mary Wordsworth containing versions of thirty poems of Wordsworth, nearly all of them published in *Yarrow Revisited*, 1835. Three of the poems appear in two versions each; two of them appear in three versions each. The following poems are present: The Dunolly Eagle; 'Most sweet it is with unuplifted eyes' (three versions); Mary Queen of Scots; To Cordelia M—; Eagles; On Revisiting Dunolly Castle; '"There!" said a Stripling, pointing with meet pride'; Cave of Staffa; Cave of Staffa II; Cave of Staffa III; Flowers on the Top of the Pillars at the Entrance of the Cave; Iona; Iona II; The River Eden, Cumberland (two versions); In the Frith of Clyde, Ailsa Crag; Tynwald Hill (three versions); By the Sea-shore; Isle of Man; On the Frith of Clyde; Nunnery; Steamboats, Viaducts, and Railways; Lowther (two versions); To the Earl of Lonsdale (two versions); 'Despond who will—*I* heard a voice exclaim'; Fancy and Tradition; Love Lies Bleeding; 'Adieu, Rydalian Laurels! that have grown'; At Bala Sala, Isle of Man; Address from the Spirit of Cockermouth Castle; The Black Stones of Iona. The notebook is the *Kendal Almanac* for 1819 and was probably carried by the Wordsworths on their tour of 1833. The book contains 84 pp. and measures $5 \times 2\frac{3}{4}$ in.

2286 Sonnet, in the hand of Mary Wordsworth, beginning 'Hark, 'tis the Thrush! undaunted, undeprest'; addressed to Mary Spring-Rice. Signed and dated by Wordsworth from Rydal Mount, Easter Sunday, 1838. 1 p., quarto.

2287 Manuscript, in an unknown hand, containing a brief account of hay-making ('The object in turning grass into hay should be, first, to make it of as good a quality as possible.'). Dated 30 June 1838 and endorsed, though probably not in Wordsworth's hand, 'Wm Wordsworth, Rydal Mount.' 2 pp., folio.

2288 Petition to the House of Commons in support of the Copyright Bill of Thomas Noon Talfourd, in the hand of John Carter, with a note in the hand of Mary Wordsworth; *c.* February 1838. 3 pp., folio.

2289 Manuscript, in an unidentified hand, of Wordsworth's The Eagle and the Dove. This is the copy sent to A. F. Rio, in Paris, who first published the poem (No. 523). Signed by Wordsworth. Postmarked 11 May 1842. 1 p., quarto.

2290 Three sonnets, in the hand of Dora Wordsworth, collectively entitled: Aspects of Christianity in America. The three are: The Pilgrim Fathers; Return to the Church in England; American Episcopacy. Each of the three is signed by Wordsworth; *c.* 1842. 1½ pp., quarto.

2291 Seven of the *Ecclesiastical Sonnets*, and alterations to be made in two others, in the hand of John Carter, enclosed in a letter to Henry Reed, 27 March 1843. The poems are: 'Bishops and Priests, blessed are ye, if deep'; The Marriage Ceremony; Thanksgiving after Childbirth; The Commination Service; Forms of Prayer at Sea; Visitation of the Sick; Funeral Service. The alterations are for: Rural Ceremony; The Liturgy. 4 pp., quarto.

2292 Sonnet, in an unidentified hand, On the Projected Kendal and Windermere Railway. Addressed from Rydal Mount, 12 October 1844, to Mrs. Swaine. 1 p., quarto.

2293 Poem entitled: To My Grandchildren; in an unidentified hand, dated from Rydal Mount, 6 June 1845, signed by Wordsworth. 4 pp., octavo.

2294 Poem now entitled: Lines Inscribed in a Copy of His Poems Sent to the Queen for the Royal Library at Windsor, written in the hand of Mary Wordsworth. The text shows several revisions and differs considerably from the printed version. Dated from the Cloisters, Westminster, 15 April 1847. Signed by both Mary and William Wordsworth. 2 pp., quarto.

2295 Power of Attorney granted by Wordsworth and William Crewdson of Kendal to William McIlvaine, Casnier of the Bank of the United States at Philadelphia to receive 'the Reimbursement of Principal of the sum of Four Thousand six hundred Dollars of six per cent Stock of 1814'. Dated 18 June 1828. Signed by Wordsworth.

2296 Manuscript in several hands, all unidentified, entitled: 'Mr. Wordsworth's Tour.' An itinerary with detailed advice on travel, inns, expenses, and the like, for a tour through the Low Countries and Germany. Undated; the paper is watermarked 1823. 7 pp., quarto.

2297 A collection of Wordsworth autographs, some of them preceded by brief excerpts from his poems. A dozen pieces.

2298 Letter to Joseph Cottle, [January 1796]. 'I have not for some time been more flattered ....' 1 p., quarto.

2299 Letter to Catherine Clarkson, [17 April 1806]. 'The contents of this letter are chiefly intended ....' 1¾ pp., quarto.

2300 Fragment of a letter to an unidentified correspondent, 27 April [1806]. 'I shall be at Grasmere in July ....' ½ p., quarto.

2301 Letter to Basil Montagu, 25 July [1806]. 'I was from home when your letter came....' With a postscript by Dorothy Wordsworth. 1 p., quarto.

2302 Letter to J. T. Tuffin, 28 September 1806. 'A long, a very long time ago ....' ½ p., quarto.

2303 Letter to [Josiah] Wade, 28 September 1806. 'I have behaved very ill in not writing to you ....' 2¼ pp., quarto.

2304 Letter to Catherine Clarkson, 11 June [1812]. 'You have most probably learned by this time ....' 2¼ pp., quarto.

2305 Letter to Catherine Clarkson, 18 June [1812]. 'This with the exception of a short note to Grasmere ....' Unsigned. 2 pp., octavo.

2306 Letter to Basil Montagu, [22 January 1813]. 'The Person who has the money to advance is a Miss Weir ....' 4 pp., quarto.

2307 Letter to Robert Blakeney, 12 June 1813. 'I did not receive your most obliging Letter ....' 3 pp., quarto.

2308 Fragment of a letter to Mr. White of Whitehaven, 22 June 1813. '...answer well for us Both....' ½ p., octavo.

2309 Fragment of a letter to an unidentified correspondent, 13 July 1813. '...they may be returned to me at some future opportunity....' 2 pp., 16mo.

2310 Letter to Robert Blakeney, 20 August 1813. 'I have had an interview with Mr. Jackson ....' 2 pp., quarto.

2311 Letter to Robert Blakeney, 1 April 1814. 'I cannot forbear writing to you on the subject of your House at Fox Gill....' 3¼ pp., quarto.

2312 Letter, in the hands of Mary and Dorothy Wordsworth, to Catherine Clarkson, [December 1814]. 'I don't know that it is quite fair to sit down ....' 3½ pp., folio.

2313 Letter to R. P. Gillies, 22 December [1814]. 'Your account of yourself distresses me. Flee from your present abode....' 3 pp., quarto.

2314 Letter to Catherine Clarkson, 25 November 1815. 'We were wholly ignorant of the death of our dear and lamented Friend ....' 3 pp., quarto.

2315 Letter to Bernard Barton, 12 January 1816. 'Though my Sister during my absence has returned thanks ....' 3½ pp., quarto.

2316 Letter to [John Scott], 21 March [1816]. 'I had packed up my little Pieces of Verse ....' Signature lacking. 2 pp., quarto.

2317 Letter to Basil Montagu, 11 May 1816. 'I am most happy to hear that R[ichar]d has executed his Will....' 2 pp., octavo.

2318 Letter to the Messrs. Longman and Co., 31 October 1816. 'Your last duly received; and I now write to say ....' 2½ pp., octavo.

2319 Letter to Henry Parry, 17 January 1817. 'I am almost ashamed to present myself before you ....' 4 pp., quarto.

2320 Letter to Mr. White of Whitehaven, 3 April [1819?] 'I learn that a fresh Coach is on the point of starting to run ....' 2¼ pp., quarto.

2321 Letter to an unidentified correspondent, 4 January 1820. 'The enclosed from some foolish Person in America arrived during my absence....' 1 p., folio.

2322 Letter to Charles Lloyd, 20 February 1822. 'I begin this letter without the usual expressions of regard ....' Transcribed by Lloyd in a letter to Thomas Noon Talfourd, 6 March 1822. The transcript is 1 p., folio.

2323 Letter to [William Stewart Rose], 28 January [1823]. 'I have to thank you for the obliging present of your translation ....' 1 p., quarto.

2324 Letter to Francis Merewether, 10 January 1825. 'You were very kind in bearing my request in mind ....' 3 pp., quarto.

2325 Letter, in the hand of Mary Wordsworth, to Jacob Fletcher, 17 January 1825. 'I should have acknowledged the receipt of your obliging communication ....' 4 pp., quarto.

2326 Letter, in the hand of Mary Wordsworth, to Jacob Fletcher, 25 February [1825]. 'Many pressing engagements have prevented an earlier acknowledgement ....' 3¼ pp., quarto.

2327 Letter, in the hand of Mary Wordsworth, to Jacob Fletcher, 6 April [1825]. 'I fear you may have been uneasy about the arrival of your Parcel ....' 3½ pp., quarto.

2328 Letter to John Brewster, 26 September 1825. 'It gives me great pleasure to comply with your request ....' 1 p., octavo.

2329 Letter to Francis Merewether, [c. 1827]. 'Long absence from home has occasioned such a press ....' 3 pp., quarto.

2330 Letter to Jacob Fletcher, 12 April 1827. 'It was gratifying to be remembered after your long ....' 2 pp., quarto.

2331 Letter to Samuel Carter Hall, 12 April 1827. 'I hasten to thank you for a Note and your valuable Present ....' 2 pp., quarto.

2332 Letter to the Messrs. Taylor & Hessey, 24 August 1827. 'Would you have the kindness to direct and forward the Enclosed to the Authors ....' ½ p., quarto.

2333 Letter to Robert Southey, [September 1827]. 'The Bearers are Gentlemen of whom I cannot say half so much ....' 1¼ pp., quarto.

2334 Fragment of a letter, in the hand of Dora Wordsworth, to Isabella Fenwick, 13 September 1827. '... & will be most happy to join you wheresoever it may be ....' ¼ p., quarto.

2335 Letter to Edward Quillinan, 9 January 1828. 'This is enclosed to Allan Cunningham with an Order for a bust ....' 3 pp., octavo.

2336 Letter to John Taylor, 30 January 1828. 'You will wonder what has become of me....' 2 pp., quarto.

2337 Letter to William Jackson, [March 1828]. 'I must scrawl you a Congratulation. You have done well ....' With a one-page note from Sara Hutchinson. 2½ pp., quarto.

2338 Letter to Barron Field, 20 June 1828. 'I am afraid you will think me very inattentive....' 1 p., quarto.

2339 Letter to George Huntly Gordon, 7 October [1828]. 'I have been long in availing myself of your kind offer....' 4 pp., octavo.

2340 Letter to George Huntly Gordon, 10 November [1828]. 'Many thanks for the care you took of the last Paquet ....' 3½ pp., quarto.

2341 Letter to George Huntly Gordon, 25 November 1828. 'How am I to thank you for your long and interesting ....' 3¼ pp., quarto.

2342 Letter to George Huntly Gordon, 15 December 1828. 'A thousand thanks—pray give yourself no more trouble ....' 4 pp., quarto.

2343 Letter to Dionysius Lardner, 12 January '1828' [for 1829]. 'I should have written to you immediately on my return from the Continent ....' With a postscript by Mary Wordsworth. 2½ pp., quarto.

2344 Letter, in the hand of Mary Wordsworth, to George Huntly Gordon, 24 January 1829. 'I employ Mrs. W's pen, being just arrived with starved fingers from Keswick ....' The last page, which was in Wordsworth's hand, was given away by Gordon and is supplied by a transcript. 5 pp., octavo.

2345 Letter to George Huntly Gordon, 29 January 1829. 'I cannot let a Post pass without thanking you ....' 4 pp., quarto.

2346 Letter to George Huntly Gordon, 26 February 1829. 'Wm left us yesterday along with his brother ....' With a two-page extract, in the hand of Dora Wordsworth, from a letter to another friend unnamed. 4 pp., octavo.

2347 Letter to Barron Field, 26 February 1829. 'It gives me great pleasure that your destiny is changed....' 2 pp., octavo.

2348 Letter to George Huntly Gordon, 20 March [1829]. 'It seems an age since I heard from you....' $3\frac{1}{2}$ pp., octavo.

2349 Letter, in the hand of Dora Wordsworth, to George Huntly Gordon, 9 April 1829. 'An inflammation in one of my eyes obliges me ....' $3\frac{1}{2}$ pp., octavo.

2350 Letter, in the hand of Dora Wordsworth, to George Huntly Gordon, 14 May 1829. 'Your letter was very welcome, it gives me much pleasure to learn ....' $9\frac{1}{4}$ pp., octavo.

2351 Letter, in the hand of Dora Wordsworth, to George Huntly Gordon, [May–June 1829?]. 'The departure of the Post will not allow me time to reply ....' $2\frac{1}{2}$ pp., octavo.

2352 Letter, in the hand of Dora Wordsworth, to George Huntly Gordon, 16 June 1829. 'Your packet was indeed welcome & we thank you cordially ....' $4\frac{1}{2}$ pp., octavo.

2353 Letter, in the hand of Dora Wordsworth, to George Huntly Gordon, 4 July [1829]. 'My letters to you have always to begin with thanks....' The last page, including the signature, is a transcript. 5 pp., octavo.

2354 Letter to George Huntly Gordon, 29 July [1829]. 'I hope you have enjoyed yourself in the Country....' 3 pp., octavo.

2355 Letter to [Joseph Cottle?], 7 August 1829. 'I deferred acknowledging the receipt of your kind Letter, till I came ....' The letter is clearly addressed to Joseph Cottle; but the name in the salutation has been inked over, and the ending runs '...and believe me, dear Mr. D, very sincerely yours ....' The letter may have been intended for 'Mr. D,' but addressed and sent to Cottle inadvertently. $2\frac{1}{2}$ pp., quarto.

2356 Letter to George Huntly Gordon, [October 1829]. 'Yesterday I reached home from Ireland where we roamed ....' With a postscript by Dorothy Wordsworth. 3 pp., quarto.

2357 Letter to George Huntly Gordon, 14 November 1829. 'I am quite at a loss what to say about Ireland....' With a postscript by Mary Wordsworth. 3 pp., quarto.

2358 Letter to George Huntly Gordon, 14 November 1829. 'I have received through your hands all the MSS of mine ....' 2 pp., octavo.

2359 Letter, in the hand of Dora Wordsworth, to George Huntly Gordon, 1 December 1829. 'You must not go to Ireland without applying to me ....' 4 pp., octavo.

2360 Letter, partly in the hand of Dora Wordsworth, to George Huntly Gordon, 16 January 1830. 'The account of Wm was satisfactory ....' 3 pp., octavo.

2361 Letter to William Jackson, [*c*. March–April 1830]. 'We congratulate you both, heartily, upon the acquisition ....' 4 pp., quarto.

2362 Letter to George Huntly Gordon, 6 April 1830. 'You are kind in noticing with thanks my rambling ....' 4 pp., octavo.

2363 Letter to George Huntly Gordon, 10 May [1830]. 'Pray get the Books as cheap as you can ....' $3\frac{1}{2}$ pp., octavo.

2364 Letter to George Huntly Gordon, 30 May [1830]. 'I am glad you approve of my determination....' With a postscript by Mary Wordsworth. $7\frac{1}{2}$ pp., octavo and $\frac{1}{2}$ p., quarto.

2365 Letter, in the hand of Mary Wordsworth, to George Huntly Gordon, [31 May 1830?]. 'Writing in haste yesterday immediately after reading William's letter ....' 3 pp., octavo.

2366 Letter to George Huntly Gordon, [July 1830]. 'Wm's Letter, I grieve to say, gives *no* account of his health ....' 4 pp., octavo.

2367 Letter to W. R. Hamilton, 9 July [1830]. 'I lose not a moment in replying to your letter ....' 2 pp., octavo.

2368 Letter to George Huntly Gordon, 10 [July 1830]. 'I am up to the ears in company and engagements....' 3 pp., octavo.

2369 Letter to George Huntly Gordon, [July–August 1830]. 'Accept my sincere thanks for so long a Letter ....' The last page, including the signature, is a transcript. $9\frac{1}{4}$ pp., octavo.

2370 Letter to George Huntly Gordon, [*c*. August 1830]. 'As Wm is on the move from Neuwied, will you be so kind as to forward ....' 3 pp., octavo.

2371 Letter to Vincent Novelle, [August–September 1830]. 'There was not the least occasion to make an apology ....' 2 pp., quarto.

2372 Letter to George Huntly Gordon, [autumn 1830]. 'How sorry we are that you have had so much trouble ....' With a postscript by Mary Wordsworth. 4 pp., octavo.

2373 Letter to George Huntly Gordon, 9 November [1830]. 'It is a long time since we had our exchange of Letters ....' 1 p., folio.

2374 Letter to T. C. Grattan, 5 January 1831. 'Your very obliging Letter, Feby 28th 1830, is now lying before ....' 3 pp., quarto.

2375 Letter to John Kenyon, 19 [January 1831]. 'I am glad my Letters found you, having begun to fear ....' 2 pp., octavo.

2376 Letter, in the hand of Edward Quillinan, to George Huntly Gordon, [April 1831]. 'Mr. Quillinan who holds the pen for me ....' 4 pp., octavo.

2377 Letter to [Allan Cunningham?], 14 April 1831. 'You will remember our talk at [Lin?] about the Busts ....' 2 pp., octavo.

2378 Letter to George Huntly Gordon, [June 1831]. 'I was glad to hear of you through the hands of your Cousin....' 4 pp., octavo.

2379 Letter to [Basil Montagu], 29 July [1831]. 'The day after I wrote my last, arrived the Selections ....' 3 pp., octavo.

2380 Letter, in the hand of Dora Wordsworth, to Robert Jones, 26 September [1831]. 'My old complaint, an inflammation in my eyes & official engagements ....' 2 pp., quarto.

2381 Letter, in the hand of Mary Wordsworth, to Francis Merewether, 29 October [1831?]. 'It was very kind of you to turn your thoughts to us ....' 4 pp., quarto.

2382 Letter, in the hand of Mary Wordsworth, to George Huntly Gordon, 16 November [1831]. 'I am glad of an opportunity, such as you have kindly allowed ....' A quarter page, including the signature, cut off. 2 pp., octavo.

2383 Letter to George Huntly Gordon, [1832?]. 'I am ashamed to trouble you so often without a word ....' 2½ pp., octavo.

2384 Letter, in the hand of Mary Wordsworth, to Mrs. John Gardner, [1832?]. 'Tho' I have had no communication with yourself, it always gives me ....' 3 pp., octavo.

2385 Letter to John Gardner, [spring 1832]. 'I have seen my Nephews Mother, and she is quite reconciled ....' 2½ pp., quarto.

2386 Letter to Lord ——, 23–4 October 1832. 'It gives me pleasure to comply with the request of your Lordship ....' With sixteen lines from *The Excursion* on a quarto page. 1½ pp., octavo.

2387 Letter to Richard Parkinson, [4 December 1832]. 'I should have thanked you earlier for the agreeable Present ....' 1½ pp., quarto.

2388 Transcript, in the hand of the recipient, of a letter to George Huntly Gordon, [1833?]. 'We have some pleasant strangers in this neighbourhood at this time ....' Gordon explains that the original 'is under a Portrait & I cannot remove it.' ½ p., octavo.

2389 Letter to Edward Moxon, [1833?]. 'I wish to make a Present of a Copy of my Selections ....' 3 pp., octavo.

2390 Letter to Robert Southey, [1833?]. 'The Bearer of this Letter is Mr. Henry Robinson (my cousin) ....' ½ p., quarto.

2391 Letter to Mary Spring-Rice, 30 January 1833. 'Understanding from my amiable Friend Miss Kinnaird that you wished ....' 4 pp., octavo.

2392 Letter to John Pagen White, 14 May 1833. 'Your courteous Letter and the accompanying Verses ....' 1½ pp., quarto.

2393 Letter, in the hand of Mary Wordsworth, to an unidentified correspondent, 12 August [1833]. 'Your obliging letter with its enclosure I did not receive till very lately ....' 2 pp., octavo.

2394 Letter, in the hand of Dora Wordsworth, to George Huntly Gordon, 24 August 1833. 'As you are so anxious for a speedy reply I regret much that I was unable ....' 4 pp., octavo.

2395 Letter, in the hand of Mary Wordsworth, to M. Montagu, 31 August [1833?]. 'You must not be hurt if in reply to your obliging letter ....' 1½ pp., quarto.

2396 Letter, in the hand of Mary Wordsworth, to Peter Cunningham, [26 September 1833]. 'It is some time since I recd your acceptable present of Drummond's Poems ....' 2 pp., octavo.

2397 Letter, in the hand of Mary Wordsworth, to Felicia Hemans, [September–October 1833]. 'So much was I pleased with both the Brothers Grave[s] that I should have been ....' 4 pp., octavo.

2398 Letter, in the hand of Mary Wordsworth, to Sir Robert Inglis, [23 November 1833]. 'My daughter having recd a note from Miss Thornton franked by you ....' 1¼ pp., quarto.

2399 Letter to Robert Perceval Graves, 11 March [1834]. 'I began a letter to you nearly a week ago ....' 4 pp., quarto.

2400 Letter to Thomas Hamilton, [1835?]. 'Mrs. Wordsworth thanks you affectionately as I do for your sympathizing ....' 1 p., quarto.

2401 Letter, in the hand of Mary Wordsworth, to Robert Perceval Graves, 20 January 1835. 'The Revd J. Fleming, Rector of Bootle & Curate of Bowness having died lately ....' 3¼ pp., quarto.

2402 Letter to Robert Montgomery, 24 March [1835?]. 'If you think my name would be of any use in the list ....' 1½ pp., quarto.

2403 Letter to Benjamin Dockray, 7 June [1835]. 'The affliction under which my family has been suffering for some time ....' 1 p., quarto.

2404 Letter to Dr. Henry Southey, 30 June [1835]. 'You will excuse I doubt not the liberty I am about to take ....' 3 pp., quarto.

2405 Letter to John Anster, 21 July [1835]. 'It is some little time since I had the honour of receiving ....' 1 p., quarto.

2406 Letter to Catherine Clarkson, 6 August 1835. 'Mrs. W— has just come with her eyes full of tears begging I would write to you ....' With a two-page letter from Gordon Wordsworth, commenting on the manuscript. $3\frac{1}{4}$ pp., quarto.

2407 Letter to Simpkin, Marshall & Co., 24 September [1835?]. 'In answer to your letter received some time ago ....' 2 pp., octavo.

2408 Letter to Messrs. Hudson & Nicholson, 11 [November 1835]. 'I am surprized to find by a letter from Longmans this morning that they have ....' 1 p., octavo.

2409 Letter, in the hand of Mary Wordsworth, to Rev. J. Green, [1836]. 'Having been from home I am sorry not to have been able ....' $1\frac{1}{2}$ p., quarto.

2410 Letter to an unidentified correspondent, [1836]. 'I hope you will not think I am taking an unwarranted liberty ....' 3 pp., octavo.

2411 Letter to R. F. Housman, 10 January 1836. 'I felt much gratified by your valuable Present ....' $2\frac{1}{2}$ pp., quarto.

2412 Letter to Francis Merewether, 7 March 1836. 'I wish I could have sent this Letter under Cover ....' Incomplete. 2 pp., quarto.

2413 Letter to Edwin Hill Handley, 18 April 1836. 'It is some time since I received a Letter from you ....' $2\frac{1}{2}$ pp., quarto.

2414 Letter to Derwent Coleridge, [May 1836]. 'I should be most glad to see you, and Mr. Marshall with whom ....' 1 p., octavo.

2415 Letter to Thomas Noon Talfourd, [May 1836]. 'Many thanks for your very kind invitation, which I hope ....' 1 p., quarto.

2416 Letter to an unidentified correspondent, 1 July 1836. 'My departure draws nigh, not for the continent but for home ....' 2 pp., quarto.

2417 Letter, in the hand of Mary Wordsworth, to the Liverpool Literary, Scientific, & Commercial Institution, 10 January 1837. 'Incessant engagements have prevented me from giving your letter ....' $1\frac{3}{4}$ pp., quarto.

2418 Letter to Strickland Cookson, [19 March 1837]. 'Will you be so kind as to answer this demand ....' 1 p., octavo.

2419 Letter to Dora Wordsworth, [25 March 1837]. 'You must have thought we were lost; I write now merely ....' 1 p., quarto.

2420 Letter to James Stephen, 5 June 1837. 'I had the pleasure of receiving by the ordinary Post yesterday ....' With a postscript by Henry Crabb Robinson. 1 p., quarto.

2421 Letter to Frances C. Mackenzie, 11 August [1837]. 'I promised myself, before we left Rome, the pleasure of writing ....' With a two-page letter, also to Miss Mackenzie, from Henry Crabb Robinson, dated 17 November 1837. 2 pp., quarto.

2422 Letter to Joseph Cottle, 19 August 1837. 'Upon returning from the Continent where I have been ....' Inserted in the Joseph Cottle Album. 3 pp., quarto.

2423 Letter to C. R. Leslie, 2 September 1837. 'I am gratified to hear of the intention to pay a tribute ....' 1 p., quarto.

2424 Letter to Sir George Beaumont, 3 September 1837. 'Allow me to thank you for your kind letter, and to express ....' 1 p., quarto.

2425 Letter to William Jerdan, 7 October [1837?]. 'Your letter of the 23d August, I did not receive till my arrival here ....' 4 pp., octavo.

2426 Letter, in the hand of Mary Wordsworth, to Thomas Spring-Rice, 17 October [1837]. 'I have deferred replying to your obliging letter, from the hope of being able ....' 7 pp., octavo.

2427 Letter, in the hand of Mary Wordsworth, to Mary Fisher, [October–November 1837]. 'I have long been in your debt ....' 4 pp., quarto.

2428 Fragment of a letter to [Thomas Noon Talfourd], [October–November 1837]. 'How sorry I am you did not return this way from Scotland!...' ½ p., octavo.

2429 Letter, in the hand of Mary Wordsworth, to Mary Fisher, 15 December [1837]. 'It would have been inconvenient to me to reply earlier ....' 4 pp., quarto.

2430 Fragment of a letter, in the hand of Mary Wordsworth, to Thomas Powell, 19 December 1837. '...the 3 poets here alluded to! I have availed myself ....' ¼ p., quarto.

2431 Letter to Edward Ferguson, 7 February 1838. 'I enclose my Sisters Receipt for the Legacy left her ....' 1 p., quarto.

2432 Letter to Horace Twiss, [April 1838?]. 'Allow me to remind you that Serjeant Talfourd's Bill ....' 1½ pp., octavo.

2433 Letter to Thomas Noon Talfourd, [14 April 1838]. 'I have not been unmindful of your Copyright Bill ....' 4 pp., quarto.

2434 Letter to Thomas Noon Talfourd, [18 April 1838]. 'Your's reached me while I was preparing rather a long letter ....' 2 pp., 16mo.

2435 Notes and fragments, partly in the hand of Mary Wordsworth, to Thomas Noon Talfourd, [c. 18 April 1838]. 'It seems therefore only to remain for me, with the view of strengthening ....' Totals 6½ pp., quarto.

2436 Letter, in the hand of Mary Wordsworth, to the Rev. Mr. Bray, 7 January [1839]. 'As I understand from my Son, that (as his Curate, for the time being at Brigham) ....' 1 p., quarto.

2437 Letter, in the hand of Mary Wordsworth, to Henry Reed, 22 February 1839. 'Your letter of the 3d of January accompanying your Reviewal of my Poems ....' 2 pp., quarto.

2438 Letter to Thomas Noon Talfourd, 8 April [1839]. 'Thanks for your Letter, which was duly received ....' 4 pp., quarto.

2439 Letter to Joseph Cottle, 26 April 1839. 'I am truly sorry not to have found you here, as Mr. Peace and I ....' 1 p., quarto.

2440 Letter to [Dr. Parry], 28 April [1839]. 'I should have been truly happy to see you to morrow as you kindly ....' 2 pp., octavo.

2441 Letter to Thomas Spring-Rice, 11 May 1839. 'I write merely to acknowledge with thanks the receipt of your Note ....' 2 pp., octavo.

2442 Letter to Henry Reed, 23 December 1839. 'The Year is upon the point of expiring ....' $3\frac{3}{4}$ pp., quarto.

2443 Letter to Thomas Spring-Rice, Lord Monteagle, 30 December [1839]. 'Your Letter, and the Enclosure, gave me, and let me add my family ....' 4 pp., octavo.

2444 Letter, in the hand of Mary Wordsworth, to Robert Perceval Graves, [c. 1840]. 'Mr. Graves will bear in mind what I said against the phrase ....' 4 pp., folio.

2445 Letter, in the hand of Mary Wordsworth, to Thomas Powell, 9 January [1840]. 'I recd your's two or three hours ago—excuse my replying to it at present ....' $2\frac{1}{2}$ pp., quarto.

2446 Letter to Cordelia [Marshall], 19 February 1840. 'If you had known how little my *promised* Letter was likely ....' 6 pp., octavo.

2447 Letter, in the hand of Mary Wordsworth, to [Robert Blakeney], 10 April [1840?]. 'You will no doubt have heard that Mr. White declines to continue ....' 2 pp., quarto.

2448 Letter, in the hand of Mary Wordsworth, to Francis Merewether, 29 April 1840. 'If you knew how few letters I write or *can* write you would not take it ill ....' 4 pp., quarto.

2449 Letter to [John Brakenridge], 23 May 1840. 'It gives me much pleasure to learn from your obliging Letter ....' $2\frac{1}{2}$ pp., quarto.

2450 Letter, in the hand of Mary Wordsworth, to Henry Reed, 26 May 1840. 'I have just received your 2d letter ....' 2 pp., quarto.

2451 Letter to John Brakenridge, 15 June 1840. 'I have the pleasure to inform you that the Crypt arrived here ....' 1½ pp., quarto.

2452 Letter to John Marshall, [September 1840?] 'Mr. Rogers and I will come to Halsteads on Thursday ....' ½ p., quarto.

2453 Letter to Henry Reed, 2 September 1840. 'I am truly thankful for your valuable Letter ....' Five lines in the hand of Mary Wordsworth; half a page in an unidentified hand; signature cut off. 1½ pp., folio.

2454 Letter, in the hand of Mary Wordsworth, to an unidentified correspondent, 10 September [1840]. 'I lose no time in thanking you for your interesting little work ....' 3 pp., octavo.

2455 Letter, in the hand of Mary Wordsworth, to Henry Reed, 14 September 1840. 'Following your good example I sent you ....' 4 pp., quarto.

2456 Letter to Thomas Powell, 22 November [1840]. 'You would perhaps hear of my late peril from the rash driving of a Coach....' 1¾ pp., quarto.

2457 Letter to Mary Spring-Rice, 28 December 1840. 'Having, my dear Friend, through a long series of years ....' 3 pp., octavo.

2458 Fragment of a letter to an unidentified correspondent, [*c.* 1841?]. '...and in case of any thing of this kind happening unfortunately ....' ½ p., octavo.

2459 Letter, in the hand of Mary Wordsworth, to [S. C. Hall], 8 January 1841. 'I was pleased to hear that you and Mrs. Hall....' 4 pp., octavo.

2460 Letter to John Wilson, 11 January 1841. 'I received the accompanying Vol: from Mr. Powell some little time ....' 2 pp., octavo.

2461 Letter, in the hand of Mary Wordsworth, to Henry Reed, 13 January 1841. 'Your most obliging letter of Oct. 30th ....' 4 pp., quarto.

2462 Letter, in the hand of Mary Wordsworth, to Viscount Mahon, 3 March 1841. 'Many thanks for your 2d letter & the extracts from Lord Russel's to you....' Heavily corrected; probably a draft. 5 pp., octavo.

2463 Letter to an unidentified correspondent, 18 March 1841. 'Your Letter was unfortunately put aside and the occasion of it slipped ....' 1 p., octavo.

2464 Letter to an unidentified correspondent, 19 April 1841. 'Your kind Letter has followed me to this place....' 2 pp., octavo.

2465 Letter to Thomas Spring-Rice, Lord Monteagle, endorsed 20 April 1841. 'Nearly a week has elapsed since your marriage, and I have often ....' 2¼ pp., octavo.

2466 Letter to Henry Reed, 15 May 1841. 'I am now on a visit alone with Mrs. Wordsworth ....' 4 pp., quarto.

2467 Letter to Sir Robert Peel, 16 June 1841. 'I regret much that I was not in the house when you did me the honor ....' 2 pp., octavo.

2468 Fragment of a letter to [William Fisher], [August 1841]. '...and my own pleasure. I do not like to address conversation for guidance ....' 4 pp., octavo.

2469 Letter to Henry Reed, 16 August 1841. 'I have just received your last very obliging letter ....' $3\frac{1}{4}$ pp., quarto.

2470 Letter, in the hand of Mary Wordsworth, to [William Fisher], 22 December [1841]. 'I rejoice exceedingly that your resolution is fixed ....' 2 pp., quarto.

2471 Letter, in the hand of Mary Wordsworth, to Christopher Wordsworth, Sr., 26 January 1842. 'I have for many years been much interested in the Matter ....' $3\frac{1}{2}$ pp., octavo.

2472 Letter, in the hand of Mary Wordsworth, to Henry Reed, 1 March 1842. 'I had purposed to write a long letter ....' 3 pp., quarto.

2473 Letter to Sir Aubrey de Vere, the elder, 31 March 1842. 'You have gratified me far beyond my deserts, Defaulter as I am ....' 6 pp., octavo.

2474 Note to Edward Moxon, 11 May 1842. 'Pray send this off to Mr. Rio without the delay of a single post.' 1 p., octavo.

2475 Letter, in the hand of Mary Wordsworth, to Henry Reed, 18 July 1842. 'Yesterday I received your kind letter ....' $4\frac{1}{2}$ pp., octavo.

2476 Letter to Henry Reed, 4 September 1842. 'Having an opportunity of sending this note ....' $3\frac{1}{2}$ pp., octavo.

2477 Letter to Martin Farquhar Tupper, 10 December 1842. 'Having received your second Series of Proverbial Philosophy ....' 2 pp., octavo.

2478 Letter to Thomas Noon Talfourd, [22 March 1843]. 'It seems attaching too much importance to the Enclosed Copy of Verses ....' Unsigned. 2 pp., octavo.

2479 Letter to Henry Reed, 27 March 1843. 'There are many things exclusive of business ....' 4 pp., quarto.

2480 Note to Henry Reed, 30 March 1843. 'I will be much obliged if you will have the enclosed Sonnets copied ....' Written on an envelope.

2481 Letter to James Montgomery, 16 April 1843. 'Allow me to ask if you are acquainted with Mr. Ebenezer Elliot ....' 2 pp., octavo.

2482 Letter to George Huntly Gordon, 17 April 1843. 'Absence from home has prevented my replying sooner ....' 2 pp., octavo.

2483 Letter to E. T. Pilgrim, 22 April 1843. 'The Poet Laureate, a Septuagenarian returns thanks to an Octogenarian Pilgrim ....' 1 p., octavo.

2484 Letter to John Taylor Coleridge, 13 May 1843. 'Having learned from the Newspapers that you have resumed ....' 2 pp., quarto.

2485 Letter to Richard Parkinson, 2 June 1843. 'It gives me pleasure to send you herewith a Drawing of Seathwaite Chapel ....' 3 pp., octavo.

2486 Letter to Henry Reed, 2 August 1843. 'I have been a discreditably long time ....' 4 pp., quarto.

2487 Letter to Sir James McGrigor, 10 August 1843. 'Remembering with gratitude the ready kindness with which you ....' 3½ pp., octavo.

2488 Letter to Christopher Wordsworth, Jr., 13 October [1843]. 'I enclose a Letter from G.H. from which you will learn ....' 3 pp., octavo.

2489 Letter to Dora Wordsworth, 14 [October 1843]. 'Why have I not written? The answer is ....' 10 pp., octavo.

2490 Letter to Christopher Wordsworth, Jr., [late 1843]. 'We are exceedingly pleased to hear that G.H. has been nominated ....' 3 pp., octavo.

2491 Letter to an unidentified correspondent, 8 February 1844. 'I have just received through Mr. Moxon my Publisher ....' 1½ pp., octavo.

2492 Letter to Thomas Powell, 22 March 1844. 'Some little Time ago we received a Stilton Cheese ....' 4 pp., octavo.

2493 Letter to Joseph Cottle, 4 April 1844. 'Your kind letter gave me much pleasure ....' Inserted in the Joseph Cottle Album. 4 pp., octavo.

2494 Letter to Richard Parkinson, 8 April [1844]. 'Accept my thanks for the 2d Edition of your Old Church Clock ....' 3 pp., octavo.

2495 Letter to Henry Reed, 5 July 1844. 'So long have I been in your debt ....' 4 pp., quarto.

2496 Letter to Richard Parkinson, 12 July 1844. 'I am glad that a 3d Edit. of the Old Church Clock is called for ....' 2½ pp., octavo.

2497 Letter to Henry Inman, 14 July 1844. 'I have just received a Letter from my highly esteemed Friend Mr. Reed ....' 2 pp., octavo.

2498 Letter to Sir Charles William Pasley, 16 November 1844. 'I am just returned home after a long ramble ....' 3 pp., octavo.

2499 Letter to [John Moultrie], [1845]. 'My Copy of the Ode in Gray's own hand-writing has ....' 2 pp., octavo.

2500 Letter to [John Holland], 4 April 1845. 'Mr. Wordsworth having just heard from his Friend Mr. C. Robinson ....' 1½ pp., octavo.

2501 Letter to Christopher Wordsworth, Jr., 10 April 1845. 'We are truly glad of the good [news] you give of your new-born ....' 3¾ pp., octavo.

2502 Letter to George Huntly Gordon, 24 June 1845. 'When I had but a glimpse of you at Mr. Moxon's I was troubled with an inflammation ....' 2 pp., octavo.

2503 Letter to Henry Reed, 1 July 1845. 'I have as usual been long in your debt ....' 4 pp., quarto.

2504 Letter to Henry Reed, 31 July 1845. 'Your Brother who is kindly coming from Liverpool ....' 4 pp., octavo.

2505 Fragment of a letter, in the hand of Mary Wordsworth, to Christopher Wordsworth, Jr., 7 August 1845. 'Pray give my blessing with a kiss to the little Maria ....' Three lines.

2506 Letter to Henry Reed, 27 September [1845]. 'The sight of your Letter was very welcome ....' 5 pp., quarto.

2507 Letter, in the hand of Mary Wordsworth, to Fred Westley, 22 December 1845. 'Mrs. W kindly allows me her hand to spare you the trouble of deciphering ....' 3½ pp., octavo.

2508 Letter to Fred Westley, [January 1846]. 'Thank you for the Book intended for the Queen....' 3 pp., 16mo.

2509 Letter to Henry Reed, 23 January 1846. 'After a delay at Liverpool under which we were not a little impatient ....' Unsigned. 4 pp., quarto.

2510 Letter to Henry Reed, 3 February [1846]. 'I was much shocked to find that my last ....' 4 pp., octavo.

2511 Letter to R. Shelton Mackenzie, 17 February 1846. 'I wish you success in your projected Magazine; but it is quite ....' 1¼ pp., octavo.

2512 Letter, in the hand of Mary Wordsworth, to [Fred Westley?], 23 February [1846]. 'The entanglement of public Affairs seems to have prevented my receiving ....' 3 pp., octavo.

2513 Letter to E. Gridlestone, 6 April [1846]. 'My Son arrived here yesterday with his Sons ....' 4 pp., octavo.

2514 Letter to [Martin Farquhar Tupper], 21 July 1846. 'Let me thank you for your *Thousand Lines*, and the accompanying Letter....' 2 pp., octavo.

2515 Letter to [Andrew McEwen?], 20 October 1846. 'You must not take it ill if I cannot answer your Letter ....' 2 pp., octavo.

2516 Letter to William Bell, 7 January 1847. 'Your Draft for 32.2.10 has been duly received, and I thank you ....' 1½ pp., octavo.

2517 Letter to Emmie Fisher, 4 March 1847. 'A single word from me I hope will not be unacceptable ....' 4 pp., 16mo.

2518 Letter, in the hand of Mary Wordsworth, to an unidentified correspondent, 27 March 1847. 'You do me justice; I never spoke with acrimony of Lord Byron ....' 2 pp., octavo.

2519 Letter to an unidentified correspondent, 25 September 1847. 'Many thanks for your prompt reply to my enquiries ....' 3 pp., octavo.

2520 Letter to [John Pringle Nichol], August 1848. 'Mr. Wordsworth is much obliged by Professor Nichol's kindness in transmitting to him Mr. Longfellow's Poem ....' $3\frac{1}{2}$ pp., octavo.

2521 Letter to [Joshua Stranger], 8 December [1848]. 'You have obliged me much by the attention which you have so readily ....' 3 pp., octavo.

2522 Letter, in the hand of Mary Wordsworth, to Edward Moxon, 19 June 1849. 'As you kindly ask if there is "any thing else you can bring for us" ....' $3\frac{1}{2}$ pp., octavo.

2523 Letter to an unidentified correspondent, 4 August 1849. 'Absence from home prevented my receiving your Letter ....' 2 pp., octavo.

2524 Letter to Lord ——, 7 September 1849. 'I much regret being obliged once again to throw myself upon your good offices ....' 3 pp., quarto.

2525 Letter, in the hand of Mary Wordsworth, to John Pringle Nichol, 15 March 1850. 'Mr. Wordsworth feels himself much obliged to Professor Nichol ....' $1\frac{1}{4}$ pp., octavo.

2526 Letter to T. E. Burton, 8 August, no year given. 'Mr. Wordsworth begs to say in answer to ....' 1 p., octavo.

2527 Letter to Mr. Fell, no date. 'Mr. Rogers my friend is here, he has got a lameness in one of his feet ....' 1 p., octavo.

2528 Letter to Mrs. Jameson, no date. 'I am truly sorry that you did not think of drawing our Gates ....' 3 pp., 16mo.

2529 Letter to Mr. Jewsbury, no date. 'I have just seen a Letter from Mr. Reynolds to Mr. S—— ....' $\frac{1}{2}$ p., quarto.

2530 Letter to [John Murray?], no date. 'If you can accommodate me with a Copy of Crabbe's Works at *Trade Price* ....' 1 p., octavo.

2531 Letter to [Henry Crabb Robinson?], no date. 'I shall be quite happy to be in South Street ....' 1 p., 16mo.

2532 Letter to [Thomas Southwood Smith?], no date. 'I am glad to learn that the Sanatorium prospers....' 1 p., 16mo.

2533 Letter, in the hand of Mary Wordsworth, to Robert Southey, no date. 'Probably you have received a Copy of the enclosed ....' 1 p., octavo.

2534 Letter to James Spedding, 1 March, no year given. 'I am about to write to you upon a small concern of my own ....' 2 pp., quarto.

2535 Letter to David Wilkie, 11 May, no year given. 'The Revd Mr. Birkett the Bearer of this, is fond of Painting ....' 1½ pp., octavo.

2536 Letter to Thomas Wilkinson, no date. 'The Bearer of this is Mr. Green of Ambleside, a very ingenious Artist ....' 1½ pp., octavo.

2537 Letter to an unidentified correspondent, 3 June, no year given. 'Innumerable and incessant engagements will, I much regret ....' 2 pp., 16mo.

2538 Letter to an unidentified correspondent, no date. 'I have strong reasons for not wishing my name to appear ....' 3 pp., 16mo.

2539 Letter to an unidentified correspondent, no date. 'If not better engaged could you breakfast with us this morning ....' 1 p., 16mo.

2540 Letter to an unidentified correspondent, no date. 'Pray thank Lady Chantrey and Mr. Weiks for their readiness ....' 3 pp., octavo.

2541 Letter, in the hand of Mary Wordsworth, to an unidentified correspondent, 22 December, no year given. 'The letter of the Warden of Merton....' 1 p., quarto.

CHARLES WORDSWORTH, Nephew of the Poet

2542 Letter to Archdeacon ——, 'Monday before Easter,' 1852. 'I am very sorry to find from your letter ....' 3 pp., octavo.

CHRISTOPHER WORDSWORTH, SENIOR

2543 Letter to Thomas Kennedy, 20 September 1830. 'I shall be much obliged by your sending me the St. James's ....' 1 p., quarto.

2544 Letter to an unidentified correspondent, [c. 1831]. 'My friend Mr. Repton the bearer of this having been lately ....' 2 pp., octavo.

2545 Letter to W. M. Heald, 30 January 1836. 'The importance of the occasion and the interest I naturally feel ....' 1 p., quarto.

2546 Letter to Thomas Kennedy, 24 October 1840. 'Be so good as forward my Tuesday next St. James's Chronicle ....' 1 p., octavo.

2547 Letter to [Thomas Kennedy], 17 September 1841. 'Be so good as send my St. James's Chronicle ....' 1 p., 16mo.

CHRISTOPHER WORDSWORTH, JUNIOR

2548 Letter to Henry Reed, 22 June 1850. 'I trust you will kindly pardon the liberty ....' 3 pp., octavo.

2549 Letter to Henry Reed, 2 September 1850. 'At present I write merely to acknowledge your great kindness ....' $2\frac{1}{2}$ pp., quarto.

2550 Letter to Henry Reed, 10 October 1850. 'I write what must be rather a hasty line ....' 4 pp., octavo.

2551 Letter to Henry Reed, 17 January 1851. 'I have to thank you for your kindness in sending ....' 2 pp., quarto.

2552 Letter to Henry Reed, 26 April 1851. 'On the next page I will add a few lines ....' 4 pp., quarto.

2553 Letter to Henry Reed, 16 March 1853. 'I received yesterday your welcome letter ....' 4 pp., quarto.

2554 Letter to Henry Reed, 4 August 1853. 'I have to thank you for your kindness ....' 3 pp., quarto.

2555 Letter to Henry Reed, 31 May 1854. 'A letter was dispatched from this place to Rydal Mount ....' 3 pp., octavo.

2556 Letter to W. L. Adye, 14 August 1865. 'I beg to offer my sincere thanks ....' $1\frac{1}{2}$ pp., octavo.

2557 Letter to J. Smallpeace, 18 March 1867. 'I beg to thank you for your kindness ....' 4 pp., octavo.

DORA WORDSWORTH

2558 Commonplace Book, entitled: *To Susan Ayling, a Memorial of Love and Affection from Dora Wordsworth*, Rydal Mount, July 7th 1824. On one leaf is pencilled, in the hand of Coleridge, what appears to be the earliest state of his ''Tis not the lily-brow I prize.' The album contains transcripts of the following poems of Wordsworth: To the Lady Fleming; 'Why, Minstrel, these untuneful murmurings' (three versions); two excerpts from *The Excursion* (one of them in the hand of Wordsworth and signed by him); Sacrament (two versions); Confirmation, Continued; Places of Worship; Pastoral Character; Baptism; Catechising; Emigrant French Clergy. These last seven poems are from the *Ecclesiastical Sonnets*. The book contains transcripts of verse by several other writers of the period, including Charles Lloyd, Robert Southey, Charles Townsend, and Hartley Coleridge. It consists of 120 pp., and measures $9 \times 7\frac{1}{4}$ in.

2559 Letter to Maryanne and Maria Jane Jewsbury, [1826]. 'Many thanks for the P.S. the Thaumatropes & the extract ....' 2 pp., quarto.

2560 Letter to Mrs. Elliot, 6 April [1827]. 'Would you gratify me by accepting ....' Enclosing a copy in the hand of Dora of Wordsworth's On Seeing a Needlecase in the Form of a Harp. 2 pp., 16mo and 3 pp., octavo.

2561 Letter to Catherine Clarkson, 29 May [1829]. 'My Mother has each day since the receipt of your letter ....' $1\frac{1}{4}$ pp., quarto.

2562 Letter to William Jackson, [April 1830]. 'You must excuse my troubling you with this note ....' $2\frac{1}{4}$ pp., octavo.

DOROTHY WORDSWORTH

2563 Poem entitled Christmas Day ('This is the day when kindred meet'). Signed and dated 5 January 1837. 1 p., quarto.

2564 Home-made notebook entitled: Travelling on the Continent; containing a record of lodgings, expenses, and like, of a continental tour. Partly in the hand of Dorothy Wordsworth. 8 pp., $9 \times 5\frac{1}{2}$ in.

2565 Notebook, parts of which are in the hand of Dorothy Wordsworth, containing information for travel on the Continent. 32 pp., $6 \times 3\frac{1}{2}$ in.

2566 A paper with the heading: Mrs. Freeman's Rout; an itinerary of a tour on the Continent. 1 p., quarto.

2567 Poem, in an unidentified hand, entitled: Written by Aunt Wordsworth for Dora W's Little Green Book ('Confiding hopes of youthful hearts'). Addressed to Helen E. Wordsworth (second wife of the poet's son John), Brigham Vicarage; *c.* 1852. $1\frac{1}{2}$ pp., octavo.

2568 Letter to Richard Wordsworth, 2 October [1807]. 'I begin to be impatient to see you, and therefore I cannot help ....' 2 pp., quarto.

2569 Letter to Mrs. Thomas Cookson, 29 August [1810]. 'I know you are not one of those who are ready to take offence ....' 4 pp., quarto.

2570 Fragment of a letter to Catherine Clarkson, 16 August 1812. 'The evening before Sara and Mary M. set off to Appleby ....' 2 pp., quarto.

2571 Letter to Josiah Wade, 27 March 1814. 'I am sure that you will at once recognize the name ....' 4 pp., quarto.

2572 Letter to Mr. White, 4 September 1818. 'I know you will excuse the liberty I am going to take ....' 2 pp., quarto.

2573 Letter to Joseph Cottle, 31 July 1828. 'In the absence of my Brother I am empowered to open letters ....' Inserted in the Joseph Cottle Album. 3 pp., quarto.

2574 Letter to George Huntly Gordon, 25 January 1829. 'Trusting that my Brother, Mr. Wordsworth of Rydal Mount has prepared ....' 1 p., quarto.

2575 Letter to George Huntly Gordon, 21 September [1829]. 'Along with the normal dispatches to my nephew William ....' 3 pp., octavo.

2576 Letter to an unidentified correspondent, 14 November [1829]. 'Mrs. Luff is very grateful for your kindness ....' 2 pp., quarto.

2577 Letter to George Huntly Gordon, [spring 1830?]. 'After my Brother had prepared the enclosed Budget of letters ....' 1½ pp., quarto.

2578 Letter to George Huntly Gordon, 25 July [1830]. 'You are so kindly disposed to serve us ....' 3 pp., octavo.

2579 Letter to Edward Ferguson, [8 October 1837]. 'A madman might as well attempt to relate the history ....' 3½ pp., quarto.

FANNY GRAHAM WORDSWORTH, Wife of
William Wordsworth, Jr.

2580 Letter to William A. Knight, 12 January, no year given. 'Many thanks, dear Professor Knight ....' 5 pp., octavo.

2581 Letter to William A. Knight, 21 January, no year given. 'I am sending you the MSS book of Poems ....' 4 pp., octavo.

HENRY WORDSWORTH (unidentified)

2582 Letter to G. W. Abbott, May 1833. 'I have been five weeks confined at home ....' 1 p., quarto.

JOHN WORDSWORTH, Father of the Poet

2583 Letter to Mr. Udale, 7 February 1777. 'Yours came in time to prevent my sending the money to Cockbridge ....' 1 p., quarto.

JOHN WORDSWORTH, Son of the Poet

2584 Letter to [William Jackson?], 7 April [1846]. 'I write to thank you for the kind communication ....' 3 pp., octavo.

2585 Letter to Edward Moxon, [1850?]. 'I wrote you a few lines the other day when we all considered my dear Father's ....' 1 p., octavo.

2586 Letter to Edward Moxon, 21 May, no year given. 'I reached Rydal on Thursday Evening ....' 3 pp., octavo.

MARY WORDSWORTH

2587 Notes entitled: Mr. Sharpe's Tour. Advice for a tour of the Continent. Undated. $1\frac{1}{4}$ pp., quarto.

2588 A fragment containing a list of fourteen books, mostly religious. Undated. 2 pp., octavo.

2589 Letter to Samuel Tilbrooke, 20 April [1816]. 'My sister being gone to pay a long mercy visit at Brathing Hall ....' With three drawings of Ivy Cottage, which was bought by Tilbrooke. 4 pp., folio.

2590 Letter to George Huntly Gordon, 28 October [1829]. 'In Mrs. Wordsworth's absence I think it right to acknowledge ....' 3 pp., octavo.

2591 Letter to George Huntly Gordon, 16 July [1830]. 'Without your sanction I continue to forward letters to William ....' 1 p., octavo.

2592 Letter to Thomas Powell, [*c.* 1 March 1837]. 'Mrs. Wordsworth takes the liberty to enclose a letter ....' $\frac{1}{2}$ p., octavo.

2593 Letter to Catherine Clarkson, 9 May [1838]. 'I am most grateful to you for the letter ....' 4 pp., quarto.

2594 Letter to Thomas Powell, [July 1838]. 'Mrs. Wordsworth, in the absence of her husband ....' 1 p., octavo.

2595 Letter to H. W. Pickersgill, 15 September [1840]. 'I have the satisfaction & pleasure to inform you that the Picture ....' $2\frac{1}{2}$ pp., octavo.

2596 Fragment of a letter to Catherine Clarkson, [April 1841?]. '...of writing to you often. We spent 10 days with my B[rothe]r & his family ....' 2 pp., octavo.

2597 Letter to an unidentified correspondent, 28 June [1841]. 'I saw Dora looking happy in her little quiet lodging ....' 4 pp., octavo.

2598 Fragment of a letter to [Henry Crabb Robinson], 16 December [1841]. 'I readily answer your call for a *letter* ....' 2 pp., octavo.

2599 Letter to Emmie Fisher, 25 April 1842. 'We do indeed, most deeply sympathize with your dear Father & Mother ....' 4 pp., octavo.

2600 Letter to Emmie Fisher, 10 December [1846]. 'I know my dear Emmie that you will forgive my tardiness ....' 8 pp., octavo.

2601 Fragment of a letter to [Emmie Fisher], [*c.* 1848–9]. '...cheerful companion, & a very useful & willing assistant to your Cousin ....' 2 pp., octavo.

2602 Letter to Edward Moxon, 29 October [1849]. 'Will you thank Mrs. Moxon for her kind note....' $2\frac{1}{2}$ pp., octavo.

2603 Fragment of a letter to Emmie Fisher, no date. 'We have the pleasure of having good tidings of the health ....' With a postscript by William Wordsworth. 1 p., octavo.

2604 Note concerning vol. 3 of Southey's History of Brazil, January 1850. 'When this Volume, upon its publication arrived from the Author, I took it with intent ....' 1 p., quarto.

WILLIAM WORDSWORTH, JUNIOR

2605 Letter to George Huntly Gordon, 12 May 1829. 'I received your welcome letter at Whitwick ....' 2½ pp., octavo.

2606 Letter to William Jackson, 23 January 1844. 'I have much pleasure in complying with your kind wish ....' 6 pp., octavo.

2607 Letter to J. M. Jones, 10 July 1865. 'I will thank you to allow the bearer, Mr. Caleb Hodgson ....' 3 pp., octavo.

2608 Letter to William A. Knight, 25 April 1882. 'I am glad to hear you have found the Journals ....' 2 pp., octavo.

2609 Letter to William A. Knight, 5 August 1882. 'In compliance with your most attentive Post card ....' 3 pp., octavo.

COLERIDGE AND HIS FAMILY

SAMUEL TAYLOR COLERIDGE

2610 Poem, now entitled: The Eolian Harp ('My pensive SARAH! thy soft cheek reclin'd'). About forty-two lines, with many revisions. Undated, but perhaps of 1795. Inserted in the Joseph Cottle Album. 2 pp., quarto.

2611 Poem: Lines Written at the King's Arms, Ross, Formerly the Residence of Mr. Kyrle, the 'Man of Ross,' Celebrated by Pope ('Richer than Misers o'er their countless hoards'). Two ten-line stanzas. Signed and dated 6 June 1795. Written in the Joseph Cottle Album. 1 p., folio.

2612 Poem, now entitled: On a Late Connubial Rupture in High Life ('I sigh, fair injured Stranger! for thy fate'). Twenty lines and a note. Signed and dated July 1796. Written in the Joseph Cottle Album. 1 p., folio.

2613 The poem entitled: To an Unfortunate Princess. Signed and dated 6 July 1796. With the following note by Susan Coates: 'This little Poem was read to my Mother by Coleridge at the moment when it was written & given to her before she left the room. I *believe* it has never been published. Southey & Coleridge were at that time (& young Humphry Davy) constant visitors at my Father's house.' Poem, 1 p., quarto; note, ½ p., quarto.

2614 Draft on Joseph Johnson, the bookseller, for £25, payable to William Remnant, dated from Hamburg, 21 September 1798.

2615 Receipt for £300 received at the hands of Joseph Cottle from 'an unknown Friend' (i.e. Thomas De Quincey). Dated 12 November 1807. Inserted in the Joseph Cottle Album.

2616 The poem The Knight's Tomb, beginning in this version: 'Where is the grave of Sir Arthur O'Relhan?' Preceded by Coleridge's note explaining that the lines were an experiment in meter and that Sir Walter Scott had published them 'but very incorrectly,' in one of his novels. Signed and dated 20 October 1824. On the back of the page are thirteen lines from his poem Youth and Age, in the hand, probably, of Sara Coleridge. 1 p., octavo.

2617 Transcript, in the hand of Anne Gillman, of a note by Coleridge on J. A. Hillhouse's poem Hadad; *c.* 1825. 3 pp., quarto.

2618 Transcript, in an unidentified hand, of Coleridge's comments on the Sacrament, Prayer, the Confession of Sin, and similar topics; *c.* 1827. 5 pp., quarto.

2619 Transcript, in the hand of Sara Coleridge, of notes written by S.T.C. in Henry Gillman's copy of The Book of Common Prayer. 7 pp., octavo.

2620 Final stanza of the poem Youth and Age. Signed and dated 18 May 1829. 1 p., 16mo.

2621 Critical notes on William Sotheby's translation of *The Iliad*; *c.* 1830. 2 pp., quarto.

2622 Transcript, in an unidentified hand, of Coleridge's Inscription for a Fountain on a Heath and of his explication of that poem; [1832]. 1½ pp., quarto.

2623 Lines 4 and 7–17 of Love's Apparition and Evanishment, with a fragment of a letter to J. G. Lockhart postmarked 6 November 1833. 1 p., quarto.

2624 Incomplete piece of prose entitled Essay on Trial Marriages. Undated. 2 pp., quarto.

2625 Transcript, in an unidentified hand, of Coleridge's notes in the British Museum's copy of *The Coming of Messiah*, by Manuel Lacunza. 4 pp., quarto and 44 pp., octavo.

2626 Comment on Mary Lamb's essay, Mrs. Leicester's School. Written on a page since torn from Henry Gillman's copy. 1½ pp. octavo.

2627 Transcript, in the hand of Sara Coleridge, of her father's notes written in a volume of *Tom Jones*. 2½ pp., quarto.

2628 Transcript, in the hand of J. H. Green, of Coleridge's note on a passage from Lucy Hutchinson's *Memoirs of the Life of Colonel Hutchinson*. 1 p., octavo.

2629 Notes on the distinction between the picturesque and the sublime ('When the whole and the parts are seen at once ....'). Undated. 2 pp., octavo.

2630 Notes on Genius, Talent, Sense, and Cleverness. Undated. 1 p., quarto.

2631 Notes on Animal Magnetism and on the unauthorized publication of Southey's *Wat Tyler*. Undated. 1 p., quarto, and 2 pp., octavo.

2632 Transcript, in the hand of Sara Coleridge, of a note found in Coleridge's room ('In the state of perfection, perhaps all other faculties may be swallowed up ....'). 1 p., octavo.

2633 Transcript, in the hand of Sara Coleridge, of a brief note on Johann Ludwig Tieck. 1 p., octavo.

2634 Fragment of a draft, perhaps of an article for *The Courier* ('The conclusion of our remarks in the Courier of Thursday ....'). 1 p., octavo.

2635 A portion of the Essay on Faith. Undated. 1 p., quarto.

2636 Thirteen lines of humorous verse ('Mon charmant, prenez gard à'). Undated. 1 p., octavo.

2637 Transcript, in the hand of Sara Coleridge, of twenty-two lines of verse on Coleridge's tea kettle ('My tiny tin, my omnium gatherum scout'). 1¼ pp., quarto.

2638 Transcript, in an unidentified hand, of 'There was a king in the North Countree', a fourteen-line parody of The Twa Sisters ending 'Take warning from this all ye young women, That ye do learn the art of swimming.' Attributed by the transcriber to 'S.T.C.'

2639 Four lines of verse entitled Inscription on a Time Piece. Signed but undated.

2640 Transcript, in an unidentified hand, of a Morning Prayer; said to be by S.T.C. 2 pp., quarto.

2641 Transcript, in an unidentified hand, of A Prayer to Be Said before a Man Begins His Work; said to be by S.T.C. 1 p., quarto.

2642 Letter to John Fellows, 13 May 1796. 'A few days ago I received thro' George Dyer a small note ....' 2 pp., quarto.

2643 Letter to John Fellows, 31 May 1796. 'The ladies, who have honored me by so delicate an act ....' With a list of subscribers. 4 pp., quarto.

2644 Letter to Joseph Cottle, 18 October 1796. 'I have no mercenary feelings, I verily believe ....' Inserted in the Joseph Cottle Album. 2 pp., quarto.

2645 Letter to Joseph Cottle, 5 November 1796. 'A Devil has got possession of my left temple, eye, cheek, jaw, throat ....' Inserted in the Joseph Cottle Album. 2 pp., octavo.

2646 Letter to J. P. Estlin, [14 January 1798]. 'After a fatiguing journey I arrived here ....' 1 p., quarto.

2647 Letter to Joseph Cottle, [24 January 1798]. 'The moment I received Mr. Wedgewood's letter, I accepted his offer ....' 1 p., quarto.

2648 Letter to Sir George Beaumont, 16 October 1803. 'I have had a large Sheet of Verses lying on my Desk ....' 4 pp., quarto.

2649 Letter to Richard Sharp, 29 January 1804. 'In case I should not be fortunate enough to find you ....' 3 pp., octavo.

2650 Letter to William Sotheby, 13 March 1804. 'Yesterday I engaged my passage to Malta on board a small ....' 3 pp., quarto.

2651 Letter to William Sotheby, 17 March 1804. 'On Thursday from 10 in the morning to 4 in the afternoon I was stretched ....' 4 pp., quarto.

2652 Letter to William Sotheby, 24 March 1804. '$\frac{1}{2}$ past 2. Consequently not 20 minutes since I quitted you ....' 3 pp., quarto.

2653 Letter to William Sotheby, 26 March 1804. 'I will fill up the Letter from Portsmouth to you with the Poem ....' 1 p., quarto.

2654 Letter to Richard Sharp, [27 March 1804]. 'Need I say, that Illness has prevented our meeting ....' 2 pp., octavo.

2655 Letter to William Sotheby, [18 April 1807]. 'When I tell you that I have but this moment left my bed ....' 2 pp., quarto.

2656 Letter to William Sotheby, [c. 8 May 1807]. 'On Wednesday noon I wrote a Letter & left it with Miss Lamb ....' 2 pp., quarto.

2657 Letter to Richard Sharp, 18 December 1807. 'A most afflicting Instance of Distress has this moment been ....' $2\frac{1}{4}$ pp., quarto.

2658 Letter to William Sotheby, [28 April 1808]. 'I esteem you; and am therefore desirous of your esteem....' 4 pp., quarto.

2659 Letter to Richard Sharp, 10 October 1809. 'This is not the time to obtrude on you ....' $3\frac{1}{2}$ pp., quarto.

2660 Letter to Richard Sharp, 24 April [1812?]. 'A more favorable Star seems rising for me ....' 3 pp., quarto.

2661 Transcript, in an unidentified hand, of an excerpt from a letter to Rev. Thomas Roberts, [c. 1813]. 'You have no conception of what my sufferings ....' Inserted in the Joseph Cottle Album. 4 pp., octavo.

2662 Letter to Mr. Kenny, [spring 1813?]. 'I have just returned from the Sea side ....' 2 pp., quarto.

2663 Fragment of a letter to Joseph Porter, [15 October 1813]. '...in 100£ within a week or 10 days at farthest....' 1½ pp., quarto.

2664 Letter to [J. J. Morgan?], [November 1813?]. 'I write to day for fear you should feel disappointed ....' 2 pp., quarto.

2665 Letter to Josiah Wade, [8 December 1813]. 'I left London the Monday before last ....' 1½ pp., quarto.

2666 Letter to J. J. Morgan, [30 June 1814]. 'This small Salmon has just this Moment been sent me ....' ¾ p., quarto.

2667 Letter to [William Lisle Bowles?], [April 1815?]. 'Health and Weather permitting, I shall enjoy the pleasure ....' 4 pp., quarto.

2668 Letter to J. M. Gutch, [August–September 1815?]. 'My accursed Letterophobia, which is always in its highest ....' 4 pp., quarto.

2669 Fragment of a letter to Lancelot Wade, [13 October 1815]. 'P.S. You know Mr. Visgar of Portland Square ....' 1 p., octavo.

2670 Letter to the Rev. T. Curtis, [*c.* 1 May 1817?]. 'The Part is at the conclusion of the first ....' 1¾ pp., octavo.

2671 Letter to C. A. Tulk, 3 December 1817. 'On my return to Highgate from Little Hampton ....' 2½ pp., quarto.

2672 Letter to C. A. Tulk, 26 January 1818. 'I need not say, that any hour passed in your society would be ....' 2½ pp., quarto.

2673 Letter to [G. Frere?], [November 1818?]. 'If the weather be not too bad I shall not fail ....' 1 p., quarto.

2674 Note to [Thomas Allsop?], 26 November 1818. 'I take the liberty of addressing a prospectus ....' ¼ p., quarto. Written on the back of p. 3 of a prospectus of Coleridge's lectures on Shakespeare.

2675 Letter to James Gillman, 20 August 1819. 'Whether from the mere intensity ....' 2¼ pp., quarto.

2676 Letter of dedication to the Lord Chief Justice Abbott, November 1819. 'The liberty, now taken in soliciting your gracious acceptance ....' 1½ pp., quarto.

2677 Letter to Thomas Allsop, 10 July 1821. 'So fully had I calculated on finding you at Highgate ....' 2 pp., octavo.

2678 Letter to Thomas Allsop, [9 February 1822]. 'It is not "my way" to sit down to a Letter, with no ....' 2 pp., quarto.

2679 Letter to William Mudford, [28 May 1822]. 'I have but this moment received your note....' 1 p., quarto.

2680 Letter to Horace Twiss, 1 July 1822. 'If I am taking an improper freedom in thus obtruding ....' 1 p., quarto.

2681 Letter to Thomas Allsop, [3 August 1822]. 'I was sadly disappointed when Mr. Watson came back without ....' With a postscript by Anne Gillman. 1½ pp., quarto.

2682 Letter to Elizabeth Aders, 26 December 1822. 'O the plague of Servants! and the Egyptian Plague of *new* ....' 3 pp., quarto.

2683 Letter to Charles Aders, [January 1823?]. 'It is a maxim with me, to make Life as continuous ....' 2½ pp., quarto.

2684 Letter to Thomas Allsop, [30 April 1823]. 'Can you give me a bed for tomorrow ....' 1 p., quarto.

2685 Letter to Mr. Gisborne, 24 August 1823. 'When I had last the pleasure of seeing you ....' 2 pp., quarto.

2686 Letter to Mr. Bohte, 9 October 1823. 'The Bearer, Mr. John Watson, is a very dear and particular Friend ....' 2 pp., quarto.

2687 Letter to Alaric Watts, [3 December 1823]. 'A very severe Cold caught by me ....' 3 pp., quarto.

2688 Letter to Mrs. J. H. Green, [7] January 1824. 'Mrs. Gillman requests me to become her ....' 1½ pp., quarto.

2689 Letter to [a Member of the Managing Committee of the London Institution], 19 February 1824. 'Your Letter of this morning occasioned the discovery of your former ....' 2 pp., quarto.

2690 Letter to George Skinner, 26 April '1820' [for 1824]. 'Mr. Gillman much regretted his absence ....' 2 pp., octavo.

2691 Letter to James Gillman, 2 November 1824. 'That so much longer an interval has passed between this and my last ....' 4 pp., quarto.

2692 Letter to James Gillman, [29 November 1824]. 'Often, even to a commonplace frequency, have the World without ....' 4 pp., quarto.

2693 Letter to [Charles Aders?], 16 January 1825. 'So stiff-necked are we in looking over our own ....' 2 pp., quarto.

2694 Transcript [in the hand of Thomas Allsop?] of a letter to [Sir Humphry Davy], [February 1825?]. 'Will you permit an old Friend, who (as you are now aware) ....' 4 pp., quarto.

2695 Letter to James Gillman, 16 October 1825. 'I have nothing to say—and too short a warning ....' Part of a leaf cut away. 3½ pp., quarto.

2696 Letter to James Gillman, 16 November 1825. 'On the receipt of your kind Letter, Mrs. Steck having in ....' 3 pp., quarto.

2697 Letter to [Charles Aders], [December 1825?]. 'Tho' it has been long since I have seen you except for a few ....' 2 pp., octavo.

2698 Letter to Derwent Coleridge, [c. 25 January 1826?]. 'Experto credes? That the most heart-withering Sorrow ....' 3 pp., 16mo.

2699 Letter to Elizabeth Aders, 3 June 1826. 'I wish that word, friend, had not been so soiled ....' 1½ pp., quarto.

2700 Letter to C. A. Tulk, 17 August 1826. 'Mr. Gillman being *called out* ....' 1¼ pp., quarto.

2701 Letter to C. A. Tulk, 20 September 1826. 'Tho' I always considered my friend Gillman as a Man of Business ....' 2½ pp., quarto.

2702 Letter to Elizabeth Aders, [c. 1 December 1826]. 'My dear Friend, and (by the privilege of silvery locks ....' 4 pp., quarto.

2703 Letter to Thomas Allsop, 1 February 1827. 'You do not know me if you think that even a week ....' 1½ pp., quarto.

2704 Letter to Henry F. Cary, May 1827. 'I have been just looking, rather staring, at Croly's Revelations ....' 4 pp., quarto.

2705 Letter to Anne Gillman, 3 May 1827. 'I received and acknowledge your this morning's Presenting both ....' 2¾ pp., octavo.

2706 Letter to S. C. Hall, 15 January 1828. 'The afflicting (humanly speaking, and to all who survive ....' 1 p., quarto.

2707 Letter to William Sotheby, [c. 5 May 1828]. 'I have to beg your pardon for the delay in answering ....' 2½ pp., octavo.

2708 Letter to James Gillman, 22 October 1828. 'That the cargo real and personal was shipped on board the Dart ....' Part of a leaf torn away. 2¼ pp., quarto.

2709 Letter to [John Anster?], [July 1829?]. 'You desire me to exclude from the consideration what cannot be excluded ....' 3½ pp., quarto.

2710 Letter to James Gillman, Jr., 10 August [1829?]. 'It will give you pleasure, I know, to receive a Letter ....' 2 pp., quarto.

2711 Letter to William Pickering, [c. 30 September 1829?]. 'I beg you ten thousand pardons ....' 1½ pp., quarto.

2712 Letter to James Gillman, Jr., [11 August 1830]. 'I was both affected and gratified by your last Letter ....' 4 pp., quarto.

2713 Letter to William Sotheby, 14 June 1831. 'The Gentleman, who will leave this at your house ....' 2 pp., quarto.

2714 Letter to Charles Stutfield, 21 August 1831. 'I thank you for your very kind letter ....' 1¾ pp., quarto.

2715 Letter to Charles Aders, 11 February 1832. 'If my memory has not deceived me or rather if my *fancy* ....' 3 pp., quarto.

2716 Letter to Messrs. Baldwin & Cradock, 29 June 1832. 'In very truth I owe an apology (I wish I could ....' 1 p., quarto.

2717 Letter to [J. B. Williams?], 12 October 1832. 'This Work has risen in public estimation ....' Written apparently on the blank leaf of a book. 1 p., octavo.

2718 Transcript, in the hand of the recipient, of a letter to Elizabeth Aders, [1833?]. 'By my idleness or oversight I have occasioned a very sweet ....' 3 pp., quarto.

2719 Letter to Thomas Pringle, [13 August 1833]. 'My only motive for wishing to learn, whether your Volume ....' 3 pp., octavo.

2720 Transcript, in the hand of Frederick Pfeffel, of a letter to Charles Aders, 18 August 1833. 'Forgive me for wasting any portion of your valuable ....' 3 pp., quarto.

2721 Letter to William Pickering, 8 April 1834. 'Be so good as to let Master Edward Parry, the Bearer ....' 1 p., octavo.

ARTHUR DUKE COLERIDGE

2722 Letter to [John T. Barker], [*c.* 1855]. 'I am unpleasantly reminded this afternoon of a long ....' 1 p., octavo.

2723 Letter to [John T. Barker], [*c.* 1855]. 'I trust you will forgive the liberty I take ....' 2 pp., octavo.

DERWENT COLERIDGE

2724 Letter to Mary Coleridge (his wife), 16 January 1831. 'Having obtained a frank from Praed for tomorrow ....' With a postscript by W. M. Praed. 2½ pp., quarto.

2725 Letter to John T. Barker, 2 June 1855. 'I have not yet had an opportunity of conferring with my relative ....' 4 pp., octavo.

GEORGE COLERIDGE

2726 Letter to Lord ——, 25 January 1801. 'About two months since I was presented with a Writ ....' 3 pp., quarto.

HARTLEY COLERIDGE

2727 Poem entitled To Wordsworth; dated Spring 1839. 'Yes mighty poet we have read thy lines.' 1 p., quarto.

JOHN TAYLOR COLERIDGE

2728 Letter to [William B. Reed], 28 March 1856. 'I am but just returned from my circuit ....' 8 pp., octavo.

SARA COLERIDGE, Wife of S.T.C.

2729 Letter to Thomas De Quincey, [*c.* 1810]. 'Permit me to return you my best thanks for your goodness ....' 2 pp., quarto.

SARA COLERIDGE, Daughter of S.T.C.

2730 A commentary on Henry Reed's *Memoir of Gray*. 6 pp., folio.

2731 A note, unaddressed, July 1827. 'Derwent says he shd be very grateful for a scrap of Mr. W's handwriting.' With a 'List of Books for Derwent.' 2 pp., octavo.

2732 Letter to an unidentified correspondent, 18 August 1847. 'Your obliging communication has just reached ....' 4 pp., octavo.

2733 Letter to Henry Reed, 21 April 1849. 'I will not wait till I can have a conference ....' 4 pp., quarto.

2734 Letter to Benjamin Bailey, 18 June 1849. 'I have deferred acknowledging the receipt of your very interesting ....' 4 pp., quarto.

2735 Letter to Benjamin Bailey, 29 June 1850. 'I began a letter to you before I left home ....' 16 pp., folio.

2736 Letter to Henry Reed, 3 July 1850. 'How many months ago did I think to write ....' 10 pp., quarto.

2737 Letter to Henry Reed, 22 July 1850. 'I was unable to despatch my letter to you ....' 2 pp., quarto.

2738 Letter to Benjamin Bailey, 30–1 October 1850. 'I am glad to learn where to send the copy of my Father's ....' 8 pp., quarto.

2739 Letter to Henry Reed, 29 November 1850. 'Many thanks to you for two most interesting volumes ....' 4 pp., quarto.

2740 Letter to Henry Reed, 19–21 May 1851. 'Your late communications have interested me ....' 14 pp., quarto.

2741 Letter to Benjamin Bailey, 2 July 1851. 'On my return home from Margate yesterday ....' 10 pp., folio.

2742 Letter to Benjamin Bailey, 1 August 1851. 'I have just finished a slow perusal of your Political Sketches ....' 4 pp., octavo.

2743 Transcript of a letter to Mr. Blackburne, 28 September [1851?]. 'Thank you, dear Mr. Blackburne ....' 1 p., quarto.

2744 Transcript of a letter to Mr. Blackburne, 13 October 1851. 'I must not omit now to thank you ....' 2 pp., quarto.

2745 Letter to Benjamin Bailey, 16 December 1851. 'I now begin to fear that it may not be in my power to peruse ....' 6 pp., quarto.

2746 Letter to Henry Reed, 22 December 1851. 'Many weeks ago I heard from Mr. Yarnall ....' 4 pp., quarto.

2747 Letter to Benjamin Bailey, 30 December 1851. 'Since I wrote the accompanying letter, I have had a little rise ....' 3 pp., quarto.

2748 Letter to Mrs. Scott, no date. 'I mean to call at your door at a Gothic hour tomorrow ....' 4 pp., 16mo.

2749 Fragment of a letter to an unidentified correspondent concerning Wordsworth's later poetry. 6 pp., octavo.

MANUSCRIPTS OF ASSOCIATIVE INTEREST

ADARE, E. R. W. WYNDHAM-QUIN, VISCOUNT

2750 Letter to William Wordsworth, 3 April 1838. 'I should have immediately replied to your letter ....' 3 pp., octavo.

2751 Letter to William Wordsworth, [May 1838]. 'I should indeed be wanting in every right feeling ....' 2 pp., octavo.

ADERS, CHARLES

2752 Letter to [William Wordsworth?], [*c*. June 1828]. 'I enclose you your Passport & Letters of introduction ....' 1½ pp., quarto.

ADERS, ELIZABETH

2753 A collection of twenty-seven letters to John T. Barker, some of which concern the sale of the Coleridge letters written to Charles and Elizabeth Aders; *c.* 1855. 65 pp., various sizes.

AGUTTER, WILLIAM

2754 An Account of the Death of the Late Mr. Henderson, Who Died at Oxford the 2d Day of November 1788. Undated. Accompanying the manuscript is an engraved portrait of John Henderson, subject of Agutter's Account and father of Richard Henderson, Joseph Cottle's tutor and adviser. Inserted in the Joseph Cottle Album. ½ p., quarto.

AGLIONBY, FRANCIS

2755 Letter to William Wordsworth, 26 March 1838. 'I feel much flattered by your remembrance of me ....' 3 pp., octavo.

ALLSOP, THOMAS

2756 Letter to S. T. Coleridge, 5 December 1818. 'I was highly gratified by your letter ....' 2¼ pp., quarto.

2757 Letter to Derwent Coleridge, [21 January 1824]. 'I have deferred writing untill I fear you will allow ....' 4 pp., quarto.

2758 Letter to S. T. Coleridge, 2 November 1825. 'I have written several letters to you and torn them up ....' 3 pp., quarto.

2759 Letter to S. T. Coleridge, no date. 'I had purposed to have walked to Highgate yester morning ....' 2 pp., quarto.

2760 Letter to S. T. Coleridge, no date. 'I am about to embark in this little process of machinery ....' 4 pp., quarto.

ALLSTON, WASHINGTON

2761 Transcript, in an unidentified hand, 'for my *still* dear friend Mrs. Gillman of Highgate,' of Washington Allston's Sonnet on the Late Samuel Taylor Coleridge. 1 p., quarto.

ARNOLD, DR. THOMAS

2762 Letter to [Derwent Coleridge], 31 December 1840. 'The very same Post which brought your Letter brought me ....' 3 pp., octavo.

ATTWOOD, MATTHIAS

2763 Letter to William Wordsworth, 30 March 1838. 'When I had the pleasure of meeting you at Lowther ....' 3 pp., octavo.

2764 Letter to William Wordsworth, 29 April 1838. 'I gave my vote with much satisfaction in support ....' 5 pp., octavo.

BAILEY, BENJAMIN

2765 Notes on Coleridge's *Essays on His Own Times*, for Sara Coleridge. 2 pp., octavo.

2766 Letter to the third Earl Grey, 10 May 1851. 'Sir J. Emerson Tennent's evidence before the Committee ....' $2\frac{1}{2}$ pp., quarto.

2767 Letter to Edward John, Lord Stanley, 13 October 1857. 'I trust you will forgive the liberty I take in sending you copies ....' 3 pp., quarto.

BARKER, JOHN T.

2768 Letter to Arthur Duke Coleridge, 18 May 1855. 'The facts of the case which Mr. Furnivall mentioned ....' 3 pp., octavo.

2769 Copy of a letter to Derwent Coleridge, 30 June 1855. 'In consequence of absence from home ....' $3\frac{1}{2}$ pp., octavo.

2770 Letter to David Masson, 16 December 1864. 'I have been prevented by domestic anxieties ....' 3 pp., octavo.

BARTON, BERNARD

2771 Letter to Edward Moxon, 12 July 1830. 'Of all the petty & dirty pieces of Criticism, or what goes for such ....' 3 pp., octavo.

2772 Letter to [Horatio Smith], 31 May 1847. 'I pray thee forgive, or at any rate patiently endure ....' 4 pp., quarto.

BEDDOES, DR. THOMAS

2773 Poem entitled: Verses on a Cornish Lady Who Was Prevailed upon to Dance with a National Cockade in 1790. Three four-line stanzas signed and dated 14 July 1796. Written in the Joseph Cottle Album.

BOWLES, CAROLINE, later Mrs. Southey

2774 Letter to Robert Southey, 21 July 1826. 'At Keswick as soon as you!...' 1 p., quarto. See also Nos. 3085–6.

BROCKEDON, WILLIAM

2775 Notes on travelling in Italy, prepared for Wordsworth and endorsed by him 'Mr. Brockendon's [*sic*] Directions.' No date. Begins: 'Travelling to Lyons from Paris in your own carriage . . . .' 4½ pp., quarto.

BROUGHAM, HENRY, later Lord Brougham

2776 Letter to [John Saunders of Plymouth], 5 July 1811. 'I take the liberty of requesting your assistance . . . .' Inserted in the Joseph Cottle Album. 3 pp., quarto.

2777 Letter to [Messrs. Saunders and Williams of Plymouth], 1 August 1811. 'I have received your letter of the 30th . . . .' Inserted in the Joseph Cottle Album. 2½ pp., quarto.

[BROWNING], ELIZABETH BARRETT

2778 Letter to [Hugh Stuart-Boyd], 26 November 1842. 'I have not sent your verses as you desired me to do . . . .' 8pp., 16mo.

BROWNING, ROBERT

2779 Letter to A. W. Colles, 11 February 1887. 'I have confessed in print long ago that I took some characteristics of Wordsworth . . . .' 2 pp., octavo.

BYRON, GEORGE GORDON, LORD

2780 Holograph of an unfinished prose story, dated 6 February 1823. 'In the year 18— a young Englishman had resided for some time in the Italian City . . . .' Bound with an envelope addressed by Byron to John Murray bearing a large, clear example of Byron's seal. 4¼ pp., quarto.

2781 Letter to R. C. Dallas, 10 September 1811. 'I rather think in one of the opening stanzas of C[hild]e H[arol]d . . . .' 1 p., quarto.

2782 Letter to J. C. Hobhouse, [1818?]. 'I hope that you or Mr. Gifford will do me the favour . . . .' 1 p., quarto.

CADELL, ROBERT

2783 Letter to Sir Robert Inglis, 7 May [1838]. 'I took upon me to submit to Serjeant Talfourd today the enclosed . . . .' 3½ pp., quarto.

CALDWELL, GEORGE

2784 Letter to Thomas Barrett Lennard, 17 March [1813]. 'I am quite ashamed when I look at the date of your letter . . . .' 4 pp., octavo.

CALLCOTT, AUGUSTUS WALL

2785 Letter to William Wordsworth, together with two long enclosures which are endorsed by Wordsworth: 'Mr Callcott's directions for works of Art in Germany' and 'Mr Hallam also on Germany.' No date; paper watermarked 1833. 2 pp., octavo and 18 pp., quarto.

CARLYLE, THOMAS

2786 Letter to Leigh Hunt, no date. 'Count Pepole, who is at present Candidate ....' 1 p., 16mo.

2787 Letter to Leigh Hunt, no date. 'I have just received a Letter from Mill ....' 1 p., octavo.

CARR, THOMAS

2788 Letter to William Wordsworth, [1838]. 'It appears to me, that the only parties interested in the Copy-right ....' 2 pp., folio.

CHESTER, JOHN

2789 Letter to Thomas Allsop, 28 September 1837. 'I herewith send you a sketch of poor Coleridge's House at Stowey ....' Enclosed is a pencil drawing of Nether Stowey. 1 p., quarto and the drawing.

CLARKE, SAMUEL

2790 Letter to John T. Barker, 4 June 1855. 'I should have replied to your note on Saturday ....' 2 pp., octavo.

2791 Letter to John T. Barker, 13 June 1855. 'I was not able to see Mr. Derwent Coleridge ....' 2 pp., octavo.

2792 Letter to John T. Barker, 14 June 1855. 'I have just got your note, which must have ....' 1 p., octavo.

2793 Letter to John T. Barker, 16 June 1855. 'My *last* note was written under the impression ....' 1½ pp., octavo.

CLARKSON, THOMAS

2794 Letter to Samuel Robinson, 21 August 1822. 'When I was with you on the 9th or 10th of May last ....' Inserted in the Joseph Cottle Album. 3 pp., quarto.

COLVIN, SIDNEY

2795 Letter to Mr. Armstrong, 12 July [1889?]. 'The Lippmanns are old friends of mine ....' 1 p., 16mo.

COTTLE, AMOS SIMON

2796 Poem: A Fable, the Glow-Worm and Grasshopper. Undated, but probably of 1796. Written in the Joseph Cottle Album. 3 pp., folio.

COTTLE, JOSEPH

2797 An album, once the property of Joseph Cottle, first publisher of *Lyrical Ballads*, containing sixty documents, some of them annotated by Cottle. The book measures 12½ × 8 in., is bound in leather, and contains seventy-nine leaves, the first of which is labelled: 'Bristol Album, 1795.' The material ranges from 1795 to 1844. The following pieces (each described under its proper alphabetical position elsewhere in this Catalogue) are present:

William Wordsworth: Remembrance of Collins, Written on the Thames near Richmond; A Grave Stone on the Floor of the Cloisters of Worcester Cathedral; a printed copy of Grace Darling; letter to Cottle, 19 August 1837; letter to Cottle, 4 April 1844. Dorothy Wordsworth: letter to Cottle, 31 July 1828. Samuel Taylor Coleridge: The Eolian Harp; Lines Written at the King's Arms, Ross; To the Princess of Wales; receipt for £300 from an unknown friend (i.e., De Quincey); letter to Cottle, 5 November 1796; letter to Cottle, 18 October 1796; transcript of an excerpt from a letter to Rev. Thomas Roberts, *c.* 1813. William Agutter: An Account of the Death of the Late Mr. Henderson. Dr. Thomas Beddoes: Verses on a Cornish Lady. Henry Brougham: letter to John Saunders, 5 July 1811; letter to Saunders and Williams, 1 August 1811. Thomas Chatterton: portrait of, engraved by Woodman from an alleged portrait by Branwhite, presented to Cottle by John Dix. Thomas Clarkson: letter to Samuel Robinson, 21 August 1822. Amos Simon Cottle: A Fable, the Glow-worm and Grasshopper. Joseph Cottle: list of the autographs in his possession. William Cowper: rhyming letter to John Newton, 12 July 1781. Thomas De Quincey: letter to Joseph Cottle, 14 October 1807. John Foster: letter to [Joseph Cottle], [November 1824]; letter to Joseph Cottle, no date. Charles Fox: two poems in Persian; To Selima; On Luxury; another poem. William Gilbert: The Aurora of Human Happiness. [James Haliburton]: The Lord's Prayer in the Batta Language. Robert Hall: letter to Joseph Cottle, 30 April 1801; letter to Joseph Cottle, 11 June 1824. Matthew Henry (1662–1714): notes for a sermon, 14 December 1693. Philip Henry (1631–96): notes for a sermon, 10 March 1656/57; notes for a sermon, no date. Charles Lloyd: Dirge Occasion'd by an Infant's Death. Robert Lovell: Sonnet on Stonehenge. [Hannah More]: letter to John Henderson, 11 April 1788. J. J. Morgan: note to Samuel Taylor Coleridge, October 1807. Mary Newton (sister of Chatterton): copy of a letter to Joseph Cottle, 17 October 1802. John Rose: Sonnet to Contentment. John Ryland, notes for sermons, November 1786. Thomas Skone: poem, transcribed by George Symes Catcott. Robert Southey: English Dactylics to a Soldier's Wife; Sonnet to Mary Cottle; two pages of the manuscript of Joan of Arc; Specimen of English Sapphics; a ticket to his lectures; The Well of St. Keyne; letter in verse to Joseph Cottle, 9 May 1800; letter to Joseph Cottle, 2 November 1806; part of a letter to Joseph Cottle,

18 June 1807; transcript of an excerpt from a letter to Joseph Cottle, no date. Anne Steele: letter to Grace Cottle, 18 May 1761. [Sir F. C. Williams]: On a Faded Cowslip Presented to Me by Anna. Unidentified writers: poem to Evening; Extempore Lines on the Vale of Oldland in Gloucestershire; excerpt from Henry Mackenzie's Man of Feeling; part of a letter to James Montgomery, quoting Henry Mackenzie on Wordsworth and Southey.

COWIE, J. N.

2798 Letter to Derwent Coleridge, 18 January 1858. 'I did not acknowledge your note at once ....' 2 pp., octavo.

COWPER, WILLIAM

2799 Letter to Rev. John Newton, 12 July 1781, in rhymed verse. 'My very dear Friend, I am going to send, what when you have read, you may scratch your head ....' This is the original manuscript of the celebrated 'Hop o' My Thumb' letter. Inserted in the Joseph Cottle Album. 1½ pp., folio.

CRESWELL, CRESSWELL

2800 Letter to William Wordsworth, [1838]. 'I beg to thank you for the very flattering note ....' 1½ pp., octavo.

DALRYMPLE, AUGUSTUS JOHN

2801 Letter to William Wordsworth, 6 April 1838. 'I have been a good deal occupied lately ....' 3½ pp., octavo.

2802 Letter to William Wordsworth, 25 April [1838]. 'Sjt. Talfourd has been speaking very eloquently ....' 2½ pp., octavo.

DARLING, GRACE

2803 Letter to Henry Birt, 14 March 1840. 'I recd your kind letter Dated 2d Inst. and am truly gratefull ....' 1 p., quarto.

DE QUINCEY, THOMAS

2804 *Notes on Wordsworth's Convention of Cintra*, with the heavily revised and much re-written draft of the 'Postscript on Sir John Moore's Letters' which comprises pp. 206–16 of De Quincey's Appendix to Wordsworth's book. The Appendix seems to be the first of De Quincey's prose to be published. Bound in full morocco under the title: *Review of the Letters of Sir John Moore*. 74 pp., quarto.

2805 Essay in the form of a letter to William Tait, editor of *Tait's Magazine*, entitled: Letter to Mr. T. concerning the Poetry of Wordsworth, and dated

16 May 1836. Not to be confused with De Quincey's essay entitled On Words-worth's Poetry, which appeared in *Tait's* in September 1845. 10 pp., quarto.

2806 The proof sheets of *Autobiography of an English Opium-eater: Recollections of Charles Lamb*; in the format of *Tait's Magazine*, June 1838. Eight double-column pages, heavily corrected and annotated in De Quincey's hand. The alterations here indicated appear neither in *Tait's* nor in the Masson edition of De Quincey's writings.

2807 Two quarto pages of manuscript, heavily altered, from De Quincey's *Autobiography*, beginning: 'Those who know Oxford are aware of the peculiar feelings which have gathered about the name and pretensions of Christ Church.' See his *Collected Writings*, Edinburgh, 1890, vol. 2, pp. 25–7.

2808 Two quarto pages of manuscript, not identified with any of De Quincey's published writing, concerning his literary life. The text begins: 'Looking back-wards through my past life, and especially with a reference to my literary experience, I may divide it into three periods.'

2809 Two quarto pages of De Quincey's remarks on Charles Lamb, most of it published in the *Collected Writings*, vol. 5, pp. 253–6. The text begins: 'On the tea-table lay a copy of Wordsworth in 2 Vols; it was the edition of Longman, printed about the time of Waterloo.'

2810 Two quarto pages, heavily revised in De Quincey's hand, concerning Robert Burns. The manuscript is without date; it begins: 'I, in this year 1801, when in the company of Dr. Currie, did not forget ....' The material has not been identified with any of De Quincey's published writings.

2811 Letter to Joseph Cottle, 14 October 1807. 'I will write for the 300£ to-morrow ....' Inserted in the Joseph Cottle Album, together with Coleridge's receipt for £300, received at the hands of Cottle from 'an unknown Friend,' i.e., De Quincey. ½ p., quarto.

2812 Letter to William Wordsworth, 1 April 1818. 'With my utmost diligence I have not been able to finish ....' ¼ p., quarto.

2813 Letter to William Wordsworth, 19 July 1829. 'I write to thank you and Mr. John Wordsworth ....' 2 pp., octavo.

EASTLAKE, C. L.

2814 Letter to Derwent Coleridge, 15 June 1853. 'Make any use of my name you please....' 2 pp., octavo.

2815 Letter to W. Richmond, 2 December 1859. 'I beg to acknowledge the receipt this day of your circular ....' 2 pp., octavo.

ELLIS, JOHN

2816 Letter to William Wordsworth, 28 April 1838. 'I have no doubt that you will hear today from other ....' 6 pp., octavo.

EVERETT, EDWARD

2817 Letter to Henry Taylor, 28 May 1850. 'It is a great while since I have written ....' 4 pp., quarto.

FENWICK, ISABELLA

2818 Letter to Henry Reed, 31 August 1853. 'I have received through Mrs. Wordsworth ....' 3 pp., quarto.

FIELDS, JAMES T.

2819 Letter to Henry Reed, 9 November 1850. 'In reply to yours of the 7th I beg to say ....' 1 p., octavo.

FORSTER, CHARLES

2820 Letter to Benjamin Bailey, 31 January 1850. 'In reply to your repeated friendly inquiries ....' 4 pp., quarto.

2821 Letter to Benjamin Bailey, 27 June 1850. 'Your full and most interesting letter of May 6 ....' $3\frac{1}{2}$ pp., quarto.

2822 Letter to [Benjamin Bailey?], 4 February 1851. 'One line of thanks for your last kind ....' 1 p., octavo.

2823 Letter to Benjamin Bailey, 31 May 1851. 'The India Mail (D.V.) must not go out ....' 4 pp., octavo.

2824 Letter to Benjamin Bailey, 1 December 1851. 'I have to thank you for your several ....' 8 pp., octavo.

2825 Letter to Benjamin Bailey, 3 February 1852. 'I write you from a sick house; this whole family ....' 3 pp., octavo.

2826 Letter to Benjamin Bailey, 5 April 1852. 'As Lord Derby is Premier, and Lord Stanley ....' 4 pp., octavo.

FOSTER, JOHN

2827 Letter to [Joseph Cottle?], [November 1824]. 'Not having heard you mention Mr. Sheppard's book ....' Inserted in the Joseph Cottle Album. 1 p., octavo.

2828 Letter to Joseph Cottle, no date. 'I had reckoned on passing a few hours with you ....' Inserted in the Joseph Cottle Album. 1½ pp., quarto.

FOX, CHARLES

2829 Two brief poems in Persian. Written in the Joseph Cottle Album, probably in 1796.

2830 Poem: To Selima. Four four-line stanzas, signed and dated 27 June 1796. Written in the Joseph Cottle Album. ½ p., folio.

2831 Poem: On Luxury. Eight lines, signed, without date but probably of 1796. Written in the Joseph Cottle Album.

2832 Poem: 'Tho' yon proud Khan with elephantine port.' Twelve lines, signed and dated July 1796. Written in the Joseph Cottle Album.

FURNIVALL, FRANCIS J.

2833 Letter to John T. Barker, [1855]. 'I have classes from 8 to 10 ....' 2 pp., octavo.

GILBERT, WILLIAM

2834 Poem: The Aurora of Human Happiness, an Ode. Signed and dated 26 May 1795. Written in the Joseph Cottle Album. 1½ pp., folio.

GILLMAN, ANNE

2835 Letter to Thomas Allsop, [post 1820]. 'The sight of your hand-writing, my dear Mr. Allsop ....' 2½ pp., quarto.

2836 Letter to Thomas Allsop, [post 1820]. 'I thank you for sending the blond but I was obliged to get some ....' 2 pp., quarto.

2837 Letter to Thomas Allsop, [post 1820]. 'I am grieved at your account of yourself ....' 3 pp., quarto.

2838 Letter to Thomas Allsop, [post 1820]. 'I should have written before, but I waited in the hope ....' 3 pp., octavo.

2839 Letter to Thomas Allsop, 12 September [1821]. 'Your letter, my very dear young friend, was most welcome ....' 2½ pp., quarto.

2840 Letter to S. T. Coleridge, 7 April, no year given. 'I was in hopes I should hear from our kind friend Mr. A ....' 3½ pp., quarto.

2841 Letter to [Thomas Allsop?], no date. 'Your affectionate little Note is lying open before me ....' 3¼ pp., octavo.

GILLMAN, JAMES

2842 Manuscript entitled: A Short Account of Mr. Coleridge's Personal Sufferings and Their Physical Causes. No date. 2 pp., octavo.

2843 Letter to Thomas Hurst, 3 January 1835. 'I should be obliged to you to send me Fraser's Magazine ....' 1 p., quarto.

GOMM, WILLIAM

2844 Letter to William Wordsworth, 30 March 1838. 'Although I am not returning so ready a reply ....' 7 pp., octavo.

GRAHAM, SIR J. R. G.

2845 Letter to William Wordsworth, 30 March 1838. 'I am disposed on any account to pay the utmost attention ....' 2 pp., octavo.

GRANVILLE, GRANVILLE LEVESON-GOWER, EARL

2846 Letter to Thomas Babington Macaulay, 15 February 1856. 'I have not lost a moment in writing to Lord Palmerston....' 1 p., octavo.

HALIBURTON (formerly BURTON), JAMES

2847 A slip entitled: The Lord's Prayer in the Batta Language by Mr. Burton. With seven lines of script. Inserted in the Joseph Cottle Album.

HALL, ROBERT

2848 Letter to Joseph Cottle, 30 April 1801. 'I return you my sincere [thanks] for the very handsome present ....' Inserted in the Joseph Cottle Album. 3 pp., quarto.

2849 Letter to Joseph Cottle, 11 June 1824. 'I have received very attentively the [second] edition of your strictures ....' Inserted in the Joseph Cottle Album. $3\frac{1}{2}$ pp., quarto.

HAMILTON, J.

2850 Letter to Mary Wordsworth, no date. 'Lady Pasley and Miss Bainbridge intended to have the pleasure ....' 3 pp., octavo.

HAMILTON, WILLIAM ROWAN

2851 Letter to Robert Southey, 10 August 1830. 'Being aware that there had been sickness ....' $2\frac{1}{2}$ pp., octavo.

HARDMAN, J.

2852 Letter to Elizabeth Aders, [*c.* 1855]. 'Mrs. Gillman, I am happy to say, is in greatly improved health ....' 1 p., octavo.

HATHERLY, WILLIAM PAGE WOOD, LORD

2853 Letter to Derwent Coleridge, 19 December 1879. 'It is long since we met and I gladly avail myself ....' 1 p., quarto.

HAZLITT, WILLIAM

2854 Letter to [William Godwin], 5 January 1806. 'I inclose this for you in a parcel conveying to Johnson ....' 1 p., quarto.

HENRY, MATTHEW (1662–1714)

2855 Notes for a sermon, in minute handwriting. Inserted in the Joseph Cottle Album. 8 pp., 16mo.

HENRY, PHILIP (1631–96)

2856 Notes for a sermon, written in minute handwriting in a home-made booklet. Dated 10 March 1656/57. With a note to Joseph Cottle from C. J. Whittuck concerning its provenance. Inserted in the Joseph Cottle Album. The notebook measures $4\frac{1}{4} \times 3$ in. and contains 16 pp. Philip Henry was the father of Matthew Henry (see above); both were dissenting clergymen.

2857 Notes for a sermon, undated, in minute handwriting. Inserted in the Joseph Cottle Album. 4 pp., 16mo.

HOOK, W. F.

2858 Letter to Derwent Coleridge, 16 September 1851. 'Your letter found me at Derwent Isle and what with climbing ....' 10 pp., octavo.

HORSMAN, EDWARD

2859 Letter to William Wordsworth, 19 April [1838]. 'I trust you will be good enough to excuse my having ....' $3\frac{1}{2}$ pp., quarto.

2860 Letter to William Wordsworth, 30 April 1838. 'I was favored with your letter on my arrival in town ....' 10 pp., octavo.

HOWARD, PHILIP

2861 Letter to William Wordsworth, 11 April 1838. 'I fear that you have deemed me wanting in attention ....' 4 pp., octavo.

HUNT, W. HOLMAN

2862 Letter to Mrs. Leslie, no date. 'I am so very sorry not to be able to accept your invitation ....' 1 p., octavo.

2863 Letter to Mrs. Derwent Coleridge, no date. 'Mr. W. Holman Hunt will have great pleasure in accepting ....' 1 p., octavo.

Written on the Thames near Richmond

How rich the wave in front, impress'd
With evening-twilights summer hues,
While, facing thus the crimson west,
The boat her magic path pursues,
Nor heeds how dark the backward stream,
Of face, a moment past, so smiling!
—And still, perhaps, with faithless gleam
Some other loiterer beguiling.

Such views the youthful bard allure,
And, thoughtless of the following gloom,
He deems their colours shall endure
Till Peace go with him to the tomb.
And such did once the *Poet bless   *Collins
Who, pouring here a later² ditty,   ²hisode on the
Could find no refuge from distress   death of Thomson
But in the milder grief of Pity.   among the last of
                                          his composition.

Remembrance! as we glide along
For him suspend the dashing oar;
And pray that never Child of Song
May know his freezing sorrows more.
How calm! how still! — the only sound
The dripping of the oar suspended!
— A moral darkness deepens round,
By virtue's holiest powers attended.

March 29. 1797 —   W. Wordsworth

An Early Manuscript Poem of Wordsworth.   No. 2797

To the Princess of Wales
written during her separation from the Prince.

I sigh, fair injur'd Stranger! for thy fate —
But what shall sighs avail thee? Thy poor Heart
'Mid all "the pomp and circumstance" of State
Shivers in nakedness. Unbidden start
Sad Recollections of Hope's garish dream
That shap'd a seraph form, & nam'd it Love,
Its hues gay-varying as the Orient Beam
Varies the neck of Cytherea's Dove.

To one soft accent of domestic joy
Poor are the Shouts that shake the high-arch'd Dome;
Those Plaudits, that thy public path annoy,
Alas! they tell thee — Thou'rt a Wretch at home!

O then retire and weep! Their very Woes
Solace the Guiltless. Drop the pearly flood
On thy sweet Infant, as the full-blown Rose
Surcharg'd with dew bends o'er its neighb'ring Bud.

And ah! that Truth some holy spell could lend
To lure thy Wanderer from the Syren's Power;
Then bid your Souls inseparably blend
Like two bright Dew-drops meeting in a Flower!

                                    S. T. Coleridge
                                        July, 1796

‡ alluding to the Plaudits with which the Princess
was received at the Opera house during her
separation.

INGLIS, SIR ROBERT

2864 Letter to William Wordsworth, 26 April 1838. 'We have *not* been defeated ....' 2 pp., octavo.

2865 Letter to William Wordsworth, 28 April 1838. 'I am extremely obliged to you for your letter ....' 3 pp., octavo.

2866 Letter to William Wordsworth, 8 May 1838. 'What do you think of the enclosed?...' 1 p., octavo.

2867 Letter to William Wordsworth, 12 May 1838. 'I could not have received your prose without an instant ....' 2½ pp., octavo.

IRTON, SAMUEL

2868 Letter to William Wordsworth, 26 March 1838. 'I fear I shall not be in the House ....' 2 pp., octavo.

JAMES, WILLIAM

2869 Letter to William Wordsworth, 26 March 1838. 'I have not yet seen Serjeant Talfourd's Bill ....' 1 p., octavo.

JOHNSTON, WILLIAM

2870 Letter to William Wordsworth, 24 April 1838. 'Having written some articles which were published ....' 3 pp., quarto.

KEATS, JOHN

2871 Stanzas xxix and xxxii of Keats's poem Isabella ('They told their Sister how with sudden speed' and 'In the mid days of Autumn, on their eves'), a part of the manuscript once in the possession of Joseph Severn, who cut it into portions. Endorsed: 'MS of Keats from J. S., Rome, Feb: 1833, T. H. Cromeck.'

KINGSLEY, CHARLES, SENIOR

2872 Letter to Derwent Coleridge, 24 March 1845. 'I trust that you will come to the vestry to *vote only* ....' 1 p., octavo.

KINGSLEY, CHARLES, JUNIOR

2873 Letter to Derwent Coleridge, 3 January 1854. 'You have of course seen the proposed address ....' 2 pp., octavo.

2874 Letter to Mrs. Derwent Coleridge, 12 December 1864. 'It is a great pleasure to me to hear from you....' 7 pp., octavo.

KNIGHT, WILLIAM ANGUS

2875 A collection of 166 letters addressed to Knight, nearly all of them concerning Wordsworth or Coleridge, by various correspondents. Among the letter-writers are the following: Ernest Hartley Coleridge (3), J. K. Quillinan (4), Gordon Graham Wordsworth (11), J. R. Tutin (8), J. Dykes Campbell (21), Edward Dowden (7), Frances Arnold, H. D. Rawnsley, Thomas Hutchinson, Florence De Quincey, Alfred Ainger, Richard Garnett, and Charles Southey.

LAMB, CHARLES

2876 Letter to Thomas Manning, [June 1800]. 'I am a Letter in your Debt, but I am scarcely rich enough ....' 1 p., folio.

2877 Letter to Mrs. Clarkson, [1807]. 'I ought to have written to you before, but I expected ....' 2¼ pp., quarto.

2878 Letter to S. T. Coleridge, [26 August 1814]. 'Let thy hungry soul rejoice. There is corn in Egypt ....' 3 pp., quarto.

2879 Letter to J. A. Hessey, [May 1825?]. 'I am very poorly indeed and fear I shall have nothing ....' ½ p., 16mo.

2880 Letter to Robert Southey, 10 August 1825. 'You'll know who this letter comes from by opening ....' Misdated 19 August in the Lucas edition of the Letters. 4 pp., quarto.

LANDOR, WALTER SAVAGE

2881 Letter to Mr. Maylor, no date. 'A few days ago I was favored by the Criticism ....' Written on a slip.

2882 Letter to an unidentified correspondent, no date. 'I am confined to my room where I have just received ....' 1 p., 16mo.

LANG, ANDREW

2883 Letter to Mrs. Baird Smith, 18 February [1896]. 'The letter is of 1829 or 1830 ....' 2 pp., octavo.

LIDDELL, HENRY T.

2884 Letter to William Wordsworth, 26 March [1838]. 'I have received your letter ....' 4 pp., octavo.

LLOYD, CHARLES, SENIOR

2885 Letter to Thomas Manning, 13 [March] 1806. 'I remember with satisfaction thy late kind visit ....' 3 pp., quarto.

LLOYD, CHARLES, JUNIOR

2886 Poem: Dirge Occasion'd by an Infant's Death. Six four-line stanzas. Signed and dated 20 October 1796. With a note by Lloyd: 'S. T. Coleridge's birth day, he being twenty-four years old.' Written in the Joseph Cottle Album. 1 p., folio.

2887 Two notebooks containing the text of Lloyd's novel entitled: *Isabel, a Domestick Tale; or, Godwin versus Godwin*. At the end appears this note: 'I finished copying this tale 24th July 1800, written either in March or April (or in both) 1789. Charles Lloyd.' The novel was published in two volumes in 1820. The notebooks measure $7\frac{1}{4} \times 4\frac{1}{2}$ in. and $7\frac{3}{4} \times 6\frac{1}{4}$ in., and contain respectively 200 pp. and 260 pp.

2888 Letter to Thomas Manning, 23 September 1798. 'The first thing which occurs to me to express is the want ....' 2 pp., quarto.

2889 Letter to Thomas Manning, 28 December 1798. 'I am taking the first moment of quietness & solitude ....' 3 pp., quarto.

2890 Letter to Thomas Manning, 6 January 1799. 'You will be surprised to see me dating from hence ....' 4 pp., quarto.

2891 Letter to Thomas Manning, 22 January 1799. 'Why have you been so long silent? ...' 4 pp., quarto.

2892 Letter to Thomas Manning, 25 January 1799. 'I should be much obliged to you if you would ....' $3\frac{1}{2}$ pp., quarto.

2893 Letter to Thomas Manning, 5 February 1799. 'I am so far on my way to Cambridge ....' 4 pp., quarto.

2894 Letter to Thomas Manning, 18 February 1799. 'At length my fathers letter, together with yours ....' 3 pp., quarto.

2895 Letter to Thomas Manning, 19 March 1799. 'Your letter though it is full of reproving criticism ....' $1\frac{1}{2}$ pp., folio.

2896 Letter to Thomas Manning, 25 March 1799. 'I have just received a letter from Wordsworth ....' 3 pp., folio.

2897 Letter to Thomas Manning, 11 April 1799. 'After a repetition of interviews for some days ....' 2 pp., folio.

2898 Letter to Thomas Manning, 28 May 1799. 'This is the first letter which I have been able to write ....' 4 pp., quarto.

2899 Letter, in an unidentified hand, to Thomas Manning, June 1799. 'You keep me in almost a cruel state of suspense ....' 3 pp., quarto.

2900 Letter to Thomas Manning, 1 June 1799. 'I am still anxiously wishing to see you here....' 3 pp., quarto.

2901 Letter, partly in the hand of Sophia Lloyd, to Thomas Manning, 3 June 1799. 'Your letter has very much affected me ....' 3 pp., quarto.

2902 Letter to Thomas Manning, 29 January 1800. 'Have you any objection to call on the British Critick ....' 3 pp., quarto.

2903 Letter to Thomas Manning, 14 April 1800. 'An evil destiny I believe awaits me ....' 4 pp., quarto.

2904 Letter to Thomas Manning, 9 May 1800. 'Sophia & I are very happily situated here ....' With a long postscript by Sophia Manning. $3\frac{1}{4}$ pp., quarto.

2905 Letter to Thomas Manning, 6 September 1800. 'I must begin with making the same request to you ....' $3\frac{1}{2}$ pp., quarto.

2906 Letter to Thomas Manning, 10 December 1800. 'Why do you never write? ...' 4 pp., quarto.

2907 Letter to Thomas Manning, 26 January [1801]. 'We were very glad to hear from you today ....' 4 pp., quarto.

2908 Letter to Thomas Manning, 5 March 1801. 'I scarcely take it kind that I never hear from you ....' With a long postscript by Sophia Lloyd. 4 pp., quarto.

2909 Letter to Thomas Manning, 31 March 1801. 'The kindness expressed in your last letter & in the note ....' 4 pp., quarto.

2910 Letter to Thomas Manning, 2 October 1801. 'I have to return you many thanks for your kind ....' 4 pp., quarto.

2911 Letter to Thomas Manning, 21 June 1802. 'I received your letter last night ....' With a long postscript by Sophia Lloyd. 4 pp., folio.

2912 Letter to Thomas Manning, 6 July 1804. 'After such a long interval of silence as ours ....' With a long postscript by Sophia Lloyd. 4 pp., quarto.

2913 Letter to Thomas Manning, 24 February 1805. 'I was indeed delighted at seeing your hand writing ....' With a long postscript by Sophia Lloyd. 4 pp., quarto.

2914 Letter to Thomas Manning, 1 April 1805. 'I am truly sorry to learn that you have been so much ....' 2 pp., quarto.

2915 Letter to [Thomas Noon Talfourd?], 6 March 1822. 'I had a letter a few days ago from Mr. Alaric A. Watts ....' Includes copies of one letter and one draft of a letter addressed by Lloyd to William Wordsworth, and also a transcript of Wordsworth's letter to Lloyd, 20 February 1822: 'I begin this letter without the usual expressions of regard ....' $6\frac{1}{2}$ pp., folio.

LLOYD, SOPHIA

2916 Letter to Thomas Manning, 26 January [1800]. 'You recollect that if Charles could not answer your letter ....' 3 pp., quarto.

2917 Letter to Thomas Manning, [*c.* 23 May 1800]. 'Your letter has certainly "surprized" me ....' 4 pp., quarto.

2918 Letter to Thomas Manning, 6 July 1800. 'Considering how prettily you complimented me in your last ....' 4 pp., quarto.

2919 Letter to Thomas Manning, 13 December 1800. 'It is quite impossible for me to make any plausible excuse ....' 3 pp., quarto.

LLOYD, THOMAS

2920 Letter to William Wordsworth, 4 April [1838]. 'I am in receipt of your letter of 2 April ....' $1\frac{1}{2}$ pp., quarto.

LOVELL, ROBERT

2921 Sonnet entitled Stonehenge. Signed and dated 30 May 1795. Written in the Joseph Cottle Album.

MACAULAY, THOMAS BABINGTON

2922 Letter to Derwent Coleridge, 15 June 1853. 'I shall be most happy to subscribe for a proof impression ....' 1 p., octavo.

2923 Letter to Derwent Coleridge, 15–16 January [1856?]. 'I hope the interview with Mr. Cowper may produce ....' $7\frac{1}{2}$ pp., octavo.

2924 Letter to Derwent Coleridge, 16 February 1856. 'As soon as you had left me I wrote to Lord Granville ....' $1\frac{1}{2}$ pp., octavo.

2925 Letter to Derwent Coleridge, 30 May 1856. 'I am truly sorry that I have an engagement which will make it ....' 1 p., octavo.

2926 Letter to Derwent Coleridge, 16 April 1859. 'I am sorry that it will be impossible for me to avail ....' 1 p., octavo.

MACMILLAN, ALEXANDER

2927 Letter to John T. Barker, 16 May 1853. 'There is no doubt that any thing of Coleridge's would have a chance ....' 1 p., octavo.

2928 Letter to John T. Barker, 23 May 1855. 'If any of the Coleridge family want to purchase these letters ....' 1 p., octavo.

2929 Letter to John T. Barker, 21 June 1864. 'The Coleridge Letters are [?] to hand ....' 1 p., octavo.

MANNING, THOMAS

2930 Draft of a letter to Charles Lloyd, no date. 'I feel some dif[fidence] in expr[essing] to you what pleasure I have received from reading your Poem ....' 2½ pp., folio.

2931 Letter to Charles Lloyd, 25 September 1798. 'Nothing gives me more sincere pleasure than the affectionate ....' 1 p., quarto.

MASSON, DAVID

2932 Letter to [John T. Barker], 2 December 1864. 'I have been reading carefully the Coleridge MSS ....' 2½ pp., octavo.

MAURICE, F. D.

2933 Letter to Derwent Coleridge, 5 May 1852. 'I was not unprepared for your tidings ....' 3 pp., octavo.

2934 Letter to Derwent Coleridge, 1 March 1853. 'I am sorry to trouble you with such a trifle ....' 3 pp., octavo.

MEAKIN, RACHEL MYERS

2935 An album, included in which are brief verses by William Wordsworth, Dora Wordsworth, and Southey, and a drawing by Dora Wordsworth of a ruin. Wordsworth's contribution is four lines from The Longest Day. On the front cover is a drawing of Gale Farm, Ambleside; on the back a drawing of No. 19 St. Saviour's Gate. Both are signed 'R. R. 1830.' The book probably belonged originally to Rachel's mother, Julia Myers, Wordsworth's cousin and ward, to whom he wrote the poem beginning 'Small service is true service while it lasts.' 22 pp., 5½ × 3½ in.

MILNES, RICHARD MONCKTON

2936 Letter to William Wordsworth, 30 March [1838]. 'If Talfourd's bill come on Wednesday the 11th I will take care ....' 2 pp., octavo.

MORE, HANNAH

2937 Letter to John Henderson (Cottle's tutor), 11 April 1788. 'Though I do not deal much in the doctrine of impulses ....' Conclusion lacking. Inserted in the Joseph Cottle Album. 4 pp., quarto.

MORGAN, J. J.

2938 Note to Samuel Taylor Coleridge, October 1807. 'The first time I have been out of the house ....' Written on a visiting card. Inserted in the Joseph Cottle Album.

NEWTON, MARY, Sister of Thomas Chatterton

2939 Copy, in an unidentified hand, of a letter to Joseph Cottle, 17 October 1802. 'I should have answered your friendly letter ....' Inserted in the Joseph Cottle Album. 3 pp., octavo.

ORD, W. H.

2940 Letter to Derwent Coleridge, 24 November [1830?]. 'I give you my most hearty thanks for your very kind ....' 4 pp., octavo.

PALGRAVE, FRANCIS

2941 Letter to Derwent Coleridge, 1 October 1852. 'I ought, long before this, to have returned ....' 3 pp., octavo.

PERCEVAL, GEORGE

2942 Letter to an unidentified correspondent, 30 March 1838. 'I have many apologies to make for allowing your letter ....' 2 pp., octavo.

PICKERSGILL, H. W.

2943 Letter to Sir Robert Peel, 26 May 1840. 'Hoping I might obtain the Portrait of Mr. Wordsworth ....' 2 pp., octavo.

POLLOCK, WILLIAM FREDERICK

2944 Letter to William Wordsworth, 26 March 1838. 'It needed not your powerful advocacy & *authority* ....' 2 pp., octavo.

2945 Letter to Derwent Coleridge, 9 June 1853. 'I called this morning at Moxon's on my way down ....' 3 pp., octavo.

PRAED, WINTHROP MACKWORTH

2946 A Valentine poem, initialed 'W. P.' and dated from Trinity College, February 1823, but in a hand other than Praed's. Enclosed is a four-page printed poem in Welsh entitled: Can Serch. 4 pp., quarto.

2947 Letter to Derwent Coleridge, 29 July 1822. 'I have just heard from S. Lutwidge who gives me so bad an account ....' 4 pp., quarto.

2948 Letter to Derwent Coleridge, 15 August 1822. 'I have been for some time anxiously hoping ....' 4 pp., quarto.

2949 Letter to Derwent Coleridge, 16 March 1824. 'There are five lines of Horace for you ....' 3 pp., quarto.

2950 Letter to Derwent Coleridge, 24 May 1824. 'I have just received your letter ....' 4 pp., quarto.

2951 Letter to Derwent Coleridge, 24 August 1824. 'You are indebted to Malden, my dear Derwent ....' 4 pp., folio.

2952 Letter to Derwent Coleridge, 10 October 1824. 'Here I am for a week ....' 3 pp., quarto.

2953 Letter to Derwent Coleridge, 1–3 April 1825. 'You will I imagine be considerably astonished ....' 4 pp., quarto.

2954 Letter to Derwent Coleridge, 16 October 1825. 'With an hope of doing C. K. a benefit ....' 2 pp., quarto.

2955 Letter to Derwent Coleridge, 27 December 1825. 'I have oceans of talk to pour forth ....' 3 pp., quarto.

2956 Letter to Derwent Coleridge, 29 December 1825. 'The coach will bring you to Newton ....' 1 p., quarto.

2957 Letter to Derwent Coleridge, 11 January 1826. 'I have been travelling to and from town ....' $2\frac{1}{2}$ pp., octavo.

2958 Letter to Derwent Coleridge, 9 February 1826. 'I have two letters of yours to answer ....' 4 pp., quarto.

2959 Letter to Derwent Coleridge, 12 May [1826]. 'I have written to Praed's this day ....' 1 p., quarto.

2960 Letter to Derwent Coleridge, 14 October 1826. 'You remember perhaps enough of my concerns ....' 4 pp., quarto.

2961 Letter to Derwent Coleridge, 3 December 1826. 'I ought not to have given you to understand ....' 4 pp., quarto.

2962 Letter to Derwent Coleridge, [October 1827?]. 'I am most truly and heartily obliged ....' 4 pp., quarto.

2963 Letter to Derwent Coleridge, 1 December 1827. 'If I could in any way continue ....' 3 pp., quarto.

2964 Letter to Derwent Coleridge, 31 December 1827. 'A very particularly rainy morning inspires me ....' 3 pp., quarto.

2965 Letter to Derwent Coleridge, 30 November [1828?]. 'Mary—you remember my old feud with you about the use of Christian ....' 3 pp., octavo.

2966 Letter to Derwent Coleridge, 17 September 1829. 'I take great shame to myself for not writing ....' 4½ pp., quarto.

2967 Letter to Derwent Coleridge, 16 November 1829. 'I have received your orders concerning the disposal ....' 6 pp., octavo.

2968 Letter to Derwent Coleridge, 4 February 1830. 'I enclose you a most melancholy letter ....' 2 pp., octavo.

2969 Letter to Derwent Coleridge, 24 April 1830. 'I am horrorstruck at the date ....' 4 pp., quarto.

2970 Letter to Derwent Coleridge, 15 May 1830. 'Your letter dated Apr 21 and favored by Geo. Berlase ....' 4 pp., quarto.

2971 Letter to Derwent Coleridge, 19 June [1830?]. 'I receive your letter this afternoon and lose no time ....' 3 pp., quarto.

2972 Letter to Derwent Coleridge, 13 October [1830?]. 'I am this minute returned from a visit ....' 5 pp., quarto.

2973 Incomplete letter to Derwent Coleridge, [15 October 1830?]. 'I thank you very much for your kind letter ....' 4 pp., octavo.

2974 Letter to Derwent Coleridge, 9 February 1831. 'My enquiries concerning your umbrella failed ....' 1 p., quarto.

2975 Letter to Derwent Coleridge, 27 February 1831. 'I do not like to start for my circuit ....' 3¼ pp., octavo.

2976 Letter to Mrs. Derwent Coleridge, 22 April 1831. 'Derwent being "so dreadfully idle," I hold it my duty ....' 6 pp., octavo.

2977 Letter to Derwent Coleridge, 24 November 1831. 'I suspect I have a pretty considerable sin ....' 1 p., quarto.

2978 Letter to Derwent Coleridge, 22 December 1831. 'In paying your £5. 6 at Stulters ....' 1 p., quarto.

2979 Letter to Derwent Coleridge, 18 January 1832. 'I have read your sad letter with more grief ....'

2980 Incomplete letter to Mrs. Derwent Coleridge, 15 April 1832. 'Oh what shall I say to excuse myself ....' 4 pp., octavo.

2981 Letter to Mrs. Derwent Coleridge, 28 June [1833]. 'Mrs. Derwent Coleridge's Lord & Master left Cambridge ....' 1 p., quarto.

2982 Letter to Derwent Coleridge, 5 May 1835. 'I wish right heartily I could be at your opening ....' 3 pp., octavo.

2983 Letter to Derwent Coleridge, 27 January 1837. 'It is long since any intercourse passed ....' 4 pp., octavo.

2984 Letter to Derwent Coleridge, 21 February 1837. 'I shall have no difficulty in handing you the cash ....' 3 pp., octavo.

2985 Letter to Derwent Coleridge, 11 May 1837. 'I had meditated a letter to you ....' 3 pp., octavo.

2986 Letter to Derwent Coleridge, 7 June 1837. 'I enclose a note ....' 4 pp., octavo.

2987 Letter to Derwent Coleridge, 29 May 1839. 'It never before was a task of mortification ....' 4 pp., octavo.

2988 Letter to Derwent Coleridge, no date. 'Susan tells me you were entertained by my report ....' With eight enclosures concerning games of chess. 1 p., quarto.

2989 Letter to Derwent Coleridge, no date. 'Thorpe is likely to refuse Moultrie's Curacy ....' 1 p., quarto.

PRICE, ROBERT

2990 Letter to William Wordsworth, 4 April [1838]. 'I shall have pleasure in paying attention to the Bill ....' $1\frac{1}{2}$ pp., octavo.

QUILLINAN, EDWARD

2991 Letter to Mr. Baker, 9 February 1816. 'I have this morning received your bill ....' 1 p., quarto.

2992 Letter to an unidentified correspondent, 21 January 1824. 'You take a jest with good humor....' 1 p., quarto.

2993 Letter to [Edward Moxon], 22 March 1843. 'Mr. Southey is at last released. He died yesterday ....' 4 pp., quarto.

REED, HENRY

2994 Transcript, in an unidentified hand, of an essay entitled: Memoir of Gray by Professor Reed. 6 pp., folio.

2995 Letter to William Wordsworth, 25 April 1836. 'It may appear to you strange ....' 3 pp., quarto. With Reed's copy of the same letter.

2996 Letter to William Wordsworth, 3 January 1839. 'It is rather more than a twelvemonth ....' 2 pp., quarto. With Reed's copy of the same letter.

2997 Letter to William Wordsworth, 7 May 1839. 'Your kind letter of the 22d of February ....' 4 pp., quarto. With Reed's copy of the same letter.

2998 Letter to William Wordsworth, 18 March 1840. 'Mr. Moxon has communicated to me ....' 3 pp., quarto. With Reed's copy of the same letter.

2999 Letter to William Wordsworth, 7 April 1840. 'A few days since I had the pleasure ....' 3 pp., quarto. With Reed's copy of the same letter.

3000 Letter to William Wordsworth, 5 August 1840. 'Your letter of 26 May reached me this morning ....' 3 pp., quarto.

3001 Letter to William Wordsworth, 17 August 1840. 'On the receipt of your letter of the 26 of May ....' 3 pp., quarto.

3002 Letter to William Wordsworth, 28 September 1840. 'Your letter of the 2d of this month arrived ....' 3 pp., quarto.

3003 Letter to William Wordsworth, 30 October 1840. 'The last steamer has brought me another letter ....' 3 pp., quarto. With Reed's copy of the same letter.

3004 Letter to William Wordsworth, 25 February 1841. 'Your letter of the 13th of January ....' 3 pp., quarto.

3005 Letter to William Wordsworth, 14 April 1841. 'The interests of your friend Miss Fenwick ....' 3 pp., quarto.

3006 Letter to William Wordsworth, 28 April 1841. 'Having written on matters of business ....' 3 pp., quarto. With Reed's copy of the same letter.

3007 Letter to William Wordsworth, 29 June 1841. 'Your letter from Taunton (May 15) I had ....' 3 pp., quarto.

3008 Letter to William Wordsworth, 29 November 1841. 'I had the pleasure some time since of receiving ....' 4 pp., quarto. With Reed's copy of the same letter.

3009 Letter to William Wordsworth, 30 March 1842. 'As it is important for me not to lose ....' 1 p., quarto. With Reed's copy of the same letter.

3010 Letter to William Wordsworth, 29 April 1842. 'After having mailed my letter to you ....' 6 pp., quarto. With Reed's copy of the same letter.

3011 Letter to William Wordsworth, 30 June 1842. 'Having promised to keep you as well advised ....' 3 pp., quarto. With Reed's copy of the same letter.

3012 Letter to William Wordsworth, 14 July 1842. 'In my letter by the steamer of the 1st ....' $2\frac{1}{2}$ pp., quarto.

3013 Letter to William Wordsworth, 29 July 1842. 'By the last Steamer I wrote you ....' 3 pp., quarto. With Reed's copy of the same letter.

3014 Letter to William Wordsworth, 15 November 1842. 'Since I last wrote to you I have had ....' 6 pp., quarto. With Reed's copy of the same letter.

3015 Letter to William Wordsworth, 15 March 1843. 'I have been waiting most anxiously in the hope ....' 4 pp., quarto.

3016 Letter to William Wordsworth, 30 March 1843. 'Agreeably to a promise in my last letter ....' 2 pp., quarto. With Reed's copy of the same letter.

3017 Letter to William Wordsworth, 29 April 1843. 'Your letter of the 27th of last month ....' 6 pp., quarto. With Reed's copy of the same letter.

3018 Letter to William Wordsworth, 30 May 1843. 'When the last Steamer sailed I omitted ....' 2½ pp., quarto. With Reed's copy of the same letter.

3019 Letter to William Wordsworth, 28 September 1843. 'In acknowledging the receipt of your letter ....' 4 pp., quarto. With Reed's copy of the same letter.

3020 Letter to William Wordsworth, 27 February 1844. 'Your last letter (Nov. 10) reached me sometime ....' 3 pp., quarto. With Reed's copy of the same letter.

3021 Letter to William Wordsworth, 29 April 1844. 'When I wrote to you about two months ago ....' 2 pp., quarto. With Reed's copy of the same letter.

3022 Letter to William Wordsworth, 24 May 1844. 'Permit me to have the pleasure of introducing ....' 1 p., quarto.

3023 Letter to William Wordsworth, 29 May 1844. 'A press of duties prevented my writing by the last ....' 3 pp., quarto. With Reed's copy of the same letter.

3024 Letter to William Wordsworth, 28 June 1844. 'I am about to ask a great favour of you ....' 3 pp., quarto. With Reed's copy of the same letter.

3025 Letter to William Wordsworth, 14 October 1844. 'Your kind letter of July reached me just as I ....' 4 pp., quarto. With Reed's copy of the same letter.

3026 Letter to William Wordsworth, 13 December 1844. 'It will, I think, be well that you should receive ....' 3 pp., quarto.

3027 Letter to William Wordsworth, 29 March 1845. 'The last letter I had the pleasure of receiving ....' 3 pp., quarto. With Reed's copy of the same letter.

3028 Draft of a letter to William Wordsworth, 31 March 1845. 'Having, in a letter sent by the Steamer, informed you ....' 1 p., octavo.

3029 Letter to William Wordsworth, 27 April 1845. 'This letter will, at my request, be handed to you ....' 1 p., quarto. With Reed's copy of the same letter.

3030 Letter to William Wordsworth, 28 August 1845. 'A few days before leaving Philadelphia ....' 4 pp., quarto. With Reed's copy of the same letter.

3031 Letter to William Wordsworth, 29 October 1845. 'I was much gratified in hearing from you ....' 4 pp., quarto. With Reed's copy of the same letter.

3032 Letter to William Wordsworth, 27 November 1845. 'I write to let you know that the Steamer ....' 3 pp., quarto. With Reed's copy of the same letter.

3033 Letter to Mary Wordsworth, 27 November 1845. 'You will gratify Mrs. Reed and me ....' 1½ pp., quarto. With Reed's copy of the same letter.

3034 Letter to William Wordsworth, 26 February 1846. 'We have been truly sorry in learning from your last ....' 3 pp., quarto. With Reed's copy of the same letter.

3035 Letter to William Wordsworth, 30 March 1846. 'Let me thank you for the kindly thoughtfulness ....' With Reed's copy of the same letter. 2 pp., quarto.

3036 Letter to William Wordsworth, 30 July 1846. 'The copy of the new Edition of your Poems ....' With Reed's copy of the same letter. 4 pp., quarto.

3037 Letter to William Wordsworth, 28 January 1847. 'I should not write to say to you ....' With Reed's copy of the same letter. 4 pp., quarto.

3038 Draft of a letter to William Wordsworth, 2 April 1849. 'Permit me to trespass on your kindness ....' 2 pp., quarto.

3039 Letter to William Wordsworth, 28 October 1849. 'I have hesitated about writing to you ....' With Reed's copy of the same letter. 2 pp., quarto.

3040 Letter to William Wordsworth, 10 December 1849. 'Permit me to express the gratification with which ....' With Reed's copy of the same letter. 3 pp., quarto.

3041 Draft of a letter to Christopher Wordsworth, Jr., 8 June 1850. 'I take the liberty of addressing you ....' 2 pp., quarto.

3042 Draft of a letter to Christopher Wordsworth, Jr., 28 October 1850. 'Not to miss the return Steamer ....' 4 pp., octavo.

3043 Draft of a letter to Christopher Wordsworth, Jr., 31 December 1850. 'Without waiting to hear from you again ....' 2 pp., octavo.

3044 Letter to Mary Wordsworth, 27 October 1852. 'Your friendly letter has been a very great ....' 4 pp., quarto.

3045 Letter to Mary Wordsworth, 6 April 1853. 'I am anxious to introduce to you ....' 1 p., octavo.

3046 Letter to Mary Wordsworth, 27 June 1853. 'I almost fear you may misunderstand my suffering ....' With a full-page note by Mary Wordsworth on one of the blank pages. 6 pp., quarto.

3047 Letter to Mary Wordsworth, 23 August 1853. 'Mrs. Reed and I have again to thank you ....' 7 pp., quarto.

3048 Letter to Mary Wordsworth, 7 February 1854. 'By the last Steamer I sent a few hurried ....' 4½ pp., quarto.

3049 Letter to Mary Wordsworth, 4 April 1854. 'I hasten to acknowledge and thank you ....' 4 pp., quarto.

REED, WILLIAM B., Brother of Henry Reed

3050 Letter to William Wordsworth, Jr., 12 October 1854. 'The public papers will inform you of the awful calamity ....' 1 p., octavo.

ROBINSON, HENRY CRABB

3051 Notes entitled: Minutes of a Tour in Holland &c 1815; and other notes of later tours on the Continent. 6 pp., quarto and 4 pp., octavo.

3052 Memorandum of places of interest to travellers in France and Italy. Undated. 2 pp., quarto.

3053 Letter to Thomas De Quincey, 12 July 1816. 'You will not have forgotten a fellow student at *our* Hall ....' 2 pp., quarto.

3054 Letter to Henry Southerne, 10 March 1824. 'I send you the article as complete as I have leisure ....' 1 p., octavo.

3055 Letter to Frances C. Mackenzie, 17 November [1837]. 'You will not suspect the *poet* of ingratitude or inattention ....' A joint letter from Robinson and Wordsworth, but the poet's part is dated 11 August 1837. Each part, 2 pp., quarto.

3056 Letter to William Wordsworth, 5 April 1838. 'This is a very short note to send so long ....' 2 pp., octavo.

3057 Letter to Mrs. Hughes, 1 March 1841. 'It would not be easy for me to express how much ....' 3 pp., octavo.

3058 Letter to an unidentified correspondent, 7 June 1845. '"All's well that ends well" and as our friend ....' 4 pp., octavo.

3059 Letter to Derwent Coleridge, 25 May 1849. 'It is reported that you are writing a memoir of your brother ....' 2½ pp., octavo.

3060 Letter to Derwent Coleridge, 31 January 1852. 'Some time back my old friend Mrs. Clarkson ....' 3 pp., octavo.

3061 Letter to Derwent Coleridge, 5 May 1852. 'There is no danger of your misunderstanding me ....' 1½ pp., octavo.

3062 Letter to Derwent Coleridge, 3 December 1852. 'I do not recollect when I have felt so mortified as I do ....' 2½ pp., octavo.

3063 Letter to Edward Tagart, 24 January 1853. 'I went today to Red Cross Street Library, expecting that you ....' 4 pp., octavo.

3064 Letter to Edward Tagart, 12 February 1853. 'When you approach my age, you may experience ....' 2½ pp., octavo.

3065 Letter to Derwent Coleridge, 9 June 1853. 'It was not in my power to attend the meeting at Moxon's ....' 2 pp., octavo.

3066 Letter to Mrs. Derwent Coleridge, 6 November [1854?]. 'I had forgotten that we had ever disputed about Mr. Reed's ....' 3 pp., octavo.

3067 Letter to Edward Tagart, 24 November 1854. 'Looking for something else, I have this morning found Mr. Turner's ....' 4 pp., 16mo.

3068 Letter to Mrs. Derwent Coleridge, 22 December 1857. 'So great is my confidence in your good nature ....' 2 pp., octavo.

3069 Letter to Derwent Coleridge, 16 November 1863. 'It will give me great pleasure if you will meet ....' 1 p., octavo.

3070 Letter to Mrs. Edward Tagart, 6 April, no year given. 'I have nothing *comfortable* to say for myself ....' 3 pp., octavo.

3071 Letter to Derwent Coleridge, 1 May, no year given. 'When I informed you that Mr. Wordsworth was expected ....' With a postscript by John Wordsworth. 1 p., octavo.

3072 Letter to Derwent Coleridge, 10 December, no year given. 'I was glad to receive your letter, not as an apology ....' 2 pp., 16mo.

3073 Letter to Edward Tagart, no date. 'Your friendly note was put into my hands just as I was setting ....' 2½ pp., octavo.

3074 Letter to Derwent Coleridge, no date. 'May I beg the favor of your company to meet a few friends ....' 1 p., octavo.

ROGERS, SAMUEL

3075 Letter to William Wordsworth, 19 April 1838. 'A thousand thanks for your very welcome letter ....' 1 p., octavo.

3076 Letter to Derwent Coleridge, 8 May 1852. 'How can I thank you for thinking of me, at such ....' 1 p., octavo.

ROSE, JOHN

3077 Sonnet: To Contentment. Signed and dated 4 August 1795. Written in the Joseph Cottle Album. ½ p., folio.

RUSSELL, JOHN FULLER

3078 A manuscript book of poems entitled: Delphi, and Other Poems; with a dedicatory poem to Robert Southey. Inserted are eight lines of verse in Southey's hand ('O thou sweet Lark. That I had wings like thee!'). 130 pp., octavo.

RYLAND, JOHN

3079 Notes for sermons, in Hebrew, Greek, and English, written in minute handwriting on narrow strips of paper. The slips are pasted together at the ends as if to form a cylinder. Dated November 1786. Three pieces. Inserted in the Joseph Cottle Album.

ST. JOHN, CYNTHIA MORGAN

3080 A collection of thirty-nine letters addressed to her, all of them concerning Wordsworth or Coleridge, from various correspondents including Thomas J. Wise (4), Ellis Yarnall (2), Edward Dowden (2), and William A. Knight (2).

SHELLEY, MARY

3081 Letter to an unidentified correspondent, Thursday [*c*. 1830]. 'I send you a cheque for a part of what I owe ....' 1 p., 16mo.

SHELLEY, PERCY BYSSHE

3082 Letter to John Gisborne [November 1820]. 'I send you the Phaedon & Tacitus ....' 1 p., quarto.

SIGORNEY, L. H.

3083 Letter to Henry Reed, 22 November 1853. 'I thank you for your last kind note ....' 1½ pp., octavo.

SKONE, THOMAS

3084 Poem, transcribed by George Symes Catcott (the Chattertonian), beginning 'From those gay Meads, where Avon leads his Train'. Eighteen four-line stanzas and a note on the author. Signed and dated 22 October 1796. Written in the Joseph Cottle Album. 3 pp., folio.

SOUTHEY, CAROLINE BOWLES

3085 Letter to the Messrs. Longman and Co., 21 March 1840. 'I have to thank you for your obliging letter ....' 1 p., octavo.

My dear Cottle

I am engaged in the Critical Review. immediately
I requested to review Amos's book — it was in other hands. I men-
-tioned it as what I much wished — & it has been transferred
to me. will you send me up the original that I may
do your brother justice. a huge parcel is just arrived —
all poetry. this is very lucky for our selections.

If you could assist me with ten pounds — I should be glad.
my expences this quarter have exceeded my income. I shall recover in
the next. a pestilence on Mr Pitt for raising the price of every thing!

send likewise my Northern Antiquities with the original Edda.
you shall know all that I review. God bless you.
                                    yrs affectionately
                                        RS.

I expected a proof to day.
Saturday 9th December.

Sent. J.C.

Handwriting of Robert Southey.   No. 3109

November the 12th, 1807, received from Mr Joseph Cottle the sum of three hundred Pound, presented to me thro' him by an unknown Friend. S. T. Coleridge Bristol.

Keswick. May 31. 1810

Pay to Mrs Coleridge . or order , fifty pounds on account of

Robert Southey.

To

Mr John Ballantyne

Edinburgh

£50.

Help for the Coleridges from Their Friends.   Nos. 2615 and 3102

3086 Letter to Bernard Barton, 20 June 1840. 'I beg you to believe I am very sensible for the kind concern ....' 3 pp., octavo.

See also No. 2774.

SOUTHEY, ROBERT

3087 Poem: English Dactylics to a Soldier's Wife. Twelve lines, signed and dated 25 May 1795. Written in the Joseph Cottle Album. 1 p., folio.

3088 Sonnet: To Mary Cottle ('Remember me, dear Lady! far away'). With a note in another hand: 'With a copy of Joan of Arc 1796 on title page.' Inserted in the Joseph Cottle Album. 1 p., folio.

3089 Two separate pages from the manuscript of Joan of Arc, with a marginal note by Cottle. Undated; probably of 1796. Inserted in the Joseph Cottle Album. 2 pp., quarto.

3090 Poem: Specimen of English Sapphics ('Cold was the night wind, drifting fast the snow fell'). Seven four-line stanzas, signed and dated 30 July 1796. Written in the Joseph Cottle Album. 1 p., folio.

3091 A hand-written ticket to his lectures, initialed. Probably of September 1796. Inserted in the Joseph Cottle Album.

3092 Poem: The Well of St. Keyne ('A well there is in the west country'), with a note of instruction to the printer. Thirteen four-line stanzas, undated but probably of about 1798. Inserted in the Joseph Cottle Album. 4 pp., octavo.

3093 A poem of thirteen lines, 'Moments there are in life, alas how few!' Undated. 1 p., octavo.

3094 A poem of eighteen lines entitled: Inscription in a Forest ('Stranger whose steps have reached this solitude'). Undated. 1 p., octavo.

3095 A prose passage, a portion apparently of The Doctor, which was published in 1837. Undated. 24 pp., quarto and octavo.

3096 A poem of seventeen lines, 'Aye love! he cried. It serves me well'. Undated. 1 p., octavo.

3097 Two home-made notebooks, stitched, each entitled 'Preaching' and containing notes on that subject. Undated. 15 pp., $6 \times 3\frac{3}{4}$ in.

3098 Home-made notebook containing quotations from various sources. Undated. 6 pp., $3\frac{3}{4} \times 4$ in.

3099 A collection of notes on a variety of subjects. Undated. Twenty-one separate leaves of various sizes.

3100 Notes on John Byrom. Undated. 2 pp., octavo.

3101 Home-made notebook, containing notes and comment on various subjects. Dated 25 May 1803. 11½ pp., 12mo.

3102 Check for £50 drawn in favor of Sara Coleridge (i.e., Mrs. Samuel Taylor Coleridge) dated 31 May 1810.

3103 Poem entitled: The Cataract of Lodore: Rhymes for the Nursery. Dated 1822. 3½ pp., octavo.

3104 Home-made notebook, stitched, containing extracts from various eighteenth-century periodicals. Undated, *c.* 1837. 13 pp., 6¼ × 4 in.

3105 Home-made notebook entitled 'Railroad Report, March 1838.' 2½ pp., 6¼ × 4¾ in.

3106 Deed of transfer, changing the assignment of Southey's *Life and Works of William Cowper* from the firm of Baldwin & Cradock to that of Salt, Hansard, Pouncy, Smith and Marshall. Dated 8 March 1839.

3107 Letter to Joseph Cottle, 26 April 1797. 'On receiving your letter (Thursday last) I went to the Swan ....' 4 pp., quarto.

3108 Letter to John May, 2 November 1797. 'I write from Bristol, a place where business and friendship ....' 3 pp., quarto.

3109 Letter to Joseph Cottle, 9 December [1797]. 'I am engaged in the Critical Review ....' 1 p., quarto.

3110 Letter to Joseph Cottle, in rhymed verse, 9 May 1800. 'Dear Cottle, d'ye see / In writing to thee / I do it in rhyme / That I may save time ....' Inserted in the Joseph Cottle Album. 4 pp., quarto.

3111 Letter to C. W. W. Wynn, [1802]. 'Mrs. Hughes's letter told me of Elmsley's death ....' 1 p., octavo.

3112 Letter to Joseph Cottle (first leaf cut away), 2 November 1806. Final paragraph begins: 'Coleridge is returned at last, considerably fatter ....' In 'double writer' (a carbon copy). Inserted in the Joseph Cottle Album. 1 p., quarto.

3113 Letter to Joseph Cottle (¾ of a leaf cut away), 18 June 1807. 'Long since I ought to have thanked you ....' Inserted in the Joseph Cottle Album. Originally 4 pp., quarto.

3114 Letter to the Messrs. Longman & Co., 12 August 1808. 'My letters (which relate to Portugal exclusively, not Spain) ....' 1½ pp., quarto.

3115 Letter to Thomas Smith, 15 August 1808. 'Both cheese and rug have at last arrived ....' 3 pp., quarto.

3116 Letter to Thomas Rees, 15 January 1809. 'D Juana de Austria the mother of Sebastian, was made Regent ....' 2½ pp., quarto.

3117 Letter to John May, [1 July 1809]. 'Your direction has been duely transmitted to the publisher ....' 4 pp., quarto.

3118 Letter to Mrs. Montagu, 19 October 1812. 'Your letter of the 13th was six days on its journey ....' $2\frac{1}{2}$ pp., quarto.

3119 Letter to R. J. M. Longmire, 25 November 1812. 'I have to thank you, Sir, for the moralized sketch ....' 1 p., quarto.

3120 Letter to J. H. Lovell, 29 July 1818. 'Mrs. Coleridge, having opened your letter in her husband's absence ....' 1 p., quarto.

3121 Letter to Wade Browne, 14 May 1819. 'You will wonder at seeing my letter dated from home ....' 3 pp., quarto.

3122 Letter to John Wilson, 27 July 1820. 'I am very glad that you have succeeded in obtaining ....' 2 pp., quarto.

3123 Letter to Sir William Knighton, 30 March 1821. 'I am greatly obliged to you for presenting my Vision ....' $2\frac{1}{2}$ pp., quarto.

3124 Letter to Major Moor, 4 December 1821. 'Immediately on the receipt of your letter I carefully packed ....' 2 pp., quarto.

3125 Letter to Alaric A. Watts, 29 August 1824. 'I have this evening received your letter ....' 2 pp., quarto.

3126 Letter to Miss Fields, 24 May 1825. 'Will you have the goodness to direct for me the note of thanks ....' $1\frac{1}{2}$ pp., octavo.

3127 Letter to Mrs. Fletcher, 30 March 1831. 'No one lived in habits of greater intimacy with Davy ....' 1 p., quarto.

3128 Letter to W. L. Bowles, 30 July 1832. 'This morning I received your St. John in Patmos ....' 4 pp., quarto.

3129 Letter to an unidentified correspondent, 16 March 1833. 'I am much obliged to Croker for his notes ....' 1 p., 16mo.

3130 Letter to an unidentified correspondent, 25 March 1834. 'My name is at your service....' 1 p., octavo.

3131 Letter to John Major, 1 September 1834. 'You would perceive by the return of the John Bull ....' 1 p., quarto.

3132 Letter to J. F. Russell, 27 July 1835. 'Sir Egerton's book ought to have satisfied you ....' $1\frac{1}{2}$ pp., quarto.

3133 Letter to Thomas Russell, 2 December 1835. 'I am much obliged to you for your communication ....' 1 p., octavo.

3134 Letter to J. F. Russell, 26 February 1837. 'Your letter has reached me just on my return home ....' $\frac{1}{2}$ p., quarto.

3135 Letter to William Turner, 29 October 1837. 'My second letter will ere this have reached your Father ....' 1½ pp., quarto.

3136 Letter to J. F. Russell, 8 March 1838. 'Your book reached me two days ago in a parcel ....' 1 p., quarto.

3137 Letter to [Robert Campbell], 5 April 1838. 'Here I am, safe, & if not absolutely sound ....' 3 pp., quarto.

3138 Letter to Thomas Wright, 5 May [1838]. 'I am obliged to you for sending me the prospectus of the Camden ....' ½ p., quarto.

3139 Letter to Robert Campbell, 6 May 1838. 'It is time that you should have some account ....' 3 pp., quarto.

3140 Letter to Robert Campbell, 4 December 1838. 'You are no doubt acquainted with the conduct of our landlord ....' 2 pp., quarto.

3141 Letter to Henry Taylor, 13 August 1839. 'Thank you my dear H. T. for the Bills which arrived ....' 1 p., octavo.

3142 Letter to Mr. Blakeney, Saturday evening, no date. 'Thank you, my dear Sir, for the hare....' 1 p., octavo.

3143 Transcript, in an unidentified hand, of an excerpt from a letter to Joseph Cottle, undated. 'When I think of yourself and sisters ....' Inserted in the Joseph Cottle Album. ½ p., octavo.

MAHON, PHILIP HENRY STANHOPE, VISCOUNT

3144 Letter to William Wordsworth, 2 May 1838. 'I am much gratified that what I said in the House ....' 1 p., octavo.

STANLEY, E. J.

3145 Letter to William Wordsworth, 26 March [1838]. 'As Lord John Russell has given notice of moving ....' 4 pp., octavo.

3146 Letter to Benjamin Bailey, 13 October 1851. 'I have received with pleasure, and read with interest ....' 3 pp., octavo.

STEELE, ANNE

3147 Letter to Grace Cottle (mother of Joseph Cottle), 18 May 1761. 'Having heard nothing of you so long ....' With a note by Cottle. Inserted in the Joseph Cottle Album. 1 p., quarto.

STERLING, JOHN

3148 Letter to Derwent Coleridge, [*c.* 1838]. 'I fancy I left a MacIntosh coat at the Star Inn ....' 3 pp., octavo.

STEVENSON, ANDREW

3149 Letter to John Kenyon, 3 April 1838. 'On returning from my walk, I found that you had returned ....' 1 p., octavo.

3150 Part of a letter to John Kenyon, 7 April [1838]. 'I send you the number of the Review containing the notice of Wordsworth's ....' 1 p., octavo.

TAIT, ARCHIBALD CAMPBELL, Bishop of London

3151 Letter to Derwent Coleridge, 6 February 1862. 'I beg to acknowledge your letter of the 5th ....' 4 pp., octavo.

3152 Letter to Derwent Coleridge, 1 July 1864. '[   ] spoke what many feel ....' 2 pp., octavo.

3153 Letter to Derwent Coleridge, 11 February 1865. 'Pray let Mr. Snow send his papers ....' 2 pp., octavo.

3154 Letter to Derwent Coleridge, 23 November 1868. 'My uncertainty of habitude has prevented your very kind ....' 2 pp., octavo.

3155 Letter to Derwent Coleridge, 9 September 1879. 'Most truly do I thank you for yr kind ....' 4 pp., octavo.

TALFOURD, THOMAS NOON

3156 Letter to the Messrs. Taylor & Hessey, 5 January 1823. 'After a delay which very pressing engagements have rendered ....' 2 pp., quarto.

3157 Letter to an unidentified correspondent, 6 May 1835. 'I have been to Reading to attend the Theatre ....' 1 p., quarto.

3158 Letter to William Wordsworth, 22 November 1837. 'I am greatly obliged and honored by your letter ....' 2 pp., quarto.

3159 Letter to William Wordsworth, 21 March 1838. 'The Second Reading of the Copyright Bill stands ....' $2\frac{1}{2}$ pp., quarto.

3160 Letter to William Wordsworth, 16 April 1838. 'I am sorry you should have been annoyed about a thing ....' $2\frac{1}{2}$ pp., quarto.

3161 Letter to William Wordsworth, 23 April 1838. 'Accept my warmest thanks for your most kind and encouraging ....' $1\frac{1}{2}$ pp., quarto.

3162 Letter to William Wordsworth, 30 April 1838. 'I am greatly obliged and delighted with your letter of today ....' $1\frac{1}{2}$ pp., quarto.

3163 Letter to William Wordsworth, 19 August 1838. 'Having arrived at the place where I hope to enjoy some repose ....' 8 pp., quarto.

3164 Letter to William Wordsworth, 22 October 1838. 'Your kind expression of a wish that I would look in ....' 3 pp., quarto.

3165 Letter to Robert Southey, 23 January 1839. 'I hope I do not presume too much on any recollection ....' $3\frac{1}{2}$ pp., quarto.

3166 Letter to William Wordsworth, 24 January 1839. 'As the Session of Parliament is now rapidly approaching ....' 4 pp., quarto.

3167 Letter to William Wordsworth, 4 February 1839. 'I return the draft of your Petition without feeling any ....' $1\frac{1}{4}$ pp., quarto.

3168 Letter to William Wordsworth, 10 July 1839. 'You might well ask in the few lines I had the pleasure ....' 2 pp., quarto.

3169 Letter to William Wordsworth, 18 August 1839. 'I cannot dispatch the inclosed letter, which Mr. Moxon ....' 3 pp., quarto.

3170 Letter to William Wordsworth, 7 May 1840. 'You will be sorry to know that I have very slender comfort ....' 4 pp., quarto.

TAYLOR, HENRY

3171 Letter to William B. Reed, 7 June 1848. 'I have not myself seen Mr. Wordsworth since ....' $3\frac{1}{2}$ pp., octavo.

TEMPLE, FREDERICK

3172 Letter to Derwent Coleridge, 25 January 1858. 'When you wrote to me about Clark, I was unable to stir ....' 2 pp., octavo.

3173 Letter to Derwent Coleridge, 21 October 1869. 'Thank you very much. I do not think ....' 2 pp., octavo.

3174 Letter to Derwent Coleridge, 4 August 1873. 'Thank you for your Sermons....' 3 pp., octavo.

THELWALL, JOHN

3175 Letter to Mr. Ridgeway, 18 January 1826. 'In the last page but one of Mr. Craddock's interesting memoirs ....' 1 p., quarto.

TICKNOR, GEORGE

3176 Letter to Henry Reed, 12 October 1852. 'Since I received your interesting note of the 5th ....' 2 pp., octavo.

3177 Letter to Henry Reed, 18 October 1852. 'I wrote to you a few days ago in reply ....' 2 pp., octavo.

3178 Letter to Henry Reed, 4 August 1853. 'I wrote to you only two days ago ....' 3 pp., octavo.

TOWNSHEND, CHAUNCEY HARE

3179 Letter to Derwent Coleridge, 1 February 1849. 'On the 3rd of Dec. 1849, I sent off to you a packet ....' 4 pp., octavo.

3180 Letter to Mrs. Derwent Coleridge, 7 [May 1855]. 'I write to say that I hope Derwent and yourself will ....' 4 pp., octavo.

3181 Letter to Derwent Coleridge, 7 May 1860. 'On my return from spending many months on the Continent ....' 4 pp., octavo.

3182 Letter to Mrs. Derwent Coleridge, 21 December 1863. 'It was very kind of you to write ....' 4 pp., octavo.

3183 Letter to Mrs. Derwent Coleridge, no date. 'It was very kind of you to write ....' 4 pp., octavo.

TRENCH, RICHARD CHEVENIX

3184 Letter to Derwent Coleridge, 15 June 1853. 'I shall esteem it a very great honor to be placed ....' 2 pp., octavo.

3185 Letter to Derwent Coleridge, 22 October 1863. 'Can you tell me whether the accompanying marginal note ....' 4 pp., 16mo.

TREVENEN, EMILY

3186 An album of 180 pages, about half of which have been used, containing verses, drawings, and silhouettes contributed by various hands. According to a note appended by Ernest Hartley Coleridge, 'This album accompanied Miss Trevenen on her Tour to the North to be present at Sara Coleridge's wedding, which took place Sept. 3, 1829.' Among the contributions are the following. Dorothy Wordsworth: Grasmere, a Fragment; Dora Wordsworth: The Bridal Band (to Sara Coleridge); Mary Wordsworth: Corn Flowers (by Edward Quillinan); Samuel Taylor Coleridge: Reply to a Lady's Question Respecting the Accomplishment Most Desirable in an Instructress (i.e., his Love, Hope, and Patience in Education); Sara Coleridge: Sonnet of a Young

Old Man (by Hartley Coleridge); Henry Nelson Coleridge: To My Bride on Her Wedding Morn; Derwent Coleridge: Sonnet; Robert Southey: verses addressed to Emily Trevenen; Edith, Bertha, and Kate Southey: by each, a transcript of one of their father's poems; Dr. Thomas Arnold: Verses Occasioned by the Dangerous Illness of Little Thomas Arnold; Mary (Mrs. Thomas) Arnold: Lines from a Mother to Her Little Girl on the Day She Was Seven Months Old—March 1st 1822; Sara Hutchinson: Epitaph in Grasmere Church to the Memory of Mrs. Quillinan (by Edward Quillinan); Mary Fletcher: Miss Trevenen's Reflexions on Seeing Mrs. Fletcher and Mr. Coleridge below a Canopy at Bilton, 19th June 1829; Rev. J. Carr: a cento, composed by William Wordsworth, from Akenside, Beattie, and Thomson; W. M. Praed: The Martyr's Prayer; John Moultrie: Epitaph in Windsor Church-yard.

The book contains several drawings, some in color, and a few silhouettes, among them those of Robert Southey and of Dora Wordsworth.

TRUMBULL, J. HAMMOND

3187 Letter to Henry Reed, Jr., 29 September 1883. 'Wordsworth's "Muccawiss" was, certainly, a Whip-poor-will ....' 2 pp., octavo.

TWISS, HORACE

3188 Letter to William Wordsworth, 28 March 1838. 'I will not fail to do "my little possible" in the subject ....' 2½ pp., octavo.

WEDGEWOOD, HENLEIGH

3189 Letter to Edward Tagart, 31 December [*c.* 1845]. 'It is extremely difficult for people in these sort of matters ....' 6 pp., quarto.

WILBERFORCE, SAMUEL

3190 Letter to Emily Trevenen, 24 March 1840. 'First let me thank you very sincerely for the kindness ....' 4 pp., octavo.

WILLIAMS, SIR F. C.

3191 Poem: On a Faded Cowslip Presented Me by Anna. Four four-line stanzas, signed 'Nobody indeed'; attributed to Williams in a note by Cottle. Undated, but probably of 1796. Written in the Joseph Cottle Album. ½ p., folio.

WILSON, JOHN

3192 Letter to an unidentified correspondent, 30 June 1842. 'This will be put into your hand by Charles Gurney ....' 2 pp., octavo.

3193 Letter to an unidentified correspondent, no date. 'I send you my List. I have placed ....' 2 pp., octavo.

WINTLE, ROBERT

3194 Letter to Martin Tupper, 12 March [*c.* 1839]. 'Many thanks for your Book, which I have read ....' 1 p., octavo.

UNIDENTIFIED AUTHORS

3195 Poem: Evening ('Give me to view yon starry studded Plain'), dated 5 June 1795, by 'an insane man at Dr. Fox's.' Transcribed in the Joseph Cottle Album. 1½ pp., folio.

3196 Poem: Extempore Lines on the Vale of Oldland in Gloucestershire ('Oldland, sweet spot with joy I greet'). Three six-line stanzas. Undated, but probably of 1795. Written in the Joseph Cottle Album.

3197 Transcript, in an unidentified hand, of an excerpt from Henry Mackenzie's *Man of Feeling*; undated, but perhaps of 1796. Inserted in the Joseph Cottle Album. 2 pp., quarto.

3198 Part of a letter to James Montgomery, in which is quoted part of a letter of Henry Mackenzie which mentions Wordsworth and Southey. Dated 24 January 1830. Inserted in the Joseph Cottle Album.

X

MISCELLANEOUS ITEMS

3199 An original portrait of Wordsworth, $11\frac{1}{2} \times 9\frac{3}{4}$ in., in oils on wood. Painted by William Shuter, in April 1798, for Joseph Cottle of Bristol.

3200 A miniature portrait, apparently of Wordsworth, oval, $2\frac{1}{2} \times 2$ in., in oils on ivory. Painted by an unidentified artist about 1800. On the back is a pencilled inscription: 'Mr [or Wm?] Wordsworth, Painted by My Husbands Father.' Presented to the Collection by the estate of the late Professor Broughton.

3201 An engraving of Wordsworth, with the original copper plate, by Thomas Landseer from a painting by R. B. Haydon. The plate measures $11\frac{3}{4} \times 9\frac{1}{2}$ in. The engraving was published in May 1831.

3202 A bust of Wordsworth, in plaster, by Frederick Thrupp, 23 in. high, dating from about 1852. Obtained from Henry Reed, to whom it was given by Isabella Fenwick, who probably received it from Mary Wordsworth.

3203 A colored drawing by Dora Wordsworth, $9\frac{1}{2} \times 6\frac{1}{4}$ in., inscribed on the back in her handwriting: 'Fluellen—the head of the Lake of Luzerne.'

3204 Wordsworth's reading glass, in a red leather case.

3205 A miniature harp, covered with green cloth and embroidered in gold and brilliants, made for Dora Wordsworth by Edith Southey, and designed to be used as a needle case. It stands $4\frac{3}{4}$ in. high. The 'strings' are a gradated series of twenty-two needles. Enclosed in a red silk case. The gift is the subject of Wordsworth's poem On Seeing a Needlecase in the Form of a Harp.

3206 A series of thirty-seven pen-and-ink drawings by Harry Goodwin, one a portrait of Wordsworth, the others illustrations of scenes from his life or his poems. Made between 1883 and 1887. Mounted, with captions and quotations in the handwriting of the artist, in a small folio album. Most of the drawings measure $7 \times 4\frac{1}{8}$ in.

INDEX

INDEX

[Figures refer to item numbers]